Ferguson's
Garden Plant Directory

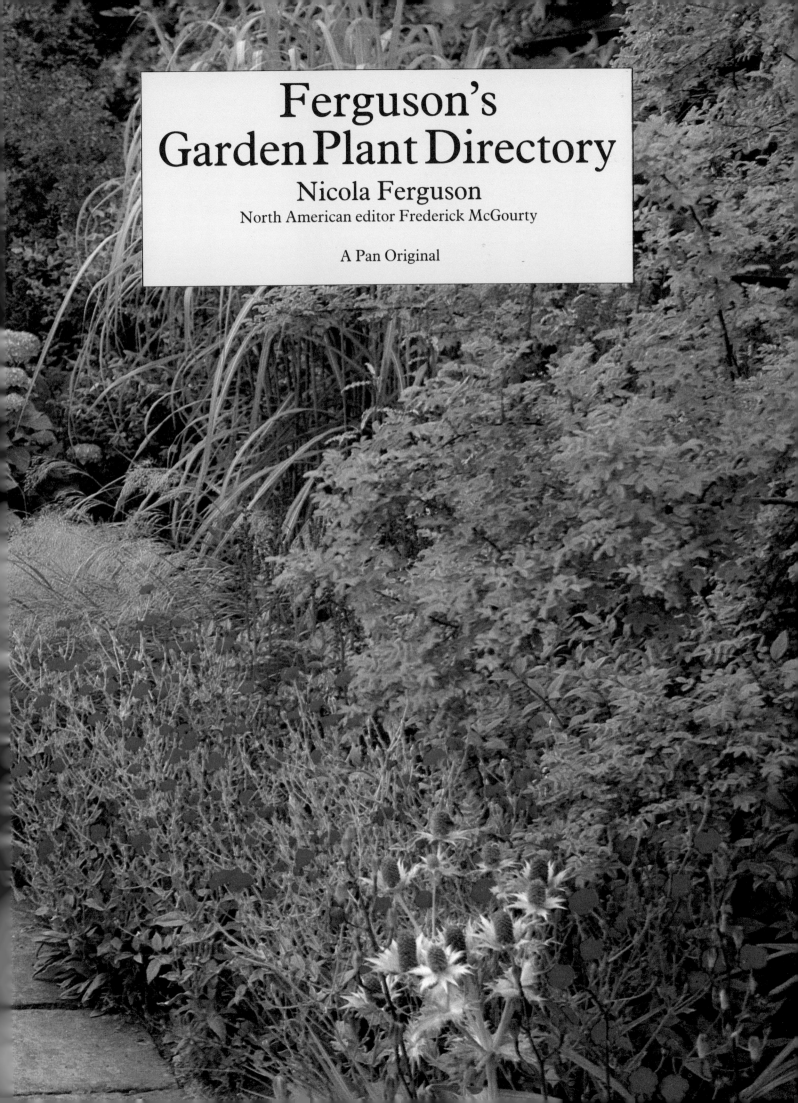

Ferguson's Garden Plant Directory

Nicola Ferguson

North American editor Frederick McGourty

A Pan Original

Nicola Ferguson was born in 1949 and brought up in Northern Ireland. She has a PhD in psychology, and she has also become an experienced gardener. She now lives with her husband and one daughter in Edinburgh, where they have a north facing, high-walled garden.

Frederick McGourty has served for 15 years as editor of the Brooklyn Botanic Garden Handbook series. He has also written pieces for the *New York Times* and the US Royal Horticultural Society Journal and other publications. He and his wife are active gardeners and Hillside, their showcase garden in Connecticut, has been the subject of a number of horticultural articles.

First published 1984 by Pan Books Ltd,
Cavaye Place, London SW10 9PG
© Nicola Ferguson 1984
hardcover ISBN 0 330 28418 5
paperback ISBN 0 330 26594 6
Photoset by Parker Typesetting Service, Leicester
Printed by Toppan Printing Co. (Singapore) Pte. Ltd

Contents

Metric conversion table

Height data for illustrated plants have been given in the text in both metric and imperial/US standard units. However, the following table will assist readers unfamiliar with the metric system when consulting the unillustrated lists of additional plants, in which metric measurements only are given.

Throughout the book, the following rounded equivalents have been used.

metres	feet	centimetres	feet/inches	
39	130	180	6	0
36	120	150	5	0
30	100	120	4	0
27	90	105	3	6
24	80	90	3	0
21	70	75	2	6
18	60	60	2	0
15	50	45	1	6
13.5	45	30	1	0
12	40	25		10
10.5	35	23		9
9	30	20		8
7.5	25	15		6
6	20	12		5
5.4	18	10		4
4.5	15	8		3
3.6	12	5		2
3	10	2		1
2.7	9			
2.4	8			
2.1	7			
1.8	6			
1.5	5			
1.2	4			
1.05	3½			

Abbreviations and symbols used in the lists

Sun and shade requirements
(For a full explanation of sun and shade categories see p. ix.)

○ sun
○ [◐] sun (or partial shade)
○ ◑ sun or partial shade
◐ [○] partial shade (or sun)
◐ partial shade
◐ ● partial or full shade

Plant name
syn. = synonym
× = recognized hybrid
★ = especially attractive plant (both in general terms, and in terms of the list in which it appears)
NA = readily available in the USA/North America only
sc NA = seldom cultivated in the USA/North America
MC in the USA/North America, a mild-climate plant which may be grown only in milder regions

Type of plant
(Abbreviations are used in conjunction, e.g. HHA = half hardy annual, SlTSh = slightly tender shrub.)

A = annual
Aq = aquatic
B = biennial
(Ba) = bamboo
Bb = bulb
C = corm
Cl = climber
Co = conifer
F = fern
(Gr) = grass
H = hardy
(Herb) = plant has culinary uses
HH = half-hardy
P = perennial
Sh = shrub
SlT = slightly tender
T = tree
Ten = tender
Tu = tuber

* = needs lime-free soil (in the case of certain plants, a neutral soil will be adequate)
E = evergreen
½E = semi-evergreen
E/½E = may be either evergreen or semi-evergreen
½E/D = may be either semi-evergreen or deciduous
(NA) = variant plant classification or flowering season in the USA/North America

The following abbreviations and symbols are used in a few lists only. The lists in which they appear are given in brackets.

≈ = suitable for shallow water; exact depth depending on species (Damp and wet soils)
√ = suitable for north-facing walls (Climbing plants)
√√ = suitable for north-facing and east-facing walls (Climbing plants)
C = particularly suitable for providing shelter in coastal gardens exposed to high wind and salt spray (Hedging plants)
✂ = foliage particularly suitable for cutting (Variegated leaves; Grey, etc. leaves; Red, etc. leaves; Yellow, etc. leaves; Decorative, green foliage)
# = only young foliage variegated or unusually coloured (Variegated leaves; Red, etc. leaves)
B = bold foliage (Decorative, green foliage)
W = evergreen leaves which change colour – usually taking on bronze or reddish hues – in late autumn and winter (Colourful autumn foliage)
also W = withered leaves which are retained during winter (Colourful autumn foliage)
(M) = mixed-coloured (red+orange, red+orange+yellow, etc.) autumn foliage (Colourful autumn foliage)
(R) = red, scarlet or pink autumn foliage (Colourful autumn foliage)
(R/B) = reddish brown or russet autumn foliage (Colourful autumn foliage)
(P) = purple autumn foliage (Colourful autumn foliage)
(Y) = yellow autumn foliage (Colourful autumn foliage)
(SH) = seed-head (Ornamental fruit)
(SP) = seed-pod (Ornamental fruit)
Dr = flowers or seed-heads suitable for drying (Cutting)

Introduction

Several years ago I acquired a garden which was mostly paths and grass. Excited by the prospect of creating something different, I settled down with gardening books and catalogues to choose some plants. However, it soon became clear that if my garden were to contain a satisfactory variety of plants, and if these plants were to be suitable for the local climate and soil, I would have to consult material that was organized in a different way.

In most gardening books and catalogues, the names of plants are followed by descriptions of characteristics and advice on cultivation. For my purposes, it would have been more useful if the characteristics (such as grey leaves or fragrant flowers) and the planting details (such as acid soil or dry shade) were given as headings and followed by lists of suitable plants. I wanted to know, for instance, what medium-sized shrubs I could grow in a heavy clay soil and what fragrant, summer-flowering climbers I could plant beside my garden seat. Often I could think of a number of possibilities, but I felt sure that I had overlooked others with which I was quite familiar.

I did find some books and catalogues that gave lists of plants for specific purposes, but these lists nearly always consisted of generic names (such as *Chrysanthemum*, *Petunia* and *Magnolia*) with no further details. This meant that I was often looking elsewhere for even the most basic information.

What I needed were lists of plants for particular purposes, where all sorts of plants were mentioned and where basic information (such as height and flower colour) about actual species and varieties was set out in a systematic form. As I was unable to find such lists, I produced them myself. I hope that you find them as useful as I do. They are intended to help anyone – expert or beginner – who wants to produce a design for a whole garden or part of a garden, or who wants to fill a particular place in their garden with a certain kind of plant.

For the knowledgeable gardener, the lists will help to jog the memory. The large number of different plants available often makes it irritatingly difficult to bring to mind all the plants that might be suitable for a particular purpose.

For the beginner, the lists will be informative, stating which plants are appropriate for certain purposes. Of course, the information which the lists give about plants does not amount to full-length description, and the lists will not design your garden for you, but they will make the whole business of choosing plants quicker, simpler and less frustrating than it can be.

Guide to the lists of plants

All the lists deal with garden plants, rather than plants that are suitable only for growing under some sort of cover. The range of garden plants is, however, enormous and if the names of all such plants were included in these lists, this book would be extremely long and not very useful. A selection of plants has, therefore, been made with two points in mind. First, the plants selected should be readily available to the ordinary gardener. (Although some slightly unusual plants appear in these lists, they are as easily obtained from most suppliers with a really wide range of general stock, as from specialists. For suppliers' addresses see p. 284.) Second, they should give a good idea of the range of height, flower colour and other characteristics of all the plants both commonly offered by seedsmen and nurseries and frequently referred to in popular gardening books.

Throughout the lists the practice of mentioning only the generic name has been avoided. If, for instance, the name *Cotoneaster*, with no further details, were given in a list of plants for chalky soils, then in height alone the commonly listed, suitable plants would range from a few centimetres/inches to well over 5 m/17 ft. The generic name alone is not, therefore, very useful information, and in all these lists examples of particular species (such as *Cotoneaster horizontalis*) and varieties or hybrids (such as *Cotoneaster* 'Cornubia') are given. The details of each plant included in these lists have been carefully checked but, gardening writers and plants being what they are, do not be dismayed to find slightly different estimates of height, flowering season and so on elsewhere.

The titles and page numbers of all the lists are given in the table of contents at the beginning of the book. Each list is preceded by a brief introduction. Many of the lists are of more general use than their titles might at first suggest. For instance, the 'Hedging' list is a good source of plants which, when they are grown as free-standing trees or shrubs, have upright, rather than wide-spreading branches (and so may be especially useful for small gardens or restricted spaces); the 'Paving' list contains numerous tidy little plants suitable for edgings to beds, borders or paths, as well as for growing between crevices in paved areas; and, while they may not be particularly adaptable, many of the plants in the 'Cutting' list have exceptionally pretty flowers that, as a bonus, last well in water.

All the lists are organized in the same way. First, each list is divided into up to six sections according to how much sun and shade the different plants require. Second, within each of these divisions, there are illustrated and unillustrated sections. (The very shortest lists – or, in some cases, a number of short sections in one list – are divided simply into illustrated and unillustrated sections in which the sun and shade requirements are noted.) In all sections, plants are arranged in order of height – beginning with the largest and ending with the smallest plant. Beneath the photographs in the illustrated sections, there are several lines of basic information about each plant. These summaries of details are followed by short descriptions with additional information. In the unillustrated sections, only the briefest of details are given and these are followed by page numbers to turn to for illustrations and fuller information. The sun and shade requirements, the division into illustrated and unillustrated sections and the summaries of details beneath the photographs are further explained and described below.

Sun and shade requirements
The six symbols used are:

○ = sun. This means that the plants mentioned must receive sun during all, or almost all, the day in the summer months; in some cases the sunniest possible position is needed, and this sort of detail is mentioned in the short descriptions beneath the illustrations.

○ [◑] = sun (or partial shade). This means that the plants mentioned prefer the conditions described under 'sun' but will do reasonably well in partial shade (that is, either in dappled shade or in positions that receive sunlight for only part of the day and are not made dark by nearby tall buildings or dense, overhanging trees).

○ ◑ = sun or partial shade. Plants in this category do equally well in either position.

◑ ○ = partial shade (or sun). This is the reverse of the situation described above in 'sun (or partial shade)'.

◑ = partial shade – as defined in 'sun (or partial shade)'.

◑ ● = partial or full shade. Many plants will do well without any sunlight. The symbol ◑ ● does not mean that all plants mentioned will do well in very dark places. A site may receive no sunshine but still be reasonably light. For those plants that bear full shade and little light there is a special list entitled 'Plants tolerant of dense shade'.

Some lists are so short that no plants appear in one or more of the headings above.

It is worth remembering that a soil's ability to retain moisture will sometimes affect the sun and shade requirements of plants growing in it. For instance, in a garden with a moisture-retentive soil, many plants will be able to stand greater exposure to sun than they could if they were grown in a light, sandy soil.

Illustrations

Every plant is illustrated once. Some plants appear in only one list; others appear in several. These last plants usually have a number of decorative features and they may be suitable for a variety of soils and sites. They are illustrated in what seems to be the most appropriate list and mentioned in the unillustrated sections of the other relevant lists. Since some plants have several features which are almost equally decorative, or they do almost equally well in more than one type of soil or site, it is important not to regard entries in the unillustrated sections of lists as necessarily inferior to the plants that are illustrated.

Arrangement in height order

Within every section of every list, plants are arranged in terms of height, with the tallest plant at the beginning and the smallest plant at the end of the section. Where several plants have the same minimum height but different maximum heights, then the plant with the largest maximum height appears first: for example, if plant A is 30-60 cm/1-2 ft high and plant B is 30-45 cm/1-1½ ft high, then plant A is placed before plant B. Where there are several plants of the same height in a section, they are arranged in alphabetical order.

Summaries of details

Except in a few cases, where extra information (such as the colour of fruits as well as flower colour) has been provided, the summaries of details, which appear immediately below the photographs, consist of six separate items of information.

Name

In each case, the main botanical name appears first. If there are any alternative botanical names these appear, in round brackets, after the main botanical name. Any common names are placed in square brackets below the botanical names. A star (★) after the botanical name or names of a plant indicates that it is, in my opinion, an especially attractive plant.

● *Main botanical names* In the lists, the names of the genus (e.g. *Clematis*) is in capital letters, the name of the species (e.g. *montana* in *Clematis montana*) is in small letters. If a species varies in the wild to the extent that it produces several distinct forms, then the names of these varieties (e.g. *rubens* in *Clematis montana rubens*) appear after the generic and specific names, in small letters; if the variety originated in cultivation, then the name (e.g. 'Tetrarose' in *Clematis montana* 'Tetrarose') appears in inverted commas. Some popular plants (for instance, roses, tulips and daffodils) have very many cultivated varieties or hybrids and these have been divided into groups (Double, Lily-flowered, etc. in the case of tulips). Where this is useful information, the group name is placed, in round brackets, after the generic name of a plant. A multiplication sign before or in the name of a plant (e.g. ×*Fatshedera lizei* or *Forsythia*× *intermedia*) means that the plant is a recognized hybrid between two genera, as in the first example, or between two species, as in the second example.

In the case of some genera and species, at least two – and sometimes dozens of – varieties and hybrids are readily available, and it has been possible to give only a selection of the whole range. To indicate this, the abbreviation 'e.g.' appears before the selected examples (for instance, *Crocus vernus* e.g. 'Striped Beauty'). If an 'e.g.' is omitted in one list, although it appears beside the same plant in other lists, this means that the plant is the only suitable one – or the only readily available suitable one – in the context of that particular list.

● *Botanical synonyms* Many plants have alternative botanical names. These names appear in round brackets and after the abbreviation ('syn.') – for synonym – in the lists. Most often, these synonyms are names which botanical research suggests are now incorrect but which are still often used in catalogues and some gardening books. Some of the synonyms are newer names which have not yet become commonly used.

● *Plants marked* ★ Each plant marked in this way is, in my opinion, especially attractive, not only in terms of the particular list in which it appears, but also from the point of view of the overall elegance and decorativeness of its various features. A few plants have so many good features that they are marked with a star in several lists (though, of course, they are illustrated in only one list).

● *Plants marked 'NA' and 'sc NA'* Plants with the letters 'NA' beside their name are readily available in the USA/North America only. Those with 'sc NA' beside their name are seldom cultivated in the USA/North America.

● *Common names* Common names appear in square brackets below all botanical names. Where no common name is given, either the plant has no common, English name, or its botanical name is better known than its common name (plants in the genus *Forsythia*, for example, are better known as such than as 'Golden Bells'). The term 'form' is used here to indicate a variety of a species, a hybrid within a genus, or a particular commercially available mixture.

Sun and shade requirements

How much sun or shade a plant requires is noted by means of a symbol (see p. vii and also p. ix) which appears below the plant's name or names.

Type of plant

Below the sun or shade requirements of a plant, there are letters which describe the type (e.g. shrub or bulb) and its hardiness. The definitions of these abbreviations, and other abbreviations used throughout the lists, are given on page vii.

The hardiness of a plant depends, to some extent, on the site and the soil as well as the climate in a particular locality. However, as a general rule:

- 'tender' means that the plant will be damaged and quickly killed by frost.
- 'half-hardy' means that, once temperatures drop below freezing, damage will probably occur; in very cold weather, all growth above ground level will be killed and the whole plant may die.
- 'slightly tender' means that, in very cold weather, superficial damage (such as the browning of leaves) will occur but the plant is unlikely to die; in the colder parts of Britain the plant may require some protection.
- 'hardy' means that, unless there are prolonged periods of very cold weather, the plant needs no special protection anywhere in the British Isles.

Since this is a practical book, a practical rather than a technical definition of the type of plant is given. Some plants are technically perennials, but they are grown as annuals or biennials. These plants appear in the lists as annuals or biennials. Where a plant's growth may vary according to climate, or where there is some dispute over its classification, variants are indicated by the use of an oblique, e.g. 'HSh/T'. '(NA)' after such a variant shows the classification applicable to the USA/North America.

Flowering season

In most of the summaries of details, the flowering season of each plant is stated. Where no information is given about flowering season and flower colour, then either the plant does not flower, or its flowers are generally considered inconspicuous. (Plants of this sort usually have some other decorative feature, such as ornamental fruit or variegated leaves, or they may be, for example, particularly useful for hedging or ground-cover.) Flowering seasons given are normally the average for the south of England. They will vary in length in certain years. Where the USA/North American flowering season differs from the British one, the variant is indicated by the abbreviation '(NA)'.

Although some plants are noted for flowering over a long period (and this may be indicated by such expressions as 'all summer'), most plants will not flower prolifically for the whole of the period stated; they will, however, normally flower during that period. Where no 'e.' (early), 'l.' (late) or 'mid' precedes a season, then it can be assumed that flowering takes place during a substantial part of the season, thought not necessarily all of it.

Flower colour

Where relevant, the flower colour of each plant is given. If two or more colours are present in a single flower, then those colours are linked with an addition sign (for example, in the case of the two snowdrops listed: 'white+green'). If a plant is sold as a mixture of colours, this is noted and the various colours are listed. Certain plants are very variable in their colour. The colours which may be produced are given in the following manner: 'white or mauve'. Finally, if a flower colour changes or fades with time, this is noted.

Height

After the flower colour, the eventual height – metric and imperial – of each plant is stated. Where applicable, these figures include the height of the flower, which in plants like herbaceous perennials may be held well above the level of the leaves. In the case of aquatic plants the figures refer to the height of the plant above water.

The range of heights given for some plants is very large and necessarily so, since eventual height is subject to many variable factors, such as the rainfall and the coldness or warmth of a particular district, the richness and moisture-retentiveness of the soil, the aspect of the site and the care with which initial planting has been carried out.

Even when a single figure is given in each column it must be taken only as an indication of height. However, it is possible to give estimates of the eventual height of plants grown in good conditions, and these are what the figures in these columns represent. (Some plants, particularly many so-called dwarf conifers, grow very slowly. The heights given for these plants in most trade catalogues indicate how large the plants will be after a number of years; the present lists give their eventual heights.)

Only two other characteristics are noted throughout the lists. First, all plants which require lime-free – or, in the case of certain plants, at least neutral – soil are marked with an asterisk. Second, all evergreen and semi-evergreen plants are marked with appropriate abbreviations (see p. vii). Semi-evergreen plants are normally evergreen, but in a cold district or during a cold winter they may lose some or all of their leaves. Plants which vary between being evergreen and semi-evergreen, or being semi-evergreen and deciduous, are also marked. Unmarked plants are deciduous. Other abbreviations and signs which appear in a few of the lists are also defined in the list of abbreviations and symbols, on p. vii.

As well as photographs and summaries of details, the illustrated sections of lists contain short descriptions of plants. These descriptions give information about, for instance, growing conditions, rates of growth, and related species and varieties. Where necessary, features such as leaves, fruits and bark are described in some detail. If no details about growing conditions have been provided, then the plant in question either has no special requirements or it is one of a large group of plants – for example, roses – the needs of which are described in all general gardening books.

After each short description, any additional lists in which the plant appears are mentioned (the list headings are given in an abbreviated form; the full titles should be referred to for more precise information). These abbreviated list headings provide a quick summary of the decorative features, possible uses, etc. of each plant.

In the unillustrated sections of lists, only the main botanical name of each plant is given. The height of the plant is also mentioned. Finally, a page number is given for an illustration and fuller information. If the plant is particularly attractive, then the symbol ★ is included.

Acknowledgements
The author and publishers would like to thank the following for kindly supplying illustrations for the book:

Heather Angel; Allwood Brothers (Hassocks) Ltd; Ardea London Ltd; A–Z Collection Ltd; Ken Beckett; Eric Brown; British Gladiolus Society; Brinsley Burbidge; Marshall Cavendish Picture Library; Eric Chrichton; Bruce Coleman Limited; de Jager; Philip Damp; D. B. Fox; Samuel Dobie & Son Ltd; J. E. Downward; Valerie Finnis; Ron and Christine Foord; E. H. Gray, Sutton's Seeds; The Iris Hardwick Library of Photographs; Pamela Harper; Hillier and Sons; Anthony Huxley; International Bloembollen Centrum; Kelway; Hazel Le Rougetel; Tania Midgley; The Natural History Museum; Natural History Photographic Agency; Natural Science Photos; Nature Photographers Ltd; Oxford Scientific Films; A. P. Paterson; Roger Phillips; Ray Proctor; Royal Horticultural Society; Martyn Rix; Kenneth Scowen; Donald Smith; Harry Smith; Peter Stiles; George Taloumis; Pamela Toler; Unwins Seeds Ltd; Michael Warren, Photos Horticultural; Tom Welsted; Michael Wright, New Leaf Books.

The author is also grateful to Seaforde Gardens, Co. Down, and to Lamb's Nurseries, Midlothian, for their assistance.

Plants suitable for shallow soils over chalk

Gardeners with very alkaline or limy – as opposed to acid – soils have to contend with the unsuitability of their soils for growing rhododendrons, camellias, most heathers and a considerable number of other plants. Gardeners with shallow soils over chalk have to deal with the additional problem of excessively free drainage. With this second type of soil many of the plants so beguilingly described as 'revelling in lime' would, in fact, be inappropriate choices; these plants enjoy the fertility of an alkaline soil, but not all of them appreciate the dryness of one through which moisture passes extremely quickly.

The plants in the following list do well, rather than survive, in both the alkalinity and the rather dry conditions of shallow soils over chalk. (Occasionally, acid soil may overlie chalk but this combination is a relatively rare one.) For areas, within a chalky garden, which are particularly dry and hot, the list entitled 'Plants suitable for dry soils in hot, sunny sites' should be consulted. Almost all the plants which appear in that list do well in alkaline soils, but there are exceptions: hybrids and varieties of the common broom, *Cytisus scoparius*, and *Berberis thunbergii* and its varieties do best in a neutral soil (that is, one which is neither alkaline nor acid), as do *Ulex europaeus* 'Plenus', a form of gorse with double flowers, and *Liriope muscari*.

Many apparently obvious candidates for inclusion do not appear in this list. Some of these plants have been excluded because they become diseased on dry soils: for instance, without constant moisture Michaelmas daisies are, in general, prone to mildew (the exception to this rule, *Aster × frikartii*, has been included as a suitable plant). Another group of favourite plants for alkaline soils are the clematis but, particularly in the case of the large-flowered hybrids, they require moisture and a good depth of soil to succeed; even the vigorous *Clematis montana* and its varieties do best in a *moist*, well-drained soil. Some plants, like annual sweet peas, the larger antirrhinums or snapdragons, and the so-called florists' chrysanthemums, rather than the border varieties of the genus, are grown almost exclusively for large blooms; these will only be produced on soils which have plenty of moisture-retentive nourishment dug into them.

Occasionally, some members of a mostly unsuitable genus sound as if they might do well in chalk soils: in general, lilies, for example, prefer or need acid soils, but *Lilium candidum*, the madonna lily, does best in an alkaline soil.

However, no lily of any sort must be allowed to dry out and, since this can be difficult to ensure on shallow soils over chalk, *Lilium candidum* is, in fact, as unsuitable as all other members of the genus for inclusion in the present list.

There are also some plants which, most discouragingly, show their dislike of a shallow, chalk soil only some considerable time after they have been planted there. On dry, chalky soils, the various japonicas and flowering quinces often produce yellow leaves after having looked healthy when younger; and, after a few years on a shallow soil, the fast-growing Leyland cypress may become top heavy and *Calocedrus decurrens* begin to lose foliage from its upper branches.

Although the fertility of alkaline soil means that even gardeners contending with chalk have a large number of suitable plants to choose from, the range of plants with certain features is rather restricted. And, of course, there are the forbidden fruits of rhododendrons, camellias and most related plants. Indeed, the main problem for many gardeners who live in areas of shallow soil over chalk is not the high alkalinity or quick drainage of their soil, but their inability to overcome a longing for, say, rhododendrons or heathers.

This longing can most easily be satisfied by growing otherwise prohibited plants in tubs, or similar containers, filled with some lime-free growing medium (see list entitled 'Trees, shrubs and climbers suitable for growing in containers' for a number of suggestions). Alternatively, certain small, manageable areas of the garden can have the alkalinity of the soil reduced and its moisture-retentiveness improved by the addition of peat and leaf-mould. In these areas the lime-tolerant, winter-flowering heaths or heathers and so on can be planted (for suitable plants see entries *not* marked with an asterisk in the 'Acid soils' list). The construction of anything other than the smallest of peat beds or walls is a more elaborate and ambitious project which only the enthusiast should attempt.

Finally, it is worth remembering that many plants associated with woodlands and acid, leaf-mouldy soils are not, in fact, adverse to alkaline conditions. The most important requirement of plants like hostas and astilbes, for example, is not acidity but moisture. By incorporating plenty of moisture-retaining substances such as garden compost, leaf-mould and peat, a range of plants even wider than the sizeable one given here can be grown in shallow soils over chalk.

PINUS nigra
[Austrian Pine]

○

type of plant: HCo
height: 21-30 m/70-100 ft
E

The Austrian pine can be planted in most soils and in several awkward sites, including exposed, seaside gardens and windy gardens on chalk; it is especially useful as a windbreak. When young it grows quickly. With age, it changes from a conical to a flat-topped tree. The very dark green of its leaves can seem somewhat gloomy in certain situations.
  Seaside.

PRUNUS (Japanese Cherry) e.g. 'Tai-Haku'★
[Great White Cherry]

○

type of plant: HT
flowering season: mid-spring
flower colour: white
height: 9-12 m/30-40 ft

The coppery colour of this vigorous and broad-headed tree's young foliage enhances the pure white of its large flowers. In autumn, the leaves are sometimes tinged with orange and yellow. Like most ornamental cherries, *P.* 'Tai-Haku' prefers a well drained, alkaline soil.
  Atmospheric pollution – Red, etc. leaves.

CERCIS siliquastrum sc NA
[Judas-tree]

○

type of plant: HT/Sh
flowering season: l. spring
flower colour: rose-purple
height: 4.5-7.5 m/15-25 ft

This slow-growing plant makes a bushy-headed tree or shrub. Although it is hardy, its flowers – which usually appear before its leaves – may be damaged by late frosts. A sheltered position is therefore advisable, and in any case good drainage is important. The seed-pods are reminiscent of mangetout or sugar peas; they often ripen to a rich, reddish purple in late summer.
  Fruit.

PRUNUS (Japanese Cherry) e.g. 'Amanogawa' (syn. *P. serrulata erecta*)

○

type of plant: HT
flowering season: spring
flower colour: pink
height: 4.5-7.5 m/15-25 ft

The strikingly narrow, upright shape of this tree is its outstanding feature. The flowers are freely produced and lightly fragrant. They usually obscure most of the young, bronze-tinged foliage. Any well drained soil is suitable, particularly if it is chalky or limy.

Atmospheric pollution – Red, etc. leaves – Fragrant flowers.

JUNIPERUS communis e.g. 'Hibernica' (syn. *J. c.* 'Stricta')
[Irish Juniper]

○

type of plant: HCo
height: 4.5-6 m/15-20 ft
E

During most of its life this conifer forms a neat and narrow column of densely packed, blue-green needles. As old age approaches, however, it becomes quite tall and much less compact. It is popular for formal plantings and as a 'focal point' in heather gardens. *J. c.* 'Compressa' (see p. 134) is a miniature version of this juniper. Both plants thrive in well drained soils, including those containing chalk or lime.

Hot, dry soils – Grey, etc. leaves.

PRUNUS (Japanese Cherry) e.g. 'Kiku-shidare Sakura' (syn. *P. serrulata rosea*)
[wrongly called Cheal's Weeping Cherry]

○

type of plant: HT
flowering season: e. spring
flower colour: pink
height: 4.5-6 m/15-20 ft

The pendant branches of this slow-growing tree are long and arching. When covered with blossom the whole plant looks like a frothy pink petticoat – a resemblance some gardeners may not find too appealing. A well drained and preferably alkaline soil is ideal. There is some bronzeness in the young leaves.

Atmospheric pollution.

FREMONTIA (syn. *Fremontodendron*) californica

○

type of plant: SITSh
flowering season: l. spring to l. summer
flower colour: yellow
height: 2.4-4.5 m/8-15 ft
E

This upright shrub is usually short-lived in Britain but, when it is grown in a sunny site against a sheltered wall, the richly coloured, waxy flowers can be quite spectacular. Freely draining soil – either alkaline or acid – promotes good growth; it also tends to prolong the life of this plant.

BUDDLEIA davidii e.g. 'Black Knight'
[form of Butterfly Bush]

○

type of plant: HSh
flowering season: midsummer to mid-autumn
flower colour: deep violet
height: 2.1-3 m/7-10 ft

Both the forms of *B. davidii* shown here are widespreading shrubs with flowers which are freely produced, sweetly scented and attractive to butterflies. Hard pruning in early spring prevents excessive 'legginess' and encourages plenty of new growth. These plants do well in light, chalky or sandy soils. *B. d.* 'Black Knight' has exceptionally dark flowers; the blooms of *B. d.* 'Royal Red' are borne in large, glowingly coloured clusters; varieties with blue, lilac or white flowers are also available.

Atmospheric pollution – Fragrant flowers.

BUDDLEIA davidii e.g. 'Royal Red'
[form of Butterfly Bush]

○

type of plant: HSh
flowering season: midsummer to mid-autumn
flower colour: red-purple
height:2.1-3 m/7-10 ft

See preceding plant.

EREMURUS robustus
[species of Foxtail Lily]
○
type of plant: HP
flowering season: l. spring to e. summer
flower colour: apricot-yellow
height: 2.1-3 m/7-10 ft

The unusual height and colour of this perennial
make it a very striking plant. In vases and rooms
that can accommodate them, the great flower
spikes are most impressive. In the garden they
usually stand spectacularly above bare earth, since
the long leaves have often withered by early
summer. *E. robustus* is at its very best in a rich
loam, but it also grows well in other well drained
soils.

   Cutting.

HIBISCUS syriacus e.g. 'Blue Bird'
[form of Rose Mallow or Tree Hollyhock]
○
type of plant: SlTSh
flowering season: midsummer to mid-autumn
flower colour: blue
height: 1.8-2.4 m/6-8 ft

Varieties of *H. syriacus* will thrive in all sorts of
fertile, well drained soils including chalky ones.
The site, however, must be warm and sheltered if
the flowers are to appear in sizeable quantities and
are not to be damaged by early frosts. Both the
cultivars shown here form bushy plants which are
covered in upright stems; *H. s.* 'Blue Bird' is a
particularly vigorous form.

   Acid soils – Atmospheric pollution –
Containers.

HIBISCUS syriacus e.g. 'Hamabo'
[form of Rose Mallow or Tree Hollyhock]
○
type of plant: SlTSh
flowering season: midsummer to mid-autumn
flower colour: pale pink+crimson
height: 1.8-2.4 m/6-8 ft

See preceding plant.

HEBE brachysiphon (syn. *H. traversii*)
○
type of plant: SlTSh
flowering season: e. summer
flower colour: white
height: 1.2-1.8 m/4-6 ft
E

The liberal sprinkling of white bottle-brushes
produced by this shrub is a familiar feature of
many seaside gardens. *H. brachysiphon* will,
however, grow well in industrial areas as well as
coastal districts. It is a neat and bushy plant which
needs no regular pruning, even when used for
hedging. In most areas of Britain, a well drained
soil and sunny site ensure survival during all but
the hardest winters.

   Seaside – Atmospheric pollution – Hedging –
Containers.

ROSA (Spinosissima Hybrid) e.g. 'Stanwell
Perpetual' ★
[form of Scotch Rose or Burnet Rose]
○
type of plant: HSh
flowering season: summer
flower colour: pink changing to white
height: 1.2-1.5 m/4-5 ft

In light soils only a limited range of roses can be
grown successfully but it includes this lovely,
graceful plant with its sweetly scented blooms
which are produced, more or less continuously,
throughout the summer. *R.* 'Stanwell Perpetual'
has a rather loose habit but, when growing well, it
makes an attractive informal hedge.

   Hedging – Fragrant flowers.

PINUS mugo pumilio
[form of Mountain Pine]
○
type of plant: HCo
height: 90-180 cm/3-6 ft
E

This prostrate form of *P. mugo* (for details of
which see p. 85) is as hardy and wind resistant as
the species. It spreads very slowly and in a fairly
open manner. Denser forms of the mountain pine
are available from specialist nurseries. They all do
well in quite a wide variety of soil types.

   Seaside – Containers.

PEROVSKIA atriplicifolia
○
type of plant: HP/Sh
flowering season: l. summer to e. autumn
flower colour: blue
height: 90-150 cm/3-5 ft

Beside the sea and in well drained – even dry – soils inland, the several good qualities of this light and graceful plant can be appreciated to the full. The grey-green leaves are attractively toothed and scented like sage; and the delicate flower spikes top elegantly curved, pale grey stems. The plant flowers over a long period.

Hot, dry soils – Grey, etc. leaves – Aromatic leaves.

ECHINOPS ritro ★
[species of Globe Thistle]
○
type of plant: HP
flowering season: summer
flower colour: blue
height: 90-120 cm/3-4 ft

The bright steely blue of this neat plant's flower heads is particularly striking combined with the almost white stems. The leaves are green above and greyish beneath; they are thistle-like. Any well drained soil is suitable. The seed-heads may be dried, but they become messy and useless for arrangements if allowed to ripen too long in the garden. The fresh flowers last well in water.

Green foliage – Cutting.

VERBASCUM × 'Gainsborough' sc NA
[form of Mullein]
○
type of plant: HP/B
flowering season: summer
flower colour: yellow
height: 90-120 cm/3-4 ft

Short-lived though these plants are, the two hybrid mulleins illustrated here are lovely enough to warrant inclusion in most large beds or borders. They prefer a light, alkaline soil and, in any case, the drainage should be good. V. × 'Gainsborough's' broad leaves are grey.

Grey, etc. leaves (V. × 'Gainsborough' only).

VERBASCUM × 'Pink Domino'
[form of Mullein]
○
type of plant: HP/B
flowering season: summer
flower colour: rose-pink
height: 90-120 cm/3-4 ft

See preceding plant.

IRIS (Bearded Hybrid) e.g. 'Dancer's Veil'
○
type of plant: HP
flowering season: e. summer
flower colour: white and purple
height: 90-105 cm/3-3½ ft

Bearded irises are classic – and very popular – garden plants, modern forms of which are available in many different colours. Some varieties, like 'Dancer's Veil', have ruffled petals; others, including 'Frost and Flame', also shown here, have upper and lower petals or other parts of their flowers which contrast strikingly in colour; and there are a number of varieties, such as the third example here, I. 'Olympic Torch', in shades of red-brown or bronze. They all make good, rather formal cut flowers. Ideally, they should be grown in a light, fertile, alkaline soil. They flower most freely when divided every few years.

Cutting.

IRIS (Bearded Hybrid) e.g. 'Frost and Flame'
○
type of plant: HP
flowering season: e. summer
flower colour: white + orange
height: 90-105 cm/3-3½ ft

See preceding plant.

IRIS (Bearded Hybrid) e.g. 'Olympic Torch'

○

type of plant: HP
flowering season: e. summer
flower colour: apricot-bronze
height: 90-105 cm/3-3½ ft

See *I*. 'Dancer's Veil', previous page.

KNIPHOFIA e.g. 'Maid of Orleans'
[form of Red Hot Poker]

○

type of plant: SlTP
flowering season: midsummer to e. autumn
flower colour: cream
height: 90-105 cm/3-3½ ft

Smaller varieties of kniphofia are now frequently listed in catalogues. This particular example is considerably shorter than, for instance, *K*. 'Royal Standard' (see p. 215); it is, however, rather less hardy. It thrives in well drained soil, and the mild, moist atmosphere of maritime districts produces especially good growth. It does not need staking.
    Cutting.

PAPAVER orientale e.g. 'Mrs Perry'
[form of Oriental Poppy]

○

type of plant: HP
flowering season: l. spring to e. summer
flower colour: salmon pink
height: 90 cm/3 ft

The beauty of the oriental poppies' flamboyant flowers justifies the rather unsightly gap left by the withering leaves in midsummer. As well as the colours shown here, there are varieties with blooms in various shades of red (see, for example, *P*. 'Marcus Perry', 75 cm/2½ ft, following page). All the readily available forms need staking. They should be grown in well drained soil. The large, solid seed-pods are attractive both when green and when dried.
    Fruit.

PAPAVER orientale e.g. 'Perry's White'
[form of Oriental Poppy]

○

type of plant: HP
flowering season: l. spring to e. summer
flower colour: white
height: 90 cm/3 ft

See preceding plant.

SALVIA haematodes

○

type of plant: HP/B
flowering season: summer
flower colour: lilac-blue
height: 90 cm/3 ft

Sage and its relations – including the somewhat short-lived plant illustrated above – grow well in soils where the drainage is good; they are especially suitable for chalky soils. The large, branching flower sprays of *S. haematodes* may become damaged in windy gardens and should, therefore, be staked. This is usually a very free-flowering plant.

LINARIA purpurea 'Canon J. Went'
[form of Toadflax]

○

type of plant: HP
flowering season: midsummer to e. autumn
flower colour: pink
height: 75-90 cm/2½-3 ft

Although the lives of individual specimens of this plant are not long, *L. p*. 'Canon J. Went' will persist in the garden by seeding itself – and coming true from seed. For this to happen, however, the soil must be light and really well drained. The whole plant has an attractive slenderness about it.
    Hot, dry soils.

SALVIA × superba

○

type of plant: HP
flowering season: summer to e. autumn
flower colour: violet-purple
height: 75-90 cm/2½-3 ft

A dense, bushy habit and a mass of richly coloured flower spikes are the main attractions of this plant which grows best in a well drained, preferably alkaline soil. The flowering season is a long one since crimson-y bracts persist after the blooms have faded. Dead-heading often results in a second crop of flowers.

ACHILLEA millefolium 'Cerise Queen'
[form of Yarrow]

○

type of plant: HP
flowering season: summer
flower colour: cerise
height: 75 cm/2½ ft

In contrast to the yellow of most yarrows there is the pale-eyed redness of this rather invasive plant. Its 8-10 cm/3-4 in wide flower heads are popular for cutting. In well drained or dry soils its roots knit into a weed-suppressing mat; this is topped by feathery, dark green foliage.

　Hot, dry soils – Ground-cover – Cutting.

ANTHEMIS tinctoria e.g. 'Grallagh Gold'
[form of Ox-eye Chamomile]

○

type of plant:HP
flowering season: summer
flower colour: golden yellow
height: 75 cm/2½ ft

Plenty of daisy-like flowers, which last well when cut, are produced by the varieties of *A. tinctoria* shown here. Although the leaves are of lesser importance than the flowers, their much-divided shape creates an attractively airy greenness beneath the blooms. As long as the soil is reasonably well drained and the site is sunny, these plants are easy to grow.

　Cutting.

ANTHEMIS tinctoria e.g. 'Wargrave Variety'
[form of Ox-eye Chamomile]

○

type of plant: HP
flowering season: summer
flower colour: creamy yellow
height: 75 cm/2½ ft

See preceding plant.

PAPAVER orientale e.g. 'Marcus Perry'
[form of Oriental Poppy]

○

type of plant: HP
flowering season: l. spring to e. summer
flower colour: orange-red
height: 75 cm/2½ ft

P. o. 'Marcus Perry' is a little shorter than some other varieties of oriental poppy, but it still needs staking if its large blooms are not to be spoilt by heavy rain or strong winds. For examples of white-flowered and pink-flowered forms of *P. orientale* and general remarks about these plants, see *P. o.* 'Mrs Perry', 90 cm/3 ft, previous page.
　Fruit.

SCABIOSA caucasica e.g. 'Clive Greaves' ★
sc NA
[form of Scabious or Pincushion Flower]

○

type of plant: HP
flowering season: summer to e. autumn
flower colour: mauve
height: 75 cm/2½ ft

A limy or chalky soil with good drainage is ideal for this plant which produces its lovely, long-stemmed flowers in profusion, especially when it is young or if it is frequently divided. It sometimes blooms from the very beginning of summer until quite late in autumn. The flowers last long in water.
　Cutting.

CARYOPTERIS × clandonensis e.g. 'Ferndown' sc NA

○

type of plant: HSh
flowering season: l. summer to e. autumn
flower colour: deep mauve
height: 60-90 cm/2-3 ft

All sorts of well drained soils suit varieties of *C.* × *clandonensis*. They thrive on chalk. The stems of these plants are rather weak and often arching but hard pruning in spring encourages strong growth. The foliage is grey-green and aromatic.

　Hot, dry soils – Grey, etc. leaves – Aromatic foliage.

CERATOSTIGMA willmottianum ★
[form of Hardy Plumbago]

○

type of plant: SlTSh
flowering season: l. summer to autumn
flower colour: bright blue
height: 60-90 cm/2-3 ft

The beautiful, clear blue of this late-flowering shrub is a treat worth waiting for. As an extra autumn attraction the leaves become tinted with red, and even the russety seed-heads are quite pleasing. The whole plant makes a rounded shape. It grows best and is least likely to die or to succumb to frost damage if given a light soil.

　Atmospheric pollution – Autumn foliage.

DICTAMNUS albus (syn. *D. fraxinella*) ★
[Burning Bush, Dittany]

○

type of plant: HP
flowering season: summer
flower colour: white
height: 60-90 cm/2-3 ft

A long-lived plant of great beauty, *D. albus* bears graceful flowers which have distinctively long and wispy stamens. The leaves are freshly and strongly aromatic and, in warm, still weather when the seed-heads are ripening, the vaporized oils surrounding the whole plant can be ignited. *D. albus* prefers an alkaline soil, but most well drained soils give good results.

　Hot, dry soils – Aromatic foliage.

HELIANTHUS annuus e.g. 'Dwarf Sungold'
[form of Sunflower]

○

type of plant: HA
flowering season: midsummer to e. autumn
flower colour: yellow
height: 60 cm/2 ft

The large flowers of this form of *H. annuus* are so fully double that to some gardeners' minds they hardly look like sunflowers at all. However, they last well in water and the whole plant is a good deal smaller than most forms of annual sunflower. For the biggest blooms and lushest growth this plant should be given a rich, moisture-retentive soil, but well drained soils of various types also produce good specimens.

　Cutting.

TULIPA (Darwin Hybrid) e.g. 'Apeldoorn'
[form of Tulip]

○

type of plant: HBb
flowering season: spring
flower colour: red
height: 60 cm/2 ft

Tulips grow well on freely draining, alkaline soils. The Darwin hybrids have big flowers and stout stems and the strong colouring of *T.* 'Apeldoorn' is also typical of many plants in this class. Darwin tulips, such as 'Clara Butt' and 'Niphetos' (see the following page), have smaller and more rounded flowers and are very popular for bedding displays. A dark-flowered tulip of this type – *T.* 'The Bishop' – is shown on p. 58. Cottage tulips, such as *T.* 'Dillenburg' (see the following page), are also used for bedding; their flowers often appear less regimented than those of the Darwin tulips.

　Hot, dry soils – Cutting (*T.* 'Dillenburg' only).

TULIPA (Darwin) e.g. 'Clara Butt'
[form of Tulip]

○

type of plant: HBb
flowering season: l. spring
flower colour: pink
height: 60 cm/2 ft

See preceding plant.

TULIPA (Cottage) e.g. 'Dillenburg'
○
type of plant: HBb
flowering season: l. spring
flower colour: salmon-orange
height: 60 cm/2 ft

See *T.* 'Apeldoorn', previous page.

TULIPA (Darwin) e.g. 'Niphetos'
[form of Tulip]
○
type of plant: HBb
flowering season: l. spring
flower colour: creamy yellow
height: 60 cm/2 ft

See *T.* 'Apeldoorn', previous page.

CENTRANTHUS (syn. *Kentranthus*) ruber
[Red Valerian]
○
type of plant: HP
flowering season: summer
flower colour: red or pink or white
height: 45-90 cm/1½-3 ft

Apart from rather sweatily scented foliage, this plant has few faults. It is ideally suited to dry, alkaline soils and in the wild is often to be found growing amongst the mortar of warm walls. The flowers are attractive to butterflies. The species typically produces deep pink blooms; a red form, *C.r.* 'Atrococcineus' (syn. *C.r.* 'Coccineus'), is sometimes available and there is also a white-flowered variety.
Hot, dry soils.

ERYNGIUM alpinum ★
○
type of plant: HP
flowering season: midsummer to e. autumn
flower colour: blue
height: 45-75 cm/1½-2½ ft

As each beautifully ruffed flower head of this plant matures, both the ruff and the central cone become suffused with steely blue. The flowers are long-lasting on the plant, and in water, and they may be successfully dried. Given good drainage, *E. alpinum* will do well in fertile and in poor soils, and the presence or absence of lime or chalk is not important.
Hot, dry soils – Cutting.

ANTHEMIS sancti-johannis
○
type of plant: HP
flowering season: summer
flower colour: orange-yellow
height: 45-60 cm/1½-2 ft

The brightly coloured flowers of this plant are usually produced in large quantities. They contrast nicely with the delicate shape and soft greyish colour of the foliage. Good drainage and sunshine are required for the most floriferous results.

CENTAUREA dealbata e.g. 'John Coutts' ★
○
type of plant: HP
flowering season: summer
flower colour: pink
height: 45-60 cm/1½-2 ft

This sturdy and vigorous plant will cover any piece of sunny, well drained and preferably alkaline ground both efficiently and decoratively. Its flowers are borne on strong stems more or less continuously throughout the summer and sometimes into autumn too.
Ground-cover – Cutting.

COREOPSIS verticillata ★
[species of Tick-seed]

○
type of plant: HP
flowering season: summer to e. autumn
flower colour: yellow
height: 45-60 cm/1½-2 ft

By far the prettiest of all the readily available
tick-seeds and longer-lived than them too,
C. verticillata has the usual mass of bright daisies,
but, unusually, the flowers are combined with
quantities of finely divided foliage. The whole
plant is neat and bushy and needs no support; it
prefers a light soil.

    Cutting.

SEDUM × 'Autumn Joy' ★
[form of Stonecrop]

○
type of plant: HP
flowering season: l. summer to mid-autumn
flower colour: rose changing to salmon pink
height: 45-60 cm/1½-2 ft

Already regarded by many as a classic garden
plant, *S. × 'Autumn Joy'* is attractive from spring
onwards when its clumps of densely packed, pale
blue-green leaves first appear. The big, flat flower
heads are good for cutting and for drying; in their
final stages they are a deep red-brown. Good
ground-cover is provided by the fleshy foliage,
particularly if this robust plant is divided every few
years. Any well drained soil is suitable and
S. × 'Autumn Joy' is quite content with poor, dry
and shallow soils.

    Hot, dry soils – Ground-cover – Grey, etc.
leaves – Cutting.

ANTIRRHINUM majus e.g. 'Little Darling'
[form of Snapdragon]

○
type of plant: HHA
flowering season: summer to mid-autumn
flower colour: mixed – red, orange, pink, yellow
height: 45 cm/1½ ft

Varieties of snapdragon like 'Little Darling',
which are really too small for cutting, will produce
flowers in quite adequate quantities and of a
reasonable size in light and dry soils. In areas
where antirrhinums are especially susceptible to
rust disease, a variety such as *A. m.* 'Rust Resistant
Mixed', 40-45 cm/15-18 in, on the following page,
should be planted.

CHEIRANTHUS cheiri e.g. 'Blood Red' sc NA
[form of Wallflower]

○
type of plant: HB
flowering season: spring to e. summer
flower colour: crimson
height: 45 cm/1½ ft

Seedsmens' catalogues list many varieties of
C. cheiri, some of them richly coloured like the
plant illustrated here. They all have a marked
preference for well drained, chalky or limy soils.
The flowers of *C. c.* 'Blood Red' have a strong, rich
scent.

    Hot, dry soils – Cutting – Fragrant flowers.

CHRYSANTHEMUM carinatum (syn.
C. tricolor) e.g. 'Monarch Court Jesters'

○
type of plant: HA
flowering season: all summer
flower colour: mixed – pink, yellow, maroon,
    white + contrasting zones
height: 45 cm/1½ ft

The large and strikingly banded flowers of this
plant remain fresh in water for at least a week.
Ideally, forms of *C. carinatum* should be given an
alkaline soil; good drainage is essential. The
variety shown above has a fairly bushy habit of
growth and is popular for summer bedding as well
as for cutting.

    Cutting.

GYPSOPHILA elegans e.g. 'Rosea'

○
type of plant: HA
flowering season: l. spring to e. autumn
flower colour: pink
height: 45 cm/1½ ft

Annual forms of *Gypsophila* are drought-tolerant
plants which do well in freely draining, alkaline
soils. Their haze of tiny blooms soften harder
outlines in flower arrangements. A widely grown
white-flowered variety of *G. elegans* is illustrated
on p. 233.

    Hot, dry soils – Cutting.

SALVIA×superba 'May Night'

○

type of plant: HP
flowering season: l. spring to summer
flower colour: dark violet
height: 45 cm/1½ ft

The exceptionally dark flowers of this dense and sturdy plant are borne over a long period. They appear a little earlier than the blooms of other *S.×superba* cultivars. All well drained soils suit this plant, though alkaline conditions are ideal.

SCABIOSA atropurpurea e.g. 'Dwarf Double Mixed'
[form of Sweet Scabious or Pincushion Flower]

○

type of plant: HA
flowering season: midsummer to e. autumn
flower colour: mixed – pink, red, lavender, blue, maroon, white
height: 45 cm/1½ ft

This very slightly scented form of sweet scabious is usually grown amongst other plants where its slender habit looks attractive rather than sparse. Chalky soils are particularly suitable, and in any case good drainage is important. The flowers remain fresh for about a week in water. There are taller varieties of this plant which may be more useful for cutting.

    Cutting.

TULIPA (Triumph) e.g. 'Korneforos'
[form of Tulip]

○

type of plant: HBb
flowering season: mid-spring
flower colour: red
height: 45 cm/1½ ft

Triumph tulips – often appearing under the heading 'mid-season tulips' in catalogues – are used almost exclusively for bedding. Their strong stems are shorter than those of the related Darwin tulips (for examples of which see above, 60 cm/2 ft). They can, therefore, be used in slightly more exposed positions, although in really windy sites their large flower heads will quickly become damaged. *T.* 'Korneforos' and other Triumph tulips need a soil that drains quickly; they do well on chalk or lime.

    Hot, dry soils.

ANTIRRHINUM majus e.g. 'Rust Resistant Mixed'
[form of Snapdragon]

○

type of plant: HHA
flowering season: summer to mid-autumn
flower colour: mixed – red, orange, white
height: 40-45 cm/15-18 in

Rust disease frequently attacks antirrhinums, sometimes turning them completely brown and always affecting their ability to flower. It is much more troublesome in some districts than others. Even rust resistant strains, such as the one shown here, may succumb to the disease in certain areas. Healthy plants grown in a light soil will, however, flower profusely and for many weeks, especially if dead-headed regularly.

CONVOLVULUS tricolor (syn. *C. minor*) e.g. 'Royal Ensign'

○

type of plant: HA
flowering season: summer
flower colour: deep blue + white + yellow
height: 30-45 cm/1-1½ ft

Sharply draining, chalky soils suit this trailing plant well. A sunny site is essential since in shade or during overcast weather, the flowers remain closed all day. In good weather they are open from early morning until late afternoon.

    Hot, dry soils.

LINARIA maroccana e.g. 'Excelsior Hybrids'
[form of Toadflax]

○

type of plant: HA
flowering season: summer
flower colour: mixed – pink, red, yellow, violet, blue
height: 30-40 cm/12-15 in

Varieties of *L. maroccana*, including the mixture shown here, are easy to grow, provided that the soil is at least reasonably well drained. Their small, snapdragon-like flowers create bright, spangled masses of colour on bushy plants.

    Hot, dry soils.

SILENE coeli-rosa (syn. *Lychnis coeli-rosa*, *Viscaria elegans*) e.g. 'Oculata Mixed'
[form of Rose of Heaven]

○

type of plant: HA
flowering season: summer
flower colour: mixed – white, pink, red, pale blue
height: 30-40 cm/12-15 in

All varieties of *S. coeli-rosa* are noted for their ability to flower very freely. *S. c.-r.* 'Oculata Mixed' has distinctive dark 'eyes' to its blooms. Some seedsmen offer selected colour forms of this strain, such as 'Blue Pearl' and 'Love', which have lavender blue and rose-coloured flowers respectively. Any well drained soil is suitable.

TULIPA (Fosteriana Hybrid) e.g. 'Madame Lefeber' (syn. *T.* 'Red Emperor')
[form of Tulip]

○

type of plant: HBb
flowering season: mid-spring
flower colour: deep red
height: 30-40 cm/12-15 in

The flowers of this strongly coloured tulip are often 15-20 cm/6-8 in wide. Unfortunately, their impressively large size makes them susceptible to damage by wind and rain. All the fosteriana hybrids do well in positions where their bulbs can become really warm and dry in summer.

Hot, dry soils.

ALLIUM moly

○

type of plant: HBb
flowering season: summer
flower colour: yellow
height: 30 cm/1 ft

In most soils, and especially in well drained ones, this plant will increase prolifically. Its bright yellow flower heads last well in water, but the whole plant has an oniony smell which can become rather too noticeable indoors. The greyish leaves begin to wither as the flowers fade.

CENTAUREA cyanus e.g. 'Jubilee Gem'
[form of Cornflower]

○

type of plant: HA
flowering season: summer to e. autumn
flower colour: blue
height: 30 cm/1 ft

Though less useful for cutting than the taller varieties of cornflower (such as *C. c.* 'Blue Diadem', see p. 255), this plant produces blooms which are longlasting in arrangements as well as in the garden. It thrives in chalky soils. *C. c.* 'Polka Dot' is a similarly sized variety with flowers in a mixture of colours, including pink, purple, blue and white. The photograph here shows *C. c.* 'Jubilee Gem' with some pale, faded flowers amongst its blue blooms.

Cutting.

CHEIRANTHUS cheiri e.g. 'Golden Bedder'
sc NA
[form of Wallflower]

○

type of plant: HB
flowering season: spring to e. summer
flower colour: golden yellow
height: 30 cm/1 ft
E

C. c. 'Golden Bedder' is an example of a dwarf variety of wallflower. It usually flowers a little earlier than its orange, scarlet and yellow-flowered counterparts (all of which have the word 'Bedder' in their varietal names). Like them, however, it is fragrant and grows best in a well drained, alkaline soil.

Hot, dry soils – Fragrant flowers.

CONVOLVULUS tricolor (syn. *C. minor*) e.g. 'Mixed'

○

type of plant: HA
flowering season: summer
flower colour: mixed – white, rose, blue + white + yellow
height: 30 cm/1 ft

This sprawling plant will be covered in flowers throughout the summer months if it is frequently and regularly dead-headed. It will grow in any well drained soil. Fertile, alkaline soils give particularly good results. The flowers close during the afternoon and remain closed all day in dull weather.

Hot, dry soils.

DIANTHUS × allwoodii e.g. 'Robin'
[form of Pink]

○

type of plant: **HP**
flowering season: **summer and e. autumn**
flower colour: **scarlet**
height: **30 cm/1 ft**
E

During its short life this plant will flower
profusely, provided it is given really well drained,
alkaline soil and full sun. It needs only light
support. A newer variety – *D.* × *a.* 'David' – also
has scarlet flowers and is generally regarded as a
more satisfactory plant than *D.* × *a.* 'Robin'.
Several *allwoodii* pinks have scented blooms; an
example of one is shown on p. 238.

Hot, dry soils – Grey, etc. leaves – Cutting.

DIANTHUS chinensis (syn. *D. sinensis*) e.g.
'Queen of Hearts'
[form of Chinese or Indian Pink]

○

type of plant: **HHA/HA**
flowering season: **midsummer to mid-autumn**
flower colour: **scarlet**
height: **30 cm/1 ft**

Single-flowered forms of the Chinese or Indian
pink are generally used for bedding. The variety
illustrated above is vigorous and well branched. It
should be given an alkaline soil for preference and
good drainage is always necessary. Its bright
blooms are unscented.

ECHIUM plantagineum (syn. *E. lycopsis*) e.g.
'Blue Bedder'
[form of Viper's Bugloss]

○

type of plant: **HA**
flowering season: **summer**
flower colour: **blue**
height: **30 cm/1 ft**

This brilliantly coloured and easily grown plant
will flower freely in almost any weather. It has a
neat bushy habit and is at its best in light, well
drained soils, although most soil types are suitable.
The following illustration shows a mixed variety of
E. plantagineum which requires the same
treatment.

Hot, dry soils.

ECHIUM plantagineum (syn. *E. lycopsis*) e.g.
'Dwarf Hybrids'
[form of Viper's Bugloss]

○

type of plant: **HA**
flowering season: **summer**
flower colour: **mixed – white, blue, pink, mauve,
    carmine**
height: **30 cm/1 ft**

See preceding plant.

HELICHRYSUM bracteatum e.g. 'Hot Bikini'
[form of Straw Flower]

○

type of plant: **HHA**
flowering season: **midsummer to e. autumn**
flower colour: **red**
height: **30 cm/1 ft**

The larger, mixed varieties of straw flower (see, for
example, *H. b.* 'Monstrosum Double Mixed',
p. 222) are very popular as dried flowers. The
papery blooms of this smaller form are good for
drying too, but the lower, bushier shape of the
whole plant makes it especially suitable for
bedding displays. A light, fertile soil is ideal.
Cutting.

IRIS (Regeliocyclus) e.g. × 'Chione'

○

type of plant: **HTu**
flowering season: **l. spring**
flower colour: **blue + buff**
height: **30 cm/1 ft**

Sunbaked, chalky soils can produce excellent,
free-flowering specimens of this plant. Dampness
leads to rotting and, since even moderate amounts
of rain during the ripening season (from
midsummer to early autumn) may be harmful,
irises in the regeliocyclus group are best grown in
dry districts only.

Hot, dry soils.

LYCHNIS × haageana
[form of Campion]

○

type of plant:HP
flowering season: summer
flower colour: orange or red or white
height: 30 cm/1 ft

For the short time that this plant is likely to last in most gardens, its sizzling flower colours will justify its inclusion. Individual plants with red or orange blooms may sometimes have foliage which is flushed with a dark, reddish colour. Well drained soils of various types are suitable.

Hot, dry soils – Cutting.

SALVIA splendens e.g. 'Blaze of Fire'

○

type of plant: HHA
flowering season: summer to e. autumn
flower colour: scarlet
height: 30 cm/1 ft

This familiar bedding plant needs a deep, rich soil for its strong stems to carry a really large number of intensely coloured flower spikes. For most purposes, however, any well drained, fertile soil will give good results. Some mixed varieties of S. splendens are also available. The colour range usually includes pink, purple and white as well as scarlet.

TULIPA (Single Early) e.g. 'Brilliant Star'
[form of Tulip]

○

type of plant: HBb
flowering season: mid-spring
flower colour: scarlet
height: 30 cm/1 ft

Often seen in pots and bowls since it forces so well, this bright tulip is also good outdoors. Although it is not a plant for windy sites, it can be grown in positions where the taller, later-flowering tulips would become decapitated. Single Early tulips come in a wide range of colours. Good drainage is essential for all varieties.

Hot, dry soils.

TULIPA (Double Early) e.g. 'Maréchal Niel'
[form of Tulip]

○

type of plant: HBb
flowering season: mid-spring
flower colour: yellow
height: 30 cm/1 ft

The fluffy but neat blooms of this tulip are attractively marked with a soft, amber colour. They are carried on short, sturdy stems and, like the flowers of many Double Early tulips, they are notably long-lasting. On heavy, ill-drained soil T. 'Maréchal Niel' will soon cease to flower and its bulbs will dwindle away even if they have been lifted each year.

Hot, dry soils.

IRIS (Bearded Hybrid) e.g. 'Carilla'

○

type of plant: HP
flowering season: l. spring
flower colour: yellow + blue
height:25-40 cm/10-15 in

All the bearded irises – including the fairly recent intermediate hybrids, such as 'Carilla' – thrive in well drained, alkaline soils. They need plenty of sun and fairly frequent division in order to produce a good number of flowers each year. Intermediate bearded irises are available in shades of blue, yellow and purple. Some red-flowered forms can be obtained and a variety with green markings is shown on p. 282.

Cutting.

SALVIA splendens e.g. 'Early Bird'

○

type of plant: HHA
flowering season: summer
flower colour: scarlet
height:25 cm/10 in

As its name implies, this plant blooms earlier than some other varieties of S. splendens. It has deep green foliage which accentuates the vividness of its flower spikes. In a rich soil S. s. 'Early Bird' will grow luxuriantly and flower profusely, but good specimens are produced on most well drained soils, including those containing chalk.

COREOPSIS tinctoria (syn. *C. bicolor, Calliopsis tinctoria*) e.g. 'Dazzler'
[form of Tick-seed]

○

type of plant: **HHA/HA**
flowering season: summer to e. autumn
flower colour: yellow + crimson
height: 23-30 cm/9-12 in

All the annual forms of *Coreopsis* are tough plants and easy to grow, particularly in a fairly light soil. The variety shown here has flowers with unusually broad bands of the two contrasting colours. It often blooms very freely and it can be induced to flower twice if sown early and dead-headed promptly.

DIANTHUS chinensis (syn. *D. sinensis*) e.g. 'Heddewigii Double Mixed' (syn. *D. heddewigii*)
[form of Chinese or Indian Pink]

○

type of plant: **HHA**
flowering season: midsummer to mid-autumn
flower colour: mixed – red, pink, white
height: 23-30 cm/9-12 in

This double-flowered form of *D. chinensis* is sometimes referred to as the Japanese pink. It makes an exceptionally good cut flower and removal of the faded blooms ensures that it lasts long in the garden too. The most suitable soil for this plant is well drained and alkaline.
  Cutting.

GAZANIA × hybrida e.g. 'Sunshine Mixed' ★
○
type of plant: **HHA**
flowering season: midsummer to mid-autumn
flower colour: mixed – orange, red, yellow, cream, bicolours
height: 23-30 cm/9-12 in

With age, the darker blooms on this plant fade to pink and white. All the flowers close in late afternoon but, when open during the next day, they are impressively large – often 8-10 cm/3-4 in wide – and beautifully coloured. These plants need good soil which is also well drained.

GYPSOPHILA paniculata e.g. 'Rosy Veil'
[form of Chalk Plant or Baby's Breath]

○

type of plant: **HP**
flowering season: all summer
flower colour: pink
height: 23-30 cm/9-12 in

The shortness of this plant's stems means that the flowers are used less often for cutting and for drying than the blooms of the more commonly seen, white-flowered varieties such as *G. p.* 'Bristol Fairy' (see p. 220). The misty, pink flower heads will, however, last well in water. All forms of *G. paniculata* thrive in sharply drained, even dry, chalky soils.
  Hot, dry soils.

CHRYSANTHEMUM parthenium (syn. *Matricaria eximia*) e.g. 'Golden Ball'

○

type of plant: **HHA**
flowering season: midsummer to e. autumn
flower colour: yellow
height: 23-30 cm/9-12 in

During its fairly short flowering season this bushy plant can become completely covered in neat, button-like flowers. Its leaves give off a sharp smell which is not particularly attractive. This is a hardy plant which may be grown in the same place for several years. However, it generally flowers better if raised, early each spring, from seed and planted out towards the beginning of summer. Almost any soil is suitable but light, alkaline soils are preferable.

PULSATILLA vulgaris (syn. *Anemone pulsatilla*)
[Pasque Flower]

○

type of plant: **HP**
flowering season: spring
flower colour: violet-purple
height: 23-30 cm/9-12 in

A rarely seen native of some English chalk uplands, the pasque flower and its various forms (including the lovely *P. v.* 'Rubra' shown right) need excellent drainage and at least some lime or chalk in the soil. Their tuffets of finely divided, hairy leaves are at their largest and densest after the flowers have faded.
  Ground-cover – Paving.

PULSATILLA vulgaris (syn. *Anemone pulsatilla*)
'Rubra' ★
[form of Pasque Flower]

○

type of plant: HP
flowering season: spring
flower colour: red
height: 23-20 cm/9-12 in

See preceding plant.

ALYSSUM saxatile e.g. 'Dudley Neville'
[form of Gold Dust]

○

type of plant: HP
flowering season: mid-spring to early summer
flower colour: buff
height:23 cm/9 in
E

Many of the named forms of *A. saxatile* have
brightly coloured flowers; the apricot-y tones of
this variety are much softer. Long, untidy tangles
of flowerless growth will soon appear on this rather
short-lived plant unless it is cut back hard each
year. When thriving, however, it produces plenty
of densely set, grey-green leaves and these can
form a thick carpet of ground-cover. Sharp
drainage and some chalk or lime are most likely to
lead to success.

 Hot, dry soils – Ground-cover – Grey, etc.
leaves.

ANTIRRHINUM majus e.g. 'Floral Carpet'
[form of Snapdragon]

○

type of plant: HHA
flowering season: summer to mid-autumn
flower colour: mixed – red, white, yellow, pink
height: 23 cm/9 in

The lowest growing varieties of antirrhinum,
including the form shown here, are quite suitable
for dry and shallow soils. Their flowers may be
smaller in these conditions than they would be on
richer soils but, since the stems are short and,
therefore, not easy to use in many arrangements,
the size of individual blooms is not very important.
Pinching out the growing tips on young plants
encourages bushiness. 'Floral Carpet' is a vigorous
strain of *A. majus* and fairly resistant to rust
disease.

 Hot, dry soils.

IBERIS umbellata e.g. 'Dwarf Fairy Mixed'
[form of Candytuft]

○

type of plant: HA
flowering season: l. spring to summer
flower colour: mixed – red, rose-pink, white,
 lavender
height:23 cm/9 in

Even in the polluted air of industrial areas and
some cities, this is an easy plant to grow. It forms a
small dome of branches topped with a mass of
flower clusters which can last up to ten days in
water. The fragrant flowers of the related *I. amara*
'Giant Hyacinth-flowered White' are, in contrast,
arranged in long spikes and they have longer stems
(the whole plant is about 40cm/15in high); they
are equally long-lasting in water.
 Paving – Cutting.

ORIGANUM hybridum

○

type of plant: SlTP
flowering season: summer
flower colour: pink
height:23 cm/9 in

Not entirely hardy, particularly if it has to contend
with winter wet, this plant nevertheless grows well
in most soils, especially those that are alkaline and
have good drainage. Its soft, grey-green leaves
blend prettily with the pinkish flowers and their
green bracts.
 Hot, dry soils – Grey, etc. leaves.

IRIS (Bearded Hybrid) e.g. 'Orchid Flare'

○

type of plant: HP
flowering season: mid-spring
flower colour: pale mauve
height: 20 cm/8 in

The newer, dwarf bearded irises flower a good deal
earlier than their more familiar, taller relations (for
examples of which see this list, 90-105 cm/3-3½ft,
above). The particular variety shown here is only
one of several possible examples of dwarf hybrids
with mauve or purplish flowers. It requires sharply
drained soil and full sun.

MUSCARI tubergenianum
[Oxford and Cambridge Grape Hyacinth]
○
type of plant: HBb
flowering season: e. spring
flower colour: light blue + dark blue
height: 20 cm/8 in

The combination of colours in this plant's dense
flower spikes accounts for the common name. As
long as the site is sunny, most well drained soils
will suit *M. tubergenianum* and it will increase
readily. Towards the end of the flowering season
the leaves can become rather untidy.

COREOPSIS grandiflora e.g. 'Goldfink' (syn.
C. g. 'Goldfinch')
[form of Tick-seed]
○
type of plant: HP
flowering season: summer
flower colour: yellow
height: 15-30 cm/6-12 in

In ordinary, or even poor, well drained soils this
plant will carry plenty of its strongly coloured
flowers for many weeks. The long-lasting blooms
have stiff stems but they are useful for only very
small arrangements.

ALLIUM ostrowskianum (syn. *A. oreophilum
ostrowskianum*)
○
type of plant: HBb
flowering season: e. summer
flower colour: purplish rose
height: 15-23 cm/6-9 in

In contrast with the neatly shaped flower heads,
the leaves of this plant are thin and drooping and,
if a good baking in the summer were not so
beneficial, *A. ostrowskianum* would look best
grown amongst other plants with quite thick
foliage. However, a little shading of the bulbs is
not harmful, as long as the soil is well drained and
the site is warm.

ALLIUM schoenoprasum
[Chives]
○
type of plant: HBb (Herb)
flowering season: summer
flower colour: lilac
height: 15-23 cm/6-9 in

It is probably best to decide early in the year
whether individual specimens of this plant are
wanted for decorative or culinary purposes, since
plenty of flowers will mean relatively few leaves.
Ideally, plants grown for their mild, onion-
flavoured foliage should be given a medium loam
and kept moist during the summer. However, the
flowers will be freely produced in lighter and drier
soils and, in most circumstances, this plant will
increase rapidly. The more impressive giant
chives, *A. s. sibiricum*, has leaves that are less well
flavoured than those of *A. schoenoprasum*.

DIANTHUS gratianopolitanus (syn. *D. caesius*)
★
[Cheddar Pink]
○
type of plant: HP
flowering season: summer
flower colour: pink
height: 15-20 cm/6-8 in
E

This outstandingly simple and beautiful plant is
also one of the longest-lived species of *Dianthus*. Its
sweetly scented flowers cover a dense carpet of
grey-green leaves. Although it is most at home in
very well drained, alkaline soils, chalk or lime is
not essential; good drainage *is*, however, and this
plant grows well in dry walls, the spaces between
paving stones and similar places.
    Hot, dry soils – Ground-cover – Paving – Grey,
etc. leaves – Fragrant flowers.

MUSCARI botryoides 'Album'
[form of Grape Hyacinth]
○
type of plant: HBb
flowering season: spring
flower colour: white
height: 15-20 cm/6-8 in

The more familiar, blue-flowered grape hyacinths
often have untidy leaves but the deep green foliage
of this plant tends to stay a little neater and it
contrasts nicely with the white flower heads. These
give out a just perceptible, sweet fragrance. Any
well drained soil is suitable.

DIANTHUS barbatus e.g. 'Wee Willie'
[form of Sweet William]

○

type of plant: HA
flowering season: summer
flower colour: mixed – red, pink, white,
 bicolours
height: 15 cm/6 in

The annual strains of sweet william, such as 'Wee
Willie', are often only very slightly scented and
their main attraction is the richness of their flower
colours. They have a preference for alkaline soils
and good drainage. Early sowing, in some warmth,
is needed for these plants to flower later the same
year.

DIANTHUS chinensis (syn. *D. sinensis*) e.g.
'Baby Doll'
[form of Chinese or Indian Pink]

○

type of plant: HHA
flowering season: midsummer to mid-autumn
flower colour: mixed – red, pink,
 white + contrasting zones
height: 15 cm/6 in

Considering the small size of this plant, the flowers
it produces are very large – at least 4 cm/1½ in
wide. Plenty of these big blooms will appear on
well drained, alkaline soils of various types but the
flowering season is lengthened considerably by
regular dead-heading.

GILIA hybrida (syn. *Leptosiphon hybridus*) e.g.
'French Hybrids'

○

type of plant: HA
flowering season: all summer
flower colour: mixed – yellow, rose, cream,
 orange, red
height: 15 cm/6 in

The number of hardy annuals that produce both
decorative flowers and attractive foliage is not
large, and plants like this form of *G. hybrida*
illustrated above are, therefore, especially
welcome. As well as delicate, long-necked blooms
these 'French Hybrids' have pretty, lobed leaves.
They are easily grown plants with a preference for
light soils.
 Paving – Green foliage.

IRIS (Bearded Hybrid) e.g. 'Bee Wings'

○

type of plant: HP
flowering season: mid-spring
flower colour: yellow + brown
height: 15 cm/6 in

The delicately marked, outer petals of this little
iris nestle amongst clumps of stiff leaves. In a very
sunny site and freely drained soil, many dwarf
bearded hybrids, including the example shown
here, will increase quite quickly, especially if they
are kept healthy and vigorous by being divided
every two or three years.

IRIS reticulata

○

type of plant: HBb
flowering season: l. winter to e. spring
flower colour: deep violet-purple
height: 15 cm/6 in

Some of the small, bulbous irises are difficult to
grow but *I. reticulata* is a most attractive exception.
Its optimistically open-armed flowers are violet
scented. They are also, unfortunately, obscured a
little by the lengthening leaves in spring. Light,
fertile soils containing some chalk or lime are ideal.
 Fragrant flowers – Winter-flowering plants.

SILENE pendula e.g. 'Dwarf Double Mixed'
[form of Catchfly]

○

type of plant: HA
flowering season: summer
flower colour: mixed – pink, salmon, scarlet,
 white
height: 15 cm/6 in

This is a very easily grown plant which will
produce a large quantity of its prettily petalled
flowers in almost any soil. Only double-flowered
forms are readily available.

SILENE schafta
[species of Campion or Catchfly]
○
type of plant: HP
flowering season: summer to e. autumn
flower colour: rosy-purple
height: 15 cm/6 in
E

With the same attractively notched petals as the preceding annual plant and just as easily grown, *S. schafta* will produce a mass of long buds, over its rather open mat of foliage, from about midsummer onwards. It prefers a light soil. In many years it will continue flowering until late autumn.

TULIPA tarda (syn. *T. dasystemon*)
[species of Tulip]
○
type of plant: HBb
flowering season: l. spring
flower colour: white + yellow
height: 15 cm/6 in

Each stem of this plant may carry as many as six distinctly marked flowers. When opened out from their creamy buds, these blooms usually measure about 4-5 cm/1½-2 in across. Full sun and sharply drained soil give the best results.
    Hot, dry soils.

TULIPA (Kaufmanniana Hybrid) e.g. 'The First' ★
[form of Water-lily Tulip]
○
type of plant: HBb
flowering season: e. spring
flower colour: cream + red
height: 15 cm/6 in

Hybrids derived from *T. kaufmanniana* are noted for their lovely colour combinations and the earliness of their flowering season. The long, red and white-edged buds of the variety shown here are carried on short, sturdy stems. The buds open out in sunshine to reveal the creamy, inner surface of each petal which is usually marked yellow at the base. In sunny sites and very well drained soils tulips of this type may be left in the ground from year to year.
    Hot, dry soils.

AUBRIETA (syn. *Aubretia*) **deltoidea e.g. 'Dr Mules'**
○
type of plant: HP
flowering season: spring
flower colour: violet-blue
height: 10-15 cm/4-6 in
E

This old and famous variety of a very well known plant provides solid blocks of deep colour in numerous gardens each spring. Where dense growth is wanted, this plant must be cut back hard after flowering. Sharp drainage and sunshine suit it well and it thrives in chalky or limy soils.
    Hot, dry soils – Ground-cover – Paving.

GERANIUM cinereum 'Ballerina'
[form of Cranesbill]
○
type of plant: HP
flowering season: l. spring to e. summer
flower colour: pale purplish pink
height: 10-15 cm/4-6 in

The dark-eyed flowers of this vigorous plant are produced over many weeks. They are beautifully veined in a deep, reddish colour but, from a distance, the overall effect is quite pale. Most well drained soils are suitable and a warm site is preferable.
    Paving.

IRIS reticulata e.g. 'Cantab'
○
type of plant: HBb
flowering season: l. winter to e. spring
flower colour: pale blue
height: 10-15 cm/4-6 in

There are various forms of *I. reticulata*, mostly with rather deep blue flowers. The variety shown above has blooms of an unusually pale, but nevertheless bright, colour which is accentuated by the orange markings on the outer petals. It lacks the beautiful, violet-like scent of the species but, like it, requires a fertile and well drained soil in order to flourish.
    Winter-flowering plants.

ALYSSUM maritimum (syn. *Lobularia maritima*)
e.g. 'Rosie O'Day'
[form of Sweet Alyssum]
○
type of plant: HA
flowering season: summer to e. autumn
flower colour: rose-pink
height: 10 cm/4 in

Chalky soils suit this plant well, but they should not be too fertile or growth will then become thin rather than cushiony and spreading. *A. m.* 'Rosie O'Day' is nearly scentless. A more recent variety – *A. m.* 'Wonderland' – has flowers of a much deeper, carmine colour. These plants respond well to dead-heading. The synonym given here is the correct botanical name, and the name more commonly used in the United States.

Hot, dry soils – Ground-cover – Paving.

GYPSOPHILA repens (syn. *G. prostrata*) ★
○
type of plant: HP
flowering season: all summer
flower colour: white
height: 8-15 cm/3-6 in
E

Entirely at home on chalk, this prostrate species of *Gypsophila* looks especially good trailing from a crevice in a dry wall. Since it grows densely and forms a fairly large mat of grassy foliage, it can be used successfully as ground-cover. A pink-flowered variety of this species is illustrated on p. 64.

Hot, dry soils – Ground-cover – Paving.

HELICHRYSUM bellidioides
[species of Everlasting Flower or Immortelle]
○
type of plant: HHP
flowering season: summer
flower colour: white
height: 8-10 cm/3-4 in
E

This is not a plant for a wet or cold garden but, given sharp drainage and plenty of sun, its rooting stems will make a tangled mat of growth, which will be covered in tiny, crisp, everlasting flowers. The leaves are silvery on their undersides only.

Ground-cover.

PHYTEUMA comosum (syn. *Physoplexis comosa*)
○
type of plant: HP
flowering season: midsummer
flower colour: purple-blue
height: 5-10 cm/2-4 in

It is probably easiest to grow this odd-looking plant in an alpine house but it will do well outdoors if provided with excellent drainage and alkaline soil. Outside, it is most frequently planted in crevices in walls.

POLYGALA calcarea
[species of Milkwort]
○
type of plant: HP
flowering season: summer
flower colour: blue
height: 5-8 cm/2-3 in
E

As a wild plant, *P. calcarea* grows on chalky grassland. Its flowers are a vivid blue and they often appear in large numbers. However, as with so many other free-flowering plants, this species can be short-lived. Its branches spread and the tufts of foliage make a fairly dense carpet of greenery.

Paving.

THYMUS serpyllum (syn. *T. drucei*) e.g.
'Coccineus'
[form of Wild Thyme]
○
type of plant: HP
flowering season: summer
flower colour: purple-crimson
height: 5 cm/2 in
½E

With its deep green, fragrant foliage and richly coloured flowers, this creeping plant is a good choice for an area of paving. It thrives in all really well drained soils, including chalky ones. Fewer unsightly patches of matted, bare stems will appear if a light clipping over is given after flowering. More vigorous varieties such as *T. s.* 'Albus' (see p. 142) make better ground-cover than this form.

Hot, dry soils – Paving – Aromatic leaves.

EDRAIANTHUS serpyllifolius (syn.
Wahlenbergia serpyllifolia)

○
type of plant: HP
flowering season: e. summer
flower colour: purple
height: 2-5 cm/1-2 in

A gritty, alkaline soil suits this plant best and, in
full sun, there will be plenty of bright purple bells
at the ends of the short stems. These tiny
branchlets lie along the ground above a fairly open
carpet of basal leaves. *E. serpyllifolius* is not usually
a long-lived plant.
   Paving.

**Additional plants, featured elsewhere in this
book, that are suitable for shallow soils over chalk**

○ sun

ULMUS × sarniensis: 21-36m (p. 90)
FAGUS sylvatica 'Purpurea': 18-27m (p. 168)
POPULUS alba: 18-27m (p. 156)
PRUNUS e.g. 'Kanzan': 7.5-10.5m (p. 91)
PINUS mugo: 3-4.5m (p. 85)
RHUS typhina: 3-4.5m (p. 190)
RHUS typhina 'Laciniata': 3-4.5m (p. 180)
YUCCA gloriosa: 2.7-3.6m (p. 56)
COLUTEA arborescens: 2.4-3m (p. 202)
LATHYRUS latifolius: 2.4-3m (p. 121)
MYRTUS communis★: 2.4-3m (p. 132)
CHIMONANTHUS praecox: 2.1-3m (p. 274)
HIBISCUS syriacus e.g. 'Woodbridge': 2.1-3m
  (p. 133)
SPARTIUM junceum: 2.1-3m (p. 56)
THUJA occidentalis e.g. 'Rheingold': 1.8-3m
  (p. 175)
EUONYMUS europaeus 'Red Cascade': 1.8-2.7m
  (p. 202)
EUONYMUS alatus: 1.8-2.4m (p. 190)
ROSA (Spinosissima Hybrid) e.g.
  'Frühlingsgold'★: 1.8-2.4m (p. 255)
FOENICULUM vulgare e.g. 'Giant Bronze':
  1.5-2.4m (p. 169)
HELIANTHUS decapetalus 'Loddon Gold': 1.5m
  (p. 213)
ROSA (Rugosa Hybrid) e.g. 'Blanc Double de
  Coubert': 1.2-1.8m (p. 129)
ROSA (Rugosa) e.g. 'Roseraie de l'Hay': 1.2-1.8m
  (p. 256)
ROSMARINUS officinalis: 1.2-1.8m (p. 196)
VERBASCUM bombyciferum: 1.2-1.8m (p. 158)
ACHILLEA 'Gold Plate': 1.2-1.5m (p. 214)
CISTUS×purpureus: 1.2-1.5m (p. 87)
ROSA (Rugosa Hybrid) e.g. 'Schneezwerg': 1.2m
  (p. 87)
WEIGELA florida 'Foliis Purpureis': 1.2m (p. 170)
KNIPHOFIA e.g. 'Royal Standard': 1.05-1.2m
  (p. 215)
JUNIPERUS×media 'Pfitzerana Aurea':
  90-180cm (p. 175)
YUCCA filamentosa★: 90-180cm (p. 57)
CENTAUREA macrocephala: 90-150cm (p. 216)
HEBE 'Midsummer Beauty': 90-150cm (p. 87)
ARTEMISIA arborescens★: 90-120cm (p. 158)
CISTUS×corbariensis: 90-120cm (p. 57)
ERYNGIUM giganteum: 90-120cm (p. 158)
EUPHORBIA wulfenii: 90-120cm (p. 158)
HELIANTHUS annuus e.g. 'Autumn Beauty':
  90-120cm (p. 217)
HELICTOTRICHON sempervirens: 90-120cm
  (p. 159)
PHLOMIS fruticosa: 90-120cm (p. 159)
IRIS (Bearded Hybrid) e.g. 'Jane Phillips'★:
  90-105cm (p. 218)
IRIS (Bearded Hybrid) e.g. 'Party Dress':
  90-105cm (p. 218)
ALLIUM aflatunense: 90cm (p. 219)
ALLIUM siculum: 90cm (p. 280)
ARTEMISIA absinthium 'Lambrook Silver':
  90cm (p. 159)
CHRYSANTHEMUM maximum e.g. 'Wirral
  Supreme': 90cm (p. 219)
COSMOS bipinnatus e.g. 'Sensation Mixed': 90cm
  (p. 219)
GYPSOPHILA paniculata e.g. 'Bristol Fairy':
  90cm (p. 220)
LAVANDULA spica: 90cm (p. 257)
SCABIOSA atropurpurea e.g. 'Cockade Mixed':
  90cm (p. 220)
STIPA calamagrostis: 90cm (p. 58)
ACHILLEA 'Coronation Gold': 75-90cm (p. 58)
ASTER×frikartii★: 75-90cm (p. 221)
COREOPSIS grandiflora e.g. 'Mayfield Giant':
  75-90cm (p. 222)
COSMOS sulphureus e.g. 'Sunset': 75-90cm
  (p. 58)
GAILLARDIA e.g. 'Wirral Flame': 75-90cm
  (p. 222)
HELICHRYSUM bracteatum 'Monstrosum
  Double Mixed': 75-90cm (p. 222)
CHRYSANTHEMUM×spectabile e.g. 'Cecilia':
  75cm (p. 222)
ERYNGIUM tripartitum: 75cm (p. 58)
STIPA pennata: 75cm (p. 223)

TULIPA (Darwin) e.g. 'The Bishop': 75cm (p. 58)
DIANTHUS e.g. 'Beauty of Cambridge': 60-90cm
  (p. 223)
DIANTHUS e.g. 'Fiery Cross': 60-90cm (p. 224)
DIANTHUS e.g. 'Harmony': 60-90cm (p. 224)
DIANTHUS e.g. 'Salmon Clove': 60-90cm
  (p. 258)
DICTAMNUS albus purpureus: 60-90cm (p. 196)
EREMURUS bungei: 60-90cm (p. 224)
HALIMIUM ocymoides: 60-90cm (p. 59)
HEBE 'Autumn Glory': 60-90cm (p. 92)
JUNIPERUS communis e.g. 'Compressa':
  60-90cm (p. 134)
KOCHIA scoparia trichophylla: 60–90cm (p. 190)
ACHILLEA ptarmica 'The Pearl': 60-75cm
  (p. 225)
CENTAUREA cyanus e.g. 'Blue Diadem':
  60-75cm (p. 225)
CHRYSANTHEMUM maximum e.g. 'Esther
  Read': 60-75cm (p. 225)
CHRYSANTHEMUM rubellum e.g. 'Clara
  Curtis': 60-75cm (p. 258)
KNIPHOFIA galpinii: 60-75cm (p. 225)
PYRETHRUM roseum e.g. 'Brenda': 60-75cm
  (p. 226)
PYRETHRUM roseum e.g. 'E. M. Robinson':
  60-75cm (p. 226)
SALVIA officinalis 'Purpurascens': 60–75cm
  (p. 170)
SAPONARIA vaccaria e.g. 'Pink Beauty':
  60-75cm (p. 226)
TULIPA (Cottage) e.g. 'Greenland'★: 60-75cm
  (p. 281)
TULIPA (Lily-flowered) e.g. 'White
  Triumphator': 60-75cm (p. 226)
ACHILLEA 'Moonshine'★: 60cm (p. 159)
ARTEMISIA dracunculus: 60cm (p. 197)
CATANANCHE caerulea: 60cm (p. 227)
CENTAUREA moschata: 60cm (p. 227)
CHRYSANTHEMUM carinatum e.g. 'Double
  Mixed': 60cm (p. 227)
COREOPSIS drummondii: 60cm (p. 228)
EUPHORBIA marginata: 60cm (p. 147)
GLADIOLUS byzantinus: 60cm (p. 228)
HYPERICUM×moserianum 'Tricolor'★:60cm
  (p. 147)
LATHYRUS latifolius: 60cm (p. 121)
LAVANDULA spica 'Vera': 60cm (p. 100)
PAPAVER nudicaule e.g. 'Champagne Bubbles'★:
  60cm (p. 229)
TULIPA (Parrot) e.g. 'Fantasy': 60cm (p. 229)
TULIPA (Darwin Hybrid) e.g. 'Gudoshnik': 60cm
  (p. 59)
THUJA plicata e.g. 'Rogersii': 45-90cm (p. 175)
LYCHNIS coronaria: 45-75cm (p. 159)
LYCHNIS coronaria 'Alba': 45-75cm (p. 160)
ANAPHALIS yedoensis: 45-60cm (p. 230)
BALLOTA pseudodictamnus: 45-60cm (p. 160)
CENTAUREA dealbata e.g. 'Steenbergii':
  45-60cm (p. 230)
CENTAUREA gymnocarpa: 45-60cm (p. 160)
DIANTHUS barbatus e.g. 'Auricula-eyed':
  45-60cm (p. 231)
DIMORPHOTHECA barberiae: 45-60cm (p. 59)
HYSSOPUS officinalis: 45-60cm (p. 197)
IRIS (Bearded Hybrid) e.g. 'Scintilla': 45-60cm
  (p. 231)
LAVANDULA spica 'Munstead': 45-60cm
  (p. 197)
SALVIA officinalis 'Tricolor'★: 45-60cm (p. 148)
SANTOLINA chamaecyparissus★: 45-60cm
  (p. 125)
SENECIO cineraria 'White Diamond': 45-60cm
  (p. 160)
ALLIUM albopilosum: 45cm (p. 232)
BRIZA maxima: 45cm (p. 233)
CHEIRANTHUS cheiri e.g. 'Cloth of Gold': 45cm
  (p. 259)
GYPSOPHILA elegans e.g. 'Covent Garden':
  45cm (p. 233)
IXIA Hybrids: 45cm (p. 233)
PYRETHRUM parthenifolium 'Aureum': 45cm
  (p. 176)
SALVIA horminum e.g. 'Blue Bouquet': 45cm
  (p. 170)

SALVIA horminum e.g. 'Monarch Bouquet
  Mixed': 45 cm (p. 234)
TULIPA (Double Late) e.g. 'Eros': 45 cm (p. 259)
TULIPA (Rembrandt) e.g. 'May Blossom': 45 cm
  (p. 234)
TULIPA (Parrot) e.g. 'Orange Favourite': 45 cm
  (p. 234)
TULIPA (Lily-flowered) e.g. 'Queen of Sheba':
  45 cm (p. 234)
CHEIRANTHUS cheiri e.g. 'Fire King': 40-45 cm
  (p. 235)
CHEIRANTHUS × allionii: 40 cm (p. 59)
CHEIRANTHUS × allionii e.g. 'Golden Bedder':
  40 cm (p. 259)
TULIPA (Greigii Hybrid) e.g. 'Oriental
  Splendour': 40 cm (p. 59)
TULIPA sylvestris: 40 cm (p. 260)
CONVOLVULUS cneorum: 30-60 cm (p. 161)
LAVANDULA spica 'Hidcote' ★: 30-60 cm
  (p. 126)
ORIGANUM majorana: 30-60 cm (p. 198)
ANAPHALIS triplinervis ★: 30-45 cm (p. 161)
BRIZA media: 30-45 cm (p. 236)
HELIPTERUM manglesii: 30–45 cm (p. 60)
HELIPTERUM roseum e.g. 'Large-flowered
  Mixed': 30-45 cm (p. 236)
IRIS (Spanish) e.g. 'King of Blues' ★: 30-45 cm
  (p. 260)
MUSCARI comosum 'Monstrosum': 30-45 cm
  (p. 237)
NEPETA × faassenii: 30-45 cm (p. 101)
CALAMINTHA nepetoides: 30-40 cm (p. 60)
GAILLARDIA pulchella e.g. 'Lollipops':
  30-40 cm (p. 237)
HERMODACTYLUS tuberosus: 30-40 cm
  (p. 282)
TULIPA (Single Early) e.g. 'General de Wet':
  30-40 cm (p. 260)
CREPIS rubra: 30 cm (p. 60)
DIANTHUS × allwoodii e.g. 'Doris' ★: 30 cm
  (p. 238)
DIANTHUS plumarius e.g. 'Mrs Sinkins': 30 cm
  (p. 261)
DIMORPHOTHECA 'Aurantica Hybrids': 30 cm
  (p. 60)
IRIS (Bearded Hybrid) e.g. 'Green Spot': 30 cm
  (p. 282)
IRIS unguicularis ★: 30 cm (p. 275)
TULIPA eichleri: 30 cm (p. 61)
TULIPA (Double Early) e.g. 'Peach Blossom':
  30 cm (p. 61)
ZAUSCHNERIA californica: 30 cm (p. 61)
LYCHNIS flos-jovis 'Hort's Variety': 25 cm
  (p. 161)
HELICHRYSUM angustifolium: 23-40 cm
  (p. 198)
TULIPA clusiana ★: 23-40 cm (p. 61)
ANTHEMIS cupaniana: 23-30 cm (p. 161)
CERATOSTIGMA plumbaginoides: 23-30 cm
  (p. 191)
HEBE × 'Carl Teschner': 23-30 cm (p. 101)
HELIANTHEMUM nummularium e.g. 'Wisley
  Pink': 23-30 cm (p. 162)
HELIANTHEMUM nummularium e.g. 'Wisley
  Primrose': 23-30 cm (p. 101)
ORIGANUM vulgare 'Aureum': 23-30 cm (p. 176)
ALYSSUM saxatile e.g. 'Citrinum': 23 cm (p. 102)
GAILLARDIA e.g. 'Goblin': 23 cm (p. 62)
HELIANTHEMUM nummularium e.g. 'Mrs
  Earle' ★: 23 cm (p. 62)
IBERIS sempervirens e.g. 'Snowflake': 23 cm
  (p. 102)
LINARIA maroccana e.g. 'Fairy Bouquet': 23 cm
  (p. 62)
SEDUM × 'Ruby Glow': 23 cm (p. 62)
DIANTHUS barbatus e.g. 'Indian Carpet':
  20-30 cm (p. 262)
THYMUS vulgaris: 20-30 cm (p. 198)
MUSCARI armeniacum e.g. 'Heavenly Blue':
  20-25 cm (p. 262)
TULIPA (Greigii Hybrid) e.g. 'Red Riding Hood':
  20 cm (p. 149)
ERYSIMUM linifolium: 15-30 cm (p. 62)
ARMERIA maritima 'Vindictive': 15-23 cm
  (p. 102)

CERASTIUM tomentosum: 15-23 cm (p. 162)
CHEIRANTHUS cheiri e.g. 'Tom Thumb
  Mixed': 15-23 cm (p. 63)
DIANTHUS deltoides: 15-23 cm (p. 140)
FESTUCA ovina 'Glauca' ★: 15-23 cm (p. 162)
HYPERICUM polyphyllum: 15-23 cm (p. 140)
SEMPERVIVUM montanum: 15-23 cm (p. 63)
THYMUS × citriodorus 'Aureus': 15-23 cm (p. 176)
ACHILLEA tomentosa: 15-20 cm (p. 102)
TANACETUM haradjanii ★: 15-20 cm (p. 162)
ALYSSUM saxatile e.g. 'Compactum': 15 cm
  (p. 63)
IRIS reticulata e.g. 'Harmony': 15 cm (p. 275)
TULIPA (Kaufmanniana Hybrid) e.g.
  'Shakespeare': 15 cm (p. 63)
PAPAVER alpinum: 10-20 cm (p. 141)
VERONICA prostrata: 10-20 cm (p. 141)
AETHIONEMA × 'Warley Rose' ★: 10-15 cm
  (p. 64)
ALYSSUM maritimum e.g. 'Little Dorrit':
  10-15 cm (p. 64)
AUBRIETA deltoidea e.g. 'Maurice Prichard':
  10-15 cm (p. 141)
SEDUM spurium e.g. 'Schorbusser Blut':
  10-15 cm (p. 141)
IRIS histrioides 'Major': 10 cm (p. 275)
SEDUM spathulifolium 'Purpureum': 10 cm
  (p. 171)
GYPSOPHILA repens rosea: 8-15 cm (p. 64)
IBERIS saxatilis: 8-15 cm (p. 64)
SAPONARIA ocymoides: 8-15 cm (p. 103)
SEMPERVIVUM arachnoideum: 8-15 cm (p. 163)
ALYSSUM maritimum e.g. 'Royal Carpet':
  8-10 cm (p. 103)
ALYSSUM montanum: 8-10 cm (p. 141)
ANTENNARIA dioica 'Rubra': 8-10 cm (p. 103)
AUBRIETA deltoidea e.g. 'Red Carpet': 8-10 cm
  (p. 103)
CROCUS imperati: 8-10 cm (p. 275)
DIANTHUS alpinus: 8-10 cm (p. 64)
DRYAS octopetala: 8-10 cm (p. 142)
ERINUS alpinus: 8-10 cm (p. 142)
IRIS danfordiae: 8-10 cm (p. 276)
SEDUM spathulifolium 'Capa Blanca' ★: 8-10 cm
  (p. 65)
PHLOX douglasii e.g. 'Boothman's Variety':
  5-10 cm (p. 142)
PHLOX subulata e.g. 'Emerald Cushion Blue':
  5-10 cm (p. 103)
PHLOX subulata e.g. 'Temiscaming': 5-10 cm
  (p. 103)
ANTHEMIS nobilis 'Treneague': 5-8 cm (p. 104)
ARMERIA caespitosa: 5-8 cm (p. 65)
ASPERULA lilaciflora caespitosa: 5-8 cm (p. 142)
POTENTILLA nitida 'Rubra': 5-8 cm (p. 163)
SEDUM acre: 5 cm (p. 65)
SILENE acaulis: 5 cm (p. 104)
THYMUS serpyllum e.g. 'Albus' ★: 5 cm (p. 142)
RAOULIA australis: 1-2 cm (p. 163)
RAOULIA lutescens: 1-2 cm (p. 104)

MALUS 'Hillieri' sc NA
[form of Flowering Crab]
○ [◑]
type of plant: HT
flowering season: l. spring
flower colour: bright pink
height: 6-7.5 m/20-25 ft

Rather later flowering and deeper in colour than
the popular Japanese crab (M. floribunda, see
p. 93), this variety has a small enough head of
slightly arching branches to be conveniently
grown as a spreading bush. However, it is
normally available as a standard with a clear stem.
Well drained, fertile soils of all types are suitable.
Flowering crabs will also tolerate moderately
heavy soils. The red fruits of M. 'Hillieri' are not
especially decorative.
  Atmospheric pollution – Fruit.

SYRINGA × josiflexa 'Bellicent' sc NA
[form of Lilac]
○ [◑]
type of plant: HSh
flowering season: l. spring to e. summer
flower colour: rose-pink
height: 3.6-4.5 m/12-15 ft

The flower clusters of this hardy and healthy shrub
are less solid in form than those produced by the
more commonly seen cultivars of S. vulgaris (for an
example of which, see the following illustration).
They are pretty even when in bud and later, when
they expand, they emit a lovely, sweet fragrance.
All lilacs need at least reasonably fertile soil. They
thrive when chalk or lime is present.
  Atmospheric pollution – Cutting – Fragrant
flowers.

SYRINGA vulgaris e.g. 'Primrose'
[form of Common Lilac]

○[◐]
type of plant: HSh
flowering season: l. spring
flower colour: pale yellow
height: 3-4.5 m/10-15 ft

This example of a single-flowered common lilac has rather smaller panicles of blooms than other, related varieties. It is only slightly fragrant. However, the flowers are freely produced on the erect branches and they are of an unusual colour. Cultivars of *S. vulgaris* need good drainage and a fertile, preferably alkaline soil. They should be regularly dead-headed.

 Atmospheric pollution – Cutting.

SYRINGA velutina (syn. *S. palibiniana, S. meyeri* 'Palibin')
[Korean Lilac]

○[◐]
type of plant: HSh
flowering season: l. spring
flower colour: lavender-pink
height: 90-150 cm/3-5 ft

The rounded form of this miniature and slow-growing lilac becomes covered in sweetly scented flower heads even when the plant is quite young. All well drained, fertile soils are suitable. Alkaline soils usually produce particularly good growth.

 Atmospheric pollution – Fragrant flowers.

PHILADELPHUS e.g. 'Manteau d'Hermine'
[form of Mock Orange]

○[◐]
type of plant: HSh
flowering season: summer
flower colour: creamy white
height: 90-120 cm/3-4 ft

Confusingly, plants of the genus *Philadelphus* are sometimes referred to as syringas, although they are quite unrelated to the plants in the preceding illustrations. This particular variety is unusually small and neat. Other popular varieties grow up to 3 m/10 ft high. They all have very sweetly scented flowers. They can be planted on most soils; those that are light and alkaline give excellent results.

 Atmospheric pollution – Hedging – Fragrant flowers.

FRITILLARIA imperialis e.g. 'Aurora'
[form of Crown Imperial]

○[◐]
type of plant: HBb
flowering season: mid-spring
flower colour: orange-red
height: 60-90 cm/2-3 ft

Fortunately, the handsome flower heads of the crown imperials are large enough to be admired from a distance. At close range, most people find their scent very unpleasant. The varieties illustrated here show the two main colours of these plants. A darker red form is also available. Rich, well drained soils are ideal and sites where the bulbs need not be moved or disturbed should be chosen.

FRITILLARIA imperialis e.g. 'Lutea Maxima'
[form of Crown Imperial]

○[◐]
type of plant: HBb
flowering season: mid-spring
flower colour: yellow
height: 60-90 cm/2-3 ft

See preceding plant.

POTENTILLA fruticosa e.g. 'Tangerine'
[form of Shrubby Cinquefoil]

○[◐]
type of plant: HSh
flowering season: e. summer to mid-autumn
flower colour: orange in shade, yellow in sun
height: 60-90 cm/2-3 ft

Most of the varieties of *P. fruticosa* have yellow flowers (see, for example, *P. f.* 'Katherine Dykes', p. 130) and even the more deeply coloured forms, including the one illustrated here, become yellower in full sun or under dry conditions. They are all easily grown plants with very long flowering seasons. Many of them form ground-covering hummocks of wiry twigs. Almost any soil will do; those with good drainage are especially suitable.

 Ground-cover – Hedging.

FILIPENDULA hexapetala (syn. *F. vulgaris*, *Spiraea filipendula*) **'Flore Pleno'**
[form of Dropwort]
○[◐]
type of plant: HP
flowering season: summer
flower colour: creamy white
height: 45-60 cm/1½-2 ft

From the bud stage onwards the branched flower heads of this plant look attractive. When dried they consist of a haze of beige bobbles. The ferny foliage covers the ground densely in most well drained or even dry soils. This plant grows well and may increase quite quickly on chalk.

Hot, dry soils – Ground-cover – Green foliage – Cutting.

ARABIS albida (syn. *A. caucasica*) **e.g. 'Rosabella'**
[form of Rock Cress or Wall Cress]
○[◐]
type of plant: HP
flowering season: all spring
flower colour: pink
height: 15-20 cm/6-8 in
E

This single-flowered variety of rock cress is less vigorous and therefore less likely to become a nuisance than, for example, the popular, white and double-flowered form (see *A. a.* 'Flore Pleno', p. 106). Its light green foliage makes tidy ground-cover. Dry, alkaline soils are especially suitable.

Hot, dry soils – Ground-cover – Paving.

CROCUS speciosus e.g. 'Albus'
○[◐]
type of plant: HBb
flowering season: autumn
flower colour: white
height: 10-15 cm/4-6 in

C. speciosus and all its readily available varieties are easily grown plants which are ideal for naturalizing in grass; they will usually increase freely in any well drained soil. When grown in grass or amongst low, evergreen ground-cover, their long-stalked flowers are supported and remain upright. In bare ground some of the blooms may flop sideways. The leaves of these bulbs are thin and grass-like; they are longest in spring. *C. s.* 'Globosus' (see below) has flowers which are rounder than those of the species.

Hot, dry soils.

CROCUS speciosus e.g. 'Globosus'
○[◐]
type of plant: HBb
flowering season: autumn
flower colour: blue
height: 10-15 cm/4-6 in

See preceding plant.

CROCUS vernus e.g. 'Queen of the Blues'
○[◐]
type of plant: HBb
flowering season: e. spring
flower colour: lavender
height: 10-15 cm/4-6 in

There are numerous varieties of the so-called Dutch crocuses. They are available in shades of yellow, blue and purple, and some white and striped forms are also listed (for further examples, see p. 67). The variety shown above is characteristically large-bloomed, free-flowering and easy to grow. All well drained soils are suitable. Sites in full sun are ideal since bulbs there will flower early. In shade the petals will open relatively infrequently.

Hot, dry soils.

CROCUS kotschyanus (syn. *C. zonatus*)
○[◐]
type of plant: HBb
flowering season: autumn
flower colour: lilac-blue
height: 8-10 cm/3-4 in

The flowers of this plant appear earlier but are smaller than those of *C. speciosus* and its varieties (see above). Each petal has an orange-gold spot at the base of its inner surface. *C. kotschyanus* is suitable for naturalizing in short grass over a freely draining soil. Its flowers are produced before its slim, green foliage.

Hot, dry soils.

FAGUS sylvatica 'Pendula'
[Weeping Beech]

○ ◑

type of plant: HT
height: 15-21 m/50-70 ft

The common beech and its numerous varieties (including this well known form with its rounded head of drooping branches) are trees for well drained soils. Damp, heavy soils are not suitable. In autumn the leaves turn a russety colour and, on small plants, they remain on the branches until spring. Specialist nurseries stock purple-leaved forms of the weeping beech.

Atmospheric pollution – Autumn foliage.

SORBUS aria
[Whitebeam]

○ ◑

type of plant: HT
flowering season: l. spring to e. summer
flower colour: white
height: 10.5-15 m/35-50 ft

In its native habitat this pyramid-shaped tree grows on limestone and chalk. However, it will do well in most soils and it is altogether a tolerant and useful plant. Its young foliage is pale and downy and borne in beautifully shaped buds. Later, the upper surfaces of the leaves become green and, finally, in autumn the foliage takes on yellow and russet tones. The bright red fruits are carried in large, hanging bunches. *S. a.* 'Lutescens' (see p. 165) is a yet more decorative variety of the species which is illustrated here in spring.

Seaside – Atmospheric pollution – Grey, etc. leaves – Autumn foliage – Fruit.

FRAXINUS excelsior 'Pendula'
[Weeping Ash]

○ ◑

type of plant: HT
height: 9-15 m/30-50 ft

The pendant branches of this tree create a humped dome of airy leaves which appear rather late in spring. The common ash and its forms, including the attractive yellow-twigged variety, *F. e.* 'Aurea', grow well in any reasonable soil whether it is light or heavy.

Clay – Seaside – Atmospheric pollution.

TAXUS baccata 'Fastigiata'
[Irish Yew]

○ ◑

type of plant: HCo
height: 9-12 m/30-40 ft
E

Pairs of this erect and columnar tree are often used as sombre sentinels in formal gardens or as a frame to a view. Individual plants can eventually become very wide-girthed, and heavy snow may open out their crowns or even damage their branches. The red fruits are poisonous. Yews will grow in most soils and they tolerate considerable dryness and deep shade.

Hot, dry soils – Dry shade – Dense shade – Hedging – Fruit.

HOHERIA sexstylosa sc NA

○ ◑

type of plant: SlTSh
flowering season: summer
flower colour: white
height: 3-4.5 m/10-15 ft
E

In mild areas or in a particularly sheltered site, this slightly unusual plant may grow into a small, upright tree. It does well on chalk but should not be allowed to become very dry. When flowering freely, its blossom can be quite spectacular – and at a time, from mid- to late summer, when relatively few shrubs are in bloom.

FORSYTHIA×intermedia 'Lynwood'

○ ◑

type of plant: HSh
flowering season: spring
flower colour: yellow
height: 2.4-3 m/8-10 ft

Few soils or sites deter the growth of forsythias. The variety shown here will thrive on chalk and in full shade as well as sun or partial shade. It has large blooms which, even in shady positions, will be freely produced along the erect branches. The flowers appear before the leaves.

Clay – Atmospheric pollution – Hedging – Cutting.

COTONEASTER 'Hybridus Pendulus'

○ ◑

type of plant: HT
flowering season: e. summer
flower colour: white
height: 2.4 m/8 ft
E, grown as a standard

When grafted on to a clear stem the long, arching growths of this very hardy shrub create an exceptionally small weeping tree. In their natural, untrained state they cover the ground quite well; they are reputed to grow most densely in partial shade. A mature specimen of this plant, grown as ground-cover, can spread about 3-3.6 m/10-12 ft wide and will be about 45 cm/1½ ft high. Like other plants of this genus, C. 'Hybridus Pendulus' produces berries which are much more decorative than its flowers. In this case the fruits are large and bright red. Almost any soil is suitable for this plant.

Clay – Ground-cover – Fruit.

PAEONIA lutea ludlowii
[form of Tree Peony/Paeony]

○ ◑

type of plant: HSh
flowering season: l. spring to e. summer
flower colour: yellow
height: 1.5-1.8 m/5-6 ft

Tree paeonies can be difficult plants but this vigorous variety is more amenable than some. It makes a large shrub which is usually a good deal wider than it is tall. Its bright green foliage is deeply divided. It thrives on chalk, particularly if the soil has been enriched with very well rotted compost; it should be sheltered from early morning sun.

Green foliage.

HYPERICUM 'Hidcote' (syn. *H. patulum* 'Hidcote') ★
[form of St John's Wort]

○ ◑

type of plant: HSh
flowering season: midsummer to mid-autumn
flower colour: yellow
height: 1.2-1.8 m/4-6 ft
½E

With the minimum of attention – just a fairly hard cutting back in spring – this rounded shrub will cover itself in large flowers for several months. The deep green leaves emit an 'oranges and lemons' fragrance which seems to be noticeable only in cool conditions. *H.* 'Hidcote' will grow in any reasonably well drained soil. It will tolerate fairly dry soils and it is a good choice for gardens on chalk.

Atmospheric pollution – Hedging.

ACANTHUS mollis latifolius
[form of Bear's Breeches]

○ ◑

type of plant: HP
flowering season: summer
flower colour: purple + white
height: 1.2 m/4 ft

This plant's spikes of purple-hooded flowers are not freely produced but the large size and strong shape of the glossy leaves are more than adequate compensation. Individual leaves are often about 45 cm/1½ ft long; they are still longer and more dramatic on the related *A. spinosus* (see p. 184). *A. m. latifolius* prefers a well drained soil but, once established, it will spread and even seed itself almost anywhere. In cold gardens it is worth protecting this plant when it is very young.

Clay – Ground-cover – Green foliage.

DEUTZIA × rosea e.g. 'Campanulata'

○ ◑

type of plant: HSh
flowering season: summer
flower colour: white + purple
height: 90-120 cm/3-4 ft

In any well drained soil this shrub will cover its long, arching branches with numerous flowers, particularly if the old wood is cut right out after the blooms have faded. *D. × rosea* itself has rose pink flowers; *D. × r.* 'Carminea' is a still deeper pink form.

Atmospheric pollution.

BERGENIA × 'Ballawley'

○ ◑

type of plant: HP
flowering season: spring
flower colour: magenta-purple
height: 30-45 cm/1-1½ ft
E

Bergenias are tough and tolerant plants which are suitable for many soils and sites. On light soils, however, some varieties become particularly colourful in autumn and winter. The large leaves of *B. × 'Ballawley'* take on reddish tones in the colder months. Throughout the year the foliage makes good ground-cover. It is also useful in flower arrangements, although the leaves of *B. cordifolia* (see p. 184) are more substantial and longer lasting.

Clay – Dry shade – Ground-cover – Green foliage – Autumn foliage.

SAXIFRAGA longifolia
[species of Saxifrage]
○ ◑
type of plant: HP
flowering season: e. summer
flower colour: white
height: 30-45 cm/1-1½ ft
E

The 'encrusted' saxifrages, of which this is an example, require very well drained soil; they have a marked preference for lime or chalk. *S. longifolia* grows especially well in crevices. Its silvery green rosettes of leaves die once they have produced their large plumes of densely packed flowers. However, some rosettes may have offsets and these can be grown on for future blooms.

Grey, etc. leaves.

MECONOPSIS cambrica
[Welsh Poppy]
○ ◑
type of plant: HP
flowering season: e. summer to e. autumn
flower colour: yellow
height: 30 cm/1 ft

This prolific self-seeder seems charming – with its fern-like leaves and lovely, simple blooms – where there is plenty of space for its offspring, but it can be a nuisance in small gardens. Nearly all plants of the genus *Meconopsis* need moist, acid soils but in Britain the Welsh poppy will grow almost anywhere; it does well on chalky soils.

ANEMONE blanda 'Mixed'
○ ◑
type of plant: HTu
flowering season: l. winter to mid-spring
flower colour: mixed – white, blue, pink
height: 10-15 cm/4-6 in

Shallow, chalky soils provide the good drainage needed by *A. blanda* and its forms. The colours in most mixtures are also available separately from nurseries specializing in bulbous plants. For an illustration of a particularly attractive, deep-blue form see p. 278.

Winter-flowering plants.

CAMPANULA cochlearifolia (syn. *C. pusilla*)
[species of Bellflower]
○ ◑
type of plant: HP
flowering season: midsummer to e. autumn
flower colour: blue
height: 10 cm/4 in

C. cochlearifolia is an easily grown and vigorous plant which is never a nuisance in the way that some other small campanulas – notably the rampant *C. poscharskyana* – certainly are. All well drained soils, including alklaline ones, are suitable.

Paving.

SAXIFRAGA × apiculata
[form of Saxifrage]
○ ◑
type of plant: HP
flowering season: spring
flower colour: yellow
height: 10 cm/4 in
E

Although the 'cushion' or kabschia saxifrages, of which this is an example, need gritty, alkaline soil and can be grown in sunny sites, they must not be allowed to become hot and dry. In warmer districts, therefore, it is advisable to plant them in partial shade. This particular hybrid is rather easier to grow than some plants of the same type. Its tiny leaves form a dense cushion of greenery.

Paving.

CAMPANULA latifolia e.g. 'Alba'
[form of Giant Bellflower]
◑ [○]
type of plant: HP
flowering season: midsummer
flower colour: white
height: 105-120 cm/3½-4 ft

The whole demeanour of this plant suggests its suitability for planting in light woodland, where the white of its flowers will be most conspicuous and where its tall, stiff stems will need no staking. Forms in various shades of blue are also available. Any fertile soil with reasonable drainage will produce good results. The very tallest and strongest specimens are usually grown on moist soils.

Cutting.

ASPLENIUM trichomanes
[Maidenhair Spleenwort]

◑

type of plant: HF
height: 8-15 cm/3-6 in
E

This little fern's tendency to establish itself in the mortar of old walls shows its liking for alkaline conditions. It seems particularly at home in cool crevices and the bright green of its young fronds can be an appealing embellishment on north-facing walls and steps as well as in paving.
   Paving – Green foliage.

Additional plants, featured elsewhere in this book, that are suitable for shallow soils over chalk

○ [◑] sun (or partial shade)
MALUS tschonoskii: 9-12 m (p. 191)
MALUS 'John Downie': 7.5-9 m (p. 203)
MALUS × robusta 'Red Siberian': 7.5-9 m (p. 203)
MALUS × floribunda: 6-9 m (p. 93)
MALUS 'Golden Hornet' ★: 6-7.5 m (p. 203)
MALUS 'Profusion' ★: 6-7.5 m (p. 171)
LAURUS nobilis: 3.6-6 m (p. 134)
SAMBUCUS nigra 'Aurea': 3.6-4.5 m (p. 176)
ARUNDINARIA japonica: 3-4.5 m (p. 182)
SYRINGA vulgaris e.g. 'Katherine Havemeyer': 3-4.5 m (p. 264)
SYRINGA vulgaris e.g. 'Madame Lemoine' ★: 3-4.5 m (p. 240)
SYRINGA vulgaris e.g. 'Souvenir de Louis Spaeth': 3-4.5 m (p. 93)
OLEARIA macrodonta: 2.4-3 m (p. 87)
PHILADELPHUS e.g. 'Virginal': 2.4-3 m (p. 93)
PHILADELPHUS coronarius: 1.8-3 m (p. 66)
OLEARIA × haastii: 1.8-2.7 m (p. 93)
SYRINGA microphylla 'Superba': 1.8-2.4 m (p. 264)
LONICERA fragrantissima: 1.8-2.1 m (p. 264)
WEIGELA florida: 1.8 m (p. 93)
EUONYMUS japonica 'Ovatus Aureus': 1.5-2.1 m (p. 150)
PHILADELPHUS e.g. 'Beauclerk' ★: 1.5-2.1 m (p. 265)
SAMBUCUS racemosa 'Plumosa Aurea': 1.5-2.1 m (p. 177)
WEIGELA e.g. 'Abel Carriere': 1.5 m (p. 48)
WEIGELA e.g. 'Bristol Ruby': 1.5 m (p. 48)
LONICERA nitida 'Baggesen's Gold': 1.2-1.8 m (p. 177)
POTENTILLA fruticosa e.g. 'Katherine Dykes': 1.2 m (p. 130)
SENECIO laxifolius ★: 90-120 cm (p. 164)
STACHYS macrantha: 45 cm (p. 105)
MATTHIOLA bicornis: 40 cm (p. 266)

POTENTILLA fruticosa mandschurica ★: 30-45 cm (p. 105)
STACHYS lanata: 30-45 cm (p. 164)
MALCOMIA maritima 'Mixed': 15-23 cm (p. 143)
ARABIS albida e.g. 'Flore Pleno': 15-20 cm (p. 106)
CROCUS vernus e.g. 'Striped Beauty': 10-15 cm (p. 67)
CROCUS vernus e.g. 'Yellow Giant': 10-15 cm (p. 67)
STACHYS lanata 'Silver Carpet' ★: 10-15 cm (p. 105)
CROCUS chrysanthus e.g. 'Blue Pearl': 8-10 cm (p. 67)
CROCUS chrysanthus e.g. 'E. A. Bowles': 8-10 cm (p. 67)
CROCUS tomasinianus 'Whitewell Purple': 8-10 cm (p. 276)
CROCUS ancyrensis: 5-8 cm (p. 276)
ACAENA buchananii: 5 cm (p. 143)
ACAENA microphylla: 5 cm (p. 106)

○ ◑ sun or partial shade
THUJA plicata: 24-36 m (p. 126)
FAGUS sylvatica: 18-27 m (p. 130)
CARPINUS betulus: 15-21 m (p. 130)
TAXUS baccata: 12-18 m (p. 126)
AESCULUS × carnea 'Briotii': 10.5-15 m (p. 50)
ACER plantanoides e.g. 'Drummondii': 9-15 m (p. 151)
SORBUS aria 'Lutescens' ★: 9-12 m (p. 165)
ACER negundo 'Variegatum': 9 m (p. 151)
CRATAEGUS monogyna: 7.5-9 m (p. 130)
ACER pseudoplatanus e.g. 'Brilliantissimum': 4.5-6 m (p. 172)
COTONEASTER 'Cornubia' ★: 4.5-6 m (p. 205)
CRATAEGUS oxyacantha e.g. 'Paul's Scarlet': 4.5-6 m (p. 95)
CRATAEGUS oxyacantha e.g. 'Plena': 4.5-6 m (p. 50)
BUXUS sempervirens: 3.6-4.5 m (p. 127)
HEDERA helix e.g. 'Hibernica': 3.6-4.5 m (p. 109)
LIGUSTRUM ovalifolium: 3.6-4.5 m (p. 127)
PRUNUS lusitanica: 3-6 m (p. 127)
CORNUS mas: 3-4.5 m (p. 276)
HOHERIA glabrata: 3-4.5 m (p. 267)
HEDERA helix e.g. 'Glacier': 3-3.6 m (p. 151)
HEDERA helix e.g. 'Gold Heart': 3-3.6 m (p. 152)
LIGUSTRUM ovalifolium 'Aureum': 2.7-3.6 m (p. 177)
BERBERIS × stenophylla ★: 2.4-3 m (p. 128)
BUXUS sempervirens e.g. 'Aureovariegata': 2.4-3 m (p. 152)
DEUTZIA scabra e.g. 'Plena': 2.4-3 m (p. 96)
FORSYTHIA × intermedia 'Spectabilis': 2.4-3 m (p. 96)
FORSYTHIA suspensa ★: 2.4-3 m (p. 50)
BERBERIS darwinii ★: 1.8-3 m (p. 205)
× OSMAREA burkwoodii: 1.8-3 m (p. 267)
COTONEASTER simonsii: 1.8-2.4 m (p. 128)
LIGUSTRUM japonicum: 1.8-2.4 m (p. 83)
AUCUBA japonica: 1.5-2.4 m (p. 83)
AUCUBA japonica e.g. 'Crotonifolia': 1.5-2.4 m (p. 136)
LONICERA × purpusii: 1.5-2.4 m (p. 267)
SYMPHORICARPOS rivularis: 1.5-2.1 m (p. 206)
WEIGELA florida 'Variegata' ★: 1.5 m (p. 152)
LONICERA nitida: 1.2-1.8 m (p. 128)
SYMPHORICARPOS × doorenbossii 'White Hedge': 1.2-1.8 m (p. 130)
DEUTZIA × elegantissima: 1.2-1.5 m (p. 268)
ACANTHUS spinosus: 90-120 cm (p. 184)
HEBE cupressoides: 90-120 cm (p. 136)
SPIRAEA × bumalda 'Anthony Waterer': 90-120 cm (p. 107)
HYPERICUM × inodorum 'Elstead': 90 cm (p. 206)
RUSCUS aculeatus: 60-90 cm (p. 84)
COTONEASTER horizontalis ★: 60 cm (p. 194)
EUPHORBIA robbiae: 45-60 cm (p. 81)
EUPHORBIA polychroma: 45 cm (p. 108)
BUXUS sempervirens 'Suffruticosa': 30-60 cm (p. 128)
RUBUS tricolor: 30-60 cm (p. 108)
COTONEASTER 'Hybridus Pendulus': 30-45 cm (p. 25)
HYPERICUM calycinum: 30-45 cm (p. 108)
BERGENIA cordifolia: 30 cm (p. 184)

BERGENIA × 'Silberlicht': 30 cm (p. 109)
SAXIFRAGA aizoon: 30 cm (p. 166)
VINCA major: 23-45 cm (p. 82)
VINCA major 'Variegata': 23-45 cm (p. 153)
HEDERA helix 'Hibernica': 23-30 cm (p. 109)
HEBE 'Pagei' ★: 15-30 cm (p. 167)
VINCA minor: 15 cm (p. 82)
VINCA minor e.g. 'Alba' ★: 15 cm (p. 111)
ANEMONE blanda 'Atrocoerulea': 10-15 cm (p. 278)
CAMPANULA garganica: 10-15 cm (p. 143)
VIOLA labradorica: 10-15 cm (p. 111)
COTONEASTER dammeri: 10 cm (p. 111)
CAMPANULA portenschlagiana: 8-15 cm (p. 112)
WALDSTEINIA ternata: 8-10 cm (p. 112)

◑ [○] partial shade (or sun)
EUONYMUS fortunei e.g. 'Silver Queen': 1.8-2.4 m (p. 137)
MAHONIA aquifolium: 90-120 cm (p. 112)
DRYOPTERIS filix-mas: 60-120 cm (p. 80)
IRIS foetidissima: 45-60 cm (p. 208)
EUONYMUS fortunei e.g. 'Silver Queen': 30-60 cm (p. 137)
EUONYMUS fortunei e.g. 'Vegetus': 30-60 cm (p. 113)
SAXIFRAGA umbrosa: 23-30 cm (p. 185)

◑ partial shade
POLYSTICHUM setiferum 'Divisilobum' ★: 75-120 cm (p. 185)
LUNARIA annua: 75 cm (p. 208)
LUNARIA annua 'Variegata': 75 cm (p. 155)
POLYSTICHUM aculeatum: 60-105 cm (p. 186)
POLYPODIUM vulgare: 15-30 cm (p. 81)
ANEMONE nemorosa: 15-23 cm (p. 55)

◑ ● partial or full shade
TAXUS baccata: 12-18 m (p. 126)
TAXUS baccata 'Fastigiata': 9-12 m (p. 24)
BUXUS sempervirens: 3.6-4.5 m (p. 127)
HEDERA helix 'Hibernica': 3.6-4.5 m (p. 109)
LIGUSTRUM ovalifolium: 3.6-4.5 m (p. 127)
LIGUSTRUM ovalifolium 'Aureum': 2.7-3.6 m (p. 177)
BUXUS sempervirens e.g. 'Aureovariegata': 2.4-3 m (p. 152)
FORSYTHIA × intermedia 'Lynwood': 2.4-3 m (p. 24)
FORSYTHIA × intermedia 'Spectabilis': 2.4-3 m (p. 96)
FORSYTHIA × suspensa ★: 2.4-3 m (p. 50)
LIGUSTRUM japonicum: 1.8-2.4 m (p. 83)
AUCUBA japonica: 1.5-2.4 m (p. 83)
AUCUBA japonica e.g. 'Crotonifolia': 1.5-2.4 m (p. 136)
PHILADELPHUS coronarius 'Aureus': 1.5-2.1 m (p. 178)
SYMPHORICARPOS rivularis: 1.5-2.1 m (p. 206)
SYMPHORICARPOS × doorenbossii 'White Hedge': 1.2-1.8 m (p. 130)
MAHONIA aquifolium: 90-120 cm (p. 112)
POLYGONATUM × hybridum ★: 75-90 cm (p. 252)
RUSCUS aculeatus: 60-90 cm (p. 84)
EUPHORBIA robbiae: 45-60 cm (p. 81)
IRIS foetidissima: 45-60 cm (p. 208)
BUXUS sempervirens 'Suffruticosa': 30-60 cm (p. 128)
RUBUS tricolor: 30-60 cm (p. 108)
SARCOCOCCA humilis: 30-60 cm (p. 273)
HYPERICUM calycinum: 30-45 cm (p. 108)
LAMIUM galeobdolon 'Variegatum': 30 cm (p. 81)
VINCA major: 23-45 cm (p. 82)
VINCA major 'Variegata': 23-45 cm (p. 153)
HEDERA helix 'Hibernica': 23-30 cm (p. 109)
VINCA minor: 15 cm (p. 82)
VINCA minor e.g. 'Alba' ★: 15 cm (p. 111)

Plants suitable for acid soils

The plants in the following list require or prefer acid soils; in some cases, a neutral soil, one that is neither acid nor alkaline, is most suitable. Although all plants, even lime-lovers such as pinks and carnations, will grow in a moderately acid soil, extreme acidity does present problems. This is because very acid soils are infertile. Even the more sheltered parts of peaty moorlands support a very limited range of plants, particularly when compared with the diversity of plant types often found in quite small areas of chalk downland. Some soils are so acid that even plants like rhododendrons cannot be grown successfully in them. It is much easier, however, to deal with extreme acidity of soil – by applying lime in some form, and other nutrients if necessary – than it is to correct extreme alkalinity. (Simple kits for testing soil acidity are readily available from garden shops.)

There are, of course, several different types of acid soil, including dry, sandy soils and heavy clay, as well as moist, woodland soils. A large proportion of the plants in this list are woodland in origin and they therefore appreciate a cool and moist, but well drained, growing medium. There are, however, some plants, such as *Indigofera gerardiana*, which prefer rather drier, acid conditions, and a few plants actually do best in dry and impoverished acid soils. Plants in the latter category include *Ulex europaeus* 'Plenus', a double-flowered form of gorse, and the hybrids and varieties of *Cytisus scoparius* (common broom).

The fact that many acid-loving plants are woodland in origin is reflected in the unusually high proportion of entries in the ◑ (partial shade) and ◑ [○] (partial shade (or sun)) categories of this list. Plants in the latter category require both a soil that does not dry out and, especially in the case of early-flowering plants, some protection from damage by spring frosts. If these plants are placed in a sunnier and more open position these requirements, which are usually easier to meet in partially shaded sites, must be borne in mind. (As a general rule the smaller-leaved rhododendrons can stand more sunshine than those with large leaves.)

Gardeners with alkaline soil often have such a longing for lime-hating plants like rhododendrons and most heathers that it is sometimes assumed that these plants are universally desirable. However, you may not wish to have a little bit of heathery moorland in your back garden, and the many rather strident hybrid rhododendrons may have convinced you that recreating a part of the Himalayas is an equally unattractive proposition. However, before dismissing all rhododendrons as ugly or dull, you should consider some of the less widely planted species of rhododendron in their remarkable variety of elegance, gracefulness and delicacy. Alternatively, you may like these plants but feel that you already have a sufficient number of them in your garden and that the introduction of some other plants would add interest. In either case, this list can be used as a source of information about suitable plants apart from the usually recommended rhododendrons, camellias, heaths and heathers – although, of course, these plants do form a substantial part of the list.

Many of the plants in this list flower sometime during the spring and early summer. If your garden consists almost entirely of plants which either require or prefer acid soil, it may seem rather lifeless for the rest of the year. All plants will grow on a moderately acid soil, and many suggestions for extending the season of interest will be found by consulting other lists in this book. However, you may wish to have plants which actually prefer or need an acid soil, in which case, looking at the 'flowering season' entry may help to solve the problem. You might also like to use this list in conjunction with, for instance, the 'Ornamental fruit' list or some of the foliage lists (many plants noted for their colourful autumn foliage are also particularly suitable for acid soils).

Finally, this list is a source of suggestions for gardeners in areas of alkaline soil who want to grow lime-hating plants – in peat beds or walls, for instance, or in containers filled with a lime-free compost. Some plants will tolerate a certain amount of lime, particularly if a good depth of moisture-retaining soil can be provided. Such plants include the winter-flowering heaths or heathers and the strawberry tree, *Arbutus unedo*; these are members of the normally lime-hating *Ericaceae* or heath family and, as such, perhaps particularly attractive to those gardening on alkaline soils.

LARIX leptolepis (syn. *L. kaempferi*)
[Japanese Larch]

○

type of plant: HCo
flowering season: e. spring
flower colour: male, yellow; female, pink
height: 24-30 m/80-100 ft

Despite its widespread use – in the wetter parts of Britain particularly – as a forestry tree, this larch also looks well when planted singly in big gardens. It grows quickly and is conically shaped. Its young, red-brown shoots become clothed in bright green leaves early in spring, and in autumn the foliage turns a russet colour. The rose-like cones are not large or conspicuous but they are pretty at close quarters. Soils which are moist and either acid or neutral suit this tree best and it will grow quite successfully on poor soils.

Autumn foliage – Bark and *twigs*.

MAGNOLIA denudata (syn. *M. conspicua*) ★
[Yulan]

○

type of plant: HT
flowering season: spring
flower colour: white
height: 7.5-9 m/25-30 ft

Even young specimens of this spreading, slow-growing tree usually carry a mass of large and outstandingly beautiful flowers. Each of these lovely blooms is freshly fragrant. Well drained, lime-free soils produce the best growth on this magnolia, and sheltered sites protect its flowers from frost damage.

Atmospheric pollution – Fragrant flowers.

EMBOTHRIUM coccineum lanceolatum
'Norquinco Valley' sc NA
[form of Chilean Fire Bush]

○

type of plant: SlT/HHT
flowering season: l. spring to e. summer
flower colour: scarlet
height: 4.5-9 m/15-30 ft
E/½E

In mild districts this plant will cover itself quite spectacularly with brilliant flowers. It makes a rather stiff, upright tree which often has several main stems branching at ground level. Moist soils are preferable.

HALESIA carolina (syn. *H. tetraptera*)
[species of Snowdrop Tree]

○

type of plant: HSh
flowering season: l. spring
flower colour: white
height: 3.6-5.4 m/12-18 ft

The wide-spreading branches of this shrub or tree
bear leaves quite late in spring and this helps to
show the numerous bunches of flowers to
advantage. The blooms are usually freely
produced and some of the longer shoots can be
removed for flower arrangements. Strange, green
fruits with 'wings' follow the flowers. This plant
grows best in a moist soil and in a site which is
sheltered from cold winds.
  Fruit – Cutting.

ERICA arborea
[Tree Heath]

○

type of plant: SlTSh
flowering season: spring
flower colour: white
height: 2.4-3.6 m/8-12 ft
*E

Specialist nurseries will offer a variety of *E.
arborea* known as *E. a. alpina*. This is a bushier
and hardier shrub than the species. Both plants
have sweetly fragrant clusters of flowers and they
both need an open but warm position. An acid soil
which remains moist throughout the spring and
summer is essential.
  Fragrant flowers.

LEPTOSPERMUM scoparium 'Nichollsii'
[form of Manuka or Tea Tree]

○

type of plant: SlTSh
flowering season: l. spring to e. summer
flower colour: red
height: 1.8-3 m/6-10 ft
*E

Except in very mild, coastal districts, this upright
and twiggy shrub should be given the shelter of a
warm wall. There its brilliantly coloured flowers
will be freely borne amongst the contrastingly
dark, purplish bronze leaves.
  Red, etc. leaves.

CALLISTEMON salignus
[species of Bottle Brush]

○

type of plant: HHSh
flowering season: e. summer
flowering colour: yellow
height: 1.8-2.4 m/6-8 ft
E

The fluffy flower spikes of this plant will appear in
reasonably large numbers only if a sheltered site is
chosen. In Britain, *C. salignus* is usually grown
against a sunny wall, as are other related species of
Callistemon which often have red or crimson
flowers.

INDIGOFERA gerardiana★ sc NA

○

type of plant: SlTSh
flowering season: midsummer to mid-autumn
flower colour: rose-purple
height: 1.2-1.8 m/4-6 ft

Although, at first glance, its ferny foliage makes it
look as if it would appreciate moisture, *I.
gerardiana* grows best in light and sandy soils that
drain quickly. During cold winters its arching top
growth may be killed, but this is a shrub that
produces new shoots very readily from the base.
Whatever the weather in the preceding winter, the
foliage does not appear until late spring.
  Green foliage.

LILIUM tigrinum splendens
[form of Tiger Lily]

○

type of plant: HBb
flowering season: l. summer to e. autumn
flower colour: orange
height: 1.2-1.5 m/4-5 ft

This variety of the tiger lily grows more strongly
than the species, but it is still prone to virus
diseases. These may not impair the flowering for a
year or two, but they will shorten the life of the
plant. Full sun, good drainage and lime-free soil
are the essential ingredients for success with tiger
lilies.

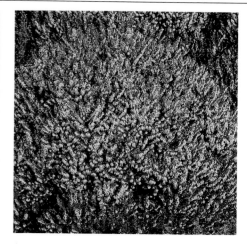

IRIS kaempferi e.g. 'Higo Strain'

○

type of plant: HP
flowering season: summer
flower colour: mixed – blue, white, purple, pink, lavender
height: 60-90 cm/2-3 ft
✳

The 20 cm/8 in flowers of this strain of iris would probably be a more common sight in gardens if *I. kaempferi* was an easier plant to grow. A rich, lime-free soil is necessary at all times of the year, and – awkwardly – this iris demands dampness during the summer but it will usually rot away if it is wet in the winter months. There is a form of *I. kaempferi* with variegated foliage (see p. 147).

Damp and wet soils.

DABOECIA cantabrica e.g. 'Alba'
[form of St Dabeoc's Heath]

○

type of plant: SITSh
flowering season: e. summer to autumn
flower colour: white
height: 60 cm/2 ft
✳ **E**

Even gardeners who shun most heaths and heathers may find the large, bell-shaped blooms of *D. cantabrica* and its cultivars attractive. The particular variety illustrated here has the usual long flowering season, and its dark green foliage and pure white flowers contrast nicely. If clipped in late autumn or spring, it will make dense ground-cover. It must have an open position. *D. cantabrica* is illustrated on p. 99.

Ground-cover.

ERICA mediterranea (syn. *E. erigena***) e.g. 'W. T. Rackliff'**
[form of Heath or Heather]

○

type of plant: SITSh
flowering season: spring
flower colour: white
height: 60 cm/2 ft
E

Varieties of *E. mediterranea* – including the densely stemmed and floriferous form shown here – can be grown in soils containing some lime or chalk. However, in all circumstances, it is important that plenty of moisture-retentive material is present. Most other varieties of this heath have flowers in shades of purple or pink.

Hedging.

ASCLEPIAS tuberosa
[species of Milkweed]

○

type of plant: HP
flowering season: summer
flower colour: orange
height: 45 cm/1½ ft
✳

After its upright stems have died back in autumn, this plant will not reappear until late spring. And indeed it may not reappear at all, since it is difficult to establish. A really warm position and a deep, sandy soil are most likely to produce successful results. The stems, with their intensely coloured flower heads, usually need light support.

CALLUNA vulgaris (syn. *Erica vulgaris***) e.g. 'Peter Sparkes' ★**
[form of Heather or Ling]

○

type of plant: HSh
flowering season: autumn
flower colour: deep pink
height: 45 cm/1½ ft
✳ **E**

Any nursery specializing in shrubs will list numerous varieties of *C. vulgaris* and several of these forms will have colourful foliage (see, for example, *C. v.* 'Gold Haze', p. 176). The leaves of the variety 'Peter Sparkes' are unexceptional, but the long racemes of double flowers are a deeper pink than normal and they look well in arrangements. A regular, spring clipping keeps this plant neat and dense.

Ground-cover – Cutting.

ERICA vagans e.g. 'Lyonesse'
[form of Cornish Heath]

○

type of plant: HSh
flowering season: l. summer to mid-autumn
flower colour: white
height: 45 cm/1½ ft
✳ **E**

Although they are rather less particular about drainage than some other heaths and heathers, varieties of *E. vagans* still require an acid soil, and an open position. Their flowers are usually pink or white (*E. v.* 'Lyonesse' is the most widely available white-flowered form). The dead blooms are an attractive brown; they persist throughout winter. All varieties of *E. vagans* make excellent ground-cover and rather wide-spreading, dwarf hedges.

Ground-cover – Hedging – Cutting.

ERICA cinerea e.g. 'C. D. Eason'
[form of Bell Heather]

○

type of plant: HSh
flowering season: midsummer to e. autumn
flower colour: deep red-pink
height: 23-30 cm/9-12 in

Of the commoner types of heath or heather,
varieties of *E. cinerea* are the ones most likely to
succeed in the drier sorts of acid soil, such as those
containing a high proportion of sand. They should
not, however, be allowed to dry out completely.
Many forms of bell heather have richly coloured
flowers. The blooms of *E. c.* 'C. D. Eason' glow
against dark foliage and even the softer colouring
of *E. c.* 'Pink Ice' (see right) is still very
conspicuous. These plants form hummocks of
growth, but varieties of *E. carnea*, *E. × darleyensis*
and *E. vagans* are denser and more effective
weed-smotherers.

ERICA cinerea e.g. 'Pink Ice'
[form of Bell Heather]

○

type of plant: HSh
flowering season: summer to e. autumn
flower colour: soft pink
height: 23 cm/9 in
*E

See preceding plant.

ERICA tetralix e.g. 'Con Underwood'
[form of Cross-leaved Heath]

○

type of plant: HSh
flowering season: summer to mid-autumn
flower colour: red
height: 23 cm/9 in
*E

The cross-leaved heaths can be grown in damp
soils as well as in those that are ordinarily
moisture-retentive. Many of these plants –
including the present example – have greyish
foliage on their upright stems. The leaves of *E. t.*
'Alba Mollis' (see p. 162) are a particularly pale,
silvery grey.
   Damp and wet soils.

IRIS innominata Hybrids

○

type of plant: HP
flowering season: e. summer
flower colour: mixed – blue, yellow, cream,
   mauve, purple, bronze, white
height: 23 cm/9 in
*E

The narrow, arching leaves of these plants form
sizeable clumps in sandy soils that contain at least
some peat or leaf-mould. The remarkable colour
range amongst hybrid strains bred from *I.
innominata* is not present in the species itself.
   Ground-cover.

LEWISIA Hybrids

○

type of plant: HP
flowering season: l. spring to midsummer
flower colour: mixed – shades of red, salmon,
   pink
height: 15-23 cm/6-9 in
E

If these lovely plants are to grow outdoors, rather
than in an alpine house, they must be given a very
well drained soil or placed in a crevice or on a slope
where any moisture will disperse quickly. These
precautions are necessary since wetness in winter
leads to rotting of the roots. A rich and preferably
acid soil produces the best results.

ERICA cinerea e.g. 'Alba Minor'
[form of Bell Heather]

○

type of plant: HSh
flowering season: summer to mid-autumn
flower colour: white
height: 15 cm/6 in
*E

The bell heathers are noted for their brilliantly
coloured flowers (see, for example, *E. c.* 'C. D.
Eason', 23-30 cm/9-12 in, above) but there are pale
forms, and some varieties, such as the plant shown
here, have white flowers. They can all be grown in
slightly drier soils than most other heaths and
heathers. Nurseries specializing in plants of this
sort will also list a few varieties of *E. cinerea* with
coloured – usually yellow or golden – foliage.
These forms tend not to flower very freely.

RHODOHYPOXIS baurii

○

type of plant: SlTP
flowering season: l. spring to e. autumn
flower colour: deep pink
height: 8-10 cm/3-4 in

When it is given a moisture-retentive soil that is also well drained, this plant will survive most British winters. A combination of coldness and wetness is more damaging than low temperatures alone. Forms of *R. baurii* with crimson or white flowers can be obtained from nurseries specializing in rock garden plants.

Additional plants, featured elsewhere in this book, that are suitable for acid soils

○ sun

PINUS radiata: 24-30 m (p. 85)
LIQUIDAMBAR styraciflua: 15-21 m (p. 189)
CHAMAECYPARIS obtusa 'Tetragona Aurea':
  7.5-10.5 m (p. 174)
CRYPTOMERIA japonica 'Elegans': 6-7.5 m
  (p. 189)
ACACIA dealbata: 4.5-7.5 m (p. 253)
MAGNOLIA grandiflora 'Exmouth': 4.5-7.5 m
  (p. 253)
ACER palmatum: 4.5-6 m (p. 190)
ACER palmatum 'Atropurpureum' ★: 3.6-4.5 m
  (p. 168)
TAMARIX pentandra: 3.6-4.5 m (p. 129)
TAMARIX tetrandra: 3-4.5 m (p. 86)
HIBISCUS syriacus e.g. 'Woodbridge': 2.1-3 m
  (p. 133)
HIBISCUS syriacus e.g. 'Blue Bird': 1.8-2.4 m
  (p. 3)
HIBISCUS syriacus e.g. 'Hamabo': 1.8-2.4 m (p. 3)
CYTISUS scoparius e.g. 'Andreanus': 1.8 cm
  (p. 57)
ACER palmatum 'Dissectum': 1.5-2.4 m (p. 180)
ACER palmatum 'Dissectum Atropurpureum':
  1.5-2.4 m (p. 133)
CYTISUS scoparius e.g. 'Firefly': 1.5-2.1 m (p. 92)
BERBERIS thunbergii: 1.5-1.8 m (p. 190)
LUPINUS arboreus: 1.5-1.8 m (p. 86)
BERBERIS thunbergii atropurpurea: 1.2-1.8 m
  (p. 169)
CYTISUS scoparius e.g. 'Cornish Cream':
  1.2-1.8 m (p. 86)
BERBERIS thunbergii 'Aurea': 90-120 cm (p. 175)
ERICA mediterranea e.g. 'Brightness': 90 cm
  (p. 125)
IRIS kaempferi e.g. 'Variegata': 60-75 cm (p. 147)
DABOECIA cantabrica: 60 cm (p. 99)

ERICA × darleyensis e.g. 'Arthur Johnson': 60 cm
  (p. 100)
GREVILLEA robusta: 60 cm (p. 181)
CRYPTOMERIA japonica 'Vilmoriniana':
  45-90 cm (p. 134)
CALLUNA vulgaris e.g. 'Gold Haze' ★: 45-75 cm
  (p. 176)
CALLUNA vulgaris e.g. 'H. E. Beale': 45-60 cm
  (p. 100)
CALLUNA vulgaris e.g. 'Robert Chapman': 45 cm
  (p. 190)
ERICA × darleyensis e.g. 'Silver Beads': 45 cm
  (p. 275)
ERICA vagans e.g. 'Mrs D. F. Maxwell': 45 cm
  (p. 100)
BERBERIS thunbergii 'Atropurpurea Nana':
  30-60 cm (p. 171)
ERICA tetralix e.g. 'Alba Mollis': 23-30 cm (p. 162)
ERICA carnea e.g. 'Springwood White' ★: 23 cm
  (p. 102)
ERICA carnea e.g. 'King George': 15-23 cm
  (p. 275)
ERICA carnea e.g. 'Vivellii': 15-23 cm (p. 191)
LITHOSPERMUM diffusum e.g. 'Heavenly
  Blue' ★: 10-15 cm (p. 102)

TROPAEOLUM speciosum
[Flame Flower]
○ [◐]
type of plant: HPCl
flowering season: summer
flower colour: scarlet
height: 3-4.5 m/10-15 ft

Gardeners in districts where the weather is cool and moist for much of the year can comfort themselves with the knowledge that only under these conditions and in an acid or neutral soil is the brilliantly coloured flame flower seen at its best. This is one of those 'two for the price of one' climbers that can be grown through another plant, so that, on a single piece of ground, there are two major periods of interest. Ideally, this plant should have cool roots with its top growth in sunshine. It often grows well facing north or east.
  Climbers – Green foliage.

KALMIA latifolia
[Calico Bush, Mountain Laurel]
○ [◐]
type of plant: HSh
flowering season: e. summer
flower colour: pink
height: 1.8-2.4 m/6-8 ft
*E

The resemblance of this plant to a rhododendron seems to account for the frequence with which partially shaded sites are recommended for its growth. In some shade – and a moist, lime-free and well drained soil – this rounded shrub will certainly produce plenty of glossy leaves, but its flowers may appear in disappointingly small numbers. Sunshine and moisture are more likely to lead to success, although this can be a shy-flowering shrub even when apparently well suited. In the United States *K. latifolia* requires shade for best performance.

DIERAMA pulcherrimum
[species of Wand Flower]
○ [◐]
type of plant: SlTC
flowering season: l. summer to e. autumn
flower colour: deep red
height: 1.2-1.5 m/4-5 ft
*E

The wiry flower stems of this plant arch beautifully and are strung at first with silver buds and then with graceful hanging bells which move in the slightest breeze. The leaves form grass-like tufts. A light, moist soil which contains little or no lime is ideal. The corms of this plant resent disturbance, but in very cold areas it is best to lift them in autumn and store them under cover until springtime.

Additional plants, featured elsewhere in this book, that are suitable for acid soils

○ [◑] sun (or partial shade)
ABIES procera: 30-39 m (p. 164)
EUCALYPTUS gunnii: 15-21 m (p. 164)
ABIES koreana: 6-9 m (p. 203)
EUCALYPTUS niphophila ★: 6-7.5 m (p. 209)
ARBUTUS unedo: 4.5-7.5 m (p. 204)
CLETHRA alnifolia 'Paniculata': 1.8 m (p. 265)
LILIUM auratum: 1.5-2.1 m (p. 265)
ULEX europaeus 'Plenus': 90-108 cm (p. 66)
ABIES balsamea 'Hudsonia': 60-90 cm (p. 135)
PRIMULA rosea 'Delight': 15 cm (p. 72)

SORBUS aucuparia
[Rowan, Mountain Ash]

○ ◑

type of plant: HT
flowering season: l. spring to e. summer
flower colour: white
height: 9-12 m/30-40 ft

Rowans are most at home on acid soils, although they will tolerate some chalk or lime if the soil is deep. Their flowers are less attractive than their bunches of orange-red fruit but these berries are, unfortunately, soon devoured by birds. As some compensation, however, the leaves become warmly coloured in mid-autumn. The central branches of *S. aucuparia* are conspicuously upright, and the overall outline is oval or roughly triangular.

Damp and wet soils – Atmospheric pollution – Autumn foliage – Fruit.

CORNUS kousa chinensis
[form of Dogwood or Cornel]

○ ◑

type of plant: HT
flowering season: e. summer
flower colour: white
height: 6-7.5 m/20-25 ft

In a rich and acid or neutral loam the tiered branches of this tree will usually be covered in a mass of flowers. Pimply, red fruits are produced in early autumn and, a little later, the leaves turn bright crimson.

Autumn foliage – Fruit.

MAGNOLIA × soulangiana

○ ◑

type of plant: HSh/T
flowering season: mid-spring
flower colour: white + rose-purple
height: 6-7.5 m/20-25 ft

The popularity of this hybrid magnolia is due not only to the reliable way in which it produces its spectacular, 12 cm/5 in wide flowers, but also to its tolerance of heavyish soils and some lime. Ideally, however, this spreading shrub or tree and its varieties (for examples of which, see p. 95) should be given an acid or neutral soil that drains well. It is important too that some shelter from frosty winds is provided, so that the flowers do not become scorched.

Clay – Atmospheric pollution – Cutting.

EUCRYPHIA × nymansensis 'Nymansay'

○ ◑

type of plant: SlTT
flowering season: l. summer to e. autumn
flower colour: white
height: 4.5-9 m/15-30 ft
E

The narrow and erect shape of this tree becomes clothed in honey-scented, white blossom at a time of the year (in gardens with acid soils, particularly) when most shrubs have finished flowering. However, it may be several years before this eye-catching display begins. *E. × n.* 'Nymansay' will tolerate some lime, but it is at its best in a light, moist soil that is either acid or neutral. It needs protection from cold winds. In mild, maritime districts this shrub may eventually exceed even the larger of the two heights given here.

Fragrant flowers.

AMELANCHIER canadensis
[Shadbush, species of Snowy Mespilus or June Berry]

○ ◑

type of plant: HSh/T
flowering season: spring
flower colour: white
height: 3-5.4 m/10-18 ft

The individual flowers of this plant are quite small and delicately shaped but they are so numerous that the overall effect is almost dazzling. At first, the leaves have a slight coppery tinge; in autumn they become suffused with mellow shades of red and yellow. *A. canadensis* forms a suckering shrub or dome-headed tree. It is easy to grow in any moist or damp, lime-free soil. The edible fruits are not particularly decorative.

Damp and wet soils – Atmospheric pollution – Autumn foliage.

CAMELLIA reticulata e.g. 'Captain Rawes'★

○ ◑

type of plant: HHSh
flowering season: l. winter to mid-spring
flower colour: red
height: 3-4.5 m/10-15 ft
*E

Even in mild areas this open, spreading shrub
needs the protection of a wall and it is often given a
sunny position to ensure that plenty of the
exceptionally large and flamboyant blooms
appear. In a warm site, however, it is especially
important to pay attention to this plant's need for a
cool, moist root run. A westerly aspect usually
gives the most satisfactory results.

Green foliage – Cutting – Winter-flowering
plants.

**RHODODENDRON (Hardy Hybrid) e.g.
'Cynthia'**

○ ◑

type of plant: HSh
flowering season: l. spring to e. summer
flower colour: rosy crimson
height: 3-3.6 m/10-12 ft
*E

This rhododendron has all the qualities that make
the so-called 'hardy hybrids' such popular plants:
it grows well in dense shade (provided that it is
given a moist, lime-free soil and its roots are
mulched with peat or leaf-mould); it has large
flower trusses which are freely produced,
particularly in sheltered, lightly shaded positions;
and it is, of course, fully hardy throughout Britain.
An example of a mauve-flowered rhododendron of
this type is shown on p. 95, and there are hardy
hybrids with pink, purple and white flowers too.

Atmospheric pollution – Dense shade.

**CHAMAECYPARIS obtusa e.g. 'Nana Gracilis'
[form of Hinoki Cypress]**

○ ◑

type of plant: HCo
height: 2.4-3 m/8-10 ft
E

Slow-growing though this conifer is, its
curvaceous sprays of dark green leaves can be
appreciated from the very earliest stages of its life.
If they are crushed, these leaves give out a sweet
smell. Peaty soils are most suitable for cultivars of
C. obtusa; they grow poorly in dry and alkaline
conditions. The form illustrated here is conically
shaped. Some other varieties have golden foliage
(see C. o. 'Tetragona Aurea', p. 174) or are
particularly small (see C. o. 'Nana', p. 136).

Aromatic leaves.

**MAGNOLIA liliiflora 'Nigra' (syn. M. ×
soulangiana 'Nigra')**

○ ◑

type of plant: HSh
flowering season: spring to e. summer
flower colour: purple
height: 2.4-3 m/8-10 ft
*

M. l. 'Nigra' is a small and bushy plant compared
with many other popular magnolias and its elegant
flowers are of an unusually rich yet soft colour. It
will grow most successfully in a well drained, acid
soil and in a site that is sheltered from cold winds.

**PICEA glauca albertiana 'Conica'
[form of White Spruce]**

○ ◑

type of plant: HCo
height: 1.8-3 m/6-10 ft
E

Even when grown in the moist, acid soils and
sheltered sites that suit them best, specimens of
this plant will reach their ultimate height only after
many years. However, their notably neat,
triangular outline and the bright green of their
young foliage will be much in evidence when they
are still very small.

Containers.

CAMELLIA × williamsii e.g. 'Donation' ★

○ ◑

type of plant: HSh
flowering season: l. winter to mid-spring
flower colour: pink
height: 1.8-2.4 m/6-8 ft
*E

This outstanding camellia produces its lovely,
formal flowers in profusion over a period of several
weeks. Like other williamsii varieties, it makes an
upright plant and its faded flowers drop from its
branches. It needs a cool, deep, lime-free soil.
Some shelter from early morning sun may be
necessary, particularly in colder districts, if the
flowers are not to become damaged during frosty
weather. However, in cold areas, a sunny position
is often needed to ripen the wood and thereby
produce blossom; a west-facing wall is ideal.

Containers – Green foliage – Winter-flowering
plants.

LUPINUS e.g. 'Russell Hybrids Mixed'
[forms of Lupin or Lupine]
○ ◑
type of plant: HP
flowering season: l. spring to e. summer
flower colour: mixed – pink, red, yellow, white,
    blue, purple
height: 90-120 cm/3-4 ft

Unless one particular colour is wanted, a mixture
of Russell hybrids is probably the best choice of
lupin for most gardens. These are large-flowered
plants which usually need little or no support.
Separate colours are available from specialist
nurseries. An example of a bicoloured lupin is
shown in the following illustration and a further
example of named varieties is given on p. 244. *L.*
'Dwarf Lulu' is a readily available strain of
shorter-growing plants (see second right). Acid or
neutral soils with good drainage produce the
longest lived lupins but, in any case, (*contd*)

LUPINUS Hybrid e.g. 'The Governor'
[form of Lupin or Lupine]
○ ◑
type of plant: HP
flowering season: l. spring to e. summer
flower colour: blue+white
height: 90-105 cm/3-3½ ft

See preceding plant.

(*contd*)
these plants are short-term perennials. They are
popular for cutting, although they do not remain
fresh for very long in water.
    Cutting.

LUPINUS Hybrid e.g. 'Dwarf Lulu'
[form of Lupin or Lupine]
○ ◑
type of plant: HP
flowering season: l. spring to e. summer
flower colour: mixed – pink, red, blue, purple,
    white
height: 60 cm/2 ft

See *L.* e.g. 'Russell Hybrids Mixed', left.

PICEA abies 'Nidiformis'
[form of Norway or Common Spruce]
○ ◑
type of plant: HCo
height: 60 cm/2 ft
E

This dense and spreading plant with its layers of
dark foliage usually lives up to its varietal name
only when it is young. By middle age, it tends to be
flat-topped and to have lost the central depression
which made it resemble a bird's nest. Spruces of all
types do best in moist, lime-free soils and their rate
of growth is fastest in sheltered positions. Varieties
of *P. abies* are tolerant of the cold, damp
conditions which heavy clay produces.
    Clay.

CALCEOLARIA integrifolia (syn. *C. rugosa***)**
e.g. 'Sunshine'
○ ◑
type of plant: HHA
flowering season: all summer
flower colour: yellow
height: 23 cm/9 in

Of the calceolarias commonly listed in seedsmen's
catalogues, this is the best form for summer
bedding. It is expensive but it flowers freely and
individual plants will be very similar in height. A
warm, well drained soil that is either acid or
neutral is ideal.

PRIMULA auricula e.g. 'Mixed Hybrids'
[form of Auricula]
○ ◑
type of plant: HP
flowering season: spring
flower colour: mixed – yellow, gold, pink, red,
    bronze, blue, purple
height: 15-23 cm/6-9 in
E

In a mixture of *P. auricula* hybrids not only the
flowers but also the leaves will vary considerably.
Some plants will have foliage which is only very
slightly grey, while the leaves of other varieties will
be quite pale. Whatever its colour, the foliage of
these plants forms good, ground-covering clumps
especially in rather acid, moisture-retentive soils.
Mixtures of so-called 'Garden Auriculas' usually
include some plants with richly scented blooms.
    Ground-cover – Fragrant flowers.

NARCISSUS cyclamineus ★
[species of Daffodil]

○ ◑

type of plant: HBb
flowering season: l. winter to e. spring
flower colour: yellow
height: 10-20 cm/4-8 in

As long as it has moisture this lovely, miniature
daffodil is quite easy to grow. It is particularly at
home in a soil that contains plenty of peat or
leaf-mould and it can be naturalized under such
conditions.

Winter-flowering plants.

> **Additional plants, featured elsewhere in this
> book, that are suitable for acid soils**
>
> ○ ◑ sun or partial shade
> TAXODIUM distichum: 21-30 m (p. 72)
> PICEA omorika: 15-21 m (p. 94)
> NYSSA sylvatica: 10.5-18 m (p. 193)
> PICEA breweriana ★: 9-15 m (p. 183)
> PICEA pungens 'Koster': 7.5-9 m (p. 166)
> MAGNOLIA × soulgangiana e.g. 'Alexandrina':
>   6-7.5 m (p. 94)
> MAGNOLIA × soulganiana e.g. 'Lennei': 6-7.5 m
>   (p. 95)
> SORBUS vilmorinii ★: 4.5-6 m (p. 205)
> EUCRYPHIA glutinosa: 3.6-5.4 m (p. 193)
> RHODODENDRON (Hardy Hybrid)
>   'Fastuosum Flore Pleno': 3-3.6 m (p. 94)
> RHODODENDRON ponticum: 3-3.6 m (p. 128)
> HAMAMELIS mollis ★: 2.4-3.6 m (p. 276)
> CORYLOPSIS willmottiae: 2.4-3 m (p. 267)
> MAGNOLIA stellata: 1.8-3 m (p. 96)
> CAMELLIA × williamsii e.g. 'J. C. Williams'
>   1.8-2.4 m (p. 135)
> CORYLOPSIS pauciflora: 1.2-1.8 m (p. 268)
> GAULTHERIA shallon: 1.2-1.8 m (p. 106)
> OSMUNDA regalis: 1.2-1.8 m (p. 73)
> VACCINIUM corymbosum: 1.2-1.8 m (p. 193)
> LUPINUS Hybrid e.g. 'My Castle': 90-105 cm
>   (p. 244)
> HYDRANGEA × 'Preziosa': 90 cm (p. 136)
> PERNETTYA mucronata e.g. 'Bell's Seedling':
>   60-90 cm (p. 206)
> PERNETTYA mucronata e.g. 'Davis Hybrids':
>   60-90 cm (p. 206)
> CHAMAECYPARIS obtusa e.g. 'Nana': 45-75 cm
>   (p. 136)
> MOLINIA caerulea 'Variegata': 45-60 cm (p. 152)
> LIRIOPE muscari: 30-45 cm (p. 80)
> PICEA mariana 'Nana': 30-45 cm (p. 137)
> VACCINIUM vitis-idaea: 15 cm (p. 111)
> CORNUS canadensis: 10-15 cm (p. 111)

**CAMELLIA japonica e.g. 'Adolphe Audusson'
★**

◑ [○]

type of plant: HSh
flowering season: l. winter to e. spring
flower colour: blood red
height: 1.8-3.6 m/6-12 ft
*E

The cooler the district, the more sun camellias
need in order to produce plenty of flowers. If
grown in a cold area, the ideal position for this
outstanding plant is on a west- or even a
south-facing wall (provided its roots can be kept
cool and moist). *C. j.* 'Adolphe Audusson' flowers
earlier and more profusely than many other related
cultivars. It grows fairly strongly and erectly.
When fully expanded, its beautiful flowers are
often 12 cm/5 in wide.

Atmospheric pollution – Containers – Green
foliage – Cutting – Winter-flowering plants.

**RHODODENDRON (AZALEA) e.g. 'Coccinea
Speciosa' ★**

◑ [○]

type of plant: HSh
flowering season: l. spring to e. summer
flower colour: orange-red
height: 1.5-2.4 m/5-8 ft
❄

The Ghent hybrids – of which this plant is an
example – are azaleas with fairly small flowers.
However, they usually bloom freely, and many of
them are very fragrant (for details of an especially
well scented cultivar see *R.* 'Narcissiflorum',
p. 271). *R.* 'Coccinea Speciosa' has a markedly
flat-topped and layered habit of growth; in autumn
its foliage glows with reds, oranges and yellows.
Well drained but moisture-retentive soils are ideal.
The Ghent hybrids are very hardy plants.

Autumn foliage.

**RHODODENDRON (AZALEA) e.g.
'Daybreak'**

◑ [○]

type of plant: HSh
flowering season: l. spring to e. summer
flower colour: orange-yellow
height: 1.5-2.4 m/5-8 ft
❄

This azalea and the ones shown in the following
two illustrations are Knap Hill hybrids. These
shrubs are noted for the rich and varied colours of
their large flowers. Specialist nurseries will list
numerous varieties (including forms with yellow
or white blooms). Some of them, like *R.*
'Berryrose', will have young leaves which are
slightly tinged with a coppery colour. Many of
them will colour well in the autumn. (The foliage
of *R.* 'Daybreak' and 'Glowing Embers' becomes
brilliant with shades of yellow, orange and red
before it falls.) These vigorous plants can *(contd)*

**RHODODENDRON (AZALEA) e.g.
'Berryrose'**

◑ [○]

type of plant: HSh
flowering season: l. spring to e. summer
flower colour: rose-pink
height: 1.5-2.1 m/5-7 ft
❄

See preceding plant.

(contd)
be grown in full sun if they are kept well watered
and their shallow roots are covered thickly with
peat or leaf-mould.

Atmospheric pollution – Autumn foliage (*R. R.*
'Daybreak' and 'Glowing Embers' only).

RHODODENDRON (AZALEA) e.g. 'Glowing Embers'

◑ [○]
type of plant: HSh
flowering season: l. spring to e. summer
flower colour: scarlet + orange
height: 1.5-2.1 m/5-7 ft
*

See *R.* 'Daybreak', preceding page.

LILIUM speciosum rubrum [form of Lily]

◑ [○]
type of plant: HHBb
flowering season: l. summer to e. autumn
flower colour: deep pink + white
height: 1.5 m/5 ft
*

This unusually late-flowering lily needs a warm, sheltered position and a freely draining, acid soil to do well outdoors. It makes an excellent cut flower, as does the related and slightly hardier *L. s. r. magnificum* (this last plant has red-spotted blooms some 15-20 cm/6-8 in wide). *L. speciosum* itself and some of its forms are very fragrant (see, for example, *L. s. album*, p. 271). All these lilies are, unfortunately, prone to virus diseases, and when infected produce few flowers.
    Cutting.

HYDRANGEA macrophylla (Hortensia) e.g. 'Altona'

◑ [○]
type of plant: SlTSh
flowering season: midsummer to e. autumn
flower colour: blue (on acid soils) changing to plum crimson
height: 1.2-1.8 m/4-6 ft

Hydrangeas of most sorts grow best on neutral or slightly acid soils which are deep, rich and moisture-retentive. In more alkaline conditions the large-flowered variety shown here will be a dark rose colour until autumn, when it will take on bluer tones. The young growths on this rounded and bushy plant can easily become damaged by frost; exposed positions are, therefore, unsuitable.
    Atmospheric pollution – Containers – Cutting.

HYDRANGEA macrophylla (Lacecap) e.g. 'Bluewave'

◑ [○]
type of plant: SlTSh
flowering season: midsummer to e. autumn
flower colour: blue
height: 1.2-1.8 m/4-6 ft

Compared with the plant in the previous illustration, the Lacecap hydrangeas are altogether less formal shrubs. They look well in natural settings, such as light woodland, where they are sheltered from frost damage and where some of them – including the present example – can become large, spreading and, eventually, ground-covering plants. (*H. m.* 'Whitewave', which is shown in the following illustration, tends to be a slightly smaller plant.) The outer, sterile florets of *H. m.* 'Bluewave' will be pink on slightly alkaline soils, and chalk or lime will also redden the inner flowers of *H. m.* 'Whitewave'. *(contd)*

HYDRANGEA macrophylla (Lacecap) e.g. 'Whitewave'

◑ [○]
type of plant: SlTSh
flowering season: midsummer to e. autumn
flower colour: white
height: 1.2-1.8 m/4-6 ft

See preceding plant.

(contd)
However, really alkaline conditions do not produce healthy hydrangeas of this type and, provided that they are fertile and moist, acid or neutral soils are much more suitable.
    Atmospheric pollution.

RHODODENDRON (AZALEA) e.g. 'Koster's Brilliant Red' ★

◑ [○]
type of plant: HSh
flowering season: l. spring
flower colour: bright orange-red
height: 1.2-1.8 m/4-6 ft
*

The Mollis azaleas – of which the plant shown here is an example – have large trusses of flowers which unfold on bare branches. Their blooms are often vividly coloured. The variety 'Koster's Brilliant Red' has a second season of brightness in autumn, when its rather unpleasantly aromatic foliage turns from green to a mixture of fiery colours. A moisture-retentive soil is important for good growth and this plant will respond well to its roots being covered with peat or leaf-mould each year.
    Autumn foliage.

RHODODENDRON (Azalea Series) kaempferi
◐[○]
type of plant: SlT/HSh
flower season: l. spring to midsummer
flower colour: salmon-pink or orange or
  brick-red
height: 1.2-1.5 m/4-5 ft
*½E/D

Individual specimens of this plant vary a good deal
in the colour of their flowers and the time of year at
which they bloom. However, they all form rather
lax shrubs which often become almost completely
covered in flowers. In a cold district or on an
exposed site all the leaves will fall in autumn. *R.
kaempferi* grows best in a cool, moist soil.

**RHODODENDRON Hybrid e.g. 'Blue
Diamond'**
◐[○]
type of plant: HSh
flowering season: mid-spring
flower colour: blue
height: 90-150 cm/3-5 ft
*E

R. 'Blue Diamond' is a slow-growing plant with
fairly upright branches. Like many small-leaved
rhododendrons it can withstand exposure to full
sun quite well. However, it needs moisture and, in
some shade, it is less likely to dry out. A shady
position will also protect its flowers (which are of a
remarkably clear blue for a rhododendron) from
frost damage. Its leaves emit an aromatic fragrance
when bruised.
  Hedging – Aromatic leaves.

RHODODENDRON Hybrid e.g. 'Elizabeth'★
◐[○]
type of plant: HSh
flowering season: spring
flower colour: scarlet-crimson
height: 90-150 cm/3-5 ft
*E

The brightly coloured, trumpet-shaped flowers of
this low and spreading rhododendron usually
appear in large numbers. Although a really well
grown specimen will be dense enough for
ground-cover, a better choice is the related and
almost prostrate *R.* 'Jenny' (see below, p. 40).
Both plants prefer a shaded site and their roots
must be kept cool and moist.

**RHODODENDRON (AZALEA) e.g. 'Blue
Danube'**
◐[○]
type of plant: SlTSh
flowering season l. spring to e. summer
flower colour: bluish violet
height 90 cm/3 ft
*½E

Compared with most other 'evergreen' azaleas, *R.*
'Blue Danube' flowers exceptionally late in the
year and its blooms, although not actually blue, are
much bluer than usual. It is advisable to give this
plant shelter from cold winds; if its roots are kept
moist (with a thick layer of peat, for example) it
can be grown in a fairly sunny position.

RHODODENDRON Hybrid e.g. 'Cilpinense'
◐[○]
type of plant: HSh
flowering season: e. spring
flower colour: pinkish white
height 90 cm/3 ft
*E

This openly branched rhododendron is a fully
hardy plant but its lovely, bell-shaped flowers are
produced so early in the year that, unless it is given
some shelter, all its blossom may be ruined by
frost. It requires the sort of moist, rich soil
appreciated by all rhododendrons.

**RHODODENDRON (AZALEA) e.g. 'Orange
Beauty'**
◐[○]
type of plant:SlTSh
flowering season: l. spring
flower colour: orange
height: 90 cm/3 ft
*½E

If planted in full sun, the colour of this azalea's
flowers will soon fade. Given some shade and
shelter and a suitably moisture-retentive soil,
however, there will usually be a mass of blossom of
a fairly strong orange shade, softened somewhat by
a tinge of salmon pink.

RHODODENDRON (AZALEA) e.g. 'Palestrina' ★

◐ [○]
type of plant: HSh
flowering season: l. spring
flower colour: white + light green
height: 90 cm/3 ft
*½E

For those gardeners who find the hot colours of many azaleas too insistent and who also dislike the main alternatives of mauves and violets, there are the white-flowered varieties, among which 'Palestrina' is outstanding. It carries its pure, cool blossom on fairly erect branches. The throat of each flower is delicately marked in green. The usual moist but open-textured soil is required.

PRIMULA pulverulenta

◐ [○]
type of plant: HP
flowering season: summer
flower colour: crimson
height: 75 cm/2½ ft

Extreme acidity does not suit most primulas but they thrive on substantial, moisture-retentive soils which are either neutral or slightly acid. The opulently coloured, pale-stemmed species shown here needs a fertile soil and, although constant wetness is unsuitable, it grows especially well near water. The excellent 'Bartley Strain' of *P. pulverulenta* (see the following illustration) produces flowers of an attractive, soft colour as an alternative to the vinous tones of the species.
    Damp and wet soils.

PRIMULA pulverulenta 'Bartley Strain'

◐ [○]
type of plant: HP
flowering season: summer
flower colour: pink
height: 75 cm/2½ ft

See preceding plant.

SKIMMIA japonica 'Rubella' (syn. *S. reevesiana* 'Rubella', *S. rubella*)

◐ [○]
type of plant: HSh
flowering season: spring
flower colour: white or pinkish
height: 60-90 cm/2-3 ft
*E

Even though this is a male form of skimmia and therefore produces no berries, its dark red flower buds are almost as conspicuous as any fruit. They decorate the dense, hummocky shape of this plant throughout the winter months and then open out into heads of fragrant flowers in early spring. There should be no lime in the soil for this slow-growing shrub which flourishes in a cool, shady position where moisture is always present.
    Atmospheric pollution – Ground-cover – Cutting – Fragrant flowers.

RHODODENDRON (AZALEA) e.g. 'Rosebud'

◐ [○]
type of plant: SlTSh
flowering season: l. spring
flower colour: rose-pink
height: 60 cm/2 ft
*½E

Most azaleas are single-flowered but there are a few forms with double or semi-double blooms. In the majority of cases, the extra petals are arranged so that it seems as if one flower is growing out of another (the semi-evergreen variety 'Blaauw's Pink' has flowers of this so-called 'hose-in-hose' type). *R.* 'Rosebud', however, has unusually full and rounded flowers which are formed in a slightly different way. They are borne on spreading branches. A sheltered but cool position is most suitable.
    Containers.

TRICYRTIS stolonifera (syn. *T. formosana stolonifera*) [species of Toad Lily]

◐ [○]
type of plant: HP
flowering season: l. summer to mid-autumn
flower colour: pale mauve
height: 60 cm/2 ft

This slender and small-flowered plant needs careful positioning if its delicate, purple-spotted blooms are not to be overlooked. It thrives in cool, shady places and peaty soils, but it must have some warmth to produce its flowers which open late in the year over a period of several weeks.

**MERTENSIA virginica
[Virginia Cowslip]**

◐[○]
type of plant: HP
flowering season: l. spring to e. summer
flower colour: blue
height: 30-60 cm/1-2 ft

No doubt the beautifully blue flowers of this perennial would be seen more commonly in shady gardens if it were not for the fact that, by late summer, not only the flowers but also the leaves and the stems of this plant have disappeared. Where the resulting gap can either be covered by another plant or is unimportant, *M. virginica* will present a particularly attractive combination of blue flowers and greyish leaves each year. It is easy to grow in any moisture-retentive and fertile soil and while it tolerates sunshine, it prefers partial or full shade.

Grey, etc. leaves – Cutting.

RHODODENDRON Hybrid e.g. 'Jenny' (syn.
R. 'Elizabeth Jenny')

◐[○]
type of plant: HSh
flowering season: spring
flower colour: bright red
height: 30-60 cm/1-2 ft
*E

On such a low bed of greenery the 8 cm/3 in wide flowers of this plant look particularly large. *R.* 'Jenny' – which is sometimes referred to as *R.* 'Creeping Jenny' – will slowly form a ground-covering hummock about 1.5 m/5 ft across, provided that it is given a moisture-retentive soil. If it is at all dry, however, its habit of growth will be quite sparse and straggly.

Ground-cover – Containers.

**PRIMULA denticulata
[Drumstick Primrose]**

◐[○]
type of plant: HP
flowering season: spring
flower colour: pale lavender blue
height: 30 cm/1 ft

In a slightly acid or neutral soil which holds moisture well, several specimens of this sturdy plant will knit together into a weed-suppressing cover of foliage. Many different forms of *P. denticulata*, with variously coloured, spherical flower heads, are available. Purple, crimson, white and lilac cultivars are easily obtained from specialist nurseries. The leaves of all forms are only partially developed when the buds open in early spring.

Ground-cover.

**PRIMULA vulgaris elatior e.g. 'Giant Bouquet'
[form of Polyanthus]**

◐[○]
type of plant: SITP
flowering season: spring
**flower colour: mixed – red, pink, yellow, blue,
  white**
height: 23-30 cm/9-12 in

Of the two mixtures of polyanthus shown in this and the following photograph, the variety 'Giant Bouquet' is the most suitable for British gardens. *P. v. e.* 'Pacific Strain' will produce its flowers freely only in a warm and sheltered site. Both varieties need a rich, moist soil. They are often grown from seed and used for spring bedding. Their flower heads, which last well in water, are carried on fairly thick stems. Seedsmen will usually list some separately coloured forms of these plants.

Cutting.

**PRIMULA vulgaris elatior e.g. 'Pacific Strain'
[form of Polyanthus]**

◐[○]
type of plant: SITP
flowering season: spring
**flower colour: mixed – red, pink, yellow, blue,
  white**
height: 23-30 cm/9-12 in

See preceding plant.

SOLDANELLA montana

◐[○]
type of plant: HP
flowering season: spring
flower colour: lavender
height: 15 cm/6 in
E

Gardeners love the fringed flowers of soldanellas but, unfortunately, slugs and snails find them attractive too and all the buds of these plants may be eaten by early spring if some precautions are not taken. A gritty but moisture-retentive soil suits all soldanellas, including the example shown above; excellent drainage also helps to deter any slimy intruders (who may be further discouraged by the application of a proprietary slug bait).

GENTIANA sino-ornata ★
[species of Gentian]

◐ [○]
type of plant: HP
flowering season: autumn
flower colour: deep blue
height: 10-15 cm/4-6 in

All gentians seem to have acquired a reputation for being difficult to grow, but the species illustrated here, and some other forms too, can be very easy, given the right conditions. *G. sino-ornata* needs a deep, acid soil that never dries out but also never becomes waterlogged. It thrives and will spread into wide, grassy mats if it is fed on a diet of very well rotted manure, light loam and leaf-mould. Areas of paving which do not become too hot can be studded with this beautiful plant, which will appreciate the coolness at its roots.

Paving.

PRIMULA vulgaris
[Primrose]

◐ [○]
type of plant: HP
flowering season: spring
flower colour: yellow
height: 10-15 cm/4-6 in

This well loved plant looks as charming in informal garden plantings as it does in the deciduous woodlands and hedgerows of Britain. If it is grown in a sheltered place, it may begin to flower as early as January. However, the common primrose is a very hardy plant which will do well almost anywhere, provided that it is given a moist and reasonably fertile soil. At its best, it will form ground-covering clumps of foliage and seed itself freely.

Ground-cover.

SCIADOPITYS verticillata
[Umbrella Pine]

◐
type of plant: HCo
height: 15-24 m/50-80 ft
*E

It is not the overall shape of this tree which gives it its common name but its tufts of leaves; these are arranged radially, like the ribs of an umbrella. *S. verticillata* grows slowly, even when given the rich, moist, acid soil which suits it best. It eventually forms a large but slender pyramid of greenery. It may occasionally be shrub-like with several main stems.

Green foliage.

RHODODENDRON arboreum e.g. 'Blood Red'

◐
type of plant: HHT
flowering season: spring
flower colour: red
height: 9-12 m/30-40 ft
*E

Although there are some hardier varieties of *R. arboreum*, none of them are quite so impressively dark-flowered as the rather tender forms such as 'Blood Red'. Only mild, moist areas – usually not far from the sea in Britain – provide the right conditions for these trees. Even in such places, a sheltered, semi-shaded site is necessary to protect the flowers (which appear only on moderately mature specimens) from frost damage. The leaves of *R. arboreum* and its forms are long; their undersides are covered in a pale grey or rust-coloured felt.

RHODODENDRON Hybrid e.g. 'Azor'

◐
type of plant: HSh/T
flowering season: e. summer
flower colour: pink
height: 3-3.6 m/10-12 ft
*E

Not all hybrid rhododendrons are as tough and tolerant as the so-called 'Hardy Hybrids' (for an example of which see *R.* 'Cynthia', p. 34). Cultivars like 'Azor', for instance, do not grow well in full sun or when exposed to cold winds. A cool, moist soil in light woodland is ideal. *R.* 'Azor' is notable for its late flowering season. It has an open, wide-spreading habit of growth.

PIERIS formosa forrestii (syn. *P. forrestii*, *Andromeda formosa*) ★

◐

type of plant: SlTSh
flowering season: spring
flower colour: white
height: 1.8-3 m/6-10 ft
*E

This is not the easiest pieris to grow but, of the readily available species and forms, it is the most beautiful and distinguished-looking. Its young leaves are a dramatic red. However, they can be easily damaged by frost, wind and sun – and especially early morning sun after a very cold night. The flower buds are also liable to damage. A sheltered site is, therefore, essential and, in addition, this slow-growing, rather rounded plant requires a moist, lime-free soil. *P.* 'Forest Flame' (see p. 173) is a smaller and hardier alternative.

Red, etc. leaves – Cutting.

RHODODENDRON augustinii

◐

type of plant: SlT/HSh
flowering season: spring
flower colour: blue
height: 1.8-3 m/6-10 ft
*E

The upright branches of this rhododendron become smothered in funnel-shaped flowers each spring. Even young plants flower freely. Individual specimens vary in the colour of their blossom, some being mauve or violet rather than blue, but there are plants that are almost true blue. The flowers that open first in spring may be spoilt by frost if the shrub is not given a sheltered, shady site. Like all rhododendrons it needs coolness and moisture at its roots.

RHODODENDRON griersonianum

◐

type of plant: SlT/HSh
flowering season: e. summer
flower colour: scarlet
height: 1.8-2.4 m/6-8 ft
*E

Nurseries with an extensive range of species rhododendrons will list this remarkably coloured plant. Although it is the parent of many hybrids, none of its offspring (which include, for example, *R.* 'Elizabeth', see above, p. 38) can match it for the brightness and clarity of its flower colour. It should be given a sheltered position where the soil stays cool and moist throughout the year.

LILIUM pardalinum
[Panther Lily, Leopard Lily]

◐

type of plant: HBb
flowering season: midsummer
flower colour: orange + orange-yellow
height: 1.5-2.1 m/5-7 ft

Opinions vary as to whether this lily should be grown in sun or shade, but since it requires constant moisture during summer, it is usually easier to manage in light shade. Ideally, the soil should be a spongy mixture of loam, leaf-mould and sand. Both the species and its readily available variety *L. p. giganteum* are vigorous plants which, if they become infected with a virus disease, are normally able to withstand the effects quite well. *L. p. giganteum* has flowers of a reddish colour and it can grow up to 2.4 m/8 ft high.

MECONOPSIS betonicifolia (syn. *M. baileyi*)
[Himalayan Blue Poppy]

◐

type of plant: HP
flowering season: summer
flower colour: rich sky blue
height: 90-120 cm/3-4 ft

Coolness and moisture are needed to produce the best growth and the most stikingly coloured specimens of this plant. An absence of lime often leads to particularly clear blue flowers. Except in ideal conditions with shelter and a rich soil, *M. betonicifolia* blooms only once, after several years, and then dies.

BEGONIA hybrida pendula e.g. 'Golden Shower'

◐

type of plant: TenTu
flowering season: summer
flower colour: golden yellow
height: 30-60 cm/1-2 ft

The arching stems of this plant make it especially suitable for growing in window boxes and hanging baskets. All pendula begonias – including mixtures such as the one shown in the following illustration – flower very freely for many weeks. A light, rich, moist soil with leaf-mould or peat produces excellent results. Tuberous begonias need moderate warmth to encourage them into growth. The tubers should be lifted and stored after the leaves begin to die. Other popular tuberous begonias include the multiflora types, which bear large quantities of fairly small flowers; the plants are normally 23-30 cm/9-12 in high.

BEGONIA hybrida pendula e.g. 'Mixed'

◖

type of plant: TenTu
flowering season: summer
flower colour: mixed – salmon, scarlet, yellow,
    orange, pink, white
height: 30-60 cm/1-2 ft

See preceding plant.

BLECHNUM spicant
[Hard Fern]

◖

type of plant: HF
height: 30-45 cm/1-1½ ft
*E

Clumps of this tough and amenable fern can be
used to cover the ground in many an
unpromisingly dry place. Its upright, fertile
fronds are, however, largest and longest (up to
75 cm/2½ ft occasionally) in moist soils. Beneath
these conspicuous fertile fronds lie rosettes of
broader, sterile fronds.
    Dry shade – Ground-cover – Green foliage.

TRILLIUM grandiflorum ★
[Wake Robin]

◖

type of plant: HP
flowering season: spring
flower colour: white
height: 30-45 cm/1-1½ ft

Trilliums grow well in woodland, where they
appreciate the coolness and the moist, leaf-mouldy
soil. The species shown here has large,
three-petalled flowers, each of which is
accompanied by a trio of leaves. It often forms
quite large clumps and it is a plant that is both
robust and beautiful.

TRILLIUM erectum

◖

type of plant: HP
flowering season: mid-spring
flower colour: purplish maroon
height: 30 cm/1 ft

In contrast to the white flowers of some trilliums
(such as *T. grandiflorum*, above), there are the rich
maroon or red petals of species like *T. erectum*. In
this case, the flowers are quite small (about half the
size of *T. grandiflorum*'s blooms); they have a most
unpleasant smell. A light, moist and humus-rich
soil is ideal.

ANDROMEDA polifolia
[Bog Rosemary]

◖

type of plant: HSh
flowering season: l. spring to e. summer
flower colour: white or pink
height: 23-30 cm/9-12 in
*E

Nurseries that specialize in heaths and heathers or
in rhododendrons will probably list this related
plant which is particularly suitable for damp, or at
least fairly moist, lime-free soils. *A. polifolia* grows
as a stiff little bush; in certain small forms the habit
is a spreading, sprawling one. There are attractive,
pale undersides to the leathery leaves. This plant
normally flowers freely.
    Damp and wet soils.

CASSIOPE tetragona

◖

type of plant: HSh
flowering season: spring
flower colour: white
height: 23-30 cm/9-12 in
*E

Although heath-like in appearance, *C. tetragona*'s
very upright, scaly-leaved stems give it a much
more distinctive and interesting appearance than
most heaths. It must be given a cool but open
position and it needs moist soil to which peat or
leaf-mould has been added. For details of a
mat-forming species of *Cassiope* which can be used
for ground-cover on rock gardens, see p. 116.

ERYTHRONIUM revolutum 'White Beauty'
(syn. *E.* × 'White Beauty') ★
◐
type of plant: HBb
flowering season: spring
flower colour: white
height: 23-30 cm/9-12 in

This much-admired plant will usually increase
into sizeable clumps if it is supplied with a moist
soil, a cool site and plenty of well rotted compost,
leaf-mould or some similar material. Its lily-like
flowers peer down at its leaves which are marbled
with purplish brown and white markings.
  Variegated leaves.

OURISIA coccinea
◐
type of plant: HP
flowering season: summer
flower colour: scarlet
height: 23 cm/9 in
E

Growing this plant well can be rather difficult since
it thrives in a cool, damp climate in spring and
summer but it needs to be dry in winter. Where
summers *and* winters are damp, it requires
overhead protection during the colder months.
However, its flowers are most delicately shaped
and vividly coloured. They are held well above the
mats of foliage.

BEGONIA semperflorens e.g. 'Flamingo'
◐
type of plant: HHA
flowering season: summer to e. autumn
flower colour: white + pink
height: 15 cm/6 in

Cultivars of *B. semperflorens* are the most popular
fibrous-rooted begonias. They need to be raised in
a moderate temperature, from seed, each year.
Their numerous flowers are produced
continuously over several months, even in a wet
summer. Most varieties, including 'Flamingo'
(shown above) and 'Organdy' (see the following
photograph), grow neatly and densely. A low
proportion of the plants in the 'Organdy' mixture
will have bronze leaves, but there are varieties,
such as *B. s.* 'Indian Maid' (see p. 173), which are
noted for their deep purple-brown foliage. All
these plants do well in porous soils with plenty of
peat or similar moisture-retentive substances.

BEGONIA semperflorens e.g. 'Organdy'
◐
type of plant: HHA
flowering season: summer to e. autumn
flower colour: mixed – red, pink, white
height: 15 cm/6 in

See preceding plant.

ERYTHRONIUM dens-canis
[Dog's-tooth Violet]
◐
type of plant: HBb
flowering season: spring
flower colour: pinkish purple
height: 10-15 cm/4-6 in

Under the shade of tall deciduous trees and in a
moist and humus-y soil this charming little plant
may increase quite quickly. Its flowers hang above
foliage which is variegated with a unique
combination of turquoise-green and purplish
brown. There are several named forms of this
plant in colours ranging from deep purple to pale
pink and white.
  Variegated leaves.

PLEIONE formosana (syn. *P. bulbocodioides*)
◐
type of plant SITP
flowering season: spring
flower colour: mauve-pink + cream
height: 10-15 cm/4-6 in

Despite being nearly hardy, this orchid needs to be
grown in a sheltered site and to be given some
overhead cover in winter if it is to flower well. The
expensive *Cypripedium reginae* (see below, p. 45) is
usually an easier orchid to deal with. The flowers
of *P. formosana* are carried on short stems; they
appear before the leaves. The plant needs to be
kept fairly dry during winter but should have
plenty of moisture in late spring and summer. A
light, peaty soil is ideal.

SHORTIA uniflora

◑

type of plant: HP
flowering season: spring
flower colour: pale pink
height: 10-15 cm/4-6 in
❊ **E**

The leaves of this plant take on a reddish tinge as they mature and this colouring is echoed in the calyces which clasp the lovely, frilled petals. Some leaves may turn completely red during the colder months. In the cool sponginess of a soil enriched with leaf-mould or peat, *S. uniflora* will grow densely and spread slowly into very decorative, small-scale ground-cover.

Ground-cover – Autumn foliage.

KIRENGESHOMA palmata ★

◑ ●

type of plant: HP
flowering season: l. summer to mid-autumn
flower colour: yellow
height: 90-120 cm/3-4 ft

The unusually tree-like leaves, the black stems and the pale thick-petalled flowers of this plant combine to produce an overall effect of rare distinction. The buds appear in early summer and need a fairly sheltered site to encourage them to open later on. This is not, however, a plant for hot places nor does it grow well in alkaline soils. A moist and peaty soil suits it best and it appreciates the dampness near streams and ponds.

Damp and wet soils – Green foliage.

CYPRIPEDIUM reginae
[species of Lady's Slipper Orchid]

◑ ●

type of plant: HP
flowering season: summer
flower colour: pink+white
height: 45 cm/1½ ft
❊

Many bulb specialists' catalogues will list this expensive but sturdy orchid. Its big-bellied flowers are accompanied by pale green, pleated leaves. Individual blooms are often 5-8 cm/2-3 in wide. A deep, moist, leafy soil suits this plant well.

Additional plants, featured elsewhere in this book, that are suitable for acid soils

◑ partial shade
RHODODENDRON sinogrande: 9 m (p. 185)
ACER japonicum 'Aureum' ★: 4.5-6 m (p. 177)
RHODODENDRON Hybrid e.g. 'Loderi King George' ★: 4.5-6 m (p. 272)
RHODODENDRON Hybrid e.g. 'Albatross': 3.6-4.5 m (p. 272)
ENKIANTHUS campanulatus: 2.4-3.6 m (p. 194)
CARDIOCRINUM giganteum: 1.8-3 m (p. 272)
RHODODENDRON lutescens: 1.8-3 m (p. 279)
FOTHERGILLA monticola: 1.8-2.4 m (p. 194)
PIERIS 'Forest Flame': 1.8-2.4 m (p. 173)
PIERIS japonica 'Variegata': 1.8-2.4 m (p. 154)
RHODODENDRON williamsianum ★: 90-150 cm (p. 138)
FOTHERGILLA gardenii: 60-90 cm (p. 194)
SMILACINA racemosa: 60-90 cm (p. 186)
ADIANTIUM pedatum 'Japonicum': 30-60 cm (p. 173)
LUZULA maxima: 30-45 cm (p. 115)
BEGONIA semperflorens e.g. 'Indian Maid': 23 cm (p. 173)
BLECHNUM penna-marina: 15 cm (p. 116)
CASSIOPE lycopodioides: 5-8 cm (p. 116)

◑ ● partial or full shade
RHODODENDRON (Hardy Hybrid) e.g. 'Cynthia': 3-3.6 m (p. 34)
RHODODENDRON (Hardy Hybrid) e.g. 'Fastuosum Flore Pleno': 3-3.6 m (p. 94)
RHODODENDRON ponticum: 3-3.6 m (p. 128)
GAULTHERIA shallon: 1.2-1.8 m (p. 106)
OSMUNDA regalis: 1.2-1.8 m (p. 73)
DRYOPTERIS cristata: 60-90 cm (p. 79)
MERTENSIA virginica: 30-60 cm (p. 73)
PODOPHYLLUM emodi: 30 cm (p. 208)
PACHYSANDRA terminalis: 23-30 cm (p. 117)
PACHYSANDRA terminalis 'Variegata': 23 cm (p. 155)
VACCINIUM vitis-idaea: 15 cm (p. 111)
CORNUS canadensis: 10-15 cm (p. 111)
GAULTHERIA procumbens: 8-15 cm (p. 118)

Plants suitable for heavy clay soils

Often, the main problem that the gardener on a heavy clay soil has to contend with is a sore back. Not only is heavy clay an inhospitable soil for many plants, but it is usually difficult and unpleasant to work. Even medium-sized lumps of such soil seem to weigh a surprising amount as one tries to lever them from their surroundings.

The problems of such an unpromising growing medium are often overlooked by gardening writers. Planting recommendations, such as 'any soil, provided it is well drained', can be the despair of gardeners who have to deal with heavy clay; even 'a moisture-retentive soil' usually means a nice, spongy, leaf-mouldy soil, rather than a slab of clammy clay.

Heavy clay soils are, generally speaking, dense and compacted, sticky when wet, often impenetrable when dry. Their compacted nature means that they incorporate little air, and water cannot easily pass through them. In airless, semi-waterlogged conditions many plants rot and die, and others form roots only slowly. Yet clay soils are, in general, rich soils. If heavy clay can have plenty of strawy manure, leaf-mould, peat, grit and so on dug into it, to open it out and lighten it, then a wide range of plants will grow in it, and often more luxuriously than in a very light, fast-draining soil. For detailed descriptions of various methods of draining and improving the structure of heavy clay, see *Gardening on Clay* by Howard Hamp Crane (published by Collingridge).

It can, however, take some considerable time before various improvement measures are completed, and the following list consists of plants that are prepared to tolerate a soil that is heavy and drains slowly. Many of these plants would be seen at their best in a well drained soil and, in almost all cases, they would become established more quickly there. However, they will grow quite satisfactorily in a heavier, less well drained medium.

All the plants in this list are hardy. Most often it is a combination of wetness and low temperatures, rather than low temperatures alone, which kills plants. In heavy clay soils, which tend to be both wet and cold, many slightly tender plants become, in effect, even less hardy. For this reason, plants such as escallonias, which are not fully hardy, but which are sometimes recommended for clay soils, do not appear in this list. The damaging effects of cold and wet combined can be overcome, to some extent, by carrying out as much planting as possible in the spring. (Plants which flower early in the year must obviously be in the ground several months beforehand and are therefore unsuitable for this treatment.)

The heaviness of many clay soils can lead not only to reduced hardiness, but also to a shortening of the lives of plants. Varieties of forget-me-not (*Myosotis alpestris*) are included in this list since they do well on heavy clay soils, but while they can be perennial plants on light or medium soils, on heavy soils they must be treated as biennials.

Most bulbous plants do not do well on heavy clay soils (only examples of the tougher – and less expensive – daffodils, for example, have been recommended as suitable). On such soils they tend to rot and to be attacked by slugs. Light, quick-draining materials, such as grit or ashes, should, ideally, be placed around the roots of all plants liable to slug damage. The menace of these pests, that feel particularly at home on a damp, badly drained soil, can also be dealt with by putting down slug bait (preferably under – for instance – small, upturned flower pots, in order to protect birds and other animals from the poison).

No attempt has been made to include all plants that might possibly grow in a heavy clay soil in this list. Fairly undemanding plants, like potentillas (shrubby cinquefoils), that have a preference for light, well drained soils have been excluded. Roses are traditionally associated with clay but, in fact, a medium loam suits most of them best, and rugosa and Scotch roses prefer an even lighter soil. No roses have been included in this list, but the really vigorous types, such as the rambler 'Wedding Day', can survive with relatively little preparation of the soil. In cases where a heavy soil is detrimental to the main decorative effect of a plant, that plant is not recommended: *Cotinus coggygria* (smoke tree or Venetian sumach) and its varieties, for example, grow satisfactorily on heavy clay, but their autumn colouring is usually disappointing there.

Several of the plants in this list require constant moisture, at least during the growing season. Where conditions are wetter than moist, the list entitled 'Plants suitable for damp and wet soils' should be consulted.

QUERCUS robur (syn. *Q. pedunculata*)
[Common Oak, English Oak]

○

type of plant: HT
height: 18-27 m/60-90 ft

This very long-lived tree eventually has a wide, rounded and fairly open crown. There is a variety – *Q.r.* 'Fastigiata' which, when young, forms a tapering column; it is available from specialist nurseries. The well known fruits are inconspicuous. Ideally, this tree should be grown in a deep, moist loam; similar soils, including stiff and heavy clays, also give good results.

ASTER novae-angliae e.g. 'September Ruby'
[form of Michaelmas Daisy]

○

type of plant: HP
flowering season: e. autumn
flower colour: ruby red
height: 1.05-1.2 m/3½-4 ft

A. novae-angliae and its varieties are tough, unfussy plants which will grow in almost any moisture-retentive soil. They appear not to be affected by the disease aster wilt, to which *A. novi-belgii* and its cultivars are particularly susceptible. *A. n.-a.* 'September Ruby' and other taller varieties usually need staking.

Damp and wet soils – Cutting.

CROCOSMIA × curtonus 'Lucifer' NA

○

type of plant: SITP
flowering season: summer
flower colour: red-orange
height: 90 cm/3 ft

Brilliantly coloured flowers appear in early or midsummer. The plants need a sheltered site in the normally colder areas of the United States, where they benefit from a winter cover of evergreen boughs. Good drainage gives particularly satisfactory results. The strap-like leaves also have some ornamental value. In Britain, this British-bred plant and relative hybrids are stocked by nurseries specializing in perennials.

HELENIUM autumnale e.g. 'Butterpat'
○
type of plant: HP
flowering season: l. summer to e. autumn
flower colour: yellow
height: 90 cm/3 ft

The three varieties of *H. autumnale* illustrated in this and the following two photographs are easy to grow in any garden soil; good drainage is not important. They are all floriferous plants, which need to be staked if the flowers are not to end up at ground level. They also need regular division to keep them blooming freely. Although they make good cut flowers their petals hang down characteristically, and in a vase this feature may not seem appealing.
    Cutting.

HELENIUM autumnale e.g. 'Coppelia'
○
type of plant: HP
flowering season: summer
flower colour: coppery orange
height: 90 cm/3 ft

See preceding plant.

HELENIUM autumnale e.g. 'Moerheim Beauty'
○
type of plant: HP
flowering season: midsummer to e. autumn
flower colour: bronze-red
height: 90 cm/3 ft

See *H. a.* 'Butterpat', second left.

ASTER novi-belgii e.g. 'Carnival'
[form of Michaelmas Daisy]
○
type of plant: HP
flowering season: autumn
flower colour: red
height: 60-75 cm/2-2½ ft

If it were not for their susceptibility to various pests and diseases, including mildew and aster wilt, the numerous varieties of *A. novi-belgii* would be outstanding garden plants. Despite the drawbacks, their large flowers, which are freely produced and often beautifully coloured, are very popular for use both in the border and as cut flowers. The taller varieties usually need staking, but there are dwarf cultivars (such as *A. n.-b.* 'Audrey' illustrated second right) which are self-supporting. A moisture-retentive soil helps to make attacks of mildew less likely.
    Damp and wet soils – Cutting.

INULA hookeri sc NA
○
type of plant: HP
flowering season: l. summer to e. autumn
flower colour: yellow
height: 60 cm/2 ft

This bushy, spreading plant grows well on clay and other soils that retain moisture. Its main attraction is the narrowness of the rays of its pale yellow flowers (which are sweetly scented but only just perceptibly so).
    Cutting.

ASTER novi-belgii e.g. 'Audrey'
[form of Michaelmas Daisy]
○
type of plant: HP
flowering season: autumn
flower colour: pale blue
height: 30-45 cm/1-1½ ft

Dwarf hybrid asters are now available in shades of blue, pink and red; an example of a white-flowered variety is illustrated on p. 70. These plants are neat and dense; they do not need staking. The example shown here is typically tidy and free-flowering. Any moistish soil produces good growth.
    Damp and wet soils – Cutting.

CHAMAECYPARIS pisifera 'Filifera' NA
[Threadleaf False Cypress]
○ [◑]
type of plant: HCo
height: 18m/60ft
E

A handsome pyramidal evergreen with lacy foliage. 'Filifera Aurea' has golden-coloured leaves and, in Britain, is more readily available than the green-leaved variety. Older specimens are especially graceful and spreading, sometimes forming a small coppice.

CERCIS canadensis NA
[American Redbird]
○ [◑]
type of plant: HT
flowering season: spring
flower colour: purple-pink
height: 7.5m/25ft

This small tree is grown especially for its flowers in early or mid-spring. It is native to the southern United States, where it is held in almost as much esteem as *Cornus florida*, the eastern flowering dogwood. *Cercis chinensis*, from China, grows usually to 1.8-2.4m/6-8ft and is shrubby. The flowers bloom simultaneously with those of *C. canadensis* but are more conspicuous.

VIBURNUM plicatum tomentosum 'Lanarth'
(**syn.** *V. tomentosum* 'Lanarth')★
[form of Japanese Snowball]
○ [◑]
type of plant: HSh
flowering season: l. spring to e. summer
flower colour: white
height: 1.8-3m/6-10ft

The outstanding feature of this shrub is its widely spreading, horizontal branches. During the flowering season this interesting and decorative habit of growth is accentuated by the 'lace-cap' flowers. Berries are not produced regularly or prolifically, but the foliage becomes nicely plummy in autumn. A moist, preferably alkaline soil suits this plant best.
   Autumn foliage.

WEIGELA e.g. 'Abel Carriere'
○ [◑]
type of plant: HSh
flowering season: l. spring to e. summer
flower colour: rose-pink
height: 1.5m/5ft

Weigelas (which are still occasionally listed under the name *Diervilla*) are easily grown shrubs that do well in almost all soils. However, they have a preference for fairly moist soil, including clays. The two hybrids illustrated here are very free-flowering; they may be kept so by quite hard pruning after the blooms have faded. *W.* 'Bristol Ruby' tends to be a more upright plant than *W.* 'Abel Carriere'. There are weigela hybrids with pale pink flowers and with white flowers.
   Chalk – Atmospheric pollution.

WEIGELA e.g. 'Bristol Ruby'
○ [◑]
type of plant: HSh
flowering season: l. spring to e. summer
flower colour: ruby-red
height: 1.5m/5ft

See preceding plant.

RUDBECKIA fulgida (syn. *R. newmannii, R. speciosa*) **'Goldsturm'**
[form of Coneflower]

○ [◐]
type of plant: HP
flowering season: l. summer to mid-autumn
flower colour: yellow
height: 75 cm/2½ ft

The large flowers of this plant are freely borne on upright stems. They have prominent central 'cones' of very dark brown and the whole effect is sprightly and shining. Any reasonable garden soil, provided it is moisture-retentive, is suitable for this plant.

 Cutting.

SOLIDAGO×hybrida e.g. **'Lemore'**
[form of Golden Rod]

○ [◐]
type of plant: HP
flowering season: l. summer to e. autumn
flower colour: primrose
height: 75 cm/2½ ft

Of a pleasantly soft yellow compared with some of the other hybrid golden rods, *S.*×*h.* 'Lemore' has flower heads which are more widely branching and less plume-like than usual. Like most plants of this genus, however, *S.*×*h.* 'Lemore' is vigorous. It prefers a fairly heavy, moist soil. However, it will do quite well in any good soil, particularly if it is lifted and divided regularly.

 Cutting.

CAMASSIA cusickii
[species of Quamash]

○ [◐]
type of plant: HBb
flowering season: summer
flower colour: lavender
height: 60-90 cm/2-3 ft

A huge bulb lurks beneath the finely petalled flowers of this plant. The strap-shaped leaves lie around rather untidily until late summer, by which time the whole plant has usually died down. *C. cusickii* seems to prefer quite heavy soils and a constant supply of moisture is important.

 Cutting.

BUXUS microphylla koreana NA

○ [◐]
type of plant: HSh
height: 60 cm/2 ft
E

This is a somewhat loose, spreading evergreen shrub with small leaves which turn olive green in winter. It is tolerant of greater cold then *Buxus sempervirens. B. microphylla* 'Compacta' ('Kingsville Dwarf') is a very dense grower, with old plants eventually growing to 45 cm/18 in.

BUPHTHALMUM salicifolium (syn. *Inula* 'Golden Beauty')

○ [◐]
type of plant: HP
flowering season: summer to mid-autumn
flower colour: yellow
height: 45-60 cm/1½-2 ft

This easily satisfied plant is clump-forming but rather lax. Although it does not look particularly attractive when staked, the flower stems need to be held upright somehow or they become so curved that it is difficult to use them in flower arrangements. However, the blooms last well in water and they are available over a very long period. Some moistness in the soil ensures good, thick growth.

 Ground-cover – Cutting.

SOLIDAGO×hybrida e.g. **'Golden Thumb'** (syn. *S.*×*h.* 'Queenie')
[form of Golden Rod]

○ [◐]
type of plant: HP
flowering season: l. summer to e. autumn
flower colour: yellow
height: 30 cm/1 ft

This is the smallest readily available solidago. It is a neat, bushy plant which needs no staking and it is altogether better behaved than the very large and voracious solidagos now less frequently listed in catalogues. Ordinary soil suits this plant, although it has some preference for moisture-retentive loams and clays.

 Cutting.

Additional plants, featured elsewhere in this
book, that are suitable for heavy clay soils

○ [◑] sun (or partial shade)
PLATANUS×hispanica: 21-30 m (p. 92)
SAMBUCUS nigra 'Aurea' 3.6-4.5 m (p. 176)
VIBURNUM opulus 'Sterile': 3.6-4.5 m (p. 70)
WEIGELA florida: 1.8 m (p. 93)
SAMBUCUS racemosa 'Plumosa Aurea'★:
    1.5-2.1 m (p. 177)
VIBURNUM opulus 'Compactum': 1.2-1.8 m
    (p. 204)
RUDBECKIA 'Goldquelle': 75-90 cm (p. 241)
SOLIDAGO×hybrida e.g. 'Goldenmosa':
    75-90 cm (p. 241)
PELTIPHYLLUM peltatum: 60-90 cm (p. 71)
CAMASSIA quamash: 45-75 cm (p. 242)
AJUGA reptans 'Atropurpurea': 10-15 cm (p. 172)

**ALNUS cordata
[Italian Alder]**

○ ◑
**type of plant: HT
flowering season: e. spring
flower colour: yellow
height: 15-24 m/50-80 ft**

Bright green, glossy leaves are the main feature of
this narrow pyramidal tree. The brown 'cones' are
conspicuous but not very decorative. In most
British gardens this alder will be the lesser of the
two heights given here and, in some cases, it may
reach only 9-12 m/30-40 ft. Though it prefers moist
growing conditions, it will tolerate quite dry soils.
For wet – rather than damp – soils the common
alder (A. glutinosa) is a better choice than
A. cordata.

   Damp and wet soils – Atmospheric pollution –
Green foliage.

**AESCULUS×carnea 'Briotii'
[form of Red Horse Chestnut]**

○ ◑
**type of plant: HT
flowering season: l. spring to e. summer
flower colour: red
height: 10.5-15 m/35-50 ft**

From a distance, this dome-headed tree's
numerous, light red flowers look most impressive;
they are less interesting on closer inspection. Only
a few conkers are produced. A.×c. 'Briotii' will
grow in most soils but the best specimens have
been planted in deep fertile loams and clays.

   Chalk – Atmospheric pollution.

**CRATAEGUS oxyacantha (syn. C. laevigata)
e.g. 'Plena'
[form of Hawthorn or May]**

○ ◑
**type of plant: HT
flowering season: l. spring
flower colour: white
height: 4.5-6 m/15-20 ft**

Though less tough than the common hawthorn
(see C. monogyna, p. 130), this spikily shaped tree
is adaptable and very hardy. It can withstand
salt-laden winds and dirty, grimy air. The red
fruits are carried in small bunches. Fungal
problems have diminished the usefulness of this
cultivar in the United States, where other
fungal-resistant selections have been popular, e.g.
'Superba', 'Winter King'.

   Chalk – Seaside – Atmospheric pollution –
Fruit.

FORSYTHIA suspensa ★

○ ◑
**type of plant: HSh
flowering season: spring
flower colour: yellow
height: 2.4-3 m/8-10 ft, 4.5 m/15 ft+against a wall**

All the readily available forsythias are easy to grow
in any soil including heavy clay. F. suspensa, with
its arching and hanging branches, has a much
more graceful habit than the more usual hybrids of
this genus. It looks especially nice fan-trained
against a wall or sprawling over a fence or low
bank. Its ability to flower quite well in full shade
makes it useful for covering gloomy north walls.

   Chalk – Atmospheric pollution – Climbers –
Cutting.

**SPIRAEA×arguta
[Bridal Wreath, Foam of May]**

○ ◑
**type of plant: HSh
flowering season: l. spring
flower colour: white
height: 1.8-2.4 m/6-8 ft**

Each of the curved stems of this rounded shrub is
covered with numerous, tightly packed flowers in
spring. The mass of blossom and the habit of
growth make this a spectacular plant during its
flowering season. S.×arguta is easily pleased,
although it has a preference for good, deep soil and
a fairly open site.

   Atmospheric pollution.

EUPATORIUM purpureum
[Joe Pye Weed]

○ ◑

type of plant: HP
flowering season: l. summer to e. autumn
flower colour: purplish pink
height: 1.2-1.8 m/4-6 ft

This is the sort of rather coarse – but impressive –
plant which is well able to cope with the exigencies
of heavy clay. Its size and habit of growth make
E. purpureum more suitable for a wild garden (or,
at least, a very large border) than a small and
carefully tended bed. It will grow in the majority of
moistish soils.

SALIX hastata 'Wehrhahnii' sc NA
[form of Willow]

○ ◑

type of plant: HSh
flowering season: spring
flower colour: silver-grey changing to yellow
height: 1.2 m/4 ft

The dark, upright branches of this shrub contrast
attractively with the numerous, very pale catkins
which are unaccompanied, at first, by any of the
greyish foliage. *S. h.* 'Wehrhahnii' is a
slow-growing plant of a rounded, spreading shape.
It is suitable for most garden soils, including
moisture-retentive ones like clay, and it does well
in damp or even wet areas of ground.
  Damp and wet soils.

POLYGONUM amplexicaule
'Atrosanguineum'
[form of Knotweed]

○ ◑

type of plant: HP
flowering season: summer to e. autumn
flower colour: deep red
height: 90-120 cm/3-4 ft

The main attraction of this plant is its long
flowering season. It produces large quantities of
flower spikes from the beginning of summer until
early autumn, or sometimes even later. Its clumps
of leaves can spread fairly quickly and it
suppresses weeds – and other, less vigorous plants
if not carefully sited – most effectively. It likes
damp or moisture-retentive soils.
  Damp and wet soils – Ground-cover.

ANEMONE × hybrida (syn. *A. × elegans*,
***A. japonica*) e.g. 'Louise Uhink' ★ sc NA**
[form of Japanese Anemone]

○ ◑

type of plant: HP
flowering season: l. summer to mid-autumn
flower colour: white
height: 90-105 cm/3-3½ ft

The beautiful flowers of all the Japanese
anemones, including the example shown here,
belie the tough and adaptable nature of these
spreading, ground-covering plants. At first, they
increase slowly and flower little but, once
established, they grow strongly. Because Japanese
anemones produce their leaves late in spring, they
are often interplanted with bulbs. They prefer a
substantial, moisture-retentive soil and will grow
well, but flower less profusely, in full shade.
  Ground-cover.

LYSIMACHIA clethroides
[species of Loosestrife]

○ ◑

type of plant: HP
flowering season: midsummer to e. autumn
flower colour: white
height: 75-90 cm/2½-3 ft

L. clethroides flowers usefully late in the gardening
year in any case, and its season of interest is
lengthened still further by its foliage turning red in
autumn. The flowers last well in water and are
attractive in arrangements because of their
graceful, arching shape. A fairly moist soil is
needed to grow this erectly stemmed plant. If the
soil is also rich, *L. clethroides* can spread quite
quickly.
  Autumn foliage – Cutting.

DORONICUM plantagineum e.g. 'Excelsum'
(syn. *D. p.* 'Harpur Crewe')
[form of Leopard's Bane]

○ ◑

type of plant: HP
flowering season: mid-spring to e. summer
flower colour: yellow
height: 75 cm/2½ ft

The yellow daisies of the doronicums bring a
foretaste of summer to the spring garden. The
particular hybrid illustrated here has exceptionally
large flowers (they are often 8 cm/3 in wide). It is
easy to grow as long as it has a heavyish,
moisture-retentive soil. In strong sun its blooms
may become paler.
  Cutting.

HEMEROCALLIS e.g. 'Marion Vaughn' ★
sc NA
[form of Day Lily]

○ ◑

type of plant: HP
flowering season: summer
flower colour: pale yellow
height: 75 cm/2½ ft

The beautiful and sweetly scented flowers of this vigorous plant are, individually, short-lived, but over the summer months one shapely bloom follows another. The leaves form a thick clump and arch elegantly. Day lilies do best in a good, moisture-retentive soil in borders or by the edge of pools.

Damp and wet soils – Ground-cover – Green foliage – Fragrant flowers.

CHAENOMELES (syn. *Cydonia*) **speciosa** (syn. *C. lagenaria*) e.g. 'Simonii' ★

○ ◑

type of plant: HSh
flowering season: spring
flower colour: scarlet
height: 60-90 cm/2-3 ft

There are few soils and sites with which cultivars of *C. speciosa* – including *C. s.* 'Simonii' – cannot cope. This particular variety is unusually low and spreading. In a sheltered spot its brilliant flowers may be produced as early as January or February. For preference, however, shallow, chalky soils should be avoided and it should be remembered that dense shade will diminish the number of flowers and subsequent golden yellow fruits produced.

Atmospheric pollution – Fruit – Cutting.

DIGITALIS grandiflora (syn. *D. ambigua*)
[species of Foxglove]

○ ◑

type of plant: HP
flowering season: summer
flower colour: yellow
height: 60-90 cm/2-3 ft

Although *D. grandiflora* lasts longer than many perennial foxgloves, it is still a fairly short-lived plant. Growing it in heavy clay usually supplies some of its needs for humus and moisture, but this treatment will not prolong its life. On the other hand, its woodland nature means that it can tolerate dry shade but, under such conditions, flowering will not be profuse.

Dry shade – Cutting.

MONARDA didyma e.g. 'Croftway Pink'
[form of Sweet Bergamont, Bee Balm or Oswego Tea]

○ ◑

type of plant: HP
flowering season: summer
flower colour: rose-pink
height: 60-90 cm/2-3 ft

This plant – and related cultivars such as *M. d.* 'Cambridge Scarlet' (see p. 199) – needs a moist, fertile soil. When growing well it produces numerous flowers in succession and the foliage forms quite a thick clump. Indeed, in ideally damp and rich soils, it can eventually become invasive. Its leaves emit a fresh, orangey smell when bruised.

Damp and wet soils – Aromatic leaves – Cutting.

LYTHRUM virgatum e.g. 'Rose Queen'

○ ◑

type of plant: HP
flowering season: midsummer to e. autumn
flower colour: rose-pink
height: 60 cm/2 ft

L. v. 'Rose Queen' is a tough and adaptable plant which can be grown almost anywhere. Really moist or boggy soils are generally considered most suitable, but heavy clay soils and moist loams give good, if not quite so luxuriant, results.

Damp and wet soils.

POLEMONIUM caeruleum
[Jacob's Ladder, Greek Valerian]

○ ◑

type of plant: HP
flowering season: l. spring to midsummer
flower colour: blue or white
height: 60 cm/2 ft

It would be misleading, perhaps, to say that the feathery leaves of this plant are decorative, but they certainly complement the numerous, dainty flowers. *P. caeruleum* tends to vary in the colour of the blooms it produces. Nurseries specializing in hardy perennials may offer selected forms. *P.* 'Sapphire', for example, has attractive, light blue flowers and it is usually listed with *P. caeruleum*. Fertile, moisture-retentive soils of various sorts produce the best growth and the longest-lived plants.

NARCISSUS (Trumpet) e.g. 'Golden Harvest'
[form of Daffodil]

○ ◑
type of plant: HBb
flowering season: e. spring
flower colour: yellow
height: 45 cm/1½ ft

Both this daffodil and the one in the following photograph are examples of old, garden varieties that grow strongly in a wide variety of soil types. They are well able to compete with other plants and so are suitable for mixed borders and for naturalizing in grass. The slight twist to the petals of N. 'Golden Harvest' helps to prevent the large flowers from looking too solid. 'Mrs R. O. Backhouse' is usually one of the cheapest pink-cupped daffodils in bulb specialists' catalogues.

NARCISSUS (Large-cupped) e.g. 'Mrs R. O. Backhouse'
[form of Daffodil]

○ ◑
type of plant: HBb
flowering season: mid-spring
flower colour: ivory + pink
height: 40 cm/15 in

See preceding plant.

PRUNELLA webbiana e.g. 'Pink Loveliness'
[form of Self-heal]

○ ◑
type of plant: HP
flowering season: all summer
flower colour: clear pink
height: 30 cm/1 ft

This plant's mat of dark green leaves makes good ground-cover in any moist soil; heavy clay is suitable as long as it does not become hard and dry in summer. P. w. 'Pink Loveliness' has a tendency to produce large numbers of self-sown and variably coloured seedlings. Dead-heading helps to keep this proclivity under control.
    Ground-cover.

NARCISSUS × 'W. P. Milner'
[form of Daffodil]

○ ◑
type of plant: HBb
flowering season: l. winter to e. spring
flower colour: yellow
height: 15-25 cm/6-10 in

While this daffodil is altogether smaller and more finely constructed than N. N. 'Golden Harvest' and 'Mrs R. O. Backhouse' (both illustrated above), it too is a robust plant and suitable for naturalizing. Unlike some miniature daffodils, it can cope with a certain amount of heaviness in the soil and it will grow well in most situations.
    Winter-flowering plants.

Additional plants, featured elsewhere in this book, that are suitable for heavy clay soils

○ ◑ sun or partial shade
TAXODIUM distichum: 21-30 m (p. 72)
CARPINUS betulus: 15-21 m (p. 130)
PICEA omorika: 15-21 m (p. 94)
SALIX × chrysocoma ★: 13.5-18 m (p. 72)
FRAXINUS excelsior 'Pendula': 9-15 m (p. 24)
CRATAEGUS monogyna: 7.5-9 m (p. 130)
SALIX daphnoides: 6-9 m (p. 210)
MAGNOLIA × soulangiana: 6-7.5 m (p. 33)
MAGNOLIA × soulangiana e.g. 'Alexandrina': 6-7.5 m (p. 95)
MAGNOLIA × soulangiana e.g. 'Lennei': 6-7.5 m (p. 95)
ACER pseudoplatanus e.g. 'Brilliantissimum': 4.5-6 m (p. 172)
COTONEASTER 'Cornubia': 4.5-6 m (p. 205)
CRATAEGUS oxyacantha e.g. 'Paul's Scarlet': 4.5-6 m (p. 95)
HEDERA colchica 'Dentata-Variegata': 4.5-6 m (p. 151)
HEDERA helix e.g. 'Hibernica': 3.6-4.5 m (p. 109)
SALIX alba 'Chermesina': 3-4.5 m (p. 210)
HEDERA helix e.g. 'Glacier': 3-3.6 m (p. 151)
HEDERA helix e.g. 'Gold Heart' ★: 3-3.6 m (p. 152)
VIBURNUM × bodnantense 'Dawn': 2.4-3.6 m (p. 276)
BERBERIS × stenophylla ★: 2.4-3 m (p. 128)
CORYLUS avellana e.g. 'Contorta': 2.4-3 m (p. 211)
FORSYTHIA × intermedia 'Lynwood': 2.4-3 m (p. 24)
FORSYTHIA × intermedia 'Spectabilis': 2.4-3 m (p. 96)
COTONEASTER 'Hybridus Pendulus': 2.4 m (p. 25)
BERBERIS darwinii: 1.8-3 m (p. 205)
VIBURNUM tinus: 1.8-3 m (p. 277)
CORNUS alba 'Elegantissima' ★: 1.8-2.7 m (p. 72)

RIBES sanguineum e.g. 'Pulborough Scarlet': 1.8-2.7 m (p. 80)
CORNUS stolonifera 'Flaviramea': 1.8-2.4 m (p. 211)
COTONEASTER simonsii: 1.8-2.4 m (p. 128)
AUCUBA japonica: 1.5-2.4 m (p. 83)
AUCUBA japonica e.g. 'Crotonifolia': 1.5-2.4 m (p. 136)
CORNUS alba 'Sibirica': 1.5-2.4 m (p. 211)
RIBES sanguineum e.g. 'King Edward VII': 1.5-2.1 m (p. 96)
SYMPHORICARPOS rivularis: 1.5-2.1 m (p. 206)
WEIGELA florida 'Variegata' ★: 1.5 m (p. 152)
CHAENOMELES speciosa e.g. 'Nivalis': 1.2-1.8 m (p. 96)
DIPSACUS fullonum: 1.2-1.8 m (p. 206)
LIGULARIA stenocephala 'The Rocket': 1.2-1.8 m (p. 73)
SYMPHORICARPOS × doorenbosii 'White Hedge': 1.2-1.8 m (p. 130)
VIBURNUM carlesii: 1.2-1.8 m (p. 268)
CHAENOMELES × superba e.g. 'Knap Hill Scarlet': 1.2-1.5 m (p. 244)
CHAENOMELES × superba e.g. 'Rowallane': 1.2-1.5 m (p. 130)
SYMPHYTUM × uplandicum: 1.2-1.5 m (p. 73)
ACANTHUS mollis latifolius: 1.2 m (p. 25)
LIGULARIA dentata 'Desdemona': 1.2 m (p. 172)
ACANTHUS spinosus: 90-120 cm (p. 184)
SPIRAEA × bumalda 'Anthony Waterer': 90-120 cm (p. 107)
LYTHRUM salicaria e.g. 'Firecandle': 90 cm (p. 74)
THALICTRUM aquilegifolium: 90 cm (p. 166)
VIBURNUM davidii ★: 90 cm (p. 206)
HEMEROCALLIS e.g. 'Pink Damask': 75-90 cm (p. 107)
POLEMONIUM foliosissimum: 75-90 cm (p. 184)
POLYGONUM bistorta 'Superbum': 75-90 cm (p. 74)
LYTHRUM salicaria e.g. 'Robert': 75 cm (p. 74)
HEMEROCALLIS e.g. 'Burning Daylight': 60-90 cm (p. 74)   *continued*

○ ◐ sun or partial shade *continued*
LYSIMACHIA punctata: 60-90cm (p. 75)
MONARDA didyma e.g. 'Cambridge Scarlet':
   60-90cm (p. 199)
RUSCUS aculeatus: 60-90cm (p. 84)
COTONEASTER horizontalis ★: 60cm (p. 194)
PICEA abies 'Nidiformis': 60cm (p. 35)
ANEMONE×hybrida e.g. 'September Charm':
   45-60cm (p. 107)
LEUCOJUM aestivum 'Gravetye': 45-60cm (p. 75)
ALCHEMILLA mollis ★: 45cm (p. 108)
DORONICUM e.g. 'Spring Beauty': 40-45cm
   (p. 249)
BERGENIA×'Ballawley': 30-45cm (p. 25)
COTONEASTER 'Hybridus Pendulus': 30-45cm
   (p. 25)
FRITILLARIA meleagris: 30-45cm (p. 75)
FRITILLARIA meleagris e.g. 'Aphrodite':
   30-45cm (p. 76)
BERGENIA cordifolia: 30cm (p. 184)
BERGENIA×'Silberlicht': 30cm (p. 109)
HEDERA helix 'Hibernica': 23-30cm (p. 109)
PRUNELLA webbiana e.g. 'Loveliness': 23cm
   (p. 110)
SYMPHYTUM grandiflorum: 23cm (p. 110)
GALANTHUS elwesii: 15-25cm (p. 277)
HEDERA colchica 'Dentato-Variegata': 15-23cm
   (p. 151)
GALANTHUS nivalis: 10-20cm (p. 278)
COTONEASTER dammeri: 10cm (p. 111)

ILEX crenata 'Helleri' NA
[form of Japanese Holly]

◐ [○]
type of plant: HSh
height: 1.2 m/4 ft
E

This is a neat, compact, dome-shaped shrub with small, dark evergreen leaves. Fruit, when produced, is black. Used frequently in home gardens and commercial plantings in the United States, where *Ilex aquifolium* is usually unsatisfactory, *I. crenata* tolerates winter cold and summer heat better than does that species.

ACONITUM napellus e.g. 'Bressingham Spire'
[form of Monkshood]

◐ [○]
type of plant: HP
flowering season: summer
flower colour: violet-blue
height: 90 cm/3 ft

A. n. 'Bressington Spire' has, as its varietal name suggests, strikingly upright flower spikes which, together with the darkness of its hooded blooms and the deep divisions of its leaves, make it an imposing plant. Moisture-retentive soils, including clay, suit varieties of *A. napellus* best. If these plants are grown in sun they need to be watered frequently in dry weather.

MYOSOTIS alpestris (syn. *M. rupicola*) e.g.
'Carmine King'
[form of Forget-me-not]

◐ [○]
type of plant: HB
flowering season: mid-spring to e. summer
flower colour: carmine-pink
height: 23 cm/9 in

As noted in the introduction to this list, varieties of *M. alpestris* do well, but are short-lived, in clay. Ideally, they should be given a moist, fertile soil which is reasonably well drained. *M.* 'Carmine King' is an upright plant and probably the most attractive of the red- or pink-flowered forget-me-nots. There are, of course, numerous blue-flowered varieties of this plant (for an example of which, see p. 144).
   Paving.

ERANTHIS hyemalis
[Winter Aconite]

◐ [○]
type of plant: HTu
flowering season: l. winter to e. spring
flower colour: yellow
height: 8-10 cm/3-4 in

The winter aconite is one of those tantalizing plants that can make large and beautiful carpets of colour once established, or can disappear without trace a couple of years after planting. Two factors which make the former state of affairs more likely are plenty of moisture (in a fairly heavy loam or clay, for example), and the use of freshly lifted tubers. By early summer this plant is no longer visible above ground.
   Winter-flowering plants.

DIGITALIS purpurea e.g. 'Foxy'
[form of Foxglove]

◐
type of plant: HB/A
flowering season: summer
flower colour: mixed – pink, rose, cream, white
height: 75-90 cm/2½-3 ft

Where the very tall flower spikes of the larger strains of foxglove would be out of scale, *D. p.* 'Foxy' could be a suitable substitute. Its colour range is slightly less wide than that of, for instance, *D. p.* 'Excelsior' (see p. 251) and its flower stems are obviously shorter, but it is still good material for cutting. It may be grown as an annual from seed sown in earliest spring under glass or indoors. It should be planted out in a moisture-retentive soil.
   Cutting.

ANEMONE nemorosa
[Wood Anemone]

◑

type of plant: HTu
flowering season: spring
flower colour: pinkish white
height: 15-23 cm/6-9 in

One of the prettiest inhabitants of British woodlands, the wood anemone is a remarkably adaptable plant. It grows well in heavy soils but it will tolerate quite dry conditions too. It looks especially attractive naturalized in grass amongst trees and large shrubs where the absence of its leaves after midsummer is not noticeable.

Chalk – Dry shade.

LEUCOJUM vernum ★
[species of Snowflake]

◑

type of plant: HBb
flowering season: l. winter to e. spring
flower colour: white
height:15-20 cm/6-8 in

L. vernum will do well in any moisture-retentive soil; the fertility of the soil is not important. Some people find that the fairly large blooms of this plant smell unattractively like hawthorn flowers, while other people find its fragrance sweet and pure.

Fragrant flowers – Winter-flowering plants.

PIERIS floribunda NA

◑ ●

type of plant; HSh
flowering season: e. spring
flower colour: white
height: 1.8 m/6 ft
*E

This is a compact grower, with horizontally borne clusters of white bell-shaped flowers in spring. It is hardier than the more common *P. japonica*, and tolerant of heavier soil at maturity.

PODOPHYLLUM peltatum NA
[Mayapple]

◑ ●

type of plant: HP
flowering season: spring
flower colour: white
height: 45 cm/1½ ft

A charming spring wild flower of the woodlands of the eastern United States. The flowers are 5 cm/2 in across, and are followed by edible yellow fruit. The foliage, which dies back in summer, is large and palmately lobed. In Britain, *P. emodi* (see p. 208) is more readily available than *P. peltatum*.

Additional plants, featured elsewhere in this book, that are suitable for heavy clay soils

◑ [○] partial shade (or sun)
MAHONIA aquifolium: 90-120 cm (p. 112)
RODGERSIA pinnata e.g. 'Superba' ★: 90-120 cm (p. 77)
RODGERSIA podophylla: 90-120 cm (p. 172)
RODGERSIA tabularis: 90-120 cm (p. 184)
DRYOPTERIS filix-mas: 60-120 cm (p. 80)
SCROPHULARIA aquatica 'Variegata': 60-90 cm (p. 153)
MENTHA spicata: 60 cm (p. 200)
TELLIMA grandiflora: 45-60 cm (p. 113)
MENTHA rotundifolia 'Variegata': 30-60 cm (p. 154)
AJUGA pyramidalis: 15-23 cm (p. 114)
MYOSOTIS alpestris e.g. 'Blue Ball': 15 cm (p. 144)
AJUGA reptans e.g. 'Burgundy Glow' ★: 10-15 cm (p. 172)
AJUGA reptans e.g. 'Variegata': 8-10 cm (p. 154)
LYSIMACHIA nummularia: 2-5 cm (p. 115)

◑ partial shade
DIGITALIS purpurea e.g. 'Excelsior Strain': 1.5 m (p. 251)
ARUNCUS dioicus: 1.2-1.8 m (p. 79)

◑ ● partial or full shade
HEDERA helix 'Hibernica': 3.6-4.5 m (p. 109)
FORSYTHIA × intermedia 'Lynwood': 2.4-3 m (p. 24)
FORSYTHIA × intermedia 'Spectabilis': 2.4-3 m (p. 96)
FORSYTHIA suspensa ★: 2.4-3 m (p. 50)
AUCUBA japonica: 1.5-2.4 m (p. 83)
AUCUBA japonica e.g. 'Crotonifolia': 1.5-2.4 m (p. 136)
SYMPHORICARPOS rivularis: 1.5-2.1 m (p. 206)
HYDRANGEA macrophylla 'Nikko Blue': 1.5 m (p. 83)
CHAENOMELES speciosa e.g. 'Nivalis': 1.2-1.8 m (p. 96)

SYMPHORICARPOS × doorenbosii 'White Hedge': 1.2-1.8 m (p. 130)
CHAENOMELES × superba e.g. 'Knap Hill Scarlet': 1.2-1.5 m (p. 244)
CHAENOMELES × superba e.g. 'Rowallane': 1.2-1.5 m (p. 130)
SYMPHYTUM × uplandicum: 1.2-1.5 m (p. 73)
MAHONIA aquifolium: 90-120 cm (p. 112)
RODGERSIA pinnata e.g. 'Superba' ★: 90-120 cm (p. 77)
RODGERSIA podophylla: 90-120 cm (p. 172)
RODGERSIA tabularis: 90-120 cm (p. 184)
ANEMONE × hybrida e.g. 'Louise Uhink' ★: 90-105 cm (p. 51)
POLYGONATUM × hybridum ★: 75-90 cm (p. 252)
DRYOPTERIS dilatata: 60-120 cm (p. 186)
CHAENOMELES speciosa e.g. 'Simonii' ★: 60-90 cm (p. 52)
DRYOPTERIS cristata: 60-90 cm (p. 79)
RUSCUS aculeatus: 60-90 cm (p. 84)
SCROPHULARIA aquatica 'Variegata': 60-90 cm (p. 153)
ANEMONE × hybrida e.g. 'September Charm': 45-60 cm (p. 107)
LAMIUM galeobdolon 'Variegatum': 30 cm (p. 81)
HEDERA helix 'Hibernica': 23-30 cm (p. 109)
SYMPHYTUM grandiflorum: 23 cm (p. 110)
LAMIUM maculatum 'Roseum': 15-23 cm (p. 117)
LAMIUM maculatum 'Aureum': 15 cm (p. 178)

Plants suitable for dry soils in hot, sunny sites

The majority of plants appreciate some sunshine, but fewer of them can withstand hot, dry conditions and occasional periods of drought. Fast-draining sandy soils, shallow soils over chalk and poor, stony soils, as well as steep, south-facing banks, and beds at the foot of sunny, sheltered walls can all be hot enough and dry enough to make many plants wilt and die. On the other hand, some plants actually enjoy such conditions: you may never see the beautiful, winter blooms of *Iris unguicularis* (Algerian iris) unless you plant it in full sun and very well drained soil, and many of those sought-after, grey-leaved plants will grow long and lanky – and become much more susceptible to frost damage – in cool, moisture-retentive soils.

Plants which do well in hot, dry sites have adapted themselves, in various ways, to the conditions prevailing there. Some of these adaptations are attractive. For instance, most plants with aromatic foliage can withstand strong sun and lack of moisture. This is because the oils which they contain become volatile in heat and produce a protective haze around the vulnerable leaf surfaces, thereby preventing the whole plant from becoming desiccated. Some plants have hairy leaves which perform the same protective function, and which make their foliage appear grey. (For the many attractive grey-leaved plants which are suitable for hot, dry sites, use this list in conjunction with the list entitled 'Plants with grey, blue-grey or "silver" leaves'.) Finally, other plants have developed thick, fleshy leaves in order to retain moisture and prevent desiccation; the popular sempervivums or houseleeks, which are so often grown in drystone walls, are examples of plants with this sort of foliage.

Some plants which can survive in dry soils and full sun do not appear in the following list. In many cases, these plants, which include border carnations and bearded hybrid irises, are grown specifically for their flowers and often for cutting. Hot, dry soils are not moist enough – and often not rich enough – to produce, large, well formed blooms in any quantity, and many gardeners would be disappointed with these plants' performance in arid conditions. A few plants have been excluded because they will not reach maximum size in dry places, and largeness is their main feature (the cotton or Scotch thistle, *Onopordum acanthium*, has been omitted on this basis). Other plants, such as *Lupinus arboreus* (tree lupin), may be rather smaller in dryish places but, in their case, size is less important than, for instance, flowers or fragrance; these plants have been included in the following list.

If moisture-retaining substances, such as peat and leaf-mould are dug into the soil, hot and rather arid sites can contain a wider range of plants than appears in this list. In addition, a good covering of foliage can do much to reduce the loss of moisture from a soil (many dense, leafy plants appear in the 'Ground-cover' list). For details of how to improve dry soils, as well as descriptions of suitable – mainly perennial – plants, see Beth Chatto's *The Dry Garden* (published by Dent).

Finally, in interpreting descriptions of the soil types suitable for different plants, it is important to remember that the words 'well drained' do not usually mean sharply drained, and that they may denote the moist, cool sponginess of peaty soils. Similarly, it is worth bearing in mind that plants which thrive in fast-draining soil and sun beside the sea, are not always suitable for a hot, dry site inland, since the general humidity of the seaside will often be missing there.

Entries for ○ [◑] *(sun (or partial shade)) and* ○ ◑ *(sun or partial shade) categories have been retained to allow cross-reference to other lists.*

GENISTA aetnensis sc NA
[Mount Etna Broom]
○
type of plant: HSh
flowering season: summer
flower colour: yellow
height: 4.5-6 m/15-20 ft

This plant's open structure of branches and rushy, green twigs is filled, in midsummer, with a mass of vanilla-scented blossom. A light, rather poor soil which drains quickly is ideal; on richer soils this shrub does not flower very freely.

Atmospheric pollution – Fragrant flowers.

YUCCA gloriosa
○
type of plant: HSh
flowering season: autumn
flower colour: creamy white, sometimes tinged red
height: 2.7-3.6 m/9-12 ft
E; leaves 1.2-2.4 m/4-8 ft high

The sharp-pointed leaves of this plant are arranged in a dramatic rosette. Older specimens have short, wrinkled trunks and, if grown in a hot site and a well drained soil, they will flower fairly regularly every few years. The great panicles of flowers may sometimes be damaged by frost in Britain. *Y. gloriosa* is a very long-lived plant which increases slowly in size.

Chalk – Seaside – Containers – Green foliage.

SPARTIUM junceum
[Spanish Broom]
○
type of plant: HSh
flowering season: summer
flower colour: yellow
height: 2.1-3 m/7-10 ft

The Spanish broom has a tendency to become lanky with age. However, sharply draining soils and full sun, as well as twice-yearly trimming of the green, rush-like twigs, helps to produce bushy plants. Strong winds, including salty sea gales, will also encourage dense growth. The pea-shaped flowers have a sweet scent and are produced over a period of several weeks.

Chalk – Seaside – Atmospheric pollution – Bark and *twigs* – Fragrant flowers.

CYTISUS scoparius e.g. 'Andreanus'
[form of Common Broom]

○

type of plant: HSh
flowering season: l. spring to e. summer
flower colour: yellow + crimson
height: 1.8 m/6 ft

There are numerous varieties of the common
broom, many of them conspicuously bicoloured
like the example illustrated here. All of them are
shrubs with upright branches and spraying twigs.
They are easy to grow and very floriferous. Their
green twigs should be cut back quite hard after
flowering. Poor, sandy soils suit these plants best.

Acid soils – Seaside – Atmospheric pollution –
Bark and *twigs*.

CYTISUS × praecox
[Warminster Broom]

○

type of plant: HSh
flowering season: spring
flower colour: pale yellow
height: 1.2-1.5 m/4-6 ft

The pendulous green branches of this shrub create
an attractive rounded shape throughout the year
but when they become covered with flowers in
spring the effect is spectacular. Unfortunately,
this great arching sheaf of blossom has a heavy,
dank smell. The most suitable soils for *C. × praecox*
have very good drainage and are not particularly
fertile.

Atmospheric pollution – Bark and *twigs*.

TEUCRIUM fruticans sc NA
[Shrubby Germander]

○

type of plant: HHSh
flowering season: summer to e. autumn
flower colour: pale blue
height: 1.2-1.5 m/4-5 ft
E

Only in mild, maritime areas can this loosely
spreading shrub be grown in an open position.
Elsewhere it needs shelter and warmth. Its
grey-green leaves and lipped flowers are carried on
white stems; the foliage is attractively aromatic.
T. fruticans requires a light, dryish soil. It is not
hardy in colder parts of the United States.

Seaside – Grey, etc. leaves – Aromatic leaves.

YUCCA filamentosa ★
[Adam's Needle]

○

type of plant: HSh
flowering season: summer
flower colour: creamy white
height: 90-180 cm/3-6 ft
E; leaves 60-75 cm/2-2½ ft high

All the cultivated yuccas are boldly shaped,
handsome plants but *Y. filamentosa* is especially
attractive, mainly because its flowers are so lovely
and its leaves are so satisfactorily broad and yet not
sharp nor too rigid. A really warm position and a
well drained soil are essential, and if this plant is
grown for its flowers as well as its leaves, the soil
must also be reasonably fertile. Compared with
Y. gloriosa (see above, p. 56), *Y. filamentosa* is
free-flowering.

Chalk – Seaside – Containers – Green foliage –
Fragrant flowers.

CISTUS × corbariensis sc NA MC
[form of Rock Rose]

○

type of plant: HSh
flowering season: summer
flower colour: white + yellow
height: 90-120 cm/3-4 ft
E

Some gardeners doubt the hardiness of this plant
and it is certainly not suitable for cold, heavy soils
and frosty places. However, grown in a very light
soil which drains rapidly and given an open, hot
and sunny position, *C. × corbariensis* will quickly
form a bushy hummock of dark, wavy leaves. Its
numerous flowers are produced in succession over
several weeks. The toughest rock rose is generally
considered to be *C. laurifolius*. It has pure white
flowers and may grow up to 180 cm/6 ft high.

Chalk – Seaside – Atmospheric pollution –
Ground-cover.

MALVA alcea 'Fastigiata'
[form of Mallow]

○

type of plant: HP
flowering season: midsummer to mid-autumn
flower colour: rose-pink
height: 90 cm/3 ft

Poor soils prolong the life of this plant and it will
flower over an exceptionally long period even
when there is little or no rain. The upright stems
usually need no staking.

PHYGELIUS capensis sc NA MC
[Cape Figwort]
○
type of plant: SlTSh/P
flowering season: midsummer to mid-autumn
flower colour: red
height: 90 cm/3 ft
E, up to 1.8 m/6 ft against a wall

In districts with cold winters, it is probably best to
regard this plant as a herbaceous perennial and to
let its top growth die and be renewed each year.
Against a sunny wall in a warm garden however, its
almost branchless stems will become woody and
persistent. *P. capensis* has a long flowering season.
It can withstand drought well. It is not hardy in
colder parts of the United States.
Cutting.

STIPA calamagrostis
○
type of plant: HP (Gr)
flowering season: summer
flower colour: green changing to buff
height: 90 cm/3 ft

The feathery plumes of this grass are often
30 cm/12 in long. They sway above a dense but
rather untidy clump of ground-covering foliage. If
cut when fully ripened, they dry well.
S. calamagrostis is one of the most attractive grasses
for light, well drained soils.
Chalk – Ground-cover – Cutting – Green
flowers.

ACHILLEA 'Coronation Gold' (syn.
A. eupatorium 'Coronation Gold', *A. filipendulina*
'Coronation Gold')
[form of Yarrow]
○
type of plant: HP
flowering season: summer
flower colour: yellow
height: 75-90 cm/2½-3 ft
½E

Where *A.* 'Gold Plate' (see p. 214) would be much
too large, this similar but altogether smaller plant
would be a good substitute. The flat flowers retain
nearly all their original colour when dried. In
winter, rosettes of feathery leaves remain. Well
drained soils of most types suit this plant.
Chalk – Cutting.

COSMOS (syn. *Cosmea*) **sulphureus e.g.**
'Sunset'
○
type of plant: HHA
flowering season: midsummer to e. autumn
flower colour: orange-red
height: 75-90 cm/2½-3 ft

Only in hot, dry places will this upright plant
flower freely for many weeks. If picked in bud, the
long-stemmed blooms last well in water.
Chalk – Green foliage – Cutting.

ERYNGIUM tripartitum ★
○
type of plant: HP
flowering season: midsummer to e. autumn
flower colour: grey-blue
height: 75 cm/2½ ft

The slender stems of this plant tend to sprawl,
particularly in fairly rich, moist soils, but its
numerous, blue, ball-like flowers make up for any
thinness or untidiness in its habit of growth. A
dryish, sandy soil and full sun suit *E. tripartitum*
best and it will tolerate short periods of drought.
The 1 cm/½ in wide flowers are useful for cutting
and drying although they look most effective when
covering the plant outdoors.
Chalk – Cutting.

TULIPA (Darwin) e.g. 'The Bishop'
[form of Tulip]
○
type of plant: HBb
flowering season: l. spring
flower colour: purple
height: 75 cm/2½ ft

This tulip is so darkly and opulently coloured that,
unless it is set amongst paler plants or given a
contrastingly light background, it may not be
very conspicuous. The same is true of an even
darker Darwin tulip, 'La Tulipe Noire' (which is,
in fact, a deep maroon-purple). Like all tulips,
these plants thrive and last longest in well drained,
preferably alkaline soils and in positions where
their bulbs can receive plenty of sun. They are of a
type of tulip which is especially popular for spring
bedding displays.
Chalk.

HALIMIUM ocymoides (syn. *Helianthemum algarvense*) sc NA MC

○

type of plant: SlTSh
flowering season: e. summer
flower colour: yellow + brown
height: 60-90 cm/2-3 ft
E

The lovely, warm combination of yellow and dark chocolate brown in its petals makes this branching, hummocky plant a distinctive member of the rock rose and sun rose family. In common with its relations, however, it needs a very well drained soil and full sun; it thrives on hot, dry banks and in seaside gardens. Its foliage is grey-green.

Chalk – Ground-cover – Containers – Grey, etc. leaves.

**TULIPA (Darwin Hybrid) e.g. 'Gudoshnik'
[form of Tulip]**

○

type of plant: HBb
flowering season: spring
flower colour: apricot-pink + orange-scarlet
height: 60 cm/2 ft

Many Darwin hybrid tulips have brightly coloured flowers (see, for example, *T.* 'Apeldoorn', p. 7) but there are several varieties in softer shades and some forms – like *T.* 'Gudoshnik' – combine soft and bright colours in their petals. All tulips of this type have very large flowers on strong stems. They do not do well on heavy, slow-draining soils; hot, dry conditions are much more suitable.

Chalk.

**DIMORPHOTHECA barberiae
[species of Cape Marigold]**

○

type of plant: SlTP
flowering season: all summer
flower colour: purplish pink
height: 45-60 cm/1½-2 ft

A sunny site is essential for this plant, first, because it is not fully hardy and, second, because only in sunshine will its flowers open wide. Its lack of hardiness also means that excellent drainage is required. (There is a smaller variety of this plant, known as *D. b.* 'Compacta', which is slightly hardier.) In ideally hot and dry conditions it will create quite a dense, spreading clump of aromatic foliage. In the United States, the plant is grown as an annual except in California.

Chalk – Ground-cover – Aromatic leaves.

**CHEIRANTHUS × allionii (syn. *Erysimum asperum*)
[Siberian Wallflower]**

○

type of plant: HB
flowering season: spring to e. summer
flower colour: orange
height: 40 cm/15 in
E

The most popular wallflowers are cultivars of *C. cheiri*, but the lesser known Siberian wallflower and its few varieties are attractive plants of denser habit and spicier scent which, usefully, flower a little later than their commoner counterparts. (While varieties of *C. cheiri* appear under 'wallflower' in seedsmen's lists, the Siberian wallflower is to be found under *Cheiranthus*). All really well drained, alkaline soils are suitable for *C. × allionii*.

Chalk – Fragrant flowers.

**TULIPA (Greigii Hybrid) e.g. 'Oriental Splendour'
[form of Tulip]**

○

type of plant: HBb
flowering season: mid-spring
flower colour: red + yellow
height: 40 cm/15 in

Although, of course, they are not very long-lasting features in the garden each year, the striped leaves of tulips like 'Oriental Splendour' can be extremely decorative. The flowers, as well as the leaves, of this particular variety are bicoloured, and some gardeners may find this altogether too 'busy' a combination. *T.* 'Red Riding Hood' (see p. 149) is a Greigii hybrid with flowers of a uniform scarlet and very darkly striped leaves. The bulbs of these plants need to be hot and dry in summer so that they will flower well the following year.

Chalk – Variegated leaves.

**CYTISUS × kewensis
[form of Broom]**

○

type of plant: HSh
flowering season: l. spring
flower colour: pale yellow
height: 30-60 cm/1-2 ft

Like all the commonly grown brooms, *C. × kewensis* flowers very freely. Its habit of growth is spreading (sometimes up to 150 cm/5 ft wide) and more or less prostrate. In sharply draining, sandy soils and full sun the layers of twigs can be dense enough to smother most weeds.

Ground-cover – Containers.

HELIPTERUM manglesii (syn. *Rhodanthe manglesii*)
[species of Everlasting Flower or Immortelle]
○
type of plant: H/HHA
flowering season: midsummer to e. autumn
flower colour: mixed – pink, white + yellow
height: 30-45 cm/1-1½ ft

H. manglesii is grown mainly for its strawy flowers which are easy to dry. It is also useful for planting in infertile soils that drain very rapidly (although it can be grown successfully under quite moist and fertile conditions too).

Chalk – Cutting.

CALAMINTHA nepetoides
○
type of plant: HP
flowering season: l. summer to e. autumn
flower colour: blue + white
height: 30-40 cm/12-15 in

This bushy plant, with its numerous upright stems, becomes a haze of palest blue towards the end of summer. It thrives in dry soils.

Chalk – Aromatic leaves.

TROPAEOLUM majus e.g. 'Golden Gleam'
[form of Nasturtium]
○
type of plant: HA
flowering season: summer to e. autumn
flower colour: yellow
height: 30-40 cm/12-15 in

Nasturtiums are such undemanding plants that it is nearly impossible not to grow them successfully. They are especially well suited to poor, dry soils, where they bloom very freely; on rich soils they tend to produce so much foliage that many of the flowers become hidden. The 'Gleam' strain of nasturtiums is noted for its vigour. The plants have semi-trailing stems and large, sweetly scented blooms (the fragrance is strongest in the yellow-flowered varieties, such as shown above).

Ground-cover – Fragrant flowers (*T. m.* 'Golden Gleam' only).

TROPAEOLUM majus e.g. 'Scarlet Gleam'
[form of Nasturtium]
○
type of plant: HA
flowering season: summer to e. autumn
flower colour: orange-red
height: 30-40 cm/12-15 in

See preceding plant.

CREPIS rubra
[species of Hawk's Beard]
○
type of plant: HA
flowering season: l. summer
flower colour: pink
height: 30 cm/1 ft

Easily grown in any soil with good drainage, this plant also performs well where there is little moisture and where the soil is infertile. Its flowers are carried on erect stems above a low rosette of foliage; they close in the afternoon.

Chalk.

DIMORPHOTHECA 'Aurantiaca Hybrids'
[form of Star of the Veldt]
○
type of plant: HHA
flowering season: summer
flower colour: mixed – white, lemon, orange, salmon, cream
height: 30 cm/1 ft

In a warm garden these plants may be treated as hardy annuals and sown, in late spring, where they are to flower. They need a light, dryish soil; their spreading habit makes them particularly suitable for covering sunny banks. The flowers close in the evening and during dull weather. Removing the faded blooms lengthens the flowering season considerably.

Chalk.

ESCHSCHOLZIA californica e.g. 'Ballerina'
[form of Californian Poppy]

○

type of plant: HA
flowering season: summer to e. autumn
flower colour: mixed – red, pink, orange, yellow
height: 30 cm/1 ft

Apart from their masses of bright blooms, the Californian poppies have decorative, blue-green leaves which are finely divided. The largest number of flowers appear on sandy soils which drain very quickly. Poor soils are suitable, provided they are light and rather dry. The mixture shown here produces fluted flowers, a few of which may be bicoloured. The blooms are open during the hours of full daylight only.

Grey, etc. leaves.

TULIPA eichleri
[species of Tulip]

○

type of plant: HBb
flowering season: spring
flower colour: scarlet
height: 30 cm/1 ft

Some of the species of tulip are easier to grow than the more commonly seen hybrids. *T. eichleri*, for example, can establish itself in sunny places and well drained soils in a way very few of the large-flowered bedding tulips could possibly match. And yet its satiny petals are just as conspicuously coloured as those of any named variety.

Chalk.

TULIPA (Double Early) e.g. 'Peach Blossom'
[form of Tulip]

○

type of plant: HBb
flowering season: mid-spring
flower colour: deep rose-pink
height: 30 cm/1 ft

This confection of pink is less susceptible to wind damage than it looks, since the long-lasting flowers are borne on fairly short stems. The Double Early tulips (of which another example appears on p. 13) are popular for spring bedding displays.

Chalk.

ZAUSCHNERIA californica MC
[Californian Fuchsia]

○

type of plant: SlTP
flowering season: l. summer to mid-autumn
flower colour: scarlet
height: 30 cm/1 ft

In full sun and with the reflected warmth from a south-facing wall, this plant will flower well and make substantial clumps of growth above spreading, underground shoots. Good drainage is essential. In Britain it is advisable to cover *Z. californica*, with bracken or straw for example, during the coldest months. The foliage of this plant is a greyish green. It is tender in the cooler parts of the United States.

Chalk – Ground-cover – Grey, etc. leaves.

TULIPA clusiana ★
[Lady Tulip]

○

type of plant: HBb
flowering season: mid-spring
flower colour: red + white
height: 23-40 cm/9-15 in

Elegantly slender in all its parts, this tulip needs a sheltered position if it is not to become damaged by wind and rain. With shelter, however, and a really well drained soil, its bulbs will ripen properly each summer and they need not be lifted and dried every year.

Chalk.

ESCHSCHOLZIA californica e.g. 'Mission Bells'
[form of Californian Poppy]

○

type of plant: HA
flowering season: summer to e. autumn
flower colour: mixed – yellow, red, orange, pink
height: 23-30 cm/9-12 in

For general remarks about the appearance and cultivation of Californian poppies see *E. c.* 'Ballerina', 30 cm/1 ft, above. The variety shown here has particularly large flowers but, as is usual with these annuals, the petals close up in dull weather, and even on sunny days they are open during the lightest part of the day only.

Grey, etc. leaves.

GAILLARDIA e.g. 'Goblin'
[form of Blanket Flower]

○

type of plant: **HP**
flowering season: **summer to mid-autumn**
flower colour: **red + yellow**
height: **23 cm/9 in**

Most of the readily available forms of perennial
blanket flower are about three times as tall as the
variety shown here. This plant will live longest and
be at its best in a light, dry soil.
Chalk.

HELIANTHEMUM nummularium (syn.
H. chamaecistus, H. vulgare) e.g. 'Mrs Earle' (syn.
'Fireball') ★
[form of Sun Rose]

○

type of plant: **HSh**
flowering season: **summer**
flower colour: **red**
height: **23 cm/9 in**
E

Double-flowered varieties of sun rose, such as
H. n. 'Mrs Earle', retain their petals until evening;
the blooms of single-flowered forms have normally
disintegrated by early afternoon. In full sun and a
very well drained soil they make dense and
spreading hummocks of ground-cover. Some
varieties have grey leaves (see, for example, *H. n.*
'Wisley Pink', p. 162).
Chalk – Ground-cover – Paving.

LINARIA maroccana e.g. 'Fairy Bouquet'
[form of Toadflax]

○

type of plant: **HA**
flowering season: **summer**
flower colour: **mixed – violet, blue, red, pink,
yellow**
height: **23 cm/9 in**

This upright but well branched plant will flower
freely in most soils. However, it thrives where the
drainage is good, and it is quite suitable for hot and
rather dry conditions.
Chalk.

SEDUM × 'Ruby Glow'
[form of Stonecrop]

○

type of plant: **HP**
flowering season: **l. summer**
flower colour: **crimson**
height: **23 cm/9 in**

The overall impression of rich colouring which
this plant gives is due not only to its flowers but
also to the purplish tints of its blue-grey leaves and
the redness of its semi-prostrate stems. *S.* × 'Ruby
Glow' is well able to withstand periods of drought,
and in dry conditions the young foliage is rarely
devoured by slugs to the extent that it is in
moisture-retentive soils.
Chalk – Ground-cover – Grey, etc. leaves.

TROPAEOLUM majus e.g. 'Empress of India'
[form of Nasturtium]

○

type of plant: **HA**
flowering season: **summer to e. autumn**
flower colour: **scarlet**
height: **23 cm/9 in**

Many of the mixtures of nasturtium offered by
seedsmen will contain some plants that have dark
green or bronze foliage. A few of these plants,
including the example shown here, can be
obtained as separate varieties. There is also a form
(*T. m.* 'Alaska Mixed') with pale green leaves
which are variegated with cream. All these rather
bushy plants are ideally suited to hot, dry, infertile
soils where they will flower freely. Moister
conditions are needed for lush foliage.
Ground-cover – Green foliage.

ERYSIMUM linifolium (syn. *Cheiranthus
linifolius*)

○

type of plant: **HB**
flowering season: **l. spring to midsummer**
flower colour: **lilac**
height: **15-30 cm/6-12 in**
E

A drystone wall provides the ideal conditions for
this plant which lives longest and flowers most
profusely in poor, sharply drained soils and full
sun. Its tufted habit of growth also makes it
suitable for short-term ground-cover at the edge of
borders and beside paths.
Chalk – Ground-cover.

CHEIRANTHUS cheiri e.g. 'Tom Thumb Mixed'
[form of Wallflower]

○

type of plant: HB
flowering season: spring to e. summer
flower colour: mixed – yellow, orange, red
height: 15-23 cm/6-9 in
E

In small gardens and windy positions dwarf wallflowers like those of the 'Tom Thumb' strain are useful alternatives to the taller varieties such as 'Blood Red' (p. 9) and 'Cloth of Gold' (p. 259). Whatever their height, these plants need a well drained and preferably alkaline soil; they will thrive on dry, sunny banks. The 'Tom Thumb' mixture is also available in separate colours. Its flowers are richly fragrant.

Chalk – Fragrant flowers.

SEMPERVIVUM montanum
[species of Houseleek]

○

type of plant: HP
flowering season: summer
flower colour: pinkish purple
height: 15-23 cm/6-9 in
E; leaves 2-5 cm/1-2 in high

Once established, this plant needs very little moisture to grow well. It is especially suitable for sunny, drystone walls, where its neat bobbles of foliage knit into dense mats.

Chalk – Paving – Green foliage.

ALYSSUM saxatile e.g. 'Compactum'
[form of Gold Dust]

○

type of plant: HP
flowering season: mid-spring to e. summer
flower colour: golden yellow
height: 15 cm/6 in
E

Plenty of sun, a very well drained soil and a good, hard pruning after the flowers have faded will keep this plant tidy and dense. Most varieties of *A. saxatile* are rather short-lived; the double-flowered form (*A. s.* 'Plenum', syn. 'Flore-pleno') tends to last longest. For a softly coloured variety of gold dust see *A. s.* 'Dudley Neville', p. 15.

Chalk – Ground-cover – Paving – Grey, etc. leaves.

CALANDRINIA umbellata ★
[Rock Purslane]

○

type of plant: HHA/HB
flowering season: summer
flower colour: crimson
height: 15 cm/6 in

C. umbellata's dazzling flower colour seems appropriate for a plant that thrives in almost parched soils and the sunniest possible positions. Several specimens of this semi-prostrate annual (it is biennial in mild areas only) will create quite good ground-cover if they are grown about 15-20 cm/6-8 in apart.

Paving.

PORTULACA grandiflora 'Double Mixed'
[form of Sun Plant]

○

type of plant: HHA
flowering season: summer to e. autumn
flower colour: mixed – yellow, white, red, pink, purple, orange
height: 15 cm/6 in

A dry soil and a warm site suit this plant well but, if it is to flower over a reasonably long period, the soil must not be too poor and stony. The stems of *P. g.* 'Double Mixed' are nearly prostrate and this habit of growth is shown off best on a sunny slope or bank.

TULIPA (Kaufmanniana Hybrid) e.g. 'Shakespeare'
[form of Water-lily Tulip]

○

type of plant: HBb
flowering season: e. spring
flower colour: salmon + apricot
height: 15 cm/6 in

This early-flowering tulip can be left in the ground for several years if it has been planted in sharply draining soil and full sun. It may even increase under such conditions. For another example of a tulip of this type see *T.* 'The First', p. 18.

Chalk.

AETHIONEMA × 'Warley Rose' ★

○

type of plant: HP
flowering season: l. spring to e. summer
flower colour: rose-pink
height: 10-15 cm/4-6 in
E

By the beginning of summer nearly all the stems of
this bushy plant are topped with clusters of pretty
flowers. A light soil with good drainage and a
position in full sun usually produce excellent
results. The foliage of this plant is a bluish grey
which complements the blue-tinged pink of the
flowers.
    Chalk – Paving – Grey, etc. leaves.

**ALYSSUM maritimum (syn. *Lobularia maritima*)
e.g. 'Little Dorrit'
[form of Sweet Alyssum]**

○

type of plant: HA
flowering season: summer to e. autumn
flower colour: white
height: 10-15 cm/4-6 in

Only the white-flowered forms of *A. maritimum*,
such as 'Little Dorrit', are as sweetly scented as the
species; the darker varieties have little or no
fragrance. All forms bloom profusely. They grow
well in sunny places and light soils. *A. m.* 'Little
Dorrit' makes a well branched hummock of
growth. Varieties that spread more widely are also
available. The synonym given here is the correct
botanical name, and the name more commonly
used in the United States.
    Chalk – Ground-cover – Paving – Fragrant
flowers.

**GYPSOPHILA repens rosea (syn.
G. prostrata rosea)**

○

type of plant: HP
flowering season: all summer
flower colour: pink
height: 8-15 cm/3-6 in
E

If placed in the crevice of a wall this trailing plant
not only has its flowers and its thick cushion of
foliage displayed to advantage, but it also obtains
the warmth and good drainage it needs. It may be
grown with equal success, however, on level
ground. *G. repens* itself is shown on p. 19; it has
white flowers.
    Chalk – Ground-cover – Paving.

**IBERIS saxatilis
[species of Candytuft]**

○

type of plant: HP
flowering season: l. spring to midsummer
flower colour: white
height: 8-15 cm/3-6 in
E

Hot, dry conditions, the grimy air of cities and
infertile soils do little to deter the performance of
this plant which will prosper in any well drained
soil. Its shrubby growth forms a dark green carpet
of ground-cover about 30-60 cm/1-2 ft wide.
    Chalk – Ground-cover – Paving.

**DIANTHUS alpinus
[species of Pink]**

○

type of plant: HP
flowering season: summer
flower colour: pink or deep rose
height: 8-10 cm/3-4 in
E

Pinks of all sizes need a soil that drains very
quickly and that is, for preference, either chalky or
limy. They also require full sun. The rock-garden
species illustrated here has surprisingly big flowers
for such a small plant; individual blooms are
sometimes 4 cm/1½ in wide. However, they lack
any scent, although some of the Allwoodii hybrids
from *D. alpinus* (which are usually listed by
seedsmen) are fragrant. All these plants are
short-lived.
    Chalk – Paving.

**MESEMBRYANTHEMUM criniflorum (syn.
Dorotheanthus bellidiflorus) ★
[Livingstone Daisy]**

○

type of plant: HHA
flowering season: summer
flower colour: mixed – pink, red, pale mauve,
    yellow, buff, white
height: 8-10 cm/3-4 in

The succulent leaves and stems of the Livingstone
daisy are indications of this plant's ability to
withstand quite long periods of drought. Light
soils, including those that are quite shallow, give
the most satisfactory results and really sunny sites
ensure that the flowers are open for as long as
possible (except in the brightest light, the blooms
remain closed). Hot, dry conditions produce
growth that is dense as well as spreading.
    Ground-cover.

SEDUM spathulifolium 'Capa Blanca' ★
[form of Stonecrop]

○
type of plant: HP
flowering season: summer
flower colours: yellow
height: 8-10 cm/3-4 in
E

This little plant produces solid mats of grey foliage which consist of numerous tightly packed rosettes of white-dusted leaves. It grows well in warm places and will spread most attractively over paving stones and bare rocks. The yellow flowers are borne on red stems. Any well drained or dryish soil is suitable. A purple-leaved form of *S. spathulifolium* is illustrated on p. 171.

Chalk – Ground-cover – Paving – Grey, etc. leaves.

ARMERIA caespitosa
[species of Thrift]

○
type of plant: HP
flowering season: l. spring to e. summer
flower colour: pink
height: 5-8 cm/2-3 in
E

When in full flower, the almost stemless blooms of this plant create a close-fitting cover for the tufts of grassy leaves. A well drained, preferably sandy soil and plenty of sunshine create the ideal conditions for growing *A. caespitosa*.

Chalk – Paving.

SEDUM acre
[Biting Stonecrop, Wallpepper]

○
type of plant: HP
flowering season: summer
flower colour: yellow
height: 5 cm/2 in
E

This easily grown and free-flowering plant looks well on top of a wall or amongst sun-baked paving stones, but it should not be allowed to mingle with rarer or more valuable plants since it may quickly engulf them.

Chalk – Paving.

Additional plants, featured elsewhere in this book, that are suitable for dry soils in hot, sunny sites

○ sun
ROBINIA pseudoacacia e.g. 'Bessoniana': 9-12 m (p. 90)
ROBINIA pseudoacacia e.g. 'Frisia': 7.5-10.5 m (p. 174)
JUNIPERUS communis e.g. 'Hibernica': 4.5-6 m (p. 2)
CYTISUS battandieri ★: 3-4.5 m (p. 254)
JUNIPERUS virginiana e.g. 'Skyrocket': 3-4.5 m (p. 132)
COLUTEA arborescens: 2.4-3 m (p. 202)
FOENICULUM vulgare e.g. 'Giant Bronze': 1.5-2.4 m (p. 169)
JUNIPERUS squamata 'Meyeri': 1.5-2.4 m (p. 157)
CYTISUS scoparius e.g. 'Firefly': 1.5-2.1 m (p. 92)
TROPAEOLUM majus 'Tall Mixed': 1.5-2.1 m (p. 121)
BERBERIS thunbergii: 1.5-1.8 m (p. 190)
LUPINUS arboreus ★: 1.5-1.8 m (p. 86)
BERBERIS thunbergii atropurpurea: 1.2-1.8 m (p. 169)
CYTISUS scoparius e.g. 'Cornish Cream': 1.2-1.8 m (p. 86)
ROSMARINUS officinalis: 1.2-1.8 m (p. 196)
ACHILLEA 'Gold Plate': 1.2-1.5 m (p. 214)
CISTUS × purpureus: 1.2-1.5 m (p. 87)
JUNIPERUS × media e.g. 'Pfitzerana Aurea': 90-180 cm (p. 175)
PEROVSKIA atriplicifolia: 90-150 cm (p. 4)
ARTEMISIA arborescens ★: 90-120 cm (p. 158)
BERBERIS thunbergii 'Aurea': 90-120 cm (p. 175)
ERYNGIUM giganteum: 90-120 cm (p. 158)
EUPHORBIA wulfenii: 90-120 cm (p. 158)
PHLOMIS fruticosa: 90-120 cm (p. 159)
ARTEMISIA absinthium 'Lambrook Silver': 90 cm (p. 159)
COSMOS bipinnatus e.g. 'Sensation Mixed': 90 cm (p. 219)

GYPSOPHILA paniculata e.g. 'Bristol Fairy': 90 cm (p. 220)
LAVANDULA spica: 90 cm (p. 257)
GAILLARDIA e.g. 'Wirral Flame': 75-90 cm (p. 222)
LINARIA purpurea 'Canon J. Went': 75-90 cm (p. 5)
ACHILLEA millefolium 'Cerise Queen': 75 cm (p. 6)
STIPA pennata: 75 cm (p. 223)
CARYOPTERIS × clandonensis e.g. 'Ferndown': 60-90 cm (p. 7)
DICTAMNUS albus ★: 60-90 cm (p. 7)
DICTAMNUS albus purpureus: 60-90 cm (p. 196)
GENISTA hispanica: 60-90 cm (p. 99)
JUNIPERUS communis e.g. 'Compressa': 60-90 cm (p. 134)
ACHILLEA ptarmica 'The Pearl': 60-75 cm (p. 225)
SALVIA officinalis 'Purpurascens': 60-75 cm (p. 170)
TULIPA (Viridiflora) e.g. 'Greenland' ★: 60-75 cm (p. 281)
TULIPA (Lily-flowered) e.g. 'White Triumphator': 60-75 cm (p. 226)
ACHILLEA 'Moonshine' ★: 60 cm (p. 159)
ARTEMISIA dracunculus: 60 cm (p. 197)
LAVANDULA spica 'Vera': 60 cm (p. 100)
TULIPA (Darwin Hybrid) e.g. 'Apeldoorn': 60 cm (p. 7)
TULIPA (Darwin) e.g. 'Clara Butt': 60 cm (p. 7)
TULIPA (Cottage) e.g. 'Dillenburg': 60 cm (p. 8)
TULIPA (Parrot) e.g. 'Fantasy': 60 cm (p. 229)
TULIPA (Darwin) e.g. 'Niphetos': 60 cm (p. 8)
CENTRANTHUS ruber: 45-90 cm (p. 8)
ERYNGIUM alpinum: 45-75 cm (p. 8)
GENISTA lydia ★: 45-75 cm (p. 92)
LYCHNIS coronaria: 45-75 cm (p. 159) *continued*

○ **sun** *continued*

LYCHNIS coronaria 'Alba': 45-75 cm (p. 160)
BALLOTA pseudodictamnus: 45-60 cm (p. 160)
CYTISUS×beanii: 45-60 cm (p. 100)
HYSSOPUS officinalis: 45-60 cm (p. 197)
JUNIPERUS horizontalis e.g. 'Glauca': 45-60 cm (p. 100)
LAVANDULA spica 'Munstead': 45-60 cm (p. 197)
RUTA graveolens 'Jackman's Blue'★: 45-60 cm (p. 160)
SALVIA officinalis 'Tricolor': 45-60 cm (p. 148)
SANTOLINA chamaecyparissus★: 45-60 cm (p. 125)
SEDUM×'Autumn Joy'★: 45-60 cm (p. 9)
CHEIRANTHUS cheiri e.g. 'Blood Red': 45 cm (p. 9)
CHEIRANTHUS cheiri e.g. 'Cloth of Gold': 45 cm (p. 259)
GYPSOPHILA elegans e.g. 'Covent Garden': 45 cm (p. 233)
GYPSOPHILA elegans e.g. 'Rosea': 45 cm (p. 9)
TULIPA (Double Late) e.g. 'Eros': 45 cm (p. 259)
TULIPA (Triumph) e.g. 'Korneforos': 45 cm (p. 10)
TULIPA (Rembrandt) e.g. 'May Blossom': 45 cm (p. 234)
TULIPA (Parrot) e.g. 'Orange Favourite': 45 cm (p. 234)
TULIPA (Lily-flowered) e.g. 'Queen of Sheba': 45 cm (p. 234)
CHEIRANTHUS cheiri e.g. 'Fire King': 40-45 cm (p. 235)
CHEIRANTHUS×allionii e.g. 'Golden Bedder': 40 cm (p. 259)
TULIPA sylvestris: 40 cm (p. 260)
BERBERIS thunbergii 'Atropurpurea Nana': 30-60 cm (p. 171)
CONVOLVULUS cneorum★: 30-60 cm (p. 161)
LAVANDULA spica 'Hidcote'★: 30-60 cm (p. 126)
CONVOLVULUS tricolor e.g. 'Royal Ensign': 30-45 cm (p. 10)
HELIPTERUM roseum e.g. 'Large-flowered Mixed': 30-45 cm (p. 236)
IRIS (Spanish) e.g. 'King of Blues': 30-45 cm (p. 260)
JUNIPERUS horizontalis e.g. 'Douglasii': 30-45 cm (p. 101)
NEPETA×faassenii: 30-45 cm (p. 101)
GAILLARDIA pulchella e.g. 'Lollipops': 30-40 cm (p. 237)
HERMODACTYLUS tuberosus: 30-40 cm (p. 282)
LINARIA maroccana e.g. 'Excelsior Hybrids': 30-40 cm (p. 10)
TULIPA (Single Early) e.g. 'General de Wet': 30-40 cm (p. 260)
TULIPA (Fosteriana Hybrid) e.g. 'Madame Lefeber': 30-40 cm (p. 11)
CHEIRANTHUS cheiri e.g. 'Golden Bedder': 30 cm (p. 11)
CONVOLVULUS tricolor e.g. 'Mixed': 30 cm (p. 11)
DIANTHUS×allwoodii e.g. 'Doris': 30 cm (p. 238)
DIANTHUS×allwoodii e.g. 'Robin': 30 cm (p. 12)
DIANTHUS plumarius e.g. 'Mrs Sinkins': 30 cm (p. 261)
ECHIUM plantagineum e.g. 'Blue Bedder': 30 cm (p. 12)
ECHIUM plantagineum e.g. 'Dwarf Hybrids': 30 cm (p. 12)
HORDEUM jubatum: 30 cm (p. 238)
IRIS (Regeliocyclus) e.g.×'Chione': 30 cm (p. 12)
IRIS unguicularis★: 30 cm (p. 275)
LYCHNIS×haageana: 30 cm (p. 13)
TULIPA (Single Early) e.g. 'Brilliant Star': 30 cm (p. 13)
TULIPA (Double Early) e.g. 'Maréchal Niel': 30 cm (p. 13)
LYCHNIS flos-jovis 'Hort's Variety': 25 cm (p. 161)
HELICHRYSUM angustifolium: 23-40 cm (p. 198)
GYPSOPHILA paniculata e.g. 'Rosy Veil': 23-30 cm (p. 14)

HELIANTHEMUM nummularium e.g. 'Wisley Pink': 23-30 cm (p. 162)
HELIANTHEMUM nummularium e.g. 'Wisley Primrose': 23-30 cm (p. 101)
ALYSSUM saxatile e.g. 'Citrinum': 23 cm (p. 102)
ALYSSUM saxatile e.g. 'Dudley Neville': 23 cm (p. 15)
ANTIRRHINUM majus e.g. 'Floral Carpet': 23 cm (p. 15)
IBERIS sempervirens e.g. 'Snowflake': 23 cm (p. 102)
ORIGANUM hybridum: 23 cm (p. 15)
THYMUS vulgaris: 20-30 cm (p. 198)
TULIPA (Greigii Hybrid) e.g. 'Red Riding Hood': 20 cm (p. 149)
ARMERIA maritima 'Vindictive': 15-23 cm (p. 102)
CERASTIUM tomentosum: 15-23 cm (p. 162)
DIANTHUS deltoides: 15-23 cm (p. 140)
FESTUCA ovina 'Glauca'★: 15-23 cm (p. 162)
THYMUS×citriodorus 'Aureus': 15-23 cm (p. 176)
ACHILLEA tomentosa: 15-20 cm (p. 102)
DIANTHUS gratianopolitanus★: 15-20 cm (p. 16)
TANACETUM haradjanii★: 15-20 cm (p. 162)
TULIPA tarda: 15 cm (p. 18)
TULIPA (Kaufmanniana Hybrid) e.g. 'The First'★: 15 cm (p. 18)
AUBRIETA deltoidea e.g. 'Dr Mules': 10-15 cm (p. 18)
AUBRIETA deltoidea e.g. 'Maurice Prichard': 10-15 cm (p. 141)
SEDUM spurium e.g. 'Schorbusser Blut': 10-15 cm (p. 141)
ALYSSUM maritimum e.g. 'Rosie O'Day': 10 cm (p. 19)
SEDUM spathulifolium 'Purpureum': 10 cm (p. 171)
GYPSOPHILA repens: 8-15 cm (p. 19)
SEMPERVIVUM arachnoideum: 8-15 cm (p. 163)
ALYSSUM maritimum e.g. 'Royal Carpet': 8-10 cm (p. 103)
ALYSSUM montanum: 8-10 cm (p. 141)
ANTENNARIA dioica 'Rubra': 8-10 cm (p. 103)
AUBRIETA deltoidea e.g. 'Red Carpet': 8-10 cm (p. 103)
CROCUS imperati: 8-10 cm (p. 275)
ERINUS alpinus: 8-10 cm (p. 142)
PHLOX douglasii e.g. 'Boothman's Variety': 5-10 cm (p. 142)
ANTHEMIS nobilis 'Treneague': 5-8 cm (p. 104)
ASPERULA lilaciflora caespitosa: 5-8 cm (p. 142)
THYMUS serpyllum e.g. 'Albus'★: 5 cm (p. 142)
THYMUS serpyllum e.g. 'Coccineus': 5 cm (p. 19)

PHILADELPHUS coronarius
[species of Mock Orange]
○ [◑]
type of plant: HSh
flowering season: summer
flower colour: creamy white
height: 1.8-3 m/6-10 ft

All the mock oranges are suitable for planting in quite light soils but *P. coronarius* should be chosen if the conditions are unusually dry. This vigorous shrub grows densely and erectly. Its flowers have a strong scent which is reminiscent of the fragrance of orange blossom; they open a little earlier than the blooms of well known, named varieties.

Chalk – Atmospheric pollution – Fragrant flowers – Cutting.

ULEX europaeus 'Plenus' sc NA MC
[form of Gorse, Furze or Whin]
○ [◑]
type of plant: HSh
flowering season: mainly spring
flower colour: yellow
height: 90-180 cm/3-6 ft
E

Not the choicest of garden plants, despite its double flowers, *U. e.* 'Plenus' is, nevertheless, so free-flowering and so well adapted to poor, dry soils that it should certainly be considered when the problem of planting an arid site arises. It makes a dense shrub with sharp, spiny shoots – which can be useful if this plant is grown as part of a hedge. Its flowers emit a sweet, vanilla-like fragrance on sunny days. Rich and very alkaline soils are not suitable for this shrub.

Acid soils – Seaside – Atmospheric pollution – Hedging – Fragrant flowers.

CROCUS vernus e.g. 'Striped Beauty'
○ [◑]
type of plant: HBb
flowering season: e. spring
flower colour: white + purple
height: 10-15 cm/4-6 in

Large-flowered crocuses like 'Striped Beauty' and 'Yellow Giant' (the latter plant is shown in the following illustration) require only a well drained soil and some sunshine to grow quite satisfactorily. They will thrive and multiply, however, in a hot, rather dry site, and full sun encourages earlier flowering. These plants are sturdy enough for naturalizing in short grass. An example of a blue-flowered crocus of this type appears on p. 23.
    Chalk.

CROCUS vernus e.g. 'Yellow Giant'
○ [◑]
type of plant: HBb
flowering season: e. spring
flower colour: golden yellow
height: 10-15 cm/4-6 in

See preceding plant.

CROCUS chrysanthus e.g. 'Blue Pearl'
○ [◑]
type of plant: HBb
flowering season: l. winter to e. spring
flower colour: pale blue
height: 8-10 cm/3-4 in

Hybrids derived from *C. chrysanthus* have flowers that are not only earlier but also smaller than the blooms of the so-called Dutch crocuses (for two examples of which, see the preceding illustrations). Both the varieties of *C. chrysanthus* shown here are free-flowering and reliable plants. There are forms of this crocus with white flowers (*C. c.* 'Snow Bunting' is outstandingly attractive) but most varieties have either blue or yellow blooms. They all grow best in well drained soils and their buds will open early in warm, sunny positions.
    Chalk – Winter-flowering plants.

CROCUS chrysanthus e.g. 'E. A. Bowles'
○ [◑]
type of plant: HBb
flowering season: l. winter to e. spring
flower colour: yellow
height: 8-10 cm/3-4 in

See preceding plant.

OENOTHERA biennis
[Evening Primrose]
○ ◑
type of plant: HB
flowering season: summer to mid-autumn
flower colour: yellow
height: 75-90 cm/2½-3 ft

Unless its ripening pods are removed, this plant will produce numerous self-sown seedlings. These would be inappropriate in a formal garden, but in rougher pieces of ground their rosettes of foliage will create quite good ground-cover of a conveniently self-perpetuating sort. The flowers of this plant emit a sweet fragrance when they open in late afternoon; they are borne in succession over an exceptionally long period. *O. biennis* will grow well in dry and infertile soils. It is not cultivated in the United States except in wild flower gardens because of its invasive traits.
    Ground-cover – Fragrant flowers.

> **Additional plants, featured elsewhere in this book, that are suitable for dry soils in hot, sunny sites**
>
> ○ [◑] sun (or partial shade)
> FILIPENDULA hexapetala 'Flore Pleno': 45-60 cm (p. 23)
> STACHYS lanata: 30-45 cm (p. 164)
> ARABIS albida e.g. 'Flore Pleno': 15-20 cm (p. 106)
> ARABIS albida e.g. 'Rosabella': 15-20 cm (p. 23)
> CROCUS speciosus e.g. 'Albus': 10-15 cm (p. 23)
> CROCUS speciosus e.g. 'Globosus': 10-15 cm (p. 23)
> CROCUS vernus e.g. 'Queen of the Blues': 10-15 cm (p. 23)
> STACHYS lanata 'Silver Carpet'★: 10-15 cm (p. 165)
> CROCUS kotschyanus: 8-10 cm (p. 23)
> CROCUS tomasinianus 'Whitewell Purple': 8-10 cm (p. 276)
> CROCUS ancyrensis: 5-8 cm (p. 276)
>
> ○ ◑ sun or partial shade
> TAXUS baccata: 12-18 m (p. 126)
> TAXUS baccata 'Fastigiata': 9-12 m (p. 24)
> BERBERIS × stenophylla★: 2.4-3 m (p. 128)
> EUPHORBIA robbiae: 45-60 cm (p. 81)
> HYPERICUM calycinum: 30-45 cm (p. 108)
> LIRIOPE muscari: 30-45 cm (p. 80)

Plants suitable for damp and wet soils (including plants suitable for shallow water)

Of all the features that can make a garden lovely, water – in some form or other – is probably the one which comes to mind most readily. Waterfalls and fountains may catch the eye, but it is the relatively still expanses of water, in ponds, lakes and slow-flowing streams, that set off plants particularly well.

The following list includes plants with which water in various forms can be surrounded: there are plants that will grow in shallow water at the edges of ponds and streams, plants that are suitable for the wet soils beside many natural areas of water, and plants that are suitable for damp soils which may or may not be near open water. This list does not deal with deep water, ornamental plants, such as water-lilies, or submerged, oxygenating plants. Plants of the latter category often have insignificant flowers and their leaves may be visible for only short periods during the year. They are, however, essential to the plant and animal life of ponds and lakes. Not only do they oxygenate the water, but they help to keep it clear and fresh, and they provide shelter and protection for fish.

Those who consider that leaves are as decorative as flowers will find that selecting plants for a water garden is a particularly enjoyable exercise. Not only do leaves grow luxuriantly in or near water, but areas of fairly still water are the perfect, reflective surfaces against which to display the good looks of beautiful foliage. Bold leaves, in particular, are shown to advantage beside water, and a considerable number of the plants in this list also appear in the 'Decorative green foliage' list. There are, for instance, the big, broad, blue-green leaves of *Hosta sieboldiana*, the strikingly upright, sword-shaped leaves of *Phormium tenax* (New Zealand flax) and its variegated and unusually coloured varieties, and the spreading, saucer-shaped leaves of *Peltiphyllum peltatum*.

Some plants may not have particularly ornamental leaves but, as a whole, they create bold shapes and look well beside water for this reason. This list includes various bamboos whose canes provide good, vertical contrast to horizontal stretches of water. Weeping willows, such as *Salix × chrysocoma*, are popular choices for large gardens with ponds or lakes for a similar reason. On a much smaller scale, upright shapes are provided by the various moisture-loving irises, and by plants like *Acorus calamus* 'Variegatus' (a variegated form of sweet flag) and *Butomus umbellatus* (flowering rush). Plants of an arching habit can also look most attractive by water: both the shuttlecock or ostrich

feather fern and day lilies, for instance, have elegantly curved leaves.

In order to allow cross-reference to other lists, plants in this list are retained in their usual sun or shade categories. However, as a very general rule, when plants that appreciate moist growing conditions are supplied with plenty of water, they can often withstand more sunshine than they could if they were grown in an ordinary border. Many of the plants in the ○ ◑ (sun or partial shade) category, and even some of those in the ◑ [○] (partial shade (or sun)) category, will do well in *full* sun when they are grown in wet or very damp soils.

The complications involved in the relationship between moisture and sunshine or shade and their effect upon plants, are discussed in Alan Bloom's *Moisture Gardening* (published by Faber and Faber – see pp. 44-6 in particular). This clear and helpful book also deals with the subject of the control of moisture. No plant likes to be submerged in water one week and left high and dry the next. Moisture-loving plants grow most successfully when the supply of water is reasonably constant. However, there are some plants, such as *Iris kaempferi* and its varieties, which are best kept dry during their dormant period. For most plants there should be plenty of moisture during the growing season at least, even if it is difficult to provide permanently damp or wet conditions.

Many of the plants in this list are often recommended as suitable subjects for growing in the ground around areas of water. Artificial pools, which nowadays are usually lined with strong, water-impervious, plastic sheeting, do not have banks which are sufficiently damp or wet to support most of these plants. However, during the construction of artificial pools, ledges and pockets can be made within them, and these can hold shallow-water plants, of which there are a number in this list.

General gardening books sometimes deal with the subject of water and bog gardens (the *Reader's Digest Illustrated Guide to Gardening*, for instance, has a section devoted to water plants and the construction of various kinds of water garden). There is also quite a wide range of publications which deal exclusively with the subject or some aspect of it, including Alan Bloom's book, mentioned above, Frances Perry's *The Garden Pool* (published by David and Charles) and *Modern Water Gardening* by Reginald Kaye (published by Faber and Faber).

METASEQUOIA glyptostroboides [Dawn Redwood]

○

type of plant: HCo
height: 18-24 m/60-80 ft

Although most soils are quite suitable for this narrowly conical tree, it grows especially fast (as much as 90 cm/3 ft a year sometimes) in rather damp but well drained conditions. Its leaves are bright green when young; in autumn they turn a pinkish or red-tinged brown.

  Atmospheric pollution – Autumn foliage.

POPULUS tremula sc NA [Aspen]

○

type of plant: HT
flowering season: l. winter to e. spring
flower colour: pinkish grey
height: 9-15 m/30-50 ft

The drawbacks to this tree are that its questing roots can damage drains and the foundations of buildings and that its fluffy seeds can be very messy. However, the way in which its leaves tremble in the slightest breeze is most attractive and there are the additional attractions of long catkins early in the year and yellow foliage in autumn. Of all the readily available poplars, the aspen is, perhaps, the most suitable for damp and wet soils. It grows quickly and becomes openly branched as it matures.

  Clay – Atmospheric pollution – Autumn foliage – Winter-flowering plants.

PHYLLOSTACHYS nigra 'Boryana' (syn. *P. boryana, P. nigra* 'Bory') **MC [form of Black Bamboo]**

○

type of plant: SlTP (Ba)
height: 2.4-3.9 m/8-13 ft
E

Moisture, shelter and sunshine will produce good clumps of this bamboo. The canes are, at first, a soft green colour; as they mature they turn yellow and become marked with purple. The upper part of each stem arches and is covered with graceful, narrow leaves.

  Green foliage – Bark and *twigs*.

FILIPENDULA rubra venusta NA
[Martha Washington Plume]
○
type of plant: HP
flowering season: summer
flower colour: pink
height: 1.8 m/6 ft

Given a moist soil in an open exposure, this becomes an almost stately plant, with clear pink plumes for several weeks in midsummer. It spreads rapidly from the roots, and division is best done every year or two. Some staking is necessary in windy sites.

BUTOMUS umbellatus
[Flowering Rush]
○
type of plant: HPAq
flowering season: summer
flower colour: rose pink
height: 60-90 cm/2-3 ft
≈

The freest flowering specimens of *B. umbellatus* are those that are planted directly in the mud of the edges of ponds and slow-moving rivers and that have their roots more or less permanently covered by shallow water. The rush-like leaves of this plant are bronze when young.
 Red, etc. leaves.

IRIS laevigata
○
type of plant: HP
flowering season: e. summer
flower colour: deep blue
height: 60 cm/2 ft
≈

Ideally, this plant should be grown in shallow water (not more than about 15 cm/6 in deep), but it will do almost equally well in a really moist soil. Its softly coloured foliage and mellow blue flowers make a particularly attractive combination. The flowers are usually 10-12 cm/4-5 in wide.

PONTEDERIA cordata
[Pickerel Weed]
○
type of plant: HPAq
flowering season: l. summer to e. autumn
flower colour: blue
height: 60 cm/2 ft
≈

Each flower stalk of this vigorous plant tends to carry a single glossy green leaf, the smoothness of which contrasts well with the numerous small petals of the flower spike. *P. cordata* needs to have its roots in water which is either still or slow-moving and about 15-23 cm/6-9 in deep.
 Green foliage.

SAGITTARIA sagittifolia 'Flore Pleno' (syn.
S. japonica 'Flore Pleno')
[form of Arrowhead]
○
type of plant: HPAq
flowering season: summer
flower colour: white
height: 60 cm/2 ft
≈

S. sagittifolia itself will grow in ponds and slow-flowing streams that are moderately deep, but the roots of this double-flowered form should be planted in only 10-15 cm/4-6 in of water. The strikingly shaped foliage of *S. s.* 'Flore Pleno' is a very pale green. Fertile conditions are needed to produce good growth and plenty of flowers.
 Green foliage.

SCHIZOSTYLIS coccinea
[Kaffir Lily]
○
type of plant: SlTP
flowering season: autumn
flower colour: scarlet
height: 45-60 cm/1½-2 ft

This vigorous plant will spread freely in rich, moist soil and in the damper, milder parts of the country. It needs frequent division. The bright blooms last for a considerable time when cut and used in flower arrangements. *S. c.* 'Mrs Hegarty' (see p. 232) is a pale pink variety of the plant shown here. In the United States this plant is grown outdoors only in mild climates.
 Cutting.

ORONTIUM aquaticum
[Golden Club]
○
type of plant: HPAq
flowering season: l. spring to e. summer
flower colour: yellow
height: 30-45 cm/1-1½ ft
≈

When grown at the margins of ponds this plant produces rounded leaves which have a bluish tinge in their colouring. The flower spikes give off a thoroughly unpleasant scent; they are borne on thick, curving stems and they appear in particualrly large numbers on fertile soils.

Grey, etc. leaves.

ASTER novi-belgii e.g. 'Snowsprite'
[form of Michaelmas Daisy]
○
type of plant: HP
flowering season: autumn
flower colour: white
height: 30 cm/1 ft

Michaelmas daisies are so frequently seen in conventional beds and borders that their suitability for damp soils – on pond and river banks, for instance – tends to get overlooked. The number of dwarf varieties of aster, such as 'Snowsprite', has increased in recent years and there are now forms with blue flowers (see, for example, *A. n.-b.* 'Audrey', p. 47), with red and with pink flowers. They are all good for cutting.

Clay – Cutting.

Additional plants, featured elsewhere in this book, that are suitable for damp and wet soils

○ sun
POPULUS nigra 'Italica': 24-36 m (p. 89)
POPULUS alba: 18-27 m (p. 156)
CORTADERIA selloana: 1.8-2.7 m (p. 212)
RHEUM palmatum e.g. 'Bowles' Crimson' ★:
  1.5-2.1 m (p. 169)
ASTER novae-angliae e.g. 'Harrington's Pink':
  1.2 m (p. 214)
ASTER novae-angliae e.g. 'September Ruby':
  105-120 cm (p. 46)
ASTER novi-belgii e.g. 'Fellowship': 90-120 cm
  (p. 217)
ASTER novi-belgii e.g. 'Marie Ballard': 90-120 cm
  (p. 219)
SALIX lanata ★: 60-120 cm (p. 159)
IRIS kaempferi e.g. 'Higo Strain': 60-90 cm (p. 30)
ASTER novi-belgii e.g. 'Carnival': 60-75 cm (p. 47)
IRIS kaempferi e.g. 'Variegata': 60-75 cm (p. 147)
LIATRIS spicata: 60-75 cm (p. 225)
GLYCERIA maxima 'Variegata': 60 cm (p. 147)
SCHIZOSTYLIS coccinea e.g. 'Mrs Hegarty' ★:
  45-60 cm (p. 232)
ASTER novi-belgii e.g. 'Audrey': 30-45 cm (p. 47)
ERICA tetralix e.g. 'Alba Mollis': 23-30 cm (p. 162)
ERICA tetralix e.g. 'Con Underwood': 23 cm
  (p. 31)

VIBURNUM opulus 'Sterile'
[Snowball, form of Guelder Rose]
○ [◐]
type of plant: HSh
flowering season: l. spring to e. summer
flower colour: creamy white
height: 3.6-4.5 m/12-15 ft

No berries are produced by this form of *V. opulus*, the main attraction of which is the conspicuously rounded shape of its pure white flowers. Soils that are permanently damp are ideal for this rather erect shrub, but any moisture-retentive soil will suit it well. Its maple-like foliage turns red in autumn. A smaller variety of *V. opulus* which bears numerous bunches of berries is illustrated on p. 204.

Clay – Autumn foliage.

SCIRPUS tabernaemontani e.g. 'Zebrinus'
sc NA
[Zebra Rush]
○ [◐]
type of plant: SlTPAq
flowering season: summer
flower colour: red-brown
height: 90-120 cm/3-4 ft
≈

The strange, horizontal markings on the stems of this plant tend to fade with age and, unless the roots are divided every year, plain green stems may outnumber those that are variegated. The zebra rush thrives in shallow water or boggy ground where the soil is fertile and slightly acid and where there is shelter from very cold winds.

Variegated leaves.

IRIS sibirica e.g. 'Perry's Blue'
○ [◐]
type of plant: HP
flowering season: summer
flower colour: rich blue
height: 90 cm/3 ft

I. sibirica and hybrids from it are adaptable plants which will flourish in sunshine and moist, fertile soils but which will also grow well under drier, slightly shadier conditions. *I. s.* 'Perry's Blue' is one of several, readily available blue-flowered varieties. There are a few white-flowered forms; 'White Swirl' (see the following illustration) has unusually large, wide-spread petals. Purple-flowered varieties are sometimes listed.

Cutting.

IRIS sibirica e.g. 'White Swirl'
○ [◐]
type of plant: HP
flowering season: summer
flower colour: white
height: 90 cm/3 ft

See preceding plant.

ZANTEDESCHIA aethiopica (syn.
Richardia africana) 'Crowborough' ★ MC
[form of Arum Lily or Lily of the Nile]
○ [◐]
type of plant: SlTTu
flowering season: summer
flower colour: white
height: 75-90 cm/2½-3 ft
≈

This particular form of the arum lily is almost
hardy, especially if it is grown in shallow water
(about 10-15 cm/4-6 in deep). If it is planted either
in moisture-retentive soil in a border or in boggy
ground, it usually needs to have its roots covered in
winter for the first few years. The supremely
elegant blooms make magnificent cut flowers. The
foliage is dark green, spear-shaped and
appropriately handsome.
    Green foliage – Cutting.

PELTIPHYLUM peltatum (syn.
Saxifraga peltata)
[Umbrella Plant]
○ [◐]
type of plant: HP
flowering season: spring
flower colour: pink
height: 60-90 cm/2-3 ft

The dwarf form of this plant, known as *P. p.*
'Nanum', is, unfortunately, not very readily
available and the species itself is large and often
invasive. However, in rich, boggy soil and beside a
sizeable pond or stream for instance, it can look
most impressive. Each of its rounded and
scalloped leaves is about 30 cm/1 ft in diameter.
The foliage makes good ground-cover. It appears
after the circular heads of pink flowers.
    Clay – Ground-cover – Green foliage.

LYSICHITUM (syn. *Lysichiton*) americanum
[wrongly called Skunk Cabbage]
○ [◐]
type of plant: HP
flowering season: spring
flower colour: yellow
height: 30-45 cm/1-1½ ft
≈; leaves, after flowers, 60-90 cm/2-3 ft high

Lit by low sun early in the year, the 30 cm/1 ft high
'flowers' of this plant look splendid, but some
gardeners consider that there is a price to pay for
this magnificence when the massive, weed-
suppressing leaves emerge later. In an informal
waterside setting, however, the foliage does not
look out of place. *L. americanum* needs a rich soil
and constant moisture. It may be grown in water
about 8 cm/3 in deep.
    Ground-cover – Green foliage.

LYSICHITUM (syn. *Lysichiton*)
camtschatcense sc NA
○ [◐]
type of plant: HP
flowering season: spring
flower colour: white
height: 23-30 cm/9-12 in
leaves, after flowers, 90 cm/3 ft high

This plant is a smaller, white-flowered version of
L. americanum (see preceding illustration). It too
has very large leaves which are produced after its
flowers and it needs the same damp or wet and
fertile conditions. However, it is not suitable for
planting in water. Its flowers emit a sweet scent.
    Ground-cover – Green foliage – Fragrant
flowers.

CALTHA palustris 'Plena'
[form of Marsh Marigold or Kingcup]
○ [◐]
type of plant: HP
flowering season: spring
flower colour: golden yellow
height: 23 cm/9 in
≈

The double-flowered form of *C. palustris* grows
well either in shallow water or in very moist
ground. The smaller, white-flowered variety, *C. p.*
'Alba' (see the following illustration), is not at its
best in water. Both plants have round, shiny leaves
which, in the case of *C. p.* 'Plena', form a
weed-smothering clump. The double flowers last
longest but *C. p.* 'Alba' often blooms for a second
time in autumn.
    Ground-cover (*C. p.* 'Plena' only).

CALTHA palustris 'Alba'
[form of Marsh Marigold or Kingcup]
○[◑]
type of plant: HP
flowering season: spring
flower colour: white
height: 15-23 cm/6-9 in

See preceding plant.

PRIMULA rosea 'Delight'
○[◑]
type of plant: HP
flowering season: spring
flower colour: deep pink
height: 15 cm/6 in

This intensely coloured plant has a reputation for being difficult to grow but, in general, it only requires a constant supply of moisture to do well. It is suitable for quite boggy ground and for the banks of streams and natural ponds. The leaves lengthen after the flowers have faded. This plant is sometimes referred to as *P. r.* 'Visser de Greer'.
   Acid soils.

TAXODIUM distichum
[Swamp Cypress, Bald Cypress]
○ ◐
type of plant: HCo
height: 21-30 m/70-100 ft

Gardeners with plenty of patience will choose this tree rather than the somewhat similar and much faster growing dawn redwood (*Metasequoia glyptostroboides*, see above, p. 68). They will be rewarded for their perseverance by finer foliage, a more attractive russety autumn colour and a broader and more shapely conical outline. Any moisture-retentive soil is suitable and this tree thrives in wet soils where its roots usually produce prominent bulges known as 'knees'.
   Acid soils – Clay – Autumn foliage.

SALIX × chrysocoma (syn. *S. alba* 'Tristis', *S. alba* 'Vitellina Pendula', *S. babylonica* 'Ramulis Aureis') ★
[Golden Weeping Willow]
○ ◐
type of plant: HT
flowering season: spring
flower colour: yellow
height: 13.5-18 m/45-60 ft

The hanging twigs and slender leaves of this very fast-growing tree create dramatic sheets of greenery. When the foliage falls, the beautiful golden yellow of the twigs is conspicuous and decorative. *S. × chrysocoma* is often planted beside water but it grows well in any soil that is reasonably deep and moisture retentive. Its broad dome of branches makes it an unsuitable tree for small gardens.
   Clay – Atmospheric pollution – Green foliage – Bark and *twigs*.

CORNUS alba 'Elegantissima' (syn. *C. a.* 'Sibirica Variegata') ★
[form of Red-barked Dogwood]
○ ◐
type of plant: HSh
height: 1.8-2.7 m/6-9 ft

Most of the dogwoods grown for their coloured stems have rather dull foliage, at least until autumn. However, *C. a.* 'Elegantissima' is attractive throughout the year: in winter there are red stems of a plummy shade (these are richly coloured and most numerous when all growths are pruned hard annually in March); in spring and summer these stems are covered in pale green and white, variegated leaves; in autumn the foliage takes on a pinkish tinge. *C. a.* 'Elegantissima' will grow in most soils but it will be lushest in damp and wet conditions.
   Clay – Atmospheric pollution – Variegated leaves – Autumn foliage – Bark and *twigs*.

LIGULARIA stenocephala 'The Rocket' (syn. *L. przewalskii* 'The Rocket', *Senecio przewalskii* 'The Rocket')

○ ◐

type of plant: HP
flowering season: midsummer to e. autumn
flower colour: yellow
height: 1.2-1.8 m/4-6 ft

Damp and wet soils suit this plant best. Its great jagged leaves are veined in purple and its 60 cm/2 ft spikes of flowers are carried on black stems. Both of these features contribute to an overall impression of handsome vigour.

Clay – Green foliage.

OSMUNDA regalis ★
[Royal Fern]

○ ◐

type of plant: HF
height: 1.2-1.8 m/4-6 ft
* ≈

As long as it has a lime-free, moisture-retentive soil this splendid fern will grow well, but it will be magnificently large and lush on the banks of a river or lake or in very shallow water. It bears a few upright, fertile fronds which, at first glance, look like flowers. Its leaves turn yellow and yellowish-brown in autumn.

Acid soils – Dense shade – Green foliage – Autumn foliage.

SYMPHYTUM×uplandicum (syn. *S. peregrinum*)
[form of Comfrey]

○ ◐

type of plant: HP
flowering season: summer
flower colour: pink changing to blue
height: 1.2-1.5 m/4-5 ft
E

The blue bells which follow pink buds on this tough and trouble-free plant make up for the coarseness of the hairy foliage. Almost any soil will do but moisture and some shade produce particularly vigorous specimens. *S.×uplandicum* can be grown in fully shaded positions.

Clay.

TYPHA angustifolia
[Lesser Reedmace, Lesser Bulrush]

○ ◐

type of plant: HPAq
height: 1.2-1.5 m/4-5 ft
brown, fruiting heads in summer; ≈

Once it has become established in the rich mud and shallow water it prefers, the lesser reedmace will start to produce brown 'bulrush' heads. It may also start to spread – with unwelcome rapidity – into large, dense colonies and it is, therefore, unsuitable for planting beside small ponds or pools. The fruiting heads are popular for dried flower arrangements. For details of the less invasive dwarf reedmace, see *T. minima*, p. 75.

Fruit.

RANUNCULUS lingua 'Grandiflora' sc NA
[form of Greater Spearwort]

○ ◐

type of plant: HP
flowering season: summer
flower colour: yellow
height: 1.2 m/4 ft

≈

Boggy ground or, preferably, shallow water (up to 30 cm/1 ft deep) should be chosen for this plant. When grown at the margin of ponds and lakes, *R. l.* 'Grandiflora' may increase quite quickly. Any underwater foliage will remain green throughout the winter.

SANGUISORBA obtusa (syn. *Poterium obtusum*)
[species of Burnet]

○ ◐

type of plant: HP
flowering season: summer
flower colour: pink
height: 1.05 m/3½ ft

The shaggy, pink bottle-brush flowers of this vigorous plant are often over 8 cm/3 in long; their stems usually need support. In really moist soil the pale green, divided leaves will be especially long and just as decorative a feature as the flowers.

Green foliage.

LYTHRUM salicaria e.g. 'Firecandle'
[form of Purple Loosestrife]
○ ◐
type of plant: HP
flowering season: midsummer to e. autumn
flower colour: rose-red
height: 90 cm/3 ft

Garden varieties of *L. salicaria*, such as the one shown here, create conspicuously shaped blazes of colour in almost any soil. Damp or wet conditions and a little shade are ideal. These plants normally flower continuously throughout the period stated above. *L. s.* 'Robert' (see second right) is rather bushier than most other forms of purple loosestrife.
   Clay.

POLYGONUM bistorta 'Superbum'
[form of Knotweed]
○ ◐
type of plant: HP
flowering season: l. spring to midsummer, and
   often l. summer to e. autumn
flower colour: pink
height: 75-90 cm/2½-3 ft

The foliage of this robust plant is, perhaps, a little too weed-like for some gardeners' tastes but it is arranged in a good, ground-covering clump and it does not look at all out of place in 'natural' waterside plantings. *P. b.* 'Superbum' will grow well in any fertile, moisture-retentive soil; it will thrive and flower freely in damp ground near water.
   Clay – Ground-cover.

LYTHRUM salicaria e.g. 'Robert'
[form of Purple Loosestrife]
○ ◐
type of plant: HP
flowering season: midsummer to e. autumn
flower colour: bright pink
height: 75 cm/2½ ft

See *L. s.* 'Firecandle', second left.

TROLLIUS ledebouri 'Golden Queen'
[form of Globe Flower]
○ ◐
type of plant: HP
flowering season: summer
flower colour: orange
height: 75 cm/2½ ft

With its mat of roots and its clump of lobed leaves, this plant will prevent most weeds from growing in or around it. A damp, boggy soil is not essential but some moisture is important. The upright stamens, in the centre of each flower, are a distinctive feature; other cultivated globe flowers (such as *T. europaeus* 'Superbus', see the following page) have much rounder blooms.
   Ground-cover – Cutting.

CYPERUS longus sc NA
[Sweet Galingale]
○ ◐
type of plant: HP
flowering season: l. summer to e. autumn
   (persisting through winter)
flower colour: reddish brown
height: 60-120 cm/2-4 ft
≈

C. longus can spread quite quickly into large, grassy masses. Its leaves and bracts are arranged in an attractive, spoke-like fashion. Where self-sown seedlings would not be a nuisance, its elegant flower heads can be left on the plant in winter but, late in the year, the foliage can look very untidy. This sedge should be planted in water about 30 cm/1 ft deep. It emits a sweet fragrance from its stems and roots.
   Green foliage – Winter-flowering plants.

HEMEROCALLIS e.g. 'Burning Daylight'
sc NA
[form of Day Lily]
○ ◐
type of plant: HP
flowering season: summer
flower colour: orange
height: 60-90 cm/2-3 ft

Day lilies are easily grown plants that thrive in both moderately moist and quite damp soils. Their clumps of arching leaves look beautiful reflected in water. As each short-lived bloom fades another opens until flowering finally stops – in late summer in the case of the example shown here. Many different cultivars of *Hemerocallis* are now available, particularly in the United States. The main colours are deep red, yellow, pink and orange.
   Clay – Ground-cover – Green foliage.

LYSIMACHIA punctata
[species of Loosestrife]

○ ◐
type of plant: HP
flowering season: summer
flower colour: yellow
height: 60-90 cm/2-3 ft

The strong flower colour and rather rough, coarse leaves of this perennial can look incongruous in borders full of daintier plants, but they seem appropriately robust and unpretentious in less formal settings. *L. punctata* is a vigorous, often invasive plant which is suitable for any moist or damp soil.

    Clay.

TROLLIUS europaeus 'Superbus' ★
[form of Globe Flower]

○ ◐
type of plant: HP
flowering season: l. spring to e. summer
flower colour: lemon yellow
height: 60-75 cm/2-2½ ft

T. e. 'Superbus' makes a lovely cut flower and a beautiful garden plant. Its shining flowers are of a satisfying rotundity; they contrast well with the lobed leaves. Damp soils suit this plant best but it will grow densely and flower freely in any soil that stays moist during warm weather.

    Ground-cover – Cutting.

LEUCOJUM aestivum 'Gravetye' ★
[form of Summer Snowflake or Loddon Lily]

○ ◐
type of plant: HBb
flowering season: l. spring
flower colour: white
height: 45-60 cm/1½-2 ft

Few bulbous plants grow well in damp soils but the Loddon lily is an outstandingly attractive exception. The form illustrated here is larger and more robust than the species. Each of its hanging flowers has tiny touches of green on the petal tips. Ordinary, moisture-retentive soils, as well as those that are damp, produce good specimens of this plant.

    Clay – Cutting.

RANUNCULUS aconitifolius 'Flore Pleno' ★
[Fair Maids of France, White Bachelor's Buttons]

○ ◐
type of plant: HP
flowering season: l. spring to e. summer
flower colour: white
height: 45-60 cm/1½-2 ft

Nurseries that specialize in perennial plants will probably list this old, double-flowered form of *R. aconitifolius*. It is not so vigorous as the species but it usually produces plenty of closely petalled flowers which remain intact and fresh-looking for a considerable time, both in the garden and when cut. Its deep green foliage covers the ground quite densely, particularly if the soil is rich, moist and not too heavy.

    Ground-cover – Cutting.

TYPHA minima
[Dwarf Reedmace, Dwarf Bulrush]

○ ◐
type of plant: HPAq
height: 45-60 cm/1½-2 ft
brown, fruiting heads in summer; ≈

Although not so invasive as some other, closely related plants, *T. minima* is still fairly strong-growing and not a good choice for very small areas of water. Its fruiting flower heads are shorter and fatter than those of the more commonly seen reedmaces. It should be planted in fertile mud under a few centimetres/inches of water.

    Fruit.

FRITILLARIA meleagris
[Snake's Head]

○ ◐
type of plant: HBb
flowering season: spring
flower colour: purple + white
height: 30-45 cm/1-1½ ft

The strange chequering characteristic of the snake's head fritillary is absent or inconspicuous on the petals of white forms such as 'Aphrodite'. However, the charming bell shape is, of course, still present and both the species and its varieties are suitable for naturalizing in short grass where there is plenty of moisture. A mixture of various colours is often easier to obtain than forms of separate colours.

    Clay.

FRITILLARIA meleagris e.g. 'Aphrodite'
[form of Snake's Head]
○ ◑
type of plant: HBb
flowering season: spring
flower colour: white
height: 30-45 cm/1-1½ ft

See preceding plant.

GEUM rivale 'Leonard's Variety' sc NA
[form of Water Avens]
○ ◑
type of plant: HP
flowering season: l. spring to summer
flower colour: pale salmon
height: 30-45 cm/1-1½ ft
E/½E

Both damp and ordinarily moist soils suit this
plant but its hairy leaves will grow most thickly in
rather boggy ground. The flowers hang prettily
from red stalks and the softly coloured petals are
enclosed in rich red calyces.
    Ground-cover.

MIMULUS luteus
[Monkey Musk]
○ ◑
type of plant: HP
flowering season: l. spring to summer
flower colour: yellow or yellow + red-brown
height: 30-45 cm/1-1½ ft (average)
height very variable: 10-60 cm/4 in-2 ft

The monkey musk produces a mass of usually
speckled flowers over lush and spreading
greenery. It is not a very long-lived plant. It should
be given a wet soil and, where convenient, its roots
should be allowed to grow into shallow water.

CAREX morrowi 'Variegata' (**syn.** *C. japonica*)
[form of Sedge]
○ ◑
type of plant: HP (Gr)
height: 23 cm/9 in
E

There is some confusion in trade catalogues over
the naming of various plants in the genus *Carex*.
Nurseries with a good range of perennials or
specialists in water and bog plants will list one or
more of these sedges with their elegantly arching
leaves and attractive, white or yellow variegations.
They all need moist growing conditions and the
present example does especially well in damp soil
near water.
    Variegated leaves.

MYOSOTIS palustris (**syn.** *M. scorpioides*)
[Water Forget-me-not]
○ ◑
type of plant: HPAq
flowering season: l. spring to summer
flower colour: blue
height: 15-30 cm/6-12 in
E ≈

The flowers of the water forget-me-not are very
small but they are produced in large numbers from
late spring until the beginning of autumn. If not
grown in water about 5-8 cm/2-3 in deep this plant
must be given a wet soil.

CALLA palustris
[Bog Arum]
○ ◑
type of plant: HPAq
flowering season: e. summer
flower colour: white
height: 15-23 cm/6-9 in
≈

This little plant can form a most attractive edge to a
pool. It needs fertile mud to grow well and its
creeping roots can be covered by up to 15 cm/6 in of
water. Red berries follow the shapely, white
flowers.
    Fruit.

MIMULUS cupreus e.g. 'Red Emperor'
[form of Monkey Flower]

○ ◐

type of plant: HP/A
flowering season: summer to e. autumn
flower colour: crimson-scarlet
height: 15 cm/6 in

Few of the monkey flowers live very long and
cultivars like *M.c.* 'Red Emperor' need to be
divided frequently or to be grown from seed or
from cuttings each year. (Although these plants
are hardy they are often treated as half-hardy
annuals and sown under glass in early spring.)
Moist soils, near pools or streams for instance, suit
M. cupreus and its offspring well.

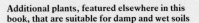

Additional plants, featured elsewhere in this
book, that are suitable for damp and wet soils

○ ◐ sun or partial shade
ALNUS cordata: 15-24 m (p. 50)
SORBUS aucuparia: 9-12 m (p. 33)
SALIX daphnoides: 6-9 m (p. 210)
AMELANCHIER canadensis: 3-5.4 m (p. 33)
SALIX alba 'Chermesina': 3-4.5 m (p. 210)
HIPPOPHAE rhamnoides: 2.4-3.6 m (p. 88)
ARUNDINARIA murielae: 1.8-3 m (p. 183)
GUNNERA manicata: 1.8-2.7 m (p. 183)
CORNUS stolonifera 'Flaviramea': 1.8-2.4 m
  (p. 211)
CORNUS alba 'Sibirica': 1.5-2.4 m (p. 211)
SYMPHORICARPOS rivularis: 1.5-2.1 m (p. 206)
GAULTHERIA shallon: 1.2-1.8 m (p. 106)
SYMPHORICARPOS × doorenbosii 'White
  Hedge': 1.2-1.8 m (p. 130)
VACCINIUM corymbosum: 1.2-1.8 m (p. 193)
ASTILBE taquetii 'Superba': 1.2 m (p. 106)
LIGULARIA dentata 'Desdemona': 1.2 m (p. 172)
SALIX hastata 'Wehrhahnii': 1.2 m (p. 51)
PHALARIS arundinacea 'Picta': 90-150 cm
  (p. 152)
POLYGONUM amplexicaule 'Atrosanguineum':
  90-120 cm (p. 51)
HEMEROCALLIS e.g. 'Pink Damask': 75-90 cm
  (p. 107)
HEMEROCALLIS e.g. 'Marion Vaughn': 75 cm
  (p. 52)
TROLLIUS × cultorum e.g. 'Orange Princess':
  75 cm (p. 246)
MONARDA didyma e.g. 'Cambridge Scarlet':
  60-90 cm (p. 199)
MONARDA didyma e.g. 'Croftway Pink':
  60-90 cm (p. 52)
LYTHRUM virgatum e.g. 'Rose Queen': 60 cm
  (p. 52)
SYMPHYTUM grandiflorum: 23 cm (p. 110)
VACCINIUM vitis-idaea: 15 cm (p. 111)

FILIPENDULA purpurea (syn. *Spiraea palmata*)

◐ [○]

type of plant: HP
flowering season: midsummer
flower colour: pink
height: 90-120 cm/3-4 ft

A rich soil that remains moist or damp throughout
the spring and summer months will produce a
great clump of good-looking leaves on this plant.
The flower stems are leafy and they make it seem as
if the flowers are sitting almost directly on top of a
mound of greenery.

Ground-cover – Green foliage – Cutting.

RODGERSIA pinnata e.g. 'Superba' ★

◐ [○]

type of plant: HP
flowering season: midsummer
flower colour: pink
height: 90-120 cm/3-4 ft

This plant's fingered leaves are often 30 cm/1 ft
wide. Their wrinkled surface somehow
accentuates the suffusion of bronze – most
noticeable when the foliage is young – through the
basic green colouring. In this form of *R. pinnata*
the flowers are a darker pink than normal. Spongy
soils that are either moist or boggy are ideal, and
there should be some shelter from cold winds.
This plant may be grown in full as well as partial
shade.

Clay – Ground-cover – Red, etc. leaves.

PRIMULA florindae ★
[Giant Himalayan Cowslip]

◐ [○]

type of plant: HP
flowering season: summer
flower colour: yellow
height: 75-120 cm/2½-4 ft

The great sprays of flowers produced by this
vigorous and beautiful primula have a sweet
fragrance. In rich, damp soils the flower stalks may
be as much as 180 cm/6 ft tall and the broad leaves
will grow thickly enough to block out most weeds.
Under such conditions this plant may also seed
itself quite freely.

Acid soils – Ground-cover – Fragrant flowers.

LOBELIA fulgens Hybrid e.g. 'Queen Victoria'
(syn. *L. cardinalis* 'Queen Victoria')

◐ [○]

type of plant: HHP
flowering season: l. summer
flower colour: red
height: 75 cm/2½ ft

As compensation for its lack of hardiness this plant
offers wonderfully vivid flowers; these are often
borne over several weeks. The foliage is a rich
red-purple. Hybrids from *L. fulgens* can either be
lifted and their roots stored under cover each
winter or they can be given protective layers of
bracken or peat in the garden during the colder
months. They all need a moist or damp soil that is
also fertile and, in warm districts, they may be
grown in a fully shaded position. They are grown
infrequently in the United States, and then mainly
as annuals.

Red, etc. leaves.

ACORUS calamus 'Variegatus'
[form of Sweet Flag]
◑[○]
type of plant: HPAq
height: 60-75 cm/2-2½ ft
≈

When bruised, all parts of this plant emit a warm, spicy scent. The upright and strongly shaped foliage looks lovely reflected in water. Each leaf has one edge coloured white or, sometimes, cream. *A.c.* 'Variegatus' is at its best growing in a few centimetres/inches of water, but damp and wet soils also suit it.

Variegated leaves – Aromatic leaves.

ASTILBE×arendsii e.g. 'White Gloria'
[form of False Goat's Beard]
◑[○]
type of plant: HP
flowering season: summer
flower colour: white
height: 60 cm/2 ft

With abundant moisture astilbes can be grown in full sun where they will probably flower particularly freely. *A.×a.* 'White Gloria' is one of several white-flowered cultivars; other popular forms are mainly in shades of red and pink. The pretty, toothed leaves make good clumps of ground-cover.

Ground-cover – Green foliage – Cutting.

HOSTA 'Thomas Hogg'
[form of Plantain Lily]
◑[○]
type of plant: HP
flowering season: summer
flower colour: lilac
height: 60 cm/2 ft

Of the many, widely available hostas with variegated leaves 'Thomas Hogg' is perhaps the toughest and easiest to grow. The upper surface of its white-edged foliage is unusually smooth and its leaves tend to emerge from the ground a little earlier than those of most other hostas. Rich soils that are either moist or damp encourage lush clumps of growth through which no weeds can penetrate.

Ground-cover – Variegated leaves.

PRIMULA beesiana
◑[○]
type of plant: HP
flowering season: e. summer
flower colour: purplish rose
height: 45-60 cm/1½-2 ft

The Candelabra primulas, which include *P. beesiana* and the plants shown in the following two illustrations, are fairly easy though not especially long-lived perennials for acid or neutral soils that are also fertile and moisture-retentive. A sunny position is suitable as long as the ground is permanently damp. The flower stalks of all primulas of this type are encircled by whorls of primrose-like flowers.

Acid soils.

PRIMULA japonica
◑[○]
type of plant: HP
flowering season: l. spring to e. summer
flower colour: purplish red
height: 45-60 cm/1½-2 ft

P. japonica and forms selected from it flower earlier than other Candelabra primulas. 'Postford White' is a particularly attractive variety, the yellow-eyed flowers of which will gleam alluringly in the dappled shade of light woodland. Both the species and the variety produce rosettes of large leaves and these can grow so thickly in really fertile, damp soils that few weeds will manage to penetrate them. (For further remarks about Candelabra primulas see the preceding plant.)

Acid soils.

PRIMULA japonica 'Postford White' ★ sc NA
◑[○]
type of plant: HP
flowering season: l. spring to e. summer
flower colour: white
height: 45-60 cm/1½-2 ft

See preceding plant.

ARUNCUS dioicus (syn. *A. sylvester*, *Spiraea aruncus*) [Goat's Beard]

◐

type of plant: HP
flowering season: e. summer
flower colour: creamy white
height: 1.2-1.8 m/4-6 ft

Damp or moist soils are ideal for this large, handsome plant but it is vigorous enough to grow well under most conditions. Its long, fern-like foliage forms a 90-120 cm/3-4 ft wide, weed-proof clump. Most nurseries will offer the male form of this plant; female plants have less elegant flower plumes but they do produce good seed-heads. There is a cut-leaved variety of *A. dioicus*, known as 'Kneiffi', which is only 90 cm/3 ft high.

Clay – Ground-cover – Green foliage.

CIMICIFUGA simplex NA [Kamchatka Snakeroot]

◐

type of plant: HP
flowering season: autumn
flower colour: white
height: 90-150 cm/3-5 ft

A stout perennial with handsomely divided foliage, *C. simplex* bears clusters of clean white flowers late in the season. They present a bottlebrush-like appearance and provide a welcome contrast to the daisy flower form of chrysanthemums and asters. The soil should be deep and moisture-retentive. In Britain, specialist nurseries may stock a related plant, *C.* 'White Pearl'.

MATTEUCCIA struthiopteris (syn. *Struthiopteris germanica*) [Ostrich Feather Fern, Shuttlecock Fern]

◐

type of plant: HF
height: 90-120 cm/3-4 ft

The beautifully symmetrical, sterile fronds of this fern are freshest and most delicate in springtime. In winter the previously inconspicuous, fertile fronds remain, looking decorative despite being dark and withered. The roots of this plant can spread quite widely, especially in the damp conditions which suit it best.

Green foliage.

HOUTTUYNIA cordata 'Plena' sc NA

◐

type of plant: HP
flowering season: summer
flower colour: white
height: 15-23 cm/6-9 in

≈

Even the double-flowered form of *H. cordata* is vigorous enough to be invasive in some rich, damp soils or in fertile mud along the margins of ponds. The leaves of this plant have a metallic sheen which is slightly more pronounced in sunny sites. (Less shade is needed if the ground is really wet or if *H. c.* 'Plena' is grown in a few centimetres/inches of water.) A strong, orangey scent is released from the foliage when it is bruised.

Ground-cover – Aromatic foliage.

DRYOPTERIS cristata [Crested Buckler Fern]

◐ ●

type of plant: HF
height: 60-90 cm/2-3 ft

✳

Nothing like as stately or as interesting as the other two ferns illustrated in this list of plants for damp and wet ground (see *Osmunda regalis*, p. 73, and *Matteuccia struthiopteris*, above), *D. cristata* is, nevertheless, quite attractive and it will tolerate dense as well as full or partial shade. Although it is a moisture-loving plant, it will grow sastisfactorily in ordinary garden soil provided that it is acid or neutral.

Acid soils – Clay – Dense shade – Green foliage.

Additional plants, featured elsewhere in this book, that are suitable for damp and wet soils

◐ [○] partial shade (or sun)
ARUNDINARIA nitida: 2.4-3 m (p. 211)
RODGERSIA podophylla: 90-120 cm (p. 172)
RODGERSIA tabularis: 90-120 cm (p. 184)
PRIMULA pulverulenta: 75 cm (p. 39)
PRIMULA pulverulenta 'Bartley Strain': 75 cm (p. 39)
SCROPHULARIA aquatica 'Variegata': 60-90 cm (p. 153)
HOSTA fortunei: 60-75 cm (p. 113)
HOSTA undulata: 60-75 cm (p. 153)
ASTILBE × arendsii e.g. 'Fanal': 60 cm (p. 184)
ASTILBE × arendsii e.g. 'Rheinland' ★: 60 cm (p. 113)
HOSTA sieboldiana ★: 60 cm (p. 167)
HOSTA fortunei 'Albopicta': 45-60 cm (p. 150)
HOSTA plantaginea: 45-60 cm (p. 271)
ONOCLEA sensibilis ★: 45-60 cm (p. 185)
ASTILBE chinensis pumila: 23-30 cm (p. 114)
NIEREMBERGIA repens ★: 5 cm (p. 144)
LYSIMACHIA nummularia: 2-5 cm (p. 115)

◐ partial shade
HOSTA fortunei 'Aurea': 45-60 cm (p. 177)
ANDROMEDA polifolia: 23-30 cm (p. 43)

◐ ● partial or full shade
SYMPHORICARPOS rivularis: 1.5-2.1 m (p. 206)
GAULTHERIA shallon: 1.2-1.8 m (p. 106)
OSMUNDA regalis ★: 1.2-1.8 m (p. 73)
SYMPHORICARPOS × doorenbosii 'White Hedge': 1.2-1.8 m (p. 130)
SYMPHYTUM × uplandicum: 1.2-1.5 m (p. 73)
KIRENGESHOMA palmata ★: 90-120 cm (p. 45)
RODGERSIA pinnata e.g. 'Superba' ★: 90-120 cm (p. 77)
RODGERSIA podophylla: 90-120 cm (p. 172)
RODGERSIA tabularis: 90-120 cm (p. 184)
LOBELIA fulgens Hybrid e.g. 'Queen Victoria': 75 cm (p. 77)
SCROPHULARIA aquatica 'Variegata': 60-90 cm (p. 153)
HOSTA fortunei: 60-75 cm (p. 113)
PODOPHYLLUM emodi: 30 cm (p. 208)
CAREX morrowi 'Variegata': 23 cm (p. 76)
SYMPHYTUM grandiflorum: 23 cm (p. 110)
VACCINIUM vitis-idaea: 15 cm (p. 111)

Plants tolerant of dry shade

The very mention of dry shade makes normally enthusiastic gardeners become as dismal and dejected as the areas in their gardens where this unfortunate combination of conditions exists. Even a little preliminary digging in a dry and shady site is a depressing exercise, particularly when it involves the rather fruitless excavation of pieces of root from a shallow layer of dusty soil. However, do not underestimate the satisfaction to be gained from conquering such an area, and making it green and interesting instead of brown and boring.

Areas of dry shade are often caused by the roots of overhanging trees sucking moisture from surrounding soil. They may also be due to walls sheltering sites from rain-bearing winds and facing directions – usually north and east – from which relatively dry winds blow. In addition, some very fast-draining soils can be almost as dry in a little shade as they are in sunshine. Whatever the cause of the problem of dry shade, however, the provision of material which retains moisture easily is the single factor most likely to lead to a solution.

This material may be farmyard manure, leaf-mould, garden compost, moss peat or a number of other substances which, when dug into dry soils, increase the amount of organic matter in them and thereby their capacity to hold water. At the very least, plants which are to be grown in dry, shady sites should be provided with generously sized planting holes, and these holes should be filled with plenty of the type of material mentioned above.

In the case of particularly dry sites which contain many tree roots, it is often worth not only lining planting holes with organic matter, but also placing a new layer of good, moisture-retentive material on top of the existing soil. This upper layer, and any subsequent dressings of leaf-mould and so on, will, in time, rot down into and amalgamate with the lower layer. This process will be hastened if the lower layer is loosened, as far as possible, before the new layer is applied.

To enable this list to be used in conjunction with other lists, the height given for each plant is the same as usual. However, two points should be borne in mind when interpreting estimates of height in the present context: first, plants may be less vigorous – and therefore smaller – than normal in dry, shady sites; second, if a site is heavily shaded, established plants may become taller than usual and rather lanky, as they are drawn upwards towards light. This lankiness can be reduced, to some extent, by occasional pinching out of the tips of the growing shoots. Regular, hard pruning is not recommended as a method of achieving bushiness, because of the reduced vigour of plants grown in dry, shady conditions.

You may also find that these inhospitable conditions result in fewer flowers and fruits than normal. Perhaps the best effect to aim for in dry, shady sites is a healthy covering of leaves. *Hedera helix* 'Hibernica' may not be a particularly decorative plant, but its large, green leaves form excellent ground-cover, even in difficult places. How successfully this ivy can cope with dry shade is shown by the plantings of it beneath wide-spreading trees in the Royal Botanic Gardens at Kew – illustrated in Graham Stuart Thomas's *Plants for Ground-Cover* (published by Dent). There it is used, by itself, in extensive sweeps. In dry, shady areas, where plants can become rather patchy, a large number of plants of a single species or variety, rather than a few specimens of several different types of plant, seems to be more successful at disguising any patchiness.

Although all the plants in the following list will tolerate dry shade when they are established, they may need to be watched carefully for signs of drought during their first few seasons. This applies particularly to the larger specimens such as *Ilex aquifolium* (common holly). Where appropriate, only the most suitable examples of a genus which will tolerate dry shade have been included: for instance, all ivies will withstand shade and dryness to some extent, but *Hedera helix* 'Hibernica' and *H. h.* 'Gold Heart' (syn. *H. h.* 'Jubilee') seem particularly well suited to these conditions. Only these two ivies have been included in the following list.

RIBES sanguineum e.g. 'Pulborough Scarlet' sc NA
[form of Flowering Currant]
○ ◑
type of plant: HSh
flowering season: spring
flower colour: deep red
height: 1.8-2.7 m/6-9 ft

R. sanguineum and its garden varieties are very tolerant plants which will thrive in well drained, fertile soils. They will also grow – with remarkable success – in dry, shady positions and in heavy clay. 'Pulborough Scarlet' is a vigorous, upright form. It will attain its ultimate height quickly and it is useful for hedging. If its stems are cut early in the year and brought indoors, the buds soon open out into white or very pale pink flowers which emit a slight, musky smell.

Clay – Atmospheric pollution – Hedging – Cutting.

LIRIOPE muscari ★
○ ◑
type of plant: HP
flowering season: l. summer to mid-autumn
flower colour: violet-blue
height: 30-45 cm/1-1½ ft
E

Any dry site, in sun or light shade, can be made to shine with the glossy, arching foliage of this plant. It needs good drainage but light soils that are also very alkaline are not suitable. *L. muscari* grows slowly and densely. Its long-lasting flower spikes are borne on dark, wiry stems.

Acid soils – Hot, dry soils – Ground-cover – Green foliage.

DRYOPTERIS filix-mas
[Male Fern]
◑ [○]
type of plant: HF
height: 60-120 cm/2-4 ft

Even thoroughly discouraging conditions, such as dry shade, shallow, chalky soils and heavy clay, seem to produce quite large and luxuriant specimens of this vigorous fern. It will seed itself in places where few other plants could be coaxed to survive. Infertile soils and sunny positions slow its growth only a little. The fronds of this fern remain green until late in the year and, with the thick roots, they make good ground-cover.

Chalk – Clay – Ground-cover – Green foliage.

DICENTRA eximia NA
[Eastern Bleeding Heart]
◐ [○]
type of plant: HP
flowering season: spring to autumn
flower colour: light pink
height: 40 cm/15 in

The ferny foliage of this hardy perennial is always attractive, and the plant always has a few flowers on it after the main surge of bloom in spring. *Dicentra eximia* is of easy culture but performs best in woody soil in light shade, where it will reseed freely. 'Luxuriant', a hybrid of western United States origin, is a deeper pink but otherwise has the same good qualities.

EPIMEDIUM × rubrum
[form of Barrenwort or Bishop's Hat]
◐ [○]
type of plant: HP
flowering season: spring
flower colour: red + yellow or white
height: 30 cm/1 ft
½E

Few plants can tolerate dry shade better than epimediums, and this is one of the most handsome kinds. The foliage, which has a red tint in spring, is pretty, and deer do not eat it as they do hosta foliage. Performance is best in a rich, retentive loam, but the plant seems to grow adequately almost anywhere. *E. × versicolor* 'Sulphureum', with yellow flowers, is as easy to grow. In autumn, *E. × rubrum*'s foliage turns a bright, pinkish red.
 Ground cover – Green foliage – Autumn foliage.

POLYPODIUM vulgare
[Common Polypody]
◐
type of plant: HF
height: 15-30 cm/6-12 in
E

The fronds of the common polypody stay green throughout winter but there is a gap, in spring, when the old foliage withers and the new foliage only just begins to emerge. Nevertheless, this fern is suitable for ground-cover and it will carpet dry soils most effectively. It may also be planted on old tree stumps or in crevices in walls. *P. v.* 'Cornubiense' is a form with lacier foliage than the species.
 Chalk – Ground-cover – Green foliage.

CYCLAMEN neapolitanum (syn.
C. hederifolium) ★
◐
type of plant: HTu
flowering season: l. summer to autumn
flower colour: pink
height: 10-15 cm/4-6 in

The beautiful, marbled leaves of this plant (and of *C. n.* 'Album', its white-flowered form) appear in autumn and die down in spring. The foliage therefore receives light underneath deciduous trees, even if these cast quite dense shade during the rest of the year. *C. neapolitanum* will grow in dry shade amongst the roots of other plants but, in such positions, it is especially important to apply a layer of leaf-mould after the leaves have died down. In cool, humus-rich, rather alkaline soils thick clumps of foliage will be produced and self-sown seedlings may appear.
 Ground-cover – Variegated leaves.

EUPHORBIA robbiae ★ sc NA MC
[species of Spurge]
◐ ●
type of plant: HP
flowering season: l. spring to e. summer
flower colour: yellow-green
height: 45-60 cm/1½-2 ft
E

This leathery leaved plant is so well equipped to deal with dry shade that its dark green rosettes may spread quite freely even around the trunks of moderately sized trees. It is suitable both for sunny sites and for densely shaded positions. If either the foliage or the flowers are cut, care must be taken that none of the poisonous juice from the stalks comes in contact with eyes or skin.
 Chalk – Dense shade – Ground-cover – Green foliage – Cutting – Green flowers.

LAMIUM galeobdolon (syn. *Galeobdolon luteum*)
'Variegatum'
[form of Yellow Archangel]
◐ ●
type of plant: HP
flowering season: e. summer
flower colour: yellow
height: 30 cm/1 ft
E

Dryness and shade help to curb the remarkable vigour of this trailing plant which, in fertile, moisture-retentive soils, can spread well over 240 cm/8 ft wide. The leaves have white markings and the central area of older foliage is tinted with bronze. The variegation is most pronounced in light shade. *L. g.* 'Variegatum' should be kept well away from less vigorous plants.
 Chalk – Clay – Dense shade – Ground-cover – Variegated leaves.

VINCA major
[Greater Periwinkle]

◐ ●

type of plant: HSh/P
flowering season: mid-spring to e. summer
flower colour: blue
height: 23-45 cm/9-18 in
E

The variegated form of this long-suffering plant is illustrated on p. 153. Both the species and its variety will grow in sun or dense shade and in poor, dry soils in gloomy places (although it is worth giving the variegated form better treatment in order to get plenty of brightly marked leaves). The stems that bear flowers are upright; other growths are prostrate, spreading and – eventually – ground-covering.

Chalk – Dense shade – Atmospheric pollution – Ground-cover.

LAMIUM maculatum 'Beacon Silver'
[form of Spotted Dead Nettle]

◐ ●

type of plant: HP
flowering season: summer
flower colour: bright pink
height: 15 cm/6 in

This strong-growing ground-cover has leaves which are almost completely silver, edged by a narrow green rim. Almost any soil seems suitable, but performance is best in one with good moisture retention. An important plant for giving a light effect in a deeply shaded area. Like all lamiums, this can be a rampant plant if left to its own devices.

Dense shade – Ground-cover – Variegated leaves.

VINCA minor
[Lesser Periwinkle]

◐ ●

type of plant: HSh/P
flowering season: e. spring to e. summer
flower colour: blue
height: 15 cm/6 in
E

Compared with *V. major* (see second left), the lesser periwinkle generally makes a denser carpet of ground-cover and grows more quickly. Like the larger species it tolerates dense shade and dryness, although sunshine and an ordinary well drained soil will produce the best results. There are many different varieties of *V. minor*: a white-flowered form is illustrated on p. 111, and there are cultivars with reddish purple flowers and double flowers; the varieties with variegated leaves tend to be rather less vigorous than the species which can become invasive.

Chalk – Dense shade – Atmospheric pollution – Ground-cover – Containers.

Additional plants, featured elsewhere in this book, that are tolerant of dry shade

◐ partial shade
ILEX aquifolium: 7.5-12 m (p. 127)
HEDERA helix 'Gold Heart' ★: 3-3.6 m (p. 152)
RIBES sanguineum e.g. 'King Edward VII': 1.5-2.1 m (p. 96)
LONICERA nitida: 1.2-1.8 m (p. 128)
POLYSTICHUM setiferum 'Divisilobum' ★: 75-120 cm (p. 185)
LUNARIA annua:75 cm (p. 208)
LUNARIA annua 'Variegata': 75 cm (p. 155)
MELISSA officinalis 'Aurea': 75 cm (p. 152)
POLYSTICHUM aculeatum: 60-105 cm (p. 186)
DIGITALIS grandiflora: 60-90 cm (p. 52)
TELLIMA grandiflora: 45-60 cm (p. 113)
BERGENIA×'Ballawley': 30-45 cm (p. 25)
BLECHNUM spicant: 30-45 cm (p. 43)
LUZULA maxima: 30-45 cm (p. 115)
BERGENIA cordifolia: 30 cm (p. 184)
BERGENIA×'Silberlicht': 30 cm (p. 109)
ENDYMION non-scriptus: 23-30 cm (p. 272)
ANEMONE nemorosa: 15-23 cm (p. 55)
WALDSTEINIA ternata: 8-10 cm (p. 112)

◐ ● partial or full shade
TAXUS baccata: 12-18 m (p. 126)
TAXUS baccata 'Fastigiata': 9-12 m (p. 24)
BUXUS sempervirens: 3.6-4.5 m (p. 127)
HEDERA helix 'Hibernica': 3.6-4.5 m (p. 109)
LIGUSTRUM ovalifolium: 3.6-4.5 m (p. 127)
LIGUSTRUM ovalifolium 'Aureum': 2.7-3.6 m (p. 177)
BUXUS sempervirens 'Aureovariegata': 2.4-3 m (p. 152)
AUCUBA japonica: 1.5-2.4 m (p. 83)
AUCUBA japonica e.g. 'Crotonifolia': 1.5-2.4 m (p. 136)
SYMPHORICARPOS rivularis: 1.5-2.1 m (p. 206)
GAULTHERIA shallon: 1.2-1.8 m (p. 106)
SYMPHORICARPOS×doorenbosii 'White Hedge': 1.2-1.8 m (p. 130)

MAHONIA aquifolium: 90-120 cm (p. 112)
PRUNUS laurocerasus e.g. 'Otto Luyken': 90 cm (p. 107)
POLYGONATUM×hybridum ★: 75-90 cm (p. 252)
×FATSHEDERA lizei: 60-90 cm (p. 136)
RUSCUS aculeatus: 60-90 cm (p. 84)
IRIS foetidissima: 45-60 cm (p. 208)
BUXUS sempervirens 'Suffruticosa': 30-60 cm (p. 128)
RUBUS tricolor: 30-60 cm (p. 108)
SARCOCOCCA humilis: 30-60 cm (p. 273)
HYPERICUM calycinum: 30-45 cm (p. 108)
VINCA major 'Variegata': 23-45 cm (p. 153)
HEDERA helix 'Hibernica': 23-30 cm (p. 109)
PACHYSANDRA terminalis ★: 23-30 cm (p. 117)
PACHYSANDRA terminalis 'Variegata': 23 cm (p. 155)
EPIMEDIUM grandiflorum 'Rose Queen': 20-30 cm (p. 117)
CONVALLARIA majalis: 15-23 cm (p. 272)
EPIMEDIUM×youngianum 'Niveum': 15-23 cm (p. 187)
LAMIUM maculatum 'Roseum': 15-23 cm (p. 117)
VACCINIUM vitis-idaea: 15 cm (p. 111)
VINCA minor e.g. 'Alba' ★: 15 cm (p. 111)
CORNUS canadensis: 10-15 cm (p. 111)

Plants tolerant of dense shade

In nearly every garden there is an area which is not only sunless and in full shade, but also so darkened by high walls or thickly leaved, overhanging trees that it is densely shaded. Many plants which will grow well against a sunless north wall will not tolerate the lack of light in such areas.

Whether you are starting to make a new garden or already have an established one, these areas of barren gloominess can be most depressing. Often the easiest solution seems to be to fill them with the rubbish bins, on the basis that nothing will grow there anyway. Yet, as the following list shows, the range of plants that will grow in dense shade is actually quite wide, and any unattractive impedimenta can easily be concealed beneath a vigorous climber, like *Clematis montana* or one of its varieties, grown over the top and three sides of a simple frame in a lighter part of the garden. (Although it is deciduous, *Clematis montana* usually retains its foliage until early winter and, once it becomes established, its stems alone form a thick, tangled mass.)

Among them, the plants in this list have many features that will brighten a gloomy corner. And, of course, it is not only flowers that will lighten dark positions.

Several of the plants in this list have variegated leaves and, although the variegation – particularly of some leaves marked with yellow – may not be so bright as it might be in lighter sites, it will be conspicuous enough to relieve the darkness of these difficult places. Glossiness of leaf can also enliven densely shaded sites and this list contains a number of plants (such as *Aucuba japonica*, *Prunus laurocerasus* 'Otto Luyken' and *Sarcococca humilis*) which have this characteristic. The contrast of different types of foliage is a rather overlooked source of interest in dark sites. Unless the site is very small, or already has contrast provided by the foliage of a large, overhanging tree, it is worth trying to choose a variety of plants rather than several that are exactly the same.

Fruits, such as the orange-red seeds of *Iris foetidissima* or the scarlet berries of *Skimmia japonica* 'Foremanii', are always a cheering sight and particularly welcome in gloomy places, although they may not be produced as prolifically there as in sunnier positions. If plants are being chosen for their ornamental fruit it is important to remember that, in the case of some species and varieties – including the female skimmia referred to above – plants of both sexes must be grown for fruit to be produced.

Many of the plants in this list are woodland in origin and are therefore suitable for planting under trees. However, a few resent being dripped upon: *Hosta fortunei*, for instance, does better in shade cast by buildings rather than shade produced by overhanging branches. The majority of these plants also tolerate dryness and appear in either the illustrated or unillustrated section of the 'Dry shade' list.

LIGUSTRUM japonicum MC
[Japanese Privet]

◑ ●

type of plant: HSh
flowering season: l. summer
flower colour: white
height: 1.8-2.4 m/6-8 ft
E

Like the well known oval-leaved privets which have been so widely used for hedging, this shrub too can make a nice, formal hedge (it does, however, need frequent clipping). It grows quickly and densely and its dark, smoothly shaped foliage is altogether more substantial than that of the commoner privets. Its flowers are not especially decorative and they have a somewhat cloying scent. *L. japonicum* can be grown in almost any soil and in sun or shade but it is not so tolerant of dry shade as *L. ovalifolium* and its cultivars.

Chalk – Atmospheric pollution – Hedging.

AUCUBA japonica (syn. *A. j. concolor*) **MC**

◑ ●

type of plant: HSh
height: 1.5-2.4 m/5-8 ft
E

So often consigned to the driest and dreariest of corners in gardens, this plant can look surprisingly attractive even in deep shade – if it is given a moisture-retentive soil. It will, however, tolerate a combination of dryness and shade. Its delicately toothed leaves are, at their best, a deep and shiny background for the bright red berries (which appear when male and female plants are grown together). A widely available, variegated form of *A. japonica* is shown on p. 136. Both these plants can be grown in sun or shade.

Chalk – Clay – Dry shade – Seaside – Atmospheric pollution – Green foliage – Fruit.

HYDRANGEA macrophylla 'Nikko Blue' NA

◑ ●

type of plant: HSh
flowering season: summer
flower colour: blue
height: 1.5 m/5 ft

A snowball type with all sterile florets, this hydrangea is dependable in flower in the colder reaches of the United States, where hydrangea buds are commonly frozen over in winter. There are no special soil requirements.

Clay.

RUSCUS aculeatus MC
[Butcher's Broom]
◐ ●
type of plant: HSh
height: 60-90 cm/2-3 ft
E

If a few female plants of this stiff, upright sub-shrub are grown beside a male plant, then large, bright red berries will be produced in autumn. The fruit normally lasts until late spring. Any soil – poor or fertile, heavy or light – will suit this plant and it can be grown successfully underneath trees and in sunny positions.

Chalk – Clay – Dry shade – Fruit.

RAMONDA myconi (syn. *R. pyrenaica*)★
◐ ●
type of plant: HP
flowering season: l. spring
flower colour: lavender
height: 10-15 cm/4-6 in
E

Cool, shady sites and light, humus-y soils suit this plant best. It is often recommended for crevices in north-facing walls where its rosette of lovely, red-fringed, wrinkled leaves can be shown to advantage. The flowers are usually lavender-blue, but seedlings may vary in the colour of their blooms.

Green foliage.

HABERLEA rhodopensis
◐ ●
type of plant: HP
flowering season: spring
flower colour: lilac
height: 10 cm/4 in
E

H. rhodopensis is related to the plant shown in the preceding illustration and it should be grown under similar conditions. Its leaves are smoother and more leathery than those of *R. myconi*.

Additional plants, featured elsewhere in this book, that are tolerant of dense shade

TAXUS baccata: 12-18 m (p. 126)
TAXUS baccata 'Fastigiata': 9-12 m (p. 24)
BUXUS sempervirens: 3.6-4.5 m (p. 127)
HEDERA helix 'Hibernica': 3.6-4.5 m (p. 109)
LIGUSTRUM ovalifolium: 3.6-4.5 m (p. 127)
RHODODENDRON (Hardy Hybrid) e.g. 'Cynthia': 3-3.6 m (p. 34)
RHODODENDRON (Hardy Hybrid) e.g. 'Fastuosum Flore Pleno': 3-3.6 m (p. 95)
RHODODENDRON ponticum: 3-3.6 m (p. 128)
FATSIA japonica ★: 2.4-3.6 m (p. 135)
SYMPHORICARPOS rivularis: 1.5-2.1 m (p. 206)
GAULTHERIA shallon: 1.2-1.8 m (p. 106)
OSMUNDA regalis: 1.2-1.8 m (p. 73)
SYMPHORICARPOS × doorenbosii 'White Hedge': 1.2-1.8 m (p. 130)
MAHONIA aquifolium: 90-120 cm (p. 112)
SKIMMIA japonica 'Foremanii' ★: 90-120 cm (p. 208)
PRUNUS laurocerasus e.g. 'Otto Luyken': 90 cm (p. 107)
POLYGONATUM × hybridum ★: 75-90 cm (p. 252)
DRYOPTERIS dilatata: 60-120 cm (p. 186)
DRYOPTERIS cristata: 60-90 cm (p. 79)
× FATSHEDERA lizei: 60-90 cm (p. 136)
SCROPHULARIA aquatica 'Variegata': 60-90 cm (p. 153)
HOSTA fortunei: 60-75 cm (p. 113)
HELLEBORUS lividus corsicus ★: 60 cm (p. 283)
EUPHORBIA robbiae ★: 45-60 cm (p. 81)
HELLEBORUS orientalis Hybrids: 45-60 cm (p. 279)
IRIS foetidissima: 45-60 cm (p. 208)
BRUNNERA macrophylla: 45 cm (p. 116)
BUXUS sempervirens 'Suffruticosa': 30-60 cm (p. 128)
RUBUS tricolor: 30-60 cm (p. 108)
SARCOCOCCA humilis: 30-60 cm (p. 273)
HELLEBORUS niger: 30-45 cm (p. 279)

HYPERICUM calycinum: 30-45 cm (p. 108)
SAXIFRAGA fortunei: 30-45 cm (p. 186)
SAXIFRAGA fortunei 'Wada's Variety': 30-45 cm (p. 173)
LAMIUM galeobdolon 'Variegatum': 30 cm (p. 81)
VINCA major: 23-45 cm (p. 82)
VINCA major 'Variegata': 23-45 cm (p. 153)
HEDERA helix 'Hibernica': 23-30 cm (p. 109)
PACHYSANDRA terminalis ★: 23-30 cm (p. 117)
PACHYSANDRA terminalis 'Variegata': 23 cm (p. 155)
SYMPHYTUM grandiflorum: 23 cm (p. 110)
CONVALLARIA majalis: 15-23 cm (p. 272)
LAMIUM maculatum 'Roseum': 15-23 cm (p. 117)
VIOLA cornuta e.g. 'Alba': 15-23 cm (p. 110)
VIOLA cornuta e.g. 'Jersey Gem': 15-23 cm (p. 143)
LAMIUM maculatum 'Aureum': 15 cm (p. 178)
LAMIUM maculatum 'Beacon Silver': 15 cm (p. 82)
VACCINIUM vitis-idaea: 15 cm (p. 111)
VINCA minor: 15 cm (p. 82)
VINCA minor e.g. 'Alba' ★: 15 cm (p. 111)
CORNUS canadensis: 10-15 cm (p. 111)
GAULTHERIA procumbens: 8-15 cm (p. 118)

Shrubs (90 cm/3 ft and over) and trees suitable for windswept seaside gardens

Those who garden inland may imagine, as they drive along some coast during their summer holidays, that a garden beside the sea must be an entirely trouble-free possession, a place where exotica flourish and ordinary plants become unrecognizably large and luxuriant. If they could see the same area in autumn and winter they might be disillusioned. An exposed coastal garden, though lovely on a calm, summer's day, can be depressingly windswept and salt-encrusted during stormy weather.

Nevertheless, it is no myth that the seaside can provide an exceptionally favourable climate in which to grow plants. The mild weather and high level of general humidity mean that slightly tender and even half-hardy plants can often be grown without protection beside the sea, and these conditions usually result in hardier plants doing outstandingly well there too. In most cases, however, this desirable state of affairs will only be reached after the problem of salt-laden wind has been dealt with.

All the plants in the following list will withstand high winds and salt spray. By doing so, not only do they themselves survive, but they also give some shelter and protection to more vulnerable plants. (Many of the plants in this list that are most suitable for providing shelter are also to be found in the 'Hedging plants' list.) Once a barrier is established in the face of salt and wind, an extremely wide range of plants can be grown in a seaside garden.

Of course, shelter can be provided by walls, but with all solid barriers there is the problem of turbulence on the leeward side, and this can cause as much damage as winds straight from the sea. Much the most satisfactory forms of shelter are those that filter wind. In very exposed positions, the plants that are intended to form the first line of defence against salt-laden winds will, themselves, need shelter when young. Temporary wattle fencing, sacking attached to stakes, or any other form of shelter which allows the passage of air, can be used to protect these and other young plants until their root systems are large enough to prevent them from being torn from the ground by strong winds.

Some of the plants in this list are rather too decorative – and expensive – to use as part of the first barrier between sea and garden. Plants that are exposed to the full brunt of wind and salt spray tend to become battered and bent; their leaves are sometimes scorched or torn; and trees in this position will often be little more than misshapen shrubs. The most practical choices for such exposed sites are the ordinary species rather than the varieties of plants.

Once a barrier against salt and wind has become established, the task of choosing small and medium-sized plants for seaside gardens presents few difficulties. Indeed, small plants that naturally hug the ground have their own, built-in protection against high winds in their habit of growth.

In deciding which of the many possible small and medium-sized plants would be most suitable for a seaside garden, it is worth bearing in mind some of the ways in which plants native to the seashore protect themselves from salt spray and high winds.

Comparatively little damage can be done to leaves which are tough and leathery: *Griselinia littoralis* has leaves of this type and it is included in this list. Certain inland plants, such as the hollies listed here, have similarly tough foliage which enables them to grow well beside the sea, even though this is not their native habitat.

Some seaside plants have foliage which is covered with tiny hairs; these hairs protect the leaf surface from being damaged by salt, and they also reduce the loss of moisture caused by wind. Many grey-leaved plants, such as *Senecio laxifolius*, grow particularly well near the sea and mainly because they have this form of protection. Very small or narrow leaves are a further form of protection against wind damage, and there are numerous seaside plants (such as *Hippophae rhamnoides*) with compact foliage in some form or other.

Finally, flexible stems are less likely to be damaged by high winds than brittle stems are. Although the white willow and its varieties may not be very commonly associated with seaside gardens, their flexible shoots and slightly hairy leaves make them eminently suitable for coastal plantings.

To allow cross-reference to other lists, average heights, which have been used elsewhere in this book, are retained here. In windswept coastal gardens, the height of some of the plants in this list may be lower than average, particularly if the plants are used to provide shelter. Generally speaking, however, plants will not be very much smaller, and some compaction by wind improves the appearance of certain plants.

For hedging plants particularly suitable for providing shelter against high winds and salt spray, see items marked 'C' in the 'Hedging plants' list.

PINUS radiata (syn. *P. insignis***) MC**
[Monterey Pine]

○

type of plant: HCo
height: 24-33 m/80-110 ft
*E

This dome-headed tree grows very rapidly and a number of young specimens can soon form an effective shelter belt, especially near the sea. Larger and older specimens transplant less successfully than young plants. The foliage of this conifer is bright green, but in the dense crown it can appear quite dark. *P. radiata* prefers a fairly acid, well drained soil. It is not winter hardy in the colder parts of the United States.
    Acid soils.

CUPRESSUS macrocarpa MC
[Monterey Cypress]

○

type of plant: HCo
height: 18-27 m/60-90 ft
E

A tolerance of salt-laden winds and an ability to grow quickly make *C. macrocarpa* particularly suitable for providing shelter in coastal areas; very cold winds tend to 'burn' and dry its resinous foliage. Mature trees may be quite wide-spreading, with horizontal branches, but young plants are columnar. *C. m.* 'Goldcrest' is a readily available, yellow-leaved form of this conifer. Any well drained soil is suitable. These plants are not winter-hardy in the colder parts of the United States.
    Aromatic leaves.

PINUS mugo (syn. *P. montana***)**
[Mountain Pine]

○

type of plant: HCo
height: 3-4.5 m/10-15 ft
E

This very hardy species of pine is usually low and spreading with gnarled branches; it can, however, be a good deal more upright. In any case, *P. mugo* will grow in both acid and alkaline soils and it will withstand strong winds. The young foliage is light green. There are various prostrate forms of this plant including *P. m. pumilio* (for details of which, see p. 3).
    Chalk.

TAMARIX tetrandra
[species of Tamarisk]

○

type of plant: HSh
flowering season: l. spring
flower colour: pale pink
height: 3-4.5 m/10-15 ft

Provided that this plant is cut back hard after flowering, it maintains its graceful arching habit but does not become too open and gangling. Its tiny, overlapping leaves, which give a feathery appearance to the whole plant, resist damage from both salt spray and polluted air. Well drained soils of all types suit *T. tetrandra* but very shallow, limy soils are best avoided.

Acid soils – Atmospheric pollution – Hedging.

ESCALLONIA macrantha ★ MC

○

type of plant: SlTSh
flowering season: summer to e. autumn
flower colour: red
height: 3 m/10 ft
E

E. macrantha is a vigorous, rounded shrub which is frequently used for hedging in coastal areas. Its pungently scented leaves are thick and leathery and well able to withstand salt spray borne on gale force winds. In colder, inland gardens this plant is often grown against a wall. It is not suitable for heavy, badly drained soils, and it does not do well in the colder regions of the United States.

Atmospheric pollution – Hedging – Aromatic leaves.

ESCALLONIA e.g. 'Apple Blossom' MC

○

type of plant: SlTSh
flowering season: summer to e. autumn
flower colour: pink + white
height: 1.8 m/6 ft
E/½E

Although this rather stiff, upright shrub grows well in coastal regions, it is not quite so robust or so suitable for full exposure to sea winds as *E. macrantha* (see previous illustration). However, most gardeners would consider that its small, shiny leaves and pretty sprays of flowers make it a more decorative garden plant than the species. Any well drained soil gives good results. It does not grow well in the colder parts of the United States.

Atmospheric pollution – Hedging – Containers – Cutting.

LAVATERA olbia 'Rosea'
[form of Bush-mallow]

○

type of plant: SlTP/Sh
flowering season: summer to mid-autumn
flower colour: pink
height: 1.8 m/6 ft

This short-lived plant produces numerous blooms over an unusually long flowering season. Its elegantly branching but tough stems withstand wind well; they should be cut down to ground level each spring. The longest lived plants are grown in well drained, rather poor soils, and a warm site is essential.

Grey, etc. leaves.

LUPINUS arboreus ★ MC
[Tree Lupin]

○

type of plant: HSh/P
flowering season: all summer
flower colour: yellow
height: 1.5-1.8 m/5-6 ft
E/½E

Part of the attraction of this plant is its obviously ephemeral nature. It quickly makes a leafy, spreading shrub and, for a few years only, produces a mass of yellow flower spikes which are very sweetly scented. Its preference is for light and poor soils, and it is so well suited to life beside the sea that it has become naturalized along parts of the southern and eastern coasts of England. There are forms of this plant with white, blue or purple flowers. In the United States it is grown mainly in California; it is tender elsewhere.

Acid soils – Hot, dry soils – Fragrant flowers.

CYTISUS scoparius e.g. 'Cornish Cream'
sc NA
[form of Common Broom]

○

type of plant: HSh
flowering season: l. spring to e. summer
flower colour: cream
height: 1.2-1.8 m/4-6 ft

The common broom, of which this variety is one of many possible examples, has a short but colourful life. It flowers very freely and, in winter, its rich green twigs look cheerfully evergreen. To extend its brief life, *C. s.* 'Cornish Cream' and similar varieties must be pruned hard after flowering and before setting seed. Alkaline soils should be avoided and really well drained, rather poor, acid soils should be chosen instead. These plants are erect with spraying, twiggy growths.

Acid soils – Hot, dry soils – Atmospheric pollution – Bark and *twigs*.

CISTUS × purpureus ★
[form of Rock Rose]

○
type of plant: SlTSh
flowering season: summer
flower colour: rose
height: 1.2-1.5 m/4-5 ft
E

Given a dry, light soil that is not too fertile, this rounded shrub will produce tough stems which make it less susceptible to damage in cold winters. It is an excellent seaside plant. Each large, tissue-thin flower is short-lived but there is a succession of blooms. The young growths are resinous and fragrant, but the foliage is a rather gloomy greyish green.

Chalk – Hot, dry soils – Atmospheric pollution – Aromatic leaves.

ROSA (Rugosa Hybrid) e.g. 'Schneezwerg' (syn. *R.* 'Snow Dwarf')
[form of Rose]

○
type of plant: HSh
flowering season: summer
flower colour: white
height: 1.2 m/4 ft

This neat and upright plant produces its richly scented flowers on and off throughout the summer and often into autumn too. Late blooms are accompanied by small but bright, orange-red hips. Its overall shape and sturdy nature make *R.* 'Schneezwerg' a good seaside plant and useful for hedging. It thrives in a light, sandy soil but any well drained soil is suitable.

Chalk – Hedging – Fruit – Fragrant flowers.

HEBE 'Midsummer Beauty' sc NA MC
○
type of plant: SlTSh
flowering season: summer
flower colour: lavender
height: 90-150 cm/3-5 ft
E

All the hebes – or shrubby veronicas as they are sometimes called – are splendid seaside and town plants. This particular cultivar has the unexpected bonus of sweetly scented flowers. Its leaves are conspicuously and attractively red-brown beneath. In a well drained soil this very free-flowering hebe will come through most British winters unscathed.

Chalk – Atmospheric pollution – Fragrant flowers.

QUERCUS ilex MC
[Holm Oak, Evergreen Oak]

○ [◑]
type of plant: SlTT
flowering season: l. spring to e. summer
flower colour: yellow
height: 15-18 m/50-60 ft
E

Fully exposed to salt-laden winds this glossy-leaved tree grows well but is usually quite small and shrub-like. In more tranquil surroundings, however, it forms a leafy, dome-headed tree of a substantial appearance and the fine corrugations of its bark are clearly visible. It responds healthily to clipping and makes an attractive formal hedge. Very cold winds and late spring frosts can 'burn' its foliage and it is best grown in mild areas and on well drained soils.

Atmospheric pollution – Hedging – *Bark and twigs*.

OLEARIA macrodonta sc NA MC
[species of Daisy Bush, New Zealand Holly]

○ [◑]
type of plant: SlTSh
flowering season: summer
flower colour: white
height: 2.4-3.6 m/8-12 ft
E

The daisy bushes are, in general, tolerant of salt-laden winds but this vigorous, upright species is even more successful in exposed seaside gardens than most of its relatives. Its attractive leaves have the double protection of leathery upper surfaces and white felting on the undersides. Although some people find the large flower heads of this shrub sweetly fragrant, the musky smell emitted by the leaves tends to be dominant. *O. macrodonta* needs a well drained soil and, in inland gardens, a warm, sheltered site.

Chalk – Hedging – Green foliage.

GRISELINIA littoralis MC
○ ◑
type of plant: SlTSh
height: 3-3.6 m/10-12 ft
E; up to 7.5 m/25 ft if very mild

In mild, coastal areas this upright shrub can form a small tree. Its copious, leathery leaves are of an unusual, fresh green – the colour of a nice, crisp eating apple. They are also highly resistant to damage from salt spray and strong winds. *G. littoralis* makes an excellent hedge or windbreak near the sea. Any fertile soil is suitable for this shrub but, in colder gardens in particular, good drainage is an advantage. There is an even less hardy, variegated form of this plant.

Hedging – Green foliage.

HIPPOPHAE rhamnoides ★
[Sea Buckthorn]
○ ◑
type of plant: HSh
height: 2.4-3.6 m/8-12 ft
sometimes up to 7.5 m/25 ft

Once fully established, this vigorous, thorny
shrub takes to seaside living so well that it sows
itself liberally in its own shelter. Plants of both
sexes must be grown for the numerous,
long-lasting and bird-resistant berries to appear.
The pale, silvery grey foliage helps to disguise the
stiff and rather coarse growth of this plant.
H. rhamnoides is grown most often on sandy and
other light, dry soils, but it does almost equally
well near water inland.

Damp and wet soils – Hedging – Grey, etc.
leaves – Fruit.

**Additional shrubs and trees, featured elsewhere
in this book, that are suitable for windswept
seaside gardens**

○ sun
PINUS nigra: 21-30 m (p. 1)
POPULUS alba: 18-27 m (p. 156)
CORDYLINE australis: 3.6-9 m (p. 180)
TAMARIX pentandra: 3.6-4.5 m (p. 129)
YUCCA gloriosa: 2.7-3.6 m (p. 56)
SPARTIUM junceum: 2.1-3 m (p. 56)
ESCALLONIA e.g. 'Donard Radiance': 1.8-2.4 m
(p. 125)
CYTISUS scoparius e.g. 'Andreanus': 1.8 m (p. 57)
CYTISUS scoparius e.g. 'Firefly': 1.5-2.1 m (p. 92)
HEBE brachysiphon: 1.2-1.8 m (p. 3)
ROSA (Rugosa Hybrid) e.g. 'Blanc Double de
Coubert' ★: 1.2-1.8 m (p. 129)
ROSA (Rugosa) e.g. 'Roseraie de l'Hay': 1.2-1.8 m
(p. 256)
ROSMARINUS officinalis: 1.2-1.8 m (p. 196)
TEUCRIUM fruticans: 1.2-1.5 m (p. 57)
PINUS mugo pumilio: 90-180 cm (p. 3)
YUCCA filamentosa: 90-180 cm (p. 57)
CISTUS×corbariensis: 90-120 cm (p. 57)
ERICA mediterranea e.g. 'Brightness': 90 cm
(p. 125)

○ [◑] sun (or partial shade)
ILEX aquifolium e.g. 'Argentea Marginata': 6-9 m
(p. 149)
EUCALYPTUS niphophila ★: 6-7.5 m (p. 209)
ILEX×altaclarensis e.g. 'Golden King': 5.4-7.5 m
(p. 149)
ARBUTUS unedo: 4.5-7.5 m (p. 204)
LAURUS nobilis: 3.6-6 m (p. 134)
PHORMIUM tenax: 3-3.6 m (p. 182)
PHORMIUM tenax e.g. 'Purpureum': 3-3.6 m
(p. 171)
PHORMIUM tenax e.g. 'Variegatum': 3-3.6 m
(p. 150)
OLEARIA×haastii: 1.8-2.7 m (p. 93)

EUONYMUS japonicus 'Ovatus Aureus':
1.5-2.1 m (p. 150)
POTENTILLA fruticosa e.g. 'Katherine Dykes':
1.2 m (p. 130)
ULEX europaeus 'Plenus': 90-180 cm (p. 66)
SENECIO laxifolius ★: 90-120 cm (p. 164)

○ ◑ sun or partial shade
SORBUS aria: 10.5-15 m (p. 24)
FRAXINUS excelsior 'Pendula': 9-15 m (p. 24)
SORBUS aria 'Lutescens': 9-12 m (p. 165)
ILEX aquifolium: 7.5-12 m (p. 127)
CRATAEGUS monogyna: 7.5-9 m (p. 130)
ILEX aquifolium e.g. 'J. C. van Tol': 6-9 m (p. 204)
ILEX aquifolium e.g. 'Bacciflava': 6-7.5 m (p. 204)
ACER pseudoplatanus e.g. 'Brilliantissimum':
4.5-6 m (p. 172)
COTONEASTER 'Cornubia': 4.5-6 m (p. 205)
CRATAEGUS oxyacantha e.g. 'Paul's Scarlet':
4.5-6 m (p. 95)
CRATAEGUS oxyacantha e.g. 'Plena': 4.5-6 m
(p. 50)
ELAEAGNUS×ebbingei: 3-4.5 m (p. 128)
SALIX alba e.g. 'Chermesina': 3-4.5 m (p. 210)
GARRYA elliptica: 2.4-4.5 m (p. 282)
BERBERIS×stenophylla ★: 2.4-3 m (p. 128)
BERBERIS darwinii: 1.8-3 m (p. 205)
VIBURNUM tinus: 1.8-3 m (p. 277)
COTONEASTER simonsii: 1.8-2.4 m (p. 128)
AUCUBA japonica: 1.5-2.4 m (p. 83)
AUCUBA japonica 'Crotonifolia': 1.5-2.4 m
(p. 136)
FUCHSIA e.g. 'Riccartonii' ★: 90-180 cm (p. 131)
HEBE cupressoides: 90-120 cm (p. 136)

◑ [○] partial shade (or sun)
EUONYMUS fortunei e.g. 'Silver Queen':
1.8-2.4 m (p. 137)

◑ ● partial or full shade
AUCUBA japonica: 1.5-2.4 m (p. 83)
AUCUBA japonica e.g. 'Crotonifolia': 1.5-2.4 m
(p. 136)

Trees, shrubs and climbers* tolerant of atmospheric pollution

Compared with a hundred or even fifty years ago, there are today relatively few town gardeners who have to contend with the problem of growing plants in a dirty, smoky atmosphere. However, unclean air is not entirely a thing of the past, and the plants for certain sites (near large groups of factories or beside busy main roads, for instance) must be chosen carefully if they are to grow healthily.

Some plants are particularly well equipped to withstand dirt and grime, and it is perhaps not surprising that a considerable number of them also withstand the damaging effects of salt spray. The following list contains several plants, such as *Escallonia macrantha*, *Quercus ilex* (holm oak or evergreen oak) and various hollies, whose tough, leathery leaves make them equally suitable for exposed, coastal sites and the polluted atmosphere of some industrial areas. Other plants, such as *Tamarix tetrandra* (a species of tamarisk), have foliage which is arranged in narrow, overlapping layers. An arrangement of this sort ensures that there is little vulnerable leaf-surface to which damaging deposits of salt or dirt can adhere. A few plants – *Spartium junceum* (Spanish broom) is an example – achieve the same end by means of having very few leaves.

Many of the plants in this list do not, however, have foliage of any of the types described above. Generally speaking, these plants are tolerant of atmospheric pollution because they are vigorous and undemanding. The ordinary, species sycamore, *Acer pseudoplatanus*, is notable for the way in which it will seed itself, even in soil which is exhausted by over-cultivation and made sour by years of exposure to polluted air. This species has some more decorative varieties which, although less vigorous, tolerate dirt and grime. One of these varieties, *A. p.* 'Brilliantissimum', which has pink, young foliage, is included in this list.

Certain members of the *Leguminosae* or pea family are able to manufacture some of their own food requirements, and this accounts for their tolerance of really poor or impoverished soils. *Colutea arborescens* (a species of bladder senna) and *Ulex europaeus* (gorse, furze or whin, a double-flowered form of which appears in this list), for example, are both members of this plant family, often seen colonizing the embankments and cuttings of disused railway lines.

In areas where the atmosphere has been polluted for many years, the soil too will be polluted. If plants have been grown in this soil over a long period, and if little nourishment has been added to it during this time, its fertility will almost certainly be very low. In such adverse conditions, only the most vigorous and undemanding plants will grow at all satisfactorily. However, the whole range of plants in this list can be grown if some improvements are made to impoverished and polluted soils. Many such soils are deficient in humus as well as chemical salts, and it is important that not only fertilizers but also humus-forming materials, such as leaf-mould and garden compost, are applied.

Even when supplied with a fertile soil, plants in very polluted areas may be smaller than normal and some evergreens may be only semi-evergreen or even deciduous. This should be borne in mind when consulting the list.

Those who deal with the planting and maintenance of sites in areas of atmospheric pollution are usually interested in the more long-lived and labour-saving plants. For this reason, the following list contains only trees, shrubs and woody, perennial climbers. However, there are herbaceous and bulbous plants, annuals, biennials and ferns that will tolerate atmospheric pollution. Plants in the genera *Coreopsis* (annual species and varieties of which are often listed as *Calliopsis*), *Dianthus* and *Iberis* are some particularly suitable subjects. In addition, the bearded hybrid irises and almost all ferns will grow remarkably well in smoky and dirty surroundings. As mentioned above, leathery leaves are a good form of protection against dirt and grime. Undemanding, medium-sized plants with foliage of this type include the various species and varieties of *Bergenia*. Plants with hairy leaves are, in contrast, not generally suitable for sites where the atmosphere is very dusty or gritty since the foliage will become clogged with particles of dirt. This is not only unsightly but also unhealthy.

In assessing plants that do not appear in this list for their ability to tolerate atmospheric pollution, some indication of vigorous growth is usually a good guide to suitable material. Of course, some plants are often directly described as vigorous: most descriptions of, for instance, the roses in this particular list draw attention to their 'vigorous' or 'strong' growth; other suitable roses will be described in similar terms. However, a tendency to self-seed, an ability to grow in poor soil and an ability to become naturalized in coarse grass are some other slightly less obvious indications of vigour.

Perennial climbers with persistent, woody stems.

POPULUS nigra 'Italica'
[Lombardy Poplar]

○

type of plant: HT
flowering season: mid-spring
flower colour: reddish
height:24-36 m/80-120 ft

Even when this tree has reached its ultimate height, it is unlikely to be much more than 4.5 m/15 ft wide. Despite its very restricted spread, however, it is quite unsuitable for planting near buildings since its roots are extensive and greedy. Several specimens of the Lombardy poplar can be used to form a fast-growing windbreak or screen and they may be grown in heavy and damp soils as well as in those with better drainage. The plant is usually short-lived in the United States because of fungal disorders.

Clay – Damp and wet soils.

TILIA platyphyllos
[Large-leaved Lime]

○

type of plant: HT
flowering season: summer
flower colour: creamy yellow
height: 24-36 m/80-120 ft

This tough and usually healthy tree has a fairly narrow, dome-shaped head. All moisture-retentive soils that are at least reasonably well drained are suitable for limes; a fertile loam is ideal. The sweet scent from the flowers of *T. platyphyllos* is attractive to bees. In Britain, nurseries sometimes offer an upright and a red-twigged form of this plant.

Fragrant flowers.

SOPHORA japonica NA
[Pagoda-tree, Scholar-tree]

○

type of plant: HT
flowering season: l. summer
flower colour: creamy white
height: 22.5 m/75 ft

This is a large, often vase-shaped tree with airy, compound foliage. The pea-like flowers, borne in showy clusters, are followed by green pods which have tight strictures separating the individual seeds. The tree is best not planted near a path because the pods, which persist until late winter, are quite slippery when they finally fall. Average soil conditions suffice. British nurseries with a wide range of trees and shrubs may stock this plant.

ULMUS ×sarniensis (syn. *U. carpinifolia sarniensis, U. wheatleyi*)
[Wheatley Elm, Jersey Elm]
○
type of plant: HT
height: 21-36 m/70-120 ft

Because it has a neat and narrowly conical head of branches, this tree is quite often used for roadside and street planting. The smaller and slower-growing variety with yellow leaves (sold under various names, including *U.×s.* 'Dicksonii') is more suitable for the average garden; it is only about 10.5-12 m/35-40 ft high. The foliage of *U.×sarniensis* turns bright yellow in autumn; in spring there are bunches of green, winged fruits amongst the new leaves. This tree is more resistant to Dutch elm disease than, for instance, *U. procera* (the English elm). Most soils are suitable.

Chalk – Autumn foliage – Fruit.

MORUS alba NA
[White Mulberry]
○
type of plant: HT
flowering season: spring
flower colour: greenish
height: 13.5 m/45 ft

Though not in the first rank of trees, this is useful in air-polluted cities or on problem soils, where choicer plants cannot be grown. The fruits may be black, red or white and, while insipid, are enjoyed by those who like to eat mulberries. It is extensively naturalized by the birds. Fruitless cultivars are sold in the western United States for street plantings. 'Pendula', once very popular, makes an interesting small, intensely sweeping tree.

TILIA×euchlora
[form of Lime]
○
type of plant: HT
flowering season: summer
flower colour: creamy yellow
height: 12-18 m/40-60 ft

T.×euchlora usually produces some pendulous branches beneath its main, rounded crown. Its leaves are glossy, and the strong, sweet scent of its flowers attracts and temporarily intoxicates bees. This tree is best grown on a loamy soil, although it will tolerate slightly drier conditions than the broad-leafed lime or linden (*T. platyphyllos*, see previous page).

Fragrant flowers.

PRUNUS avium 'Plena' sc NA
[form of Gean, Wild Cherry or Mazzard]
○
type of plant: HT
flowering season: l. spring
flower colour: white
height: 12-13.5 m/40-45 ft

The long-stalked, double flowers of this tree are very freely produced; they appear as the leaves are expanding. *P. a.* 'Plena' should be given a well drained soil. In autumn, its globular head of branches is often covered in yellow and red-tinged foliage.

Autumn foliage.

CATALPA bignonioides
[Indian Bean Tree]
○
type of plant: HT
flowering season: summer
flower colour: white + purple
height: 9-13.5 m/30-45 ft

The Indian bean tree and its decorative, yellow-leaved variety (see next page) thrive in sheltered, town gardens. Their big, bold leaves do not unfold until early summer, when they are accompanied by sweetly fragrant flowers. In autumn, very slender seed-pods – which may be over 30 cm/1 ft long – ripen to a reddish brown colour. These plants grow best in a good, moisture-retentive soil. The species forms a spreading, rounded tree.

Green foliage – Fruit.

ROBINIA pseudoacacia e.g. 'Bessoniana'
sc NA
[form of False Acacia or Black Locust]
○
type of plant: HT
flowering season: e. summer
flower colour: creamy white
height: 9-12 m/30-40 ft

R. pseudoacacia itself has thorny branches but this broad-headed variety is generally free of sharp spines. Its branches are, however, brittle and this makes it an unsuitable plant for windy sites. False acacias thrive in urban and industrial areas and in well drained or dry soils. *R. p.* 'Bessoniana' produces long tassels of lightly scented flowers amongst its ferny foliage. Another round-headed form, *R. p.* 'Inermis', rarely flowers. *R. p.* 'Frisia' has bright yellow foliage; it is illustrated on p. 174.

Hot, dry soils – Green foliage – Fragrant flowers.

CATALPA bignonioides 'Aurea' ★
[form of Indian Bean Tree]

○

type of plant: HT
flowering season: summer
flower colour: white + purple
height: 7.5-12 m/25-40 ft

Catalpas are late breaking into leaf but, in the case of this yellow-leaved variety, this is an advantage since it means that the unusual colour of the foliage is retained for longer than normal. *C. b.* 'Aurea' loses only a little of its bright yellowness by late summer. It is an excellent plant for a town garden. When cut right back in late winter or spring each year, it forms a large shrub. (For general remarks about the Indian bean tree, see *C. bignonioides*, previous page.)

Yellow, etc. leaves – Fruit.

PRUNUS (Japanese Cherry) e.g. 'Kanzan' (syn.
P. Kwanzan, P. 'Sekiyama', *P. serrulata*
purpurascens)

○

type of plant: HT
flowering season: mid-spring
flower colour: purplish pink
height: 7.5-10.5 m/25-35 ft

The frothy, pink flowers of *P.* 'Kanzan' are, briefly, an eye-catching, springtime sight in British suburbs. The blossom is borne on stiffly upright branches amongst red-tinged, young foliage; there is some autumn colour. A well drained and preferably alkaline soil is most suitable.

Chalk – Red, etc. leaves.

LABURNUM×watereri 'Vossii' (syn.
L.×'Vossii')

○

type of plant: HT
flowering season: l. spring to e. summer
flower colour: yellow
height: 6-9 m/20-30 ft

The heavy, hanging flower trusses of this laburnum are often 30 cm/1 ft long. They are suspended from the arching tips and subsidiary twigs of the rather erect branches, and they are followed by small quantities of pods containing poisonous seeds. A light, sweet scent is emitted from the blossom; it is more noticeable in the evening than during the day. Almost any soil will suit this plant but well drained, reasonably deep soils are ideal.

MORUS nigra sc NA
[Common Mulberry, Black Mulberry]

○

type of plant: HT
height: 6-9 m/20-30 ft

Female black mulberries bear dark, edible fruits but these are not decorative and it is the large dome of branches and the eventually gnarled appearance of the leaning trunk – or trunks – which make this tree an interesting feature of a large garden. It needs a deep, fertile soil, especially if crops of fruit are wanted.

PRUNUS dulcis (syn. *P. amygdalus,*
P. communis)
[Common Almond]

○

type of plant: HT
flowering season: spring
flower colour: pink
height: 6-9 m/20-30 ft

Young specimens of *P. dulcis* have quite upright branches but mature trees are broader and more spreading. The flowers are large and, since they open early in spring, some shelter from cold winds is advisable. In the majority of British gardens, fruit is set, but it does not often ripen completely. Well drained soils of most sorts are suitable for this plant. Flowers are usually killed by spring frosts in cooler parts of the United States.

CEANOTHUS×'Gloire de Versailles' sc NA

○

type of plant: HSh
flowering season: midsummer to mid-autumn
flower colour: powder blue
height: 1.5-2.1 m/5-7 ft

Unlike the evergreen ceanothuses, in Britain the deciduous forms, such as 'Gloire de Versailles', do not need the protection of a sunny wall (although they will flourish and grow very tall there). Provided the site is fairly warm they are quite suitable for open beds and borders. *C.×*'Gloire de Versailles' should have its rather open growths pruned very hard each spring and it should be given a well drained, preferably neutral soil. Its flowers are sweetly but not very strongly scented. It is not reliably hardy in the colder parts of the United States.

Fragrant flowers.

CYTISUS scoparius e.g. 'Firefly' sc NA
[form of Common Broom]

○

type of plant: HSh
flowering season: l. spring to e. summer
flower colour: yellow + scarlet
height: 1.5-2.1 m/5-7 ft

Plants as tough – and as nearly leafless – as the popular varieties of common broom come to little harm in the dirty air of certain urban and industrial areas. These shrubs need an acid or neutral soil that is very well drained and their arching green twigs should be pruned hard after the numerous flowers have faded. Poor soils are quite suitable. There are several hybrids, including the present example, with strikingly bicoloured flowers.

Acid soils – Hot, dry soils – Seaside – Bark and *twigs*.

ROSA (Hybrid Tea) e.g. 'Peace' ★
[form of Rose]

○

type of plant: HSh
flowering season: summer to mid-autumn
flower colour: pale yellow
height: 1.2-1.8 m/4-6 ft

This famous rose is tough, vigorous and bushy. Its pink-edged blooms are large (often 10 cm/4 in wide) and, despite their lack of pronounced fragrance, they are popular for cutting. A well dug, fertile loam suits most roses best, but strong-growing varieties like 'Peace' will tolerate heavier and slightly lighter soils. Many other, vigorous, hybrid tea roses will do well in districts with a polluted atmosphere.

Cutting.

ROSA (Floribunda) e.g. 'Evelyn Fison' sc NA
[form of Rose]

○

type of plant: HSh
flowering season: summer to mid-autumn
flower colour: scarlet
height: 75-105 cm/2½-3½ ft

The strongest growing floribunda roses, including the example shown here, do well in large cities and industrial areas. 'Evelyn Fison' is noted for its generous clusters of flowers which remain brightly coloured even in full sun. A rich, loamy soil is ideal for this plant.

HEBE × 'Autumn Glory' sc NA MC

○

type of plant: SlTSh
flowering season: midsummer to autumn
flower colour: violet
height: 60-90 cm/2-3 ft
E

All the hebes are excellent plants for town or seaside gardens. *H*. × 'Autumn Glory' is only one example from quite an extensive range of widely available forms and species. It may be used for ground-cover, though its upright and rather sparse habit of growth means that individual specimens must be planted close to one another. The foliage has a slight purplish tinge which is most noticeable in the young leaves. Well drained soils of various types suit this plant.

Chalk – Ground-cover.

GENISTA lydia ★
[species of Broom]

○

type of plant:HSh
flowering season: l. spring to e. summer
flower colour: yellow
height: 45-75 cm/1½-2½ ft

The curved, grey-green twigs of *G. lydia* look especially attractive hanging over the edge of a low wall or covering a steep, sunny bank. This short-lived and very free-flowering plant can also be grown in a large container. In open ground its semi-prostrate branches may spread over 1.5 m/5 ft wide. Sharply drained and infertile soils produce the largest quantities of blossom.

Hot, dry soils – Ground-cover – Containers – Bark and *twigs*.

PLATANUS × hispanica (syn. *P*. × *acerifolia*,
***P*. × *hybrida*)**
[London Plane]

○ [◑]

type of plant: HT
height: 21-30 m/70-100 ft

The mottled trunks and high, domed crowns of London planes are familiar sights in many European cities. The foliage of *P*. × *hispanica* is variable but more or less maple-like; it turns yellow and yellowy orange in autumn. This long-lived tree thrives in deep, moist loams; it does not grow well on dry or shallow soils.

Clay – Green foliage – Autumn foliage – *Bark and twigs*.

MALUS floribunda
[Japanese Crab]
○ [◐]
type of plant: HT
flowering season: l. spring
flower colour: pink changing to white
height: 6-9 m/20-30 ft

Not all flowering crabs bear decorative fruit and *M. floribunda* is grown more for its mass of red-budded flowers and its wide head of semi-pendulous branches than for its 'apples' which are small and yellow. Well drained, fertile soils of all types suit the Japanese crab which will also tolerate moderately heavy clay.

Chalk – Fruit.

SYRINGA vulgaris e.g. 'Souvenir de Louis Spaeth'
[form of Common Lilac]
○ [◐]
type of plant: HSh
flowering season: l. spring
flower colour: deep wine-red
height: 3-4.5 m/10-15 ft

The popular varieties of *S. vulgaris* are vigorous plants which will grow well in urban and industrial districts, although not in the cities of the eastern United States, where there are high levels of ozone and sulphur dioxide. *S. v.* 'Souvenir de Louis Spaeth' is an especially strong and robust form with rather spreading branches. The scent of its flowers is not so attractive as that of some other lilacs (such as *S. v.* 'Katherine Havemeyer', see p. 264). A fertile soil is needed for the greedy roots of all varieties of *S. vulgaris*.

Chalk – Cutting – Fragrant flowers.

PHILADELPHUS e.g. 'Virginal'
[form of Mock Orange]
○ [◐]
type of plant: HSh
flowering season: summer
flower colour: white
height: 2.4-3 m/8-10 ft

The tall, strong-growing variety of mock orange illustrated here has exceptionally large clusters of very fragrant, pure white, double flowers. It has an upright habit of growth. There are smaller forms of *Philadelphus*, such as 'Manteau d'Hermine' (see p. 22), and several cultivars have single rather than double flowers (see, for example, *P.* 'Beauclerk', p. 265). All these plants do well in a wide variety of soil types but they thrive where good drainage is available. They are excellent shrubs for town and city gardens.

Chalk – Cutting – Fragrant flowers.

OLEARIA × haastii sc NA MC
[form of Daisy Bush]
○ [◐]
type of plant: HSh
flowering season: summer
flower colour: white
height: 1.8-2.7 m/6-9 ft
E

The leaves of this rounded plant are protected against both salt spray and smoky, grimy air by having white-felted undersides and tough, smooth upper surfaces. *O. × haastii* is a wind-resistant shrub and suitable for fully exposed gardens close to the sea. It flowers very freely; the blossom has a musky, hawthorn-like scent. Any well drained soil is suitable. In the United States it is hardy mainly in California and the Pacific Northwest.

Chalk – Seaside – Hedging.

WEIGELA florida
○ [◐]
type of plant: HSh
flowering season: l. spring to e. summer
flower colour: rose-pink
height: 1.8 m/6 ft

Two well-known hybrids from *W. florida* and other species are shown on p. 48. *W. florida* itself is a tough, trouble-free plant with slightly arching branches. It will produce plenty of flowers in most soils and sites but sunshine and a fertile, moisture-retentive soil give the best results. A few nurseries still list weigelas under the name *Diervilla*.

Chalk – Clay.

Additional trees, shrubs and climbers, featured elsewhere in this book, that are tolerant of atmospheric pollution

○ sun
LIRIODENDRON tulipifera: 21-30 m (p. 179)
FAGUS sylvatica 'Purpurea': 18-27 m (p. 168)
POPULUS alba: 18-27 m (p. 156)
GINKGO biloba ★: 18-24 cm (p. 189)
METASEQUOIA glyptostroboides: 18-24 cm (p. 68)
POPULUS tremula: 9-15 m (p. 68)
GLEDITSCHIA triacanthas 'Sunburst': 9-12 m (p. 174)
PRUNUS (Japanese Cherry) e.g. 'Tai-Haku' ★: 9-12 cm (p. 1)
ROBINIA pseudoacacia 'Frisia': 7.5-10.5 m (p. 174)
MAGNOLIA denudata ★: 7.5-9 m (p. 28)
PRUNUS cerasifera: 6-7.5 m (p. 129)
PRUNUS subhirtella e.g. 'Autumnalis': 6-7.5 m (p. 274)
ROSA (Rambler) e.g. 'Wedding Day': 6-7.5 m (p. 120)
PRUNUS cerasifera 'Pissardii': 6 m (p. 168)
MAGNOLIA grandiflora 'Exmouth' ★: 4.5-7.5 m (p. 253)
PRUNUS (Japanese Cherry) e.g. 'Amanogawa': 4.5-7.5 m (p. 2)
GENISTA aetnensis: 4.5-6 m (p. 56)
PRUNUS (Japanese Cherry) e.g. 'Kiku-shidare Sakura': 4.5-6 m (p. 2)
PYRUS salicifolia 'Pendula' ★: 4.5-6 m (p. 157)
ROSA (Rambler) e.g. 'Albertine': 4.5 m (p. 120)
ROSA wichuraiana: 4.5 m (p. 101)
RHUS typhina: 3-4.5 m (p. 190)
RHUS typhina 'Laciniata': 3-4.5 m (p. 180)
TAMARIX tetrandra: 3-4.5 m (p. 86)
ESCALLONIA macrantha: 3 m (p. 86)
COLUTEA arborescens: 2.4-3 m (p. 202)
BUDDLEIA davidii e.g. 'Black Knight': 2.1-3 m (p. 2)
BUDDLEIA davidii e.g. 'Royal Red': 2.1-3 m (p. 2)   *continued*

○ sun *continued*
HIBISCUS syriacus e.g. 'Woodbridge': 2.1-3 m (p. 133)
SPARTIUM junceum: 2.1-3 m (p. 56)
ROSA (Rambler) e.g. 'Albertine': 2.1 m (p. 120)
ESCALLONIA e.g. 'Donard Radiance': 1.8-2.4 m (p. 125)
HIBISCUS syriacus e.g. 'Blue Bird': 1.8-2.4 m (p. 3)
HIBISCUS syriacus e.g. 'Hamabo': 1.8-2.4 m (p. 3)
CYTISUS scoparius e.g. 'Andreanus': 1.8 m (p. 57)
ESCALLONIA e.g. 'Apple Blossom': 1.8 m (p. 86)
BERBERIS thunbergii: 1.5-1.8 m (p. 190)
BERBERIS thunbergii atropurpurea: 1.2-1.8 m (p. 169)
CYTISUS×praecox: 1.2-1.8 m (p. 57)
CYTISUS scoparius e.g. 'Cornish Cream': 1.2-1.8 m (p. 86)
HEBE brachysiphon: 1.2-1.8 m (p. 3)
ROSA (Rugosa Hybrid) e.g. 'Blanc Double de Coubert': 1.2-1.8 m (p. 129)
ROSA (Hybrid Tea) e.g. 'Pascali': 1.2-1.8 m (p. 213)
ROSA (Rugosa) e.g. 'Roseraie de l'Hay': 1.2-1.8 m (p. 256)
CISTUS×purpureus: 1.2-1.5 m (p. 87)
ROSA (Hybrid Tea) e.g. 'Wendy Cussons': 1.2-1.5 m (p. 256)
WEIGELA florida 'Foliis Purpureis': 1.2 m (p. 170)
ROSA (Hybrid Tea) e.g. 'Prima Ballerina': 1.05-1.35 m (p. 256)
HEBE 'Midsummer Beauty': 90-150 cm (p. 87)
BERBERIS thunbergii 'Aurea': 90-120 cm (p. 175)
CISTUS×corbariensis: 90-120 cm (p. 57)
CERATOSTIGMA willmottianum: 60-90 cm (p. 7)
GENISTA hispanica: 60-90 cm (p. 99)
HYPERICUM×moserianum 'Tricolor'★: 60 cm (p. 147)
ROSA wichuraiana: 45 cm (p. 101)
BERBERIS thunbergii 'Atropurpurea Nana': 30-60 cm (p. 171)
HEBE×'Carl Teschner': 23-30 cm (p. 101)

HYPERICUM polyphyllum: 15-23 cm (p. 140)

○ [◐] sun (or partial shade)
EUCALYPTUS gunnii: 15-21 m (p. 164)
QUERCUS ilex: 15-18 m (p. 87)
MALUS tschonoskii: 9-12 m (p. 191)
JASMINUM officinale: 9 m (p. 264)
MALUS 'John Downie': 7.5-9 m (p. 203)
MALUS×robusta 'Red Siberian': 7.5-9 m (p. 203)
ILEX aquifolium e.g. 'Argentea Marginata'★: 6-9 m (p. 149)
EUCALYPTUS niphophila: 6-7.5 m (p. 209)
MALUS 'Gold Hornet'★: 6-7.5 m (p. 203)
MALUS 'Hillieri': 6-7.5 m (p. 21)
MALUS 'Profusion'★: 6-7.5 m (p. 171)
ILEX×altaclarensis e.g. 'Golden King': 5.4-7.5 m (p. 149)
ARBUTUS unedo: 4.5-7.5 m (p. 204)
SAMBUCUS nigra 'Aurea': 3.6-4.5 m (p. 176)
SYRINGA×josiflexa 'Bellicent': 3.6-4.5 m (p. 21)
SYRINGA vulgaris e.g. 'Katherine Havemeyer': 3-4.5 m (p. 264)
SYRINGA vulgaris e.g. 'Madame Lemoine'★: 3-4.5 m (p. 240)
SYRINGA vulgaris e.g. 'Primrose': 3-4.5 m (p. 22)
PHORMIUM tenax: 3-3.6 m (p. 182)
PHORMIUM tenax e.g. 'Purpureum': 3-3.6 m (p. 171)
PHORMIUM tenax e.g. 'Variegatum': 3-3.6 m (p. 150)
ELAEAGNUS pungens 'Maculata'★: 2.4-3 m (p. 150)
OSMANTHUS heterophyllus: 1.8-3 m (p. 126)
PHILADELPHUS coronarius: 1.8-3 m (p. 66)
OSMANTHUS delavayi★: 1.8-2.4 m (p. 264)
SYRINGA microphylla 'Superba': 1.8-2.4 m (p. 264)
CLETHRA alnifolia 'Paniculata': 1.8 m (p. 265)
EUONYMUS japonicus 'Ovatus Aureus': 1.5-2.1 m (p. 150)
PHILADELPHUS e.g. 'Beauclerk'★: 1.5-2.1 m (p. 265)

WEIGELA e.g. 'Abel Carriere': 1.5 m (p. 48)
WEIGELA e.g. 'Bristol Ruby': 1.5 m (p. 48)
ULEX europaeus 'Plenus': 90-180 cm (p. 66)
SYRINGA velutina: 90-150 cm (p. 22)
PHILADELPHUS e.g. 'Manteau d'Hermine': 90-120 cm (p. 22)
SENECIO laxifolius★: 90-120 cm (p. 164)

AESCULUS indica sc NA
[Indian Horse Chestnut]
○ ◐
type of plant: HT
flowering season: summer
flower colour: white
height: 21-30 m/70-100 ft

The shiny leaves and the elegant, domed outline of this tree make it a more decorative plant than the common horse chestnut (*A. hippocastanum*) which is so widely grown in Britain. However, it lacks the commoner plant's subtle but early, autumn colour in its foliage. A deep, fertile soil suits *A. indica* best.

PICEA omorika
[Serbian Spruce]
○ ◐
type of plant: HCo
height: 15-21 m/50-70 ft
E

The Serbian spruce is a variable plant. The best forms of it are very narrow and spire-shaped with curved branches which have upswept tips. The cones of all forms are quite small but of a beautiful dark purple colour when young. *P. omorika* is extremely hardy and it will grow in cold, heavy clays. It does well even in very acid soils and in areas with moderately polluted air.

Clay – Acid soils – Fruit.

DAVIDIA involucrata
[Pocket-handkerchief Tree, Dove Tree, Ghost Tree]

○ ◐
type of plant: HT
flowering season: l. spring
flower colour: cream
height: 12-15 m/40-50 ft

Specimens of *D. involucrata* are usually about ten years old before they begin to produce the strange looking petal-like bracts which earn the plant its various common names. More mature trees have domed heads of rather upright branches. The foliage is a bright green. In autumn the egg-shaped fruits become mottled with a russet colour. Fertile, moisture-retentive soils are most suitable for this plant.

Fruit.

MAGNOLIA × soulangiana e.g. 'Alexandrina'

○ ◑

type of plant: **HSh/T**
flowering season: **mid-spring**
flower colour: **white + rose-purple**
height: **6-7.5 m/20-25 ft**

The two forms of *M.* × *soulangiana* shown here are as reliably free-flowering, from a fairly early age, as *M.* × *soulangiana* itself (for an illustration of which, see p. 33). *M.* × *s.* 'Alexandrina' differs from the typical plant in the deep purple flush at the base of each of its blooms. It is often a dense, branching shrub and occasionally a small tree. *M.* × *s.* 'Lennei' (see right) is nearly always spreading and shrub-like. It has larger, darker flowers and a slightly later flowering season than normal. Its blooms are sweetly scented. *M. soulangiana* and its forms tolerate lime and heavy clay but the ideal soil for these plants is deep, well drained and either acid or neutral. All spring-flowering (*contd*)

MAGNOLIA × soulangiana e.g. 'Lennei'

○ ◑

type of plant: **HSh/T**
flowering season: **mid-spring**
flower colour: **rose-purple + white**
height: **6-7.5 m/20-25 ft**

See preceding plant.

(*contd*)
magnolias are liable to have their blooms damaged by frost and wind if they are grown in exposed positions.

Acid soils – Clay – Cutting – Fragrant flowers (*M.* × *s.* 'Lennei' only).

BETULA pendula 'Youngii'
[Young's Weeping Birch]

○ ◑

type of plant: **HT**
height: **5.4-7.5 m/18-25 ft**

The lower branches of this tree touch the ground, so it is not until autumn that the silvery bark of older specimens becomes noticeable. Before the leaves fall they turn a greenish gold which some people find attractive. *B. p.* 'Youngii' can be planted in any soil, but the best canopy of weeping growth will be produced on reasonably deep and fertile loams.

Bark and twigs.

CRATAEGUS oxyacantha (syn. *C. laevigata*) e.g. 'Paul's Scarlet' (syn. 'Coccinea Plena') [form of Hawthorn or May]

○ ◑

type of plant: **HT**
flowering season: **l. spring**
flower colour: **scarlet**
height: **4.5-6 m/15-20 ft**

The double-flowered forms of *C. oxyacantha* are more decorative than the common hawthorn (see *C. monogyna*, p. 130) but they are not quite so outstandingly hardy and robust. Nevertheless, they grow very well in towns and cities and in windswept gardens beside the sea. They make more or less round-headed trees. The strongly coloured flowers of *C. o.* 'Paul's Scarlet' have no scent but the white, double-flowered form shown on p. 50 has a cloying, sweet fragrance.

Chalk – Clay – Seaside.

PYRACANTHA coccinea 'Lalandei'
[form of Firethorn]

○ ◑

type of plant: **HSh**
flowering season: **e. summer**
flower colour: **white**
height: **3.6-4.5 m/12-15 ft**
E

The flower heads of pyracanthas are only moderately attractive but the splendid bunches of berries which follow them are very decorative and they appear in large numbers even in sites facing north or east. *P. c.* 'Lalandei' is a vigorous variety. It should be given plenty of room to grow since cutting it back severely will diminish the amount of berries produced. It can be used for thorny hedging and it is altogether a very tough and adaptable plant. Most soils, including chalky (limy) ones of a reasonable depth, suit firethorns.

Hedging – Fruit.

RHODODENDRON (Hardy Hybrid) e.g. 'Fastuosum Flore Pleno'

○ ◑

type of plant: **HSh**
flowering season: **l. spring to e. summer**
flower colour: **mauve**
height: **3-3.6 m/10-12 ft**
***E**

As long as they have a fairly well drained, lime-free soil, the so-called 'hardy hybrid' rhododendrons will grow almost anywhere. They tolerate full sun (if their roots are covered with leaf-mould or peat) and dense shade, and they are much more successful as town plants than most other rhododendrons. The form illustrated here has large, long-lasting flowers; it grows a little faster than some hardy hybrids. Rhododendrons of this type are available with red, white, pink and purple flowers.

Acid soils – Dense shade.

DEUTZIA scabra (syn. *D. crenata*) e.g. 'Plena'

○ ◑

type of plant: HSh
flowering season: summer
flower colour: white flushed rose-purple
height: 2.4-3 m/8-10 ft

This plant is sometimes sold under the name 'Pride of Rochester'. It has upright branches covered in peeling bark and its flowers are very freely produced (provided late spring frosts have not damaged the buds and any old stems have been cut right back to ground level each year). Well drained soils of various types suit this shrub which will grow healthily in districts with polluted air.

Chalk – *Bark* and twigs.

FORSYTHIA×intermedia 'Spectabilis'

○ ◑

type of plant: HSh
flowering season: spring
flower colour: yellow
height: 2.4-3 m/8-10 ft

Amongst a group of hybrids noted for the reliability and freedom with which they produce their flowers, *F.×i.* 'Spectabilis' is exceptionally floriferous. Its erect branches are often almost completely covered in blossom and only the oldest wood is bare. If picked in bud early in the year the flowers will open indoors. Any soil and almost all sites are suitable for this shrub. It will flower quite well even in full shade. The leaves are produced after the blossom has faded.

Chalk – Clay – Hedging – Containers – Cutting.

MAGNOLIA stellata

○ ◑

type of plant: HSh/T
flowering season: spring
flower colour: white
height: 1.8-3 m/6-10 ft

The star magnolia, as *M. stellata* is sometimes called, grows slowly, usually in the form of a rounded bush, and rarely exceeds 3 m/10 ft; it is, therefore, suitable for small gardens. Its lightly fragrant flowers appear on plants which are only two or three years old. Since the buds begin to open very early in spring they are liable to frost damage (cold, windy sites aggravate this problem). A deep, loamy soil which contains little or no lime will produce the best specimens of this plant.

Acid soils – Fragrant flowers.

RIBES sanguineum e.g. 'King Edward VII'
[form of Flowering Currant]

○ ◑

type of plant: HSh
flowering season: spring
flower colour: crimson
height: 1.5-2.1 m/5-7 ft

Dry , shady corners in town gardens often contain a flowering currant or two which will usually be growing well and producing quite a sizeable amount of hanging blossom. Better growth and more flowers appear in sunny sites and well drained but moisture-retentive soils. *R. s.* 'King Edward VII' is a slightly smaller form of the species with the usual upright growths on spreading main branches. If its bud-covered stems are brought indoors, the flowers will have white or very pale pink petals when they expand. There is a slight musky smell to the blossom.

Clay – Dry shade – Hedging – Cutting.

CHAENOMELES (syn. *Cydonia*) **speciosa** (syn. *C. lagenaria*) e.g. 'Nivalis'
[form of Japonica or Japanese Quince]

○ ◑

type of plant: HSh
flowering season: spring
flower colour: white
height: 1.2-1.8 m/4-6 ft

Most forms of *C. speciosa*, including the one shown here, grow rather openly and they usually look best trained against a wall (when they may be over 3.6 m/12 ft high). All japonicas are very hardy plants which are suitable for any soil (although extremely alkaline conditions are best avoided). They do well on cold, sunless walls. An unusually low-growing variety of *C. speciosa*, with scarlet flowers, is illustrated on p. 52 and there are other forms with pink flowers. Yellow, edible fruits ripen in late summer and early autumn.

Clay – Fruit – Cutting.

KERRIA japonica
[Jew's Mallow]

○ ◑

type of plant: HSh
flowering season: spring
flower colour: orange-yellow
height: 1.2-1.8 m/4-6 ft

The double-flowered form of *K. japonica* (see p. 243) is a more popular garden plant than the species but it lacks the species' natural grace. Both plants are tough. They are easy to grow and will sucker quite freely in most soils and in either sun or full shade. Their slim branches are bright green.

Bark and *twigs* – Cutting.

Additional trees, shrubs and climbers, featured elsewhere in this book, that are tolerant of atmospheric pollution

○ ◐ sun or partial shade

FAGUS sylvatica: 18-27m (p. 130)
ALNUS cordata: 15-24m (p. 50)
CARPINUS betulus: 15-21m (p. 130)
FAGUS sylvatica 'Pendula': 15-21m (p. 24)
PARTHENOCISSUS quinquefolia: 15-21m (p. 192)
HYDRANGEA petiolaris★: 15-18m (p. 122)
PARTHENOCISSUS tricuspidata 'Veitchii': 15m (p. 192)
SALIX×chrysocoma★: 13.5-18m (p. 72)
BETULA pendula: 12-18m (p. 210)
BETULA pendula 'Dalecarlica': 12-18m (p. 210)
AESCULUS×carnea 'Briotii': 10.5-15m (p. 50)
SORBUS aria: 10.5-15m (p. 24)
ACER griseum: 10.5-12m (p. 210)
ACER platanoides e.g. 'Drummondii': 9-15m (p. 151)
FRAXINUS excelsior 'Pendula': 9-15m (p. 24)
SORBUS aria 'Lutescens': 9-12m (p. 165)
SORBUS aucuparia: 9-12m (p. 33)
ACER negundo 'Variegatum': 9m (p. 151)
ILEX aquifolium: 7.5-12m (p. 127)
CRATAEGUS monogyna: 7.5-9m (p. 130)
ARALIA elata: 6-10.5m (p. 183)
ILEX aquifolium e.g. 'J. C. van Tol': 6-9m (p. 204)
SALIX daphnoides: 6-9m (p. 210)
ILEX aquifolium e.g. 'Bacciflava': 6-7.5m (p. 204)
MAGNOLIA×soulangiana: 6-7.5m (p. 33)
ACER pseudoplatanus e.g. 'Brilliantissimum': 4.5-6m (p. 172)
COTONEASTER 'Cornubia': 4.5-6m (p. 205)
CRATAEGUS oxyacantha e.g. 'Plena': 4.5-6m (p. 50)
HEDERA canariensis 'Variegata': 4.5-6m (p. 151)
HEDERA colchica 'Dentata-Variegata': 4.5-6m (p. 151)
ROSA (Climber) e.g. 'Mme Alfred Carrière': 4.5-6m (p. 123)
BUXUS sempervirens: 3.6-4.5m (p. 127)
HEDERA helix e.g. 'Hibernica': 3.6-4.5m (p. 109)
LIGUSTRUM ovalifolium: 3.6-4.5m (p. 127)
PYRACANTHA 'Orange Glow': 3.6-4.5m (p. 205)
PYRACANTHA rogersiana 'Flava': 3.6-4.5m (p. 127)
AMELANCHIER canadensis: 3-5.4m (p. 33)
ELAEAGNUS×ebbingei: 3-4.5m (p. 128)
SALIX alba 'Chermesina': 3-4.5m (p. 210)
HEDERA helix e.g. 'Glacier': 3-3.6m (p. 151)
HEDERA helix e.g. 'Gold Heart'★: 3-3.6m (p. 152)
RHODODENDRON (Hardy Hybrid) e.g. 'Cynthia': 3-3.6m (p. 34)
RHODODENDRON ponticum: 3-3.6m (p. 128)
LIGUSTRUM ovalifolium 'Aureum': 2.7-3.6m (p. 177)
GARRYA elliptica★: 2.4-4.5m (p. 282)
FATSIA japonica★: 2.4-3.6m (p. 135)
BERBERIS×stenophylla: 2.4-3m (p. 128)
BUXUS sempervirens e.g. 'Aureovariegata': 2.4-3m (p. 152)
FORSYTHIA×intermedia 'Lynwood': 2.4-3m (p. 24)
FORSYTHIA suspensa★: 2.4-3m (p. 50)
BERBERIS darwinii: 1.8-3m (p. 205)
KERRIA japonica 'Pleniflora': 1.8-3m (p. 243)
×OSMAREA burkwoodii: 1.8-3m (p. 267)
VIBURNUM tinus: 1.8-3m (p. 277)
CORNUS alba 'Elegantissima'★: 1.8-2.7m (p. 72)
RIBES sanguineum e.g. 'Pulborough Scarlet': 1.8-2.7m (p. 80)
CORNUS stolonifera 'Flaviramea': 1.8-2.4m (p. 211)
COTONEASTER simonsii: 1.8-2.4m (p. 128)
LIGUSTRUM japonicum: 1.8-2.4m (p. 83)
SPIRAEA×arguta: 1.8-2.4m (p. 50)
LEYCESTERIA formosa: 1.8m (p. 211)
AUCUBA japonica: 1.5-2.4m (p. 83)
AUCUBA japonica e.g. 'Crotonifolia': 1.5-2.4m (p. 136)
CORNUS alba 'Sibirica': 1.5-2.4m (p. 211)
SYMPHORICARPOS rivularis: 1.5-2.1m (p. 206)
WEIGELA florida 'Variegata'★: 1.5m (p. 152)
HYPERICUM 'Hidcote'★: 1.2-1.8m (p. 25)

SYMPHORICARPOS×doorenbosii 'White Hedge': 1.2-1.8m (p. 130)
CHAENOMELES×superba e.g. 'Knap Hill Scarlet': 1.2-1.5m (p. 244)
CHAENOMELES×superba e.g. 'Rowallane': 1.2-1.5m (p. 130)
DEUTZIA×elegantissima: 1.2-1.5m (p. 268)
ROSA (Floribunda) e.g. 'Iceberg'★: 1.2-1.5m (p. 244)
DAPHNE mezereum: 90-150cm (p. 277)
DEUTZIA×rosea e.g. 'Campanulata': 90-120cm (p. 25)
HEBE cupressoides: 90-120cm (p. 136)
SPIRAEA×bumalda 'Anthony Waterer': 90-120cm (p. 107)
HYPERICUM×inodorum 'Elstead': 90cm (p. 205)
PRUNUS laurocerasus e.g. 'Otto Luyken': 90cm (p. 107)
CHAENOMELES speciosa e.g. 'Simonii'★: 60-90cm (p. 52)
×FATSHEDERA lizei: 60-90cm (p. 136)
PERNETTYA mucronata e.g. 'Bell's Seedling': 60-90cm (p. 206)
PERNETTYA mucronata e.g. 'Davis Hybrids': 60-90cm (p. 206)
COTONEASTER horizontalis★: 60cm (p. 194)
HYDRANGEA petiolaris★: 60cm (p. 122)
BUXUS sempervirens 'Suffruticosa': 30-60cm (p. 128)
HYPERICUM calycinum: 30-45cm (p. 108)
PARTHENOCISSUS quinquefolia: 30cm (p. 192)
VINCA major: 23-45cm (p. 82)
VINCA major 'Variegata': 23-45cm (p. 153)
HEDERA helix 'Hibernica': 23-30cm (p. 109)
PARTHENOCISSUS tricuspidata 'Veitchii': 23cm (p. 192)
HEBE 'Pagei'★: 15-30cm (p. 167)

HEDERA canariensis 'Variegata': 15-23cm (p. 151)
HEDERA colchica 'Dentata-Variegata': 15-23cm (p. 151)
VINCA minor: 15cm (p. 82)
VINCA minor e.g. 'Alba'★: 15cm (p. 111)
COTONEASTER dammeri: 10cm (p. 111)

CAMELLIA japonica e.g. 'Contessa Lavinia Maggi' sc NA MC

◐ [○]
type of plant: HSh
flowering season: spring
flower colour: white or pale pink+deep pink
height: 1.8-3.6m/6-12ft
*E

Cultivars of *C. japonica* are some of the most elegant plants for city gardens and the striped flowers of varieties like 'Contessa Lavinia Maggi' do not look out of place in formal, urban surroundings. All these plants have thick, leathery leaves and flowers mainly in shades of pink or red (there are also white-flowered forms). They need a moist, peaty soil and, in cold districts, enough warmth to produce plenty of buds. Their blooms are susceptible to frost damage and east-facing sites are, therefore, generally unsuitable.

Acid soils – Containers – Green foliage.

RHODODENDRON (AZALEA) e.g. 'Cecile'

◐ [○]
type of plant: HSh
flowering season: l. spring to e. summer
flower colour: salmon-pink
height: 1.5-2.1m/5-7ft
*

Of all the azaleas, those – like the variety 'Cecile' – that are classified as Knap Hill hybrids are the most suitable for districts with polluted air. These plants grow strongly – even in full sun, if they are given a moisture-retentive soil and their roots are covered with leaf-mould or peat. They are available in a wide range of colours (for further examples see pp. 36 and 37) and their flowers are larger than the blooms of most other azaleas. Some Knap Hill hybrids have young foliage which is a coppery colour and the leaves of many forms are brightly coloured in autumn.

Acid soils.

**HYDRANGEA macrophylla (Hortensia) e.g.
'Générale Vicomtesse de Vibraye' (syn. *H. m.*
'Vibraye') sc NA**

◑[○]
type of plant: SlTSh
flowering season: midsummer to e. autumn
flower colour: rose or blue
height: 1.2-1.8 m/4-6 ft

The solid, formal flowers of mop-headed
hydrangeas associate well with buildings and look
appropriately opulent in large tubs. On the neutral
or acid soils which suit it best, *H. m.* 'Générale
Vicomtesse de Vibraye' will produce large
numbers of sky-blue blooms over its rounded mass
of foliage. On more alkaline soils the flowers will
be pink. The plant needs a rich, moist soil to which
plenty of humus has been added if necessary, and
it also requires a slightly sheltered position to
minimize frost damage to its young shoots.

Acid soils – Containers – Cutting.

**Additional trees, shrubs and climbers, featured
in this book, that are tolerant of
atmospheric pollution**

◑[○] partial shade (or sun)
PARTHENOCISSUS henryana★: 7.5-9m (p. 153)
MAHONIA×'Charity': 2.1-3m (p. 278)
MAHONIA japonica★: 2.1-3m (p. 271)
CAMELLIA japonica e.g. 'Adolphe Audusson'★:
  1.8-3.6m (p. 36)
CAMELLIA japonica e.g. 'Alba Simplex': 1.8-3m
  (p. 137)
RHODODENDRON luteum: 1.8-3m (p. 194)
EUONYMUS fortunei e.g. 'Silver Queen':
  1.8-2.4m (p. 137)
RHODODENDRON (AZALEA) e.g.
  'Daybreak': 1.5-2.4m (p. 36)
RHODODENDRON (AZALEA) e.g.
  'Berryrose': 1.5-2.1m (p. 36)
RHODODENDRON (AZALEA) e.g. 'Glowing
  Embers': 1.5-2.1m (p. 36)
HYDRANGEA macrophylla (Hortensia) e.g.
  'Altona': 1.2-1.8m (p. 37)
HYDRANGEA macrophylla (Lacecap) e.g.
  'Bluewave': 1.2-1.8m (p. 37)
HYDRANGEA macrophylla (Hortensia) e.g.
  'Madame E. Mouillière': 1.2-1.8m (p. 137)
HYDRANGEA macrophylla (Lacecap) e.g.
  'Whitewave': 1.2-1.8m (p. 37)
SKIMMIA japonica: 90-150cm (p. 271)
MAHONIA aquifolium: 90-120cm (p. 112)
SKIMMIA japonica 'Foremanii': 90-120cm
  (p. 208)
SKIMMIA japonica 'Rubella'★: 60-90cm (p. 39)
EUONYMUS fortunei e.g. 'Silver Queen':
  30-60cm (p. 137)
EUONYMUS fortunei e.g. 'Vegetus': 30-60cm
  (p. 113)
PARTHENOCISSUS henryana★: 15cm (p. 153)

◑ ● partial or full shade
BUXUS sempervirens: 3.6-4.5m (p. 127)
HEDERA helix 'Hibernica': 3.6-4.5m (p. 109)
LIGUSTRUM ovalifolium: 3.6-4.5m (p. 127)
RHODODENDRON (Hardy Hybrid) e.g.
  'Cynthia': 3-3.6m (p. 34)
RHODODENDRON (Hardy Hybrid) e.g.
  'Fastuosum Flore Pleno': 3-3.6m (p. 94)

RHODODENDRON ponticum: 3-3.6m (p. 128)
LIGUSTRUM ovalifolium 'Aureum': 2.7-3.6m
  (p. 177)
FATSIA japonica★: 2.4-3.6m (p. 135)
BUXUS sempervirens e.g. 'Aureovariegata':
  2.4-3m (p. 152)
FORSYTHIA×intermedia 'Lynwood': 2.4-3m
  (p. 24)
FORSYTHIA×intermedia 'Spectabilis': 2.4-3m
  (p. 96)
FORSYTHIA suspensa★: 2.4-3m (p. 50)
KERRIA japonica 'Pleniflora': 1.8-3m (p. 243)
LIGUSTRUM japonicum: 1.8-2.4m (p. 83)
AUCUBA japonica: 1.5-2.4m (p. 83)
AUCUBA japonica e.g. 'Crotonifolia': 1.5-2.4m
  (p. 136)
PHILADELPHUS coronarius 'Aureus': 1.5-2.1m
  (p. 178)
SYMPHORICARPOS rivularis: 1.5-2.1m (p. 206)
CHAENOMELES speciosa e.g. 'Nivalis':
  1.2-1.8m (p. 96)
KERRIA japonica: 1.2-1.8m (p. 96)
SYMPHORICARPOS×doorenbosii 'White
  Hedge': 1.2-1.8m (p. 130)
CHAENOMELES×superba e.g. 'Knap Hill
  Scarlet': 1.2-1.5m (p. 244)
CHAENOMELES×superba e.g. 'Rowallane':
  1.2-1.5m (p. 130)
MAHONIA aquifolium: 90-120cm (p. 112)
SKIMMIA japonica 'Foremanii': 90-120cm
  (p. 208)
PRUNUS laurocerasus e.g. 'Otto Luyken': 90cm
  (p. 107)
CHAENOMELES speciosa e.g. 'Simonii'★:
  60-90cm (p. 52)
×FATSHEDERA lizei: 60-90cm (p. 136)
BUXUS sempervirens 'Suffruticosa': 30-60cm
  (p. 128)
SARCOCOCCA humilis: 30-60cm (p. 273)
HYPERICUM calycinum: 30-45cm (p. 108)
VINCA major: 23-45cm (p. 82)
VINCA major 'Variegata': 23-45cm (p. 153)
HEDERA helix 'Hibernica': 23-30cm (p. 109)
VINCA minor: 15cm (p. 82)
VINCA minor e.g. 'Alba'★: 15cm (p. 111)

Plants suitable for ground-cover

The current popularity of plants whose foliage covers the ground more or less densely is due only in part to their often neat, compact shapes and the natural look which collections of them can give to sites where they are the main components. Of equal, or usually greater, importance is the fact that their habits of growth normally ensure that weeds are smothered and that, therefore, maintenance work is reduced to a minimum. Ground-cover plants can also help to conserve moisture in the soil and so cut down the need for artificial watering. In addition, many of them are useful for binding loose soils together.

Since the reduction of maintenance work is often the main reason for growing ground-cover plants, this list deals chiefly with perennial plants of various types. However, some annuals and biennials have been included. These are either labour-saving self-seeders, such as the evening primrose (*Oenothera biennis*), which are probably best reserved for the less formal parts of gardens, or bedding plants, such as the varieties of *Alyssum maritimum*, which may prove useful in filling gaps among permanent features, particularly in newly planted sites.

Unless a gently undulating carpet of very similarly sized plants is the effect that is actually required, it is best to avoid the temptation of planting only the quickest maturing material. Both trees and larger shrubs introduce variety to ground-cover schemes which can be monotonous unless particular attention has been paid to contrasts of such features as height, leaf form and colour, and habit of growth.

The term 'ground-cover' may conjure up visions of nothing but hummocks of foliage. However, this list contains plants of many other shapes too, and all of them cover the ground well. There are, for instance, plants that form mats of foliage, such as the familiar *Stachys lanata* (commonly called lamb's tongue, lamb's ear and similar names) and its non-flowering variety *S. l.* 'Silver Carpet'; there are plants whose habit of growth is either upright, like *Romneya coulteri*, or arching, like the varieties of day lily; and there are plants, such as rosemary and *x Fatshedera lizei* that sprawl loosely over the ground.

Even among these few examples of plants of different shapes, there is considerable variety of leaf form and colour. For instance, *x Fatshedera lizei*'s ivy-like leaves are deep green and glossy, while *Stachys lanata*'s pointed, oval foliage is silvery grey and woolly.

The most useful source of information about ground-cover plants and their habits of growth, leaf forms and colours, and much else, is Graham Stuart Thomas's *Plants for Ground-Cover* (published by Dent). The range of plants described in this authoritative work is wider and it includes more unusual items than the present comparatively simple list could deal with. It also includes information about large and often slow-growing shrubs which eventually form good ground-cover, and one chapter is devoted to plants which are suitable for really large areas.

When planning any scheme which involves ground-cover plants, it is important to remember that some of these plants are very rapid spreaders. A plant which increases quickly may, at first, seem attractive to the owner of a new garden. However, after a few years, attempts to prevent a whole area becoming invaded by a single species or variety, such as *Gaultheria shallon* or *Lamium galeobdolon* 'Variegatum', may prove difficult and time-consuming. Plants which are invasive do, of course, have their uses, particularly in large areas, but they are often a nuisance in small and even average-sized gardens. Any reference, in general descriptions, to a plant being 'rampant' or 'invasive' should be noted, and the long-term implications should be taken into consideration.

If ground-cover plants are to be successful labour-savers in the garden they must be provided, at the outset, with soil which has been cleared of weeds and is well dug. In this medium they have the best chance of making a weed-proof layer of foliage within a fairly short period. Once established, ground-cover plants can suppress weed seedlings but, with a very few exceptions, they are unable to control perennial weeds which are already in the soil.

Despite the warnings above, most ground-cover plants are neither invasive nor difficult to grow, and the initial preparation of the soil can be made quite easy with the help of weedkillers and, where required, mechanical cultivators. Nor should the selection of ground-cover plants be difficult since there are plants of this type for every site and soil.

PRUNUS tenella (syn. *P. nana*) 'Fire Hill'
[form of Dwarf Russian Almond]

○

type of plant: HSh
flowering season: mid-spring
flower colour: rosy crimson
height: 60-120 cm/2-4 ft

Clustered along the erect growths of this spreading plant are numerous, delicate blooms; slender leaves open fully when the flowering season is over. *P. t.* 'Fire Hill' helps to prevent weed growth by forming a thicket of stems which increases – in a fairly restrained manner – by means of underground shoots. This shrub has a preference for alkaline soils but, although good drainage is important, a very shallow soil is not suitable.

Containers.

GENISTA hispanica
[Spanish Gorse]

○

type of plant: HSh
flowering season: e. summer
flower colour: yellow
height: 60-90 cm/2-3 ft

The green stems of this drought-resistant shrub create a dense, humpy globe of ground-cover. This is a very free-flowering plant in most conditions, but particularly large numbers of blooms are produced on light and poor soils.

Hot, dry soils – Atmospheric pollution – Bark and *twigs*.

DABOECIA cantabrica
[St Dabeoc's Heath]

○

type of plant: SlTSh
flowering season: e. summer to autumn
flower colour: rose-purple
height: 60 cm/2 ft
*E

St Dabeoc's heath is a naturally dense and hummocky plant which will remain thick and neat if clipped after flowering or in spring. It produces its exceptionally large, bell-shaped blooms over a long period. There are various purple or pink varieties of this plant and an example of a white-flowered form appears on p. 30.

Acid soils.

ERICA × **darleyensis (syn.** *E. mediterranea hybrida*) **e.g. 'Arthur Johnson'** ★ **MC [form of Heath or Heather]**

○

type of plant: HSh
flowering season: l. autumn to l. spring
flower colour: rose-pink
height: 60 cm/2 ft
E

This outstanding variety of heather is a vigorous, mound-forming plant which blooms profusely over a number of months and makes excellent ground-cover. Its flower sprays are long and slender and useful for flower arrangements in winter. *E.* × *darleyensis* and its cultivars will tolerate some alkaline soils; they will not grow satisfactorily on shallow, chalky (limy) soils.

　Acid soils – Containers – Cutting – Winter-flowering plants.

LAVANDULA spica (syn. *L. officinalis*) **'Vera'** ★ **[Dutch Lavender]**

○

type of plant: HSh
flowering season: l. summer to e. autumn
flower colour: lavender blue
height: 60 cm/2 ft
E

Of the readily available forms of lavender, this variety is the most effective ground-cover. However, like all lavenders, it benefits from a good clipping over once the cleanly scented flowers have faded. Its neat, rounded shape is covered with grey leaves which also have the characteristic, well scrubbed fragrance of lavender. *L. s.* 'Vera' is easy to grow in any soil that drains freely.

　Chalk – Hot, dry soils – Hedging – Containers – Grey, etc. leaves – Aromatic leaves – Fragrant flowers.

CALLUNA vulgaris (syn. *Erica vulgaris*) **e.g. 'H. E. Beale' [form of Heather or Ling]**

○

type of plant: HSh
flowering season: autumn
flower colour: pink
height: 45-60 cm/1½-2 ft
***E**

Its tall sprays of flowers, its vigour and its late flowering season all account for this plant's long-standing popularity. It forms a spreading hummock which covers the ground well, particularly if it is clipped regularly each spring.

　Acid soils – Cutting.

CYTISUS × **beanii [form of Broom]**

○

type of plant: HSh
flowering season: l. spring
flower colour: golden yellow
height: 45-60 cm/1½-2 ft

The closely packed twigs of this semi-prostrate plant create a mound of ground-covering growth which becomes swathed in yellow during the flowering season. However, the particular yellow of this plant is not to every gardener's taste since, in large quantities especially, it can be a fairly forceful colour. Very alkaline soils and those with bad drainage should be avoided since they shorten the life of this already short-lived shrub.

　Hot, dry soils.

JUNIPERUS horizontalis e.g. 'Glauca' ★ **[form of Creeping Juniper]**

○

type of plant: HCo
height: 45-60 cm/1½-2 ft
E

This wide-spreading conifer makes excellent ground-cover with its long branches densely set with steely blue-green needles. As a young plant, *J. h.* 'Glauca' hugs the ground tightly. In time, however, it forms mounds of foliage which can make it rather more attractive than some of the completely prostrate varieties. Like most junipers, this plant thrives in any well drained soil. Many cultivars of *J. horizontalis* are available in the United States. Best known are 'Bar Harbor' and 'Wilton'.

　Hot, dry soils – Grey, etc, leaves.

ERICA vagans e.g. 'Mrs D. F. Maxwell' ★ **[form of Cornish Heath]**

○

type of plant: HSh
flowering season: l. summer to mid-autumn
flower colour: cerise
height: 45 cm/1½ ft
***E**

Even when the deeply coloured blooms of this plant have faded, the rich, warm brown of its dead flower heads continues to be decorative throughout the winter. *E. v.* 'Mrs D. F. Maxwell' is a notably neat and dense variety, but all forms of Cornish heath are of a thickset, hummocky nature and make good ground-cover. They do better than most heaths and heathers on a heavyish soil.

　Acid soils – Hedging – Cutting.

ROSA wichuraiana
[species of Rose]

○

type of plant: HSh
flowering season: l. summer
flower colour: white
height: 45 cm/1½ ft
½E

The trailing stems of this vigorous rose root as they spread and, together with the dark, shiny leaves, they create a large, ground-covering carpet. The flowers are small but deliciously apple-scented. Nurseymen dealing in a wide range of roses will probably stock several prostrate or ground-covering forms, such as *R.* 'Max Graf' and *R.* × *paulii*. All these roses should be given a rich, open-textured soil. *R. wichuraiana* may also be grown upright – e.g. over a wall or pergola.

Atmospheric pollution – Climbers – Fragrant flowers.

JUNIPERUS horizontalis e.g. 'Douglasii'
[form of Creeping Juniper]

○

type of plant: HCo
height: 30-45 cm/1-1½ ft
E

Similar in many respects to *J. h.* 'Glauca' (see previous page), this plant has foliage of a greyer blue-green which becomes tinged with purple in the colder months. It tends not to build up into mounds of growth but to remain very flat; it may need the tips of its shoots pinched back occasionally to make it thick and dense.

Hot, dry soils – Grey, etc. leaves – Autumn foliage.

NEPETA × **faassenii** (syn. *N. mussinii*)
[form of Catmint]

○

type of plant: HP
flowering season: l. spring to e. autumn
flower colour: blue
height: 30-45 cm/1-1½ ft
½E

Cats seem to derive some strange pleasure from rolling in this plant but, provided they have not inflicted too much damage, and provided that the stems have been cut right back in spring, *N.* × *faassenii* forms a good, ground-covering clump of grey-green leaves. The flowers are produced over an exceptionally long period. A rather musty, mint-like smell is emitted by the foliage. *N.* × *f.* 'Six Hills Giant' is a larger and hardier version of *N.* × *faassenii*; it does not require such a well drained soil as the type plant.

Chalk – Hot, dry soils – Grey, etc. leaves.

HEBE × **'Carl Teschner'**

○

type of plant: SlTSh
flowering season: summer
flower colour: purple
height: 23-30 cm/9-12 in
E

The neatness of this plant makes it suitable both for growing in a tub or similar container, and for use as ground-cover. It forms a hummock of slightly grey foliage and it may be twice as wide as it is high. It often flowers profusely. *H.* × 'Carl Teschner' is not a plant for a very cold garden or badly drained soil.

Chalk – Atmospheric pollution – Containers.

HELIANTHEMUM nummularium (syn. *H. chamaecistus, H. vulgare*) **e.g. 'Wisley Primrose' sc NA**
[form of Sun Rose]

○

type of plant: HSh
flowering season: summer
flower colour: yellow
height: 23-30 cm/9-12 in
E

In general, the sun roses make good ground-cover, especially if they are chopped back ruthlessly after flowering. *H. n.* 'Wisley Primrose' is a dense and strong-growing variety with large flowers and grey-green foliage. The flowers shed their petals in the afternoon but numerous buds provide a succession of blooms. Helianthemums thrive in well drained – even dry – soils and warm, sunny sites.

Chalk – Hot, dry soils – Paving – Grey, etc. leaves.

PENSTEMON newberryi

○

type of plant: SlTSh
flowering season: midsummer
flower colour: purplish rose
height: 23-30 cm/9-12 in
E

For the size of shrub, *P. newberryi*'s flowers are large – almost too large, perhaps, so that the balance of flowers and foliage is upset. The tiny leaves and branches of this plant usually knit into a fairly dense mat which is covered with intensely coloured blooms in summer. A well drained soil is necessary for successful growth and some protection from cold winds may also be needed in exposed gardens.

Paving.

ALYSSUM saxatile e.g. 'Citrinum' (syn. *A. s.* 'Silver Queen')
[form of Gold Dust]

○

type of plant: HP
flowering season: mid-spring to e. summer
flower colour: pale yellow
height: 23 cm/9 in
E

This is a paler but still brightly coloured version of that mainstay of rock gardens, border edges and dry walls: *Alyssum saxatile*. Both the species and its varieties are plants that grow strongly, for a short time at least; they can, therefore, be used to cover largish areas. However, they soon become lanky if not cut back hard after flowering. The leaves of *A. s.* 'Citrinum' are grey-green and covered in short hairs.

Chalk – Hot, dry soils – Grey, etc. leaves.

ERICA carnea e.g. 'Springwood White' ★
[form of Heath or Heather]

○

type of plant: HSh
flowering season: winter to e. spring
flower colour: white
height: 23 cm/9 in
E

The tight little carpets created by *E. carnea* and its offspring make most efficient ground-cover. The variety 'Springwood White' is often regarded as one of the best of all heathers with its long flower spikes and its particularly dense and spreading habit of growth. It, like other *E. carnea* cultivars, is more lime-tolerant than other plants of the genus, but it will not grow well in very dry, chalky (limy) soils.

Acid soils – Containers – Winter-flowering plants.

IBERIS sempervirens 'Snowflake'
[form of Candytuft]

○

type of plant: HP
flowering season: l. spring to e. summer
flower colour: white
height: 23 cm/9 in
E

Spreading neatly and eventually widely, *I. s.* 'Snowflake' will thrive in various inhospitable circumstances including poor soils, sun-baked dry walls and dirty, grimy town gardens. The flower heads of this variety are large and pure white; they need to be removed from the plant as they fade to ensure that plenty of blooms are produced over a long period.

Chalk – Hot, dry soils – Paving.

ARMERIA maritima 'Vindictive' sc NA
[form of Sea Pink or Thrift]

○

type of plant: HP
flowering season: l. spring to midsummer
flower colour: deep rose-pink
height: 15-23 cm/6-9 in
E

This deeply coloured variety of the familiar sea pink holds its long-lasting flowers well above a dense and grassy cushion of foliage. It looks especially nice grown beside stone, either on a rock garden, in between slabs of paving or on a dry wall. Dry places in general suit it well.

Chalk – Hot, dry soils – Paving – Cutting.

ACHILLEA tomentosa
[species of Yarrow]

○

type of plant: HP
flowering season: summer
flower colour: yellow
height: 15-20 cm/6-8 in
E

Many gardeners are familiar with the great flat heads of the border achilleas (such as *A.* 'Gold Plate'). This plant is on an altogether smaller scale but it has a similar taste for well drained and alkaline soils and plenty of sun. Its carpet of fern-like foliage makes a labour-saving edge to borders. *A. tomentosa* is also suitable for dry, hot spots on rock gardens.

Chalk – Hot, dry soils.

LITHOSPERMUM diffusum e.g. 'Heavenly Blue' ★

○

type of plant: HSh
flowering season: summer
flower colour: deep blue
height: 10-15 cm/4-6 in
*E

Although at first glance this plant may appear to be some difficult gentian, it is, in fact, fairly easy to grow. Given a well drained, acid or neutral soil and a sunny site, it covers itself in a mass of flowers and its prostrate stems often form a ground-covering carpet. If necessary, the density of growth can be improved by a light clipping after flowering. There is a less widely available form – *L. d.* 'Grace Ward' – which is more vigorous and has flowers of a more intense colour than *L. d.* 'Heavenly Blue'.

Acid soils – Paving.

**SAPONARIA ocymoides
[Rock Soapwort]**

○

**type of plant: HP
flowering season: summer
flower colour: bright pink
height: 8-15 cm/3-6 in**

Efficient though this vigorous, trailing plant is at
suppressing most weeds, it can prove an
over-energetic inhabitant of small and well tended
rock gardens. Nurserymen specializing in alpine
plants may stock the better behaved and denser
varieties S. o. 'Compacta' and S. o. 'Compacta
Rubra'. S. ocymoides's tendency to spread widely
(up to 75 cm/2½ ft) may be controlled, to some
extent, by planting it between paving stones or in
the crevices between stones in a wall.
 Chalk – Paving.

**ALYSSUM maritimum (syn. *Lobularia maritima*)
e.g. 'Royal Carpet'
[form of Sweet Alyssum]**

○

**type of plant: HA
flowering season: summer to e. autumn
flower colour: deep purple
height: 8-10 cm/3-4 in**

At least in the early stages of their short lives and in
not too rich a soil, varieties of A. maritimum form
dense, bushy plants. Those cultivars which have
white flowers (such as A. m. 'Little Dorrit', see
p. 64) are also fragrant, but this spreading
purple-flowered form is scentless. Flowering will
be particularly profuse if the faded blooms are
removed regularly. The synonym given here is the
correct botanical name, and the name more
commonly used in the United States.
 Chalk – Hot, dry soils – Paving.

ANTENNARIA dioica 'Rubra' ★

○

**type of plant: HP
flowering season: l. spring to e. summer
flower colour: rose-red
height: 8-10 cm/3-4 in
E**

This carpeting plant spreads slowly, rooting as it
goes, until its grey leaves cover an area of about
30 sq cm/1 sq ft. In a newer variety, A. d. 'Aprica',
the leaves are as close set as those of A. d. 'Rubra'
but they are bright and silvery and the flowers are
white. These plants must have good drainage to
grow well.
 Chalk – Hot, dry soils – Paving – Grey, etc.
leaves.

**AUBRIETA (syn. *Aubretia*) deltoidea e.g. 'Red
Carpet'**

○

**type of plant: HP
flowering season: spring
flower colour: deep red
height: 8-10 cm/3-4 in
E**

During the flowering season, the greyish leaves of
this mat-forming plant become smothered in
richly coloured blooms. If it is to be kept neat and
dense, the whole plant must be cut back after the
flowers have faded. It flourishes in well drained,
limy soil and it is a popular choice for the top of
drystone walls.
 Chalk – Hot, dry soils – Paving.

**PHLOX subulata e.g. 'Emerald Cushion Blue'
[form of Moss Phlox]**

○

**type of plant: HP
flowering season: spring
flower colour: light blue
height: 5-10 cm/2-4 in
E**

These two floriferous plants make dense,
wide-spreading mats of tiny leaves. The variety
P. s. 'Emerald Cushion Blue' has attractive, light
green foliage, while the flowers of P. s.
'Temiscaming' (see following photograph) are of
eye-opening vividness. Any reasonably fertile,
well drained soil suits P. subulata and its varieties
and they are especially neat and dense if they are
trimmed each year.
 Chalk – Paving.

**PHLOX subulata e.g. 'Temiscaming' sc NA
[form of Moss Phlox]**

○

**type of plant: HP
flowering season: spring
flower colour: bright red
height: 5-10 cm/2-4 in
E**

See preceding plant.

ANTHEMIS nobilis 'Treneague'
[form of Common Chamomile]

○

type of plant: HP
height: 5-8 cm/2-3 in
E

Where grass would get parched and frazzled, this non-flowering form of chamomile will probably thrive and produce creeping mats of finely divided foliage. It is also useful as a substitute lawn in dry, sunny places that, for some reason or other, are difficult to mow, since it normally requires clipping – or mowing in large areas – only once, or perhaps twice, a year. Its leaves emit a rather fruity smell when trodden upon, but *A. n.* 'Treneague' will not take the heavy wear and tear that some grasses are able to withstand.

Chalk – Hot, dry soils – Paving – Aromatic foliage.

SILENE acaulis
[Moss Campion]

○

type of plant: HP
flowering season: l. spring to e. summer
flower colour: pink
height: 5 cm/2 in
E

This plant's tiny tufts of foliage are packed closely together into a light green carpet which spreads by rooting. In a very sharply drained soil and full sun this carpet of leaves may be covered by another, floral one. However, *S. acaulis* is often rather shy-flowering. It does not grow well in the United States.

Chalk – Paving.

RAOULIA lutescens

○

type of plant: HP
flowering season: l. spring to e. summer
flower colour: lemon yellow
height: 1-2 cm/½-1 in
E

Both the flowers and the grey-green leaves of this plant are very small but they often cover an area well over 30 sq cm/1 sq ft. The leaves are arranged in tiny rosettes which form a tight, ground-hugging mat. *R. lutescens* needs sharply drained soil and some moisture to be seen at its best.

Chalk – Paving – Grey, etc. leaves.

Additional plants, featured elsewhere in this book, that are suitable for ground-cover

○ sun
RHEUM palmatum e.g. 'Bowles' Crimson': 1.5-2.1 m (p. 169)
ROMNEYA coulteri: 1.5-2.1 m (p. 256)
DAPHNE odora 'Aureomarginata': 1.2-1.8 m (p. 146)
ROSMARINUS officinalis: 1.2-1.8 m (p. 196)
JUNIPERUS×media e.g. 'Pfitzerana Aurea': 90-180cm (p. 175)
CISTUS×corbariensis: 90-120cm (p. 57)
CAMPSIS radicans: 90cm (p. 119)
PENNISETUM alopecuroides: 90cm (p. 220)
STIPA calamagrostis: 90cm (p. 58)
ACHILLEA millefolium 'Cerise Queen': 75cm (p. 6)
CROCOSMIA masonorum: 75cm (p. 233)
SALIX lanata★: 60-120cm (p. 159)
HALIMIUM ocymoides: 60-90cm (p. 59)
HEBE 'Autumn Glory': 60-90cm (p. 92)
SALVIA officinalis 'Purpurascens': 60-75cm (p. 170)
DABOECIA cantabrica e.g. 'Alba': 60cm (p. 30)
GLYCERIA maxima 'Variegata': 60cm (p. 147)
LATHYRUS latifolius: 60cm (p. 121)
LIMONIUM latifolium: 60cm (p. 228)
CALLUNA vulgaris e.g. 'Gold Haze': 45-75cm (p. 176)
GENISTA lydia★: 45-75cm (p. 92)
BALLOTA pseudodictamnus: 45-60cm (p. 160)
CENTAUREA dealbata e.g. 'John Coutts': 45-60cm (p. 8)
DIMORPHOTHECA barberiae: 45-60cm (p. 59)
HYSSOPUS officinalis: 45-60cm (p. 197)
RUTA graveolens 'Jackman's Blue': 45-60cm (p. 160)
SALVIA officinalis 'Tricolor': 45-60cm (p. 148)
SANTOLINA chamaecyparissus: 45-60cm (p. 125)
SEDUM×'Autumn Joy': 45-60cm (p. 9)

SENECIO cineraria 'White Diamond': 45-60cm (p. 160)
CALLUNA vulgaris e.g. 'Peter Sparkes': 45cm (p. 30)
CALLUNA vulgaris e.g. 'Robert Chapman': 45cm (p. 190)
ERICA×darleyensis e.g. 'Silver Beads': 45cm (p. 275)
ERICA vagans e.g. 'Lyonesse': 45cm (p. 30)
BERBERIS thunbergii 'Atropurpurea Nana': 30-60cm (p. 171)
CONVOLVULUS cneorum: 30-60cm (p. 161)
CYTISUS×kewensis: 30-60cm (p. 59)
ANAPHALIS triplinervis: 30-45cm (p. 161)
IRIS graminea: 30-45cm (p. 260)
TROPAEOLUM majus e.g. 'Golden Gleam': 30-40cm (p. 60)
TROPAEOLUM majus e.g. 'Scarlet Gleam': 30-40cm (p. 60)
IRIS unguicularis: 30cm (p. 275)
VERONICA incana: 30cm (p. 161)
ZAUSCHNERIA californica: 30cm (p. 61)
ANTHEMIS cupaniana: 23-30cm (p. 161)
CERATOSTIGMA plumbaginoides: 23-30cm (p. 191)
HELIANTHEMUM nummularium e.g. 'Wisley Pink': 23-30cm (p. 162)
ORIGANUM vulgare 'Aureum': 23-30cm (p. 176)
PENSTEMON menziesii: 23-30cm (p. 139)
PULSATILLA vulgaris: 23-30cm (p. 14)
PULSATILLA vulgaris 'Rubra': 23-30cm (p. 15)
SATUREIA montana 'Coerulea': 23-30cm (p. 198)
ALYSSUM saxatile e.g. 'Dudley Neville': 23cm (p. 15)
HELIANTHEMUM nummularium e.g. 'Mrs Earle'★: 23cm (p. 62)
IRIS innominata Hybrids: 23cm (p. 31)
PHLOX amoena: 23cm (p. 139)
SEDUM×'Ruby Glow': 23cm (p. 62)
TROPAEOLUM majus e.g. 'Empress of India': 23cm (p. 62)
THYMUS vulgaris: 20-30cm (p. 198)

ERYSIMUM linifolium: 15-30cm (p. 63)
CERASTIUM tomentosum: 15-23cm (p. 162)
DIANTHUS deltoides: 15-23cm (p. 140)
ERICA carnea e.g. 'King George': 15-23cm (p. 275)
ERICA carnea e.g. 'Vivellii': 15-23cm (p. 191)
FESTUCA ovina 'Glauca': 15-23cm (p. 162)
HYPERICUM polyphyllum: 15-23cm (p. 140)
DIANTHUS gratianopolitanus★: 15-20cm (p. 16)
TANACETUM haradjanii★: 15-20cm (p. 162)
ALYSSUM saxatile e.g. 'Compactum': 15cm (p. 63)
VERONICA prostrata: 10-20cm (p. 141)
ALYSSUM maritimum e.g. 'Little Dorrit': 10-15cm (p. 64)
ANDROSACE lanuginosa: 10-15cm (p. 163)
ARENARIA montana: 10-15cm (p. 141)
AUBRIETA deltoidea e.g. 'Dr. Mules': 10-15cm (p. 18)
AUBRIETA deltoidea e.g. 'Maurice Prichard': 10-15cm (p. 141)
SEDUM spurium e.g. 'Schorbusser Blut': 10-15cm (p. 141)
ALYSSUM maritimum e.g. 'Rosie O'Day': 10cm (p. 19)
SEDUM spathulifolium 'Purpureum': 10cm (p. 171)
GYPSOPHILA repens: 8-15cm (p. 19)
GYPSOPHILA repens rosea: 8-15cm (p. 64)
IBERIS saxatilis: 8-15cm (p. 64)
DRYAS octopetala: 8-10cm (p. 142)
HELICHRYSUM bellidioides: 8-10cm (p. 19)
MESEMBRYANTHEMUM criniflorum: 8-10cm (p. 64)
SEDUM spathulifolium 'Capa Blanca'★: 8-10cm (p. 65)
PHLOX douglasii e.g. 'Boothman's Variety': 5-10cm (p. 142)
POTENTILLA nitida 'Rubra': 5-8cm (p. 163)
THYMUS serpyllum e.g. 'Albus': 5cm (p. 142)
RAOULIA australis: 1-2cm (p. 163)

POTENTILLA 'Elizabeth'
[form of Shrubby Cinquefoil]

○ [◑]
type of plant: HSh
flowering season: e. summer to mid-autumn
flower colour: yellow
height: 75-90 cm/2½-3 ft

An unusually long flowering season and an obliging nature are combined in this shrub with a neat, weed-smothering habit of growth. The numerous twigs create a dense hummock which often spread 1.2-1.5 m/4-5 ft wide. Flowering may begin in late spring and the blooms are normally produced in large quantities. This plant is still sometimes sold as *P. arbuscula* or *P. fruticosa arbuscula*. It makes a very floriferous, informal hedge which needs no pruning. Any soil with reasonable drainage is suitable.

   Hedging.

CROCOSMIA × crocosmiiflora (syn. *Montbretia crocosmiiflora*) **e.g. 'Citronella'**
[form of Common Montbretia]

○ [◑]
type of plant: SITC
flowering season: summer
flower colour: lemon yellow
height: 60-75 cm/2-2½ ft

This variety of common montbretia is less hardy than some of the newer hybrids but its sprays of flowers are large and shapely and not too stridently coloured. Its sheaves of foliage suppress most weeds, but where a really energetic ground-coverer of similar appearance is wanted, then the orange-flowered common montbretia – *C. × crocosmiiflora* – should be chosen. A well drained soil which retains moisture in summer is required for both the species and the variety and a sheltered site is necessary for *C. × c.* 'Citronella'.

   Cutting.

GERANIUM pratense e.g. 'Mrs Kendall Clarke' sc NA
[form of Meadow Cranesbill]

○ [◑]
type of plant: HP
flowering season: summer
flower colour: pale blue
height: 60-75 cm/2-2½ ft

The lovely leaves of this clump-forming plant cover the ground thickly and decoratively. In autumn they become brightly coloured. Almost any reasonably well drained soil is suitable and, when growing well, this plant seeds itself prolifically. The long stalks may need some support.

   Green foliage – Autumn foliage.

HEUCHERA sanguinea e.g. 'Scintillation' ★
[form of Coral Bells]

○ [◑]
type of plant: HP
flowering season: l. spring to midsummer
flower colour: bright pink + coral
height: 60 cm/2 ft
E

Over a bed of densely packed leaves, the tiny but brilliantly coloured flowers of this plant hover on slim, strong stems. To be seen at their best, *H. sanguinea* cultivars need frequent division; the divided pieces should be planted quite deeply in soil which is both well drained and fertile.

   Cutting.

STACHYS macrantha (syn. *S. grandiflora, Betonica grandiflora, B. macrantha*)

○ [◑]
type of plant: HP
flowering season: l. spring to midsummer
flower colour: purple
height: 45 cm/1½ ft
E

This easily grown plant makes a mat of wrinkly leaves and produces sturdy whorls of flowers above a ground-covering base. *S. m.* 'Rosea' has rose pink flowers.

   Chalk.

POTENTILLA fruticosa mandschurica ★
[form of Shrubby Cinquefoil]

○ [◑]
type of plant: HSh
flowering season: e. summer to mid-autumn
flower colour: white
height: 30-45 cm/1-1½ ft

As free-flowering and as good at preventing weed growth as the many related varieties of shrubby potentillas, *P. f. mandschurica* has the added attraction of grey foliage. It makes a low and spreading shrub. A more upright, less readily available variety, *P. f.* 'Vilmoriniana', has distinctly silvery foliage and creamy white flowers. Both these plants are easy to grow.

   Chalk – Grey, etc. leaves.

ARABIS albida (syn. *A. caucasica*) e.g. 'Flore Pleno'
[form of Rock Cress or Wall Cress]
○ [◑]
type of plant: HP
flowering season: all spring
flower colour: white
height: 15-20 cm/6-8 in
E

This is not a plant for a very small rock-garden but, given enough room – and it will probably have a spread of at least 45 cm/1½ ft – its mat of softly coloured foliage can be appreciated both as ground-cover and as an attractive setting for the long-lasting flowers. It thrives in any sunny spot and does particularly well in dry soils.
  Chalk – Hot, dry soils – Paving.

GERANIUM dalmaticum
○ [◑]
type of plant: HP
flowering season: e. summer
flower colour: pink
height: 12.5 cm/5 in

A charming little ground-coverer with glossy, refined foliage and large, 2 cm/1 in flowers for the plant height. No special care seems necessary provided average garden soil is given. 'Album', with white flowers, is less vigorous.
  Green foliage.

ACAENA microphylla
○ [◑]
type of plant: HP
height: 5 cm/2 in

The tiny leaves of this plant knit together into a prostrate mat of bronzed greenery. Large red burrs succeed the inconspicuous flowers. In a well drained soil and full sun *A. microphylla* may spread over 60 cm/2 ft wide. Its small leaves and spiny fruits contrast nicely with paving stones.
  Chalk – Paving – Red, etc. leaves – Fruit.

Additional plants, featured elsewhere in this book, that are suitable for ground-cover

○ [◑] sun (or partial shade)
POTENTILLA fruticosa e.g. 'Katherine Dykes': 1.2 m (p. 130)
SENECIO laxifolius★: 90-120 cm (p. 164)
PELTIPHYLLUM peltatum: 60-90 cm (p. 71)
POTENTILLA fruticosa e.g. 'Tangerine': 60-90 cm (p. 22)
CROCOSMIA × crocosmiiflora e.g. 'Jackanapes': 60-75 cm (p. 241)
GERANIUM pratense e.g. 'Album': 60-75 cm (p. 183)
BUPHTHALMUM salicifolium: 45-60 cm (p. 49)
FILIPENDULA hexapetala: 45-60 cm (p. 23)
HEUCHERA sanguinea e.g. 'Red Spangles': 45-60 cm (p. 242)
LYSICHITUM americanum: 30-45 cm (p. 71)
STACHYS lanata: 30-45 cm (p. 164)
LYSICHITUM camtschatcense: 23-30 cm (p. 71)
CALTHA palustris 'Plena': 23 cm (p. 71)
ARABIS albida e.g. 'Rosabella': 15-20 cm (p. 23)
AJUGA reptans 'Atropurpurea': 10-15 cm (p. 172)
STACHYS lanata 'Silver Carpet'★: 10-15 cm (p. 165)
ACAENA buchananii: 5 cm (p. 143)

GAULTHERIA shallon MC
○ ◑
type of plant: HSh
flowering season: l. spring to e. summer
flower colour: pale pink
height: 1.2-1.8 m/4-6 ft
*E

This invasive, thicket-forming plant is probably best reserved for rough ground-cover under trees – where it feels most at home in any case. It suckers and spreads freely in moist and damp soils but it will also tolerate dry shade. The purple berries are covered with an attractive bloom and some birds, including pheasants, find them appetizing.
  Acid soils – Damp and wet soils – Dry shade – Dense shade – Fruit.

ASTILBE taquetii 'Superba'
[form of False Goat's Beard]
○ ◑
type of plant: HP
flowering season: l. summer
flower colour: magenta
height: 1.2 m/4 ft

This magnificent plant is rather taller and a good deal later in flowering than the more commonly seen varieties of *A. × arendsii* (for one example of which, see p. 113). The dark foliage makes good ground-cover in any moisture-retentive or damp soil.
  Damp and wet soils – Green foliage – Cutting.

TSUGA canadensis 'Pendula'
[form of Eastern Hemlock]
○ ◑
type of plant: HCo
height: 90-180 cm/3-6 ft
E

The pendulous tips of this slow-growing conifer eventually touch the ground and the whole plant takes on a mounded, bushy appearance. In maturity, it may be over 3.6 m/12 ft wide. The young foliage is a bright and fresh green. This variety of *T. canadensis* is more lime-tolerant than some plants of its genus, but, ideally, it should be grown in an acid, sandy soil.

SPIRAEA × bumalda 'Anthony Waterer'
○ ◑
type of plant: HSh
flowering season: summer
flower colour: crimson
height: 90-120 cm/3-4 ft

The young leaves of this plant are sometimes marked with cream and pink but the sizeable flower heads and the dense, hummocky habit of growth are more conspicuous and reliable attractions. *S. × b.* 'Gold Flame' is a newer cultivar which regularly produces bright gold and orange foliage. *S. × b.* 'Anthony Waterer' will grow healthily in most soils and sites; it should be pruned very hard in spring.

Chalk – Clay – Atmospheric pollution – Hedging – Containers – Variegated leaves.

PRUNUS laurocerasus e.g. 'Otto Luyken' ★
[form of Cherry Laurel or Common Laurel]
○ ◑
type of plant: HSh
flowering season: e. summer
flower colour: white
height: 90 cm/3 ft
E

The frequent use of this plant in large, public ground-cover schemes probably means that its virtues are often belittled. However, its good features do include attractively upright tips to the more or less prostrate branches, pleasing, shiny leaves and an ability to grow well in various unpromising sites and almost any soil, provided that it is not too alkaline. The berries are at first red and then black. *P. l.* 'Otto Luyken' makes a dense, low-growing hedge which needs little attention.

Dry shade – Dense shade – Atmospheric pollution – Hedging – Fruit.

HEMEROCALLIS e.g. 'Pink Damask'
[form of Day Lily]
○ ◑
type of plant: HP
flowering season: summer
flower colour: pink
height: 75-90 cm/2½-3 ft

Once planted, day lilies can be left undisturbed for some considerable time, during which their sheaves of arching foliage will form large, weed-proof clumps. Each flower lasts for only one day but numerous buds open in succession. This particular variety grows strongly and flowers freely. It is only one of many possible examples from a range of hybrids which is constantly increasing. Fertile, moisture-retentive soils suit day lilies best and they grow lushly by water.

Clay – Damp and wet soils – Green foliage.

EUPHORBIA griffithii 'Fireglow' sc NA
[form of Spurge]
○ ◑
type of plant: HP
flowering season: e. summer
flower colour: orange-red
height: 60-90 cm/2-3 ft

The intensely coloured bracts of this bushy, spreading perennial remain bright and colourful for several weeks. The leaves have pink midribs which are discernible and attractive at close range. This species of spurge is not as tolerant of dry soils as some of its near relatives. It is not, however, a fussy plant and most well drained soils are suitable.

ANEMONE × hybrida (syn. *A. × elegans*,
***A. japonica*) e.g. 'September Charm'**
[form of Japanese Anemone]
○ ◑
type of plant: HP
flowering season: l. summer to mid-autumn
flower colour: pink
height: 45-60 cm/1½-2 ft

After a year or two of settling into its new home, this variety of Japanese anemone will start to produce plenty of flowers over spreading clumps of foliage. In full shade there will be fewer blooms but the plant will still do well. Good, moisture-retentive soil ensures the densest and most effectively weed-suppressing growth. 'September Charm' is a smaller and neater plant than many other varieties of *A. × hybrida* (for an example of a taller-growing cultivar, see p. 51).

Clay.

GERANIUM × 'Johnson's Blue'
[form of Cranesbill]
○ ◐
type of plant: HP
flowering season: summer
flower colour: blue
height: 45-60 cm/1½-2 ft

The beautiful, blue flowers and lovely, light leafiness of this plant go together with such density of growth that weeding amongst the stems and stalks is usually quite unnecessary. Any well drained soil suits this plant, but it is not at its best in very dry places.
　Green foliage.

ALCHEMILLA mollis ★
[Lady's Mantle]
○ ◐
type of plant: HP
flowering season: summer
flower colour: yellow-green
height: 45 cm/1½ ft

Now, apparently, one of the essential ingredients of any British garden, this almost too good-natured plant has indeed many admirable qualities. Its copious, ground-covering foliage is an unusual velvety green; its airy sprays of tiny flowers are a delight both in the garden and when cut; and it will grow almost anywhere – including places where it is not wanted, since it can be a prolific self-seeder. If the flower heads seem untidy towards the end of their season, the whole plant can be razed to the ground and there will soon be fresh, new leaves.
　Clay – Green foliage – Cutting – Green flowers.

EUPHORBIA polychroma (syn. *E. epithymoides*) ★
[species of Spurge]
○ ◐
type of plant: HP
flowering season: spring
flower colour: yellow
height: 45 cm/1½ ft

One of the cheering sights of springtime, this brightly coloured plant makes neat, self-supporting domes of greenery. Its flower heads are good for cutting, but the stem tips must either be singed or dipped in boiling water for a few minutes to stop the harmful, milky juices from flowing. In autumn, the leaves often become tinged with an unusual mixture of pink, yellow and apricot. *E. polychroma* thrives in any fertile soil with reasonable drainage.
　Chalk – Autumn foliage – Cutting.

GERANIUM endressii e.g. 'Wargrave Pink'
[form of Cranesbill]
○ ◐
type of plant: HP
flowering season: summer
flower colour: salmon-pink
height: 45 cm/1½ ft

This vigorous plant forms a spreading clump of attractive, light green foliage. It is happy in sun or light shade but lushest and most ground-covering in a cool position and a well drained but moisture-retentive soil. There are other pink-flowered varieties of this plant (including *G. e.* 'A. T. Johnson', see the following page).
　Green foliage.

RUBUS tricolor sc NA
[species of Ornamental Bramble]
○ ◐
type of plant: HSh
flowering season: midsummer
flower colour: white
height: 30-60 cm/1-2 ft
E/½E

The outstanding vigour of this plant is reminiscent of the energy of its relative, the bramble or blackberry of hedgerows. However, compared with that common species, its leaves and flowers are more decorative, its stems are bristly rather than thorny and it has a very much denser habit of growth. Its rooting carpet of stems can easily expand by 1.8 m/6 ft in a season. It grows anywhere. Red, edible fruits are produced only occasionally.
　Chalk – Dry shade – Dense shade.

HYPERICUM calycinum
[Rose of Sharon, Aaron's Beard]
○ ◐
type of plant: HSh
flowering season: summer to e. autumn
flower colour: yellow
height: 30-45 cm/1-1½ ft
E/½E

Rose of Sharon may be all too common a sight and its flowers may be rather too large for its overall size, but few plants are so colourful and accommodating in so many unpromising places. It makes an ever-widening mass of erect stems which suppress weeds most successfully, and especially so if the whole plant is cut back severely every few years. Intermittent trimming also helps to keep this plant dense.
　Chalk – Hot, dry soils – Dry shade – Dense shade – Atmospheric pollution.

VERONICA gentianoides
[species of Speedwell]

○ ◑

type of plant: HP
flowering season: l. spring to e. summer
flower colour: pale blue
height: 30-45 cm/1-1½ ft

The low-growing foliage of this plant is
overtopped by tall spikes of flowers and the
difference in height is attractive and conspicuous.
The leaves are arranged in rosettes which knit
together into a mat. There is a form of this plant
with creamy white markings on its foliage; it is less
vigorous than the species. Both plants need a
fertile, well drained soil.

GERANIUM endressii e.g. 'A. T. Johnson' ★
[form of Cranesbill]

○ ◑

type of plant: HP
flowering season: summer
flower colour: pink
height: 30-40 cm/12-15 in

Like the related but stronger variety of *G. endressii*
illustrated on the previous page, this plant makes
excellent ground-cover, particularly in lightly
shaded sites. It too has pretty foliage.
  Green foliage.

BERGENIA × 'Silberlicht' (syn. *B.* × 'Silver
Light') ★

○ ◑

type of plant: HP
flowering season: spring
flower colour: white changing to pink
height: 30 cm/1 ft
E

Nearly all the bergenias (which have, in the past,
been included in the genera *Saxifraga* and
Megasea) are good ground-cover plants. This fairly
recent hybrid is notable for its white flowers;
typically, bergenia flowers are some shade of pink
or purple. Its leaves are dark and fairly small. The
plant and its relatives are easy to grow in any soil;
they are useful, small evergreens for limy areas.
  Chalk – Clay – Dry shade – Green foliage.

GEUM × borisii
[form of Avens]

○ ◑

type of plant: HP
flowering season: l. spring to summer
flower colour: orange-red
height: 30 cm/1 ft
E/½E

Smaller than the familiar varieties of *G. chiloense*,
this species also has a denser clump of foliage
beneath its bright flowers. When several
specimens are planted quite closely together they
cover the ground thickly. Ordinary, garden soil of
moderate fertility suits this plant; it grows and
flowers well if divided frequently.

CAMPANULA carpatica
[species of Bellflower]

○ ◑

type of plant: HP
flowering season: summer
flower colour: blue or mauve or white
height: 23-30 cm/9-12 in

This tough, clump-forming plant suppresses most
weeds in a very floriferous and decorative fashion.
Its flowers are large and the variability of their
colour is accounted for by the fact that several
forms are often sold under the name of the species
alone. Nurseries specializing in rock plants will
usually list selected forms in separate colours.
Good, well drained soils suit these plants best.

HEDERA helix 'Hibernica' (syn. *H. hibernica*)
[Irish Ivy]

○ ◑

type of plant: HCl
height: 23-30 cm/9-12 in
E, grown as ground-cover

There are many ivies with interesting foliage, but
this plain-leaved variety is the one to choose where
vigorous, undemanding ground-cover is needed.
It is one of the best plants of its type for growing in
dry shade underneath trees. Nor is the foliage to be
despised since, in a healthy state, the big glossy
leaves are quite attractive. To encourage rooting,
stones or bent pieces of wire should be used to pin
down the stems. This self-clinging plant can, of
course, be grown upwards as well as along the
ground. It is suitable for north- and east-facing
walls.
  Chalk – Clay – Dry shade – Dense shade –
Atmospheric pollution – Climbers.

GERANIUM sanguineum
[Bloody Cranesbill]

○ ◑

type of plant: HP
flowering season: summer to e. autumn
flower colour: crimson
height: 23 cm/9 in

The delicately cut leaves of this plant look pretty not only in spring and summer but also in autumn, when they very often become richly coloured. The vivid flowers are produced over a long period; a few blooms may appear right up until the final weeks of the year. In addition to all these good features, *G. sanguineum* is also an excellent ground-cover plant which will form a spreading hummock of foliage in any reasonably fertile and well drained soil. The variety *G. s. lancastriense* is similar to the species; it has pink flowers on shorter stalks.

Green foliage – Autumn foliage.

POLYGONUM affine 'Donald Lowndes' ★
sc NA
[form of Knotweed]

○ ◑

type of plant: HP
flowering season: summer to e. autumn
flower colour: deep pink
height: 23 cm/9 in

A long flowering season, attractively russety leaves in autumn and winter, and a completely weed-proof, carpet-like habit of growth are all points in this plant's favour. A possible drawback is its tendency to be a little too energetic in really fertile, moist soil. *P. a.* 'Darjeeling Red' – a more richly coloured form of the species – is an even worse offender in this respect and it should be excluded from small gardens.

Autumn foliage.

PRUNELLA webbiana e.g. 'Loveliness'
[form of Self-heal]

○ ◑

type of plant: HP
flowering season: all summer
flower colour: pale violet
height: 23 cm/9 in

Like its counterpart *P. w.* 'Pink Loveliness' (see p. 53), this plant has leaves which cover the ground quite thickly, especially if it is given constant moisture. When growing happily, however, it may seed itself liberally, though dead-heading can prevent too many seedlings appearing.

Clay.

SYMPHYTUM grandiflorum
[species of Comfrey]

○ ◑

type of plant: HP
flowering season: spring
flower colour: cream
height: 23 cm/9 in
E

Hardly an exquisite embellishment to a garden, *S. grandiflorum* is, however, useful in certain places, including the ground beneath shrubs and trees. As long as the soil is not dry, it will creep densely and rapidly, soon forming an impenetrable carpet of foliage. It thrives near water.

Clay – Damp and wet soils – Dense shade.

VIOLA cornuta e.g. 'Alba'
[form of Horned Violet]

○ ◑

type of plant: HP
flowering season: l. spring to summer
flower colour: white
height: 15-23 cm/6-9 in
E

V. c. 'Alba' is one of the strongest-growing forms of horned violet. Its tufts of foliage root as they spread into dense clumps. If, after flowering, the flower stems and any other long shoots are cut back, a second crop of flowers usually appears. Well drained, moisture-retentive soils and generally cool conditions produce the best growth. The very slight, sweet scent of this plant is most easily perceived at dusk.

Dense shade – Paving.

CHIASTOPHYLLUM oppositifolium (syn.
Cotyledon oppositifolia, C. simplicifolia)

○ ◑

type of plant: HP
flowering season: summer
flower colour: yellow
height: 15 cm/6 in
E

The squeakily succulent leaves of this plant are packed together into a close mat. As they age they often turn a vivid red, particularly if the plant has been grown in full sun. *C. oppositifolium* is not, however, suitable for hot, dry sites; it grows most densely if given some moisture and shade.

Autumn foliage.

VACCINIUM vitis-idaea
[Cowberry]

○ ◐

type of plant: HSh
flowering season: e. summer
flower colour: white or pink
height: 15 cm/6 in
*E

Apart from a dislike of alkaline soils, this is a most accommodating plant. The neat little leaves become bronzed in winter and at all times they are part of a spreading, weed-suppressing carpet. The red berries are long-lasting and edible. Although it will tolerate dryness and shade, *V. vitis-idaea* should ideally be planted in an open site and given a moisture-retentive soil that has been enriched with humus.

Acid soils – Damp and wet soils – Dry shade – Dense shade – Autumn foliage – Fruit.

VINCA minor e.g. 'Alba' ★
[form of Lesser Periwinkle]

○ ◐

type of plant: HSh/P
flowering season: e. spring to e. summer
flower colour: white
height: 15 cm/6 in
E

Though not so invasive as *V. minor* itself (for details of which, see p. 82), this is still a vigorous plant which, after a couple of years, will start to make good ground-cover (and after five or six years may be something of a nuisance in the garden). It will grow anywhere, in any soil, although well drained soils are preferable. There are many varieties of *V. minor*: some have variegated leaves, others produce paler or redder flowers than the species.

Chalk – Dry shade – Dense shade – Atmospheric pollution – Containers.

CORNUS canadensis (syn. *Chamaepericlymenum canadense*)
[species of Dogwood or Cornel]

○ ◐

type of plant: HP/Sh
flowering season: e. summer
flower colour: white + greenish purple
height: 10-15 cm/4-6 in
*

In light woodland and fairly moist, peaty soil this plant spreads quickly into a carpet of erect stems topped, at first, with radiating leaves alone and then with leaves and white, flower-like bracts. From time to time, red berries follow some of these bracts. In autumn (and in sun, or partial rather than full shade) the leaves become wine-coloured. This plant will grow satisfactorily in dry shade.

Acid soils – Dry Shade – Dense shade – Autumn foliage.

POLYGONUM vacciniifolium MC
[species of Knotweed]

○ ◐

type of plant: HP
flowering season: l. summer to mid-autumn
flower colour: pink
height: 10-15 cm/4-6 in
E

This very free-flowering species of knotweed is easy to grow in most soils and has all the vigour usually associated with plants of its genus. It looks especially good if its long, crimson, mat-forming stems are allowed to trail over a wall or boulder. Whereas some knotweeds have leaves that are somewhat flaccid and dull in colour, *P. vacciniifolium*'s foliage is neat and a rich, shining green. This is not a plant for small spaces; it may sometimes spread over 90 cm/3 ft wide.

VIOLA labradorica
[species of Violet]

○ ◐

type of plant: HP
flowering season: spring
flower colour: mauve
height: 10-15 cm/4-6 in
E

V. labradorica may have no scent, but its ability to make purple-tinted mats of foliage and to cover these with pretty flowers, even in quite dry places, is compensation enough. Ideally, this plant should be given cool, slightly moist conditions but its toughness and vigour usually ensure that it spreads without any difficulty in most soils and sites.

Chalk – Paving – Red, etc. leaves.

COTONEASTER dammeri ★

○ ◐

type of plant: HSh
flowering season: e. summer
flower colour: white
height: 10 cm/4 in
E

The range of ground-covering cotoneasters has widened considerably in the last few years, but *C. dammeri* remains one of the best plants of its sort. It will spread by approximately 45-60 cm/1½-2 ft a year into a large, really close-knit mat of glossy, green foliage. The red berries, which are much more decorative than the flowers, are only quite attractive to birds. This plant will grow well in many different types of soil.

Chalk – Clay – Atmospheric pollution – Fruit.

CAMPANULA portenschlagiana (syn.
C. muralis)
[species of Bellflower]

○ ◑
type of plant: HP
flowering season: midsummer to e. autumn
flower colour: bluish mauve
height: 8-15 cm/3-6 in
E

This very invasive plant should be reserved for
areas where no other, weaker plants could be
enveloped in and suffocated by its spreading mass
of densely packed leaves. Its exuberance can be
controlled to some extent by planting it in crevices
either in walls or in paving. *C. portenschlagiana* is
not too particular about the soil and site it is to
grow in, though it does have a preference for good
drainage.

Chalk – Paving.

WALDSTEINIA ternata (syn. *W. trifolia*) ★

○ ◑
type of plant: HP
flowering season: spring
flower colour: yellow
height: 8-10 cm/3-4 in
E

The pretty leaves of this plant overlap one another
until, after a year or two, they form a
ground-hugging layer of foliage. For so decorative
a plant – with its yellow, strawberry flowers and its
dark green leaves contrasting most satisfactorily –
it is remarkably unfussy. The foliage sometimes
becomes bronzed in winter.

Chalk – Dry shade – Green foliage.

**Additional plants, featured elsewhere in this
book, that are suitable for ground-cover**

○ ◑ sun or partial shade
GUNNERA manicata: 1.8-2.7 m (p. 183)
OSMUNDA regalis: 1.2-1.8 m (p. 73)
ACANTHUS mollis latifolius: 1.2 m (p. 25)
PHALARIS arundinacea 'Picta': 90-150 cm
  (p. 152)
ACANTHUS spinosus: 90-120 cm (p. 184)
POLYGONUM amplexicaule 'Atrosanguineum':
  90-120 cm (p. 51)
ANEMONE×hybrida e.g. 'Louise Uhink'★:
  90-105 cm (p. 51)
VIBURNUM davidii: 90 cm (p. 206)
OENOTHERA biennis: 75-90 cm (p. 67)
POLYGONUM bistorta 'Superbum': 75-90 cm
  (p. 74)
HEMEROCALLIS e.g. 'Marion Vaughn': 75 cm
  (p. 52)
MELISSA officinalis 'Aurea': 75 cm (p. 152)
TROLLIUS×cultorum e.g. 'Orange Princess':
  75 cm (p. 246)
TROLLIUS ledebouri 'Golden Queen': 75 cm
  (p. 74)
×FATSHEDERA lizei: 60-90 cm (p. 136)
HEMEROCALLIS e.g. 'Burning Daylight':
  60-90 cm (p. 74)
PERNETTYA mucronata e.g. 'Bell's Seedling':
  60-90 cm (p. 206)
PERNETTYA mucronata e.g. 'Davis Hybrids':
  60-90 cm (p. 206)
PHYSALIS franchetii: 60-90 cm (p. 207)
TROLLIUS europaeus 'Superbus': 60-75 cm
  (p. 75)
CLEMATIS montana: 60 cm (p. 122)
CLEMATIS montana rubens: 60 cm (p. 122)
CLEMATIS montana e.g. 'Tetrarose': 60 cm
  (p. 122)
CLEMATIS orientalis: 60 cm (p. 122)
CLEMATIS tangutica: 60 cm (p. 123)
COTONEASTER horizontalis: 60 cm (p. 194)
HYDRANGEA petiolaris★: 60 cm (p. 122)
JASMINUM nudiflorum: 60 cm (p. 277)
VITIS coignetiae: 60 cm (p. 192)
EUPHORBIA robbiae: 45-60 cm (p. 81)
RANUNCULUS aconitifolius 'Flore Pleno':
  45-60 cm (p. 75)
BERGENIA×'Ballawley': 30-45 cm (p. 25)
COTONEASTER 'Hybridus Pendulus': 30-45 cm
  (p. 25)
GEUM rivale 'Leonard's Variety': 30-45 cm (p. 76)
LIRIOPE muscari: 30-45 cm (p. 80)
BERGENIA cordifolia: 30 cm (p. 184)
PARTHENOCISSUS quinquefolia: 30 cm (p. 192)
PRUNELLA webbiana e.g. 'Pink Loveliness':
  30 cm (p. 53)
VINCA major: 23-45 cm (p. 82)
VINCA major 'Variegata': 23-45 cm (p. 153)
DAPHNE cneorum 'Eximia': 23-30 cm (p. 269)
PARTHENOCISSUS tricuspidata 'Veitchii':
  23 cm (p. 192)
HEBE 'Pagei': 15-30 cm (p. 167)
HEDERA canariensis 'Variegata': 15-23 cm
  (p. 151)
HEDERA colchica 'Dentata-Variegata': 15-23 cm
  (p. 151)
PRIMULA auricula e.g. 'Mixed Hybrids':
  15-23 cm (p. 35)
VIOLA cornuta e.g. 'Jersey Gem': 15-23 cm
  (p. 143)
VINCA minor: 15 cm (p. 82)
VIOLA odorata e.g. 'Princess of Wales': 15 cm
  (p. 270)

**MAHONIA aquifolium
[Oregon Grape]**

◑ [○]
type of plant: HSh
flowering season: spring
flower colour: yellow
height: 90-120 cm/3-4 ft
E

The thickets of upright stems and glossy, spiny
leaves which this suckering plant slowly creates
make good ground-cover. *M. aquifolium* is
particularly useful underneath the dripping leaves
of trees and in their shade. It also makes a nice,
informal hedge or barrier. It will grow almost
anywhere. The leaves may become red or bronze
in winter. The blue-black berries are an additional
decorative feature.

Chalk – Clay – Dry shade – Dense shade –
Atmospheric pollution – Hedging – Containers –
Green foliage – Autumn foliage – Fruit – Cutting.

**RHODODENDRON (AZALEA) e.g.
'Hinomayo'**

◑ [○]
type of plant: HSh
flowering season: spring
flower colour: clear pink
height: 90-120 cm/3-4 ft
✳½E

This vigorous azalea covers the ground well with
spreading branches. Its spectacularly floriferous
nature makes it a good plant for a tub or pot,
although if it is grown in a container particular
attention must be paid to keeping the soil
constantly moist. This plant also needs some
shelter from cold winds and late frosts which may
damage its new growth.

Acid soils – Containers.

RHODODENDRON (AZALEA) e.g. 'Addy Wery' sc NA

◑ [○]
type of plant: SlTSh
flowering season: l. spring
flower colour: orange-scarlet
height: 90 cm/3 ft
*½E

If several specimens of this large-flowered azalea are planted closely together a good, ground-covering group can be formed. When individual plants eventually become too large, they can easily be moved to another site, as quite mature shrubs. The leaves that remain on this plant in winter take on attractive coppery tints. A partially shaded site preserves the brilliant flower colour and lessens the likelihood of frost and wind damage.

Acid soils – Autumn foliage.

HOSTA fortunei
[species of Plantain Lily]

◑ [○]
type of plant: HP
flowering season: summer
flower colour: lilac
height: 60-75 cm/2-2½ ft

More workaday than some of its variegated relations, *H. fortunei* is, nevertheless, attractive with its long-stalked, ribbed leaves packed solidly into a weed-proof clump. It grows most luxuriantly in a rich, damp soil; partial or full shade tends to ensure that the moist conditions that this plant enjoys are maintained even during sunny weather. *H. fortunei*'s flowers are carried well above its foliage.

Damp and wet soils – Dense shade – Green foliage.

ASTILBE×arendsii e.g. 'Rheinland' ★
[form of False Goat's Beard]

◑ [○]
type of plant: HP
flowering season: summer
flower colour: pink
height: 60 cm/2 ft

Apart from their provision of excellent ground-cover, especially in damp and boggy soils, the astilbes in general have lovely, ferny foliage and nice, strong-stemmed plumes of flowers. The seed-heads of the latter may either be left standing to decorate the garden in winter or be cut for use indoors. *A.×a.* 'Rheinland' flowers earlier than many astilbe hybrids. *A.×a.* 'Peach Blossom' is a taller, light pink variety.

Damp and wet soils – Green foliage – Cutting.

TELLIMA grandiflora ★

◑ [○]
type of plant: HP
flowering season: mid-spring to e. summer
flower colour: pale green changing to pink
height: 45-60 cm/1½-2 ft
E

The spreading clumps of scalloped leaves produced by this plant let few weeds get past the seedling stage. In winter the foliage becomes mottled with brown or, if it has been grown in sun, pink. Unfortunately, slugs find the leaves very attractive. Ideally, *T. grandiflora* should be given a moisture-retentive soil and a shady site, where it may seed itself quite freely. It is, however, also suitable for quite dry positions. The purple-leaved form of this plant – *T. g.* 'Purpurea' – is becoming more readily available.

Clay – Dry shade – Green foliage – Autumn foliage – Green flowers.

EUONYMUS fortunei (syn. *E. radicans*) e.g. 'Vegetus' ★

◑ [○]
type of plant: HSh
height: 30-60 cm/1-2 ft
E

For ground-cover purposes, this is one of the best of the increasingly popular *E. fortunei* cultivars. It has a trailing, carpeting habit of growth. Although it does not produce variegated leaves like, for example, *E. f.* 'Silver Queen' (see p. 137), it does bear numerous, bright orange seeds in creamy capsules. It will grow in a wide variety of soil types and it can be persuaded to climb nearby supports. However, it is probably best when allowed to sprawl along the ground.

Chalk – Atmospheric pollution – Containers – Fruit.

DICENTRA formosa

◑ [○]
type of plant: HP
flowering season: l. spring to e. summer
flower colour: pink
height: 30-45 cm/1-1½ ft

A cool and shady site suits this plant perfectly. Under such conditions it produces quantities of graceful, ferny foliage which cover an area of about 60 sq cm/2 sq ft. Some nurseries stock the much darker-flowered *D. f.* 'Adrian Bloom'.

Green foliage.

RHODODENDRON impeditum
◑[○]
type of plant: HSh
flowering season: spring
flower colour: purplish blue
height: 30 cm/1 ft
˙E

This dwarf rhododendron is thickly clothed in
1 cm/½ in long, grey-green leaves. It is dense and
dome-shaped and it covers the ground closely.
Like many rhododendrons with small leaves,
R. impeditum is tolerant of an open, sunny
position, provided that the soil is moisture-
retentive. This is normally a very free-flowering
plant.
  Acid soils – Containers – Grey, etc. leaves.

ASTILBE chinensis pumila
[form of False Goat's Beard]
◑[○]
type of plant: HP
flowering season: midsummer to e. autumn
flower colour: rose-purple
height: 23-30 cm/9-12 in

At the other end of the scale from *A. taquetii*
'Superba' (see p. 106) and considerably smaller
than almost all the *A. × arendsii* cultivars (for an
example of which, see p. 184) is this plant with its
neat, dense carpet of feathery leaves. Like most
astilbes it thrives in moisture-retentive and damp
soils, and it is a good bog plant.
  Damp and wet soils – Green foliage.

AJUGA pyramidalis
[Pyramidal Bugle]
◑[○]
type of plant: HP
flowering season: l. spring
flower colour: blue + purple
height: 15-23 cm/6-9 in
E

Not a foliage plant like the popular forms of
A. reptans, the pyramidal bugle is, however,
similarly ground-covering and with much more
conspicuous flowers. These nestle between the
spiralling purple bracts and are of a strikingly
bright blue. A moisture-retentive soil is essential
for good, thick growth.
  Clay.

LOBELIA erinus e.g. 'Cambridge Blue'
◑[○]
type of plant: HHA
flowering season: l. spring to e. autumn
flower colour: light blue
height: 15 cm/6 in

The compact forms of lobelia shown in this and the
following two photographs are suitable for
short-term ground-cover. They grow into dense
hemispheres of foliage and are very free-flowering
plants. *L. r.* 'Rosamund' is a departure from the
classic lobelia colouring of cultivars like
'Cambridge Blue' and 'Crystal Palace'. The last
variety has dark, bronzy leaves to accompany its
deep blue flowers. A moderately rich, moist soil
and some shelter (usually in the form of dappled
shade) produce good growth. There are trailing
varieties of this plant, such as *L. e.* 'Sapphire' for
use in window boxes, hanging baskets and (*contd*)

LOBELIA erinus e.g. 'Crystal Palace'
◑[○]
type of plant: HHA
flowering season: l. spring to e. autumn
flower colour: dark blue
height: 15 cm/6 in

See preceding plant.

(contd)
similar containers.
  Paving – Red, etc. leaves (*L. e.* 'Crystal Palace'
only).

LOBELIA erinus e.g. 'Rosamund'
◑[○]
type of plant: HHA
flowering season: l. spring to e. autumn
flower colour: red + white
height: 15 cm/6 in

See *L. e.* 'Cambridge Blue', left.

PRIMULA×pruhoniciana (syn. *P.×juliana*)
'Wanda'

◑ [○]
type of plant: HP
flowering season: spring
flower colour: crimson-purple
height: 10 cm/4 in

P.×p. 'Wanda' carries richly coloured flowers just
above its clump-forming, dark green leaves. It is a
popular and early-flowering plant (some blooms
may appear before the onset of spring) which is
easily established in any reasonably fertile,
moisture-retentive soil. It often increases quickly
but, in any case, individual plants may be expected
to spread about 30-45 cm/1-1½ ft wide.

Acid soils.

LYSIMACHIA nummularia
[Creeping Jenny]

◑ [○]
type of plant: HP
flowering season: summer
flower colour: yellow
height: 2-5 cm/1-2 in
E

In the wild, this plant is found in damp, shady
places and for the lushest growth and longest,
trailing stems, these conditions should be imitated
in the garden. However, a drier soil and some sun
produces denser leafiness and, therefore, better
ground-cover. Wherever it is grown this plant is
likely to spread widely (up to 90 cm/3 ft or so). *L. n.*
'Aurea' is a yellow-leaved and less vigorous variety
of the species.

Clay – Damp and wet soils.

**Additional plants, featured elsewhere in this
book, that are suitable for ground-cover**

◑ [○] partial shade (or sun)
ANGELICA archangelica: 1.2-2.4 m (p. 199)
SKIMMIA japonica: 90-150 cm (p. 271)
FILIPENDULA purpurea: 90-120 cm (p. 77)
RODGERSIA pinnata e.g. 'Superba'★: 90-120 cm
  (p. 77)
RODGERSIA podophylla: 90-120 cm (p. 172)
RODGERSIA tabularis: 90-120 cm (p. 184)
SKIMMIA japonica 'Foremanii': 90-120 cm
  (p. 208)
RHODODENDRON (AZALEA) e.g.
  'Hinodegiri': 90 cm (p. 137)
PRIMULA florindae: 75-120 cm (p. 77)
DRYOPTERIS filix-mas: 60-120 cm (p. 80)
SKIMMIA japonica 'Rubella': 60-90 cm (p. 39)
HOSTA undulata★: 60-75 cm (p. 153)
ASTILBE×arendsii e.g. 'Fanal': 60-75 cm (p. 184)
ASTILBE×arendsii e.g. 'White Gloria': 60 cm
  (p. 78)
ASTRANTIA major: 60 cm (p. 283)
ASTRANTIA maxima: 60 cm (p. 251)
HOSTA sieboldiana★: 60 cm (p. 167)
HOSTA 'Thomas Hogg': 60 cm (p. 78)
ANTHERICUM liliago: 45-60 cm (p. 251)
HOSTA fortunei 'Albopicta': 45-60 cm (p. 154)
HOSTA plantaginea: 45-60 cm (p. 271)
IRIS foetidissima: 45-60 cm (p. 208)
ONOCLEA sensibilis: 45-60 cm (p. 185)
×HEUCHERELLA 'Bridget Bloom': 45 cm
  (p. 251)
EUONYMUS fortunei e.g. 'Silver Queen':
  30-60 cm (p. 137)
MENTHA rotundifolia 'Variegata': 30-60 cm
  (p. 154)
RHODODENDRON Hybrid e.g. 'Jenny':
  30-60 cm (p. 40)
EPIMEDIUM×rubrum: 30 cm (p. 81)
PRIMULA denticulata: 30 cm (p. 40)
SAXIFRAGA umbrosa: 23-30 cm (p. 185)
CONVALLARIA majalis: 15-23 cm (p. 272)
LONICERA japonica 'Aureoreticulata': 15-20 cm
  (p. 153)
LONICERA japonica halliana★: 15-20 cm (p. 270)
LONICERA periclymenum 'Belgica': 15-20 cm
  (p. 270)
LONICERA periclymenum 'Serotina': 15-20 cm
  (p. 271)
LOBELIA erinus e.g. 'String of Pearls': 15 cm
  (p. 144)
PARTHENOCISSUS henryana: 15 cm (p. 153)
AJUGA reptans e.g. 'Burgundy Glow': 10-15 cm
  (p. 172)
PRIMULA vulgaris: 10-15 cm (p. 41)
AJUGA reptans e.g. 'Variegata': 8-10 cm (p. 154)
NIEREMBERGIA repens: 5 cm (p. 144)

LUZULA maxima (syn. *L. sylvatica*)
[species of Woodrush]

◑
type of plant: HP
flowering season: l. spring to e. summer
flower colour: buff
height: 30-45 cm/1-1½ ft
E

This plant makes very good ground-cover in the
wilder and rougher parts of gardens; it should not
be allowed to encroach upon more decorative
plants that are weaker than itself. Its vigour means
that it can cope with a wide variety of growing
conditions, but acid, moisture-retentive soils suit
it best. Nurseries with a good selection of grasses
and grass-like plants may stock the less invasive,
variegated form of this rush.

Acid soils – Dry shade.

GERANIUM macrorrhizum e.g. 'Album'★
[form of Cranesbill]

◑
type of plant: HP
flowering season: l. spring to midsummer
flower colour: pinkish white
height: 30-40 cm/12-15 in
½E

G. m. 'Album' is an outstandingly effective
smotherer of weeds about which no apologies as to
lack of decorativeness need be made. Some of the
leaves, including those on the flower stalks, are
deciduous; they become brightly coloured in most
autumns. In winter, only the evergreen leaves
remain and they form a dense, fairly low carpet of
cover. All the leaves are strongly aromatic. The
blush colour of the flowers is perfectly
complemented by the soft red of the surrounding
calyces and the fresh green of the foliage.

Autumn foliage – Aromatic leaves.

OMPHALODES cappadocica

◑

type of plant: HP
flowering season: l. spring to e. summer
flower colour: clear blue
height: 15-23 cm/6-9 in

Although otherwise rather unremarkable, this is
an eye-catching plant when in bloom. Its
spreading clumps of foliage are an appropriately
unobtrusive background for the beautiful blue of
its flowers which are produced over a number of
weeks. This is a woodland plant which prefers a
peaty, moisture-retentive soil in dappled shade.
Paving.

BLECHNUM penna-marina MC

◑

type of plant: HF
height: 15 cm/6 in
E

Both decorative and useful, this dainty little fern
grows densely enough to prevent most weeds from
appearing in its midst. It holds its fertile fronds
erectly above slowly spreading roots which are
most at home in acid or neutral soils and moist,
cool sites.

Acid soils – Paving – Green foliage.

CASSIOPE lycopodioides

◑

type of plant: HSh
flowering season: spring
flower colour: white
height: 5-8 cm/2-3 in
*E

As a change from the more usual heaths and
heathers, there is this related plant. Its close-knit
mat of prostrate stems and overlapping, scaly
leaves covers the ground well. Gardeners who live
in the cooler, damper parts of the country have the
right conditions for growing this plant. A
lime-free, humus-y soil is essential.
Acid soils.

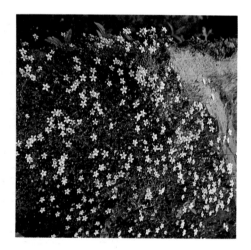

**ARENARIA balearica
[species of Sandwort]**

◑

type of plant: HP
flowering season: l. spring to e. summer
flower colour: white
height: 2-5 cm/1-2 in
E

A. balearica is a welcome exception to the general
rule that small, mat-forming plants require full
sun and a dry soil. This plant actually prefers
partial shade and some moisture (although the
drainage must be good). It grows well when
covering a north-facing rock or low wall. It is also
suitable for planting in the crevices between
paving stones since it can be walked on quite
frequently without any ill effect.
Paving.

**Additional plants, featured elsewhere in this
book, that are suitable for ground-cover**

◑ partial shade
ARUNCUS dioicus: 1.2-1.8 m (p. 79)
RHODODENDRON williamsianum★: 90-150 cm
(p. 138)
POLYSTICHUM setiferum 'Divisilobum':
75-120 cm (p. 185)
ATHYRIUM filix-femina: 75 cm (p. 185)
POLYSTICHUM aculeatum: 60-105 cm (p. 186)
MILIUM effusum 'Aureum'★: 60-90 cm (p. 177)
SMILACINA racemosa: 60-90 cm (p. 186)
HOSTA fortunei 'Aurea': 45-60 cm (p. 177)
BLECHNUM spicant: 30-45 cm (p. 43)
GERANIUM macrorrhizum e.g. 'Ingwersen's
Variety': 30-40 cm (p. 200)
POLYPODIUM vulgare: 15-30 cm (p. 81)
HOUTTUYNIA cordata 'Plena': 15-23 cm (p. 79)
CYCLAMEN neopolitanum: 10-15 cm (p. 81)
SHORTIA uniflora: 10-15 cm (p. 45)

BRUNNERA macrophylla (syn.
Anchusa myosotidiflora)★

◑ ●

type of plant: HP
flowering season: l. spring to e. summer
flower colour: blue
height: 45 cm/1½ ft

The glorious, bright blue of this plant shines out
from the shaded sites where it grows most
luxuriantly and seeds itself most prolifically. Its
large, rough leaves are attractive in spring but both
in the less readily available, variegated form and in
the species itself, they become coarser and
shabbier as the year progresses. However, they
remain good ground-cover throughout their
growing season. This plant needs a moist soil and
in dry, shady sites the clumps of foliage are much
smaller and less dense.

Dense shade – Green foliage – Cutting.

PACHYSANDRA terminalis ★

◐ ●

type of plant: HSh
flowering season: mid-spring
flower colour: white
height: 23-30 cm/9-12 in
*E

P. terminalis makes a neat, ground-covering carpet of attractively arranged leaves. Apart from its dislike of limy soils, it is a very tolerant plant which will do well even underneath trees and large shrubs. Its stems do sometimes become too sprawling in dense shade, but pinching out the growing tips usually rectifies this fault. There is a variegated form of this sub-shrub (see p. 155). The flowers of both plants are not particularly decorative but they do have a sweet fragrance.

 Acid soils – Dry shade – Dense shade – Green foliage – Fragrant flowers.

PULMONARIA angustifolia
[Blue Cowslip, species of Lungwort]

◐ ●

type of plant: HP
flowering season: spring
flower colour: royal blue
height: 23-30 cm/9-12 in

This lungwort can grow so lustily in a cool, moist corner that it may interfere with other, nearby plants. In general, however, it presents few problems and it solves others by covering the ground well with its clumps of dark leaves. In bud, the flowers are a pretty pink which blends nicely with the pure, bright blue of the open blooms.

TIARELLA cordifolia ★
[Foam Flower]

◐ ●

type of plant: HP
flowering season: l. spring to e. summer
flower colour: white
height:23-30 cm/9-12 in
E

During autumn and winter the virtually evergreen leaves of this surface-spreading plant become suffused with bronze, the colour extending outwards from the veins of the foliage. In a moisture-retentive soil and shaded site these leaves form a dense, weed-excluding carpet. In drier sites this plant grows less thickly, but it is usually satisfactory beneath trees and shrubs if some moisture is present.

 Green foliage – Autumn foliage.

EPIMEDIUM grandiflorum (syn.
E. macranthum) **'Rose Queen'**
[form of Barrenwort or Bishop's Hat]

◐ ●

type of plant: HP
flowering season: l. spring to e. summer
flower colour: deep pink
height: 20-30 cm/9-12 in
E/½E

E. g. 'Rose Queen' has unusually large, deeply coloured flowers (see p. 187 for an illustration of the flowers of a barrenwort). In spring the leaves are reddish; in autumn they become bronzed. This plant will tolerate dry shade but it is best in a reasonably moist soil. It takes a year or two to become established, after which it continues to grow fairly slowly.

 Dry shade – Red, etc. leaves – Green foliage – Autumn foliage – Cutting.

LAMIUM maculatum 'Roseum'
[form of Spotted Dead Nettle]

◐ ●

type of plant: HP
flowering season: l. spring to e. summer
flower colour: pink
height: 15-23 cm/6-9 in
E

Very much less invasive than the notorious – but sometimes useful – *L. galeobdolon* 'Variegatum' (see p. 81), this plant spreads its small, white-striped leaves neatly over about 45 sq cm/1½ sq ft. Its flowers are a clearer, less strident colour than those of most red- or pink-flowered dead nettles. *L. m.* 'Roseum' grows well in any soil; it can be kept dense and tidy by being cut right back after flowering.

 Clay – Dry shade – Dense shade – Variegated leaves.

PHLOX stolonifera alba NA

◐ ●

type of plant: HP
flowering season: spring
flower colour: white
height: 15 cm/6 in

This plant forms prostrate ground-cover and is excellent for shaded banks. 'Blue Ridge' is icy blue, 'Pink Ridge' a soft lavender pink. Average garden soil is sufficient, but chalk should be avoided.

OMPHALODES verna
[Blue-eyed Mary]

◐ ●

type of plant: HP
flowering season: spring
flower colour: clear blue + white
height: 10-15 cm/4-6 in

In moist, well drained soils the long-stalked leaves of *O. verna* make fairly good ground-cover. A tendency to invasiveness can usually be checked by placing this plant in a woodland setting and giving it some grass to compete with. In certain years, the small, white-eyed flowers may appear before the beginning of spring.

GAULTHERIA procumbens★
[Partridge Berry, Creeping Wintergreen, Checkerberry]

◐ ●

type of plant: SlTSh
flowering season: summer
flower colour: white or pinkish
height: 8-15 cm/3-6 in
⁕E

As dense and as effective a ground-coverer as, for instance, *Cotoneaster dammeri* (see p. 111), this spreading shrub is, unfortunately, rather fussier about the growing conditions it requires. It is not suitable for limy or heavy soils and ideally it should have a constant supply of moisture retained by, for instance, leaf-mould or peat. Both the bright red, edible berries and the glossy leaves of this plant have the medicinal smell of wintergreen.

  Acid soils – Dense shade – Aromatic leaves – Fruit.

Additional plants, featured elsewhere in this book, that are suitable for ground-cover

◐ ● partial or full shade
GAULTHERIA shallon: 1.2-1.8 m (p. 106)
OSMUNDA regalis: 1.2-1.8 m (p. 73)
MAHONIA aquifolium: 90-120 cm (p. 112)
RODGERSIA pinnata e.g. 'Superba'★: 90-120 cm
  (p. 77)
RODGERSIA podophylla: 90-120 cm (p. 172)
RODGERSIA tabularis: 90-120 cm (p. 184)
SKIMMIA japonica 'Foremanii': 90-120 cm
  (p. 208)
ANEMONE×hybrida e.g. 'Louise Uhink'★:
  90-105 cm (p. 51)
PRUNUS laurocerasus e.g. 'Otto Luyken'★: 90 cm
  (p. 107)
POLYGONATUM×hybridum: 75-90 cm (p. 252)
DRYOPTERIS dilatata: 60-120 cm (p. 186)
×FATSHEDERA lizei: 60-90 cm (p. 136)
HOSTA fortunei: 60-75 cm (p. 113)
JASMINUM nudiflorum: 60 cm (p. 277)
ANEMONE×hybrida e.g. 'September Charm':
  45-60 cm (p. 107)
EUPHORBIA robbiae: 45-60 cm (p. 81)
HELLEBORUS orientalis Hybrids: 45-60 cm
  (p. 279)
IRIS foetidissima: 45-60 cm (p. 208)
RUBUS tricolor: 30-60 cm (p. 108)
SARCOCOCCA humilis: 30-60 cm (p. 273)
HYPERICUM calycinum: 30-45 cm (p. 108)
LAMIUM galeobdolon 'Variegatum': 30 cm (p. 81)
TIARELLA wherryi: 25-40 cm (p. 187)
VINCA major: 23-45 cm (p. 82)
VINCA major 'Variegata': 23-45 cm (p. 153)
HEDERA helix 'Hibernica': 23-30 cm (p. 109)
PULMONARIA saccharata: 23-30 cm (p. 155)
PACHYSANDRA terminalis 'Variegata': 23 cm
  (p. 155)
SYMPHYTUM grandiflorum: 23 cm (p. 110)
CONVALLARIA majalis: 15-23 cm (p. 272)
VIOLA cornuta e.g. 'Alba': 15-23 cm (p. 110)
VIOLA cornuta e.g. 'Jersey Gem': 15-23 cm
  (p. 143)
CHIASTOPHYLLUM oppositifolium: 15 cm
  (p. 110)
LAMIUM maculatum 'Aureum': 15 cm (p. 178)
LAMIUM maculatum 'Beacon Silver': 15 cm
  (p. 82)
VACCINIUM vitis-idaea: 15 cm (p. 111)
VINCA minor: 15 cm (p. 82)
VINCA minor e.g. 'Alba'★: 15 cm (p. 111)
CORNUS canadensis: 10-15 cm (p. 111)

Climbing plants (including shrubs needing support in order to grow upright)

Some beautiful and popular plants are climbers. The remarkable range of that most popular genus of climbers, *Clematis*, contains an impressive variety of flower colours and shapes, and there must be a climbing or rambling rose to suit nearly every site.

Considering the overall size which many climbers achieve, they take up surprisingly little space on the ground. For this reason, they are especially useful for providing both height and sizeable blocks of colour in small gardens. In such gardens, the branches and roots of the majority of small-sized trees and medium-sized shrubs consume too much valuable space. A really vigorous climber such as *Parthenocissus quinquefolia* (Virginia creeper) will, however, usually produce a limited depth of growth on its support, yet it can easily reach the top of a three-storeyed building.

Climbing plants are, perhaps, most commonly used to clothe bare walls or fences. In small, walled gardens the wall-space can exceed the area of the garden itself. By covering the walls with climbers the amount and variety of vegetation are significantly increased. When surrounding a garden with climbers in this manner, it is worth bearing in mind that plants, including other nearby climbers, that bloom profusely or that have interesting foliage can be set off particularly well by a plain, green-leaved climber. *Hedera helix* 'Hibernica' (Irish ivy), for example, has inconspicuous flowers, and its big, bold leaves are a uniform dark green, but it provides a most satisfactory contrast to 'busier' variegated leaves and more exotic flowers.

Even though some climbers can grow to remarkable heights, there is no need to reserve them for very large walls. Most climbing plants can be cut back quite successfully and kept within bounds in this way. Many plants will adapt themselves to lower supports by, for instance, building up mounds of growth upon themselves. Alternatively, vigorous climbers, including the so-called mile-a-minute or Russian vine, can be allowed to run rampantly over, for example, large balconies or unsightly garages, where they will produce curtains of exuberant foliage.

So many of the most popular climbing plants are long-lived that annual climbers are often overlooked. Sweet peas can make as pretty and as fragrant a screen as most scented, climbing roses; the leaves of *Humulus scandens* 'Variegatus' (a form of hop) are just as attractive as the foliage of some variegated ivies; and the fruits borne by ornamental gourds are as interesting, in their own way, as *Clematis tangutica*'s fluffy seed-heads. The short lifespan and rapid growth of annual climbers are obvious advantages in circumstances where a covering or screen is wanted quickly but not permanently.

Apart from covering walls and fences and screening unsightly objects, climbers are often used to cover pergolas or arches. They are less frequently seen growing through other plants. Yet this can be a method of achieving particularly dramatic combinations of flower colour, or of enlivening a plant which, by itself, is rather dull or has a very limited season of interest. (Climbers should not be grown through shrubs and trees – or other climbers – that are much less vigorous than themselves, in case the weaker plants should suffer.) Some climbing plants also make good ground-cover, provided they are given some initial support or encouraged to root by having their shoots pegged down. (For suitable plants see the 'Ground-cover' list.)

Although many climbing plants require wires or netting for support, there are some climbers that produce suckers or aerial roots which cling to surfaces. Self-clinging plants in this list are: *Campsis radicans*, *Euonymus fortunei* 'Silver Queen', all varieties of *Hedera* (ivy), and all species and varieties of *Parthenocissus*.

As usual, figures denote ultimate heights. Most climbers can, however, be easily contained, and many will adapt themselves to quite low walls, fences, etc.

WISTERIA sinensis (syn. *W. chinensis*)
[Chinese Wisteria]

○
type of plant: HCl
flowering season: l. spring to e. summer
flower colour: violet-blue
height: 18-30 m/60-100 ft

Good nurseries sometimes offer specimens of this plant which have been trained as standards. They make most attractive – but expensive – small trees (usually not more than about 1.5 m/5 ft high). Given only normal pruning, however, *W. sinensis* will twine its way high up trees and house walls. It needs a rich moist soil, and some shelter to protect its flower buds from frost damage.

Clay – Containers (*when grown as a standard*) – Fragrant flowers.

CAMPSIS radicans
[species of Trumpet Creeper or Trumpet Vine]

○
type of plant: SITCl
flowering season: l. summer to e. autumn
flower colour: orange + red
height: 12 m/40 ft

The various species and forms of trumpet creeper must have a really warm site to become established fairly quickly and to flower at all well. Their stems are equipped with aerial roots which will cling to the surface of walls. *C. radicans* is a vigorous plant when grown in rich soil and a sunny position. It can be used for ground-cover, on hot – but not dry – banks and similar places, where it will be about 90 cm/3 ft high.

Ground-cover.

PASSIFLORA caerulea MC
[Common Passion Flower]

○
type of plant: HHCl
flowering season: summer to e. autumn
flower colour: white + purple
height: 6-9 m/20-30 ft

The interesting flowers of this vigorous climber are, unfortunately, not very long-lasting. They tend to be produced over quite a long period but only a few blooms appear at any one time. They are slightly scented. A well drained, rather poor soil suits this plant and it should be given a warm position. It will cling to support such as wire netting by means of tendrils. Its orange fruits rarely ripen in British gardens.

Containers.

ROSA (Rambler) e.g. 'Wedding Day'
[form of Rose]

○

type of plant: HCl
flowering season: summer
flower colour: white
height: 6-7.5 m/20-25 ft

R. 'Wedding Day' is sometimes classified as a climber and occasionally as a 'musk rambler'. It grows very strongly and may be trained into mature and established trees. Its flowers open from yellow buds; they have the rich, strong scent of orange-blossom. An even more vigorous climber is the white-flowered *R. filipes* 'Kiftsgate'. Both these plants are far too large and wide-spreading for small gardens. Ideally, they should be grown in well cultivated, fertile loams.

   Atmospheric pollution – Fragrant flowers.

ROSA (Climber) e.g. 'New Dawn' ★
[form of Rose]

○

type of plant: HCl
flowering season: summer
flower colour: silvery pink
height: 4.5-6 m/15-20 ft

This moderately vigorous rose blooms almost continuously during the summer months with two main flushes of flowers early and late in the season. It has a light, sweet fragrance. Its very thorny, rambler-like growths are best trained over pergolas, pillars and similar supports rather than tied against walls. A well drained, moisture-retentive and fertile soil suits this plant best.

   Cutting – Fragrant flowers.

SOLANUM crispum 'Glasnevin' (syn. *S. c.* 'Autumnale') sc **NA MC**
[form of Chilean Potato Tree]

○

type of plant: SlTSh
flowering season: e. summer to mid-autumn
flower colour: bluish purple + yellow
height: 4.5-6 m/15-20 ft
½E

The long stems of this scrambling shrub need to be tied to wires or to a trellis to keep them upright. They are sometimes killed by frost in cold districts, although the plant itself will survive all but the most severe British winters (provided it is given a warm, sheltered site and a well drained soil in the first place). This particular variety of *S. crispum* has an exceptionally long flowering season. The largest number of blooms appear in early summer and at the very beginning of autumn.

   Containers.

ROSA (Rambler) e.g. 'Albertine'
[form of Rose]

○

type of plant: HCl
flowering season: summer
flower colour: pale pink
height: 4.5 m/15 ft

Like many ramblers, *R.* 'Albertine' is susceptible to mildew, particularly if it is grown against a wall. Plants treated as free-standing bushes or trained over pergolas and arches are much less troubled by this fungal disease. (As a bush, *R.* 'Albertine' grows about 2.1 m/7 ft high and sprawls widely.) This vigorous rose produces richly fragrant flowers, the overall colour of which is made up of two shades of pink – one darker than the other.

   Atmospheric pollution – Cutting – Fragrant flowers.

COBAEA scandens
[Cup and Saucer Plant, Cathedral Bells]

○

type of plant: HHACl
flowering season: midsummer to mid-autumn
flower colour: purple + green
height: 3-6 m/10-20 ft

The remarkable speed with which this plant grows makes it useful for covering even quite large areas for a short time. It will attach itself to wire netting and other forms of support by means of tendrils. The 5-8 cm/2-3 in long flowers are, at first, greenish white and then deep purple; the saucer-like calyces at the base of the fused petals remain green throughout the flowering season. *C. s.* 'Alba' is a variety with very pale green blooms. These plants need a well drained soil and they will grow fastest in a sheltered site.

   Cutting.

ECCREMOCARPUS scaber
[Chilean Glory Flower]

○

type of plant: HHA/PCl
flowering season: summer to e. autumn
flower colour: orange-red
height: 3-4.5 m/10-15 ft
½E/D

Only in the mildest areas of Britain will this rapid climber produce persistent, woody stems. Elsewhere its top growth will usually die in winter and be renewed each spring. *E. scaber* is often treated as an annual. However it is grown, it should be given a light but moisture-retentive soil and support should be provided for its tendrils to cling to. It normally produces large numbers of brightly coloured, tubular flowers.

IPOMOEA rubro-caerulea (syn. *I. tricolor*, *Pharbitis tricolor*) e.g. 'Heavenly Blue'
[form of Morning Glory]

○

type of plant: HHACl
flowering season: midsummer to e. autumn
flower colour: blue
height: 2.4-3 m/8-10 ft

The beautiful sky-blue of this twining climber is the colour most often associated with morning glory, but there are also a few forms with pink and with striped flowers, and some varieties, such as 'Scarlet O'Hara', have red blooms. Unless these plants are warm and sheltered they do not grow or flower well, but under suitable conditions they usually climb rapidly and bloom profusely over a long period. A light, fertile soil is ideal.

Containers.

LATHYRUS latifolius
[Everlasting Pea, Perennial Pea]

○

type of plant: HPCl
flowering season: summer to e. autumn
flower colour: red or white or violet
height: 2.4-3 m/8-10 ft

The flowers of the perennial pea are a good deal simpler and less frilled than those of the more commonly seen varieties of annual, sweet pea; they are usually a purplish pink or red and always scentless. Well drained soils of various types are suitable and *L. latifolius* is especially vigorous in a fertile soil. Its tendrilled growths, which die back each winter, may be allowed to sprawl along the ground, where they will form a wide, entwined mass, covered with soft green foliage and about 60 cm/2 ft high.

Chalk – Ground-cover – Containers – Cutting.

LATHYRUS odoratus e.g. 'Winston Churchill'
[form of Sweet Pea]

○

type of plant: HACl
flowering season: summer to e. autumn
flower colour: crimson
height: 1.8-3 m/6-10 ft

British seed catalogues list many different varieties of sweet pea. *L. o.* 'Winston Churchill' is a brightly coloured form with fluted petals but little or no scent. (Two especially fragrant varieties are shown on p. 255.) Mixtures as well as separate colours are readily available and vigorous varieties, such as 'Galaxy Mixed' (see p. 213), can be used to cover fences and trellis-work. All sweet peas make excellent cut flowers. These plants climb by means of tendrils and they will grow most strongly in well dug, fertile soils.

Containers – Cutting.

TROPAEOLUM majus e.g. 'Tall Mixed'
[form of Nasturtium]

○

type of plant: HACl
flowering season: summer to e. autumn
flower colour: mixed – red, orange, yellow
height: 1.5-2.1 m/5-7 ft

Many of the most popular forms of nasturtiums are low-growing, trailing plants but a few climbing varieties can also be obtained. The climbing forms have leaf-stalks which will clasp supports such as canes and wires. All forms of *T. majus* are very easily grown plants that flower particularly well in poor, dry soils. Both the trailing and the climbing types can be used to cover hot, sunny banks.

Hot, dry soils.

THUNBERGIA alata 'Mixed'
[form of Black-eyed Susan]

○

type of plant: HHACl
flowering season: summer to e. autumn
flower colour: mixed – cream, orange,
  buff + dark brown
height: 90-180 cm/3-6 ft

This twining plant is often included in the greenhouse section of seed catalogues and, if it is to be grown outdoors, it needs a sheltered position in full sun. Any well drained soil is suitable. Forms of *T. alata* can be planted in hanging baskets as well as trained up canes and similar supports.

TROPAEOLUM peregrinum (syn. *T. canariense*)
MC
[Canary Creeper]

○ [◐]

type of plant: HACl
flowering season: summer to e. autumn
flower colour: yellow
height: 1.8-3 m/6-10 ft

√

The pale, lobed leaves of this fast-growing climber make a pretty background for the fringed flowers. As long as the site is fairly sheltered, *T. peregrinum* can be grown on a north wall, although there will be even more blooms in sunnier positions. A well drained, fertile soil that does not dry out too readily suits this plant best. Its subsidiary stalks need some sort of support around which to coil themselves.

Green foliage.

HYDRANGEA petiolaris ★

○ ◑
type of plant: HCl
flowering season: summer
flower colour: white
height: 15-18 m/50-60 ft
√

Ideally, this self-clinging climber should be grown on a wall that faces west and it should be given a fertile, moisture-retentive soil. However, it is a tough and vigorous plant that will do quite well in most sites and soils. It usually takes some time to become established. Its aerial roots will fasten themselves into soil if given some initial encouragement. When grown as ground-cover *H. petiolaris* will slowly thicken into a 60 cm/2 ft high carpet of rich green foliage. In autumn the leaves turn clear yellow before falling.

Atmospheric pollution – Ground-cover – Autumn foliage.

POLYGONUM baldschuanicum MC
[Russian Vine, Mile-a-Minute]

○ ◑
type of plant: HCl
flowering season: midsummer to e. autumn
flower colour: white
height: 12-15 m/40-50 ft
√√

Established specimens of the Russian vine can grow over 4.5 m/15 ft in a single season and this makes them useful for covering unattractive sheds and similar, large, ugly objects. The rampant, twining growths withstand very hard pruning. *P. baldschuanicum* can be planted in any soil, although its famously fast growth will begin soonest under reasonably well drained and fertile conditions.

CLEMATIS montana

○ ◑
type of plant: HCl
flowering season: l. spring
flower colour: white
height: 6-10.5 m/20-35 ft
√

Sunny or partially shaded sites are equally suitable for *C. montana* and its varieties but a combination of shade at the roots and sun on the upper growth produces the best results. A moist, fertile and preferably alkaline soil is ideal and encourages these very vigorous climbers to grow quickly only a year or two after planting. Both *C. montana* itself and its pink-flowered variety, *C. m. rubens* (see right), have vanilla-scented flowers. The young leaves of the latter plant are a purplish bronze colour. *C. m.* 'Tetrarose' (see second right) has slightly larger flowers than normal; its new *(contd)*

CLEMATIS montana rubens

○ ◑
type of plant: HCl
flowering season: l. spring to e. summer
flower colour: pink
height: 6-10.5 m/20-35 ft
√

See preceding plant.

(contd)
foliage is less colourful than that of *C. m. rubens*. All these plants have twining leaf-stalks which will attach themselves easily to support such as wire netting. *C. montana* and its forms can also make large, tangled mats of ground-cover about 60 cm/2 ft high and over 3 m/10 ft wide.

Ground-cover – Red, etc. leaves (*C. m. rubens* only) – Fragrant flowers (*C. montana* and *C. m. rubens* only).

CLEMATIS montana e.g. 'Tetrarose'

○ ◑
type of plant: HCl
flowering season: l. spring to e. summer
flower colour: lilac-pink
height: 6-10.5 m/20-35 ft
√

See *C. montana*, left.

ROSA (Climber) e.g. 'Mme Alfred Carrière' ★
[form of Rose]

○ ◑
type of plant: HCl
flowering season: summer
flower colour: white
height: 4.5-6 m/15-20 ft
✓

The main flowering season of this very hardy rose
is summer but its richly fragrant blooms will
continue to appear in small numbers until
mid-autumn. In sunshine and a suitably fertile and
well cultivated soil this plant will grow vigorously
and bloom profusely. It will also perform well on a
north wall, provided that it is not so cold and
exposed that the wood has little chance to ripen.

Atmospheric pollution – Fragrant flowers.

CLEMATIS tangutica ★
○ ◑
type of plant: HCl
flowering season: l. summer to mid-autumn
flower colour: yellow
height: 4.5-5.4 m/15-18 ft
✓

Unlike most clematis, this vigorous species has
two major seasons of interest since both its flowers
and its long-lasting seed-heads are beautiful.
Given twigs for its tendrils to twine around,
C. tangutica will make good ground-cover, with its
long, slender stems eventually knitting into a
60 cm/2 ft high mass of greenery. A fertile,
moisture-retentive soil suits this plant best. When
it is grown upright, its roots should be in shade and
its branches in full light.

Ground-cover – Containers – Fruit.

CLEMATIS orientalis
[Orange-peel Clematis]

○ ◑
type of plant: HCl
flowering season: l. summer to mid-autumn
flower colour: yellow
height: 3.6-5.4 m/12-18 ft
✓

C. orientalis is similar to the plant shown in the
previous illustration but its leaves are greyer and
its petal-like sepals are thicker and reminiscent of
rind – hence the common name. It should be
cultivated in the same way as *C. tangutica* and it too
can be used for ground-cover. Its seed-heads are
silky and silvery grey. In very cold gardens a north
wall is not suitable for this plant and it will only
flower well in warmer positions.

Ground-cover – Containers – Fruit.

ROSA (Climber) e.g. 'Danse du Feu'
[form of Rose]

○ ◑
type of plant: HCl
flowering season: summer
flower colour: scarlet
height: 3.6 m/12 ft
✓✓

The deeply coloured blooms of this rose are most
shapely soon after opening; later they flatten and
their petals curl somewhat. Early summer is the
main flowering season but sizeable quantities of
blooms are produced on and off for several
months. Although flowering will be freest in sunny
positions, this is one of the best, readily available
climbing roses for north and east walls. It should
be given a well prepared, fertile soil.

Cutting.

CLEMATIS (Large-flowered Hybrid) e.g.
'Jackmanii Superba'

○ ◑
type of plant: HCl
flowering season: midsummer to e. autumn
flower colour: dark violet-purple
height: 2.4-4.5 m/8-15 ft

C. 'Jackmanii Superba' needs to be placed in a
prominent position if the velvety darkness of its
flowers is not be 'lost' amongst brighter colours. It
is a vigorous plant and, in common with other
large-flowered, hybrid clematis, it requires a rich,
preferably alkaline soil. It is important to shade the
roots of all these climbers from direct sunlight, but
they flower most profusely when their upper
branches are in full sun; their twining leaf-stalks
need support, such as netting, to cling to. *C.*
'Lasurstern' (see right) has large and beautifully
shaped blooms, the colour of which is enhanced by
white stamens. The strong-growing *(contd)*

CLEMATIS (Large-flowered Hybrid) e.g.
'Lasurstern' ★ MC

○ ◑
type of plant: HCl
flowering season: e. summer to mid-autumn
flower colour: purple-blue
height: 2.4-4.5 m/8-15 ft

See preceding plant

(contd)
and highly popular cultivar *C.* 'Nelly Moser' (see
next page) retains the pink markings on its large
blooms longest when it is grown facing north. *C.*
'Ville de Lyon' (see next page) does not have
especially large flowers but they are very brightly
coloured. A large-flowered, hybrid clematis with
double, white blooms is shown on p. 135.

Containers.

CLEMATIS (Large-flowered Hybrid) e.g. 'Nelly Moser'

○ ◑

type of plant: HCl
flowering season: l. spring to e. autumn
flower colour: pale mauve + deep pink
height: 2.4-3.6 m/8-12 ft
√

See *C.* 'Jackmanii Superba', previous page.

CLEMATIS (Large-flowered Hybrid) e.g. 'Ville de Lyon'

○ ◑

type of plant: HCl
flowering season: midsummer to mid-autumn
flower colour: crimson
height: 2.4-3.6 m/8-12 ft

See *C.* 'Jackmanii Superba', previous page.

CLEMATIS macropetala ★

○ ◑

type of plant: HCl
flowering season: l. spring to e. summer
flower colour: violet-blue
height: 2.4-3 m/8-10 ft
√

Although the flowers of this clematis are much less than half the size of the great, wide blooms of hybrids like 'Nelly Moser' (see second left), they are conspicuous and charming and the plants themselves are easy to grow. No regular pruning is needed. *C. macropetala* is a vigorous, bushy species. (For general comments about the cultivation of clematis, see *C.* 'Jackmanii Superba' on the previous page.)

CLEMATIS alpina (syn. *Atragene alpina*)

○ ◑

type of plant: HCl
flowering season: spring
flower colour: violet-blue
height: 1.2-1.8 m/4-6 ft
√

Many clematis look particularly attractive when grown through another plant, such as an evergreen shrub or a climbing rose. In some cases, however, the clematis overwhelms its host. This is rarely a problem with *C. alpina* which is a much less vigorous plant than, for instance, *C. macropetala* (see above). There are a few varieties of *C. alpina*, one of which has white flowers, but they are not very readily available. (For an outline of the cultivation of clematis, see *C.* 'Jackmanii Superba' on the previous page.)

LONICERA × brownii 'Fuchsoides' [form of Scarlet Trumpet Honeysuckle]

◑ [○]

type of plant: SlTCl
flowering season: l. spring and l. summer
flower colour: orange-scarlet
height: 3-4.5 m/10-15 ft
½ E/D, √

The climbing honeysuckles thrive in light shade and in moisture-retentive soils that are rich and of a rather spongy texture. Their roots should always be positioned out of direct sunlight. A few of these twining climbers, including *L. × brownii* 'Fuchsoides', lack any scent. They do, however, have very vividly coloured flowers. *L. × brownii* 'Fuchsoides' grows best in mild areas of Britain. It flowers most profusely during the earlier of the two seasons stated above.

Hedging plants

So many hedges provide shelter and privacy in such an unobtrusive way that the fact that they can be striking and attractive features in themselves is often overlooked. Of course, in some cases an unobtrusive screen or barrier is most suitable. However, one does not need to go to the lengths of elaborate topiary to produce a hedge that is decorative as well as useful.

The majority of the plants in the following list have conspicuous flowers, and a flowering hedge can, at its best, be an impressive sight. Sometimes, species or varieties are mixed: for example, different varieties of escallonia are popular choices for a mixed, flowering hedge.

A number of the plants in this list bear fruits which are as decorative as any flowers, and mixed hedges can be produced with these plants too. In many cases, the production of fruit and flowers is reduced – at least to some extent – by regular clipping. Where plenty of fruit and flowers are wanted, plants should, ideally, be grown as parts of informal hedges or screens.

Certain varietal names in this list indicate that variegated or unusually coloured foliage is an important decorative feature of some hedging plants: *Ilex aquifolium* 'Argentea Marginata', for example, is a form of common holly which has leaves edged with creamy white. There are also plants with purple leaves, plants with yellow leaves, and grey-leaved plants, and all of them can make a quite conventionally shaped hedge more than usually interesting.

All the plants in the following list can be used as informal screens or edgings which require either a minimum amount of trimming or, where necessary, only the usual pruning. Some plants are also suitable for closely clipped, formal hedges: *Lonicera nitida*, privet, yew, box, holly, Portugal laurel and common beech, for example, will all withstand frequent trimming.

Plants are a more satisfactory form of shelter from wind than solid barriers, such as walls, which often produce areas of harmful turbulence. In very exposed areas wind will cause serious structural damage to many plants; it will dry out both plants and soil; and it will reduce temperatures. All of this makes it difficult to establish young plants.

Evergreen hedges suitable for lessening the effects of cold winds in particular are mentioned in connection with winter-flowering plants (see p. 274). Some deciduous plants for the same purpose are: *Fagus sylvatica* and *F. s.*

'Purpurea', *Hippophae rhamnoides*, *Tamarix pentandra* and *T. tetrandra*.

Salt-laden winds present an especially difficult problem. Plants marked 'C' in this list are suitable as a front line of defence against strong winds in coastal districts. Even these plants may become bent and battered in exceptionally exposed positions, but they will survive.

Some gardens may need to be protected from damage by trespassers and livestock rather than wind. There are a number of prickly or thorny hedging plants that are especially suitable for this purpose and they include *Crataegus monogyna*, *Ilex aquifolium* and some of its varieties, *Hippophae rhamnoides* and the taller species and varieties of *Berberis*.

In the following list evergreen and deciduous plants are dealt with separately. If a hedge is being grown to provide privacy or to screen some unsightly object or unattractive view, then plants of the former type are usually the best choice, but established deciduous hedging plants can create almost as dense a screen with their twigs and branches alone as evergreen foliage does.

Hedges that are used to enclose and conceal may often need to be fast-growing. An indication of the rate of growth of larger plants is shown as 'height after six years' for plants grown as part of more or less formal hedges.

In small gardens particularly, it is important to bear in mind two of the drawbacks of hedges: first, hedges take up room, and second, they draw moisture and nutrients from the soil around them so that few plants can be placed close to them.

Detailed instructions about how to prepare ground for hedging and how to plant and maintain hedges are included in all good general gardening books. There is also a helpful Royal Horticultural Society pamphlet entitled *Hedges and Screens*, by F. W. Shepherd (Wisley handbook No. 17).

The clipping involved in producing formal hedges alters considerably the eventual height of some plants. This is particularly true in the case of the larger shrubs and trees. In the list below, two sets of heights have been given for each plant whose normal minimum height is more than 3 m/10 ft: the eventual height if the plant is grown as part of an informal screen or edging; and the height that the plant may be expected to reach after six years if it is trained as part of a more or less formal hedge.

Evergreen hedging plants

ESCALLONIA e.g. 'Donard Radiance' sc NA MC

○   ✕

type of plant: SlTSh
flowering season: summer to e. autumn
flower colour: red
height: 1.8-2.4 m/6-8 ft
E/½E

The upright varieties of escallonia, such as 'Donard Radiance', are especially suitable for hedging, but all the popular hybrids are densely branched shrubs. They have attractive, small flowers. In mild areas, escallonias are evergreen. When used for hedging, individual plants should be set about 75 cm/2½ ft apart and trimmed after their flowers have faded. Well drained soils of various types are suitable. In the United States, they grow satisfactorily only on the west coast.

Seaside – Atmospheric pollution – Containers – Cutting.

ERICA mediterranea (syn. *E. erigena*) e.g. 'Brightness' ★ sc NA MC
[form of Heath or Heather]

○

type of plant: SlTSh
flowering season: mid-spring to e. summer
flower colour: rose-pink
height: 90 cm/3 ft

Gardeners with a moisture-retentive, acid soil can use the taller-growing and fairly erect varieties of some heaths and heathers for hedging. *E. m.* 'Brightness' will remain bushily cone-shaped if it is clipped lightly after flowering. When grown as part of a hedge, plants should be set not more than 30 cm/1 ft apart. A white-flowered form of *E. mediterranea* is illustrated on p. 30. Both these plants will tolerate slightly alkaline conditions but they do not do well in shallow, dry soils.

Acid soils – Seaside.

SANTOLINA chamaecyparissus (syn. *S. incana*)★
[species of Lavender Cotton or Cotton Lavender]

○

type of plant: HSh
flowering season: summer
flower colour: yellow
height: 45-60 cm/1½-2 ft

The button-like flowers of this plant must be sacrificed if a really neat, dense mound of silvery foliage is wanted. Hard pruning each spring is essential if *S. chamaecyparissus* is used for hedging or edging (in which case young plants should be placed about 30-45 cm/1-1½ ft apart). A soil that drains quickly will also help thick growth. The feathery foliage has a pleasant, pungent aroma.

Chalk – Hot, dry soils – Ground-cover – Containers – Grey, etc. leaves – Aromatic leaves.

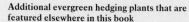

LAVANDULA spica (syn. *L. officinalis*)
'Hidcote' (syn. 'Nana Atropurpurea')★
[form of Old English Lavender]

○

type of plant: HSh
flowering season: summer to e. autumn
flower colour: deep violet
height: 30-60 cm/1-2 ft

Hedges of lavender look neat and flower well only if they are grown on light soils and clipped twice a year (after the blooms have faded, and again in spring). Even when treated in this way, they normally need replacing after six or seven years. *L. s.* 'Hidcote' is a naturally neat plant with exceptionally dark, but not especially fragrant flower spikes. Its aromatic foliage is grey-green with a silvery cast. When used for hedging individual plants should be spaced about 30 cm/1 ft apart.

Chalk – Hot, dry soils – Containers – Grey, etc. leaves – Aromatic leaves – Fragrant flowers.

OSMANTHUS heterophyllus (syn.
O. aquifolium, O. ilicifolius)

○ [◐]
type of plant: SlTSh
flowering season: autumn
flower colour: white
height: 1.8-3 m/6-10 ft

This prickly shrub will slowly make a dense and fairly wide hedge. It bears small, tubular flowers which are sweetly and strongly scented; these do not appear in large numbers unless the plant is allowed to grow freely. (When *O. heterophyllus* is used for hedging it needs an annual, spring clipping.) Most well drained soils are suitable. Young plants should be set approximately 45-60 cm/1½-2 ft apart if they are to form the basis of a hedge.

Atmospheric pollution – Fragrant flowers.

Additional evergreen hedging plants that are featured elsewhere in this book
Heights given are for plants grown as informal screens or edgings; † indicates height after six years if the plant is trained as part of a formal hedge.

○ sun
PITTOSPORUM tenuifolium: 1.8-2.4 m†,
  4.5-7.5 m (p. 180)
ESCALLONIA macrantha★: 3 m (p. 86) C
ESCALLONIA e.g. 'Apple Blossom': 1.8 m (p. 86)
HEBE brachysiphon: 1.2-1.8 m (p. 3) C
ROSMARINUS officinalis: 1.2-1.8 m (p. 196)
LAVANDULA spica: 90 cm (p. 257)
ERICA mediterranea e.g. 'W. T. Rackliff': 60 cm
  (p. 30)
LAVANDULA spica 'Vera': 60 cm (p. 100)
HYSSOPUS officinalis: 45-60 cm (p. 197)
LAVANDULA spica 'Munstead': 45-60 cm
  (p. 197)
RUTA graveolens 'Jackman's Blue': 45-60 cm
  (p. 160)
ERICA vagans e.g. 'Lyonesse': 45 cm (p. 30)
ERICA vagans e.g. 'Mrs D. F. Maxwell': 45 cm
  (p. 100)

○ [◐] sun (or partial shade)
QUERCUS ilex: 1.2-1.5 m†, 15-18 m (p. 87) C
ILEX aquifolium e.g. 'Argentea Marginata'★:
  1.8-2.4 m†, 6-9 m (p. 149)
ILEX × altaclarensis e.g. 'Golden King': 1.2-1.8
  m†, 5.4-7.5 m (p. 149)
LAURUS nobilis: 1.5-1.8 m†, 3.6-6 m (p. 134)
OLEARIA × macrodonta: 2.4-3.6 m (p. 87) C
ELAEAGNUS pungens 'Maculata': 2.4-3 m
  (p. 150)
OLEARIA × haastii: 1.8-2.7 m (p. 93) C
OSMANTHUS delavayi: 1.8-2.4 m (p. 264)
EUONYMUS japonicus 'Ovatus Aureus':
  1.5-2.1 m (p. 150)
LONICERA nitida 'Baggesen's Gold': 1.2-1.8 m
  (p. 177)
ULEX europaeus 'Plenus': 90-180 cm (p. 66) C
SENECIO laxifolius: 90-120 cm (p. 164) C

THUJA plicata (syn. *T. lobbii*)
[Western Red Cedar]

○ ◐

type of plant: HCo
height after six years: 2.4-3 m/8-10 ft
height as screen: 24-36 m/80-120 ft

The western red cedar grows almost as quickly as × *Cupressocyparis leylandii* (see right) but it is less widely used for screens and hedges. It is normally quite successful on rather shallow, chalky soils. However, deep, moisture-retentive soils produce the fastest growth. Hedges of this conifer should have their fruit-scented foliage trimmed – preferably with secateurs – in summer. Young plants for hedging need to be spaced about 60 cm/2 ft apart. When left untrimmed, *T. plicata* has a narrowly conical outline.

Chalk – Aromatic leaves.

×CUPRESSOCYPARIS leylandii
[Leyland Cypress]

○ ◐

type of plant: HCo
height after six years: 3-3.6 m/10-12 ft
height as screen: 21-30 m/70-100 ft

× *C. leylandii* is famous for its rapid rate of growth. It is a vigorous plant and, if the speed with which it can reach a substantial size has been underestimated, it may be cut back quite hard. It can be used for formal hedging – in which case shaping and clipping should be carried out in late summer. Alternatively, this conifer can be grown as a single specimen or as part of an informal screen; unclipped, it makes a broad column of greenery with a pointed top. A less vigorous, yellow-leaved form, known as × *C. l.* 'Castlewellan', is one of several readily available varieties of this plant. Any well drained soil is suitable, as long as it is of a reasonable depth.

TAXUS baccata
[Common Yew]

○ ◐

type of plant: HCo
height after six years: 1.2-1.8 m/4-6 ft
height as screen: 12-18 m/40-60 ft

Although it grows quite slowly, at least when young, the common yew makes a supremely formal, long-lived hedge. All well drained soils suit this very hardy plant. When left unclipped, it eventually makes a round-headed tree with horizontal branches. Hedges of yew should be trimmed annually in late summer; their constituent plants need to be placed about 60 cm/2 ft apart. Nearly every part of the common yew is poisonous. The red berries are usually decorative at close quarters only.

Chalk – Hot, dry soils – Dry shade – Dense shade – Fruit.

CHAMAECYPARIS lawsoniana e.g. 'Green
Hedger'★ MC
[form of Lawson Cypress]

○ ◑

type of plant: HCo
height after six years: 1.5-1.8 m/5-6 ft
height as screen: 12-15 m/40-50 ft

Specialist nurseries in Britain offer dozens of
varieties of Lawson cypress, some of which grow
very erectly and so are particularly suitable for
hedging. *C. l.* 'Green Hedger' forms a narrow,
elongated pyramid of upright branches and bright
green foliage. Several specimens can be grown as a
screen or, when set approximately 60 cm/2 ft apart
and trimmed in late summer, they can be used to
make a dense, formal hedge. This conifer needs a
moist soil with good drainage if it is to grow well.

ILEX aquifolium
[Common or English Holly]

○ ◑

type of plant: HT
height after six years: 1.8-2.4 m/6-8 ft
height as screen: 7.5-12 m/25-40 ft
C

I. aquifolium is armed with very sharply spined
leaves and although they make a hedge
impenetrable, they also make pruning and
trimming awkward. Young hedging specimens
need to be planted not more than 60 cm/2 ft apart.
Few berries will appear on the female plants if
pruning is undertaken each year. *I. aquifolium* is
altogether a tough and hardy plant which grows
well in most soils. Left unpruned, it eventually
makes a tree with a roughly pyramidal outline.

Dry shade – Seaside – Atmospheric pollution –
Fruit.

BUXUS sempervirens
[Common or English Box]

○ ◑

type of plant: HSh
height after six years: 1.5-1.8 m/5-6 ft
height as screen: 3.6-4.5 m/12-15 ft

A thick, formal hedge can be made from this
glossy-leaved shrub. It is also suitable for topiary.
Box hedges need to be trimmed once a year in
spring or, preferably, late summer and they should
be made up of young plants spaced about
45 cm/18 in apart. Left untrimmed, the common
box will slowly form an irregularly rounded head
of branches on a clear stem. Its inconspicuous, but
sweetly fragrant flowers are not produced in large
numbers when it is used for hedging. Any soil suits
B. sempervirens; it thrives on chalk. A variegated
form of box is shown on p. 152.

Chalk – Dry shade – Dense shade – Atmospheric
pollution – Fragrant flowers.

LIGUSTRUM ovalifolium
[Oval-leaved Privet]

○ ◑

type of plant: HSh
flowering season: summer
flower colour: white
height after six years: 1.2-1.8 m/4-6 ft
height as screen: 3.6-4.5 m/12-15 ft
E/½E

L. ovalifolium usually needs trimming three times
a year if it is to make a really neat hedge. A further
drawback is the way in which its roots draw
nourishment and moisture from a very wide area of
surrounding soil. However, this is an adaptable
plant. The more decorative, golden privet
(*L. o.* 'Aureum') is shown on the right of this
photograph and on p. 177. The spacing of plants
for hedges should be about 45 cm/18 in.

Chalk – Dry shade – Dense shade –
Atmospheric pollution.

PYRACANTHA rogersiana (syn. *P. crenulata
rogersiana*) 'Flava'★
[form of Firethorn]

○ ◑

type of plant: HSh
flowering season: e. summer
flower colour: white
height after six years: 1.8-2.4 m/6-8 ft
height as screen: 3.6-4.5 m/12-15 ft

Cultivars of *P. rogersiana*, including the
yellow-berried form shown here, are especially
suitable for hedging since they have an erect habit
of growth. However, most pyracanthas make
good, thorny hedges. If they are pruned only
lightly or trimmed occasionally they will produce
plenty of red, orange or yellow berries; when
sheared regularly each summer they bear little
fruit. Individual plants should be set about
60 cm/2 ft apart in well drained soil.

Atmospheric pollution – Fruit.

PRUNUS lusitanica
[Portugal Laurel]

○ ◑

type of plant: HSh/T
flowering season: e. summer
flower colour: white
height: 3-6 m/10-20 ft

In mild areas, free-standing specimens of this
plant will form substantial trees with layers of
spreading branches. Most usually, however, the
Portugal laurel is a wide, dense shrub. Because its
glossy leaves are fairly large, this plant needs to be
pruned, rather than clipped, if a neat, formal
shape is wanted. The same is true of the faster
growing, but much less lime-tolerant cherry laurel
(*P. laurocerasus*), a small form of which is
illustrated on p. 107. *P. lusitanica* has sweetly
scented flowers. Hedging or screening plants
should be placed about 90-120 cm/3-4 ft apart.

Chalk – Fragrant flowers.

ELAEAGNUS × ebbingei ★

○ ◑

type of plant: HSh
height: 3-4.5 m/10-15 ft
C

This vigorous and very wind tolerant plant will quickly form a thick screen of leathery leaves. Its foliage is a greyish beige colour below and an unusual olive green above. The young leaves are covered with silvery grey marks. Mature shrubs produce tiny, white flowers which have a sweet, penetrating fragrance. In spring there are orange fruits, but these are generally not very decorative. All well drained soils suit this plant and it tolerates quite dry conditions. It often spreads well over 2.4 cm/8 ft wide.

Seaside – Atmospheric pollution – Green foliage – Fragrant flowers.

RHODODENDRON ponticum

○ ◑

flowering season: l. spring to e. summer
flower colour: mauve-purple
height: 3-3.6 m/10-12 ft
*, sometimes up to 6 m/20 ft

Many rhododendrons are more beautiful than this very common plant, but few of them are quite so easily grown or so tough, hardy and adaptable. *R. ponticum* is best treated as an informal screen or windbreak. (If it is pruned hard, few of the rather variably coloured flowers will appear.) In mild districts of Britain, and on suitably moist and acid soils, this plant becomes tree-like. When used for screening, young specimens should be set approximately 1.2 m/4 ft apart.

Acid soils – Dense shade – Atmospheric pollution.

BERBERIS × stenophylla ★ sc NA MC
[form of Barberry]

○ ◑

type of plant: HSh
flowering season: spring
flower colour: yellow
height: 2.4-3 m/8-10 ft

This dense and prickly shrub produces thickets of stems and a mass of elegantly arching twigs. In spring, the yellow flowers are very freely produced and, if this plant is used for hedging, it should be pruned lightly after the sprays of blossom have faded. *B.* × *stenophylla* is more successful on dry soils than some other, evergreen barberries, but it also grows well on heavy clay. Hedging plants need to be spaced about 60 cm/2 ft apart. This shrub thrives near the sea, even in quite exposed positions.

Chalk – Clay – Hot, dry soils – Seaside – Atmospheric pollution.

COTONEASTER simonsii ★

○ ◑

type of plant: HSh
flowering season: e. summer
flower colour: white
height: 1.8-2.4 m/6-8 ft
½E

C. simonsii is only semi-evergreen, but this is not a serious drawback since, when the leaves fall, the large, orange-red berries – which cling closely to the erect stems – are particularly well displayed. These berries normally last throughout the winter. *C. simonsii* is not suitable for formal hedging. When used for screens and informal hedges, individual plants should be spaced about 50 cm/20 in apart. All ordinary garden soils are suitable.

Chalk – Clay – Seaside – Atmospheric pollution – Fruit.

LONICERA nitida
[species of Shrubby Honeysuckle]

○ ◑

type of plant: HSh
height: 1.2-1.8 m/4-6 ft

When allowed to grow freely, this shrub produces long, branching shoots and these give the plant a rather spiky appearance. *L. nitida* is, however, used almost exclusively for hedging and, if it is clipped at least twice a year, its very small, shiny leaves form a dense mass of smart-looking greenery. Attended to less frequently, hedges of this fast-growing plant soon begin to look untidy. Young plants should be spaced about 30 cm/1 ft apart. They will grow in almost any soil, although good drainage is an advantage.

Chalk – Dry shade.

BUXUS sempervirens 'Suffruticosa'
[form of Common or English Box]

○ ◑ .

type of plant: HSh
height: 30-60 cm/1-2 ft

Hedges of this very slow-growing form of box can be used to enclose herb gardens and similar, rather formal collections of plants. The annual, spring or summer trimming of such low hedges can, however, be an awkward business. All forms of the common box are tolerant of a wide range of soil types, but they have a preference for well drained, alkaline conditions. Closely clipped specimens bear only a few, sweetly scented flowers. The spacing for hedges of *B. s.* 'Suffruticosa' should be about 23 cm/9 in apart.

Chalk – Dense shade – Dry shade – Atmospheric pollution – Containers – Fragrant flowers.

TSUGA heterophylla (syn. *T. albertiana*)
[Western Hemlock]

◐ [○]
type of plant: HCo
height after six years: 2.4-3 m/8-10 ft
height as screen: 24-39 m/80-130 ft

Planted about 60 cm/2 ft apart and trimmed annually (once established, but more frequently at first), young specimens of this conifer can rapidly make a handsome hedge. They will only grow really well, however, in mild, moist or even wet areas and they require deep, acid, loamy soil. Untrimmed plants are cone-shaped with slightly drooping, topmost shoots. In the United States, they are satisfactory only in the Pacific Northwest.
Acid soils.

Deciduous hedging plants

Additional evergreen hedging plants that are featured elsewhere in this book
Heights given are for plants grown as informal screens or edgings; † indicates height after six years if the plant is trained as part of a formal hedge.

○ ◐ sun or partial shade
CHAMAECYPARIS lawsoniana e.g. 'Allumii': 2.4 m†, 12-15 m (p. 165)
TAXUS baccata 'Fastigiata': 1.2-1.8 m†, 9-12 m (p. 24)
CHAMAECYPARIS lawsoniana e.g. 'Columnaris': 1.8-2.4 m†, 6-9 m (p. 166)
ILEX aquifolium e.g. 'J. C. van Tol': 1.8-2.4 m†, 6-9 m (p. 204)
ILEX aquifolium e.g. 'Bacciflava': 1.8-2.4 m†, 6-7.5 m (p. 205)
PYRACANTHA coccinea 'Lalandei': 1.8-2.4 m†, 3.6-4.5 m (p. 95)
PYRACANTHA 'Orange Glow': 1.8-2.4 m†, 3.6-4.5 m (p. 205)
GRISELINIA littoralis: 3-3.6 m (p. 87) C
LIGUSTRUM ovalifolium 'Aureum': 2.7-3.6 m (p. 177)
BUXUS sempervirens e.g. 'Aureovariegata': 2.4-3 m (p. 152)
BERBERIS darwinii: 1.8-3 m (p. 205)
×OSMAREA burkwoodii: 1.8-3 m (p. 267)
VIBURNUM tinus: 1.8-3 m (p. 277)
LIGUSTRUM japonicum: 1.8-2.4 m (p. 83)
HYPERICUM 'Hidcote': 1.2-1.8 m (p. 25)
PRUNUS laurocerasus e.g. 'Otto Luyken' ★: 90 cm (p. 107)

◐ [○] partial shade (or sun)
RHODODENDRON Hybrid e.g. 'Praecox': 1.2-1.5 m (p. 278)
RHODODENDRON e.g. 'Blue Diamond': 90-150 cm (p. 38)
MAHONIA aquifolium: 90-120 cm (p. 112)

◐ ● partial or full shade
TAXUS baccata: 1.2-1.8 m†, 12-18 m (p. 126)
TAXUS baccata 'Fastigiata': 1.2-1.8 m†, 9-12 m (p. 24)
BUXUS sempervirens: 1.5-1.8 m†, 3.6-4.5 m (p. 127)
LIGUSTRUM ovalifolium: 1.2-1.8 m†, 3.6-4.5 m (p. 127)
RHODODENDRON ponticum: 3-3.6 m (p. 128)
LIGUSTRUM ovalifolium 'Aureum': 2.7-3.6 m (p. 177)
BUXUS sempervirens e.g. 'Aureovariegata': 2.4-3 m (p. 152)
LIGUSTRUM japonicum: 1.8-2.4 m (p. 83)
MAHONIA aquifolium: 90-120 cm (p. 112)
PRUNUS laurocerasus e.g. 'Otto Luyken' ★: 90 cm (p. 107)
BUXUS sempervirens 'Suffruticosa': 30-60 cm (p. 128)

PRUNUS cerasifera
[Cherry Plum, Myrobalan]

○
type of plant: HT
flowering season: e. spring
flower colour: white
height after six years: 2.4-3 m/8-10 ft
height as screen: 6-7.5 m/20-25 ft

The deep green leaves of *P. cerasifera* are sometimes combined with the purple foliage of *P. c.* 'Pissardii' (see p. 168) in a mixed hedge. Both plants produce lovely, simple flowers and, if a flowering hedge is wanted, pruning should be carried out in late spring. These are vigorous trees, round-headed in their natural state, and when used for informal screens they should be grown about 1.5 m/5 ft apart; hedging plants need to be about 60 cm/2 ft apart. Most well drained soils suit *P. cerasifera*.
Atmospheric pollution.

TAMARIX pentandra
[species of Tamarisk]

○
type of plant: HSh
flowering season: l. summer to e. autumn
flower colour: rose-pink
height after six years: 1.8-2.4 m/6-8 ft
height as screen: 3.6-4.5 m/12-15 ft
C

Whether this shrub is grown as part of an informal hedge or screen or planted as a solitary specimen within a garden, it needs to be pruned hard each year. Left unpruned, its arching branches quickly become long and ungainly. Young plants set approximately 60 cm/2 ft apart in well drained, preferably acid soil can make an excellent windbreak near the sea. The feathery foliage of this shrub is composed of numerous, small, scale-like leaves.
Acids soils – Seaside – Green foliage.

ROSA (Rugosa Hybrid) e.g. 'Blanc Double de Coubert' ★
[form of Rose]

○
type of plant: HSh
flowering season: summer
flower colour: white
height: 1.2-1.8 m/4-6 ft

Rugosa roses need little or no attention, even when they are grown as informal hedges. If necessary, they may be pruned lightly in spring and this treatment will ensure that plenty of flowers appear. *R.* 'Blanc Double de Coubert' is a dense and prickly plant with crinkled leaves which turn yellow in autumn. Its flowers are clove-scented. Plants grown about 90-120 cm/3-4 ft apart will knit into a sturdy, wind-resistant barrier. Rugosa roses thrive in light soils.
Chalk – Seaside – Atmospheric pollution – Autumn foliage – Cutting – Fragrant flowers.

POTENTILLA fruticosa e.g. 'Katherine Dykes'
[form of Shrubby Cinquefoil]
○ [◐]
type of plant: HSh
flowering season: e. summer to mid-autumn
flower colour: pale yellow
height: 1.2 m/4 ft

Cultivars of *P. fruticosa* make very floriferous, informal hedges. The variety 'Katherine Dykes' often starts to flower in late spring and continues to bloom freely until well into autumn. This occurs only in areas with cool summers, as in Britain and the northern reaches of the United States. It produces a thick mass of twigs on arching stems. When used for hedging, individual specimens should be spaced about 60-75 cm/2-2½ ft apart. Any soil is suitable, particularly if it is well drained.

Chalk – Seaside – Ground-cover.

FAGUS sylvatica
[Common or European Beech]
○ ◐
type of plant: HT
height after six years: 1.5-2.4 m/5-8 ft
height as screen: 18-27 m/60-90 ft
plants under 3 m/10 ft, withered leaves retained during winter

Provided that time and trouble have been taken over creating a solid, bushy base, a mature hedge of beech can look very handsome. Young plants should be spaced about 50 cm/1½ ft apart; they should be cut back, quite hard, for the first two years. If trimming is carried out in summer, russety, withered leaves cover the plants until springtime. The common beech naturally forms a magnificent, broad-leaved tree. All soils that are well drained suit *F. sylvatica* and its various forms.

Chalk – Atmospheric pollution – Autumn foliage.

CARPINUS betulus ★
[Common or European Hornbeam]
○ ◐
type of plant: HT
flowering season: spring
flower colour: yellowish green
height after six years: 1.5-2.4 m/5-8 ft
height as screen: 15-21 m/50-70 ft
plants under 3 m/10 ft, withered leaves retained during winter

An attractive hedging plant in its own right, hornbeam is often used as a substitute for beech in gardens with heavy soil. It requires much the same treatment as beech (see comments on the preceding plant). Its foliage turns yellow in autumn and then becomes pale brown. Grown as a tree, hornbeam produces a broad pyramidal head of branches, and it has a fluted, grey bark.

Chalk – Clay – Atmospheric pollution – Autumn foliage – *Bark* and twigs – Green flowers.

CRATAEGUS monogyna sc NA
[Common or European Hawthorn, May, Quick]
○ ◐
type of plant: HT
flowering season: l. spring
flower colour: white
height after six years: 1.5-2.1 m/5-7 ft
height as screen: 7.5-9 m/25-30 ft
C

The common hawthorn is outstanding as a seaside windbreak and its general toughness accounts for its widespread use, in Britain, as a hedging plant. If clipped preferably twice a year in summer, it forms an impenetrable barrier of thorny twigs, but few of the heavily scented flowers or the red fruits are produced. Young plants should be set out at 30 cm/1 ft intervals. Almost any soil is suitable. *C. m.* 'Stricta' is a columnar form.

Chalk – Clay – Seaside – Atmospheric pollution – Fruit.

SYMPHORICARPOS × doorenbosii 'White Hedge'
[form of Snowberry]
○ ◐
type of plant: HSh
height: 1.2-1.8 m/4-6 ft

In winter, this shrub's thicket of slender, upright twigs is decorated with clusters of white berries. These fruits ripen in mid-autumn. They appear in particularly large numbers if the plant is grown in a fairly light position, but even in dry and deeply shaded places some berries will be produced. *S.* × *d.* 'White Hedge' is a very adaptable plant and suitable for any soil and site. Specimens for hedging should be spaced about 45 cm/1½ ft apart. Established hedges need to be trimmed twice during the summer months.

Chalk – Clay – Damp and wet soils – Dry shade – Dense shade – Atmospheric pollution – Fruit.

CHAENOMELES (syn. *Cydonia*) × superba e.g. 'Rowallane'
[form of Flowering Quince]
○ ◐
type of plant: HSh
flowering season: spring
flower colour: red
height: 1.2-1.5 m/4-5 ft

This very hardy plant can be grown as a free-standing shrub, or it may be trained against a wall (when it will exceed the heights given here); it also makes a bushy hedge which is rather wide for its height. It will produce plenty of its large blooms in most soils and sites, including fully shaded areas. Very alkaline soils are not suitable. Hedges should be made up of specimens spaced about 90-120 cm/3-4 ft apart; they should be pruned in late autumn or winter. This shrub's golden-yellow fruits can be used to make jelly.

Clay – Atmospheric pollution – Fruit – Cutting.

FUCHSIA 'Riccartonii' (syn. *F. magellanica* 'Riccartonii')★

○ ◐
type of plant: SlTSh
flowering season: midsummer to mid-autumn
flower colour: scarlet + violet
height: 90-180 cm/3-6 ft

The hardier and more vigorous varieties of fuchsia, such as the readily available plant shown here, will grow into large plants (well over 240 cm/8 ft) in mild, moist districts. Elsewhere, hard frosts may cut them to the ground each winter and they will be much smaller and usually less free-flowering. *F.* 'Riccartonii' is commonly used for informal hedges and screens in the warmer, maritime districts of Britain. Its straight, slightly splaying branches usually need no trimming. Individual plants should be grown about 60 cm/2 ft apart in a moisture-retentive but well drained soil.

   Seaside.

Additional deciduous hedging plants that are featured elsewhere in this book
Heights given are for plants grown as informal screens or edgings; † indicates height after six years if the plant is trained as part of a formal hedge.

○ sun
FAGUS sylvatica 'Purpurea': 1.5-2.4 m†, 18-27 m (p. 168)
PRUNUS cerasifera 'Pissardii': 2.4-3 m†, 6 m (p. 168)
TAMARIX tetrandra: 3-4.5 m (p. 86) C
ROSA (Spinosissima Hybrid) e.g. 'Frühlingsgold': 1.8-2.4 m (p. 255)
ROSA (Hybrid Musk) e.g. 'Penelope': 1.8 m (p. 256)
BERBERIS thunbergii: 1.5-1.8 m (p. 190)
BERBERIS thunbergii atropurpurea: 1.2-1.8 m (p. 169)
ROSA (Rugosa) e.g. 'Roseraie de l'Hay': 1.2-1.8 m (p. 256)
ROSA (Spinosissima Hybrid) e.g. 'Stanwell Perpetual': 1.2-1.5 m (p. 3)
ROSA (Rugosa Hybrid) e.g. 'Schneezwerg': 1.2 m (p. 87)
BERBERIS thunbergii 'Aurea': 90-120 cm (p. 175)
ROSA gallica 'Versicolor': 90-120 cm (p. 218)

○ [◐] sun (or partial shade)
SYRINGA microphylla 'Superba': 1.8-2.4 m (p. 264)
PHILADELPHUS 'Manteau d'Hermine': 90-120 cm (p. 22)
POTENTILLA 'Elizabeth'★: 75-90 cm (p. 105)
POTENTILLA fruticosa e.g. 'Tangerine': 60-90 cm (p. 22)

○ ◐ sun or partial shade
HIPPOPHAE rhamnoides★: 2.4-3.6 m (p. 88) C
FORSYTHIA × intermedia 'Lynwood': 2.4-3 m (p. 24)
FORSYTHIA × intermedia 'Spectabilis': 2.4-3 m (p. 96)

RIBES sanguineum e.g. 'Pulborough Scarlet': 1.8-2.7 m (p. 80)
RIBES sanguineum e.g. 'King Edward VII': 1.5-2.1 m (p. 96)
ROSA (Floribunda) e.g. 'Iceberg'★: 1.2-1.5 m (p. 244)
SPIRAEA × bumalda 'Anthony Waterer': 90-120 cm (p. 107)

◐ ● partial or full shade
FORSYTHIA × intermedia 'Lynwood': 2.4-3 m (p. 24)
FORSYTHIA × intermedia 'Spectabilis': 2.4-3 m (p. 96)
SYMPHORICARPOS × doorenbosii 'White Hedge': 1.2-1.8 m (p. 130)
CHAENOMELES × superba e.g. 'Rowallane': 1.2-1.5 m (p. 130)

Trees, shrubs and climbers suitable for growing in containers

All you may require of the following list is that it helps you decide how to fill a pair of tubs or pots by your front door. On the other hand, you may be the owner of one of an increasingly large number of gardens which consist entirely of plants grown in ornamental containers. In all these cases, the usual recommendations, such as zonal geraniums and trailing lobelias, are unlikely to produce enough large, woody or permanent material for your purposes.

Most trees, shrubs and climbers will grow well in containers. The main exceptions to this general rule are, first, large plants with fleshy roots and, second, plants that require a very moist growing medium. In the latter case, the need for frequent watering usually makes these plants impractical choices.

Of the many plants that are possible subjects for containers, the appearance of some makes them more suitable than others. Growing a plant in a container tends to draw attention to its weak points as well as its strong points. What seemed such an attractive plant in a well filled border, can often look rather uninteresting in a smartly painted tub all of its own.

Many of the plants in this list have unusually coloured or interestingly shaped leaves. Even in the case of the deciduous trees, shrubs and climbers, attractive foliage is decorative for a substantial part of the year. Although the leaves of some plants take on spectacular colours in autumn, this dramatic display is usually short-lived, and it is best to make sure that the plants have some additional, decorative feature.

Other plants in this list, such as the common box and the sweet or bay laurel, have leaves which are not especially ornamental, but they will withstand frequent clipping. A plant that has been trimmed into an unusual shape can be just as striking as a mass of colourful leaves or flowers. The natural habitat of some plants, including the junipers listed here, makes them suitable for the same, rather formal settings that standard bay trees and clipped specimens of box are usually found in.

If the sole decorative quality of a plant is its blossom, then this should be really outstanding for the plant to look well in a container. Plants with large and flamboyant flowers are obvious choices but the various brooms, for example, are also suitable since their small flowers are produced in very large quantities. Indeed, the restriction of roots in containers often results in unusually large quantities of fruit and flowers on many plants.

The selection of plants suitable for growing in containers in shady positions is quite large. It includes rhododendrons and camellias, which will not tolerate alkaline soils. Growing these shrubs in containers filled with a lime-free compost is usually the most convenient solution to the problem of longing to grow these plants but having a thoroughly unsuitable soil in which to do so.

Growing plants in containers is also a solution to the main problem of gardening in a particularly cold area: if half-hardy plants are grown in tubs or large pots, they can be lifted into a cool greenhouse, or some other light and mainly frost-free place, during the colder months.

A few plants, such as winter jasmine and *Forsythia × intermedia* 'Spectabilis', which will grow quite healthily in sun and shade, have been excluded from the ◑ ● (partial or full shade) category in this list because they do not usually flower well in shade.

Information about preparing containers for planting and maintaining plants grown in containers will be found in several general gardening books and in, for example, Leslie John's *Plants in Tubs, Pots, Boxes, and Baskets* (published by David and Charles) and Judith Berrisford's *Window Box and Container Gardening* (published by Faber and Faber). In the United States, the subject is covered in the Brooklyn Botanic Garden handbook, *Gardening in Containers* (Brooklyn Botanic Garden, Brooklyn, NY).

In the coldest parts of the United States very few plants in containers can be left out over winter. The rule is to select especially hardy plants and then protect with evergreen boughs or salt hay bound on top and around the sides.

The heights given here are – unless otherwise stated – for plants grown normally in open ground. Plants that are large can have their growth in containers restricted by fairly frequent root pruning. The height of small and medium-sized plants is not altered substantially when grown in containers.

JUNIPERUS virginiana e.g. 'Skyrocket'
[form of Pencil Cedar]

○

type of plant: HCo
height: 3-4.5 m/10-15 ft
E

The unusually narrow, columnar shape of this juniper makes it suitable for planting in tubs in rather formal surroundings. Like other conifers of similar outline, it is also popular for providing a contrast in height and shape in beds of heather. Its foliage is a bluish grey. All well drained soils, including those that are quite dry, produce good specimens of this plant.

Hot, dry soils – Grey, etc. leaves.

CHAMAECYPARIS lawsoniana e.g. 'Ellwood's Gold'
[form of Lawson Cypress]

○

type of plant: HCo
height: 2.4-3.6 m/8-12 ft
E

By midsummer the yellow-green of this conifer's foliage has faded to an unexceptional green. However, *C. l.* 'Ellwood's Gold' is of such a neat, pillar-like form that it is a conspicuous plant throughout the year. It needs a position in full sun, both to produce a yellowness in its leaves and to preserve this colouring for as long as possible. Cultivars of *C. lawsoniana* thrive in moist, well drained soils.

Yellow, etc. leaves.

MYRTUS communis★ MC
[Common Myrtle]

○

type of plant: HHSh
flowering season: summer
flower colour: white
height: 2.4-3 m/8-10 ft
E

The common myrtle is a dense, glossy-leaved shrub with spicily aromatic foliage and sweet-scented flowers. It is suitable for growing outdoors in mild areas only and, even in these regions, it requires a warm, sheltered site, preferably against a wall. In colder gardens it is best to grow *M. communis* in some sort of container which can be brought under cover in winter. The purple-black berries are not produced regularly nor are they very decorative.

Chalk – Aromatic leaves – Fragrant flowers.

HIBISCUS syriacus e.g. 'Woodbridge'
[form of Rose Mallow or Tree Hollyhock]
○
type of plant: SlTSh
flowering season: midsummer to mid-autumn
flower colour: rosy pink
height: 2.1-3 m/7-10 ft

Although, individually, the flowers of this dense, upright plant are short-lived, a succession of blooms is produced over a long period. The lengthy flowering season and the showiness of the flowers make *H. s.* 'Woodbridge' and other, related varieties good tub plants which will perform particularly well in sheltered sites and rich soils.

Chalk – Acid soils – Atmospheric pollution.

LATHYRUS odoratus e.g. 'White Ensign'
[form of Sweet Pea]
○
type of plant: HACl
flowering season: summer to e. autumn
flower colour: white
height: 1.8-3 m/6-10 ft

Because they take up so little ground space, sweet peas – including the example shown here – are particularly suitable for growing alongside other, smaller and more spreading plants in tubs and pots. However, their need for a rich, moisture-retentive soil must be attended to in these circumstances as well as in open beds and borders. *L. o.* 'White Ensign' is fragrant but not outstandingly so, and if a really strongly scented sweet pea is wanted then blue-flowered varieties such as 'Noel Sutton', or lavender-flowered forms such as 'Leamington', should be chosen.

Climbers – Cutting.

ABUTILON megapotamicum
○
type of plant: HHSh
flowering season: e. summer to mid-autumn
flower colour: yellow + red
height: 1.8-2.4 m/6-8 ft
E

If grown in a container this half-hardy shrub can easily be given the winter protection (in a cool greenhouse, for instance) that it needs in all but the mildest areas. A warm, sheltered site and a well drained soil are essential. Since the slender stems of this plant are lax and spreading, some support must be given to enable them to grow upright.

Climbers.

ACER palmatum 'Dissectum Atropurpureum'★
[form of Japanese Maple]
○
type of plant: HSh
height: 1.5-2.4 m/5-8 ft

In time, this expensive but most attractive plant forms a spreading heap of feathery leaves. Its foliage is maroon-purple in spring and summer, and red in autumn. *A. p.* 'Dissectum Atropurpureum' needs a moist soil that is acid or neutral if it is to grow well. It should also be given shelter from cold winds and early morning frost.

Acid soils – Red, etc. leaves – Autumn foliage.

LIPPIA citriodora (syn. *Aloysia citriodora,*
*A. triphylla***)**
[Lemon-scented Verbena]
○
type of plant: HHSh
flowering season: l. summer
flower colour: pale mauve
height: 1.5-1.8 m/5-6 ft

This shrub is often cut down to ground level by frost. It will form a rather loose framework of permanent branches only in really mild districts or when grown in a tub or pot and moved under cover in winter. A beautifully fresh, lemon fragrance is emitted by the leaves when they are pinched or crushed. Sheltered, sunny sites and well drained soils suit this shrub best.

Aromatic leaves.

WISTERIA floribunda e.g. 'Macrobotrys' (syn.
*W. multijuga***)**
[form of Japanese Wisteria]
○
type of plant: HCl
flowering season: l. spring to e. summer
flower colour: lilac
height: 90-150 cm/3-5 ft
grown as a standard; normally 6-9 m/20-30 ft high

W. f. 'Macrobotrys' is a vigorous, twining climber which is usually grown up house walls, over pergolas and arches and, occasionally, through trees. It can also be trained as a standard – with a single stem and a spreading head of growth – when it looks especially attractive in a large tub. The pendant clusters of flowers can be up to 90 cm/3 ft long and they have a sweet, vanilla-like scent. Ideally, this plant should be given a sheltered position and a soil which retains moisture easily.

Clay – Climbers – Fragrant flowers.

JUNIPERUS communis 'Compressa'
[form of Common Juniper]

○

type of plant: HCo
height: 60-90 cm/2-3 ft
E

Where the Irish juniper (*J. c.* 'Hibernica', see p. 2) would be too large, this similarly shaped, but much slower growing variety could be used. Its narrow column of foliage is a silvery blue-grey. *J. c.* 'Compressa' remains very small for so long that it is quite suitable for planting in trough gardens and window-boxes as well as in larger containers. It flourishes on chalk and in all well drained soils, and it will tolerate short spells of drought.

Chalk – Hot, dry soils – Grey, etc. leaves.

PUNICA granatum 'Nana' MC
[form of Pomegranate]

○

type of plant: HH/TenSh
flowering season: summer to e. autumn
flower colour: reddish scarlet
height: 60-90 cm/2-3 ft

This neat, rounded shrub does not usually produce any fruit, except in very warm regions or when grown in a greenhouse. However, its beautifully coloured blooms more than compensate for this shortcoming. *P. g.* 'Nana' has a long flowering season, and this makes it a particularly good tub or pot plant. If it is grown in some sort of container there is also the advantage of being able easily to give it shelter in the colder months of the year.

CRYPTOMERIA japonica 'Vilmoriniana'
[form of Japanese Cedar]

○

type of plant: HCo
height: 45-90 cm/1½-3 ft
E

The solid, green globe of this extremely slow-growing conifer turns a rich reddish-purple in winter. Its slow growth rate, tidy shape and winter colour all make *C. j.* 'Vilmoriniana' suitable for planting in various types of container. It must be remembered, however, that in all circumstances this plant should have plenty of moisture, especially when young.

Acid soils – Autumn foliage.

ROSA (Miniature) e.g. 'Perla de Montserrat'
sc NA
[form of Rose]

○

type of plant: HSh
flowering season: summer
flower colour: pink
height: 30-40 cm/12-15 in

Even quite small window-boxes can have roses growing in them if miniature varieties, such as the two examples illustrated above and right, are chosen. However, there must be a reasonable depth of fertile, well drained soil, and full sun is essential. Only very light pruning is needed. Some varieties of miniature rose are available as standards.

ROSA (Miniature) e.g. 'Yellow Doll' sc NA
[form of Rose]

○

type of plant: HSh
flowering season: summer
flower colour: yellow changing to ivory
height: 30 cm/1 ft

In common with other yellow-flowered miniature roses, the petals of this delicately fragrant plant fade to a quite pale colour in strong sunlight. (For general remarks, see preceding plant.)

Fragrant flowers.

LAURUS nobilis MC
[Sweet Bay, Bay Laurel]

○ [◗]

type of plant: SlTSh (Herb)
height: 1.5-1.8 m/5-6 ft
E, grown as a standard; normally 3.6-6 m/12-20 ft high

This upright, pyramidal shrub is often used to form mop-headed standards for planting in tubs. Treated in this way, it needs frequent trimming in summer. However, it can also be allowed to grow freely, when the only pruning it will require is the removal of frost-damaged leaves and stems. The warmly aromatic foliage of *L. nobilis* is particularly susceptible to 'burning' in cold winds, although it tolerates the milder, salt-laden breezes of the seaside remarkably well. This shrub should be grown in a well drained soil.

Chalk – Seaside – Hedging – Aromatic leaves.

ABIES balsamea 'Hudsonia'
[form of Balsam Fir]

○ [◑]
type of plant: HCo
height: 60-90 cm/2-3 ft
E

As long as this slow-growing conifer is kept well watered, it will flourish in tubs and pots. The resinous foliage is banded with white underneath, and the whole plant is of a neat, rounded shape.

Acid soils – Aromatic leaves.

Additional trees, shrubs and climbers, featured elsewhere in this book, that are suitable for growing in containers

○ sun
PASSIFLORA caerulea: 6-9 m (p. 119)
SOLANUM crispum 'Glasnevin': 4.5-6 m (p. 120)
CORDYLINE australis: 3.6-9 m (p. 180)
YUCCA gloriosa: 2.7-3.6 m (p. 56)
HUMULUS scandens 'Variegatus': 2.4-3 m (p. 146)
IPOMOEA rubro-caerulea e.g. 'Heavenly Blue': 2.4-3 m (p. 121)
LATHYRUS latifolius: 2.4-3 m (p. 121)
LATHYRUS odoratus e.g. 'Air Warden': 1.8-3 m (p. 212)
LATHYRUS odoratus e.g. 'Leamington': 1.8-3 m (p. 255)
LATHYRUS odoratus e.g. 'Mrs R. Bolton': 1.8-3 m (p. 212)
LATHYRUS odoratus e.g. 'Noel Sutton': 1.8-3 m (p. 255)
LATHYRUS odoratus e.g. 'Winston Churchill': 1.8-3 m (p. 121)
ESCALLONIA e.g. 'Donard Radiance': 1.8-2.4 m (p. 125)
HIBISCUS syriacus e.g. 'Blue Bird': 1.8-2.4 m (p. 3)
HIBISCUS syriacus e.g. 'Hamabo': 1.8-2.4 m (p. 3)
LATHYRUS odoratus e.g. 'Galaxy Mixed': 1.8-2.4 m (p. 213)
ESCALLONIA e.g. 'Apple Blossom': 1.8 m (p. 86)
ACER palmatum 'Dissectum': 1.5-2.4 m (p. 180)
HEBE brachysiphon: 1.2-1.8 m (p. 3)
ROSMARINUS officinalis: 1.2-1.8 m (p. 196)
WEIGELA florida 'Foliis Purpureis': 1.2 m (p. 170)
PINUS mugo pumilio: 90-180 cm (p. 3)
YUCCA filamentosa ★: 90-180 cm (p. 57)
CHAMAECYPARIS lawsoniana e.g. 'Minima Aurea' ★: 90-150 cm (p. 175)
WISTERIA sinensis: 90-150 cm (p. 119)
WISTERIA sinensis 'Alba': 90-150 cm (p. 253)
BERBERIS thunbergii 'Aurea': 90-120 cm (p. 175)
CISTUS×corbariensis: 90-120 cm (p. 57)

PRUNUS tenella 'Fire Hill': 60-120 cm (p. 99)
HALIMIUM ocymoides: 60-90 cm (p. 59)
ERICA×darleyensis e.g. 'A. Johnson': 60 cm (p. 100)
HYPERICUM×moserianum 'Tricolor': 60 cm (p. 147)
LAVANDULA spica 'Vera': 60 cm (p. 100)
GENISTA lydia ★: 45-75 cm (p. 92)
RUTA graveolens 'Jackman's Blue': 45-60 cm (p. 160)
SANTOLINA chamaecyparissus ★: 45-60 cm (p. 125)
ERICA×darleyensis e.g. 'Silver Beads': 45 cm (p. 275)
BERBERIS thunbergii 'Atropurpurea Nana': 30-60 cm (p. 171)
CYTISUS×kewensis: 30-60 cm (p. 59)
LAVANDULA spica 'Hidcote': 30-60 cm (p. 126)
HEBE×'Carl Teschner': 23-30 cm (p. 101)
ERICA carnea e.g. 'Springwood White' ★: 23 cm (p. 102)
ERICA carnea e.g. 'King George': 15-23 cm (p. 275)
ERICA carnea e.g. 'Vivellii': 15-23 cm (p. 191)
HYPERICUM polyphyllum: 15-23 cm (p. 140)

○ [◑] sun (or partial shade)
JASMINUM officinale: 9 m (p. 264)
VITIS vinifera 'Purpurea': 6 m (p. 171)
PHORMIUM tenax: 3-3.6 m (p. 182)
PHORMIUM tenax e.g. 'Purpureum': 3-3.6 m (p. 171)
PHORMIUM tenax e.g. 'Variegatum': 3-3.6 m (p. 150)
ELAEAGNUS pungens 'Maculata' ★: 2.4-3 m (p. 150)
SYRINGA vulgaris e.g. 'Katherine Havemeyer': 1.8-2.4 m (p. 264)
SYRINGA vulgaris e.g. 'Madame Lemoine': 1.8-2.4 m (p. 240)
EUONYMUS japonicus 'Ovatus Aureus': 1.5-2.1 m (p. 150)
EUCALYPTUS gunnii ★: 1.5-1.8 m (p. 164)

CLEMATIS (Large-flowered Hybrid) e.g. 'Duchess of Edinburgh'

○ ◑
type of plant: HCl
flowering season: l. spring to e. summer
flower colour: white
height: 2.4-4.5 m/8-15 ft

The spectacular blooms of all the large-flowered hybrid clematis make these climbers attractive plants for growing in containers. The double-flowered forms – such as the example illustrated here – are particularly eye-catching. All hybrid clematis like a substantial, limy soil, with shade at their roots and sun on their upper growth. Another double-flowered clematis which can be acquired quite easily is the violet-purple 'Vyvyan Pennell'. As a very young plant, this variety tends to produce single flowers but, in maturity, it becomes fully and flamboyantly double.

Climbers.

FATSIA japonica (syn. *Aralia sieboldii*) ★ MC
[False Castor Oil Plant]

○ ◑
type of plant: SlTSh
flowering season: autumn
flower colour: cream
height: 2.4-3.6 m/8-12 ft
E

Often seen growing in large tubs – in town gardens particularly – this sparsely branched shrub is noted for its big, handsome leaves (some of these leaves may be up to 40 cm/15 in wide). Although *F. japonica* will grow in dense shade, it may have to be given a warm, sheltered position in cold districts, especially if more than just a few of the heads of creamy flowers are to appear.

Dense shade – Atmospheric pollution – Green foliage.

CAMELLIA×williamsii e.g. 'J. C. Williams' MC

○ ◑
type of plant: HSh
flowering season: midwinter to mid-spring
flower colour: pale pink
height: 1.8-2.4 m/6-8 ft
E

The *williamsii* varieties of camellias have the advantage, over the *japonica* cultivars, of shedding their flowers when the petals have faded. This feature is particularly useful if the plants are to be grown in tubs or pots, where dead blossom would appear very unsightly. *C.×w*. 'J. C. Williams' forms a fairly upright, rather open shrub. Like all camellias, it needs cool, moist, lime-free soil; in cold districts, it should receive sun for most of the day, to ensure there are plenty of flowers.

Acid soils – Green foliage – Winter-flowering plants.

AUCUBA japonica e.g. 'Crotonifolia' (syn. *A.j.* 'Crotonoides')
[form of Spotted Laurel]

○ ◑

type of plant: HSh
height: 1.5-2.4 m/5-8 ft
E

It is now more or less obligatory to pour scorn on this tough, bushy plant which will put up with so much and demand so little. However, when grown in good soil and given at least some sun to brighten the yellow in its leaves, this shrub can look quite handsome. *A.j.* 'Variegata', for example, is lightly speckled with yellow, and a form with yellow centres to its leaves can be obtained from specialist nurseries. *A.j.* 'Crotonifolia' is a male plant, but *A.j.* 'Variegata' is female and will bear red berries when fertilized by a male.

Chalk – Clay – Dry shade – Seaside – Atmospheric pollution – Variegated leaves.

HEBE cupressoides MC

○ ◑

type of plant: HSh
flowering season: e. summer
flower colour: pale blue
height: 90-120 cm/3-4 ft
E

Often mistaken, when not in flower, for a dwarf conifer, this dense, rounded shrub looks well in a tub (at least when young or middle-aged and really neat). Its leaves have the warm scent of cedar wood. The whipcord hebes – of which this is an example – are amongst the hardiest plants in this genus. It is, however, safest to give them a well-drained soil and, in colder districts, a fairly sunny site. *H. armstrongii* is another, readily available whipcord hebe; it has interestingly stringy, 'old gold' foliage.

Chalk – Seaside – Atmospheric pollution – Green foliage – Aromatic leaves.

HYDRANGEA × 'Preziosa' (syn. *H. serrata* 'Preziosa')

○ ◑

type of plant: SlTSh
flowering season: midsummer to e. autumn
flower colour: pink changing to crimson
height: 90 cm/3 ft

This compact variety of hydrangea produces its brightly coloured flowers over a long period. It has leaves which become tinged with purple in autumn and, in spring, the young foliage may be similarly coloured. These various seasons of interest make it one of the best hydrangeas for growing in tubs. However, when it is grown in a container, care must be taken over watering, since this plant must not be allowed to dry out. An acid soil is most suitable.

Acid soils – Autumn foliage.

×FATSHEDERA lizei★ MC

○ ◑

type of plant: SlTSh
height: 60-90 cm/2-3 ft
E, up to 2.4 m/8 ft against a wall

A shapely, glossy leaf and a tolerance of difficult conditions are the main features of this plant. It can be grown either as a sprawling shrub or, given support of some sort, as a climber. It rarely flowers outdoors. There is a rather less common and less hardy, variegated form of this plant with pale cream edges to its leaves.

Dry shade – Dense shade – Atmospheric pollution – Ground-cover – Climbers – Green foliage.

FUCHSIA Hybrid e.g. 'Mrs Popple' sc NA

○ ◑

type of plant: SlTSh
flowering season: midsummer to mid-autumn
flower colour: scarlet + violet
height: 60-90 cm/2-3 ft
can be grown as standard: 90-120 cm/3-4 ft high

Since they flower so profusely and for so long, many of the hybrid fuchsias make ideal tub or pot plants. The variety illustrated here grows strongly. It has arching stems. In most districts, frosts will kill its top growth each winter, but new shoots will come readily from the base in the following spring. Whether grown in a container or in open ground, the plant should be given a cool, moist and, preferably, neutral soil. It should be planted deeply and mulched regularly.

CHAMAECYPARIS obtusa e.g. 'Nana'
[form of Hinoki Cypress]

○ ◑

type of plant: HCo
height: 45-75 cm/1½-2½ ft
E

The mossy foliage of this very slow-growing conifer is arranged in such a way as to create an almost frilly effect. When crushed, the leaves emit a sweet, resinous smell. The overall shape of this plant is a fat, squat cone, the neatness and density of which is well suited to tubs and other containers. *C. obtusa* and its cultivars appreciate fairly moist growing conditions.

Acid soils – Aromatic leaves.

PICEA mariana (syn. *P. nigra*) 'Nana' ★
[form of Black Spruce]

○ ◖

type of plant: HCo
height: 30-45 cm/1-1½ ft
E

The radiating shoots of this conifer are covered
with small, blue-grey needles and the overall
impression is of a tight little blue bun. *P. m.* 'Nana'
is ideal for planting in troughs and sinks since it
grows so very slowly, but care must be taken not to
let it dry out.

   Acid soils – Grey, etc. leaves.

FUCHSIA Hybrid e.g. 'Tom Thumb' sc NA

○ ◖

type of plant: SlTSh
flowering season: midsummer to mid-autumn
flower colour: violet+scarlet
height: 30 cm/1 ft
can be grown as standard: 90-120 cm/3-4 ft high

This free-flowering variety is the smallest, readily
available fuchsia that is suitable for growing
outdoors. (For general remarks about growth and
cultivation, see *F*. 'Mrs Popple' on the previous
page.)

CAMELLIA japonica e.g. 'Alba Simplex'

◖ [○]

type of plant: HSh
flowering season: l. winter to e. spring
flower colour: white
height 1.8-3 m/6-10 ft
* E

All varieties of *C. japonica* make good tub plants,
although those with a markedly spreading habit
(for example, *C. j.* 'Lady Clare') are probably less
suitable than the upright types, such as *C. j.* 'Alba
Simplex'. Despite being more weather-resistant
than some camellias, the flowers of this plant
should be given protection from early morning sun
since, after a frost, this can reduce the petals to
limp, brown rags. Camellias require plenty of
moisture. When grown in tubs they should be
given regular draughts of rainwater.

   Acid soils – Atmospheric pollution – Green
foliage – Winter-flowering plants.

EUONYMUS fortunei (syn. *E. radicans*) e.g.
'Silver Queen'

◖ [○]

type of plant: HSh/Cl
height: 1.8-2.4 m/6-8 ft
E, grown as climber

There are now a number of variegated forms of
E. fortunei. The variety illustrated here is widely
available. When grown against a wall it will
produce self-clinging shoots. Otherwise, it is
bushy and hummock-shaped and about
30-60 cm/1-2 ft high. The decorative foliage has a
creamy yellow cast when young; when mature, the
leaf margins become white and they are sometimes
tinged with pink in cold weather. The related
variety 'Emerald 'n' Gold' has green and deep
yellow foliage. It too makes good ground-cover.
Both these plants grow in most soils.

   Chalk – Atmospheric pollution – Ground-cover
– Climbers – Variegated leaves.

HYDRANGEA macrophylla (Hortensia) e.g.
'Madame E. Mouillière' ★ sc NA

◖ [○]

type of plant: SlTSh
flowering season: midsummer to e. autumn
flower colour: white
height: 1.2-1.8 m/4-6 ft

The mop-headed hydrangeas are classic tub plants
and *H. m.* 'Madame E. Mouillière' is generally
regarded as the best white hydrangea of this type.
It flowers continuously during the period stated
and makes a bushy, well branched plant. It grows
best in a rich, slightly acid soil and a sheltered site;
its roots should be cool and moist. In semi-shade,
the flowers of this plant fade eventually to a
greenish colour; in sun, they take on pinkish tones
as they age.

   Acid soils – Atmospheric pollution – Cutting.

RHODODENDRON (AZALEA) e.g.
'Hinodegiri'

◖ [○]

type of plant: SlTSh
flowering season: spring
flower colour: crimson
height: 90 cm/3 ft
* ½ E

In winter, the leaves of this slow-growing Kurume
azalea become bronze-green. However, the main
season of interest is spring, when the brightly
coloured flowers appear in profusion. *R.*
'Hinodegiri' is a dense and tidy plant and this
makes it particularly suitable both for
ground-cover and for growing in containers. All
semi-evergreen azaleas of this type should be given
shelter from cold winds; they also require moist,
acid soil.

   Acid soils – Ground-cover – Autumn foliage.

RHODODENDRON williamsianum ★

◑

type of plant: SlT/HSh
flowering season: mid-spring
flower colour: pink
height: 90-150 cm/3-5 ft
* **E**

This rhododendron's flowers are so outstandingly
pretty that they deserve to be shown off in a pot or
tub or in a prominent position in the garden. The
plant itself is neat and domed and, in addition to
the lovely flowers, there is the attractive
brown-bronze of the young leaves. Unfortunately,
these young growths are susceptible to frost
damage. A sheltered site is, therefore, as
important as the lime-free soil and moist root-run
required by all rhododendrons.

Acid soils – Ground-cover – Red, etc. leaves.

**Additional trees, shrubs and climbers, featured
elsewhere in this book, that are suitable for
growing in containers**

○ ◑ sun or partial shade
HEDERA canariensis 'Variegata': 4.5-6 m (p. 151)
HEDERA colchica 'Dentata-Variegata': 4.5-6 m
   (p. 151)
CLEMATIS tangutica: 4.5-5.4 m (p. 123)
CLEMATIS orientalis: 3.6-5.4 m (p. 123)
HEDERA helix e.g. 'Glacier': 3-3.6 m (p. 151)
HEDERA helix e.g. 'Gold Heart' ★: 3-3.6 m (p. 152)
CLEMATIS (Large-flowered Hybrid) e.g.
   'Jackmanii Superba': 2.4-4.5 m (p. 123)
CLEMATIS (Large-flowered Hybrid) e.g.
   'Lasurstern': 2.4-4.5 m (p. 123)
CLEMATIS (Large-flowered Hybrid) e.g. 'Nelly
   Moser': 2.4-3.6 m (p. 124)
CLEMATIS (Large-flowered Hybrid) e.g. 'Ville de
   Lyon': 2.4-3.6 m (p. 124)
BUXUS sempervirens e.g. 'Aureovariegata':
   2.4-3 m (p. 152)
CORYLUS avellana 'Contorta': 2.4-3 m (p. 211)
FORSYTHIA × intermedia 'Spectabilis': 2.4-3 m
   (p. 96)
PICEA glauca albertiana 'Conica': 1.8-3 m (p. 34)
VIBURNUM tinus: 1.8-3 m (p. 277)
CAMELLIA × williamsii e.g. 'Donation' ★:
   1.8-2.4 m (p. 34)
CHOISYA ternata: 1.8-2.4 m (p. 243)
WEIGELA florida 'Variegata': 1.5 m (p. 152)
SPIRAEA × bumalda 'Anthony Waterer':
   90-120 cm (p. 107)
VIBURNUM davidii ★: 90 cm (p. 206)
PERNETTYA mucronata e.g. 'Bell's Seedling':
   60-90 cm (p. 206)
PERNETTYA mucronata e.g. 'Davis Hybrids':
   60-90 cm (p. 206)
JASMINUM nudiflorum: 60 cm (p. 277)
BUXUS sempervirens 'Suffruticosa': 30-60 cm
   (p. 128)
DAPHNE cneorum 'Eximia': 23-30 cm (p. 269)
HEBE 'Pagei' 15-30 cm (p. 167)

VINCA minor: 15 cm (p. 82)
VINCA minor e.g. 'Alba': 15 cm (p. 111)

◑ [○] partial shade (or sun)
LONICERA japonica 'Aureoreticulata': 7.5-9 m
   (p. 153)
LONICERA japonica halliana: 7.5-9 m (p. 270)
PARTHENOCISSUS henryana: 7.5-9 m (p. 153)
MAHONIA × 'Charity': 2.1-3 m (p. 278)
MAHONIA japonica ★: 2.1-3 m (p. 271)
CAMELLIA japonica e.g. 'Adolphe Audusson' ★:
   1.8-3.6 m (p. 36)
CAMELLIA japonica e.g. 'Contessa Lavinia
   Maggi': 1.8-3.6 m (p. 97)
HYDRANGEA macrophylla (Hortensia) e.g.
   'Altona': 1.2-1.8 cm (p. 37)
HYDRANGEA macrophylla (Hortensia) e.g.
   'Générale Vicomtesse de Vibraye': 1.2-1.8 m
   (p. 98)
MAHONIA aquifolium: 90-120 cm (p. 112)
RHODODENDRON (AZALEA) e.g.
   'Hinomayo': 90-120 cm (p. 112)
RHODODENDRON (AZALEA) e.g. 'Rosebud':
   60 cm (p. 39)
EUONYMUS fortunei e.g. 'Silver Queen':
   30-60 cm (p. 137)
EUONYMUS fortunei e.g. 'Vegetus': 30-60 cm
   (p. 113)
RHODODENDRON Hybrid e.g. 'Jenny':
   30-60 cm (p. 40)
RHODODENDRON impeditum: 30 cm (p. 114)

◑ ● partial or full shade
FATSIA japonica ★: 2.4-3.6 m (p. 135)
BUXUS sempervirens e.g. 'Aureovariegata':
   2.4-3 m (p. 152)
AUCUBA japonica e.g. 'Crotonifolia': 1.5-2.4 m
   (p. 136)
MAHONIA aquifolium: 90-120 cm (p. 112)
× FATSHEDERA lizei ★: 60-90 cm (p. 136)
BUXUS sempervirens 'Suffruticosa': 30-60 cm
   (p. 128)

Plants suitable for crevices in paving

Perhaps it is not surprising that some of the most enviably attractive gardens have a terrace or paved area of some sort as their main feature. Inert, plain surfaces often set off leaves in all their variety much more effectively than either a somewhat haphazard collection of yet more leaves or an ill-kempt lawn. Plants grown within a paved area, in the crevices between pieces of paving material, are not only shown to advantage there, but they also have the effect of softening the appearance of the paving and linking it with any plants that surround it; in addition, they lessen the problem of weeds in paving.

The plants selected for the following list are low-growing since most terraces and paved areas are too small for it to be convenient to grow larger plants within them. Larger plants can be grown at the margins of paved areas, and it is worth considering subjects with bold foliage for this purpose as they often form the most effective contrast with plain surfaces. (For plants with bold, green leaves, see entries marked 'B' in list entitled 'Plants with decorative, green foliage'.) Only in an extensive area of paving are larger, upright specimens needed to relieve the monotony of a flat surface, and these are probably most conveniently grown in tubs or other ornamental containers.

Most of the plants which are suitable for crevices in paving enjoy sun and well drained soil. These requirements are easily met on any terrace which has been properly laid and which is used as a place to sit in the sun. The choice of plants which are suitable for shady terraces is less extensive, but even here quite a varied selection of plants, including some of the smaller ferns, can be grown.

No bulbous plants appear in this list since their unsightly, dying foliage, which feeds them for their flowering the following year, is not easily concealed on paving. However, crocuses, squills, and small daffodils, for instance, can certainly look attractive between paving stones. Small bulbs of this sort may be grown through some other plant in order to disguise their dying leaves, but, in this case, plenty of nutritious soil should be provided to support the two types of plant.

Many alpine plants are particularly suitable for paved areas. Some, however, like a few of the rock jasmines, have been excluded from this list because, although they might look attractive in gaps between paving, they need protection from winter wet, and this is obviously inconvenient on an ordinary terrace.

Leaves, as well as flowers, can enhance the particular characteristics of different paving materials. While many of the plants in this list have green foliage, there are a number with grey leaves and *Thymus × citriodorus* 'Aureus' is a yellow-leaved form of lemon-scented thyme. (For other plants with aromatic foliage that are suitable for planting in paving crevices, this list should be used in conjunction with the 'Plants with aromatic leaves' list.)

Although all the plants in the following list are suitable for crevices in paving, most of them will not stand up to having garden furniture placed upon them often or being walked on very frequently. A few plants, such as *Arenaria balearica*, a species of sandwort, and the non-flowering, but aromatic, variety of common chamomile, *Anthemis nobilis* 'Treneague', will withstand moderate wear and tear quite satisfactorily. In general, however, the plants in this list are best grown in parts of paved areas that are left relatively undisturbed.

EUPHORBIA myrsinites NA
[species of Spurge]

○
type of plant: **HP**
flowering season: **spring**
flower colour: **yellow**
height: **30 cm/1 ft**
E

Rope-like stalks of thick greyish leaves are characteristic of this rock garden plant. Because the stems bend over and become open at the base late in the season, the plant is best displayed hanging over a wall. Rich moist soil should be avoided. In Britain, nurseries with a really wide range of perennials or rock garden plants will stock *E. myrsinites*.
Grey, etc. leaves.

PENSTEMON menziesii

○
type of plant: **SITSh**
flowering season: **e. summer**
flower colour: **violet-purple**
height: **23-30 cm/9-12 in**
E

Good drainage and shelter from north and east winds usually ensure that this plant survives all but the coldest of British winters. The 2 cm/1 in long flowers are carried in tight sprays on shoots which are normally semi-erect but which sometimes trail.
Ground-cover.

PHLOX amoena

○
type of plant: **HP**
flowering season: **l. spring to e. summer**
flower colour: **reddish purple or deep pink or white**
height: **23 cm/9 in**
E

Individual specimens of this plant vary a good deal in the colour of their freely produced blooms, but a red-tinged purple and a deep pink are the most common shades. Full sun and well drained soil are necessary and, under these conditions, there will be plenty of blooms and the small, almost leathery leaves may form quite wide carpets. Nurseries specializing in rock garden plants often offer a form of *P. amoena* which has silvery markings on its foliage.
Ground-cover.

DIANTHUS deltoides
[Maiden Pink]
○

type of plant: HP
flowering season: summer
flower colour: red or pink or white
height: 15-23 cm/6-9 in
E

Almost all summer long this plant's clump of
spraying growth is covered in a mass of small,
scentless blooms. Varieties of *D. deltoides* with
deeply coloured flowers have dark green or
coppery foliage, but they tend to grow less strongly
than the paler forms. An alkaline soil which drains
freely is ideal for these plants; they will thrive on
drystone walls, as well as in crevices in paving or as
edgings to borders.

Chalk – Hot, dry soils – Ground-cover.

HYPERICUM polyphyllum sc NA
[species of St John's Wort]
○

type of plant: HSh
flowering season: summer to e. autumn
flower colour: yellow
height: 15-23 cm/6-9 in
E

Although its dense mound of upright and trailing
stems and blue-green leaves is rarely more than
23 cm/9 in high, *H. polyphyllum* produces rich
yellow flowers some 4 cm/1½ in wide. This plant is
easily grown in any well drained soil. *H. p.*
'Sulphureum' is a form with pale yellow blooms.

Chalk – Atmospheric pollution – Ground-cover
– Containers – Grey, etc. leaves.

LEONTOPODIUM alpinum
[Edelweiss]
○

type of plant: HP
flowering season: summer
flower colour: white
height: 15-23 cm/6-9 in

The overall, soft greyness both of the strange
flower heads and of the woolly foliage of this plant
give it its subdued charm. In cultivation the
edelweiss is sometimes short-lived, but it is not
difficult to grow provided that it has plenty of sun
and a well drained soil. It often looks most
attractive on top of a drystone wall.

Grey, etc. leaves.

LIMNANTHES douglasii★
[Poached Egg Flower]
○

type of plant: HA
flowering season: all summer
flower colour: yellow+white
height: 15-23 cm/6-9 in

Once it has been given the conditions it likes best –
coolness and moisture at its roots and sunshine on
its spreading clump of foliage – this plant will
usually seed itself from year to year. Its
requirements are most easily met by sowing it
initially in the crevices between paving stones and
in other places where its roots will always be
shaded. Its flowers have a light, sweet fragrance
and they are attractive to bees.

Fragrant flowers.

ASTER alpinus
[species of Michaelmas Daisy]
○

type of plant: HP
flowering season: midsummer
flower colour: lavender-blue
height: 15 cm/6 in

This miniature relative of the well known
Michaelmas daisies is much less trouble to grow
and keep healthy than the more highly bred
members of its family. Nurseries with a large
selection of rock garden plants will stock various
forms of *A. alpinus*, some with purplish rather than
blue flowers, but all of them rather spreading in
their habit of growth. Any well drained soil that is
not too dry will suit these plants.

VERBENA×hybrida e.g. 'Sparkle Mixed'
○

type of plant: HHA
flowering season: summer to mid-autumn
flower colour: mixed – blue, white, red, purple,
    pink+white
height: 15 cm/6 in

If this low, spreading plant is grown in areas of
paving that receive full sun, the warmth and
shelter there will make it flower particularly freely.
Its palest blooms emit a soft, sweet, clove-like
scent.

Fragrant flowers.

PAPAVER alpinum★
[Alpine Poppy]
○
type of plant: HB/P
flowering season: summer
flower colour: mixed – white, yellow, orange,
orange-red
height: 10-20 cm//4-8 in

Studded with the bright blossom of the alpine poppy, even the greyest areas of paving can look cheerful. And the crevices between paving stones are exactly the sort of places in which self-sown seedlings of this short-lived plant are likely to appear. Wherever it is grown, however, *P. alpinum* needs good drainage. Its grey-green leaves are arranged in tufts at the base of its slender flower stalks.

    Chalk – Grey, etc. leaves.

VERONICA prostrata (syn. *V. rupestris*)
[species of Speedwell]
○
type of plant: HP
flowering season: l. spring to e. summer
flower colour: blue
height: 10-20 cm/4-8 in

V. prostrata's mat of small leaves often becomes completely obscured by bright blue flowers. Various forms of this easily grown and fairly vigorous plant are available: most of them have flowers in some shade of blue, but there is a pink-flowered variety and *V. p.* 'Alba' has white blooms. These plants can spread up to 45 cm/1½ ft wide. Their upright flower spikes contrast well with the flatness of paving.

    Chalk – Ground-cover.

ARENARIA montana
[species of Sandwort]
○
type of plant: HP
flowering season: l. spring to e. summer
flower colour: white
height: 10-15 cm/4-6 in
E

Ideally, *A. montana* should have a soil that is moist but, at the same time, very well drained. Although this can be a difficult combination to maintain in beds and borders, it is often already present in the crevices between paving stones. The leaves and stalks of this plant form a dense mat of growth. (A smaller, related species – *A. balearica* – is illustrated on p. 116; it needs more shade than *A. montana*, and it has the advantage of being able to grow well even if it is walked on quite regularly.)

    Ground-cover.

AUBRIETA (syn. *Aubretia*) deltoidea e.g.
'Maurice Prichard'★
○
type of plant: HP
flowering season: spring
flower colour: pink
height: 10-15 cm/4-6 in
E

The many popular forms of aubrieta are, perhaps, most often seen trailing from the top of low walls but they also look well in the crevices between paving stones. *A. d.* 'Maurice Prichard' is a vigorous variety and typically floriferous. Its blooms are a rather paler colour than usual. When they have faded, the whole plant – which will spread up to 50 cm/20 in wide in time – should be cut back hard if it is grown in paving or for ground-cover. A very well drained, alkaline soil suits aubrietas best.

    Chalk – Hot, dry soils – Ground-cover.

SEDUM spurium e.g. 'Schorbusser Blut' (syn.
***S. s.* 'Dragon's Blood')**
[form of Stonecrop]
○
type of plant: HP
flowering season: summer
flower colour: deep red
height: 10-15 cm/4-6 in
E

The rather loose rosettes of foliage and the tangled stems of this plant knit into a rooting, ground-covering mat. Certain forms of *S. spurium* flower only rarely and are grown for their leaf colour: *S. s.* 'Green Mantle' has leaves of a soft green colour, and the variety 'Ruby Mantle' has rich red foliage. All these carpeting plants are easy to grow in any well drained soil and they will thrive even in very dry places.

    Chalk – Hot, dry soils – Ground-cover.

ALYSSUM montanum
○
type of plant: HP
flowering season: l. spring to e. summer
flower colour: yellow
height: 8-10 cm/3-4 in
E

Most of the smaller alyssums look well either tucked into crevices between paving stones or grown on top of drystone walls. *A. montanum* has the bright yellow flowers characteristic of plants in this genus and, as usual, it needs to be cut back after flowering to keep it neat and floriferous. The flower heads emit a sweet scent. All well drained soils suit this plant.

    Chalk – Hot, dry soils – Fragrant flowers.

ANDROSACE sarmentosa chumbyi
[form of Rock Jasmine]
○

type of plant: HP
flowering season: l. spring to e. summer
flower colour: deep pink
height: 8-10 cm/3-4 in

The rock jasmines are not the easiest of plants to
grow well since they require a very sharply drained
soil and, in the case of the European species
particularly, protection from winter wet.
A. sarmentosa is an Asian species and probably the
least difficult, commonly available plant in the
genus. *A. s. chumbyi* is a robust variety of
A. sarmentosa with woolly rosettes of foliage that
can spread quite widely. It often needs no
overhead protection in winter.

DRYAS octopetala★
○

type of plant: HP
flowering season: l. spring to midsummer
flower colour: white
height: 8-10 cm/3-4 in
E

If the trailing stems of this plant lie across
sun-baked stones, then an especially large number
of the lovely, anemone-like flowers are likely to
appear. These blooms are followed by fluffy
seed-heads. The tiny leaves of *D. octopetala*
resemble those of the oak and, together with the
prostrate stems, they cover the ground quite
densely. This plant needs good drainage.

　　Chalk – Ground-cover – Fruit.

ERINUS alpinus
○

type of plant: HP
flowering season: l. spring to midsummer
flower colour: pink
height: 8-10 cm/3-4 in
E

E. alpinus produces such a mass of bright blossom
that it is not surprising that individual specimens
are rather short-lived. However, this plant will,
conveniently, seed itself in any sunny piece of
ground where the drainage is good; it grows
especially well in the crevices of walls and between
paving stones. There are varieties of *E. alpinus*
with red, clear pink and white flowers.

　　Chalk – Hot, dry soils.

PHLOX douglasii e.g. 'Boothman's Variety'
sc NA
○

type of plant: HP
flowering season: l. spring to e. summer
flower colour: mauve
height: 5-10 cm/2-4 in
E

Although they are less popular than the varieties of
P. subulata (for two examples of which see p. 103),
forms of *P. douglasii* such as 'Boothman's Variety'
are attractive plants and almost as easy to grow.
However, they do require a very well drained soil
and plenty of warmth (conditions which are
usually present on drystone walls and in the
crevices between paving stones); they are able to
withstand periods of drought. The leaves of these
plants create dense, hummocky carpets of
ground-cover.

　　Chalk – Hot, dry soils – Ground-cover.

ASPERULA lilaciflora caespitosa sc NA
○

type of plant: SITP
flowering season: summer
flower colour: pink
height: 5-8 cm/2-3 in

This very small plant, which spreads only
10-15 cm/4-6 in wide, needs a gritty soil and a
position in full sun. Unless the drainage around its
roots is good, it may die in cold, wet winters. Its
starry flowers normally appear in large numbers.

　　Chalk – Hot, dry soils.

THYMUS serpyllum (syn. *T. drucei*)
e.g. 'Albus'★
[form of Wild Thyme]
○

type of plant: HP
flowering season: summer
flower colour: white
height: 5 cm/2 in
½E

T. serpyllum and its forms are ideal plants for small
areas of paving, where anything taller would be
obtrusive. Where the stems of *T. s.* 'Albus' touch
soil they will root and provide dense ground-cover
(particularly if they are trimmed after the flowers
have faded). The foliage emits a not particularly
strong, aromatic fragrance. All well drained soils
suit the wild thymes. (A red-flowered form of
T. serpyllum is illustrated on p. 19.)

　　Chalk – Hot, dry soils – Ground-cover –
Aromatic leaves.

GENTIANA septemfida
[species of Gentian]
○ [◑]
type of plant: HP
flowering season: summer
flower colour: deep blue
height: 20-30 cm/8-12 in

Some specimens of this plant produce flowers of undistinguished colouring but, at their best, the clustered blooms are a beautiful, deep blue. *G. septemfida* is easy to grow if it is given a rich, spongy, moisture-retentive soil which never dries out. If it is planted in a gap between paving stones, quite a deep hole should be excavated.

MALCOMIA maritima 'Mixed'
[form of Virginia Stock]
○ [◑]
type of plant: HA
flowering season: l. spring to e. autumn
flower colour: mixed – lilac, pink, red, white
height: 15-23 cm/6-9 in

Virginia stock is a sweetly scented plant which is extremely easy to grow. It should be sown where it is to flower, and the cracks between slabs of paving on a sunny terrace are particularly congenial positions. Many seedsmen's catalogues list separate colour forms of *M. maritima*.

Chalk – Fragrant flowers.

ACAENA buchananii MC
○ [◑]
type of plant: HP
height: 5 cm/2 in

The flowers of this mat-forming plant are insignificant, but they are followed, in late summer, by decorative, amber-yellow burrs. The somewhat similar *A. microphylla* (see p. 106) produces numerous large, red fruits. Both these plants thrive in well drained soils and sunny sites, and they look especially attractive in areas of paving. *A. buchananii* has greyish green foliage.

Chalk – Ground-cover – Grey, etc. leaves – Fruit.

VIOLA cornuta e.g. 'Jersey Gem'
[form of Horned Violet]
○ ◑
type of plant: HP
flowering season: l. spring to summer
flower colour: violet-blue
height: 15-23 cm/6-9 in
E

The horned violets grow neatly and thickly and they have a long flowering season (which can often be lengthened still further by cutting the plants back after the first flush of blooms has faded). *V. c.* 'Jersey Gem' is a deeply coloured form; a white-flowered variety is illustrated on p. 110. If these plants are grown in sunny positions their roots, at least, must be kept cool. The horned violets are only very slightly scented.

Dense shade – Ground-cover.

CAMPANULA garganica
[species of Bellflower]
○ ◑
type of plant: HP
flowering season: summer
flower colour: blue
height: 10-15 cm/4-6 in

Setting this plant amongst stone – either in a wall or in an area of paving – draws attention to the attractive way in which its flower stems radiate from a central bunch of leaves. Only a few of these leaves are normally visible in summer, since *C. garganica* is a very free-flowering plant. It is easy to grow and can spread over 30 cm/1 ft wide in fertile, well drained soils.

Chalk.

GERANIUM subcaulescens (syn. *G. cinereum subcaulescens*)
[species of Cranesbill]
○ ◑
type of plant: HP
flowering season: summer to e. autumn
flower colour: crimson
height: 10-15 cm/4-6 in

The very bright colour of this plant's petals is intensified both by the almost black centres of the flowers and by the cool, soft green of the foliage. The flowers are about 2 cm/1 in wide and they are produced at the end of rather lax stems, in large numbers and over many weeks (they often begin to open at the end of spring). Any soil with reasonably good drainage will suit *G. subcaulescens*.

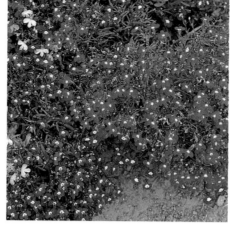

MYOSOTIS alpestris (syn. *M. rupicola*) e.g. 'Blue Ball'★
[form of Forget-me-not]

◐[○]
type of plant: HB/P
flowering season: mid-spring to e. summer
flower colour: blue
height: 15 cm/6 in

In damp, lightly shaded areas of paving this short-lived plant will cover its appropriately neat clump of leaves with a rounded cap of rich blue flowers. It is a popular plant for spring bedding and often used in combination with tulips. A pink-flowered form of forget-me-not is shown on p. 54. Both these plants will grow well in heavy soils for a limited period, but better drainage produces longer lived specimens. Plenty of moisture is essential for good growth.
    Clay.

LOBELIA erinus e.g. 'String of Pearls'

◐[○]
type of plant: HHA
flowering season: l. spring to e. autumn
flower colour: mixed – white, light blue, dark blue, pink, red
height: 15 cm/6 in

Lobelias are seen most frequently in summer bedding schemes. Provided the soil is sufficiently moisture-retentive and fertile, they can be planted in sunny sites and used to carpet the ground beneath roses. They grow neatly and densely and they have a long flowering season. They make pretty tufts of growth between paving stones. Blue-flowered lobelias (see p. 114) are particularly popular, but some mixtures like 'String of Pearls' are also available and the trailing varieties of lobelia are suitable for window boxes and hanging baskets.
    Ground-cover.

IONOPSIDIUM acaule
[Violet Cress]

◐[○]
type of plant: HA
flowering season: e. summer to e. autumn
flower colour: lilac
height: 5–8 cm/2-3 in

This little plant will usually seed itself from year to year, but it is unlikely to become a nuisance. It is easy to grow, particularly in those soils that retain moisture easily. Since it is very small and neat, it may be planted in troughs and window boxes, as well as in crevices between paving stones and along the edges of borders.

NIEREMBERGIA repens (syn. *N. rivularis*) ★

◐[○]
type of plant: HP
flowering season: summer
flower colour: white
height: 5 cm/2 in

Surrounded by an area of plain paving, the elegance and simplicity of this plant's lovely flowers can be fully appreciated. As long as its roots are cool and moist – beneath paving stones or gravel, for instance, or in rather damp ground – *N. repens* will grow well. It will thrive in sunshine if plenty of moisture is available and, when flourishing, its mat of stems and leaves may spread over 60 cm/2 ft wide.
    Damp and wet soils – Ground-cover.

SAXIFRAGA oppositifolia
[species of Saxifrage]

◐[○]
type of plant: HP
flowering season: spring
flower colour: shades of pink or purple
height: 2 cm/1 in
E

S. oppositifolia and its various forms (of which the easiest to grow is *S. o.* 'Splendens') flower earlier than many other saxifrages, but they are apt to be short-lived unless treated carefully. They need a soil that is both gritty and moisture-retentive, since they must not dry out in summer but wetness in winter will harm them. Leaf-mould and peat should be added to the gritty soil, and ideal positions are light, but cool crevices in drystone walls or paving. Good specimens of these plants produce numerous flowers over their mats of tiny leaves.

SAXIFRAGA×'Elizabethae'★
[form of Saxifrage]

◐
type of plant: HP
flowering season: spring
flower colour: yellow
height: 5–8 cm/2–3 in
E

Exposure to full sun, particularly at midday, can easily scorch this hybrid saxifrage and cause it permanent damage. It begins to flower – often prolifically – in earliest spring. Its leaves form flat cushions of greenery. A very well drained soil containing limestone chippings and leaf-mould suits this plant best, and it flourishes in narrow crevices in walls and paving.

SAXIFRAGA×'Pixie' sc NA
[example of a Mossy Saxifrage]

◗

type of plant: HP
flowering season: spring
flower colour: red
height: 5-8 cm/2-3 in
E

The so-called 'mossy' saxifrages, including
hybrids such as 'Pixie', are much easier to grow
than most of the other plants of their genus. They
will thrive in any reasonable, moisture-retentive
soil and they often make quite wide,
ground-covering mats or carpets of soft foliage.
Other hybrid saxifrages of this type include 'Peter
Pan', which has clear pink flowers, and the
white-flowered 'Pearly King'.

**Additional plants, featured elsewhere in this
book, that are suitable for crevices in paving**

○ sun
HELIANTHEMUM nummularium e.g. 'Wisley
　Pink': 23-30 cm (p. 162)
HELIANTHEMUM nummularium e.g. 'Wisley
　Primrose': 23-30 cm (p. 101)
PENSTEMON newberryi: 23-30 cm (p. 101)
PULSATILLA vulgaris: 23-30 cm (p. 14)
PULSATILLA vulgaris 'Rubra': 23-30 cm (p. 15)
HELIANTHEMUM nummularium e.g. 'Mrs
　Earle' ★: 23 cm (p. 62)
IBERIS sempervirens e.g. 'Snowflake': 23 cm
　(p. 102)
IBERIS umbellata e.g. 'Dwarf Fairy Mixed': 23 cm
　(p. 15)
THYMUS vulgaris: 20-30 cm (p. 196)
ARMERIA maritima 'Vindictive': 15-23 cm
　(p. 102)
SEMPERVIVUM montanum: 15-23 cm (p. 63)
THYMUS×citriodorus 'Aureus': 15-23 cm (p. 176)
DIANTHUS gratianopolitanus ★: 15-20 cm (p. 16)
TANACETUM 'Amani' ★: 15-20 cm (p. 162)
ALYSSUM saxatile e.g. 'Compactum': 15 cm
　(p. 63)
CALANDRINIA umbellata: 15 cm (p. 63)
GILIA hybrida e.g. 'French Hybrids': 15 cm (p. 17)
AETHIONEMA × 'Warley Rose' ★: 10-15 cm
　(p. 64)
ALYSSUM maritimum e.g. 'Little Dorrit':
　10-15 cm (p. 64)
AUBRIETA deltoidea e.g. 'Dr Mules': 10-15 cm
　(p. 18)
GERANIUM cinereum 'Ballerina': 10-15 cm
　(p. 18)
LITHOSPERMUM diffusum e.g. 'Heavenly
　Blue' ★: 10-15 cm (p. 102)
ALYSSUM maritimum e.g. 'Rosie O'Day': 10 cm
　(p. 19)
SEDUM spathulifolium 'Purpureum': 10 cm
　(p. 171)

GYPSOPHILA repens: 8-15 cm (p. 19)
GYPSOPHILA repens rosea: 8-15 cm (p. 64)
IBERIS saxatilis: 8-15 cm (p. 64)
SAPONARIA ocymoides: 8-15 cm (p. 103)
ALYSSUM maritimum e.g. 'Royal Carpet':
　8-10 cm (p. 103)
ANTENNARIA dioica 'Rubra': 8-10 cm (p. 103)
AUBRIETA deltoidea e.g. 'Red Carpet': 8-10 cm
　(p. 103)
DIANTHUS alpinus: 8-10 cm (p. 64)
SEDUM spathulifolium 'Capa Blanca' ★: 8-10 cm
　(p. 65)
PHLOX subulata e.g. 'Emerald Cushion Blue':
　5-10 cm (p. 103)
PHLOX subulata e.g. 'Temiscaming': 5-10 cm
　(p. 103)
ANTHEMIS nobilis 'Treneague': 5-8 cm (p. 104)
ARMERIA caespitosa: 5-8 cm (p. 65)
POLYGALA calcarea: 5-8 cm (p. 19)
SEDUM acre: 5 cm (p. 65)
SILENE acaulis: 5 cm (p. 104)
THYMUS serpyllum e.g. 'Coccineus': 5 cm (p. 19)
EDRAIANTHUS serpyllifolius: 2-5 cm (p. 20)
RAOULIA australis: 1-2 cm (p. 163)
RAOULIA lutescens: 1-2 cm (p. 104)

○ [◖] sun (or partial shade)
ARABIS albida e.g. 'Flore Pleno': 15-20 cm
　(p. 106)
ARABIS albida e.g. 'Rosabella': 15-20 cm (p. 23)
ACAENA microphylla: 5 cm (p. 106)

○ ◖ sun or partial shade
VIOLA cornuta e.g. 'Alba': 15-23 cm (p. 110)
VIOLA odorata e.g. 'Princess of Wales': 15 cm
　(p. 270)
VIOLA labradorica: 10-15 cm (p. 111)
CAMPANULA cochlearifolia: 10 cm (p. 26)
SAXIFRAGA × apiculata: 10 cm (p. 26)
CAMPANULA portenschlagiana: 8-15 cm (p. 112)

◖ [○] partial shade (or sun)
SAXIFRAGA umbrosa: 23-30 cm (p. 185)
MYOSOTIS alpestris e.g. 'Carmine King': 23 cm
　(p. 54)
LOBELIA erinus e.g. 'Cambridge Blue': 15 cm
　(p. 114)
LOBELIA erinus e.g. 'Crystal Palace': 15 cm
　(p. 114)
LOBELIA erinus e.g. 'Rosamund': 15 cm (p. 114)
GENTIANA sino-ornata ★: 10-15 cm (p. 41)

◖ partial shade
OMPHALODES cappadocica: 15-23 cm (p. 116)
BLECHNUM penna-marina: 15 cm (p. 116)
ASPLENIUM trichomanes: 8-15 cm (p. 26)
ARENARIA balearica: 2-5 cm (p. 116)

◖ ● partial or full shade
VIOLA cornuta e.g. 'Alba': 15-23 cm (p. 110)
VIOLA cornuta e.g. 'Jersey Gem': 15-23 cm
　(p. 143)

Plants with variegated leaves

Some gardeners love every variegated leaf they see; others consider all variegated foliage an abhorrent perversion of nature. Yet, considering the very large differences in types of variegation, it is surprising that the subject of variegated leaves should be quite such a divisive one.

Many gardeners will be familiar with the sort of variegation which consists of a margin of either white or yellow around the green centre of a leaf. The width and general effect of this margin can, however, vary considerably: for instance, the big, bold leaves of the ivy called *Hedera canariensis* 'Variegata' (syn. *H. c.* 'Gloire de Marengo') have large, irregular margins of grey and white, while each leaf of *Daphne odora* 'Aureomarginata' is edged with the narrowest line of cream. The former plant's leaves certainly deserve the epithet 'striking', but the daphne's foliage is of an altogether more subdued and delicate sort.

In some plants the margin of the leaf is green and the centre of the leaf contains the contrasting colour. This second colour may be yellow, as it is in *Hedera helix* 'Gold Heart' (syn. *H. h.* 'Jubilee'), or white – as in *Hosta undulata* – or even red or pink or bronze as it is in the mixed varieties of *Coleus blumei*.

Margins or centres of contrasting colour do not, however, exhaust the range of types of variegation. Some plants, such as *Arum italicum* 'Pictum' and one of the honeysuckles, *Lonicera japonica* 'Aureoreticulata', have networks of yellow or white veining across the green background of their leaves. In several cases, the networks look less like veining than marbling: the foliage of a number of cyclamens is variegated in this way. There are also plants whose leaves are spotted or mottled with another colour: the much maligned spotted laurels, such as *Aucuba japonica* 'Crotonifolia', fall into this category, but so too do the leaves of the dog's tooth violet with their unusual, brown markings and the leaves of several water-lilies with their splashes of maroon. Some plants with long, thin leaves are striped with another colour. Occasionally, the stripes form bands across the leaves: *Miscanthus sinensis* 'Zebrinus' and *Scirpus tabernaemontani* 'Zebrinus' both have this type of variegation.

Despite the fact that not all variegated leaves consist of strident splotches of white on green, there will be some gardeners who feel that anything other than plain green foliage looks unnatural in a garden. These gardeners may, however, acknowledge that variegated leaves are often important components of flower arrangements. The plants in the following list which have foliage that is particularly useful for cutting have been marked with a sign in the final line of information. Some variegated foliage does not make good cut material because it does not last well in water. There are also a few plants, such as the daphne mentioned above, so slow-growing that they are not practical sources of cut foliage. Many bulbous plants, including the tulips in this list, should have only a very few of their leaves picked since the foliage feeds the bulbs for next year's flowers.

An excellent source of information about all types of foliage for cutting is Sybil Emberton's *Garden Foliage for Flower Arrangement* (published by Faber and Faber). Many of the less readily available plants with variegated leaves, which have had to be excluded from this list, are described in this book and the suppliers from which they can be purchased are also noted.

When choosing variegated plants, remember that, in some cases, the variegation tends to fade during the growing season: the leaves of *Hosta fortunei* 'Albopicta', *Iris kaempferi* 'Variegata' and *Melissa officinalis* 'Aurea' are at their best in spring and early summer. Remember too that the variegated versions of plants tend to produce fewer and often smaller flowers than their green-leaved counterparts (although, with spectacular foliage, it is, perhaps, an advantage to have less conspicuous blossom). If any plant with variegated foliage produces plain green shoots as, for instance, the variegated form of box elder, *Acer negundo* 'Variegatum', sometimes does, these shoots should be cut out or the whole plant will, in time, revert to the normal green colouring.

Variegated plants are often described as difficult to place in a garden, and indeed the bolder leaf patterns can easily overshadow nearby, but less flamboyant, foliage. Bear in mind, however, the distance from which the plants are to be seen. Many of the larger trees and shrubs are generally viewed from a distance, and the markings on their individual leaves are less important than the very general effect that the contrasting colour has upon the whole plant. When you go to choose a variegated plant it can be most helpful to take even quite small pieces of the foliage of any plants which will be growing near it in your garden. You can then better imagine whether the variegated plant is going to overwhelm its prospective neighbours. Even holding a colour photograph of the plant in front of existing plants can give some idea of how it might appear *in situ*.

Most of the variegated plants which appreciate shade have white markings on their leaves. Where plants do well in either sun or shade, the brightness of the variegation – both yellow and white – is often greatest in sunshine, but the usually drier conditions of sunnier sites will mean less foliage and smaller individual leaves.

HUMULUS scandens (syn. *H. japonicus*) 'Variegatus'
[form of Hop]

○

type of plant: HACl
leaves variegated with white
height: 2.4-3 m/8-10 ft

Most of the annual climbers grow very rapidly – and *H. s.* 'Variegatus' is no exception – but few of them have anything other than rather dull foliage. However, even the plain green leaves of *H. scandens* itself are attractively shaped, and the variegated form makes a highly decorative, temporary screen of twining stems and white-splashed foliage. Neither of these plants is difficult to grow, but for the very fastest increase in size they need a rich soil and a continuous supply of moisture.

Climbers – Containers.

DAPHNE odora 'Aureomarginata' ★

○

type of plant: SlTSh
flowering season: midwinter to e. spring
flower colour: purple + white
leaves variegated with cream
height: 1.2-1.8 m/4-6 ft
E

The elegantly tapered leaves of this plant have thin, cream margins and, from a distance, these markings have a subtle, enlivening effect upon the overall appearance of the shrub. *D. o.* 'Aureomarginata' grows slowly but it eventually makes quite a wide, spreading mound of foliage. Its flowers are richly fragrant (when the blooms are open, only the inner, pale surface of the petals is visible). This plant needs a fertile soil, to which peat or leaf-mould have, ideally, been added.

Ground-cover – Fragrant flowers – Winter-flowering plants.

ZEA mays e.g. 'Gracillima Variegata'
[form of Ornamental Maize]

○

type of plant: HHA (Gr)
leaves variegated with white
height: 60-90 cm/2-3 ft

Even this relatively small ornamental maize is a striking plant in its handsome stripes, and it needs to be set amongst other plants that are strongly coloured or boldly shaped if it is not to look oddly tropical and out of place. It also requires a rich, moist soil and a warm site to do well.

IRIS kaempferi 'Variegata'

○

type of plant: HP
flowering season: summer
flower colour: violet-purple
leaves variegated with white
height: 60-75 cm/2-2½ ft
✳✂

Not all gardeners who admire the leaves of this iris can provide the right conditions for growing the plant. It must have a lime-free soil that is damp or, at least, moist, and it also needs a position in full sun. The markings on its foliage deepen as summer approaches and, by the time most of the flowers have opened, the ribbed leaves are a uniform green. The somewhat similar *I. laevigata* 'Variegata' also needs a damp, or even wet soil, but it is a lime-tolerant plant. (Photographed in early summer.)

Acid soils – Damp and wet soils.

EUPHORBIA marginata
[Snow-on-the-Mountain]

○

type of plant: HA
leaves variegated with white
height: 60 cm/2 ft
✂

The light green leaves of this bushy annual become edged and veined in white as they mature. They are popular for flower arranging, but the milky juices from their stems can be harmful, and the tips of the stalks should be singed or scalded immediately after cutting. Some shelter and a well drained soil create the most suitable conditions for this plant.

Chalk.

GLYCERIA maxima 'Variegata' (syn.
G. aquatica 'Folliis-variegatis')

○

type of plant: HP (Gr)
flowering season: summer
flower colour: creamy green
leaves variegated with yellow
height: 60 cm/2 ft

The lushest and leafiest specimens of this grass grow in wet soil or in a few centimetres/inches of water. However, such is its vigour that *G. m.* 'Variegata' will grow quite satisfactorily in drier places, and in ordinary, moisture-retentive garden soils its creeping roots are unlikely to become very invasive. The new leaves are tinged with deep pink. Later in the year, open panicles of flowers appear; these are carried well above the foliage.

Damp and wet soils – Ground-cover – Green flowers.

HYPERICUM × moserianum 'Tricolor' ★
sc NA
[form of St John's Wort]

○

type of plant: SlTSh
flowering season: summer to autumn
flower colour: yellow
leaves variegated with white, pink
height: 60 cm/2 ft
½E

This hypericum needs a more sheltered site than other commonly grown plants in its genus. When flourishing, its arching shoots make quite good ground-cover. The leaves of this plant are variegated in a particularly pretty combination of white, green and pink. However, some gardeners may consider that the arrival of the large yellow flowers creates an altogether too 'busy' effect. Any well drained soil is suitable.

Chalk – Atmospheric pollution – Containers.

IRIS pallida 'Argenteo-variegata' (syn. *I. p.*
'Variegata') ★

○

type of plant: HP
flowering season: e. summer
flower colour: light blue
leaves variegated with white
height: 60 cm/2 ft
✂

The stripes of white on the blue-green leaves of this iris are striking enough in themselves, but the arrangement of the foliage in slightly arching fans accentuates these markings still further. *I. p.* 'Argenteo-variegata' should be given a well drained, fertile soil; frequent division will keep it strong and healthy. The flowers of this plant are less attractive than the leaves, but they do emit a sweet, vanilla-like scent. A rarer form, *I. p.* 'Aureo-variegata' has yellow stripes on its foliage.

Fragrant flowers.

AMARANTHUS tricolor
[Joseph's Coat]

○

type of plant: HHA
leaves variegated with red, yellow
height: 45-60 cm/1½-2 ft

In Britain, *A. tricolor* needs a warm, sheltered site and a deep, rich soil if it is to grow well outdoors. Seed catalogues will list various forms of this bushy plant, including 'Illumination' and 'Molten Fire'. The first variety has bronze, red and yellow leaves, while the foliage of 'Molten Fire' is coppery crimson and scarlet.

SALVIA officinalis 'Tricolor' ★
[form of Common Sage]

○

type of plant: SlTSh (Herb)
flowering season: summer
flower colour: purple
leaves variegated with white, pinkish purple
height: 45-60 cm/1½-2 ft
E/½E

Many popular herbs have varieties with interestingly coloured foliage and they are often as aromatic as the plain-leaved species. *S. o.* 'Tricolor' emits the sharp scent characteristic of common sage; its leaves are a strikingly decorative mixture of grey-green, white and pink-purple, with some bright pink and red also present. This neat, hummocky plant will thrive, for many years, in light soil and full sun.

Chalk – Hot, dry soils – Ground-cover – Aromatic leaves.

PELARGONIUM × hortorum (Tricolor) e.g. 'A Happy Thought' sc NA
[form of Geranium]

○

type of plant: TenP
flowering season: e. summer to mid-autumn
flower colour: magenta
leaves variegated with cream
height: 40-45 cm/15-18 in

Some of the bedding 'geraniums', so popular in British public gardens, have very boldly marked foliage, none more so than the so-called Tricolor types, of which the variety 'A Happy Thought' is a fairly subdued example, while 'Mr Henry Cox' (see below) has leaves banded in a surprising *mélange* of dark and light green, two shades of red and cream. The markings on the leaves of Zonal geraniums most often consist of broad, circular 'horseshoes' of bronze or maroon (see, for example, the varieties 'Cherie' and *(contd)*

PELARGONIUM × hortorum (Zonal) e.g. 'Caroline Schmidt' sc NA
[form of Zonal Geranium or Horseshoe Geranium]

○

type of plant: TenP
flowering season: e. summer to mid-autumn
flower colour: red
leaves variegated with white
height: 40-45 cm/15-18 in

See preceding plant.

(contd)
'Gustav Emich', below). Occasionally, these plants have white or cream margins to their leaves (see *P. × h.* 'Caroline Schmidt', above). Some varieties are so faintly marked that they have, in effect, plain, green foliage. All the pelargoniums shown here produce rounded flower heads (in the case of the varieties 'Cherie' and *(contd)*

PELARGONIUM × hortorum (Zonal) e.g. 'Cherie' sc NA
[form of Zonal Geranium or Horseshoe Geranium]

○

type of plant: TenP
flowering season: e. summer to mid-autumn
flower colour: salmon pink
leaves variegated with bronze
height: 40-45 cm/15-18 in

See *P. × h.* 'A Happy Thought', above.

(contd)
'Gustav Emich', these are more decorative than the zoned leaves). When used for summer bedding, these tender plants must be given a well drained soil and a position in full sun. They are often re-propagated from cuttings – which root very easily – each year.

PELARGONIUM × hortorum (Zonal) e.g. 'Gustav Emich' sc NA
[form of Zonal Geranium or Horseshoe Geranium]

○

type of plant: TenP
flowering season: e. summer to mid-autumn
flower colour: scarlet
leaves variegated with bronze
height: 40-45 cm/15-18 in

See *P. × h.* 'A Happy Thought', above.

PELARGONIUM × hortorum (Tricolor) e.g. 'Mr Henry Cox' (syn. *P. × h.* 'Mrs Henry Cox') sc NA
[form of Geranium]

○

type of plant: TenP
flowering season: e. summer to mid-autumn
flower colour: pale pink
leaves variegated with cream, red
height: 40-45 cm/15-18 in

See *P. × h.* 'A Happy Thought', above.

COLEUS blumei e.g. 'Carefree Mixture'

○

type of plant: HHA
leaves variegated with red, yellow, maroon,
pink, bronze
height: 30-45 cm/1-1½ ft

Certain strains of *C. blumei*, including the mixture shown here, produce naturally well branched, bushy plants which require no pinching out of their central growing tips. The 'Carefree' plants have small, lobed leaves often edged in shades of green that are almost as bright as the brilliant reds and pinks which predominate. If grown outdoors, rather than in a greenhouse, varieties of *C. blumei* must have a really warm, sheltered site.

PELARGONIUM peltatum 'L'Elegante'
[form of Ivy-leaved Geranium]

○

type of plant: TenP
flowering season: e. summer to mid-autumn
flower colour: white
leaves variegated with white turning purple
height: 30-40 cm/12-15 in

The succulent leaves of this trailing plant have their neat, ivy-like shape accentuated by white margins. Particularly as autumn approaches, the foliage often becomes flushed with a pale, pinkish purple colour and this is most noticeable in the white part of each leaf. *P. peltatum* and its various named forms, both plain-leaved and variegated, need full sun and a well drained soil when grown outdoors; they are able to withstand periods of drought. Since they are tender perennials, they must be either overwintered in a greenhouse or raised from cuttings each year.

TULIPA (Greigii Hybrid) e.g. 'Red Riding Hood'
[form of Tulip]

○

type of plant: HBb
flowering season: mid-spring
flower colour: scarlet
leaves variegated with brownish purple
height: 20 cm/8 in

All the Greigii hybrid tulips have leaves which are striped in brown, maroon or a brownish purple. *T.* 'Red Riding Hood' has especially heavy markings on its blue-green foliage and, although these are only ephemeral features of the springtime garden, they are attractive, both in themselves and as a background to the bright scarlet flowers. Soils that drain quickly give the best results with all types of tulips.

Chalk – Hot, dry soils.

NYMPHAEA e.g. × 'Marliacea Chromatella'
sc NA
[form of Water-lily]

○

type of plant: HPAq
flowering season: summer to e. autumn
flower colour: pale yellow
leaves variegated with reddish brown
height: 10-15 cm/4-6 in

The flowers of a water-lily always outshine its leaves but, in certain cases, the colour of the blooms is enhanced by the markings on the foliage. *N.* × 'Marliacea Chromatella' has shapely petals of pale yellow and these look especially beautiful against the purple-mottled leaves. This moderately vigorous hybrid needs water about 45-60 cm/1½-2 ft deep. Its roots should be planted in fertile mud. Once established, this water-lily may produce an excessive amount of leaves, unless it is divided from time to time.

ILEX aquifolium e.g. 'Argentea Marginata'★
[form of Common or English Holly]

○ [◐]
type of plant: HT
leaves variegated with creamy white
height: 6-9 m/20-30 ft
E ✕

The common holly is the source of numerous varieties, several of which have variegated leaves. *I. a.* 'Argentea Marginata' is, at first, bushy; after many years, it grows into a tree of roughly pyramidal outline. It will bear large quantities of red berries if pollinated by a male plant. In a sunny position the markings on its leaves are clear and bright. Most soils are suitable. When used for hedging, individual plants should be set about 45 cm/1½ ft apart. Established hedges which are trimmed each year bear few berries.

Seaside – Atmospheric pollution – Hedging – Fruit.

ILEX × altaclarensis e.g. 'Golden King' (syn.
I. aquifolium 'Golden King') **sc NA**
[form of Holly]

○ [◐]
type of plant: HT
leaves variegated with yellow
height: 5.4-7.5 m/18-25 ft
E ✕

Despite its masculine name, *I.×a.* 'Golden King' is a female holly and it will produce red berries if pollinated by a male plant. Its main feature is its yellow-variegated foliage which is, conveniently, almost devoid of prickles. Particularly when young, this is a very slow-growing plant, but it eventually makes a small and fairly broad-headed tree. It will grow in most soils and sites, but sunshine brightens the variegation of its leaves. (See preceding plant for notes on holly hedges.)

Seaside – Atmospheric pollution – Hedging – Fruit.

PHORMIUM tenax e.g. 'Variegatum' MC
[form of New Zealand Flax]
○ [◐]
type of plant: SlTSh/P
flowering season: summer
flower colour: dull red
leaves variegated with cream
height: 3-3.6 m/10-12 ft
E ✕ , leaves 1.5-1.8 m/5-6 ft high

The striping on the leaves of this and some other
phormiums with similar foliage varies both within
a single plant and between plants. However, the
best forms produce clumps of rigid, well marked
leaves and, in maturity, heads of flowers on soaring
stems. A light but moisture-retentive or damp soil
suits this plant best. In cold districts, the crowns of
phormiums should be protected during the winter
months.

Damp and wet soils – Seaside – Atmospheric
pollution – Containers.

ELAEAGNUS pungens 'Maculata' ★
○ [◐]
type of plant: HSh
leaves variegated with yellow
height: 2.4-3 m/8-10 ft
E ✕

The glistening brightness of this shrub's leaves can
cheer up a winter garden more effectively than
many a winter-flowering plant. Unfortunately,
some of the angular, red-brown shoots produce
plain, green foliage and, if these shoots are not
removed at once, the whole spreading shrub turns
green in time. *E. p.* 'Maculata' will grow in most
soils, including those of reasonable depth over
chalk. The foliage of this shrub is very popular for
cutting and it lasts well in water. Tiny flowers
appear in autumn; they have a sweet scent.

Atmospheric pollution – Hedging – Containers
– Fragrant flowers.

ACTINIDIA kolomikta
○ [◐]
type of plant: SlTCl
flowering season: e. summer
flower colour: white
leaves variegated with pink, white
height: 1.8-3.6 m/6-12 ft

The extraordinary, icing sugar colours which this
twining climber develops during its growing
season seem to be most regularly produced on
specimens planted against warm walls and in good,
loamy soils. However, this is one of those wayward
plants that sometimes fails to perform as it should,
even when apparently well treated. Each of the
basically dark green leaves is about 15 cm/6 in long.
Climbers.

EUONYMUS japonicus 'Ovatus Aureus' (syn.
E. j. 'Aureovariegatus')
○ [◐]
type of plant: HSh
leaves variegated with yellow
height: 1.5-2.1 m/5-7 ft
E ✕

There are a number of variegated forms of
E. japonicus, all of them dense, bushy shrubs with
fairly upright shoots and – if planted in full sun –
very brightly marked leaves. They grow well both
by the sea and in large cities and, although they
have a preference for alkaline conditions, almost
any soil gives good results. *E. j.* 'Ovatus Aureus'
can be used for hedging (either alone or together
with the plain-leaved and faster growing species);
it needs to be trimmed annually, in spring.

Chalk – Seaside – Atmospheric pollution –
Hedging – Containers.

MISCANTHUS sinensis (syn. *Eulalia japonica*)
'Zebrinus'
○ [◐]
type of plant: HP (Gr)
flowering season: mid-autumn
flower colour: pinkish brown
leaves variegated with yellow
height: 1.2-1.8 m/4-6 ft

Few plants have horizontally banded foliage (but,
for another example, see *Scirpus tabernaemontani*
'Zebrinus', p. 70) and this grass is, therefore, as
odd as it is decorative. And it is indeed decorative
for, from a distance, its arching clumps of leaves
look as if they are shimmering with small flecks of
light. (The bars of yellow which create this effect
become most distinct towards the middle of
summer.) *M. s.* 'Zebrinus' flowers regularly, but
the more conventionally variegated *M. s.*
'Gracillimus' (see right) rarely produces any flower
heads. However, it is, if anything, a more *(contd)*

MISCANTHUS sinensis (syn. *Eulalia japonica*)
'Gracillimus' ★
○ [◐]
type of plant: HP (Gr)
leaves variegated with white
height: 75-150 cm/2½-5 ft

See preceding plant.

(contd)
elegant plant, with white stripes on a soft,
grey-green background. Both these grasses are
easily grown in any soil that does not become too
dry in summer.

Additional plants, featured elsewhere in this
book, that have variegated leaves

○ sun
TULIPA (Greigii Hybrid) e.g. 'Oriental
Splendour': 40 cm (p. 59)

○ [◑] sun (or partial shade)
SCIRPUS tabernaemontani e.g. 'Zebrinus':
90-120 cm (p. 70)
CYCLAMEN cilicium: 8-10 cm (p. 266)

ACER platanoides 'Drummondii'
[form of Norway Maple]

○ ◑

type of plant: HT
flowering season: mid-spring
flower colour: yellow
leaves variegated with white
height: 9-15 m/30-50 ft

An exceptionally neat edging of white emphasizes
the sharp, clean shape of this tree's foliage. Any
shoots which produce leaves without this edging
should be removed promptly. All
moisture-retentive soils suit this broad-headed,
variegated form of the Norway maple, but it will
also grow quite satisfactorily in rather shallow,
chalky soils.

Chalk – Atmospheric pollution.

ACER negundo 'Variegatum' (syn. *A. n.*
'Argenteovariegatum')
[form of Box Elder]

○ ◑

type of plant: HT
leaves variegated with white
height: 9 m/30 ft

A. n. 'Variegatum' is a much more openly
branched tree than the plant shown in the
preceding photograph and its ash-like foliage is
altogether more blotchily marked. It is sometimes
induced to grow as a large shrub by being cut back
hard every year. Any green-leaved suckers which
appear must be removed at once. This plant is
particularly at home in a moist soil, but it is tough
and adaptable and, therefore, easy to grow almost
anywhere.

Chalk – Atmospheric pollution.

HEDERA canariensis 'Variegata' (syn. *H. c.*
'Gloire de Marengo') **MC**
[form of Ivy]

○ ◑

type of plant: SITCl
leaves variegated with grey, white
height: 4.5-6 m/15-20 ft
E ✂

To become established quickly and to colour well,
this large-leaved, self-clinging climber should be
given a sunny position; it will, however, grow
quite adequately in shadier sites. In late autumn
and winter, the foliage often takes on a bronzed
appearance and the leaf edges turn pink. When
pegged down into soil *H. c.* 'Variegata' knits into a
carpet about 15-23 cm/6-9 in high. Any soil that
does not become too cold and wet in winter is
suitable for this ivy.

Atmospheric pollution – Ground-cover –
Climbers – Containers – Autumn foliage.

HEDERA colchica 'Dentata-Variegata'
[form of Ivy]

○ ◑

type of plant: HCl
leaves variegated with grey, yellow
height: 4.5-6 m/15-20 ft
E ✂

Of all the readily available ivies, *H. colchica* has the
largest leaves. In the form illustrated here,
individual leaves are often well over 15 cm/6 in
long. The aerial roots of this plant will cling to
walls (all aspects are suitable) and similar
supports, but they will also affix themselves to any
piece of soil they have been encouraged to lie
across. When grown as ground-cover, *H. c.*
'Dentata-Variegata' soon builds up into a mass of
leaves and stems about 15-23 cm/6-9 in high. Any
soil, including clay, will suit this ivy.

Clay – Atmospheric pollution – Ground-cover –
Climbers – Containers.

HEDERA helix e.g. 'Glacier'
[form of Common or English Ivy]

○ ◑

type of plant: HCl
leaves variegated with white
height: 3-3.6 m/10-12 ft
E ✂

Among the dozens of cultivated varieties of the
common ivy, the two moderately vigorous
climbers illustrated in this and the following
photograph give some idea of the wide difference
in appearance between these plants. 'Glacier'
produces small leaves with elegantly elongated
central lobes, and its combination of soft
grey-greens pland white is a particularly pretty one.
In comparison, 'Gold Heart' has foliage which is
altogether more striking: its leaves are larger,
thicker and more rounded, and the central areas of
bright yellow contrast strongly with the rich, dark
green margins. This last plant is (*contd*)

HEDERA helix e.g. 'Gold Heart' (syn. *H. h.* 'Jubilee')★
[form of Common or English Ivy]
○ ◐
type of plant: HCl
leaves variegated with yellow
height: 3-3.6 m/10-12 ft
E ✕

See preceding plant.
(*contd*)
remarkably tolerant of dry shade, but both varieties will grow in any soil – and in any site, including a north- or east-facing wall. A year or so after planting, these climbers will cling, by means of aerial roots, to flat surfaces. They can be used for ground-cover, but more vigorous ivies provide denser cover more quickly.

Chalk – Clay – Dry shade (*H. h.* 'Gold Heart' only) – Atmospheric pollution – Climbers – Containers.

BUXUS sempervirens e.g. 'Aureovariegata'
[form of Common or English Box]
○ ◐
type of plant: HSh
leaves variegated with yellow
height: 2.4-3 m/8-10 ft
E ✕

When set approximately 30 cm/1 ft apart, individual specimens of variegated box can be used to make formal hedges which, in maturity, need trimming once a year. In the case of the present example, the natural overall shape is a rather open one. Box will grow well in most soils, and it will flourish where chalk or lime is present. The forms with variegated foliage are brightest in sunny or partially shaded positions, but they will still be conspicuously coloured in full shade. The tiny flowers of these shrubs are sweetly scented.

Chalk – Dry shade – Atmospheric pollution – Hedging – Containers – Fragrant flowers.

WEIGELA florida 'Variegata'★
○ ◐
type of plant: HSh
flowering season: l. spring to e. summer
flower colour: pale pink
leaves variegated with cream
height: 1.5 m/5 ft
✕

This well branched, slightly arching shrub is easy to grow. The very best results are produced on soils which do not dry out too readily. Each of the tapered leaves has a broad, cream margin which later fades to white and which may become tinged with pink in autumn. This plant is deciduous but the foliage is often retained until early winter. The leaves last very well in water. (A few catalogues still list weigelas under the name *Diervilla*.)

Chalk – Clay – Atmospheric pollution – Containers.

PHALARIS arundinacea 'Picta'
[Gardener's Garters, Ribbon Grass]
○ ◐
type of plant: HP (Gr)
flowering season: summer
flower colour: creamy green or purplish
leaves variegated with cream
height: 90-150 cm/3-5 ft

Any gardener installing this very attractive grass amongst other, more precious plants must be prepared for some grubbing out in future, for this is a very vigorous plant with invasive, underground roots. Where there is plenty of room, its energetic nature can be appreciated. In damp, fertile soils especially, it will spread lustily and create large areas of ground-cover. Its naturally drooping foliage is smartest in spring and early summer.

Damp and wet soils – Ground-cover.

MELISSA officinalis 'Aurea'
[Golden Balm]
○ ◐
type of plant: HP (Herb)
leaves variegated with yellow
height: 75 cm/2½ ft

In spring the foliage of the golden balm is basically yellow with a suffusion of bright green along the main veins of each leaf. If allowed to flower, this plant soon becomes almost entirely green. It is, therefore, often cut back hard in early summer, and it will respond to this treatment by producing a fresh set of erect and bushy shoots with well coloured, pungently aromatic foliage. Most soils suit this plant. A few nurseries stock a form of balm with unvariegated, yellow leaves. It needs a shadier position than *M. o.* 'Aurea'.

Dry shade – Ground-cover – Aromatic leaves.

MOLINIA caerulea 'Variegata'
○ ◐
type of plant: HP (Gr)
flowering season: e. autumn
flower colour: purplish
leaves variegated with cream
height: 45–60 cm/1½-2 ft

M. caerulea itself grows in damp, acid soils of very low fertility, but this strikingly variegated form will flourish only if it is given less frugal treatment. In autumn, the tussocks of leaves, as well as the haze of flower spikes fade to a beautiful pale beige colour.

Acid soils.

VINCA major 'Variegata' (syn. *V. m.* 'Elegantissima')
[form of Greater Periwinkle]

○ ●
type of plant: HSh/P
flowering season: mid-spring to e. summer
flower colour: blue
leaves variegated with cream
height: 23-45 cm/9-18 in
E

The variegated form of the greater periwinkle will put up with all the difficulties that the green-leaved species will. It is, however, so much more decorative than the species that it deserves a position with a reasonable amount of light and not too dry a soil. It slowly forms a rather bumpy, ground-covering carpet of foliage and trailing shoots.

Chalk – Dry shade – Dense shade – Atmospheric pollution – Ground-cover.

Additional plants, featured elsewhere in this book, that have variegated leaves

○ ● sun or partial shade
LIGUSTRUM ovalifolium 'Aureum': 2.7-3.6m (p. 177)
CORNUS alba 'Elegantissima': 1.8-2.7m (p. 72)
AUCUBA japonica e.g. 'Crotonifolia': 1.5-2.4m (p. 136)
SPIRAEA×bumalda 'Anthony Waterer': 90-120cm (p. 107)
CAREX morrowi 'Variegata': 23cm (p. 76)
HEDERA canariensis 'Variegata': 15-23cm (p. 151)
HEDERA colchica 'Dentata-Variegata': 15-23cm (p. 151)

LONICERA japonica 'Aureoreticulata'
[form of Honeysuckle]

● [○]
type of plant: HCl
leaves variegated with yellow
height: 7.5-9 m/25-30 ft
E/½E ✕

In most summers, only a very few, sweetly scented flowers appear on this honeysuckle. With plenty of sun, the foliage will be particularly bright; partial shade and moisture are, however, probably better for the overall health of the plant. The twining growths of *L. j.* 'Aureoreticulata' need some support in order to climb. When used for ground-cover, a carpet of tangled stems and more upright shoots, about 15-20 cm/6-8 in high, is eventually formed. This honeysuckle may be grown on a north wall, provided it is fairly sheltered.

Ground-cover – Climbers – Containers.

PARTHENOCISSUS henryana (syn. *Vitis henryana*)★

● [○]
type of plant: SlTCl
leaves variegated with white, pink
height: 7.5-9 m/25-30 ft

P. henryana has leaflets about 8 cm/3 in long. In partial shade, their basic colour is a dark, bronzish green (which turns red in autumn) and the main veins are very pale. This vigorous climber will cling, by means of adhesive tendrils, to flat surfaces, a year or two after planting. It is suitable for north walls. It can also be grown horizontally, given some twigs to adhere to initially, when it will reach a height of about 15 cm/6 in. A good, loamy soil suits this plant best.

Atmospheric pollution – Ground-cover – Climbers – Containers – Autumn foliage.

SCROPHULARIA aquatica 'Variegata' (syn. *S. nodosa* 'Variegata') sc NA
[form of Figwort or Water Betony]

● [○]
type of plant: HP
leaves variegated with cream
height: 60-90 cm/2-3 ft
E

Even in densely shaded positions, the variegation on this plant's leaves remains creditably bright. *S. a.* 'Variegata' is, however, best when grown in partial shade – and when given a rich, moist soil. It will also flourish in damp and boggy ground. The dark, stiff stems must have their topknots of tiny, brown flowers removed if the whole plant is not to become untidy and rather bare.

Clay – Damp and wet soils – Dense shade.

HOSTA undulata (syn. *H. undulata undulata*)★
[species of Plantain Lily]

● [○]
type of plant: HP
flowering season: l. summer
flower colour: pale lilac
leaves variegated with white
height: 60-75 cm/2-2½ ft
✕

Nearly all hostas are popular with flower arrangers, but the twisted foliage of *H. undulata* seems to have a special attraction. *H. fortunei* 'Albopicta' (see next page) is at its most beautifully butter-coloured in spring; its older leaves are two shades of green. Nurseries with a wide range of perennials will list up to a dozen variegated hostas. Fertile, moisture-retentive soils are essential for hearty growth and great, ground-covering clumps of leaves.

Damp and wet soils – Ground-cover.

HOSTA crispula NA
[species of Plantain Lily]
◐ [○]
type of plant: HP
flowering season: summer
flower colour: lavender
leaves variegated with cream
height: 60 cm/2 ft
✕

This excellent hosta has creamy silver variegation which holds up better in partly sunny sites than the marking on other hostas. The leathery, tapering leaves are about 30 cm/1 ft long in well grown specimens. A moisture-retentive soil gives best results. This plant is one of the best of its kind and can be obtained in Britain from most nurseries with a wide range of perennials.

HOSTA fortunei 'Albopicta'
[form of Plantain Lily]
◐ [○]
type of plant: HP
flowering season: summer
flower colour: lilac
leaves variegated with yellow
height: 45-60 cm/1½-2 ft
✕

See *H. undulata*, previous page.

MENTHA rotundifolia 'Variegata'
[form of Apple Mint or Round-leaved Mint]
◐ [○]
type of plant: HP (Herb)
flowering season: midsummer to e. autumn
flower colour: mauve
leaves variegated with creamy white
height: 30-60 cm/1-2 ft

The little, wrinkled leaves of this mint emit a sharp, but also very slightly musty smell when crushed and, for culinary purposes, *M. rotundifolia* itself is more satisfactory, since its scent is fresh and clean. *M. r.* 'Variegata' is not as invasive as the species, but in cool, moist and fertile soil its rather curving stems will grow densely enough to block out most weeds.

Clay – Ground-cover – Aromatic leaves.

ARUM italicum 'Pictum' (syn.
A. italicum italicum)★
◐ [○]
type of plant: HTu
flowering season: spring
flower colour: cream
leaves variegated with grey, cream
height: 30-45 cm/1-1½ ft
✕

This plant saves all its best efforts for the second half of the year. After the short-lived flowers have faded, thick spikes of orange-red berries begin to ripen and, in autumn, remarkably resilient, pale-veined leaves appear in succession and last until early summer. The most conspicuously marked foliage is produced in sunny positions, but this plant needs coolness and moisture at its roots, which may be easier to maintain in partial shade.
  Fruit.

AJUGA reptans 'Variegata'
[form of Bugle]
◐ [○]
type of plant: HP
flowering season: l. spring to e. summer
flower colour: blue
leaves variegated with cream
height: 8-10 cm/3-4 in
E/½E

Two other varieties of *A. reptans*, one with red and one with purplish leaves, are illustrated on p. 172. *A. j.* 'Variegata' is less vigorous than either of these plants. Its grey-green and cream foliage forms a close carpet in moist soils; in dry soils it does not provide weed-proof cover.
  Clay – Ground-cover.

PIERIS japonica (syn. *Andromeda japonica*)
'Variegata'
◐
type of plant: HSh
flowering season: spring
flower colour: white
leaves variegated with creamy white
height: 1.8-2.4 m/6-8 ft
*E ✕

The young leaves of this pieris are only lightly tinged with pink. For really strong red colouring, a variety such as *P. formosa forrestii* (see p. 42) should be chosen. It is important to give this dense, slow-growing shrub a sheltered site, or its variegated leaves and its hanging bunches of flowers may easily be damaged (while still in bud, sometimes) by frost and wind. It must also have a moist, lime-free soil.
  Acid soils – Cutting.

LUNARIA annua (syn. *L. biennis*) 'Variegata'
[form of Honesty]

◗

type of plant: HB
flowering season: l. spring to midsummer
flower colour: crimson
leaves variegated with cream
height: 75 cm/2½ ft

This variegated form of honesty produces the flat and papery seed-pods which are such familiar ingredients of dried flower arrangements: Its foliage is, however, a good deal more striking than that of the plain-leaved species, particularly in spring and early summer when the variegation is boldest. Well drained soils of most sorts suit this robust, thickset plant and it will grow quite successfully in dry shade.
    Chalk – Dry shade – Fruit.

CYCLAMEN repandum

◗

type of plant: SITTu
flowering season: spring
flower colour: rose-pink
leaves variegated with silver
height: 10-15 cm/4-6 in

The leaves of this cyclamen vary in shape, but they all bear beautiful, silvery markings. Under ideal conditions – which include well drained, leaf-mouldy soil and a really sheltered site – the sweet-scented flowers are produced in large numbers. The flowers and foliage appear at approximately the same time.
    Fragrant flowers.

POLYGONATUM odoratum (syn. *P. falcatum*) 'Variegatum' NA
[Variegated Japanese Solomon's Seal]

◗ ●

type of plant: HP
flowering season: spring
flower colour: creamy white
height: 90 cm/3 ft

An elegant plant, it is grown mainly for its green and cream foliage, though the small bell-shaped flowers along the leaf stalks have a special grace in spring. Humus-y, moisture-retentive soil gives the best results. It forms a ground-cover in time.

PULMONARIA saccharata
[species of Lungwort]

◗ ●

type of plant: HP
flowering season: spring
flower colour: pink changing to blue
leaves variegated with white
height: 23-30 cm/9-12 in
E/½E

The splotchy markings on the leaves of this lungwort do not coincide with everyone's idea of decorative variegation. However, in broken shade – and *P. saccharata* does not object to being grown underneath trees – these markings can create an appropriately dappled effect. The leaves of this plant are long and, where there is a constant supply of moisture in spring and summer, they form substantial, ground-covering clumps. In fertile soils, *P. saccharata* may spread quite freely.
    Ground-cover.

PACHYSANDRA terminalis 'Variegata'

◗ ●

type of plant: HSh
flowering season: mid-spring
flower colour: white
leaves variegated with white
height: 23 cm/9 in
E

Neatly margined in white, the slightly twisted leaves of this plant will eventually cover the ground as effectively as the plain, green foliage of *P. terminalis* itself (see p. 117). As long as it is provided with a lime-free soil and some shade, *P. t.* 'Variegata' will grow satisfactorily and it may be planted in dry places underneath trees. Its spikes of tiny flowers have a sweet scent.
    Acid soils – Dry shade – Dense shade – Ground-cover –Fragrant flowers.

Additional plants, featured elsewhere in this book, that have variegated leaves

◗ [○] partial shade (or sun)
EUONYMUS fortunei e.g. 'Silver Queen': 1.8-2.4 m (p. 137)
ACORUS calamus 'Variegatus': 60-75 cm (p. 78)
HOSTA 'Thomas Hogg': 60 cm (p. 78)
×HEUCHERELLA 'Bridget Bloom': 45 cm (p. 251)
EUONYMUS fortunei e.g. 'Silver Queen': 30-60 cm (p. 137)
LONICERA japonica 'Aureoreticulata': 15-20 cm (p. 153)
PARTHENOCISSUS henryana★: 15 cm (p. 153)

◗ partial shade
ERYTHRONIUM revolutum 'White Beauty'★: 23-30 cm (p. 44)
CYCLAMEN neapolitanum★: 10-15 cm (p. 81)
ERYTHRONIUM dens-canis: 10-15 cm (p. 44)
CYCLAMEN europaeum: 8-10 cm (p. 273)

◗ ● partial or full shade
BUXUS sempervirens e.g. 'Aureovariegata': 2.4-3 m (p. 152)
AUCUBA japonica e.g. 'Crotonifolia': 1.5-2.4 m (p. 136)
SCROPHULARIA aquatica 'Variegata': 60-90 cm (p. 153)
LAMIUM galeobdolon 'Variegatum': 30 cm (p. 81)
PODOPHYLLUM emodi: 30 cm (p. 208)
VINCA major 'Variegata': 23-45 cm (p. 153)
CAREX morrowi 'Variegata': 23 cm (p. 76)
LAMIUM maculatum 'Roseum': 15-23 cm (p. 117)
LAMIUM maculatum 'Beacon Silver': 15 cm (p. 82)

Plants with grey, blue-grey or 'silver' leaves

Grey leaves are sometimes associated with an off-puttingly rarefied taste in garden design. Yet, of all the plants with foliage that is regarded as unusual, those with grey leaves enjoy the most general popularity. As well as a few slightly unusual plants and some recent introductions, the following list contains many plants that, in one form or other, have been popular for generations. There are, for example, pinks and lavenders and those favourites of cottage gardens *Lychnis coronaria* (rose campion) and *Stachys lanata* (lamb's tongue, lamb's ear, etc.).

Plants of a fairly wide range of foliage colours are included under the general heading of this list. Many grey leaves are, in fact, a greyish green of some sort, while foliage of a really pale, almost white grey is usually described as 'silver' (although the hairiness of most pale grey leaves means that they bear little resemblance to silver as a metal). A kind of greyness is also present in leaves described as 'blue'. This is true even of plants such as *Juniperus squamata* 'Meyeri', a form of juniper which can have foliage of unusually intense blue.

The colour of some so-called grey leaves can be difficult to describe accurately. For example, *Rosa rubrifolia* (syn. *R. ferruginea*) appears both in this list and in the list devoted to plants with red, purple or bronze leaves. The foliage of this rose is such a subtle mixture of purplish grey and greyish purple that to confine it to only one list would have been misleading. There are several other plants in this list whose leaf colour defies precise description.

What all these different and elusive colours have in common, however, is an ability to lighten and brighten both gardens and indoor arrangements. It is, perhaps, grey foliage more than any other single feature, which makes modern plantings of shrubs so much less oppressive than Victorian shrubberies.

The colour alone of greyish leaves is a useful source of contrast in planting schemes, particularly in schemes that consist mainly of plants with interesting foliage. Often, when there seems to be no green-leaved plant which will differ sufficiently in habit, leaf size and so on from existing material, a grey-leaved plant can solve the problem most satisfactorily. Grey leaves also set off some flower colours particularly well. In certain cases, the attractively contrasting flowers and foliage are borne on the same plant. For example, *Lychnis coronaria* has flowers of a really strong pink-red that looks especially decorative against this plant's own silvery grey foliage. Both in the garden and in the house a similarly successful contrast can be achieved by placing *Pyrethrum roseum* 'Brenda', with its bright cerise flowers, beside some medium-sized,

grey-leaved plant, such as the shrub *Senecio laxifolius*.

However, it is not only the colour of greyish foliage which makes it attractive and useful. The leaves of the plants in this list differ considerably in size, texture and shape. These differences become particularly important in planting schemes that are made up entirely of plants with grey, grey-blue or silver leaves. Although schemes of this type can look beautiful, they can also have an uninteresting, blurred appearance. This unsatisfactory flatness is less likely to arise if careful attention has been paid to conspicuous contrasts in the size, texture and shape of leaves.

A number of grey-leaved plants, including *Helichrysum angustifolium* (curry plant), *Artemisia arborescens* and *Achillea* 'Moonshine' (a form of yarrow), have small leaves or leaves that are finely divided. In contrast, there are, for example, the unusually big, pointed leaves of *Verbascum bombyciferum* (a species of mullein) and the large, lobed leaves of *Macleaya microcarpa* 'Kelway's Coral Plume' (a form of plume poppy). In shady sites the broad, blue-green foliage of *Hosta sieboldiana* would contrast well with the numerous leaflets of *Thalictrum aquilegifolium* (a species of meadow rue which will grow in either sun or partial shade).

In addition to the differences in size and shape described above, there is quite a wide range of leaf texture among the plants in this list. The foliage of many grey-leaved plants is covered with hairs. In some cases these hairs are not particularly noticeable, but in other cases they create a conspicuous felt or woolliness. Plants in this list that have hairy leaves include *Salix lanata* (woolly willow), *Senecio cineraria* 'White Diamond' and *Stachys lanata* (lamb's tongue, etc.). A few plants, such as *Senecio laxifolius* and *Populus alba* (white poplar or abele), are felted most noticeably on the undersides of their leaves. In a breeze, the white backs of *Populus alba*'s leaves become conspicuous and, from a distance, the whole tree then has a most attractive silvery look. (Some green-leaved plants, notably the olearias or daisy bushes, also have white, felted undersides.)

The smoothness of many of the blue-grey leaves in this list means that they contrast well, both in texture and colour, with the hairiest leaves, which tend to be silvery green or grey. Smooth foliage that is also fleshy is a particularly good foil to felted or woolly leaves. *Hebe* 'Pagei', *Sedum* × 'Autumn Joy' and *S.* × 'Ruby Glow' all have attractive, fleshy leaves which, apart from looking decorative in the garden, make unusual cut foliage which lasts well in water.

CEDRUS atlantica glauca★
[Blue Cedar]

○

type of plant: HCo
height: 21-30 m/70-100 ft
E

As a young tree, this plant is of a rather narrow pyramidal shape, but it broadens as it matures. Its beautiful blue foliage has cones more or less to match, although on large, old trees they are not immediately visible amongst the upper branches. This conifer will grow in well drained soils of all types, including chalky and limy soils as long as they are not shallow.
  Fruit.

POPULUS alba
[White Poplar, Abele]

○

type of plant: HT
height: 18-27 m/60-90 ft

This fast-growing, sometimes suckering tree has a domed, open head. It is quite often rather smaller than indicated here, particularly when it produces several main stems. Its young leaves are entirely covered with white down. The more mature foliage is dark grey-green above and white-felted below; it turns yellow in autumn. *P. alba* is remarkably tolerant of salt-laden winds. Its wide-spreading, shallow roots can cause serious damage to foundations and drainage systems.
  Chalk – Clay – Damp and wet soils – Seaside – Atmospheric pollution – Autumn foliage.

CUPRESSUS glabra (syn. *C. arizonica bonita*)
[Smooth Arizona Cypress]

○

type of plant: HCo
height: 13.5-18 m/45-60 ft
E

C. glabra forms a conical mass of blue-grey foliage. It grows fairly quickly and, at least in the early stages of its life, it should be sheltered from cold winds. It thrives in moisture-retentive, loamy soils. The purplish brown cones of this conifer are not particularly decorative, but the peeling, purple and yellow bark is conspicuous and interesting.
  Bark and twigs.

JUNIPERUS scopulorum NA
[Western Red-cedar]

○

type of plant: HCo
height: 7.5 m/25 ft
E

Although there are spreading forms, this usually makes a small columnar tree with silvery or light-green foliage. It is particularly drought-tolerant. Cultivars include 'Blue Heaven', 'Cologreen' and 'Pathfinder'.

PYRUS salicifolia 'Pendula'★
[form of Willow-leaved Pear]

○

type of plant: HT
flowering season: spring
flower colour: white
height: 4.5-6 m/15-20 ft

The combination of silvery grey foliage and a weeping habit makes this plant both decorative and desirable in many gardeners' eyes. The leaves are palest in spring; by midsummer their upper surfaces have become grey-green. Despite its elegant appearance this tree is tough and it will do well in any reasonably well drained garden soil.

Atmospheric pollution.

ABUTILON vitifolium

○

type of plant: SITSh
flowering season: l. spring to midsummer
flower colour: mauve
height: 3-6 m/10-20 ft
½E

Only in very mild areas will this rather short-lived shrub reach the greater of the two heights given here. Elsewhere it will be smaller and quite sparsely branched – even when given an appropriately well drained soil and a sheltered position. The attractively lobed leaves of this plant are covered with tiny white hairs.

ROSA rubrifolia (syn. *R. ferruginea*)
[species of Rose]

○

type of plant: HSh
flowering season: e. summer
flower colour: pink
height: 1.8-2.4 m/6-8 ft

The foliage of this rose is a subtle mixture of grey and purple. This colouring is complemented by the maroon stems, which are long and lax and almost thornless. Clusters of dark red hips follow the rather small, but pretty flowers. Full sun and a good, rich soil help to produce plenty of well coloured leaves.

Red, etc. leaves – Fruit.

BUDDLEIA fallowiana 'Alba' sc NA

○

type of plant: HHSh
flowering season: all summer
flower colour: cream-white
height: 1.5-2.4 m/5-8 ft

Like most buddleias, this bushy plant has fragrant flowers. However, in this case, the main attraction is the foliage, which is a very pale grey. *B. f.* 'Alba' grows most strongly in really well drained soils and sheltered sites. The flowers are cream coloured (with tiny orange markings), and not pure white as some trade catalogues would suggest.

Fragrant flowers.

JUNIPERUS squamata 'Meyeri'
[form of Juniper]

○

type of plant: HCo
height: 1.5-2.4 m/5-8 ft
E, eventually 4.5-6 m/15-20 ft high

This surprisingly blue juniper forms an erect, rather spiky plant. Its colour is often most intense at the ends of the branches and it is made even more conspicuous by the tendency of these growing tips to arch forwards and downwards. Any well drained soil suits this plant but it must have full sun for the benefit of its foliage colour.

Hot, dry soils.

ONOPORDUM acanthium
[Cotton Thistle, Scotch Thistle]
○
type of plant: HB/P
flowering season: summer
flower colour: purple
height: 1.5-1.8 m/5-6 ft
✂

Basically an elegant and imposing – and very
prickly – thistle, *O. acanthium* is popular with
flower arrangers both for its flowers and for its pale
grey leaves. The latter are large and covered in
cobwebby hairs. A rich soil produces the largest
plants, but any well drained soil is suitable. If the
flowers are pinched out, this plant becomes a
short-lived perennial.
    Cutting.

VERBASCUM bombyciferum★
[species of Mullein]
○
type of plant: HB/P
flowering season: summer
flower colour: yellow
height: 1.2-1.8 m/4-6 ft
E

The huge, felted leaves of this plant are more
attractive than the flowers. For this reason, the
flowers are often removed when immature, and
V. bombyciferum is grown as a perennial.
Individual leaves may be as much as 40 cm/15 in
long; if their stems are placed initially in hot water
they last well when cut. This plant is sometimes
sold under the name *V.* 'Broussa'. It should be
grown in well drained soil.
    Chalky.

SEQUOIA sempervirens 'Adpressa' (syn. *S. s.*
'Albospica') **MC**
**[form of Californian Redwood or Coast
Redwood]**
○
type of plant: HCo
height: 90-180 cm/3-6 ft
E, eventually very large: 15-24 m/50-80 ft high;
    young shoots cream at first

Only when pruned every few years can this slightly
unusual conifer be grown in a small or
medium-sized garden. However, this is the
treatment it normally receives and it produces
bushy plants on which the contrast between
mature, green foliage and creamy, young shoots is
very noticeable. The young leaves gradually
become a greyer colour as they age, until they
eventually turn green. *S. s.* 'Adpressa' grows best
in a moist soil; it does not do well in cold, windy
gardens.

ARTEMISIA arborescens★
○
type of plant: SlTSh
height: 90-120 cm/3-4 ft
½E, to 2.4 m/8 ft against a wall

The leaves of this plant are so beautifully silvered
and filigreed that it is tempting to overlook its
rather tender constitution and to grow it regardless
of whether it can be given a suitably light and
free-draining soil and a sheltered enough position.
Under the right conditions, however,
A. arborescens produces loose bunches of stems
which carry plenty of foliage and this is not only
lovely to look at but also strongly and refreshingly
scented.
    Chalk – Hot, dry soils – Aromatic leaves.

ERYNGIUM giganteum
○
type of plant: HB
flowering season: l. summer to e. autumn
flower colour: silvery blue
height: 90-120 cm/3-4 ft
✂

Once it has produced its neat cones of flowers,
E. giganteum dies. However, it seeds itself freely in
well drained soils and, therefore, there can always
be a good supply of the spiky, silvery blue leaves
which make such long-lasting cut material.
    Chalk – Hot, dry soils – Cutting.

EUPHORBIA wulfenii (syn. *E. veneta*) **MC**
[species of Spurge]
○
type of plant: HP/HHP (NA)
flowering season: l. spring to midsummer
flower colour: yellow-green
height: 90-120 cm/3-4 ft
E ✂

All the smartest planting schemes seem to include
this shrubby perennial with its dramatic columns
of blue-green leaves. This is not to imply,
however, that it is difficult to grow for, apart from
adequate drainage and sun, all this plant needs is
some shelter from wind. It is densest and bushiest
if, after flowering, the flower stems are completely
removed. Both the foliage and the flowers are
popular for cutting, but the poisonous juices of
this plant can irritate – and even damage – eyes and
skin with which they come in contact.
    Chalk – Hot, dry soils – Cutting – Green flowers.

HELICTOTRICHON sempervirens (syn. *Avena candida*)

○

type of plant: HP (Gr)
flowering season: summer
flower colour: silvery grey
height: 90-120 cm/3-4 ft
E ✕, leaves 30-45 cm/1-1½ ft high

Although the flowers of this dense, clump-forming grass are carried on quite tall stems, for most of the year the plant consists of a much lower tuft of bright, blue-grey foliage. Unlike some grasses, *H. sempervirens* does not spread invasively into neighbouring plants. The most vivid leaf colouring will be produced on well drained soils.

Chalk – Cutting.

PHLOMIS fruticosa
[Jerusalem Sage]

○

type of plant: SlTSh
flowering season: summer
flower colour: yellow
height: 90-120 cm/3-4 ft
E

The curving shape of this plant's leaves sets off their grey-green woolliness nicely (although some plants of this species seem to have less wavy leaves than others). Since it likes a sandy soil and a mild climate, *P. fruticosa* does well in maritime districts, but the brittleness of its vigorous, sprawling stems makes it unsuitable for very windy sites. Despite its common name, this shrub has foliage which is only very slightly aromatic.

Chalk – Hot, dry soils.

ARTEMISIA absinthium 'Lambrook Silver'
[form of Wormwood]

○

type of plant: HP
flowering season: summer
flower colour: yellow
height: 90 cm/3 ft

Dry soil and full sun ensure that the deeply divided leaves of this sub-shrubby plant are a really pale silver-green and strongly aromatic. Although less distinguished than the foliage, the flowers of *A. a.* 'Lambrook Silver' have their own charm; they are carried in long, slender spikes and interspersed with tiny, grey leaves.

Chalk – Hot, dry soils – Aromatic leaves.

SALIX lanata★
[Woolly Willow]

○

type of plant: HSh
flowering season: spring
flower colour: yellow
height: 60-120 cm/2-4 ft

S. lanata is a most attractive exception to the general rule that grey-leaved plants need well drained soils. This spreading, slow-growing willow is very hardy and it actually prefers a cool, moist soil. The silver-green of its felted foliage contrasts well with its large, plump catkins.

Clay – Damp and wet soils – Ground-cover.

ACHILLEA 'Moonshine'★
[form of Yarrow]

○

type of plant: HP
flowering season: summer
flower colour: yellow
height: 60 cm/2 ft
E

The filigree foliage of this perennial is only one of its attractive features. Conspicuously flat-headed flowers appear above its grey-green leaves and they make an interesting shape in any collection of plants; they are also excellent for cutting and drying. All well drained soils suit *A.* 'Moonshine'.

Chalk – Hot, dry soils – Cutting.

LYCHNIS coronaria (syn. *Agrostemma coronaria*)
[Rose Campion]

○

type of plant: HP
flowering season: l. summer to e. autumn
flower colour: bright pink-red
height: 45-75 cm/1½-2½ ft

Both *L. coronaria* and its white-flowered variety (which is shown in the next illustration) do well and live longest on dry soils. The flannel grey leaves seem almost to intensify the brilliance of the species' flowers, while they have the effect of increasing the coolness of the blooms of *L. c.* 'Alba'. Unless regularly dead-headed, *L. coronaria* can produce an awkwardly large number of self-sown seedlings.

Chalk – Hot, dry soils – Cutting.

LYCHNIS coronaria (syn. *Agrostemma coronaria*)
'Alba'
[form of Rose Campion]

○

type of plant: HP
flowering season: l. summer to e. autumn
flower colour: white
height: 45-75 cm/1½-2½ ft

See preceding plant.

BALLOTA pseudodictamnus

○

type of plant: SlTP
flowering season: midsummer
flower colour: mauve
height: 45-60 cm/1½-2 ft
E/½E ✕

Regarded variously as a perennial and as a shrub, *B. pseudodictamnus* forms a clump of sprawling stems which are covered in silver-grey leaves. The flowers are often considered to spoil the effectiveness of the foliage. In cold, wet winters *B. pseudodictamnus* may die, and it is, therefore, best to give it a soil with good – or sharp – drainage.
Chalk – Hot, dry soils – Ground-cover.

CENTAUREA gymnocarpa

○

type of plant: HHP
height: 45-60 cm/1½-2 ft

Few plants can rival the dramatic cascade of large, silvery, fern-like leaves of this sub-shrubby perennial. However, its lack of hardiness means that *C. gymnocarpa* often needs to be treated as a half-hardy annual or over-wintered in a greenhouse. In any case, it must have a sharply drained soil and full sun. Pinching out the flowering shoots prevents the unattractive blooms from forming.
Chalk.

RUTA graveolens 'Jackman's Blue' ★
[form of Rue]

○

type of plant: HSh
flowering season: summer
flower colour: yellow
height: 45-60 cm/1½-2 ft
E ✕

Laciness combined with a really blue-green colouring makes this form of rue a particularly fine foliage plant. Full sun is needed to get the bluest leaves, and hard pruning is required to maintain a neat, dense and rounded shape. The strange, dry pungency of the leaves is not to everyone's liking and it seems odd, nowadays, that this should once have been such a popular herb for flavouring.
Hot, dry soils – Ground-cover – Hedging – Containers – Aromatic leaves.

SENECIO cineraria (syn. *Cineraria maritima*)
'White Diamond'

○

type of plant: SlTP/HHA
flowering season: summer
flower colour: yellow
height: 45-60 cm/1½-2 ft
E ✕

If a very pale grey leaf is wanted, either in the garden or for cutting, this sub-shrub is well worth considering. It may be raised from seed each year. In mild areas, it can be grown permanently outdoors. When treated as a perennial, it makes a bushy, spreading hummock which can be kept dense by hard pruning in late spring. It should be given a soil that drains freely.
Chalk – Ground-cover.

SISYRINCHIUM striatum MC

○

type of plant: HP
flowering season: summer
flower colour: pale yellow
height: 45 cm/1½ ft
E

Although primarily grown for its pretty flowers, with their tiny, hairline markings of purple, this plant also has nice, grey-green leaves which, in quantity, contrast well with plants of a more rounded or spreading habit. *S. striatum* is easy to grow and seeds itself readily in almost any soil.

CONVOLVULUS cneorum MC

○

type of plant: **HHSh**
flowering season: **l. spring to summer**
flower colour: **white**
height: **30-60 cm/1-2 ft**
E

The silvered leafiness of this hummocky plant is accentuated by beautifully simple, silky blooms. *C. cneorum* will survive most winters in inland and moderately cold gardens if it is grown in a dry soil and full sun.

Chalk– Hot, dry soils – Ground-cover.

ANAPHALIS triplinervis★
[species of Pearly Everlasting]

○

type of plant: **HP**
flowering season: **l. summer**
flower colour: **white**
height: **30-45 cm/1-1½ ft**

This clump-forming perennial has numerous grey-green, ribbed leaves, and it is agreeably easy to please. Indeed, far from demanding a perfectly drained soil as so many grey-leaved plants do, *A. triplinervis* droops and loses foliage from the lower parts of its stems if it is very dry. The flowers of this plant are everlasting and a bright addition to dried flower arrangements.

Chalk – Ground-cover – Cutting.

ARTEMISIA schmidtiana 'Nana' NA
[Silver Mound]

○

type of plant: **HP**
flowering season: **l. summer**
flower colour: **inconspicuous**
height: **30 cm/1 ft**

One of the most widely planted grey-leaved perennials, forming an attractive mound of finely cut foliage in spring. Often loose in growth habit late in summer. Best in colder climates, in dry, poor soil. British nurseries specializing in small plants or unusual perennials may stock this plant. In the British Isles, it is normally less than half the height given here.

VERONICA incana
[species of Speedwell]

○

type of plant: **HP**
flowering season: **summer**
flower colour: **deep purple-blue**
height: **30 cm/1 ft**

V. incana is easily grown in all medium or light, garden soils. It soon forms a sprawling clump of elegantly pointed, 'silver'-grey leaves below its dark, spiky flowers.

Ground-cover.

LYCHNIS flos-jovis 'Hort's Variety'
[form of Flower of Jove]

○

type of plant: **HP**
flowering season: **summer**
flower colour: **pink**
height: **25 cm/10 in**

The arrangement of this plant's grey and woolly foliage in small, upright bunches makes it useful for contrasting with plants whose leaves are held more or less horizontally. In this variety of *L. flos-jovis* the flowers are a good, clear pink; the flowers of the species are, variably, red or red-purple. Any well drained soil suits this plant.

Chalk – Hot, dry soils.

ANTHEMIS cupaniana

○

type of plant: **HP**
flowering season: **summer**
flower colour: **white**
height: **23-30 cm/9-12 in**
E/½E

When grown in a well drained soil and cut back hard after flowering, this plant makes wide-spreading and dense mats of pale, silvery grey leaves. These leaves are very finely divided and they have a pungent scent. The sparkling white flowers are produced in succession almost all summer long.

Chalk – Ground-cover – Aromatic leaves.

ERICA tetralix 'Alba Mollis' (syn. *E. t.* **'Mollis')
[form of Cross-leaved Heath]**

○

**type of plant: HSh
flowering season: summer to e. autumn
flower colour: white
height: 23-30 cm/9-12 in**
*E

For gardeners who like their heaths and heathers
to have interestingly coloured foliage, but who find
the orange- and yellow-leaved varieties of these
plants much too obtrusive and gaudy, there are the
gentler attractions of *E. t.* 'Alba Mollis'. This
shrub has upright stems topped with crinkled,
white flowers and covered in whorls of silvery grey
leaves. It must be given a fairly moist, lime-free
soil. Other, easily available cultivars of *E. tetralix*
have foliage which is greyish green rather than
grey.

　Acid soils – Damp and wet soils.

HELIANTHEMUM nummularium (syn.
H. chamaecistus, H. vulgare) e.g. **'Wisley Pink'**
[form of Sun Rose]

○

**type of plant: HSh
flowering season: summer
flower colour: pink
height: 23-30 cm/9-12 in**
E

This variety of sun rose has distinctly grey leaves;
the foliage of some other forms of *H. nummularium*
is green or grey-green. *H. n.* 'Wisley Pink' is
vigorous and quick-growing, but it requires
cutting back after flowering to keep it neat and
dense and hummocky. It is a most floriferous
plant. The blooms shed their petals during the
afternoon, but a succession of buds opens
throughout a substantial part of the summer. Good
drainage and a sunny site produce the best growth.

　Chalk – Hot, dry soils – Ground-cover – Paving.

**RANUNCULUS gramineus
[species of Buttercup]**

○

**type of plant: HP
flowering season: l. spring to midsummer
flower colour: yellow
height: 23–30 cm/9-12 in**

Like the common buttercup, this plant has
beautiful shiny petals. Unlike the weed, however,
it is tidy and compact and, when grown on a rock
garden, its grassy, grey-green foliage contrasts
well with the hummocks and mats produced by so
many other small plants.

**CERASTIUM tomentosum
[Snow-in-Summer]**

○

**type of plant: HP
flowering season: l. spring to e. summer
flower colour: white
height: 15-23 cm/6-9 in**
E

To describe this silvery plant as 'effective
ground-cover' is something of an understatement,
since it is so vigorous that it can easily cover other
small plants with its dense mats of foliage.
However, *C. tomentosum* does have it uses, and it is
a thoroughly self-sufficient plant in very dry and
virtually uncultivated sites.

　Chalk – Hot, dry soils – Ground-cover.

FESTUCA ovina 'Glauca' (syn. *F. glauca*)★

○

**type of plant: HP (Gr)
flowering season: summer
flower colour: purplish
height: 15-23 cm/6-9 in**
E ✕

In a light soil and full sun this plant forms dense,
bristly tufts of remarkably blue foliage. Although
it grows slowly, *F. o.* 'Glauca' should be lifted and
divided every other year to ensure that plenty of
new and well coloured leaves are produced.

　Chalk – Hot, dry soils – Ground-cover.

TANACETUM haradjanii (syn. *T. densum*
'Amani', *Chrysanthemum haradjanii*)★

○

**type of plant: HP
flowering season: summer
flower colour: yellow
height: 15-20 cm/6-8 in**
E

A plant to be viewed at close quarters,
T. haradjanii has beautiful, grey leaves which are
very small and exactly like tiny feathers. When
bruised, these leaves emit a delicious, sharp scent.
Given a warm position and a freely draining soil,
this plant soon forms a mounded carpet of foliage.
The groundsel-like flowers are usually removed so
that they do not detract from the beauty of the
leaves.

　Chalk – Hot, dry soils – Ground-cover – Paving
– Aromatic leaves.

ANDROSACE lanuginosa
[species of Rock Jasmine]
○
type of plant: HP
flowering season: summer to e. autumn
flower colour: pink
height: 10-15 cm/4-6 in
E

Although the trailing stems of this rather difficult plant are sufficiently numerous to form quite a dense, ground-covering mat, *A. lanuginosa* is at its best when grown in a vertical crevice. In such a position, the strings of cool 'silver'-green leaves and the pretty, pink flowers are shown to advantage and the whole plant can easily be given the sharp drainage it needs.

Ground-cover.

SEMPERVIVUM arachnoideum
[Cobweb Houseleek]
○
type of plant: HP
flowering season: summer
flower colour: rose-red
height: 8-15 cm/3-6 in
E, leaves 1-2 cm/½-1 in high

The fleshy leaves of this drought-resistant plant have delicate cats' cradles of cobwebby hairs strung across their tips. These hairs give the plant a silvery appearance. In contrast to many plants of this genus, the flowers as well as the leaves of this species are attractive.

Chalk – Hot, dry soils.

OXALIS adenophylla
○
type of plant: HP
flowering season: l. spring to e. summer
flower colour: pink
height: 8 cm/3 in

O. adenophylla is a well behaved relative of some troublesome weeds. Its folded, clover-like leaflets form an attractive grey-green base from which the blushing flowers rise. With peat or leaf-mould added, any well drained soil suits this plant.

POTENTILLA nitida 'Rubra'
[form of Cinquefoil]
○
type of plant: HP
flowering season: summer
flower colour: deep pink
height: 5-8 cm/2-3 in
E

Although this particular variety of *P. nitida* flowers more freely than the species, it is still not a prolific producer of blooms. However, the brightness of its mat-forming, silvery leaves and the contrast between the foliage and the strong pink flowers more than makes up for the scarcity of blooms.
P. n. 'Rubra' needs sharply drained, gritty soil.
Chalk – Ground-cover.

RAOULIA australis
○
type of plant: HP
height: 1-2 cm/½-1 in
E

The minute leaves of *R. australis* make a dense mat of silvery greyness. Tiny, stemless flowers appear in summer; they are pale yellow and generally considered insignificant. Despite needing a very well drained soil, this plant must not be allowed to dry out completely. It grows slowly enough to be suitable for planting in troughs and sinks.
Chalk – Ground-cover – Paving.

Additional plants, featured elsewhere in this book, that have grey, blue-grey or 'silver' leaves

○ sun
ACACIA dealbata: 4.5-7.5 m (p. 253)
JUNIPERUS communis 'Hibernica': 4.5-6 m (p. 2)
CYTISUS battandieri★: 3-4.5 m (p. 254)
JUNIPERUS virginiana 'Skyrocket': 3-4.5 m (p. 132)
LAVATERA olbia 'Rosea': 1.8 m (p. 86)
ROMNEYA coulteri: 1.5-2.1 m (p. 256)
TEUCRIUM fruticans: 1.2-1.5 m (p. 57)
PEROVSKIA atriplicifolia: 90-150 cm (p. 4)
VERBASCUM × 'Gainsborough': 90-120 cm (p. 4)
LAVANDULA spica: 90 cm (p. 257)
CARYOPTERIS × clandonensis e.g. 'Ferndown': 60-90 cm (p. 7)
DIANTHUS (Border Carnation) e.g. 'Beauty of Cambridge': 60-90 cm (p. 223)
DIANTHUS (Border Carnation) e.g. 'Fiery Cross': 60-90 cm (p. 224)
DIANTHUS (Border Carnation) e.g. 'Harmony' 60-90 cm (p. 224)
DIANTHUS (Border Carnation) e.g. 'Salmon Clove': 60-90 cm (p. 258)
HALIMIUM ocymoides: 60-90 cm (p. 59)
JUNIPERUS communis 'Compressa': 60-90 cm (p. 134)
LAVANDULA spica 'Vera': 60 cm (p. 100)
ANAPHALIS yedoensis: 45-60 cm (p. 230)
JUNIPERUS horizontalis e.g. 'Glauca': 45-60 cm (p. 100)
SANTOLINA chamaecyparissus: 45-60 cm (p. 125)
SEDUM × 'Autumn Joy'★: 45-60 cm (p. 9)
LAYIA elegans: 40-45 cm (p. 253)
LAVANDULA spica 'Hidcote': 30-60 cm (p. 126)
ORIGANUM majorana: 30-60 cm (p. 198)
ARCTOTIS × hybrida e.g. 'Large-flowered Hybrids': 30-45 cm (p. 236)
JUNIPERUS horizontalis e.g. 'Douglasii': 30-45 cm (p. 101)
NEPETA × faassenii: 30-45 cm (p. 101)   *continued*

○ sun *continued*
ORONTIUM aquaticum: 30-45 cm (p. 70)
DIANTHUS×allwoodii e.g. 'Doris'★:30 cm (p.238)
DIANTHUS×allwoodii e.g. 'Robin': 30 cm (p. 12)
DIANTHUS plumarius e.g. 'Mrs Sinkins': 30 cm (p.261)
ESCHSCHOLZIA californica e.g. 'Ballerina': 30 cm (p.61)
EUPHORBIA myrsinites: 30 cm (p. 139)
ZAUSCHNERIA californica: 30 cm (p.61)
HELICHRYSUM angustifolium: 23-40 cm (p. 198)
ESCHSCHOLZIA californica e.g. 'Mission Bells': 23-30 cm (p.61)
HELIANTHEMUM nummularium e.g. 'Wisley Primrose': 23-30 cm (p.101)
ALYSSUM saxatile e.g. 'Citrinum': 23 cm (p.102)
ALYSSUM saxatile e.g. 'Dudley Neville': 23 cm (p.15)
ORIGANUM hybridum: 23 cm (p.15)
SEDUM×'Ruby Glow': 23 cm (p.62)
HYPERICUM polyphyllum: 15-23 cm (p. 140)
LEONTOPODIUM alpinum: 15-23 cm (p. 140)
DIANTHUS gratianopolitanus: 15-20 cm (p.16)
ALYSSUM saxatile e.g. 'Compactum': 15 cm (p.63)
PAPAVER alpinum: 10-20 cm (p.141)
AETHIONEMA×'Warley Rose': 10-15 cm (p.64)
ANTENNARIA dioica 'Rubra': 8-10 cm (p.103)
SEDUM spathulifolium 'Capa Blanca': 8-10 cm (p.65)
RAOULIA lutescens: 1-2 cm (p.104)

ABIES procera (syn. *A. nobilis***)**
[Noble Fir]
○ [◖]
type of plant: HCo
height: 30-39 m/100-130 ft
*E

This magnificent conifer grows rapidly in areas of high rainfall and fairly quickly elsewhere. Its upswept, blue-green needles cover the branches densely. In maturity, this tree has a rather open, pyramidal head on a long trunk. The yellowish-brown cones are remarkably large (up to 25 cm/10 in high) and they may appear on quite young plants.

Acid soils – Fruit.

MACLEAYA (syn. *Bocconia***) microcarpa e.g.**
'Kelway's Coral Plume'
[form of Plume Poppy]
○ [◖]
type of plant: HP
flowering season: summer
flower colour: buff tinged pink
height: 1.5-2.4 m/5-8 ft

The great, lobed leaves of this vigorous and sometimes invasive plant contrast beautifully with the plumes of tiny flowers. The foliage is grey-green above and conspicuously veined. This plant will be seen at its robust best if grown in good, deep soil and a sunny position.

EUCALYPTUS gunnii
[Cider Gum]
○ [◖]
type of plant: SlTSh/HHSh (NA)
flowering season: summer
flower colour: white
height: 1.5-1.8 m/5-6 ft
*E ✕, pruned and grown as shrub for juvenile foliage, normally 15-21 m/50-70 ft high

E. gunnii will only produce its bright, silvery blue, juvenile foliage if all its shoots are cut right back each year. Left to its own devices it very quickly makes a slender, open-headed tree, with grey-brown bark that peels to reveal cream-coloured wood. Acid or, at least, neutral soils appear to produce the best growth. The foliage is strongly aromatic.

Acid soils – Atmospheric pollution – Containers – Aromatic leaves – *Bark* and twigs.

SENECIO laxifolius★
○ [◖]
type of plant: HSh/HHSh (NA)
flowering season: summer
flower colour: yellow
height: 90-120 cm/3-4 ft
E ✕

S. laxifolius is one of the most reliable and adaptable grey-leaved shrubs in Britain. Specimens of this plant that are pruned fairly hard each spring form dense mounds of grey-green leaves which have very thin, white margins and white undersides. This shrub grows successfully – and neatly – when exposed to salt-laden winds. Its flowers are not, perhaps, its best feature and the flowering shoots are often pinched out. A well drained soil and sun suit this shrub best, but it is easily grown in most soils and situations.

Chalk – Seaside – Atmospheric pollution – Ground-cover – Hedging.

STACHYS lanata (syn. *S. olympica***)**
[Lamb's Tongue, Lamb's Ear, Lamb's Lug, etc.]
○ [◖]
type of plant: HP
flowering season: midsummer
flower colour: purple
height: 30-45 cm/1-1½ ft
E ✕

The soft and furry foliage of this mat-forming plant is as nice to feel as it is to look at. The leaves are large for the height of the foliage overall, and some gardeners consider that their appearance is spoilt by the spikes of woolly-stemmed flowers. To ensure that no – or few – flowers are produced, either *S. lanata* itself can be divided each year, or the excellent, non-flowering variety, *S. l.* 'Silver Carpet' (see next page), can be used. Wetness at the roots in winter can lead to poor growth.

Chalk – Hot, dry soils – Ground-cover.

STACHYS lanata (syn. *S. olympica*) '**Silver Carpet**'★
[form of Lamb's Tongue, Lamb's Ear, Lamb's Lug, etc.]

○ [◐]
type of plant: HP
height: 10-15 cm/4-6 in
E ✕

See preceding plant.

Additional plants, featured elsewhere in this book, that have grey, blue-grey or 'silver' leaves

○ [◐] sun (or partial shade)
EUCALYPTUS niphophila★: 6-7.5 m (p. 209)
ASPHODELINE lutea: 90 cm (p. 265)
POTENTILLA fruticosa mandschurica: 30-45 cm (p. 105)
ACAENA buchananii: 5 cm (p. 143)

CHAMAECYPARIS lawsoniana e.g. '**Triomphe de Boskoop**'
[form of Lawson Cypress]

○ ◐
type of plant: HCo
height: 18-21 m/60-70 ft
E

The slightly drooping young shoots of this large and quick-growing form of Lawson cypress are a most attractive, pale grey-blue. The older foliage is a less remarkable blue-green. Overall, the plant forms an open-headed cone with a single main stem. *C. lawsoniana* and its many varieties will grow in most soils, but the fastest and strongest growth is where moisture and good drainage are present.

CHAMAECYPARIS lawsoniana e.g. '**Allumii**'
[form of Lawson Cypress]

○ ◐
type of plant: HCo
height: 12-15 m/40-50 ft
E

Elderly specimens of this spire-shaped tree sometimes have broad bases but, more usually, *C. l.* 'Allumii' remains slender throughout its life. Its general habit makes it suitable for narrow hedging. The foliage of this conifer is blue-green. For the cultivation of *C. lawsoniana* and its varieties, see the preceding plant. (The photograph here shows young specimens used for hedging.)
   Hedging.

SORBUS aria '**Lutescens**'★
[form of Whitebeam]

○ ◐
type of plant: HT
flowering season: l. spring to e. summer
flower colour: white
height: 9-12 m/30-40 ft

A more decorative tree than *S. aria* itself, *S. a.* 'Lutescens' has a fairly upright, pyramidal habit and young leaves which are exceptionally pale. The creamy down on the upper surfaces of the foliage disappears by midsummer and the leaves are then grey-green above and grey below. *S. a.* 'Lutescens' grows well in a variety of soils and situations. It is particularly at home on chalk. The scarlet berries ripen in early autumn.
   Chalk – Seaside – Atmospheric pollution – Autumn foliage – Fruit.

CHAMAECYPARIS lawsoniana e.g. '**Fletcheri**'
[form of Lawson Cypress]

○ ◐
type of plant: HCo
height: 7.5-10.5 m/25-35 ft
E

C. l. 'Fletcheri' looks like several columnar trees growing close together. Its foliage is soft and mossy and a greyish blue-green; in winter it becomes tinged with bronze. This conifer grows quite slowly and it may be planted on rock-gardens, as long as it is realized that its ultimate height eventually – after about thirty or forty years – makes it unsuitable for such places. (For the cultivation of this plant, see *C. l.* 'Triomphe de Boskoop', above.)
   Autumn foliage.

PICEA pungens 'Koster' (syn. *P. p.* 'Kosteriana') [form of Blue Spruce]

○ ◑

type of plant: HCo
height:7.5-9 m/25-30 ft
E

Overall, this tree is narrowly conical but it has an irregular outline which is created by the main branches growing more or less horizontally. The bluest foliage is produced on the youngest shoots; older leaves are darker and more nearly blue-green. *P. p.* 'Koster' and other silvery blue varieties of the blue spruce, such as *P. p.* 'Hoopsii' and *P. p.* 'Moerheimii', need moist, preferably lime-free soils and, ideally, some shelter.

　Acid soils.

CHAMAECYPARIS lawsoniana e.g. 'Columnaris' (syn. *C. l.* 'Columnaris Glauca') [form of Lawson Cypress]

○ ◑

type of plant: HCo
height: 6-9 m/20-30 ft
E

Although not a particularly small conifer, *C. l.* 'Columnaris' is often planted in small gardens because its very slender, cylindrical habit means that it takes up little ground space. Its blue-green foliage has a greyish cast. When several specimens are planted together, this tree makes a good screen in the same way as the narrow, upright Lombardy poplar does. (For the cultivation of this plant, see *C. l.* 'Triomphe de Boskoop' on the previous page.)

　Hedging.

CHAMAECYPARIS lawsoniana e.g. 'Ellwoodii' [form of Lawson Cypress]

○ ◑

type of plant: HCo
height: 3.6-4.5 m/12-15 ft
E

Where *C. l.* 'Columnaris' (see left) would be too tall a plant, the similar, but much smaller and slower growing *C. l.* 'Ellwoodii' can be used. The leaves of this variety are grey-green and feathery. By training a single leading shoot upwards against a cane, a particularly well shaped specimen of this plant can be produced. (For general remarks about the cultivation of *C. lawsoniana* and its varieties, see *C. l.* 'Triomphe de Boskoop' on the previous page.)

THALICTRUM aquilegifolium [species of Meadow Rue]

○ ◑

type of plant: HP
flowering season: l. spring to midsummer
flower colour: mauve or purple
height: 90 cm/3 ft
✂

The fluffy flowers of this clump-forming perennial are popular both for fresh and for dried flower arrangements. However, the shiny, grey-blue foliage is at least as attractive as the flowers and certainly daintier. This species of meadow rue should be given a good, moist soil.

　Clay – Cutting.

VERONICA spicata 'Minuet' [form of Speedwell]

○ ◑

type of plant: HP
flowering season: summer
flower colour: pink
height: 45 cm/1½ ft

This plant inherits the greyness in its foliage from *V. incana* (see p. 161 for details). Its neat appearance and the uprightness of its dense flower spikes make it a good choice for planting at the front of a bed or border. Most fertile soils are suitable for *V. spicata* and its varieties (which are available in white and various shades of blue and pink, though only a few have greyish leaves); a moisture-retentive soil gives the most satisfactory results.

SAXIFRAGA aizoon (syn. *S. paniculata*) [species of Saxifrage]

○ ◑

type of plant: HP
flowering season: e. summer
flower colour: white
height: 30 cm/1 ft
E

The leaves of *S. aizoon* make a tight little carpet of silvery green rosettes, above which slim-stalked flowers appear from time to time. Nurseries specializing in alpine plants will usually list dwarf forms and forms with yellow or pink flowers. Very good drainage is needed for these plants to grow successfully.

　Chalk.

HEBE 'Pagei' (syn. *H. pageana, H. pinguifolia*
'Pagei')★

○ ◑
type of plant: HSh
flowering season: l. spring to e. summer
flower colour: white
height: 15-30 cm/6-12 in
E

Spraying outwards from a central point and
covered in neat, blue-grey leaves, the stems of this
shrub form the basis of a good, ground-covering
plant. Each of these stems is finished off with a
cluster of flowers and, apart from the main
flowering season given here, there may be a few
blooms in late summer too. *H.* 'Pagei' requires a
well drained soil. In cold areas, good drainage
helps to ensure that this plant survives particularly
severe winters.

Chalk – Atmospheric pollution – Ground-cover
– Containers.

HOSTA sieboldiana (syn. *H. glauca*)★
[species of Plantain Lily]

◑ [○]
type of plant: HP
flowering season: summer
flower colour: palest lilac
height: 60 cm/2 ft
✂

H. sieboldiana has magnificent, blue-green foliage
covered in a pale, greyish bloom. The individual
leaves are large (up to 30 cm/1 ft wide in moist, rich
soil) and beautifully ribbed. The form known as
H. s. elegans has leaves which are even larger and
bluer than those of the species. The flowers of
H. sieboldiana are unobtrusive; they only just
overtop the foliage. This plant is lushest near
water, but it grows well in good, moisture-
retentive soil.

Damp and wet soils – Ground-cover.

CHAMAECYPARIS pisifera e.g. 'Boulevard'
(syn. *C. p.* 'Cyaneoviridis')
[form of Sawara Cypress]

◑
type of plant: HCo
height: 2.4-4.5 m/8-15 ft
E

The silvery blue of this conifer's drooping young
shoots is most intense in partial shade. The whole
plant has a conical outline and a bushy habit of
growth. In autumn, the soft, feathery leaves
become tinged with purple. *C. p.* 'Boulevard' is at
its best in a fairly moist soil.

Autumn foliage.

**Additional plants, featured elsewhere in this
book, that have grey, blue-grey or 'silver' leaves**

○ ◑ sun or partial shade
SORBUS aria: 10.5-15 m (p. 24)
SORBUS hupehensis: 9-12 m (p. 193)
SALIX alba 'Chermesina': 3-4.5 m (p. 210)
HIPPOPHAE rhamnoides: 2.4-3.6 m (p. 88)
PAEONIA mlokosewitschii: 60 cm (p. 247)
CYNOGLOSSUM amabile: 45-60 cm (p. 248)
PICEA mariana 'Nana': 30-45 cm (p. 137)
SAXIFRAGA longifolia: 30-45 cm (p. 26)

◑ [○] partial shade (or sun)
DICENTRA spectabilis: 45-75 cm (p. 251)
MERTENSIA virginica: 30-60 cm (p. 40)
RHODODENDRON impeditum: 30 cm (p. 114)

◑ ● partial or full shade
MERTENSIA virginica: 30-60 cm (p. 40)

Plants with red, purple or bronze leaves

Dramatic though the autumn leaves of some plants are, their beauty is usually short-lived. The plants in the following list have leaves which provide some of the colours associated with autumn foliage, at seasons when most leaves are green; in certain cases, this unusual colouring is present for a considerable number of months in the year. Many of these plants also have the advantage of being useful sources of cut foliage, which the dying leaves of autumn are not.

If you are unfamiliar with a plant in this list do not rely upon either its varietal name or descriptions in catalogues to give you an accurate idea of its colouring. The varietal name of *Berberis thunbergii atropurpurea*, for example, should indicate that this is a plant with dark purple leaves. Its foliage is, indeed, quite dark, but its colour is more a mixture of brown, red and bronze than purple. In catalogues, the term 'purple' would appear to be used most often to describe coppery colours and colours that are mixtures of purple and bronze or red. These colours can be most attractive, but they are not what many people would think of as purple. Most of the plants in this list are also included in Sybil Emberton's *Garden Foliage for Flower Arrangement* (published by Faber and Faber) and this is a good source of more useful descriptions of leaf colour.

Certain plants have foliage which is unusually coloured only when it is young. Sometimes the colour is a bonus to, for instance, already attractively shaped leaves, as it is with the various epimediums (barrenworts or bishop's hats). In certain cases, however, the young leaves are of such a striking colour that, even if their display is short-lived, they are the main decorative feature of the plant. Both the examples of pieris in this list are grown almost entirely for the really brilliant red of their leaves in spring, and the pink, young foliage of *Acer pseudoplatanus* 'Brilliantissimum' is the only decorative feature which distinguishes it from the frequently despised sycamore, of which it is a form. In some cases, the unusually coloured young leaves set off the flowers, which are produced at the same time, particularly well. *Rhododendron lutescens'* early, yellow blossom looks especially attractive among the shiny bronze of its young leaf-growth, and the white flowers of the Japanese cherry called 'Tai-Haku' are similarly enhanced by the coppery colour of its spring foliage.

Very young leaves, however beautifully coloured, do not, unfortunately, make particularly good cut material. With some preliminary conditioning (details of which appear in most books dealing with flower arrangement), fairly immature foliage can be made to last quite well in water. However, leaves which are unusually coloured when just unfolding and for a short time afterwards are really best regarded as features with which the garden, rather than indoor arrangements, can be decorated.

As usual in these foliage lists, very slow-growing or small plants have not been recommended as suitable for cutting. The purple sage, *Salvia officinalis* 'Purpurascens', has been suggested for this purpose because, although it is not large, it responds well to cutting which counteracts a tendency to unattractive legginess.

This list does not include plants with leaves that are some shade of red or bronze on their undersides only. In a few cases, this colouring is quite noticeable: the leaves of *Hebe* 'Midsummer Beauty', for instance, are backed fairly conspicuously with a reddish colour. There are also a number of rhododendrons, such as *R. arboreum* and its varieties, and some magnolias, including *M. grandiflora* 'Exmouth', with leaves which have a brownish felting on their undersides. The most convenient way of showing these leaves to advantage is to include them in flower or foliage arrangements; their ornamental qualities are usually not quite conspicuous enough to make them significant decorative features of gardens.

For plants with leaves which take on red, purple or bronze tints during winter see entries marked 'W' in the 'Colourful autumn foliage' list.

For plants with leaves marbled, mottled or otherwise marked – rather than suffused – with bronze, brown or purple see the 'Variegated leaves' list.

**FAGUS sylvatica e.g. 'Purpurea'
[Purple Beech]**

○

**type of plant: HT
height: 18-27 m/60-90 ft**

✕

The colour of plants sold under this name varies a little, but all forms have young leaves that are pink or pale red and mature foliage that is a dark mahogany-purple. The copper beech (*F. s.* 'Cuprea') is a less commonly planted tree with redder leaves. Grown naturally, *F. s.* 'Purpurea' makes an impressively wide-spreading tree. This plant can also be used for hedging (see *Fagus sylvatica*, p. 130). All well drained soils are suitable. Small specimens of the purple beech retain their withered, russet-coloured leaves until spring.

Chalk – Atmospheric pollution – Hedging – Autumn foliage.

**PRUNUS cerasifera e.g. 'Pissardii' (syn. *P. c.* 'Atropurpurea')
[Purple-leaved Plum]**

○

**type of plant: HT
flowering season: e. spring
flower colour: pink
height: 6 m/20 ft**

✕

'Pissardii' is the most popular purple-leaved variety of *P. cerasifera*, although the very dark form known as 'Nigra' is also readily available. Both plants are used for hedging, sometimes in conjunction with *P. cerasifera* itself (see p. 129 for details). Left untrimmed, they grow into round-headed trees. The young leaves of *P. c.* 'Pissardii' are coppery; more mature foliage is a brownish purple colour. These plants should be given a well drained soil.

Atmospheric pollution – Hedging.

**ACER palmatum 'Atropurpureum' ★
[form of Japanese Maple]**

○

**type of plant: HT/Sh
height: 3.6-4.5 m/12-15 ft**

In spring, the beautiful leaves of this slow-growing tree are a bronzish pink; as they age, they deepen to a maroon colour; and in autumn they turn scarlet. *A. p.* 'Atropurpureum' eventually forms a small tree with a graceful, rather spreading outline. It should be grown in a moist, but well drained and, preferably, acid soil. A sheltered site is essential. The most easily available, large-sized maples with purple-red leaves are varieties of *A. platanoides*, mature specimens of which are 12 m/40 ft high.

Acid soils – Autumn foliage.

CORYLUS maxima 'Purpurea'
[Purple-leaf Filbert]

○

type of plant: HSh
flowering season: l. winter to e. spring
flower colour: purple
height: 3 m/10 ft

This vigorous, spreading shrub is normally pruned hard – after flowering – every other year, in order to produce plenty of new shoots with rich purple-red leaves. The nuts, as well as the catkins, of this form of filbert are suffused with purple, but they are neither large nor decorative. Most soils, including heavy, compacted clays, are suitable.

Clay – Winter-flowering plants.

COTINUS coggygria (syn. *Rhus cotinus*) e.g.
'Royal Purple'
[form of Smoke Tree or Venetian Sumach]

○

type of plant: HSh
flowering season: summer
flower colour: purplish
height: 2.4-3 m/8-10 ft

The dark purple leaves of this rounded shrub are arranged in whorls along fairly upright, slightly curving branches; in autumn, they turn red. *C. coggygria* itself becomes more or less enveloped in clouds of tiny flowers but the varieties with purple foliage bloom more sparsely. Poor, sandy soils increase the likelihood both of good foliage colour and of sizeable quantities of flower plumes (on *C. c.* 'Royal Purple' the latter become pink as seed-heads are formed).

Autumn foliage – Fruit.

FOENICULUM vulgare e.g. 'Giant Bronze'
[form of Common Fennel]

○

type of plant: HP (Herb)
flowering season: midsummer to mid-autumn
flower colour: yellow
height: 1.5-2.4 m/5-8 ft

There are various dark-leaved forms of the pungently aromatic common fennel. In the light soils and sunny places that suit them best, these plants will seed themselves freely. Some gardeners prefer to pinch out the flower buds each year, in order to prevent a mass of seedlings appearing. This treatment also tends to increase the amount of gossamer-fine foliage produced.

Chalk – Hot, dry soils – Aromatic leaves.

RHEUM palmatum e.g. 'Bowles' Crimson'★
sc NA
[form of Ornamental Rhubarb]

○

type of plant: HP
flowering season: e. summer
flower colour: red
height: 1.5-2.1 m/5-7 ft
leaves 90 cm/3 ft high, #

Even when mature and only faintly tinged with red, the foliage of this plant is most impressive. In rich, damp soils, individual leaves 90 cm/3 ft wide will not be uncommon, and they will form huge, weed-smothering clumps. The young foliage emerges as a crumpled mass of very bright red, acquiring more purplish tones as it expands. Until the branching flower panicles appear, this redness is retained on the undersides of the leaves.

Clay – Damp and wet soils – Ground-cover – Green foliage.

BERBERIS thunbergii atropurpurea
[form of Barberry]

○

type of plant: HSh
flowering season: spring
flower colour: yellow
height: 1.2-1.8 m/4-6 ft
✕

Most purple-leaved barberries have a considerable amount of reddish brown in their colouring and *B. t. atropurpurea* is no exception. The stiff branches of this dense, rounded shrub are fearsomely prickled and they can be trained to form an impenetrable hedge. On informally grown plants, the flowers are followed by scarlet berries. In autumn, the foliage turns red. *B. thunbergii* and its varieties have a preference for acid or neutral soils, but they are basically unfussy plants.

Acid soils – Clay – Hot, dry soils – Atmospheric pollution – Hedging – Autumn foliage – Fruit.

ATRIPLEX hortensis 'Rubra'
[form of Orach or Mountain Spinach]

○

type of plant: HA
flowering season: summer
flower colour: reddish
height: 1.2-1.5 m/4-5 ft
✕

Seed catalogues usually list several ornamental varieties of vegetable (sometimes in the vegetable section, sometimes amongst the flower seeds). They usually include cabbages with frilled, pink-variegated foliage, kale with purple-green leaves and this or a similar form of orach (which is occasionally listed under 'Swiss Chard'). All varieties of *A. hortensis* need a deep, rich, moisture-retentive soil for really lush growth. Their stem-ends should be boiled briefly before the foliage is used in arrangements.

WEIGELA florida 'Folliis Purpureis'

○

type of plant: HSh
flowering season: l. spring to e. summer
flower colour: pink
height: 1.2 m/4 ft

This slow-growing shrub needs a position in full sun. If it is planted in even quite light shade, its purple-flushed leaves are an uninteresting, dark, brownish green. Fertile soils of various types will produce good specimens of *W. f.* 'Folliis Purpureis' (which may appear under the name *Diervilla* in certain catalogues), but it will thrive when it remains moist throughout the spring and summer months.

Chalk – Clay – Atmospheric pollution – Containers.

RICINUS communis 'Gibsonii' ★
[form of Castor Oil Plant]

○

type of plant: HHA
height: 90-120 cm/3-4 ft

The large and boldly shaped leaves of this plant are borne on thick, reddish stems and, particularly when young, the foliage has an opulent, red-bronze sheen. Panicles of insignificant flowers are produced in midsummer. These ripen into spiny, red fruits which contain poisonous seeds. A rather light, humus-rich loam suits this plant best.

Fruit.

SALVIA officinalis 'Purpurascens'
[Purple Sage]

○

type of plant: SlTSh (Herb)
flowering season: summer
flower colour: purple
height: 60-75 cm/2-2½ ft
E/½E ✕

Clipped lightly in spring and grown in a well drained, dryish soil, this bushy plant will remain neat throughout the year and it will survive most British winters completely unscathed. Its leaves are, at first, purple; with age, they acquire grey overtones and the combination of colours is a most attractive one. The foliage is pungently aromatic. However, the plain-leaved, common sage emits a stronger scent.

Chalk – Hot, dry soils – Ground-cover – Aromatic leaves.

PERILLA frutescens 'Folliis Atropurpurea Laciniata'

○

type of plant: HHA
height: 60 cm/2 ft

The darkness of this annual's foliage is exceptional and many a plant with *atropurpurea* in its name would look pale and distinctly un-purple in comparison. When bruised, the glistening, crinkled leaves emit a warm fragrance. This plant should be given a fertile, well drained soil and a position in full sun. *P. f.* 'Atropurpurea' is the typical purple-leaved *Perilla* with leaf shape much like *Hydrangea macrophylla*. *P. f.* 'Crispa' (*nankinensis*) is the cut-leaved purple form. They have much the same use, except that the *P. f.* 'Atropurpurea' is a considerably larger plant (to 1.2-1.5 m/4-5 ft). It is also a prolific seeder.

Aromatic leaves.

SEDUM maximum 'Atropurpureum'
[form of Stonecrop]

○

type of plant: HP
flowering season: l. summer to mid-autumn
flower colour: pink
height: 45-60 cm/1½-2 ft

This sedum grows rather more openly than some other well known border plants of the same genus. Although it needs a well drained soil, it must also have some moisture. Its branching stems are a brighter colour than its thick, fleshy leaves which are, in fact, maroon-brown rather than purple. The flowers last well in water, and the seed-heads are an attractive, rich brown.

Chalk – Cutting.

SALVIA horminum e.g. 'Blue Bouquet'
[form of Clary]

○

type of plant: HA
flowering season: summer
flower colour: purple-blue
height: 45 cm/1½ ft
bracts purple-blue and particularly like true leaves

The bracts of *S. h.* 'Blue Bouquet' are so leaf-like that, for many purposes, this erectly stemmed annual may be regarded as a foliage plant. When dried, these bracts remain brightly coloured for several months. Most seed catalogues list forms of *S. horminum* with pink and red as well as with blue bracts, and mixtures of colours are also easily available (for an illustration of a mixed variety, see p. 234). All these plants should, for preference, be grown in a light, fertile soil.

Cutting.

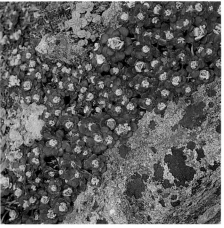

BERBERIS thunbergii 'Atropurpurea Nana' ★
[form of Barberry]

○

type of plant: HSh
flowering season: spring
flower colour: yellow
height: 30-60 cm/1-2 ft

B. t. 'Atropurpurea Nana' is so neatly and densely bun-shaped that, if a number of specimens are planted about 45 cm/1½ ft apart, they will slowly grow into completely weed-proof cover. Throughout spring and summer, the leaves of this slightly thorny shrub are a purplish red-bronze; in autumn, they turn dark purple-mahogany before falling. In autumn too, there are bright scarlet fruits. Most soils suit this plant, but it will not thrive in very alkaline conditions.

Acid soils – Clay – Hot, dry soils – Atmospheric pollution – Ground-cover – Containers – Autumn foliage – Fruit.

DAHLIA 'Redskin'

○

type of plant: HHA
flowering season: midsummer to mid-autumn
flower colour: mixed – lilac, red, yellow, orange, scarlet
height: 40 cm/15 in

It is, first and foremost, the wide range of flower colours – many of them exceptionally rich and dark – and the late flowering season that make dahlias so popular, but a few of these plants have the added attraction of dark, bronzed foliage. The 'Redskin' strain of bedding dahlias produces blooms about 8 cm/3 in wide. These plants need no staking. They grow most satisfactorily in moderately fertile, moisture-retentive soils, and they are easily raised from seed.

SEDUM spathulifolium 'Purpureum'
[form of Stonecrop]

○

type of plant: HP
flowering season: summer
flower colour: golden yellow
height: 10 cm/4 in
E

As spring and summer progress, each of this plant's reddish purple rosettes of foliage becomes increasingly whitened, in its centre at least, by a dusting of waxy powder. *S. s.* 'Purpureum' will make a close mat of leaves in any soil that drains quickly, and it is especially suitable for hot, dry places.

Chalk – Hot, dry soils – Ground-cover – Paving.

MALUS 'Profusion'
[form of Flowering Crab]

○ [◐]

type of plant: HT
flowering season: l. spring
flower colour: wine red
height: 6-7.5 m/20-25 ft
#

A rich, purplish red colour suffuses the flowers and the foliage of this broadly open-headed tree, but the copious blossom soon fades to pink and the mature leaves are a bronzed green. However, during its short period of springtime glory, this is a very decorative small tree. In autumn, dark, brown-red fruits ripen in large quantities. *M.* 'Profusion' will grow quite well in most soils, but good drainage and plenty of well rotted compost or manure produce especially vigorous specimens.

Chalk – Atmospheric pollution – Fruit.

VITIS vinifera 'Purpurea' ★ sc NA MC
[Teinturier Grape, form of Grape Vine or Wine Grape]

○ [◐]

type of plant: HCl/HHCl (NA)
height: 6 m/20 ft

Each 10-15 cm/4-6 in wide leaf on this tendrilled climber is, at first, claret red, deepening, by autumn, to a dark reddish purple. Only against a warm, sheltered wall and in deep, fertile, moisture-retentive soil will the Teinturier grape grow well and reach the height given here. In less favourable conditions, it may be only 3 m/10 ft high. The bunches of grapes ripen to a very dark purple-black colour, but they rarely taste sweet.

Climbers – Containers – Autumn foliage – Fruit.

PHORMIUM tenax e.g. 'Purpureum' MC
[form of New Zealand Flax]

○ [◐]

type of plant: SlTSh/P
flowering season: summer
flower colour: dull red
height: 3-3.6 m/10-12 ft
E ✕, leaves 1.5-1.8 m/5-6 ft high

Amongst the eye-catching bunch of sword shapes produced by this plant there are leaves of varying lengths, and they are all very long-lasting when cut and placed in water. This variety of *P. tenax* is less hardy than some, and a sheltered position and winter protection of the roots are essential in a cold district. Moist or damp soils with a fairly open texture suit this plant best. Mature specimens in warm positions will produce high heads of flowers quite regularly.

Damp and wet soils – Seaside – Atmospheric pollution – Containers.

AJUGA reptans 'Atropurpurea'
[form of Bugle]

○ [◐]

type of plant: HP
flowering season: l. spring to e. summer
flower colour: deep blue
height: 10-15 cm/4-6 in
E/½E

Full sun brings out the richest leaf colour on this creeping plant, but, if the foliage is to form a dense, ground-covering carpet, the roots must be fairly moist. Other varieties of *A. reptans* with red, purple or bronze leaves include 'Burgundy Glow' (see below), which has cream edges to its red-suffused foliage, and 'Multicolor' (syn. 'Rainbow'). The leaves of this last plant are an unusual mixture of metallic green, pale yellow and pink.

Clay – Ground-cover.

NYMPHAEA e.g. × 'James Brydon'
[form of Water-lily]

○ [◐]

type of plant: HPAq
flowering season: summer to e. autumn
flower colour: red
height: 10-15 cm/4-6 in
#

This very free-flowering plant can be grown in water up to 90 cm/3 ft deep, but it will also flourish in as little as 15 cm/6 in of water. In both cases, its roots should be in rich, loamy mud and its upper growths should not, for preference, be shaded. The young leaves are maroon. More mature foliage is only faintly mottled, although a purplish colour may be retained around the leaf edges in some instances.

Green foliage.

ACER pseudoplatanus 'Brilliantissimum'
[form of Sycamore]

○ ◐

type of plant: HT
height: 4.5-6 m/15-20 ft
#young leaves pink

Like the common sycamore, of which it is a variety, *A. p.* 'Brilliantissimum' is an easily grown plant. Its young leaves are shrimp pink but, by the beginning of summer, yellower tones become predominant and the fully mature foliage is pale green. This tree grows slowly, producing a rounded head of branches on a short trunk, so that, amongst other plants, it looks like a large shrub.

Chalk – Clay – Seaside – Atmospheric pollution.

LIGULARIA dentata (syn. *L. clivorum*, *Senecio clivorum*) **'Desdemona'**

○ ◐

type of plant: HP
flowering season: midsummer to e. autumn
flower colour: orange
height: 1.2 m/4 ft

The stems, as well as the leaves, of this plant are suffused with a dark, purplish bronze colour which becomes less purple and more metallic as the summer progresses. The undersides of the leaves are maroon. Damp and boggy conditions suit this plant best, but it will grow robustly in all fertile, moisture-retentive soils.

Clay – Damp and wet soils.

RODGERSIA podophylla

◐ [○]

type of plant: HP
flowering season: summer
flower colour: cream
height: 90-120 cm/3-4 ft

The young leaves of this rodgersia are maroon-bronze. As it expands, the foliage turns green and, particularly in sunny sites, it becomes bronze for a second time in summer. However, a position which receives sun for a substantial part of the day is suitable only if plenty of moisture is available. *R. podophylla* flourishes in damp and boggy soils that are also fertile. Under ideal conditions, which include some shelter from cold winds, the leaves of this plant are usually well over 30 cm/1 ft wide. *R. podophylla* is suitable for fully, as well as partially, shaded sites.

Clay – Damp and wet soils – Ground-cover.

AJUGA reptans e.g. 'Burgundy Glow'★
[form of Bugle]

◐ [○]

type of plant: HP
flowering season: l. spring to e. summer
flower colour: blue
height: 10-15 cm/4-6 in
E/½E, leaves edged with cream

This particular form of *A. reptans* has leaves which are basically green and cream but which are overlaid with a suffusion of bright pink and clear wine-red. Cold weather intensifies the foliage colour. In soils that retain moisture easily, this plant makes excellent ground-cover. (A purple-leaved variety of *A. reptans* is illustrated above).

Clay – Ground-cover – Autumn foliage.

PIERIS (syn. *Andromeda*) 'Forest Flame'

◑

type of plant: HSh
flowering season: spring
flower colour: white
height: 1.8-2.4 m/6-8 ft
*E# ✕

The young foliage of this dense and slow-growing shrub is a bright, pinkish red which later fades to pink and then cream. The mature leaves are green. *P. formosa forrestii* (see p. 42) has even brighter, more intensely scarlet young shoots. Shelter from frost and icy winds is most important. For gardeners who do not have the lime-free, moisture-retentive soil necessary for growing these shrubs, there is *Photinia × fraseri* 'Red Robin' (which has recently become much more widely available). The young leaves of this 3 m/10 ft high shrub are bronzy red rather than scarlet.

   Acid soils – Cutting.

**ADIANTUM pedatum 'Japonicum'★
[form of Maidenhair Fern]**

◑

type of plant: HF
height: 30-60 cm/1-2 ft
#

Both in their youthful, copper-coloured state and when they have expanded and become green, the fronds of this fern are exceptionally pretty. They are arranged in flattish fans on top of dark, wiry stems. A moist, leafy soil suits this plant best, and a sheltered position ensures that its delicate foliage remains undamaged.

   Acid soils – Green foliage.

BEGONIA semperflorens e.g. 'Indian Maid'

◑

type of plant: HHA
flowering season: summer to e. autumn
flower colour: scarlet
height: 23 cm/9 in

Many of the named varieties of *B. semperflorens* have bronze or purplish brown foliage to accompany their numerous, long-lasting, weather-resistant flowers. Some of these plants, like *B. s.* 'Indian Maid', have very brightly coloured blooms, but there are pale pink and white varieties with bronze foliage, and a few seedsmen offer mixtures of dark-leaved begonias. Popular United States cultivars include 'Gin' (deep pink), 'Vodka' (red), 'Whiskey' (white). All these plants need a light, moisture-retentive soil which contains plenty of peat or well rotted compost.

   Acid soils.

**SAXIFRAGA fortunei 'Wada's Variety'
[form of Saxifrage]**

◑ ●

type of plant: SITP
flowering season: autumn
flower colour: white
height: 30-45 cm/1-1½ ft

The interestingly bitty flowers of this plant are produced in larger quantities on *S. fortunei* itself (see p. 186), but the species lacks the attractive bronze sheen of the variety's foliage. On the variety, the stalks and the undersides of the leaves are a bright mahogany-crimson. Coolness and shelter produce the best growth on these plants, protecting them and their late flowers from frost and wind damage.

   Dense shade.

Additional plants, featured elsewhere in this book, that have red, purple or bronze leaves

○ sun
PRUNUS (Japanese Cherry) e.g. 'Tai-Haku':
   9-12 m (p. 1)
PRUNUS (Japanese Cherry) e.g. 'Kanzan':
   7.5-10.5 m (p. 91)
PRUNUS sargentii★: 7.5-9 m (p. 189)
PRUNUS (Japanese Cherry) e.g. 'Amanogawa':
   4.5-7.5 m (p. 2)
LEPTOSPERMUM scoparium 'Nichollsii':
   1.8-3 m (p. 29)
ROSA rubrifolia: 1.8-2.4 m (p. 157)
ACER palmatum 'Dissectum Atropurpureum':
   1.5-2.4 m (p. 133)
DAHLIA (Decorative) 'David Howard': 1.05 m
   (p. 214)
BUTOMUS umbellatus: 60-90 cm (p. 69)

○ [◑] sun (or partial shade)
CERCIDIPHYLLUM japonicum: 15-18 m
   (p. 191)
ACAENA microphylla: 5 cm (p. 106)

○ ◑ sun or partial shade
PARTHENOCISSUS tricuspidata 'Veitchii': 15 m
   (p. 192)
CLEMATIS montana rubens: 6-10.5 m (p. 122)
PARTHENOCISSUS tricuspidata 'Veitchii':
   23 cm (p. 192)
VIOLA labradorica: 10-15 cm (p. 111)

◑ [○] partial shade (or sun)
RODGERSAI pinnata 'Superba': 90-120 cm (p. 77)
LOBELIA fulgens Hybrid e.g. 'Queen Victoria':
   75 cm (p. 77)
ASTILBE × arendsii e.g. 'Fanal': 60 cm (p. 184)
LOBELIA erinus 'Crystal Palace': 15 cm (p. 114)

◑ partial shade
PIERIS formosa forrestii★: 1.8-3 m (p. 42)
RHODODENDRON lutescens: 1.8-3 m (p. 279)
RHODODENDRON williamsianum★: 90-150 cm
   (p. 138)

◑ ● partial or full shade
RODGERSIA pinnata 'Superba': 90-120 cm (p. 77)
RODGERSIA podophylla: 90-120 cm (p. 172)
LOBELIA fulgens Hybrid e.g. 'Queen Victoria':
   75 cm (p. 77)
PODOPHYLLUM emodi: 30 cm (p. 208)
EPIMEDIUM grandiflorum 'Rose Queen':
   20-30 cm (p. 117)
EPIMEDIUM × youngianum 'Niveum': 15-23 cm
   (p. 187)

Plants with yellow or yellow-green leaves

Yellow leaves are so closely associated with unhealthy plants by some gardeners, that they can never look at a perfectly healthy example of – for instance – one of the heathers or lings with yellow foliage, without feeling that some nice, green leaves would be preferable. Yet, to those gardeners who have a penchant for foliage in general, and unusually coloured foliage in particular, plants with yellow leaves are an especially attractive source of one of the warmer and more vitalizing colours.

Yellow-leaved plants are frequently included in the sort of planting schemes that rely upon contrasts between different textures and colours for their main decorative effect. Often, a convenient way of introducing some kinds of contrast into such schemes, is to use yellow-leaved plants. Although the range of easily available plants that have yellow foliage is not large, there are enough variations in height, leaf shape and so on to satisfy most requirements. If you are particularly interested in growing plants with yellow leaves, it is worth consulting the catalogues of various specialist nurseries; many of the most widely offered shrubs and trees, for instance, have unusual, yellow-leaved varieties.

Plants with yellow leaves are popular amongst flower arrangers, again as sources of contrasting material, especially in arrangements which consist entirely of foliage. When used with flowers, yellow leaves provide a lighter background than most green foliage does, and they can look very attractive with blooms of rather delicate colours – including the greens and yellowish greens so sought after by flower arrangers. As usual in these lists dealing with decorative foliage, plants which are particularly useful for cutting are marked; most of the plants not marked are either so small or so slow-growing that they could only provide very limited supplies of cut foliage.

A plant may be described as having yellow leaves, but it is important to remember that the colour of its leaves may change during the growing season. The foliage of some plants, such as *Milium effusum* 'Aureum' and *Hosta fortunei* 'Aureum', is at its most yellow in spring and early summer; by midsummer the leaves have become a light, yellowish green. Some conifers and heathers or lings with yellow leaves take on richer, usually redder colours in late autumn and winter; plants of this type also appear in the list entitled 'Plants with colourful autumn foliage'.

The amount of sunshine a yellow-leaved plant receives also effects the colouring of its foliage. Generally speaking, plants with tough, evergreen leaves require full sun for their foliage to be seen at its brightest and best. There are, however, some plants with yellow leaves – such as *Acer japonicum* 'Aureum', a form of maple – which become scorched in sunshine. As a very general rule, yellow leaves that can withstand plenty of sun are yellowest and brightest in positions of full exposure, while shade often has the effect of prolonging the period during which yellow hues are predominant in the foliage. One plant, *Ligustrum ovalifolium* 'Aureum' (golden privet) appears in two sun-shade categories in this list: in sun or partial shade some leaves are yellow-green or lime-yellow and others are variegated green and yellow (this plant also appears in the 'Variegated foliage' list); in shadier positions there is a higher proportion of single coloured leaves and these are of a yellowish green; full sun produces the highest percentage of variegated leaves.

Finally, there are, of course, differences in colouring between the various plants in this list in any case. Some of the conifers have foliage of a deepish bronzy-gold, while *Lamium maculatum* 'Aureum', for instance, has white markings on its leaves and the overall effect is one of pale yellow.

For foliage variegated with yellow see list entitled 'Plants with variegated leaves'.

GLEDITSCHIA (syn. *Gleditsia*) triacanthos 'Sunburst'★
[form of Honey Locust]

○

type of plant: HT
height 9-12 m/30-40 ft

Unlike many yellow-leaved plants, this broad-headed tree grows quite quickly. It is sometimes treated as a shrub and if it is pruned hard each year it produces a particularly large number of young shoots with bright foliage. The attractively shaped leaves do not unfurl until late in spring and they remain yellow during most of the summer, becoming greener as they mature. In autumn, long, twisted, bean-like pods ripen to a shiny red-brown. This tree grows well in sheltered town gardens where it is not so liable to wind damage. Any fertile, well drained soil is suitable.

Atmospheric pollution – Fruit.

CHAMAECYPARIS obtusa e.g. 'Tetragona Aurea'
[form of Hinoki Cypress]

○

type of plant: HCo
height: 7.5-10.5 m/25-35 ft
E

There are numerous very small and slow-growing forms of *C. obtusa* (see, for example, *C. o.* 'Nana', p. 136), some of which are of a similar, gold-green colour to the plant shown here. This conifer bears its tightly packed and sweetly resinous foliage along branches which create a spiky outline overall. It grows fairly slowly, even in the damper areas of Britain and in the moist, peaty soils which suit it best.

Acid soils – Aromatic leaves.

ROBINIA pseudoacacia 'Frisia'
[form of False Acacia or Black Locust]

○

type of plant: HT
flowering season: e. summer
flower colour: creamy white
height: 7.5-10.5 m/25-35 ft

The brittle branches of this upright tree are set with red thorns. In mid-spring, bright yellow leaflets unfurl and they retain their colour until late summer, when the foliage turns an almost equally attractive, fresh yellow-green. Young specimens of this plant (which can be cut back frequently to form shrubs) do not flower, but softly fragrant tassels of blossom may appear on older trees. *R. p.* 'Frisia' can be grown in light, dry soils, but its foliage will be of better quality when more moisture is present.

Hot, dry soils – Atmospheric pollution – Fragrant flowers.

THUJA occidentalis e.g. 'Rheingold' ★
[form of White Cedar or American Arbor-vitae]

○
type of plant: HCo
height: 1.8-3 m/6-10 ft
E

In autumn and winter, when many yellow-leaved plants are an unremarkable green, the orange tones in this conifer's rich gold foliage become particularly pronounced. *T. o.* 'Rheingold' is usually dense and broadly conical in shape. It grows slowly. Any well drained soil will give satisfactory results but a moist loam is ideal. When crushed, the leaves of this plant emit a fresh, fruity smell.

 Chalk – Autumn foliage – Aromatic leaves.

JUNIPERUS × media e.g. 'Pfitzerana Aurea'
[form of Juniper]

○
type of plant: HCo
height: 90-180 cm/3-6 ft
E

The young leaves of this juniper are bright yellow. By early winter, the yellowness has almost completely disappeared, but, even in its green state, this is a striking plant. Its conspicuous main branches (which may, eventually, cover an area of at least 2.4 sq m/8 sq ft) have arching tips and elegant, hanging branchlets. All junipers thrive in a wide range of soils; good drainage gives particularly satisfactory results.

 Chalk – Hot, dry soils – Ground-cover.

CHAMAECYPARIS lawsoniana e.g. 'Minima Aurea' ★
[form of Lawson Cypress]

○
type of plant: HCo
height: 90-150 cm/3-5 ft
E

This conifer's 'feathers' of golden yellow and yellow-green remain brightly coloured throughout most of the year. The plant is dense and cone-shaped and it grows very slowly. It is especially suitable for long-term planting in tubs and on rock gardens. A moisture-retentive soil with good drainage suits it best.

 Containers.

THUJA orientalis e.g. 'Aurea Nana'
[form of Chinese Arbor-vitae]

○
type of plant: HCo
height: 90-150 cm/3-5 ft
E

Vertical fans of flattened foliage envelop this slow-growing conifer in a soft, gold-green haze in early summer. During the rest of the year, the colouring is predominantly green. *T. o.* 'Aurea Nana' retains its neat, dense, oval shape throughout its life. Moist, loamy soils produce the best specimens of this plant.

BERBERIS thunbergii 'Aurea'
[form of Barberry]

○
type of plant: HSh
flowering season: spring
flower colour: yellow
height: 90-120 cm/3-4 ft

Towards the end of summer, the leaves of this plant become pale green, but, up until that time, they are a very bright, acid yellow (a colour which is enhanced by the reddish twigs). Since late frosts and icy winds can easily damage the young foliage, a sheltered site is important. Given some protection, however, this slow-growing cultivar of *B. thunbergii* will grow well in most soils (those that are acid or neutral are particularly suitable). Small, scarlet fruits appear in autumn.

 Acid soils – Clay – Hot, dry soils – Atmospheric pollution – Hedging – Containers – Fruit.

THUJA plicata (syn. *T. lobbii*) 'Rogersii' (syn. 'Aurea Rogersii')
[form of Western Red Cedar]

○
type of plant: HCo
height: 45-90 cm/1½-3 ft
E

There is an excellent form of *T. plicata*, known as 'Zebrina', with foliage attractively banded in yellow and green but, since it ultimately makes a large tree, varieties such as 'Rogersii' tend to be more widely planted. All the yellow-leaved forms of the western red cedar have bright winter foliage. *T. p.* 'Rogersii' is richly bronze-yellow or gold throughout the year. Its fruit-scented foliage is densest on mature specimens (in maturity, plants have a broadly pyramidal outline). This conifer will grow in quite dry and shallow soils, though moister conditions are preferable.

 Chalk – Aromatic leaves.

CALLUNA vulgaris (syn. *Erica vulgaris*) e.g.
'Gold Haze'★
[form of Heather or Ling]

○

type of plant: HSh
flowering season: l. summer to e. autumn
flower colour: white
height: 45-75 cm/1½-2½ ft
*E

Nurseries with a wide range of heaths and heathers
will list several varieties of *C. vulgaris* with yellow
foliage. Some of these plants may become red or
orange in winter (see, for example *C. v.* 'Robert
Chapman', p. 190). The leaves of *C. v.* 'Gold Haze'
are greenish yellow at first, deepening to a bright
gold-yellow in late summer and autumn. When
clipped lightly each spring and grown in an open
position, this plant makes good ground-cover.

Acid soils – Ground-cover.

PYRETHRUM parthenifolium (syn.
P. parthenium, Chrysanthemum parthenium)
'Aureum'
[form of Feverfew]

○

type of plant: HHA/HP
flowering season: midsummer to e. autumn
flower colour: white
height: 45 cm/1½ ft
✕, leaves 15 cm/6 in high

The small, white, daisy-like flowers of this plant
are often removed at an early stage in their growth,
particularly when the lime-yellow leaves are to be
used as an edging to summer bedding schemes.
Other yellow-leaved varieties of *P. parthenifolium*
are readily available, mainly from seedsmen. They
are all easy to grow in light, well drained soils. The
second synonym given here is the correct botanical
name, more commonly used in the United States.

Chalk.

ORIGANUM vulgare 'Aureum'
[form of Common Marjoram]

○

type of plant: SITP (Herb)
height: 23-30 cm/9-12 in
E/½E

Even when the bright yellow of its new foliage has
faded (first to an unusual khaki-green colour and
then to plain mid-green), this sweetly aromatic
plant is attractive. Its leaves encircle the fairly
upright, closely packed stems at short intervals
giving an overall impression of neatness and
density. Any soil with reasonably good drainage
will suit this plant. In very hot, dry conditions the
edges of its leaves may become scorched.

Chalk – Ground-cover – Aromatic leaves.

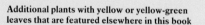

**Additional plants with yellow or yellow-green
leaves that are featured elsewhere in this book**

○ sun
CATALPA bignonioides 'Aurea': 7.5-12 m (p. 91)
CHAMAECYPARIS lawsoniana e.g. 'Ellwood's
Gold': 2.4-3.6 m (p. 132)
CALLUNA vulgaris e.g. 'Robert Chapman': 45 cm
(p. 190)

THYMUS✕citriodorus 'Aureus'
[form of Lemon-scented Thyme]

○

type of plant: HSh (Herb)
flowering season: summer
flower colour: pale mauve
height: 15-23 cm/6-9 in
E

The two most common forms of lemon-scented
thyme are the golden-leaved variety shown here
and *T.✕c.* 'Silver Queen'. The latter plant has very
pale cream markings on its grey-green leaves. Both
varieties form dense little bushes if they are grown
in full sun and a light soil and if they are cut back
quite hard after flowering.

Chalk – Hot, dry soils – Paving – Aromatic
leaves.

SAMBUCUS nigra 'Aurea'
[Golden Elder]

○ [◐]

type of plant: HSh
flowering season: e. summer
flower colour: white
height: 3.6-4.5 m/12-15 ft

Of the two forms of elder shown here, *S. racemosa*
'Plumosa Aurea' (see next page) is the most
decorative, with its elegantly slender, fringed
leaves, but *S. nigra* 'Aurea' is the fastest growing
and generally the most robust. The leaves of both
plants will be brightest in sun but, especially in the
case of *S. r.* 'Plumosa Aurea', a sunny position can
lead to scorching of the leaf margins. This damage
is less likely to occur if the soil is either moist or
damp. The golden elder's unpleasantly scented
flowers are followed by black berries; *S. r.*
'Plumosa Aurea' produces scarlet fruits. Both
shrubs can be cut back hard in early (*contd*)

SAMBUCUS racemosa 'Plumosa Aurea'★
[form of Elder]

○ [◑]
type of plant: HSh
flowering season: mid-spring
flower colour: yellowish white
height: 1.5-2.1 m/5-7 ft

See preceding plant.

(*contd*)
spring to encourage plenty of new shoots (on which the foliage will be particularly well coloured; mature leaves are yellow-green or green). This pruning usually leads to an irregularly rounded outline.

Chalk – Clay – Damp and wet soils – Atmospheric pollution (*S. nigra* 'Aurea' only) – Fruit.

LONICERA nitida 'Baggesen's Gold' sc NA
[form of Shrubby Honeysuckle]

○ [◑]
type of plant: HSh
height: 1.2-1.8 m/4-6 ft
E ✕

This yellow-leaved variety of *L. nitida* can, like the species, be used for formal hedging. However, it grows rather slowly and, since its foliage is so attractive for most of the year, it is usually planted as a single specimen in mixed borders. Overall, this shrub has a dense habit of growth but it often sends out quite long shoots. While these give an unruly appearance to hedges, they seem to enhance the prettiness of informally grown plants. Full sun is needed for good colouring, but in dry soils a little shade may be necessary to prevent scorching of the foliage.

Chalk – Hedging.

LIGUSTRUM ovalifolium 'Aureum'
[Golden Privet]

○ ◑
type of plant: HSh
flowering season: summer/e. summer (NA)
flower colour: white
height: 2.7-3.6 m/9-12 ft
E/½E ✕

Hedges of this plant – which need to be clipped three times a year if they are to remain neat and tidy – are a common sight. However, golden privet also makes an attractive, free-standing shrub with an open network of twigs on fairly upright branches. In sun, its leaves have yellow margins and green central areas; in full shade a uniform yellow-green predominates. Plants in light shade have a mixture of plain and variegated leaves. *L. o.* 'Aureum' can be grown in any soil.

Chalk – Dry shade – Atmospheric pollution – Hedging – Variegated leaves.

ACER japonicum 'Aureum'★
[form of Maple]

◑
type of plant: HT/Sh
height: 4.5-6 m/15-20 ft

For many years, this beautiful maple will be a small, rounded shrub, but it eventually forms an elegant tree with layers of its lovely foliage borne on more or less horizontal branches. As well as some shade, this plant must have moisture at its roots and shelter from cold winds, or else the margins of its many-lobed leaves will become brown and brittle and unsightly. When the young foliage first begins to expand, it is a sharp, greenish yellow. However, the colour soon deepens and softens, and it remains a sunny mid-yellow all summer. In some cases, the leaves have an attractive red margin. The autumn colouring of this plant is not exceptional.

Acid soils.

MILIUM effusum 'Aureum'★
[Bowles' Golden Grass]

◑
type of plant: HP (Gr)
flowering season: l. spring to e. summer
flower colour: yellow
height: 60-90 cm/2-3 ft
✕

All visible parts of this clump-forming grass are suffused, in spring and early summer, with a beautiful, bright, greenish yellow. Partial shade and moisture produce sharp colouring and strong growth. The loose panicles of flowers may be used in fresh and in dried arrangements. They are usually held well above the leaves, most of which will be not more than 30 cm/1 ft high.

Ground-cover – Cutting.

HOSTA fortunei 'Aurea'
[form of Plantain Lily]

◑
type of plant: HP
flowering season: summer
flower colour: lilac
height: 45-60 cm/1½-2 ft
✕

Cool, moist conditions are essential for growing this plant. Its young leaves are an attractive pale yellow, but they are also thin-textured. This lack of substance means that they are apt to wilt and to become brown and puckered at the edges if they are exposed to strong sun or if the roots of the plant are dry. The foliage is yellowest in spring; it becomes gradually greener during the summer months. Well grown specimens of this hosta produce quite large, dense clumps of foliage.

Damp and wet soils – Ground-cover.

Additional plants with yellow or yellow-green leaves that are featured elsewhere in this book

◑ ● partial or full shade
LIGUSTRUM ovalifolium 'Aureum': 2.7-3.6 m
(p. 177)

PHILADELPHUS coronarius 'Aureus'
[form of Mock Orange]

◑ ●

type of plant: HSh
flowering season: summer/l. spring (NA)
flower colour: creamy white
height: 1.5-2.1 m/5-7 ft

The plain green *P. coronarius* will flourish in dry
soils and sunny sites but this yellow-leaved variety
needs at least some moisture and shade to do well.
In full sun, its young leaves are certainly very
brightly coloured, but they soon turn green and
they often develop unsightly, brown 'scorch'
marks. Shade produces a greener and longer
lasting colour. The flowers of this dense, rather
twiggy shrub have a powerful, sweet fragrance.

Chalk – Atmospheric pollution – Fragrant
flowers.

LAMIUM maculatum 'Aureum'
[form of Spotted Dead Nettle]

◑ ●

type of plant: HP
flowering season: l. spring to e. summer
flower colour: mauve-pink
height: 15 cm/6 in
E/½E

In moisture-retentive soil, this variety of
L. maculatum will grow densely enough to be
useful for ground-cover on a small scale. It spreads
less widely and less rapidly than its green-leaved
counterparts, but its white-striped, greenish
yellow foliage makes it a much brighter and more
decorative plant.

Clay – Dense shade – Ground-cover.

Plants with decorative, green foliage

It might seem as if it could only be the shape of a green leaf which would make it decorative. However, there are green leaves that are interestingly textured, impressively sized and – perhaps unexpectedly – of rather unusual shades. All these decorative qualities can, of course, enhance a beautiful leaf shape.

Plants with interestingly textured, green foliage include the ground-covering *Viburnum davidii* which has leaves that are marked into distinct sections by three longitudinal veins, almost in the way that a piece of lightly padded material is partitioned by lines of stitching. In contrast to this leaf texture there is, on the one hand, foliage which is much more intricately veined: the leaves of *Tellima grandiflora*, for example, are reminiscent of pieces of crumpled paper which have been only partly straightened out; on the other hand, there is the very smooth foliage of certain green-leaved plants, such as water-lilies, camellias and many rhododendrons.

Griselinia littoralis' leaves, in addition to being pleasingly smooth, are of an unusual, fresh yellowish green. Other plants with light green foliage include the popular *Alchemilla mollis* (lady's mantle), whose leaves are a velvety lime-green, and *Onoclea sensibilis* (sensitive fern), which has fronds of a most attractive paleness. Exceptionally dark green leaves, such as those of the variety of nasturtium called 'Empress of India', can also be attractive.

Although all the plants in this list have foliage which is some shade of green, many of them have leaves which are more exotically coloured for limited periods during the year. For example, the mature foliage of *Rheum palmatum* 'Bowles' Crimson' is dark green, but its young leaves are red. (This plant also appears in the 'Red, purple or bronze leaves' list; the red colouring is retained, to some extent, on the backs of the mature leaves.) The species of tellima referred to above is one of a number of plants that take on bronzish brown hues in winter, and there are also plants, such as *Liriodendron tulipifera* (tulip tree), *Rhus typhina* (stag's horn sumach) and various maples, which appear both in this list and in the 'Colourful autumn foliage' list.

An interesting texture or an unusual shade of green can make a leaf decorative, but so too can exceptional size. In suitably moist and rich growing conditions *Gunnera manicata* produces massive leaves, some of which may be up to 3 m/10 ft wide. The foliage of trees like *Paulownia tomentosa* and *Catalpa*

bignonioides (Indian bean tree) is on a rather smaller scale, but it is still unusually large. All three of these plants create a bold decorative effect. (*Paulownia tomentosa* is sometimes pruned very hard in order to encourage the production of particularly large leaves; pruned specimens of this sort are occasionally used as bedding plants.) Conversely, a few plants have leaves which are decorative because they are miniature versions of the foliage of some other plants. This list includes *Berberis darwinii*, a species of barberry, which has dark green, holly-like leaves that are often less than 2 cm/1 in long.

Bold foliage can denote either very large leaves as in *Gunnera manicata*, mentioned above, or leaves whose striking appearance is due more to their clear-cut, sculptural shape than their size. Plants with leaves of a conspicuous and well defined form include the bergenias, whose foliage is rounded and solid, *Acanthus spinosus*, which has deeply incised, dark green leaves, and *Yucca filamentosa*, which is equipped with rigid, sword-shaped leaves. All these plants have foliage of a sufficiently strong shape to look well in extensive areas of paving and at the base of large walls.

To provide contrast to bold foliage, plants with delicate leaves may be chosen. Many of the ferns in this list have beautifully divided fronds which create a light and lacy effect. There are also larger plants with delicate, fern-like foliage: *Sorbus vilmorinii* (a species of rowan or mountain ash), for example, has leaves which consist of up to twenty-five individual leaflets. The narrow leaves of most grasses are an additional source of light and delicate foliage that contrasts well with more solidly shaped leaves. All grasses are marked '(Gr)' after 'type of plant'; they appear in various lists in this book, including those dealing with variegated and unusually coloured foliage.

The leaves of a few plants in this list are not perhaps very decorative in themselves, but their habit of growth or the way in which they are arranged on branches or stems show them to such advantage that the overall effect is decorative. The leaves of day lilies, for example, are not of remarkable shape or colour, but they grow in an elegantly arching way. Similarly, the individual leaves of *Picea breweriana* (Brewer's weeping spruce) are not decorative, but, in conjunction with the hanging branchlets of this tree, they create highly ornamental curtains of foliage.

LIRIODENDRON tulipifera
[Tulip Tree]

○

type of plant: HT
flowering season: summer
flower colour: yellowish green
height: 21-30 m/70-100 ft

The strangely shaped leaves of this tree – each one looking as if it were lacking a central lobe – are lime-green for most of the year, until autumn, when they turn yellow. On deep, moist soils this plant grows quickly, and mature specimens have high, domed heads with thick main branches. Ten years or so after planting, the tulip tree begins to produce its unusual flowers. These are most attractive at close quarters.

  Atmospheric pollution – Autumn foliage – Green flowers.

KOELREUTERIA paniculata★
[Goldenrain Tree]

○

type of plant: HT
flowering season: summer
flower colour: yellow
height: 9-15 m/30-50 ft

In Britain, the outstanding feature of this tree is usually its foliage, since its flowers tend to be rather sparsely produced, except in mild areas or after very warm summers. Each leaf is about 30 cm/1 ft long and composed of numerous leaflets (as many as fifteen in some cases). The foliage turns yellow in autumn (when there may also be showers of red-tinged fruits). *K. paniculata* should be given a well drained, loamy soil and a sheltered position. Mature trees are broadly round-headed.

  Autumn foliage – Fruit.

PAULOWNIA tomentosa (syn. *P. imperalis*)

○

type of plant: SlTT
flowering season: l. spring
flower colour: pale blue
height: 9-12 m/30-40 ft
leaves largest if pruned hard, B

When allowed to grow freely, *P. tomentosa* is a rounded, openly branched tree and its heart-shaped leaves are about 20-25 cm/8-10 in long. The sweetly scented flowers appear on older plants only and, in Britain, the winter flower buds are easily damaged by frost. It is sometimes cut back to ground level each year, when it will be about 1.8-2.4 m/6-8 ft high and flowerless but equipped with leaves two or three times the normal size (which are liable to be torn to pieces in windy gardens). However it is grown, this plant needs a deep, fertile soil and a sheltered site.

  Fragrant flowers.

ERIOBOTRYA japonica MC
[Loquat]
○
type of plant: HH/SlTSh
flowering season: autumn
flower colour: white
height: 4.5-7.5 m/15-25 ft
E, B

Even with a south-facing wall to grow against, the loquat very rarely produces any fruit in Britain. However, its flowers are richly scented and its thick, glossy leaves are large (up to 30 cm/1 ft long) and handsome. A light soil suits this plant best. In the United States, fruit is produced only in the warmer soils.

　Fragrant flowers.

PITTOSPORUM tenuifolium MC
○
type of plant: SlTSh/T
height: 4.5-7.5 m/15-25 ft
E ✕

The wavy edges to this plant's olive green leaves are a common feature of many florists' arrangements. In the garden, *P. tenuifolium* makes a dense, oval-shaped bush. After a number of years, it develops a short trunk. It may be used for hedging in mild areas, when it usually needs pruning or shearing twice a year. Gardeners in colder districts should give this plant a sheltered site and a well drained soil. Although they are small and dark and borne close to the black stems, the flowers of this shrub are very sweetly scented, particularly in the evening. *P. t.* 'Silver Queen' has white margins to its pale green leaves.

　Hedging – Fragrant flowers.

SOPHORA tetraptera MC
[Kowhai]
○
type of plant: SlTSh/T/HHSh/T (NA)
flowering season: l. spring
flower colour: yellow
height: 4.5-7.5 m/15-25 ft

Young plants of this shrub produce few flowers on their slender, weaving branches and, in the early stages of its life, *S. tetraptera*'s foliage is its only decorative feature. However, the leaves are composed of numerous, small leaflets which create an attractively insubstantial effect. When the hanging bunches of flowers do appear, they are followed by long, thin, yellow seed-pods. This is a plant for warm and sheltered gardens and mild districts only. It needs a well drained, loamy soil.

　Fruit.

CORDYLINE australis MC
[Cabbage Tree]
○
type of plant: HHT
flowering season: e. summer
flower colour: creamy white
height: 3.6-9 m/12-30 ft
E, B

The topknots of 60-90 cm/2-3 ft long leaves which *C. australis* produces on its erect branches give an oddly subtropical look to gardens and public parks in the mildest areas of Britain. Mature specimens of this plant may also bear large panicles of sweetly scented flowers. Strong winds that carry *warm* air will not damage this tree (which should be grown in a fertile soil with good drainage). If planted in a large tub, it may be moved under cover during the winter months in cold districts.

　Seaside – Containers – Fragrant flowers.

RHUS typhina 'Laciniata'
[form of Stag's Horn Sumach]
○
type of plant: HSh/T
flowering season: summer
flower colour: yellowish green
height: 3-4.5 m/10-15 ft

All the stag's horn sumachs (so called because of the forked, antler-like arrangement of their branches) have brilliantly coloured foliage in autumn. *R. t.* 'Laciniata' looks attractive in spring and summer too, with its numerous, deeply toothed leaflets. Female plants bear spikes of red fruit. A light soil is necessary for the richest orange-and-yellow autumn colour. This shrub will produce exceptionally long leaves if it is cut back to ground level each year, in spring.

　Chalk – Atmospheric pollution – Autumn foliage – Fruit.

ACER palmatum 'Dissectum'
[form of Japanese Maple]
○
type of plant: HSh
height: 1.5-2.4 m/5-8 ft

The foliage of this very slow-growing shrub is composed of bright green, slender leaflets which are finely divided. In outline, the plant is rounded, and the leaves hang in light, feathery layers from spreading branches. As shown in the photograph above, the foliage turns bronzish yellow in autumn. *A. p.* 'Dissectum' should, for preference, have an acid or neutral soil in which its roots will remain cool and moist. A sheltered position is also advisable, in order to protect the foliage from being damaged by cold winds. A purple-leaved form of this plant is shown on p. 133.

　Acid soils – Containers – Autumn foliage.

RICINUS communis 'Zanzibarensis'
[form of Castor Oil Plant]

○
type of plant: HHA
height: 1.2-1.8 m/4-6 ft
B

Given a light, rich soil and kept well watered in dry weather, this plant will produce leaves some 23 cm/9 in wide. The foliage colour is a particularly fresh, light green. Inconspicuous, green flowers are followed by red fruits (which contain poisonous seeds).

Fruit.

NICANDRA physaloides
[Apple of Peru, Shoo Fly Plant]

○
type of plant: HA
flowering season: midsummer to e. autumn
flower colour: pale violet + white
height: 75-90 cm/2½-3 ft

Although this vigorous, bushy plant has attractive flowers and fruit, its deeply toothed foliage is its most striking feature. The flowers open fully for only a few hours each day and the small – and inedible – 'apples', with their lantern-like bracts, are more decorative in dried arrangements than on the plant. *N. physaloides* will be lushest and leafiest in a moist, fertile soil, but it will grow quite satisfactorily under less favourable conditions.

Fruit.

GREVILLEA robusta
[Silk Oak, Silk Bark Oak]

○
type of plant: TenT
height: 60 cm/2 ft
*, **greenhouse tree used as bedding plant**

G. robusta appears in the greenhouse section of most seedsmens' catalogues. When grown outdoors, it is usually raised from seed and treated as a temporary, bedding plant. It needs a really warm, sheltered site. The young leaves of this plant are slightly bronzed.

Acid soils.

INCARVILLEA delavayi

○
type of plant: HP
flowering season: summer
flower colour: rose-pink
height: 60 cm/2 ft

The deep green, divided foliage of this perennial is of a sufficiently strong shape not to be completely outshone by the large, thick-stalked flowers. After dying down in autumn, *I. delavayi* does not reappear until late spring. The fleshy roots should be planted in fertile, well drained soil, and their position should be marked to prevent unintentional damage during the long, dormant season.

NIGELLA damascena e.g. 'Persian Jewels'
[form of Love-in-a-Mist]

○
type of plant: HA
flowering season: summer
flower colour: mixed – blue, pink, white, purple,
rose-red
height: 45-60 cm/1½-2 ft

Each of this plant's pretty flowers is surrounded by slender, green bracts and set above a haze of thread-like foliage. The flowers last well in water and the red-striped seed-pods are attractive in dried arrangements. In Britain, the brightly blue-flowered 'Miss Jekyll' is a particularly popular variety of *N. damascena*. It is illustrated on p. 232.

Cutting.

EICHHORNIA crassipes (syn. *E. speciosa*)
[Water Hyacinth]

○
type of plant: HHPAq
flowering season: summer
flower colour: pale violet
height: 15-23 cm/6-9 in

This floating plant needs to be potted up in wet soil and stored in a heated greenhouse during the colder months of the year. Although its flowers – which look, but do not smell like hyacinths – are its main attraction, the smoothly shaped, glossy leaves, with their bloated stems, are also handsome. *E. crassipes* can be grown in water up to 45 cm/18 in deep. Its roots should have access to fertile mud.

NYMPHAEA e.g.×'Escarboucle'
[form of Water-lily]

○
type of plant: HPAq
flowering season: summer to e. autumn
flower colour: red
height: 10-15 cm/4-6 in
B

Once the beautiful flowers of water-lilies appear, the leaves of these plants seem of little importance. However, the large size of the leaves, their almost circular shape and, if the plants are not overcrowded, their extreme flatness make them a bold background. The foliage of N.× 'Escarboucle' is a uniform green, but some water-lilies have maroon or purplish markings on their leaves (see, for example, N.× 'Marliacea Chromatella', p. 172, and N.× 'James Brydon', p. 149).

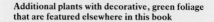

Additional plants with decorative, green foliage that are featured elsewhere in this book

○ sun
GINKGO biloba: 18-24 cm (p. 189)
LIQUIDAMBAR styraciflua★: 15-21 m (p. 189)
CATALPA bignonioides: 9-13.5 m (p. 90)
ROBINIA pseudoacacia e.g. 'Bessoniana': 9-12 m (p. 90)
MAGNOLIA grandiflora 'Exmouth'★: 4.5-7.5 m (p. 253)
ACER palmatum: 4.5-6 m (p. 190)
AZARA microphylla: 3.6-4.5 m (p. 254)
TAMARIX pentandra: 3.6-4.5 m (p. 129)
RHUS typhina: 3-4.5 m (p. 190)
YUCCA gloriosa: 2.7-3.6 m (p. 56)
PHYLLOSTACHYS nigra 'Boryana': 2.4-3.9 m (p. 68)
RHEUM palmatum e.g. 'Bowles' Crimson': 1.5-2.1 m (p. 169)
INDIGOFERA gerardiana: 1.2-1.8 m (p. 29)
YUCCA filamentosa★: 90-180 cm (p. 57)
ECHINOPS ritro: 90-120 cm (p. 4)
COSMOS bipinnatus e.g. 'Sensation Mixed': 90 cm (p. 219)
COSMOS sulphureus e.g. 'Sunset': 75-90 cm (p. 58)
KOCHIA scoparia trichophylla★: 60-90 cm (p. 190)
PELARGONIUM quercifolium: 60-90 cm (p. 197)
PELARGONIUM graveolens: 60 cm (p. 197)
PONTEDERIA cordata: 60 cm (p. 69)
SAGITTARIA sagittifolia 'Flore Pleno': 60 cm (p. 69)
NIGELLA damascena e.g. 'Miss Jekyll': 45-60 cm (p. 232)
HELIOTROPIUM peruvianum e.g. 'Royal Marine': 45 cm (p. 259)
TROPAEOLUM majus 'Empress of India': 23 cm (p. 62)
SEMPERVIVUM montanum: 15-23 cm (p. 63)

GILIA hybrida e.g. 'French Hybrids': 15 cm (p. 17)
NYMPHAEA e.g. 'Marliacea Albida': 10-15 cm (p. 263)
NYMPHAEA e.g.× 'Sunrise': 10-15 cm (p. 263)

TRACHYCARPUS fortunei (syn. *T. excelsa, Chamaerops excelsa*) **MC**
[Chusan Palm]

○ [◐]
type of plant: SITT
flowering season: e. summer
flower colour: yellow
height: 3-9 m/10-30 ft
E, B

The fans of pleated and fringed foliage produced by this slow-growing tree are sometimes over 1.2 m/4 ft wide. Like *Cordyline australis* (see p. 180), the Chusan palm is grown mainly in the warmer parts of Britain, where the mildness of the climate allows other plants of subtropical appearance to flourish. Although it is hardier than *Cordyline australis*, it is much less wind-resistant, and it needs a sheltered site to grow well.

ARUNDINARIA japonica (syn. *Pseudosasa japonica*)
[species of Bamboo]

○ [◐]
type of plant: HP (Ba)
height: 3-4.5 m/10-15 ft
E

Thickets of this bamboo can spread at alarming speed, particularly in moist or damp and fertile soils. They are probably best used to create large screens or to cover extensive, informally planted areas of ground. The leaves are decorative *en masse* only. They are liable to become damaged by cold winds, and a site with some shelter is, therefore, advisable. The canes of this plant are olive green.

Chalk – Damp and wet soils – Bark and *twigs*.

PHORMIUM tenax **MC**
[New Zealand Flax]

○ [◐]
type of plant: SITSh/P
flowering season: summer
flower colour: dull red
height: 3-3.6 m/10-12 ft
E✕, leaves 1.5-1.8 m/5-6 ft high, B

Although it lacks the spectacular colouring of some of its cultivars (for examples of which see pp. 150 and 171), *P. tenax* is, nevertheless, a very striking plant. Its rigid leaves form a great, spiky bunch of slightly blue-grey foliage. Ideally, *P. tenax* should be given a moist, loamy soil. Damp soils that do not become waterlogged are also suitable. Some protection of the crown and roots may be necessary in cold districts. In warm districts, established plants flower regularly.

Damp and wet soils – Seaside – Atmospheric pollution – Containers.

MACLEAYA (syn. *Bocconia*) **cordata**
[species of Plume Poppy]

○ [◐]
type of plant: HP
flowering season: midsummer to e. autumn
flower colour: white
height: 1.5-2.4 m/5-8 ft
B

The basically circular outline of each of this plant's
large leaves is broken by indentations which
themselves are rounded; *M. microcarpa* and its
variety 'Kelway's Coral Plume' (see p. 164) have
similar foliage of a greyer green. *M. cordata* is
slightly less vigorous than either of these plants,
but its underground roots may still spread quite
widely in deep, rich, loamy soils.

GERANIUM pratense e.g. 'Album'
[form of Meadow Cranesbill]

○ [◐]
type of plant: HP
flowering season: summer
flower colour: white
height: 60-75 cm/2-2½ ft

The true geraniums and their cultivated varieties
include many plants with exceptionally pretty
foliage. Most of them make very good ground-
cover (see pp. 108-10 and 115 for further
examples; a pale blue counterpart of the plant
shown here is illustrated on p. 105). *G. pratense*
'Album' forms a clump of deeply divided,
slim-lobed leaves which often colour well in
autumn. Like other meadow cranesbills, it is a
fairly tall plant that may need staking. Most well
drained soils are suitable.

Ground-cover – Autumn foliage.

PICEA breweriana★
[Brewer's Weeping Spruce]

○ ◐
type of plant: HCo
height: 9-15 m/30-50 ft
E

The weeping habit of this conifer takes several
years to develop, but established specimens often
have hanging branchlets which are over 60 cm/2 ft
long. Young plants grow very slowly and are
broadly pyramidal in shape. Their outline may
become more columnar as they mature. A deep,
acid, moisture-retentive soil and some shelter from
cold winds provide the ideal conditions in which to
grow this beautiful plant.

Acid soils.

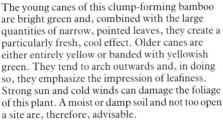

ARALIA elata
[Japanese Angelica Tree]

○ ◐
type of plant: HSh/T
flowering season: l. summer to e. autumn
flower colour: white
height: 6-10.5 m/20-35 ft
B

A. elata is a shrubby, suckering plant, except in
mild districts, where it may form a small, openly
branched tree. It grows quickly when given a rich,
moist soil and a sheltered site. The bold,
horizontally held foliage appears late in spring.
When fully expanded, some of the leaves may be as
much as 1.5 m/5 ft long and 90 cm/3 ft wide.

Atmospheric pollution.

ARUNDINARIA murieliae (syn.
Sinarundinaria murieliae)
[species of Bamboo]

○ ◐
type of plant: HP (Ba)
height: 1.8-3 m/6-10 ft
E

The young canes of this clump-forming bamboo
are bright green and, combined with the large
quantities of narrow, pointed leaves, they create a
particularly fresh, cool effect. Older canes are
either entirely yellow or banded with yellowish
green. They tend to arch outwards and, in doing
so, they emphasize the impression of leafiness.
Strong sun and cold winds can damage the foliage
of this plant. A moist or damp soil and not too open
a site are, therefore, advisable.

Damp and wet soils – Bark and *twigs*.

GUNNERA manicata MC

○ ◐
type of plant: SlTP
flowering season: l. spring to e. summer
flower colour: green
height: 1.8-2.7 m/6-9 ft
B

The flowers of this plant are thick, cone-like
structures about 60-90 cm/2-3 ft high, but they
seem small and insignificant when the huge, lobed
leaves expand above them. *G. manicata* is usually
grown in damp or boggy ground near water and, in
these circumstances, leaves over 1.8 m/6 ft wide are
not uncommon. Slightly drier conditions are also
suitable, as long as the soil is deep and fertile.
Because the crowns and leaf buds of this plant are
liable to be damaged by frost, they should have a
protective covering of leaves in winter.

Damp and wet soils – Ground-cover – Green
flowers.

PAEONIA suffruticosa (syn. *P. moutan*) e.g.
'Mrs William Kelway'
[form of Tree Peony/Paeony or Moutan]
○ ◑
type of plant: HSh
flowering season: l. spring to e. summer
flower colour: white
height: 1.5-1.8 m/5-6 ft

In addition to their large and dramatic blooms,
tree paeonies produce handsome, divided foliage.
Cultivars of *P. suffruticosa* tend to have leaves that
are not very deeply lobed. Their flowers, which
may be red or pink as well as white, are about
15-20 cm/6-8 in wide. Although these shrubs are
hardy, their young growths can easily be damaged
by frost. And whole plants may be killed by one or
other of the diseases to which tree paeonies are
susceptible. The best growth is produced on deep,
well drained, moisture-retentive soils.

ACANTHUS spinosus ★ MC
[species of Bear's Breeches]
○ ◑
type of plant: HP/SITP (NA)
flowering season: summer
flower colour: purple + white
height: 90-120 cm/3-4 ft
B

The foliage of *A. spinosus* arches upwards and
outwards, and this habit of growth emphasizes the
length and fierce, jagged prickliness of the
individual leaves (some of which may be over
60 cm/2 ft long). The hooded flowers are
splendidly bold material for large arrangements,
and the seed-heads are also attractive. Almost any
soil suits this plant, but it will become established
and start to seed itself most quickly in soils that
drain well.

    Chalk – Clay – Ground-cover – Cutting.

POLEMONIUM foliosissimum
○ ◑
type of plant: HP
flowering season: l. spring to e. autumn
flower colour: blue
height: 75-90 cm/2½-3 ft

Throughout their long flowering season, this
plant's clusters of rich, mauvish blue blooms are
held erectly above a bed of feathery foliage.
Substantial, moisture-retentive soils suits
P. foliosissimum best; it is short-lived in light and
infertile soils.

    Clay.

BERGENIA cordifolia
○ ◑
type of plant: HP
flowering season: spring
flower colour: mauve-pink
height: 30 cm/1 ft
E ✕ B

Bergenia leaves of various shapes and sizes are
popular with flower arrangers. The circular,
wavy-edged foliage of *B. cordifolia* is particularly
long-lasting when cut. It is mid-green for most of
the year, but in late autumn and winter it often
acquires a reddish purple tinge. Each leaf is about
20 cm/8 in in diameter. This plant will grow and
make solid clumps of ground-covering foliage in
almost any soil, needing little or no attention.

    Chalk – Clay – Dry shade – Ground-cover –
Autumn foliage.

RODGERSIA tabularis
◑ [○]
type of plant: HP
flowering season: midsummer
flower colour: white
height: 90-120 cm/3-4 ft
B

Especially when young, the shallowly dished
leaves of this moisture-loving plant are a bright,
pale green. The dense flower heads are carried
about 45-60 cm/1½-2 ft above the foliage. In rich,
damp soils and sheltered sites, some clumps of *R.
tabularis* may produce leaves over 90 cm/3 ft wide.
In drier conditions, a fully shaded position may
help to keep this plant moist and cool.

    Clay – Damp and wet soils – Ground-cover.

ASTILBE ✕ arendsii e.g. 'Fanal'
[form of False Goat's Beard]
◑ [○]
type of plant: HP
flowering season: summer
flower colour: deep red
height: 60 cm/2 ft

The leaves of astilbes are generally regarded as
handsome adjuncts to the flowers, rather than
decorative features in their own right. Some
dark-flowered forms, including the example
shown here, have foliage which is reddish bronze
when young and a deep, slightly coppery green
when mature. In these cases, the leaves and flowers
are more nearly equal partners. All the *A. ✕
arendsii* hybrids need moist or damp soil to grow
well. They make excellent ground-cover. Their
seed-heads are almost as attractive as their flowers.

    Damp and wet soils – Ground-cover – Red, etc.
leaves – Cutting.

ONOCLEA sensibilis★
[Sensitive Fern]

◑ [○]
type of plant: HF
height: 45-60 cm/1½-2 ft
B

This fern's boldly incised, sterile fronds turn
brown during the first frost of autumn – hence the
common name. Up until that time, they are a
beautiful, pale green. The fertile fronds, which are
less conspicuous, bear bead-like spores from
midsummer onwards. O. sensibilis is a vigorous
plant which can spread very widely. Its roots and
foliage make good ground-cover in all soils that
remain permanently moist or damp. Plenty of
moisture is especially important if this fern is
grown in full sun.
    Damp and wet soils – Ground-cover.

SAXIFRAGA umbrosa
[London Pride]

◑ [○]
type of plant: HP
flowering season: l. spring to e. summer
flower colour: pink
height: 23-30 cm/9-12 in
E

London pride is easy to grow in most soils,
although its rosettes of leathery, spoon-shaped
leaves will be largest in cool, moist, shady places.
Whether this plant is shaded or in an open
position, however, its foliage will be closely
packed and, generally, weed-proof. Single plants
may spread over 40 cm/15 in wide. The cloud-like
mass of tiny flowers is in marked contrast to the
thickset appearance of the foliage.
    Chalk – Ground-cover – Paving.

RHODODENDRON sinogrande MC

◑
type of plant: SlTT/Sh
flowering season: mid-spring
flower colour: cream + crimson
height: 9 m/30 ft
*E, B

Some of the large-leaved rhododendrons have
foliage of remarkable size and appearance.
Unfortunately, many of these expensive plants are
not easy to grow well. R. sinogrande needs a
sheltered site and is at its best in regions of high
rainfall and few frosts, where its grey-backed,
strikingly veined leaves may be 75 cm/2½ ft long.
It is often seen as a large, wide-spreading, openly
branched shrub rather than a tree. Small
specimens tend not to produce many flowers.
    Acid soils.

CIMICIFUGA racemosa★
[Black Snake Root]

◑
type of plant: HP
flowering season: summer
flower colour: white
height: 1.2-1.5 m/4-5 ft

A clump of this plant's deeply divided foliage,
though rarely spreading more than about
60 cm/2 ft wide, can be quite a striking sight, and
the soft-scented flower spikes are elegantly long
and slim in contrast. A cool, moist soil suits this
plant best.
    Cutting – Fragrant flowers.

POLYSTICHUM setiferum 'Divisilobum'★
[form of Soft Shield Fern]

◑
type of plant: HF
height: 75-120 cm/2½-4 ft
E/½E

The plants shown in this and the following two
photographs coincide with most people's idea of
how a fern should look (although see
Phyllitis scolopendrium and its variety, on the
following page, for ferns of a quite different
appearance). P. setiferum 'Divisilobum' is one of
several beautiful forms of soft shield fern with
more than usually lacy foliage. Its large fronds
spread spirally from a central crown. As its
common name suggests, the foliage of
P. aculeatum (see the following page) is tough and
leathery. This fern makes clumps of dark, shining
greenery. Athyrium filix-femina (see right) has
foliage of a much lighter colour, borne (contd)

ATHYRIUM filix-femina
[Lady Fern]

◑
type of plant: HF
height: 75 cm/2½ ft

See preceding plant.

(contd)
in graceful, arching fronds. It needs a moist soil.
The other two ferns will grow well in dry and in
moist conditions.
    Chalk (P. s. 'Divisilobum' and P. aculeatum
only) – Dry shade (P. s. 'Divisilobum' and
P. aculeatum only) – Ground-cover.

POLYSTICHUM aculeatum
[Hard Shield Fern]

◐

type of plant: HF
height: 60-105 cm/2-3½ ft
E

See *P. setiferum* 'Divisilobum', previous page.

SMILACINA racemosa
[False Spikenard, species of False Solomon's Seal]

◐

type of plant: HP
flowering season: l. spring to e. summer
flower colour: creamy white
height: 60-90 cm/2-3 ft

The stems of this slightly unusual plant are erect and form small thickets at ground level, but they arch attractively near their fluffy-flowered tips. The broad, light green leaves cover the stems well and form a dense clump of foliage. A leafy soil and a cool site provide the ideal conditions for this plant. The fragrance of its flowers is light and sweet.

Acid soils – Ground-cover – Fragrant flowers.

PHYLLITIS scolopendrium (syn. *Asplenium scolopendrium, Scolopendrium vulgare*)
[Hart's-tongue]

◐

type of plant: HF
height: 30-45 cm/1-1½ ft
E

The hart's-tongue fern thrives in chalky soils that are moist and that contain plenty of leaf-mould or well rotted compost. In drier places, the upright, strap-shaped fronds will be smaller and less richly coloured. The neat frills of *P. s.* 'Crispum' (see below) make it a very decorative plant but, in its own way, the almost completely unruffled smoothness of the species is just as pleasing.

PHYLLITIS scolopendrium (syn. as in preceding plant) **'Crispum'** ★
[form of Hart's-tongue]

◐

type of plant: HF
height: 30-45 cm/1-1½ ft
E

See preceding plant.

DRYOPTERIS dilatata
[Broad Buckler Fern]

◐ ●

type of plant: HF
height: 60-120 cm/2-4 ft

The broadness and fine divisions of this fern's foliage are accentuated by the spreading, arching habit of growth. This is an easily grown plant, though not quite so tolerant of dryness and infertile soils as the ubiquitous male fern (see *Dryopteris filix-mas*, p. 80).

Clay – Dense shade – Ground-cover.

SAXIFRAGA fortunei
[species of Saxifrage]

◐ ●

type of plant: SlTP
flowering season: autumn
flower colour: white
height: 30-45 cm/1-1½ ft

S. fortunei's constellations of lopsided stars appear late in the year and they need to be sheltered from rough autumn weather. Shelter (with some shade and a moist, humus-rich soil) will also encourage the production of good quantities of the softly gleaming, red-backed leaves which can become 'scorched' – as they are in the photograph above – by cold winds. The foliage is often regarded as being even more attractive than the flowers. A bronze-leaved variety of this plant is illustrated on p. 173.

Dense shade.

TIARELLA wherryi

◐ ●

type of plant: HP
flowering season: l. spring to l. summer
flower colour: white
height: 25-40 cm/10-15 in
E

Compared with the more commonly grown
T. cordifolia (see p. 117), this is a neater, less
spreading plant. Its lobed leaves are a soft green
which becomes overlaid with bronze or red in
winter; they form tidy clumps. *T. wherryi* grows
well in light woodland, or wherever its roots can be
kept cool and moist and its upper growth remains
shaded.

Ground-cover – Autumn foliage.

EPIMEDIUM × youngianum 'Niveum' (syn.
E. niveum)★
[form of Barrenwort, Bishop's Hat]

◐ ●

type of plant: HP
flowering season: spring
flower colour: white
height: 15-23 cm/6-9 in
½E ✕

All the epimediums have their sprays of tiny
flowers complemented by cleanly shaped, pointed
leaves. Although many of these plants can be used
for ground-cover, *E.×y.* 'Niveum' is too small for
that purpose. It does, however, grow densely,
especially in moisture-retentive soils. Its young
leaves are suffused with a pale, bronze colour;
later, the foliage is entirely green; and in autumn it
takes on reddish tints.

Dry shade – Red, etc. leaves – Autumn foliage –
Cutting.

**Additional plants with decorative, green foliage
that are featured elsewhere in this book**

○ [◐] sun (or partial shade)
PLATANUS×hispanica: 21-30 m (p. 92)
ARBUTUS unedo: 4.5-7.5 m (p. 204)
TROPAEOLUM speciosum: 3-4.5 m (p. 32)
OLEARIA macrodonta: 2.4-3.6 m (p. 87)
TROPAEOLUM peregrinum: 1.8-3 m (p. 121)
ZANTEDESCHIA aethiopica 'Crowborough':
  75-90 cm (p. 71)
MORINA longifolia: 60-90 cm (p. 241)
PELTIPHYLLUM peltatum: 60-90 cm (p. 71)
GERANIUM pratense e.g. 'Mrs Kendall Clarke':
  60-75 cm (p. 105)
FILIPENDULA hexapetala 'Flore Pleno':
  45-60 cm (p. 23)
LYSICHITUM americanum: 30-45 cm (p. 71)
LYSICHITUM camtschatcense: 23-30 cm (p. 71)
GERANIUM dalmaticum: 12.5 cm (p. 106)
NYMPHAEA e.g.×'James Brydon': 10-15 cm
  (p. 172)
AZOLLA caroliniana: 2-5 cm (p. 192)

○ ◐ sun or partial shade
ALNUS cordata: 15-24 m (p. 50)
VITIS coignetiae★: 15-24 m (p. 192)
SALIX×chrysocoma: 13.5-18 m (p. 72)
BETULA pendula 'Dalecarlica': 12-18 m (p. 210)
SORBUS vilmorinii★: 4.5-6 m (p. 205)
CAMELLIA reticulata e.g. 'Captain Rawes':
  3-4.5 m (p. 34)
ELAEAGNUS×ebbingei: 3-4.5 m (p. 128)
GRISELINIA littoralis: 3-3.6 m (p. 87)
FATSIA japonica★: 2.4-3.6 m (p. 135)
BERBERIS darwinii: 1.8-3 m (p. 205)
CAMELLIA×williamsii e.g. 'Donation':
  1.8-2.4 m (p. 34)
CAMELLIA×williamsii e.g. 'J. C. Williams':
  1.8-2.4 m (p. 135)
CHOISYA ternata: 1.8-2.4 m (p. 243)
AUCUBA japonica: 1.5-2.4 m (p. 83)
PAEONIA×lemoinei e.g. 'Souvenir de Maxime
  Cornu': 1.5-1.8 m (p. 267)
PAEONIA lutea ludlowii: 1.5-1.8 m (p. 25)
LIGULARIA stenocephala 'The Rocket':
  1.2-1.8 m (p. 73)
OSMUNDA regalis: 1.2-1.8 m (p. 73)
THALICTRUM dipterocarpum: 1.2-1.8 m
  (p. 243)
ACANTHUS mollis latifolius: 1.2 m (p. 25)
ASTILBE taquetii 'Superba': 1.2 m (p. 106)
SANGUISORBA obtusa: 1.05 m (p. 73)
HEBE cupressoides: 90-120 cm (p. 136)
PAEONIA lactiflora e.g. 'Festiva Maxima': 90 cm
  (p. 268)
PAEONIA lactiflora e.g. 'Sarah Bernhardt': 90 cm
  (p. 268)
VIBURNUM davidii★: 90 cm (p. 206)
HEMEROCALLIS e.g. 'Pink Damask': 75-90 cm
  (p. 107)
PAEONIA lactiflora e.g. 'White Wings': 75-90 cm
  (p. 193)
PHLOX paniculata 'Hampton Court': 75-90 cm
  (p. 245)
HEMEROCALLIS e.g. 'Marion Vaughn': 75 cm
  (p. 52)
PAEONIA lactiflora e.g. 'Karl Rosenfeld': 75 cm
  (p. 245)
CYPERUS longus: 60-120 cm (p. 74)
×FATSHEDERA lizei★: 60-90 cm (p. 136)
HEMEROCALLIS e.g. 'Burning Daylight':
  60-90 cm (p. 74)
PAEONIA officinalis e.g. 'Alba Plena': 60-75 cm
  (p. 246)
PAEONIA officinalis e.g. 'Rosea Plena': 60-75 cm
  (p. 246)
PAEONIA officinalis e.g. 'Rubra Plena': 60-75 cm
  (p. 246)
COTONEASTER horizontalis: 60 cm (p. 194)
VITIS coignetiae★: 60 cm (p. 192)
EUPHORBIA robbiae: 45-60 cm (p. 81)
GERANIUM×'Johnson's Blue': 45-60 cm (p. 108)
ALCHEMILLA mollis★: 45 cm (p. 108)
GERANIUM endressii e.g. 'Wargrave Pink': 45 cm
  (p. 108)
BERGENIA×'Ballawley': 30-45 cm (p. 25)
LIRIOPE muscari: 30-45 cm (p. 80)

GERANIUM endressii e.g. 'A. T. Johnson':
  30-40 cm (p. 109)
BERGENIA×'Silberlicht': 30 cm (p. 109)
GERANIUM sanguineum: 23 cm (p. 110)
WALDSTEINIA ternata: 8-10 cm (p. 112)

◐ [○] partial shade (or sun)
ARUNDINARIA nitida: 2.4-3 m (p. 211)
MAHONIA×'Charity': 2.1-3 m (p. 278)
MAHONIA japonica ★: 2.1-3 m (p. 271)
CAMELLIA japonica e.g. 'Adolphe Audusson':
  1.8-3.6 m (p. 36)
CAMELLIA japonica e.g. 'Contessa Lavinia
  Maggi': 1.8-3.6 m (p. 97)
CAMELLIA japonica e.g. 'Alba Simplex': 1.8-3 m
  (p. 137)
FILIPENDULA purpurea: 90-120 cm (p. 77)
MAHONIA aquifolium: 90-120 cm (p. 112)
SKIMMIA japonica 'Foremanii': 90-120 cm
  (p. 208)
DRYOPTERIS filix-mas: 60-120 cm (p. 80)
HOSTA fortunei: 60-75 cm (p. 113)
ASTILBE×arendsii e.g. 'Rheinland': 60 cm
  (p. 113)
ASTILBE×arendsii e.g. 'White Gloria': 60 cm
  (p. 78)
HOSTA plantaginea: 45-60 cm (p. 271)
IRIS foetidissima: 45-60 cm (p. 208)
TELLIMA grandiflora: 45-60 cm (p. 113)
DICENTRA formosa: 30-45 cm (p. 113)
EPIMEDIUM×rubrum: 30 cm (p. 81)
ASTILBE chinensis pumila: 23-30 cm (p. 114)

◐ partial shade
SCIADOPITYS verticillata: 15-24 m (p. 41)
ARUNCUS dioicus: 1.2-1.8 m (p. 79)
MATTEUCCIA struthiopteris: 90-120 cm (p. 79)
ADIANTUM pedatum 'Japonicum'★: 30-60 cm
  (p. 173)
BLECHNUM spicant: 30-45 cm (p. 43)
POLYPODIUM vulgare: 15-30 cm (p. 81)
BLECHNUM penna-marina: 15 cm (p. 116)
ASPLENIUM trichomanes: 8-15 cm (p. 27)
CYCLAMEN coum: 8-10 cm (p. 279)

◐ ● partial or full shade
FATSIA japonica★: 2.4-3.6 m (p. 135)
AUCUBA japonica: 1.5-2.4 m (p. 83)
OSMUNDA regalis: 1.2-1.8 m (p. 73)
KIRENGESHOMA palmata★: 90-120 cm (p. 45)
MAHONIA aquifolium: 90-120 cm (p. 112)
RODGERSIA tabularis: 90-120 cm (p. 184)
SKIMMIA japonica 'Foremanii': 90-120 cm
  (p. 208)
POLYGONATUM×hybridum: 75-90 cm (p. 252)
DRYOPTERIS cristata: 60-90 cm (p. 79)
×FATSHEDERA lizei★: 60-90 cm (p. 136)
HOSTA fortunei: 60-75 cm (p. 113)
HELLEBORUS lividus corsicus: 60 cm (p. 283)
EUPHORBIA robbiae: 45-60 cm (p. 81)
IRIS foetidissima: 45-60 cm (p. 208)
BRUNNERA macrophylla: 45 cm (p. 116)
PACHYSANDRA terminalis: 23-30 cm (p. 117)
TIARELLA cordifolia: 23-30 cm (p. 117)
EPIMEDIUM grandiflorum 'Rose Queen':
  20-30 cm (p. 117)
RAMONDA myconi: 10-15 cm (p. 84)

Plants with colourful autumn foliage (including plants with evergreen leaves which change colour in late autumn and winter)

If your garden is small and you would like to grow plants that have colourful autumn foliage, do not be deterred either by the fact that many large trees have beautifully coloured leaves in autumn, or by the assumption that all plants with spectacular foliage in autumn are dull during the rest of the year.

There are large trees with attractive autumn foliage, and they include many of the unusual conifers that have deciduous leaves. However, there are also many small trees and medium-sized shrubs that have brightly coloured leaves in autumn: for example, there is the particularly dramatic stag's horn sumach (*Rhus typhina*), the brilliantly coloured *Berberis thunbergii* (a species of barberry) and almost all its varieties and, for those who garden on acid soils, there is a wide choice of deciduous azaleas with leaves that turn scarlet and orange in autumn. Some of the smaller, evergreen conifers, such as certain forms of *Juniperus horizontalis* (creeping juniper), assume bronze, purplish or red hues in the colder months, and thereby add interest to the garden in both autumn and winter. Herbaceous plants, the overwhelming majority of which are small or medium-sized, are a source of colourful autumn foliage that is often overlooked. Yet, some paeonies and geraniums or cranesbills, for example, have leaves just as attractively coloured in autumn as the foliage of many shrubs and trees.

All the plants mentioned above are considerably smaller than, for instance, the larger maples and mountain ashes which are conventionally associated with brilliant autumn colour. These smaller plants are obviously suitable for small gardens, but they are also useful in large gardens, where groups of plants with colourful autumn foliage can be formed. In such gardens, tall trees which colour well in autumn can look even more striking if they are surrounded by smaller plants that also assume attractive colours in the same season.

Groupings of autumn foliage plants can be based on a dramatic conglomeration of reds and oranges, or plants with clear yellow autumn leaves can be used as a contrast to more vividly coloured material. An indication of the autumn colour of all the deciduous leaved plants in this list has been given, to assist those who wish to plan autumn foliage schemes on however large or small a scale.

Chosen carefully, the constituents of such schemes will be interesting not only in autumn. In the following list there are plants with foliage attractive in other seasons: for example, *Liquidambar styraciflua* (sweet gum) has leaves which are most elegantly five-lobed from spring to leaf-fall, and the Japanese maples with deeply cut, fern-like leaves, such as *Acer palmatum* 'Dissectum', have striking foliage for most of the year. The evergreen plants with burnished leaves in late autumn and winter can provide permanent, solid shapes in mainly deciduous plantings.

Many of the plants in this list are grown as much for their flowers as for their well coloured autumn foliage. The list also contains plants with ornamental fruit, and there are a few plants which have aromatic leaves.

When selecting positions within a garden for plants with colourful autumn foliage, a number of points should be borne in mind. First, windy sites are not suitable, since dying autumn leaves are particularly easily blown off plants.

Secondly, sunshine, even if it is broken by dappled shade or present for only a short time each day, enhances the colours of most autumn leaves. Of course, many plants with colourful autumn foliage are not suitable for very sunny positions, and consideration for the general health of these plants should take precedence over any desire to have their autumn colours brilliantly lit. However, plants that appear in both the ○ ◑ (sun or partial shade) and ◑ ● (partial or full shade) categories elsewhere in this book have been omitted from the latter category in this particular list. Generally speaking, some sunshine is required to produce – as well as to show off – the best autumn colourings; plants which will grow equally well in sun, partial shade and full shade are, therefore, more likely to become attractively coloured in autumn if they are given more exposed positions.

A poor, rather than a rich, soil also tends to encourage the production of more vivid autumn colouring. However, even if you grow a plant in poorish soil and full sun, you will find that the intensity of its autumn colouring will vary from year to year. Lastly, cool colours can heighten the effect of foliage that turns to fiery shades in autumn. A mass of bright red leaves may look more dramatic seen across an expanse of lawn, than at close quarters.

LARIX decidua (syn. *L. europaea*)
[European Larch, Common Larch]

○
type of plant: HCo
flowering season: e. spring
flower colour: male – yellow; female – red or pale green
height: 24-36 m/80-120 ft
(Y)

Before the leaves fall from this deciduous conifer in late autumn, they turn rich yellow – having emerged in spring a particularly bright green. Like many larches, *L. decidua* grows quickly. Its conical head of branches broadens considerably with age. Most soils suit this vigorous tree, but it will not flourish if its roots are very dry or wet.

ACER rubrum NA
[Red Maple]

○
type of plant: HT
flowering season: e. spring
flower colour: red
height: 22.5 m/75 ft
(R)

An attractive, round-headed or occasionally pyramidal tree. Best results occur when it is planted in moist soil, though the tree performs well under average garden conditions. Autumn leaf colour is early, usually an excellent red.

ACER saccharum NA
[Sugar Maple]

○
type of plant: HT
flowering season: spring
flower colour: green-yellow
height: 22.5 m/75 ft
(M)

An oval-shaped tree of considerable beauty in autumn when the large leaves assume tints of orange-red and yellow. Sugar maple provides the backbone of autumn colour in New England. A shallow rooted tree, it is susceptible to salt damage and should not be planted near to highways where salt is used to melt ice. A number of cultivars have been named, including columnar sorts.

QUERCUS palustris NA
[Pin Oak]

○

type of plant: HT
flowering season: spring
flower colour: yellowish green
height: 22.5 m/75 ft
*(R)

This is an attractive tree with deeply cut foliage that often turns a good deep red in autumn. Dense shade is cast, especially by the lower branches, which are pendulous except in the cultivar 'Sovereign'. The tree is moisture-tolerant. Neutral or alkaline soils should be avoided.

Clay.

GINKGO biloba★
[Maidenhair Tree]

○

type of plant: HCo
height: 18-24 m/60-80 ft
(Y)

When young, this tree grows slowly and is rather narrow, but it broadens and becomes pyramidal with age. Its unusual leaves are like tiny fans with single notches in their curved edges; they are a fresh, light green in spring and summer, and butter-yellow in autumn. *G. biloba* will grow in all well drained soils, but the best results are obtained by planting it in full sun and in a deep, fertile soil. After hot summers, female trees produce fruits which give off a most unpleasant smell as they decay.

Atmospheric pollution – Green foliage.

LIQUIDAMBAR styraciflua★
[Sweet Gum]

○

type of plant: HT
height: 15-21 m/50-70 ft
* (M)

At its best, the autumn foliage of this tree is spectacular. However, there are differences between individual plants, and the colouring is also affected by soil and by the weather in the preceding seasons. On good specimens, the maple-like leaves (which are attractively shaped whether or not they colour well) turn red, orange, and purple in autumn. At this time of the year too, the foliage becomes fragrantly aromatic. Acid soils that are, preferably, moist and loamy suit this tree best and encourage it to produce good colours. The outline of *L. styraciflua* changes with time from a pyramid to a narrow dome.

Acid soils – Green foliage – Aromatic leaves.

PRUNUS sargentii (syn. *P. serrulata sachalinensis*)★
[species of Ornamental Cherry]

○

type of plant: HT
flowering season: spring
flower colour: pink
height: 7.5-9 m/25-30 ft
(M)

Brilliant reds and oranges suffuse the leaves of this tree unusually early in autumn. In spring, the clusters of flowers are accompanied by bronze-red young foliage. Overall, this cherry's rather open head of branches creates a rounded shape. Any well drained soil is suitable, though slightly alkaline conditions are ideal.

Red, etc. leaves.

CRYPTOMERIA japonica 'Elegans'
[form of Japanese Cedar]

○

type of plant: HCo
height: 6-7.5 m/20-25 ft
E, W

The feathery foliage of this particular form of Japanese cedar looks attractive all the year round, but especially so when it turns purplish or coppery red in late autumn and winter. By the time it has reached a height of 6 m/20 ft or so, *C. j.* 'Elegans' is usually rather unstable, and some old specimens grow with their trunks lying on the ground and their branches standing erect. On plants where the bark is easily visible, the red-brown, peeling strips are a minor attraction. This tree should be sheltered from wind and given a moist, slightly acid soil. At its tidiest, it is bushily pyramidal. It is not hardy in the colder parts of the United States.

Acid soils – *Bark* and twigs.

CRATAEGUS phaenopyrum NA
[Washington Hawthorn]

○

type of plant: HT
flowering season: l. spring
flower colour: white
height: 6 m/20 ft
(M)

This is a rounded tree with interesting horizontal branches. The cluster of small white flowers in spring are handsome, but the red fruits are the main attraction. They ripen in autumn and sometimes last until spring. Autumn leaf colour is orange to scarlet. The tree is densely thorny. It is widely planted in cities.

Fruit.

ACER palmatum
[Japanese Maple]
○
type of plant: HT/Sh
height: 4.5-6 m/15-20 ft
(M)

All the Japanese maples are expensive trees or shrubs and not easy to grow well. The plain, green-leaved species, illustrated here, is the cheapest and most vigorous of these plants. It often forms a rounded, spreading shrub, but, in favourable conditions, it will develop a trunk and become an elegant small tree. Its leaves are most attractively lobed and pointed; in autumn they turn predominantly red and orange. Both the species and its varieties need a light, preferably acid soil that is also cool and moist, and they should be planted in a sheltered position. In recent years many cultivars have been named.

Acid soils – Green foliage.

RHUS typhina
[Stag's Horn Sumach]
○
type of plant: HSh/T
height: 3-4.5 m/10-15 ft
(M)

The hanging leaflets of this suckering, flat-topped plant become orange and red in autumn. After the foliage has fallen, the stark, antler-like pattern of the branches is fully visible. Female plants produce spikes of red fruits at approximately the same time as the leaves begin to colour. When cut back completely each year, *R. typhina* has very large leaves – about 45 cm/18 in long in some cases. It should be planted in a light soil and full sun for the best autumn colour. A cut-leaved cultivar of the stag's horn sumach is illustrated on p. 180.

Chalk – Atmospheric pollution – Green foliage – Fruit.

EUONYMUS alatus
○
type of plant: HSh
height: 1.8-2.4 m/6-8 ft
(R)

The red-seeded fruits of this shrub may not appear either regularly or in large numbers (unless, perhaps, when several plants are grown near each other). The chief attraction is the bright, pinkish scarlet of the leaves in autumn. *E. alatus* thrives on chalk and grows well in most soils. Its stiff, spreading branches have corky 'wings' – flat and about ½ cm/¼ in wide – attached to them.

Chalk – Fruit – Bark and *twigs*.

BERBERIS thunbergii
[species of Barberry]
○
type of plant: HSh
flowering season: spring
flower colour: yellow
height: 1.2-1.8 m/4-6 ft
(R)

This thorny shrub and its varieties have well coloured autumn foliage. In the case of the species, the leaves turn bright red at about the same time as a mass of small, scarlet berries becomes fully ripe. *B. thunbergii* forms a rounded shrub with somewhat arching branches. It makes a good, fairly wide-spreading hedge which generally requires trimming once a year, in winter. Most soils suit this plant although very alkaline conditions should be avoided.

Acid soils – Clay –Hot, dry soils – Atmospheric pollution – Hedging – Fruit.

KOCHIA scoparia trichophylla (syn.
K. trichophylla)★
[Burning Bush, form of Summer Cypress]
○
type of plant: HHA
height: 60-90 cm/2-3 ft
(R)

Even before its foliage changes from very fresh, light green to rich crimson, the summer cypress is a striking plant. Its neat, almost prim, egg-like shape may account for the frequency with which it is grown as part of a 'hedge' at the back of bedding schemes or dotted regularly amongst other annuals. This plant also looks well, however, when mixed with perennials in less formal layouts. Any well drained soil gives satisfactory results. The largest specimens are raised from seed sown under glass early in spring. Sowing the seed in open ground produces plants of the height given above.

Chalk – Green foliage.

CALLUNA vulgaris (syn. *Erica vulgaris*) e.g.
'Robert Chapman'
[form of Heather or Ling]
○
type of plant: HSh
flowering season: l. summer to e. autumn
flower colour: purple
height: 45 cm/1½ ft
*E, W

Several of the popular, yellow-leaved varieties of *C. vulgaris*, including the form shown here, become orange or red in winter. Before it deepens to a vivid red in cold weather, the foliage of *C. v.* 'Robert Chapman' is, first of all, gold – in spring – and then an apricot-y mixture of bronze, yellow and orange. This plant is a dense, ground-covering hummock of growth when it is clipped each spring and when it is grown well away from walls, hedges and overhanging branches.

Acid soils – Ground-cover – Yellow, etc. leaves.

Additional plants with colourful autumn foliage that are featured elsewhere in this book

○ sun
LARIX leptolepis: 24-30 m (p. 28)
ULMUS × sarniensis: 21-36 m (p. 90)
LIRIODENDRON tulipifera: 21-30 m (p. 179)
FAGUS sylvatica 'Purpurea': 18-27 m (p. 168)
POPULUS alba: 18-27 m (p. 156)
METASEQUOIA glyptostroboides: 18-24 cm (p. 68)
PRUNUS avium 'Plena': 12-13.5 m (p. 90)
KOELREUTERIA paniculata: 9-15 m (p. 179)
POPULUS tremula: 9-15 m (p. 68)
CRATAEGUS × lavallei 'Carrierei': 6 m (p. 201)
ACER palmatum 'Atropurpureum' ★: 3-4.5 m (p. 168)
RHUS typhina 'Laciniata': 3-4.5 m (p. 180)
COTINUS coggygria e.g. 'Royal Purple': 2.4-3 m (p. 169)
THUJA occidentalis e.g. 'Rheingold': 1.8-3 m (p. 175)
EUONYMUS europaeus 'Red Cascade': 1.8-2.7 m (p. 202)
CALLICARPA bodinieri giraldii: 1.8 m (p. 202)
ACER palmatum 'Dissectum': 1.5-2.4 m (p. 180)
ACER palmatum 'Dissectum Atropurpureum': 1.5-2.4 m (p. 133)
BERBERIS thunbergii atropurpurea: 1.2-1.8 m (p. 169)
ROSA (Rugosa Hybrid) e.g. 'Blanc Double de Coubert': 1.2-1.8 m (p. 129)
ROSA (Rugosa) e.g. 'Roseraie de l'Hay': 1.2-1.8 m (p. 256)
CERATOSTIGMA willmottianum: 60-90 cm (p. 7)
CRYPTOMERIA japonica 'Vilmoriniana': 45-90 cm (p. 134)
BERBERIS thunbergii 'Atropurpurea Nana': 30-60 cm (p. 171)
JUNIPERUS horizontalis e.g. 'Douglasii': 30-45 cm (p. 101)

CERATOSTIGMA plumbaginoides (syn.
Plumbago larpentae)
[species of Hardy Plumbago]

○
type of plant: SITP
flowering season: midsummer to autumn
flower colour: deep blue
height: 23-30 cm/9-12 in
(R)

In autumn, when the bright, deep blue flowers of this spreading, rooting plant may be at their height, the leaves turn red and crimson. *C. plumbaginoides* can, however, be something of a disappointment, with few flowers and the dullness of its leaves – in their green state – all too apparent. It is at its best in warm districts and in a position of full sun. It needs a light, well drained soil.

Chalk – Ground-cover.

ERICA carnea 'Vivellii'
[form of Heath or Heather]

○
type of plant: HSh
flowering season: l. winter to e. spring
flower colour: deep carmine
height: 15-23 cm/6-9 in
E, W

The deep and vivid flowers of *E. c.* 'Vivellii' are set amongst dark foliage which becomes bronze towards the end of the year. Like most forms of *E. carnea*, this particularly richly coloured variety is a dense, carpeting plant and, therefore, good for ground-cover. However, it grows rather more slowly than some varieties. It may be planted in chalky soils, as long as the usual requirements for some moisture and an open position are taken into account.

Acid soils – Ground-cover – Containers – Winter-flowering plants.

CERCIDIPHYLLUM japonicum
○ [◐]
type of plant: HT
height: 15-18 m/50-60 ft
(M)

Despite being hardy, this elegantly round- or oval-headed tree should be given a sheltered position – amongst other trees at the edge of light woodland, for example. With shelter of this sort its young leaves, which are, briefly, bright red, are less likely to be damaged by frosts and cold winds. In autumn, the foliage may colour well, mainly in shades of red and yellow. Alkalinity inhibits the production of good autumn colour, and the ideal soil for this tree is a moist, well drained, neutral or slightly acid loam. In Britain, this plant may sometimes have several stems and grow not more than about 6-7.5 m/20-25 ft high. In the United States, ultimate height may be over 21 m/70 ft.

Red, etc. leaves.

MALUS tschonoskii
[species of Flowering Crab]
○ [◐]
type of plant: HT
flowering season: l. spring
flower colour: white tinged pink
height: 9-12 m/30-40 ft
(R)

The fruits of this species of flowering crab are not decorative and the chief attractions are, first, the red and purplish bronze autumn colour of the foliage and, secondly, the narrow, pyramidal habit of growth. Any fertile, well drained soil will suit this tree.

Chalk – Atmospheric pollution.

EUONYMUS alatus 'Compactus' NA
[Compact Winged Euonymus]
○ [◐]
type of plant: HSh
flowering season: l. spring to e. summer
flower colour: greenish
height: 1.8 m/6 ft
(R)

A dense growing shrub with corky bark and, in autumn, reddish fruits containing orange seeds, the autumn leaf colour of this plant is variable, but usually it is the most outstanding red-to-pink of any hardy shrub. It also lasts a long time. The shrub is not particular about soil.

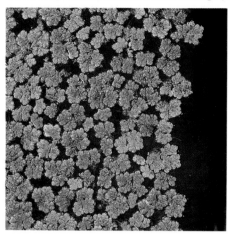

AZOLLA caroliniana
[species of Fairy Moss]
○[◑]
type of plant: SlTPAq
height: 2-5 cm/1-2 in
(R)

In some years, the pretty, moss-like foliage of this
floating plant will, as usual, turn red in autumn,
but no new, pale green leaves will emerge in
spring. *A. caroliniana* grows best in shallow ponds,
since these warm quickly in spring and summer;
however, they also become very cold in severe
winters. As a precaution, some plants can be kept
in a cool greenhouse during the coldest months.
  Green foliage.

**Additional plants with colourful autumn foliage
that are featured elsewhere in this book**

○[◑] sun (or partial shade)
PLATANUS×hispanica: 21-30 m (p. 92)
VITIS vinifera 'Purpurea': 6 m (p. 171)
VIBURNUM opulus 'Sterile': 3.6-4.5 m (p. 70)
VIBURNUM plicatum tomentosum 'Lanarth'★:
  1.8-3 m (p. 48)
VIBURNUM opulus 'Compactum': 1.2-1.8 m
  (p. 204)
GERANIUM pratense e.g. 'Album': 60-75 cm
  (p. 183)
GERANIUM pratense e.g. 'Mrs Kendall Clarke':
  60-75 cm (p. 105)

VITIS coignetiae★
[species of Ornamental Vine]
○◑
type of plant: HCl
height: 15-24 m/50-80 ft
(M)

The extreme vigour of this plant makes it
unsuitable for small gardens, but where a large
wall or even a tall tree needs covering, then this
magnificent, tendrilled climber can look splendid.
Its leaves are big (up to 30 cm/1 ft in diameter),
with reddish beige, felted undersides and richly
coloured in autumn. (The brightest colours are
produced on plants facing south or west, but other
aspects are almost equally suitable.) If its shoots
are pegged down, *V. coignetiae* can also be used to
cover large areas of ground. Treated in this way, it
will grow about 60 cm/2 ft high. This plant needs a
deep, fertile, moisture-retentive soil.
  Ground-cover – Climbers – Green foliage.

PARTHENOCISSUS quinquefolia (syn.
Vitis hederacea)
[Virginia Creeper]
○◑
type of plant: HCl
height: 15-21 m/50-70 ft
(R)

Both *P. quinquefolia* (shown above, just beginning
to turn colour) and *P. tricuspidata* 'Veitchii' (see
right) are famous for the brilliance of their autumn
foliage. Before they fall, the leaves of the first plant
turn crimson-scarlet; those of the second plant
become blood red (having emerged, in spring, a
purplish bronze). These vigorous climbers are
suitable for walls of any aspect. *P. quinquefolia* is
not quite such a close-clinging plant as
P. tricuspidata 'Veitchii', and when it is used for
ground-cover it makes a looser and slightly higher
mass of growth (about 30 cm/1 ft high as against
23 cm/9 in). Both plants need a *(contd)*

PARTHENOCISSUS tricuspidata 'Veitchii'
(**syn.** *Ampelopsis veitchii, Vitis inconstans*
'Purpurea')
[form of Boston Ivy]
○◑
type of plant: HCl
height: 15 m/50 ft
(R)

See preceding plant.

(contd)
good depth of fertile soil to become established
quickly. Once they are growing well, usually a year
or two after planting, they will attach themselves
to walls and similar surfaces by means of adhesive
tendrils. *P. quinquefolia* looks particularly
attractive when grown through a tall tree.
  Atmospheric pollution – Ground-cover –
Climbers – Red, etc, leaves (*P. tricuspidata*
'Veitchii' only).

NYSSA sylvatica
[Tupelo]
○ ◖
type of plant: HT
height: 10.5-18 m/35-60 ft
* (M)

Young specimens of this slow-growing tree are attractively pyramidal in shape, but older specimens have a less decorative, broadly columnar outline. The main attraction in either case is, however, the brilliant red and orange colouring of the leaves in autumn. In Britain, *N. sylvatica* does not often exceed the lesser of the two heights given here. It is best when grown in a moist, acid loam.

Acid soils.

SORBUS hupehensis★
[species of Rowan or Mountain Ash]
○ ◖
type of plant: HT
flowering season: l. spring to e. summer
flower colour: white
height: 9-12 m/30-40 ft
(R)

Many rowans have good autumn foliage, but the blue-green leaflets of this species turn an exceptionally clear red (bettered only, perhaps, by the brilliant scarlet of *S. sargentiana*). Before the foliage turns colour, bunches of pale berries have already ripened to white or pale pink, and these will remain on the tree until the end of the year at least. Most well drained soils suit this fairly upright tree but shallow, chalky soils shorten its life.

Grey, etc, leaves – Fruit.

EUCRYPHIA glutinosa (syn. *E. pinnatifolia*)★
○ ◖
type of plant: SlTSh/T
flowering season: summer
flower colour: white
height: 3.6-5.4 m/12-18 ft
*½E/D (M)

In mild areas and in moist, acid soils, this unusually hardy species of eucryphia often becomes crowded with white blossom. However, this is a slow-growing plant, and its beautiful, slightly fragrant flowers seldom appear in large quantities on specimens less than several years old. Towards the end of autumn, the dark, glossy foliage turns splendidly orange and red. If this upright plant is given a position in full sun, it is particularly important that its roots remain cool and moist.

Acid soils.

PARROTIA persica
○ ◖
type of plant: HSh/T
flowering season: l. winter to e. spring
flower colour: crimson
height: 3-5.4 m/10-18 ft
(M)

Although the little, tufted, winter flowers of this plant are pleasing, the brilliant reds and rich ambers of the autumn foliage are much more spectacular. Most often, *P. persica* is seen as a wide-spreading shrub with almost horizontal, somewhat drooping branches. However, some large plants may become tree-like or they can have their lower branches removed to reveal the attractive, grey-and-green-mottled, peeling bark. Fertile, well drained soils of all types produce satisfactory results, but moisture and acidity seem to lead to particularly good autumn colour.

Bark and twigs – Winter-flowering plants.

VACCINIUM corymbosum
[Swamp Blueberry, High-bush Blueberry]
○ ◖
type of plant: HSh
flowering season: l. spring to e. summer
flower colour: white or pink
height: 1.2-1.8 m/4-6 ft
* (R)

There are varieties of *V. corymbosum* which produce heavy crops of berries suitable for pie- and jam-making. Although it fruits, the species is often grown as a purely ornamental plant. Its outstanding feature is its bright red and crimson autumn foliage. This shrub is usually open and wide-spreading with long shoots (the wartiness and downy covering of which are minor attractions). It needs a moist, lime-free soil and an open site. It grows well in damp ground.

Acid soils – Damp and wet soils – Fruit – Bark and *twigs*.

PAEONIA lactiflora (syn. *P. albiflora*) e.g. 'White Wings'
[form of Peony/Paeony]
○ ◖
type of plant: HP
flowering season: e. summer
flower colour: white + yellow
height: 75-90 cm/2½-3 ft
(M)

Among the dozens of varieties of *P. lactiflora* listed by specialist growers, there will be many, like the variety shown here, with leaves that colour well in autumn. Even in good years, however, the autumn foliage of these perennials will be of secondary importance to their flowers. All these plants are long-lived. They thrive in deep, well drained soils that are fertile and moisture-retentive.

Green foliage – Cutting.

COTONEASTER horizontalis ★
[Fish-bone Cotoneaster]

○ ◐

type of plant: HSh
flowering season: e. summer
flower colour: pinkish white
height: 60 cm/2 ft
up to 2.4 m/8 ft against a wall, (R)

This splendid, all-round shrub may be allowed to form a spreading, ground-covering heap of fish-bone branches, or it may be planted against a wall. In autumn, the leaves turn a most attractive mixture of burnt orange and crimson and rows of red berries ripen. Any soil suits this shrub and it will grow well against walls of any aspect.

Chalk – Clay – Atmospheric pollution – Ground-cover – Climbers – Green foliage – Fruit – Bark and *twigs*.

RHODODENDRON luteum (syn. *R. flavum*,
Azalea pontica) ★

◐ [○]

type of plant: HSh
flowering season: l. spring to e. summer
flower colour: yellow
height: 1.8-3 m/6-10 ft
* **(M)**

Very hardy and easy to grow, this upright, suckering shrub has foliage which becomes strikingly coloured, mainly in rich shades of red, in autumn. Its funnel-shaped flowers emit a honey-sweet fragrance and are almost as pleasing, in their own way, as the autumn leaves. Ideally, this plant should be given a moist, spongy soil but, provided no chalk or lime is present, it will tolerate slightly drier conditions than most azaleas.

Acid soils – Atmospheric pollution – Fragrant flowers.

CORNUS florida NA
[Eastern Flowering Dogwood]

◐

type of plant: HT
flowering season: spring
flower colour: white
height: 7.5 m/25 ft
(R)

This is a very attractive, small tree with conspicuous, flower-like bracts. Bright red fruits, eaten by the birds, appear in late summer. Autumn leaf colour is usually a good red, and the winter twig outline is outstanding. There are many cultivars. They include 'Cloud Nine' (white bracts), 'Cherokee Chief' (ruby red bracts) and 'Welchii' (green, white and pink foliage, white flowers). In Britain, specialist nurseries may stock one of these forms or the variety known as *rubra* (pink and white bracts).

ENKIANTHUS campanulatus ★

◐

type of plant: HSh
flowering season: l. spring
flower colour: creamy yellow + red
height: 2.4-3.6 m/8-12 ft
* **(M)**

Charming though they are, the flowers of this shrub are, individually, small, and their neat, bell shape and pretty colouring can be appreciated most easily in arrangements indoors. The autumn foliage, however, is fierily brilliant and a prominent feature even at a distance outdoors. Little bead-like seed-pods ripen at the same time as the leaves turn colour; they are attractive when dried. This erectly branched shrub will grow best in sheltered, dappled shade and in a moisture-retentive, leaf-mouldy soil.

Acid soils – Cutting.

FOTHERGILLA monticola

◐

type of plant: HSh
flowering season: l. spring
flower colour: white
height: 1.8-2.4 m/6-8 ft
* **(M)**

Both *F. monticola* and the much smaller, more upright species shown in the following photograph are slow-growing plants for peaty, acid soils and lightly shaded positions. Both species produce fragrant, 'bottle-brush' flowers. Their leaves compensate for a fairly late arrival in spring by becoming brightly coloured in autumn.
F. gardenii's dying foliage is orange-red and crimson, while *F. monticola* turns a glowing mixture of red, crimson, orange and gold. *F. major* is a species which closely resembles *F. monticola*.

Acid soils – Fragrant flowers.

FOTHERGILLA gardenii (syn. *F. alnifolia*,
F. carolina)

◐

type of plant: HSh
flowering season: spring
flower colour: white
height: 60-90 cm/2-3 ft
* **(R)**

See preceding plant.

Additional plants with colourful autumn foliage that are featured elsewhere in this book

○ ◐ sun or partial shade
TAXODIUM distichum: 21-30 cm (p. 72)
FAGUS sylvatica: 18-27 m (p. 130)
CARPINUS betulus: 15-21 m (p. 130)
FAGUS sylvatica 'Pendula': 15-21 m (p. 24)
HYDRANGEA petiolaris: 15-18 m (p. 122)
SORBUS aria: 10.5-15 m (p. 24)
ACER griseum: 10.5-12 m (p. 210)
SORBUS aria 'Lutescens': 9-12 m (p. 165)
SORBUS aucuparia: 9-12 m (p. 33)
CHAMAECYPARIS lawsoniana 'Fletcheri':
    7.5-10.5 m (p. 165)
SORBUS 'Joseph Rock': 7.5-9 m (p. 204)
CORNUS kousa chinensis: 6-7.5 m (p. 33)
HEDERA canariensis 'Variegata': 4.5-6 m (p. 151)
SORBUS vilmorinii: 4.5-6 m (p. 205)
AMELANCHIER canadensis: 3-5.4 m (p. 33)
HAMAMELIS mollis: 2.4-3.6 m (p. 276)
CORYLOPSIS willmottiae: 2.4-3 m (p. 267)
CORYLUS avellana e.g. 'Contorta': 2.4-3 m
    (p. 211)
CORNUS alba 'Elegantissima': 1.8-2.7 m (p. 72)
CORNUS alba 'Sibirica': 1.5-2.4 m (p. 211)
CORYLOPSIS pauciflora: 1.2-1.8 m (p. 268)
OSMUNDA regalis: 1.2-1.8 m (p. 73)
VIBURNUM carlesii: 1.2-1.8 m (p. 268)
HYDRANGEA × 'Preziosa': 90 cm (p. 136)
LYSIMACHIA clethroides: 75-90 cm (p. 51)
HYDRANGEA petiolaris: 60 cm (p. 122)
PAEONIA mlokosewitschii: 60 cm (p. 247)
VITIS coignetiae★: 60 cm (p. 192)
EUPHORBIA polychroma: 45 cm (p. 108)
BERGENIA × 'Ballawley': 30 cm (p. 25)
BERGENIA cordifolia: 30 cm (p. 184)
PARTHENOCISSUS quinquefolia: 30 cm (p. 192)
GERANIUM sanguineum: 23 cm (p. 110)
PARTHENOCISSUS tricuspidata 'Veitchii':
    23 cm (p. 192)
POLYGONUM affine 'Donald Lowndes': 23 cm
    (p. 110)
HEDERA canariensis 'Variegata': 15-23 cm
    (p. 151)
CHIASTOPHYLLUM oppositifolium: 15 cm
    (p. 110)
VACCINIUM vitis-idaea: 15 cm (p. 111)
CORNUS canadensis: 10-15 cm (p. 111)

◐ [○] partial shade (or sun)
CELASTRUS orbiculatus: 9 m (p. 207)
PARTHENOCISSUS henryana★: 7.5-9 m (p. 153)
RHODODENDRON (AZALEA) e.g. 'Coccinea
    Speciosa': 1.5-2.4 m (p. 36)
RHODODENDRON (AZALEA) e.g.
    'Daybreak': 1.5-2.4 m (p. 36)
RHODODENDRON (AZALEA) e.g. 'Glowing
    Embers': 1.5-2.1 m (p. 36)
RHODODENDRON (AZALEA) e.g. 'Koster's
    Brilliant Red'★: 1.2-1.8 m (p. 37)
MAHONIA aquifolium: 90-120 cm (p. 112)
RHODODENDRON (AZALEA) e.g. 'Addy
    Wery': 90 cm (p. 113)
RHODODENDRON (AZALEA) e.g.
    'Hinodegiri': 90 cm (p. 137)
TELLIMA grandiflora: 45-60 cm (p. 113)
EPIMEDIUM × rubrum: 30 cm (p. 81)
PARTHENOCISSUS henryana★: 15 cm (p. 153)
AJUGA reptans 'Burgundy Glow': 10-15 cm
    (p. 172)

◐ partial shade
CHAMAECYPARIS pisifera 'Boulevard':
    2.4-4.5 m (p. 167)
GERANIUM macrorrhizum e.g. 'Album':
    30-40 cm (p. 115)
GERANIUM macrorrhizum e.g. 'Ingwersen's
    Variety': 30-40 cm (p. 200)
SHORTIA uniflora: 10-15 cm (p. 45)

◐ ● partial or full shade
TIARELLA wherryi: 25-40 cm (p. 187)
TIARELLA cordifolia: 23-30 cm (p. 117)
EPIMEDIUM grandiflorum 'Rose Queen':
    20-30 cm (p. 117)
EPIMEDIUM × youngianum 'Niveum'★:
    15-23 cm (p. 187)

Plants with aromatic leaves

Like the fragrance of one flower, the scent of a single leaf can be perceived quite differently by different people. Indeed, some leaves which are generally considered pleasantly aromatic, smell distinctly unpleasant to a few people. Because the same scent can be so differently interpreted, the following list does not contain very precise descriptions of the aromas emitted by the foliage of the various plants.

In any case, such aromas can be difficult to describe. There are some plants whose leaves smell very like other flowers or fruits: for instance, the leaves of *Lippia citriodora* are – as the specific name suggests – strongly lemon-scented, while the smell of the leaves of the western red cedar (*Thuja plicata*) and its varieties are often likened to pineapple. However, many plants have very distinctively aromatic leaves which can only really be described in terms of themselves.

Perhaps the easiest way to enjoy the scents of aromatic leaves is to grow a few of the plants in this list beside a garden seat. Although the foliage of some plants exudes its fragance freely, especially on a warm day, the leaves of most aromatic plants must be bruised before the scent is perceptible, and a garden seat is a comfortable place to carry out this pleasant task. (The leaves of the majority of conifers need to be crushed, rather than bruised, for their mainly resinous scents to be smelt, and for this reason only particularly attractive and strongly scented examples have been included in this list.)

Small aromatic plants, like *Anthemis nobilis* 'Treneague', a form of common chamomile, can be grown in gaps between paving, where they will exude their scent when trodden upon and crushed (although they should not be planted in positions where they would be subjected to hard wear). *Thymus serpyllum*, wild thyme, and its varieties are often recommended for this purpose too, but these plants are much less aromatic than the more commonly grown garden thyme and, if they are to be planted for their aromatic leaves, it is best to smell their foliage before buying them. *Anthemis nobilis* 'Treneague' can also be used to make a fragrant lawn which needs little mowing.

Many paved areas and garden seats are in sunny positions, and these suit the majority of plants with aromatic leaves. There are, however, a number of plants of this sort which actually prefer a shaded site: for instance, both the mints listed here grow well in partial shade, and some of the yellow-leaved varieties of culinary herbs – such as the yellow-leaved form of *Melissa* or balm – are at their best in lightly shaded positions where their leaves will not become scorched.

Aromatic leaves can also be enjoyed indoors. Several of the plants in this list are, of course, grown primarily for use in the kitchen. As in the other lists, these plants, and plants which may be ornamental but which are also useful in cooking, are marked '(Herb)' under 'type of plant'. There are now many ornamental varieties of culinary herbs and this list includes variegated sage and mint, purple sage, and golden-leaved balm and thyme. All these plants are as attractive in the garden and in flower arrangements as they are useful in the kitchen. The dried leaves of some other plants, such as *Lippia citriodora* and the many species pelargoniums with scented leaves, are often used in pot pourri and in sachets for linen and clothes cupboards.

For a survey of a large number of scented plants, including plants with aromatic leaves, Roy Genders' *Scented Flora of the World: An Encyclopaedia* (published by Granada in Mayflower Books) should be consulted.

**ROSMARINUS officinalis
[Common Rosemary]**

○

**type of plant: HSh (Herb)/SlTSh (NA)
flowering season: l. spring
flower colour: lavender blue
height: 1.2-1.8 m/4-6 ft
E**

In time, this plant usually produces branches which sprawl along the ground and from which the shoots, with their strongly aromatic foliage, rise erectly. Rosemary thrives in full sun and well drained, even dry soils. It may occasionally be killed in severe winters. 'Miss Jessop's Upright' is generally considered the best rosemary for hedging. In the United States, these plants need winter cover north of Washington DC.

Chalk – Hot, dry soils – Seaside – Ground-cover – Hedging – Containers.

**ALLIUM tuberosum NA
[Garlic Chives]**

○

**type of plant: HP (Herb)
flowering season: l. summer
flower colour: white
height: 75 cm/2½ ft**

Clusters of white, star-shaped flowers appear after the midsummer surge of bloom in the garden. This perennial herb is a pleasant accompaniment to heleniums, heliopsis and early chrysanthemums. The strap-like leaves may be used in the kitchen in the way that chives can.

**DICTAMNUS albus purpureus (syn.
D. fraxinella ruber)
[form of Burning Bush or Dittany]**

○

**type of plant: HP
flowering season: summer
flower colour: purplish pink
height: 60-90 cm/2-3 ft**

So powerfully aromatic is this plant that, on hot, still days in late summer its enveloping haze of vaporized oils can sometimes be ignited. These freshly scented oils normally protect the plant from the desiccating effects of strong sun and inadequate moisture. *D. a. purpureus* is, therefore, well equipped to deal with hot, dry conditions, although it will thrive in any well drained, preferably alkaline soil. *D. albus* itself, which has white flowers, is illustrated on p. 7. Both the species and variety are long-lived plants.

Chalk – Hot, dry soils.

PELARGONIUM quercifolium
[Oak-leaved Geranium]

○

type of plant: TenP
flowering season: mid-spring to e. summer
flower colour: pink+purple
height: 60-90 cm/2-3 ft

The oak-like leaves of *P. quercifolium* emit a fresh, pungent smell when bruised. Other scented-leaved geraniums include species that smell of peppermint, of roses (*P. graveolens*, see second right) and of lemons. *P. quercifolium* is a fairly upright plant. Since it needs to be under cover in winter (except in the very mildest districts), it is most conveniently grown in pots. It requires a well drained, fertile compost and a sunny position.

Green foliage.

ARTEMISIA dracunculus
[Tarragon]

○

type of plant: SITP (Herb)
height: 60 cm/2 ft

Like a number of plants in this list, *A. dracunculus* is grown almost exclusively for culinary purposes (although it will often make an appearance in decorative herb gardens, and the slimness of its leaves is a moderately attractive feature). The French variety of tarragon has the best flavoured leaves. They are hot and have an unusual mixture of sweet and slightly bitter tastes. This plant needs a light or dry soil and full sun, preferably in a sheltered position.

Chalk – Hot, dry soils.

PELARGONIUM graveolens
[Rose Geranium]

○

type of plant: TenP
flowering season: e. summer to mid-autumn
flower colour: pink
height: 60 cm/2 ft

Of the various species of 'geranium' with aromatic leaves *P. graveolens* is the most readily available. It is a spreading plant, with densely set, rose-scented foliage. It needs to be brought under cover in winter if there is any danger of frost.

Green foliage.

HYSSOPUS officinalis
[Hyssop]

○

type of plant: HP (Herb)
flowering season: midsummer to e. autumn
flower colour: blue
height: 45-60 cm/1½-2 ft
½E

The narrow leaves of this shrubby perennial have a mint-like fragrance. They are used in cooking, but not very commonly so. Since its upright stems grow densely and bushily, this plant makes quite good ground-cover (especially if it is cut back quite hard each spring). Hyssop can also be used to form a low hedge, which needs to be trimmed annually, early in the year, to keep it thick and neat. Full sun and well drained soil are essential. The flowers of this plant are attractive to bees and butterflies.

Chalk – Hot, dry soils – Ground-cover – Hedging.

LAVANDULA spica (syn. *L. officinalis*)
'Munstead'
[form of Old English Lavender]

○

type of plant: HSh
flowering season: summer to e. autumn/
**   e. summer to autumn (NA)**
flower colour: deep blue
height: 45-60 cm/1½-2 ft
E

L. spica and its forms, including the variety shown here, have foliage and flowers which are warmly and cleanly fragrant. The scent tends to be particularly pronounced on light, chalky soils and in full sun, and these conditions (along with at least one trim a year) also encourage neat, dense growth. Lavenders make attractive hedges, but their lack of longevity is a drawback.

Chalk – Hot, dry soils – Hedging – Fragrant flowers.

OCIMUM basilicum
[Sweet Basil]

○

type of plant: HHA (Herb)
flowering season: l. summer
flower colour: white
height: 30-60 cm/1-2 ft

The sweet, strong flavour of this plant's foliage seems to have a special affinity with the taste of tomatoes, although the leaves are also used in various soups and salads. A warm and sheltered site and a light, rich soil are needed for good growth. Sweet basil should be watered freely during periods of drought but kept rather dry at other times.

ORIGANUM majorana
[Sweet Marjoram, Knotted Marjoram]

○

type of plant: HHA (Herb)
flowering season: summer to e. autumn
flower colour: mauve or white
height: 30-60 cm/1-2 ft

A decorative, golden-leaved form of common
marjoram (*O. vulgare*) is illustrated on p. 176.
Although the leaves of that plant are sweetly
aromatic, the foliage of *O. majorana* is generally
considered to have a better, spicier flavour which it
retains well when it is dried. Sweet marjoram is
most often used in stuffings and sausages. It
requires a well drained, fertile soil and full sun.

Chalk – Grey, etc. leaves.

HELICHRYSUM angustifolium★
[Curry Plant]

○

type of plant: SITP
flowering season: summer
flower colour: yellow
height: 23-40 cm/9-15 in
E/½E

On warm days, the needle-fine, pale grey foliage of
this plant gives off a strong smell of curry. In
cooler weather, the leaves need to be pinched
before they emit their unmistakable aroma. Really
well drained or dry soil and a site in full sun
produce neat specimens of this plant, in which the
rather erect stems grow closely together.

Chalk – Hot, dry soils – Grey, etc. leaves.

SATUREIA hortensis
[Summer Savoury]

○

type of plant: HA (Herb)
flowering season: midsummer to e. autumn
flower colour: lilac
height: 23-30 cm/9-12 in

Summer savoury is grown purely for the slightly
bitter, thyme-like flavour of its leaves, which are
traditionally associated with broad beans, but
which can also be used in various fish and egg
dishes and in soups. The much shrubbier, but
similarly scented winter savoury (see below)
makes quite a decorative plant, particularly in the
well coloured, dwarf form illustrated here. Its
mass of dark-leaved twigs covers the ground
densely. Both types of savoury need soil that is well
drained.

Ground-cover (*S. montana* 'Coerulea' only).

SATUREIA montana 'Coerulea'
[form of Winter Savoury]

○

type of plant: HP/Sh (Herb)
flowering season: l. summer to mid-autumn
flower colour: lilac-blue
height: 23-30 cm/9-12 in
½E

See preceding plant.

PHACELIA campanularia

○

type of plant: HA
flowering season: summer
flower colour: gentian blue
height: 23 cm/9 in

Tucked in amongst the nasturtiums and poppies
so brightly illustrated in the 'hardy annual' section
of most seedsmen's catalogues, is this fast-growing
plant with flowers of an unusually bright blue. Its
spreading stems bear leaves which are fragrant
when pinched or crushed. Well drained soils of
most types are suitable.

THYMUS vulgaris
[Common Thyme, Garden Thyme]

○

type of plant: HSh (Herb)
flowering season: e. summer
flower colour: pale mauve
height: 20-30 cm/8-12 in
E

Even the ordinary, green-leaved thyme is an
attractive plant. And not only because of the
strong, pungent fragrance of its tiny leaves which
are so widely used in cooking. Its neat, dense habit
of growth makes it suitable for ground-cover and,
particularly when young, it can become covered in
flowers. Common thyme may be planted in any
soil that drains well, but it thrives in light or
dryish, alkaline soils. *T. v.* 'Aureus' is a variety
with yellow-green leaves.

Chalk – Hot, dry soils – Ground-cover – Paving.

TAGETES tenuifolia (syn. *T. signata*) e.g. 'Paprika'
[form of Marigold]

○
type of plant: HHA
flowering season: midsummer to e. autumn
flower colour: red
height: 15-23 cm/6-9 in

Some marigolds have leaves that emit a distinctly unpleasant smell when they are bruised, but the finely divided foliage of *T. tenuifolia* and its varieties is sweetly citrus-scented. Of the two cultivars illustrated here, 'Golden Gem' (see below) is particularly vigorous, but both plants will grow strongly and thickly in most well drained soils. Poor soils often give quite satisfactory results, and they may encourage these free-flowering plants to produce exceptionally large numbers of their charming, single blooms. Unlike other marigolds, varieties of (*contd*)

TAGETES tenuifolia (syn. *T. signata*) e.g. 'Golden Gem'
[form of Marigold]

○
type of plant: HHA
flowering season: midsummer to e. autumn
flower colour: golden yellow
height: 15 cm/6 in

See preceding plant.

(*contd*)
T. tenuifolia tend to be listed under their botanical, rather than their common name in British catalogues.

Additional plants with aromatic leaves that are featured elsewhere in this book

○ sun
CALOCEDRUS decurrens: 24-39 m (p. 201)
CUPRESSUS macrocarpa: 18-27 m (p. 85)
LIQUIDAMBAR styraciflua: 15-21 m (p. 189)
CHAMAECYPARIS obtusa e.g. 'Tetragona Aurea': 7.5-10.5 m (p. 174)
ESCALLONIA macrantha: 3 m (p. 85)
MYRTUS communis ★: 2.4-3 m (p. 132)
THUJA occidentalis e.g. 'Rheingold': 1.8-3 m (p. 175)
FOENICULUM vulgare e.g. 'Giant Bronze': 1.5-2.4 m (p. 169)
LIPPIA citriodora: 1.5-1.8 m (p. 133)
CISTUS × purpureus: 1.2-1.5 m (p. 87)
TEUCRIUM fruticans: 1.2-1.5 m (p. 57)
PEROVSKIA atriplicifolia: 90-150 cm (p. 4)
ARTEMISIA arborescens ★: 90-120 cm (p. 158)
ARTEMISIA absinthium 'Lambrook Silver': 90 cm (p. 159)
LAVANDULA spica: 90 cm (p. 257)
CARYOPTERIS × clandonensis e.g. 'Heavenly Blue': 60-90 cm (p. 7)
DICTAMNUS albus ★: 60-90 cm (p. 7)
SALVIA officinalis 'Purpurascens': 60-75 cm (p. 170)
LAVANDULA spica 'Vera': 60 cm (p. 100)
PERILLA frutescens e.g. 'Folliis Atropurpurea Laciniata': 60 cm (p. 170)
THUJA plicata e.g. 'Rogersii': 45-90 cm (p. 175)
DIMORPHOTHECA barberiae: 45-60 cm (p. 59)
RUTA graveolens 'Jackman's Blue': 45-60 cm (p. 160)
SALVIA officinalis 'Tricolor' ★: 45-60 cm (p. 148)
SANTOLINA chamaecyparissus ★: 45-60 cm (p. 125)
LAVANDULA spica 'Hidcote' ★: 30-60 cm (p. 126)
NEPETA × faassenii: 30-45 cm (p. 101)
CALAMINTHA nepetoides: 30-40 cm (p. 60)
ANTHEMIS cupaniana: 23-30 cm (p. 161)
ORIGANUM vulgare 'Aureum': 23-30 cm (p. 176)
THYMUS × citriodorus 'Aureus': 15-23 cm (p. 176)
TANACETUM haradjanii ★: 15-20 cm (p. 162)
ANTHEMIS nobilis 'Treneague': 5-8 cm (p. 104)
THYMUS serpyllum 'Albus': 5 cm (p. 142)
THYMUS serpyllum e.g. 'Coccineus': 5 cm (p. 19)

○ [◑] sun (or partial shade)
EUCALYPTUS gunii ★: 15-21 m (p. 164)
EUCALYPTUS niphophila: 6-7.5 m (p. 209)
LAURUS nobilis: 3.6-6 m (p. 134)
ARTEMISIA lactiflora: 1.2-1.5 m (p. 240)
ABIES balsamea 'Hudsonia': 60-90 cm (p. 135)
MORINA longifolia: 60-90 cm (p. 241)

MONARDA didyma e.g. 'Cambridge Scarlet'
[form of Sweet Bergamot, Bee Balm or Oswego Tea]

○ ◑
type of plant: HP
flowering season: summer
flower colour: crimson-red
height: 60-90 cm/2-3 ft

Most plants with aromatic foliage require a soil that drains quickly, but varieties of *M. didyma* will flower freely and grow vigorously only if their roots are moist throughout the growing season. The leaves of these plants have a strong, fresh fragrance; they are occasionally used to make a hot drink or they may be added to tea. *M. d.* 'Cambridge Scarlet' is a popular variety; forms with less strongly coloured flowers include 'Croftway Pink' (see p. 52). In damp, fertile soils these plants may form clumps of considerable size.

Clay – Damp and wet soils – Cutting.

ANGELICA archangelica

◑ [○]
type of plant: HB/P (Herb)
flowering season: summer
flower colour: green
height: 1.2-2.4 m/4-8 ft

Angelica lives longest if its emerging flower heads are removed. However, there are many gardeners who appreciate the round heads of green flowers just as much as the strong, fresh fragrance of the leaves. If allowed to flower and if grown in a moist, loamy soil, this plant produces a thick mass of seedlings which, when mature, will exclude most weeds. Green, crystallized stems of angelica are frequently used to decorate cakes and other sweet foods.

Ground-cover – Green flowers.

Additional plants with aromatic leaves that are featured elsewhere in this book

○ ◑ sun or partial shade
THUJA plicata: 24-30 m (p. 126)
CHAMAECYPARIS obtusa e.g. 'Nana Gracilis': 2.4-3 m (p. 34)
CHOISYA ternata: 1.8-2.4 m (p. 243)
HEBE cupressoides: 90-120 cm (p. 136)
MELISSA officinalis 'Aurea': 75 cm (p. 152)
MONARDA didyma e.g. 'Croftway Pink': 60-90 cm (p. 52)
CHAMAECYPARIS obtusa e.g. 'Nana': 45-75 cm (p. 136)

◑ [○] partial shade (or sun)
RHODODENDRON Hybrid e.g. 'Praecox': 1.2-1.5 m (p. 278)
RHODODENDRON Hybrid e.g. 'Blue Diamond': 90-150 cm (p. 38)
ACORUS calamus 'Variegatus': 60-75 cm (p. 78)
MENTHA rotundifolia 'Variegata': 30-60 cm (p. 154)

◑ partial shade
GERANIUM macrorrhizum e.g. 'Album' ★: 30-40 cm (p. 115)
HOUTTUYNIA cordata 'Plena': 15-23 cm (p. 79)

◑ ● partial or full shade
GAULTHERIA procumbens: 8-15 cm (p. 118)

MENTHA spicata
[Common Mint, Spearmint]

◑ [○]
type of plant: HP (Herb)
flowering season: midsummer to e. autumn
flower colour: mauve
height: 60 cm/2 ft

Nurseries specializing in herbs will list many different species and varieties of mint (including the variegated form of *M. rotundifolia* illustrated on p. 154). *M. spicata* is the species most commonly grown for use in cookery, although the leaves of the plain, green-leaved apple mint are often regarded as having a particularly fine flavour. Both these plants emit a clean fragrance from their leaves, the former plant smelling more pungent than the latter. They require a moist soil and, unless their roots are restricted, they are likely to become very invasive.

Clay.

GERANIUM macrorrhizum e.g. 'Ingwersen's Variety'
[form of Cranesbill]

◑
type of plant: HP
flowering season: l. spring to midsummer
flower colour: pink
height: 30-40 cm/12-15 in
½**E**

The lobed leaves of this weed-proof plant give out a strong, refreshing scent even when only lightly bruised. In many autumns, the taller, deciduous foliage assumes bright colours before dying. A cool, moist soil and dappled shade provide the ideal conditions for growing this perennial, but it is robust enough to do well in most types of moisture-retentive soils and even in quite sunny sites. An exceptionally attractive, very pale pink form of *G. macrorrhizum* is illustrated on p. 115.

Ground-cover – Autumn foliage.

Plants with ornamental fruit

Fruits are distinctive and welcome features of both gardens and indoor arrangements since their shapes usually differ quite markedly from the shapes of flowers and foliage, and most of them ripen at a time when the main flowering season is passed. We may miss the blossoms of spring and summer, but the fruits of autumn have their own special attraction.

The following list contains plants which bear fruits of many kinds including berries, burrs, pods and cones. Some of these fruits are edible as well as ornamental: for example, the various Japanese and flowering quinces and the flowering crabs, particularly *Malus* 'Golden Hornet' and *M.* 'John Downie', produce fruits which make excellent jellies.

All the plants in this list that have ornamental seed-pods and seed-heads are marked with appropriate abbreviations. Where the contents of the pod, rather than the pod itself, are decorative no seed-pod abbreviation appears. Additional plants with ornamental seed-heads of various types appear in the list entitled 'Plants with flowers suitable for cutting'; there they are marked 'Dr'. (The flowers of the plants with ornamental seed-pods and seed-heads in the following list are generally regarded as unsuitable for cutting.)

All the conifers in this list, with the exception of the yews, *Taxus baccata* and *T. b.* 'Fastigiata', bear characteristically dry fruits or cones. Most of the remaining plants carry berries or berry-like fruits.

Since over two-thirds of the plants listed here have conspicuous flowers, information about flowering season and flower colour has been retained. Nearly all the fruits of these plants ripen in late summer or autumn. Some fruits persist longer than others: the berries of most species and varieties of, for example, snowberries, barberries, hollies and skimmias usually last throughout the winter. However, some other plants bear fruits which seem to be particularly attractive to birds and, especially in country gardens, cotoneasters and pyracanthas, for instance, may be stripped of their ripe berries.

Although many fruits of these plants are some shade of red, the range of colours is by no means limited to this end of the spectrum. A number of plants carry blue or purple fruits, and some of these are quite striking in the intensity of their colour. Hollies and pyracanthas, which are normally associated with red or orange-red berries, have varieties which bear attractive yellow fruits. Other plants in this list produce white, orange, green, brown and black fruits. Together with the range of forms – from the long, thin seed-pods of the Indian bean tree (*Catalpa bignonioides*) to the globular burrs of *Acaena microphylla* and the feathery seed-heads of *Clematis tangutica* – the range of colours provides interestingly varied material for both house and garden.

For maximum effect, the background against which fruit will be viewed most often should be at least consistent, so that all parts of the fruiting plant or group of plants are equally conspicuous. How well the fruit stands out will also be affected by the colour of the background and the degree to which this contrasts with the colour of the fruit. Of course, some plants – mainly evergreens – provide their own contrasting background of foliage.

Before buying any plant for its fruit, it is important to check whether it is self-fertilizing. This information is particularly significant if only one plant of a certain species or variety is to be grown or if individual plants of one kind are to be grown some considerable distance apart. Many plants are self-fertilizing, but others have male and female flowers on separate plants which need to be placed near each other for fertilization and subsequent fruit production to take place. For instance, female plants of *Hippophae rhamnoides* (sea buckthorn) will produce berries only if they are grown near male plants. This is also true of most species and varieties of holly although, of the examples listed here, *Ilex aquifolium* 'J. C. van Tol' will berry without a male tree being nearby.

There are, of course, plants that do not appear in this list but which do nevertheless bear fruits. Many of these plants produce fruits that are so inconspicuous that they cannot be described as ornamental; others fruit only when the plants are quite mature; and some plants, like lily of the valley, cannot be relied upon to fruit regularly or, like the common passion flower, will fruit only after an exceptionally long, hot summer. Finally, some plants with interesting fruit are, unfortunately, not readily available and they have been excluded for this reason.

For additional plants with ornamental seed-heads of various types, see entries marked 'Dr' in list entitled 'Plants with flowers suitable for cutting'.

Any plant which appears in both the ◐ ○ (partial or full shade) section and one or other of the preceding sections will usually produce the most abundant crops of fruit when grown in the least shady, suitable position.

CALOCEDRUS decurrens (syn.
Libocedrus decurrens)
[Incense Cedar]

○
type of plant: HCo
fruit colour: yellow
height: 24-39 m/80-130 ft
E

In most parts of Britain, this conifer forms a strikingly tall, thin column of rich green foliage. It needs a deep, moisture-retentive soil in order to grow well for many years; in shallow soils and windy sites it tends to acquire a rather sparsely branched crown. Inconspicuous, female flowers ripen into small, but often numerous, bright yellow fruits. These are borne at the tips of the flattened, fan-like foliage which smells strongly of incense.
    Aromatic leaves.

CEDRUS libani
[Cedar of Lebanon]

○
type of plant: HCo
fruit colour: bluish brown
height: 21-30 m/70-100 ft
E

Young specimens of this cedar do not have the flat-topped crown characteristic of mature trees, but the branches are held horizontally from a fairly early age. After many years, large, fat cones, with a bluish or purplish cast, appear amongst the dark foliage. This conifer, which eventually forms a large and majestic tree, should be given a deep, well drained soil, enriched with plenty of leaf-mould or compost during the initial planting.

CRATAEGUS × lavallei 'Carrierei' NA
[form of Hawthorn]

○
type of plant: HT
flowering season: spring
flower colour: white
fruit colour: red
height: 6 m/20 ft

This is one of the best hawthorns. An easily grown tree, it has glossy, dark green, oval, foliage, and, in spring, pretty clusters of white flowers 2 cm/1 in across. The large red fruit colours in autumn and frequently persists until late winter. In Britain, this plant may be obtained from nurseries with a wide range of trees and shrubs.
    Autumn foliage.

CUCURBITA pepo e.g. 'Sutton's Ornamental'
sc NA
[form of Ornamental Gourd]

○

type of plant: HHACl
flowering season: l. summer to e. autumn
flower colour: orange-yellow
fruit colour: mixed – green, yellow, orange
height: 4.5-6 m/15-20 ft

Very few annual climbers produce fruits of any interest, but the various mixtures and selections of *C. pepo* bear inedible but decorative gourds in a remarkable range of shapes, sizes, textures and colours. All of them may be dried for winter decoration. The plants are usually grown upright, when some support should be provided for their tendrils to cling to, but they may also be used to cover warm slopes. Full-sun and a rich soil produce the most rapid growth and the most gourds.

Climbers.

CLERODENDRON (syn. *Clerodendrum*)
trichotomum

○

type of plant: SlTSh
flowering season: l. summer to autumn
flower colour: white
fruit colour: blue + crimson
height: 3-4.5 m/10-15 ft

The sweetly scented flowers of this shrub are clasped by persistent, red calyces which turn deep crimson in autumn and provide a luxuriously coloured background for the vivid turquoise-blue berries. Although the branches of this plant are rather sparse, the thick foliage produces a bushy appearance. Well drained soil and a warm, sheltered site are essential for the best results.

Fragrant flowers.

COLUTEA arborescens
[species of Bladder Senna]

○

type of plant: HSh
flowering season: all summer
flower colour: yellow
fruit colour: red or copper
height: 2.4-3 m/8-10 ft
(SP)

This vigorous, loosely branched shrub will grow in almost any soil. After a long flowering season, inflated seed-pods appear, ripening from pale green to a reddish or coppery colour. *C. arborescens* responds well to having its older branches removed fairly regularly, in winter or in earliest spring.

Chalk – Clay – Hot, dry soils – Atmospheric pollution.

ROSA moyesii 'Geranium'★
[form of Rose]

○

type of plant: HSh
flowering season: e. summer
flower colour: crimson
fruit colour: orange-red
height: 2.1-2.4 m/7-8 ft

R. moyesii makes such a big, arching shrub that its slightly smaller variety, 'Geranium', is often a better choice for the average-sized garden. The intensely coloured, single flowers of this rose (which seem scarlet in certain lights) are not long-lasting, but they are followed by large quantities of curvaceously shaped fruits. These are often about 5 cm/2 in long. *R. m.* 'Geranium' should, ideally, be given a fertile, well prepared, loamy soil, but it is sufficiently vigorous to tolerate less favourable conditions.

EUONYMUS europaeus 'Red Cascade'
[form of Common Spindle Tree]

○

type of plant: HSh/T
fruit colour: red + orange
height: 1.8-2.7 m/6-9 ft

Even this notably free-fruiting form of the common spindle tree will benefit from being planted in groups, so that the maximum amount of cross-pollination can take place. In most circumstances, however, its arching branches will become wreathed in hanging clusters of red, orange-seeded fruits. At approximately the same time as the fruits ripen, the mid-green leaves turn dark, purplish crimson. All reasonably well drained soils suit this plant; it is particularly at home on chalk.

Chalk – Autumn foliage.

CALLICARPA bodinieri giraldii (syn.
***C. giraldiana*)**

○

type of plant: SlTSh
fruit colour: purple
height: 1.8 m/6 ft

Thick conglomerations of light violet-purple berries glisten on the erect shoots of this shrub throughout autumn and early winter. In autumn too, the previously uninteresting foliage becomes tinged with a variety of colours, including a purplish mauve not unlike the colour of the fruits. This plant needs a sunny position, not only to ripen its wood and so to protect it from frost damage, but also to show off its berries to advantage. It should be given a fertile soil and, where possible, several specimens should be grown in a group to ensure that good crops of fruit are set.

Autumn foliage.

ZEA mays e.g. 'Rainbow'
[form of Ornamental Maize]

○

type of plant: HHA (Gr)
fruit colour: red + orange + yellow + purple
height: 1.2-1.8 m/4-6 ft

The ornamental varieties of maize or sweet corn
either have unusually coloured foliage (see, for
example, *Z. m.* 'Gracillima Variegata', p. 146), or
they produce cobs which differ from the edible
type in shape or colouring. The speckled cobs of
Z. m. 'Rainbow' cannot be eaten, but there is a
form of maize, known as 'Strawberry Corn', with
rounded, almost blackberry-coloured cobs which
are edible. Most commonly, however, it too is
grown purely for decorative purposes. The fruits
of both these plants may be dried. All forms of
Z. mays need a rich soil and a warm, sheltered site
in full sun. They must be watered well during dry
weather.

MALUS 'John Downie' sc NA
[form of Flowering Crab]

○ [◑]

type of plant: HT
flowering season: l. spring/spring (NA)
flower colour: white
fruit colour: orange + red
height: 7.5-9 m/25-30 ft

Of all the popular forms of flowering crab, 'John
Downie' produces the best-flavoured fruit for
making crab-apple jelly. It usually crops heavily.
Although it is basically an upright tree, it spreads
with age and, on mature specimens, the branches
arch slightly. *M. ×robusta* 'Red Siberian' (see
right) makes a broader tree than 'John Downie',
even from an early age. Its long-stalked fruits are
round and exceptionally long-lasting, often
remaining on the tree until mid-winter. However,
they are less suitable for making into jelly than the
fruits of 'John Downie'. Both these trees *(contd)*

MALUS × robusta 'Red Siberian' ★
[form of Flowering Crab]

○ [◑]

type of plant: HT
flowering season: spring
flower colour: white or pinkish
fruit colour: scarlet
height: 7.5-9 m/25-30 ft

See preceding plant.

(contd)

bear large quantities of slightly scented blossom in
spring. They will flourish in any fertile, well
drained soil and grow quite satisfactorily in all but
the heaviest and wettest of clays.

Chalk – Atmospheric pollution.

ABIES koreana
[Korean Fir]

○ [◑]

type of plant: HCo
flowering season: l. spring
flower colour: male – red-brown then yellow;
    female – red or pink or green
fruit colour: blue changing to brown
height: 6-9 m/20-30 ft
E

Specimens of this bushy, pyramidally shaped tree
as little as seven or eight years old may bear quite
large numbers of cones, about 8 cm/3 in long,
amongst the stout 'sausages' of dark green,
silver-backed foliage. In certain years, the female
flowers are so freely produced on the upper
branches that they are a conspicuous and
decorative feature. Neutral or slightly acid soils
suit this conifer best.

Acid soils.

CELASTRUS scandens NA
[American Bittersweet]

○ [◑]

type of plant: HCl
fruit colour: orange + yellow
height: 7.5 m/25 ft or more

This is an attractive vine in autumn when the
orange and yellowish fruit ripen. Fruits are borne
on terminal shoots, not in the leaf axils as in
C. orbiculatus. The latter, from the East, is a
vigorous grower which has become widely
naturalized in the United States. It is readily
available in Britain (for illustration and comments,
see p. 207).

MALUS 'Golden Hornet' ★
[form of Flowering Crab]

○ [◑]

type of plant: HT
flowering season: l. spring/spring (NA)
flower colour: white
fruit colour: yellow
height: 6-7.5 m/20-25 ft

The bright yellow fruits of this flowering crab
usually stay thickly clustered on the branches until
well into winter. These crab-apples make a good
jelly (although their flavour is not so fine as that of
M. 'John Downie's' fruits; see above). At first, this
tree has an erect habit of growth, but as it matures,
its head of branches opens and spreads into a neat,
oval shape which is rather wider at the top than the
bottom. For a brief outline of the soils suitable for
growing this plant, see the final sentence in the
comments on *M.* 'John Downie'.

Chalk – Atmospheric pollution.

ARBUTUS unedo★ MC
[Strawberry Tree]

○ [◐]
type of plant: HT/Sh/HHT/Sh (NA)
flowering season: l. autumn
flower colour: white or pink
fruit colour: red
height: 4.5-7.5 m/15-25 ft
E

Both the heather-like flowers and the round fruits of this plant are produced in autumn, the fruits having ripened from the previous year's flowers. Before they become red, the rotund 'strawberries' are a warm, red-speckled yellow. In mild, damp areas *A. unedo* is a bushy, broad-headed tree; elsewhere it forms a rounded shrub. It has a preference for, but does not require, acid or neutral soil.

Acid soils – Seaside – Atmospheric pollution – Green foliage.

VIBURNUM opulus e.g. 'Compactum'
[form of Guelder Rose]

○ [◐]
type of plant: HSh
flowering season: l. spring to e. summer
flower colour: white
fruit colour: red
height: 1.2-1.8 m/4-6 ft

This small and very free-fruiting form of the wild guelder rose grows densely and has a spread roughly equal to its height. It thrives in moist or damp soils. The lace-cap flowers are pretty, but in autumn the lobed leaves turn scarlet and rosy red and, above all, there is the glowing, translucent red of the bunched berries. 'Xanthocarpum' is a less widely available variety of *V. opulus*; its fruit are a pinkish yellow.

Clay – Damp and wet soils – Autumn foliage.

Additional plants with ornamental fruit that are featured elsewhere in this book

○ sun
ULMUS × sarniensis: 21-36 m (p. 90)
CEDRUS atlantica glauca ★: 21-30 m (p. 156)
KOELREUTERIA paniculata: 9-15 m (p. 179)
CATALPA bignonioides: 9-13.5 m (p. 90)
GLEDITSCHIA 'Sunburst': 9-12 m (p. 174)
CATALPA bignonioides 'Aurea': 7.5-12 m (p. 91)
CRATAEGUS phaenopyrum: 6 m (p. 189)
CERCIS siliquastrum: 4.5-7.5 m (p. 1)
SOPHORA tetraptera: 4.5-7.5 m (p. 180)
HALESIA carolina: 3.6-5.4 m (p. 29)
RHUS typhina: 3-4.5 m (p. 190)
RHUS typhina 'Laciniata': 3-4.5 m (p. 180)
COTINUS coggygria e.g. 'Royal Purple': 2.4-3 m (p. 169)
EUONYMUS alatus: 1.8-2.4 m (p. 190)
ROSA rubrifolia: 1.8-2.4 m (p. 157)
ROSA (Hybrid Musk) e.g. 'Penelope': 1.8 m (p. 256)
BERBERIS thunbergii: 1.5-1.8 m (p. 190)
ROSA (Hybrid Musk/Modern Shrub) e.g. 'Will Scarlet': 1.5-1.8 m (p. 213)
BERBERIS thunbergii atropurpurea: 1.2-1.8 m (p. 169)
RICINUS communis e.g. 'Zanzibarensis': 1.2-1.8 m (p. 181)
ROSA (Rugosa Hybrid) e.g. 'Schneezwerg': 1.2 m (p. 87)
BERBERIS thunbergii 'Aurea': 90-120 cm (p. 175)
RICINUS communis e.g. 'Gibsonii': 90-120 cm (p. 170)
PAPAVER orientale e.g. 'Mrs Perry': 90 cm (p. 5)
PAPAVER orientale e.g. 'Perry's White': 90 cm (p. 5)
NICANDRA physaloides: 75-90 cm (p. 181)
PAPAVER orientale e.g. 'Marcus Perry': 75 cm (p. 6)
BERBERIS thunbergii 'Atropurpurea Nana': 30-60 cm (p. 171)
DRYAS octopetala: 8-10 cm (p. 142)

○ [◐] sun (or partial shade)
ABIES procera: 30-39 m (p. 164)
ILEX aquifolium e.g. 'Argentea Marginata'★: 6-9 m (p. 149)
MALUS floribunda: 6-9 m (p. 93)
MALUS 'Hillieri': 6-7.5 m (p. 21)
MALUS 'Profusion': 6-7.5 m (p. 171)
VITIS vinifera 'Purpurea': 6 m (p. 171)
ILEX × altaclarensis e.g. 'Golden King': 5.4-7.5 m (p. 149)
SAMBUCUS nigra 'Aurea': 3.6-4.5 m (p. 176)
SAMBUCUS racemosa 'Plumosa Aurea': 1.5-2.1 m (p. 177)
ACAENA buchananii: 5 cm (p. 143)
ACAENA microphylla: 5 cm (p. 106)

SORBUS 'Joseph Rock' sc NA
[form of Rowan or Mountain Ash]

○ ◐
type of plant: HT
flowering season: l. spring
flower colour: creamy white
fruit colour: yellow
height: 7.5-9 m/25-30 ft

Long after they have ripened from a creamy colour to a rich, orange-tinted yellow, the fruits of this erectly branched tree are still hanging, unmolested by birds. At all stages of their development, these berries contrast well with the fern-like foliage. They begin to deepen in colour towards the end of summer and, when they have become bright yellow, the leaves turn orange-red, caramel and coppery purple. This neatly made tree may be planted in most soils, but it grows best in neutral or slightly acid loams.

Autumn foliage.

ILEX aquifolium e.g. 'J. C. van Tol' (syn. *I. a.* 'Polycarpa')
[form of Common or English Holly]

○ ◐
type of plant: HT
fruit colour: red
height: 6-9 m/20-30 ft
E

Almost all hollies bear male and female flowers on separate plants, and groups or, at least, pairs of both sexes must be grown if regular crops of berries are wanted. *I. a.* 'J. C. van Tol' is a readily available, self-fertile variety which will bear plenty of red fruits each year, even if no other holly is planted nearby. However, it will carry outstandingly heavy crops of fruit if a male plant is close, since this will assist fertilization. *I. a.* 'Bacciflava' (see following page) will produce its unusually coloured berries *only* when pollinated by a male plant. It has a denser, more *(contd)*

ILEX aquifolium e.g. 'Bacciflava' (syn. *I. a.* 'Fructo-luteo')
[form of Common or English Holly]

○ ◑

type of plant: HT
fruit colour: yellow
height: 6-7.5 m/20-25 ft
E

See preceding plant.

(contd)
pyramidal habit of growth than *I. a.* 'J. C. van Tol', and its leaves are sharply spined. 'J. C. van Tol''s almost total lack of prickles, as well as its rather narrow shape, makes it particularly suitable for hedging. Unfortunately, when either of these hollies is trimmed or pruned each year, it rarely produces many berries. Both these plants grow slowly. They will do well in most soils.

    Seaside – Atmospheric pollution – Hedging.

COTONEASTER 'Cornubia'★

○ ◑

type of plant: HSh
flowering season: e. summer
flower colour: white
fruit colour: red
height: 4.5-6 m/15-20 ft
½E

The long branches of this shrub arch and spread over a considerable area and the plant is usually as wide as it is high. It is sometimes grown with a clear main stem. In autumn, it bears great, heavy crops of large berries on short twigs. This impressive plant will thrive in all reasonably fertile soils. Among the many cotoneasters with decorative fruit, *C.* 'Cornubia' often retains its berries for an exceptionally long time – sometimes well into winter. Further illustrations of berried cotoneasters are shown on pp. 25, 128 and 194.

    Chalk – Clay – Seaside – Atmospheric pollution.

SORBUS vilmorinii★
[species of Rowan or Mountain Ash]

○ ◑

type of plant: HSh/T
flowering season: l. spring to e. summer
flower colour: white
fruit colour: rose-red changing to palest pink
height: 4.5-6 m/15-20 ft

Whether it grows shrubbily or forms a small tree, *S. vilmorinii* produces a dense, rounded head of rather pendulous branches. Although most rowans have attractive foliage, the numerous small leaflets of this slow-growing species create an especially light and delicate effect. In autumn, the leaves turn a bronzy mixture of purple and red. When the foliage is still green, the berries are rosy red; they change, gradually, to the palest of pinks and hang on the tree until late autumn. A deep soil that is either neutral or acid suits this plant best.

    Acid soils – Green foliage – Autumn foliage.

PYRACANTHA 'Orange Glow'
[form of Firethorn]

○ ◑

type of plant: HSh
flowering season: e. summer
flower colour: white
fruit colour: orange-red
height: 3.6-4.5 m/12-15 ft
E

This vigorous, rather upright plant is often trained against a wall (when it may exceed the heights given here by 1.5-2.4 m/5-8 ft). Even when facing north or east, it will produce heavy crops of thickly clustered berries. Very thorny hedging can be made from this plant, but if it is sheared hard every year it will bear relatively few berries. All soils that are, at least, moderately well drained suit pyracanthas. A yellow-berried variety is illustrated on p.127

    Atmospheric pollution – Hedging.

BERBERIS darwinii★
[species of Barberry]

○ ◑

type of plant: HSh/SlTSh (NA)
flowering season: spring
flower colour: orange-yellow
fruit colour: dark blue
height: 1.8-3 m/6-10 ft
E

Both the flowers and the fruits of *B. darwinii* are borne in large quantities amongst the tiny, gleaming, holly-like leaves. Apart from a few wayward stems, this dense and prickly shrub is neatly shaped. It makes an excellent, informal hedge or screen (which should be pruned, rather than trimmed, after the flowers have faded). Any soil that does not become very dry suits this slow-growing shrub.

    Chalk – Clay – Seaside – Atmospheric pollution – Hedging – Green foliage.

TAXUS cuspidata NA
[Japanese Yew]

○ ◑

type of plant: HCo
fruit colour: red
height: 1.5-6 m/5-20 ft
E

This plant is hardy in the northern United States where, except in the case of *T. b.* 'Reparta', *T. baccata* cannot be grown successfully over the long term. Depending on the form, Japanese yew is a small pyramidal tree with upright branches, or a spreading shrub of varying height. Many cultivars have been named and are widely used in landscaping. They benefit from an occasional application of dalomitic limestone. Like other yews, they dislike poor drainage. 'Hicksii', a cultivar derived from *T. cuspidata × T. baccata*, resembles Irish yew but is considerably hardier. 'Hatfieldii' is similar but makes a better hedge.

SYMPHORICARPOS rivularis (syn.
S. albus laevigatus)
[Snowberry]
○ ◐
type of plant: HSh
fruit colour: white
height: 1.5-2.1 m/5-7 ft

S. rivularis' tolerance of difficult conditions means that this shrub is often planted in dark and dry places. In such circumstances, its thickets of slender, upright stems usually have only a light sprinkling of big, white berries. In any reasonably fertile and moisture-retentive soil, however (and in a sunny or lightly shaded place), there will usually be large crops of fruits. These will remain on the bushes until the final weeks of winter. *S. rivularis* tends to sucker in most soils, and it may do so very freely where the ground is permanently damp.

Chalk – Clay – Damp and wet soils – Dry shade – Dense shade – Atmospheric pollution.

DIPSACUS fullonum
[Fuller's Teazel]
○ ◐
type of plant: HB
flowering season: l. summer to autumn
flower colour: rosy-purple
fruit colour: brown
height: 1.2-1.8 m/4-6 ft
(SH)

The large, bristly seed-heads of this biennial are not, perhaps, quite decorative enough for the majority of beds and borders, but they dry well, and a big group of teazels can look most attractive in an informal setting. All moisture-retentive soils suit this plant, and it will usually seed itself from year to year. In flower, it is visited by bees; when its seeds are ripe, it attracts various birds, including goldfinches.

Clay.

HYPERICUM × inodorum 'Elstead' (syn.
H. elatum 'Elstead') **sc NA**
[form of St John's Wort]
○ ◐
type of plant: HSh
flowering season; summer to e. autumn
flower colour: yellow
fruit colour: red
height: 90 cm/3 ft
½E

Unfortunately, this shrub is prone to rust disease, and many nurseries do not stock it for this reason. In good health, however, *H. × i.* 'Elstead' flowers freely and produces numerous clusters of slender, upright, pink-red berries on its erect stems. Although it grows well on shallow, chalky soils, rust is less likely to be a problem in moister conditions. This shrub needs to be cut back hard, in early spring, to keep it fairly dense and bushy.

Chalk – Atmospheric pollution.

VIBURNUM davidii ★
○ ◐
type of plant: HSh
flowering season: e. summer
flower colour: white
fruit colour: bright blue
height: 90 cm/3 ft
E

Even if there is room for only a single specimen of this shrub in a garden, it is still worth growing. While at least two plants – one male and one female – must be present for large amounts of berries to appear, the neat, close cap of deeply veined leaves is a satisfying sight in itself. This slow-growing shrub is often about twice as wide as it is high. It makes good ground-cover in all fertile, moisture-retentive soils, and it looks splendid, when young, in really large tubs.

Clay – Ground-cover – Containers – Green foliage.

PERNETTYA mucronata e.g. 'Bell's Seedling'
sc NA MC
○ ◐
type of plant: HSh
flowering season: l. spring to e. summer
flower colour: white
fruit colour: red
height: 60-90 cm/2-3 ft
***E**

Although *P. m.* 'Bell's Seedling' is, in theory, self-fertilizing, it will fruit far more freely and regularly if one male plant is grown with one or more female plants. The same mixture of sexes is necessary with the multi-coloured 'Davis Hybrids' (see right). Both forms are spreading, sometimes invasive plants with upright stems. They make dense, ground-covering thickets of growth, especially when young and when grown in full sun. Their tiny, bell-shaped flowers are less conspicuous than their fruits which *(contd)*

PERNETTYA mucronata e.g. 'Davis Hybrids'
sc NA MC
○ ◐
type of plant: HSh
flowering season: l. spring to e. summer
flower colour: white
fruit colour: mixed – pink, red, white, purple
height: 60-90 cm/2-3 ft
***E**

See preceding plant.

(contd)
ripen in autumn and persist until spring. Both these shrubs should be given a moisture-retentive soil to which peat or leaf-mould has been added.

Acid soils – Atmospheric pollution – Ground-cover – Containers.

PHYSALIS franchetii (syn.
P. alkekengi franchetii)
[Chinese Lantern]

○ ◑
type of plant: HP
fruit colour: orange-red
height: 60-75 cm/2-2½ ft
(SP)

This familiar ingredient of dried flower
arrangements is an invasive plant with
underground roots that spread quickly in most
soils. The papery, lantern-like seed-pods ripen in
early autumn and keep their colour well when
dried; they are also attractive when still green.
P. franchetii makes rather untidy ground-cover
and does not merit too prominent a position in the
garden.
Ground-cover.

GEUM montanum
[species of Avens]

○ ◑
type of plant: HP
flowering season: l. spring to midsummer
flower colour: yellow
fruit colour: beige
height: 23 cm/9 in
E (SH)

The chief glory of this tufted plant is its mass of
2 cm/1 in wide flowers, but the fluffy, feathery
seed-heads which follow are also charming. Any
soil with reasonable drainage is suitable but cool,
leafy soils give particularly good results.

Additional plants with ornamental fruit that are
featured elsewhere in this book

○ ◑ sun or partial shade
PICEA omorika: 15-21 m (p. 94)
TAXUS baccata: 12-18 m (p. 126)
DAVIDIA involucrata: 12-15 cm (p. 94)
SORBUS aria: 10.5-15 m (p. 24)
SORBUS aria 'Lutescens' ★: 9-12 m (p. 165)
SORBUS aucuparia: 9-12 m (p. 33)
SORBUS hupehensis: 9-12 m (p. 193)
TAXUS baccata 'Fastigiata': 9-12 m (p. 24)
ILEX aquifolium: 7.5-12 m (p. 127)
CRATAEGUS monogyna: 7.5-9 m (p. 130)
CORNUS kousa chinensis: 6-7.5 m (p. 33)
CRATAEGUS oxyacantha e.g. 'Plena': 4.5-6 m
   (p. 50)
CLEMATIS tangutica: 4.5-5.4 m (p. 123)
CLEMATIS orientalis: 3.6-5.4 m (p. 123)
PYRACANTHA coccinea 'Lalandei': 3.6-4.5 m
   (p. 95)
PYRACANTHA rogersiana 'Flava': 3.6-4.5 m
   (p. 127)
GARRYA elliptica: 2.4-4.5 m (p. 282)
HIPPOPHAE rhamnoides ★: 2.4-3.6 m (p. 88)
COTONEASTER 'Hybridus Pendulus': 2.4 m
   (p. 25)
COTONEASTER simonsii: 1.8-2.4 m (p. 128)
LEYCESTERIA formosa: 1.8 m (p. 211)
AUCUBA japonica: 1.5-2.4 m (p. 83)
CHAENOMELES speciosa e.g. 'Nivalis':
   1.2-1.8 m (p. 96)
GAULTHERIA shallon: 1.2-1.8 m (p. 106)
SYMPHORICARPOS × doorenbosii 'White
   Hedge': 1.2-1.8 m (p. 130)
VACCINIUM corymbosum: 1.2-1.8 m (p. 193)
CHAENOMELES × superba e.g. 'Knap Hill
   Scarlet': 1.2-1.5 m (p. 244)
CHAENOMELES × superba e.g. 'Rowallane':
   1.2-1.5 m (p. 130)
TYPHA angustifolia: 1.2-1.5 m (p. 73)
DAPHNE mezereum: 90-150 cm (p. 277)
PRUNUS laurocerasus e.g. 'Otto Luyken': 90 cm
   (p. 107)
CHAENOMELES speciosa e.g. 'Simonii':
   60-90 cm (p. 52)
RUSCUS aculeatus: 60-90 cm (p. 84)
CLEMATIS orientalis: 60 cm (p. 123)
CLEMATIS tangutica: 60 cm (p. 123)
COTONEASTER horizontalis ★: 60 cm (p. 194)
PAEONIA mlokosewitschii: 60 cm (p. 247)
TYPHA minima: 45-60 cm (p. 75)
COTONEASTER 'Hybridus Pendulus': 30-45 cm
   (p. 25)
CALLA palustris: 15-23 cm (p. 76)
VACCINIUM vitis-idaea: 15 cm (p. 111)
COTONEASTER dammeri: 10 cm (p. 111)

CELASTRUS orbiculatus (syn. *C. articulatus*)

◑ [○]
type of plant: HCl
fruit colour: orange + scarlet
height: 9 m/30 ft

Each small, scarlet fruit of this climber is, at first,
enclosed in a light brown capsule. In autumn, this
covering splits and the inner, yellowish orange
surface provides a bright background for the
shining seeds. As the fruits are ripening, the leaves
of this vigorous, twining plant turn yellow. All
moisture-retentive soils suit *C. orbiculatus*, and it
can be used to cover walls of any aspect. It looks
well growing into a tree. Both sunny and lightly
shaded positions produce strong specimens of this
plant, but some shade appears to heighten the
colouring of its fruits. Plants of *C. orbiculatus*
offered for sale are usually self-fertile, but there are
some male and female forms too.
Climbers – Autumn foliage.

ILEX opaca NA
[American Holly]

◑ [○]
type of plant: HT
fruit colour: red
height: 9 m/30 ft
E

This is an attractive, broad-leaved evergreen tree
with dull green leaves. Female plants that have
been pollinated bear persistent red fruit. Although
American holly cannot survive the winters of the
coldest parts of the United States, it is the hardiest
broad-leaved evergreen tree. It is also more
adaptable to summer heat than *I. aquifolium*.

ILEX cornuta NA
[Chinese Holly]

◐[○]
type of plant: HSh
fruit colour: red
height: 1.8 m/6 ft
E

Glossy evergreen leaves with sharp, three-pointed tips are characteristic of this holly, which tolerates summer heat better than almost any other kind. Red fruits are borne on plants with female flowers without pollination. 'Burfordii', which lacks the three-pointed tip, is the standard cultivar. Chinese holly is not hardy in the colder parts of the United States.

SKIMMIA japonica 'Foremanii' (syn.
S. foremanii)★

◐[○]
type of plant: HSh
flowering season: spring
flower colour: creamy white
fruit colour: scarlet
height: 90-120 cm/3-4 ft
E

S. j. 'Foremanii' is often described as self-fertile. It is, in fact, female and it requires a male plant (for example, see p. 271) in order to bear fruit. Its almost scentless flowers are less decorative than its fruits which persist throughout the winter months. The plant itself forms a dense mound of broad, leathery leaves. It thrives in cool, moist, loamy soils. This slow-growing shrub may be planted in deep shade.
    Dense shade – Atmospheric pollution – Ground-cover – Green foliage.

IRIS foetidissima
[Stinking Iris, Gladdon, Gladwyn Iris]

◐[○]
type of plant: HP
flowering season: e. summer
flower colour: lilac + yellowish green
fruit colour: red
height: 45-60 cm/1½-2 ft
E

In autumn, the yawning seed-pods of this iris are filled with bright berries; the preceding flowers are much less impressive. *I. foetidissima* will produce thick clumps of dark, arching leaves in any soil and in all but the sunniest of sites. There is a beautiful variegated form of this plant. It seldom bears fruit, and is not very widely available.
    Chalk – Dry shade – Dense shade – Ground-cover – Green foliage.

LUNARIA annua (syn. *L. biennis*)
[Honesty]

◐
type of plant: HB
flowering season: l. spring to midsummer
flower colour: lilac-purple
fruit colour: silvery
height: 75 cm/2½ ft
(SP)

The flat, oval seed-pods of this plant are frequently used in dried arrangements. More unusually, they are picked while still green and mixed with fresh flowers. Any well drained soil will suit *L. annua* and, although it will not grow so stoutly in dry, shady conditions, it will normally be quite as satisfactory there as in less difficult conditions. A variegated form of honesty is show on p. 155.
    Chalk – Dry shade.

PODOPHYLLUM emodi★

◐●
type of plant: HP
flowering season: l. spring to e. summer
flower colour: white
fruit colour: red
height: 30 cm/1 ft

The lovely, simple flowers of this plant sit on top of deeply lobed leaves which are, at first, folded close to the stems and mottled with reddish bronze markings. From late summer onwards, bright red fruits begin to ripen. They are oval and up to 5 cm/2 in long. A spongy soil, moist or damp and containing plenty of peat, leaf-mould or similar substances suits this plant best.
    Acid soils – Damp and wet soils – Variegated leaves.

Additional plants with ornamental fruit that are featured elsewhere in this book

◐[○] partial shade (or sun)
LONICERA periclymenum 'Belgica': 4.5-6 m (p. 270)
LONICERA periclymenum 'Serotina': 4.5-6 m (p. 270)
SKIMMIA japonica: 90-150 cm (p. 271)
MAHONIA aquifolium: 90-120 cm (p. 112)
EUONYMUS fortunei 'Vegetus': 30-60 cm (p. 113)
ARUM italicum 'Pictum' ★: 30-45 cm (p. 154)
LONICERA periclymenum 'Belgica': 15-20 cm (p. 270)
LONICERA periclymenum 'Serotina': 15-20 cm (p. 270)

◐ partial shade
LUNARIA annua 'Variegata': 75 cm (p. 155)

◐● partial or full shade
TAXUS baccata: 12-18 m (p. 126)
TAXUS baccata 'Fastigiata': 9-12 m (p. 24)
AUCUBA japonica: 1.5-2.4 m (p. 83)
SYMPHORICARPOS rivularis: 1.5-2.1 m (p. 206)
CHAENOMELES speciosa e.g. 'Nivalis': 1.2-1.8 m (p. 96)
GAULTHERIA shallon: 1.2-1.8 m (p. 106)
SYMPHORICARPOS × doorenbosii 'White Hedge': 1.2-1.8 m (p. 130)
CHAENOMELES × superba e.g. 'Knap Hill Scarlet': 1.2-1.5 m (p. 244)
CHAENOMELES × superba e.g. 'Rowallane': 1.2-1.5 m (p. 130)
MAHONIA aquifolium: 90-120 cm (p. 112)
SKIMMIA japonica 'Foremanii' ★: 90-120 cm (p. 208)
PRUNUS laurocerasus e.g. 'Otto Luyken': 90 cm (p. 107)
CHAENOMELES speciosa e.g. 'Simonii': 60-90 cm (p. 52)
RUSCUS aculeatus: 60-90 cm (p. 84)
IRIS foetidissima: 45-60 cm (p. 208)
SARCOCOCCA humilis: 30-60 cm (p. 273)
VACCINIUM vitis-idaea: 15 cm (p. 111)
GAULTHERIA procumbens: 8-15 cm (p. 118)

Plants with ornamental bark and twigs (including the canes of bamboos)

While most plants are considered in terms of their flowers or leaves, there are some trees and shrubs the bark and twigs of which are particularly attractive. These features are, of course, especially prominent during winter and, although the list of winter-flowering plants may seem the obvious place to look for attractive plants for the colder months, the following list contains some of the more unusual components of the interesting winter garden.

This list is divided into two sections: the first section is made up of plants with ornamental bark; the second section contains plants which produce attractive twigs. Strictly speaking, it is the bark which makes many of the plants in the twigs section interesting. However, the term 'bark' is reserved here for the outer covering of the trunk or main stems of a plant, while the term 'twigs' refers to the smaller branches and younger shoots of a plant.

Among the more familiar plants with ornamental bark are birches such as *Betula pendula* and its varieties. If your garden is large enough, the silvery trunks of these trees look particularly striking in groups, and against a dark background of, for instance, glossy-leaved evergreens. A lighter background, such as a buff-coloured stone wall, or a stretch of grass, provides a more satisfactory contrast to trees, like the paper-bark maple (*Acer griseum*), which have dark brown trunks. When choosing plants with ornamental bark it is worth bearing in mind that this feature may only become prominent when the tree or shrub is quite mature; for instance, the bark of *Eucalyptus niphophila* and *Parrotia persica* peels on older specimens only.

In contrast, it is often the youngest growth which is the most interesting in plants with ornamental twigs. The stems of both *Salix alba* 'Chermesina' (a form of white willow) and the varieties of *Cornus alba* (a species of dogwood), for example, are most brightly coloured when young. To ensure that plenty of new growth is produced each year, plants of this type should be pruned hard every other spring. This severe pruning does, of course, tend to make plants smaller and shrubbier than they would be naturally. However, since coloured stems are the main attraction in these cases, the heights given in these lists are for specimens which have been cut back frequently. (As an added attraction, some varieties of *Cornus alba* have variegated foliage and this makes them interesting in summer as well as winter; an example – *C. a.* 'Elegantissima' – has been included in this list.)

Coloured twigs look attractive not only in the garden but also cut and brought indoors. Both indoors and outdoors the shiny, red stems of *Cornus alba* 'Sibirica' and the greenish yellow stems of *C. stolonifera* 'Flaviramea' are a particularly striking combination.

Plants with green twigs may not be as dramatic as the red- and yellow-twigged varieties mentioned above, but they too are attractive, both growing and as material for cutting. In the garden, they can give an evergreen effect to plants which are in fact deciduous, while the rush-like stems of shrubs such as the hybrids and varieties of common broom (*Cytisus scoparius*) are a good substitute for cut foliage during winter.

If you find ornamental bark and twigs particularly attractive features, there are a number of plants which do not appear in this list but which do have these characteristics. Although these plants (such as the white-stemmed *Rubus cockburnianus*, and *Prunus serrula* with its polished and peeling bark) may be frequently referred to by gardening writers who deal with the subject of bark and twigs, you will probaby find that only nurseries which carry a really wide range of shrubs and trees will stock them.

A good source of information about other plants with attractive bark and twigs is H. G. Hillier's *Manual of Trees and Shrubs* (published by David and Charles). This gives a list of suitable plants, descriptions of which appear in the main text of the book. In addition, Roger Phillips's *Trees in Britain, Europe and North America* (published by Pan Books) contains a number of excellent illustrations of the bark of trees. Many of these trees have not been included in this list, either because they are not often offered for sale, or because they are not generally regarded as having ornamental bark. However, you may find them attractive or interesting and, in the case of the more unusual trees, worth searching for.

Bark

CRYPTOMERIA japonica NA
[Japanese Cedar]

○
type of plant: H/SlTCo
height: 22.5 m/75 ft
E, bark red-brown, peeling

The Japanese cedar makes a tall, usually narrow tree with attractive, shedding cinnamon-coloured bark. An important forest tree in its homeland, it performs best in the warmer parts of the United States. Many of the cultivars are less hardy than the species itself. In the British Isles, smaller forms of this plant (for example, see p. 189) are more popular than the species.

JUGLANS nigra NA
[Black Walnut]

○
type of plant: HT
height: 22.5 m/75 ft
bark dark brown, ridged

This is a large tree with compound leaves and dark coloured bark. The nuts, which have a musky taste, are produced in greenish-yellow husks that can be a nuisance on the lawn. The trees perform best in soils that are not excessively acidic. The roots emit a substance called juglone, which is toxic to many kinds of plants.

EUCALYPTUS niphophila ★ MC
[Snow Gum]

○ [◐]
type of plant: HT/SlTT (NA)
flowering season: summer
flower colour: white
height: 6-7.5 m/20-25 ft
* E, bark mottled, peeling

Once established, *E. niphophila* may increase by up to 1.2 m/4 ft each year. Plants grown on moist, acid soils and sheltered from cold winds seem to grow particularly fast. The long, aromatic adult leaves are carried on twigs that are red in winter and pale blue-white in spring. The trunk or trunks and main branches are beautifully mottled creamy white and grey.

Acid soils – Seaside – Atmospheric pollution – Grey, etc. leaves – Aromatic leaves – Bark and *twigs*.

BETULA pendula
[Silver Birch]

○ ◑
type of plant: HT
height: 12-18 m/40-60 ft
bark silvery, peeling

The silver birch and many of its varieties, including *B. p.* 'Dalecarlica' (see right), are rather open, narrow-headed trees with slender trunks which become pale-barked with age. *B. p.* 'Dalecarlica' tends to develop this feature a little earlier than the species and, as an additional attraction, it has deeply cut, feathery leaves. The pendulous branchlets of these trees create a light and graceful effect, and most silver birches can be planted in quite small gardens without seeming too large or dominant. Their leaves turn a subdued green-gold in autumn. Nurseries specializing in trees and shrubs will stock other birches with decorative bark, such as the paper *(contd)*

BETULA pendula 'Dalecarlica'★
[Swedish Birch]

○ ◑
type of plant: HT
height: 12-18 m/40-60 ft
bark silvery, peeling

See preceding plant.

(contd)
birch (*P. papyrifera*) and the very pale-stemmed *B. jacquemontii*. All these trees grow best on loam, but they will tolerate a very wide range of soil conditions.
　Atmospheric pollution – Green foliage (*B. p.* 'Dalecarlica' only).

ACER griseum★
[Paper-bark Maple]

○ ◑
type of plant: HT
height: 10.5-12 m/35-40 ft
bark reddish brown, peeling

The main branches and trunk of this slow-growing, and usually very expensive tree are covered in large, russet-coloured strips of old bark which roll back to reveal new bark beneath. For a brief period, late in spring, the young leaves are chocolate coloured; in autumn, the foliage turns scarlet and orange. The upright branches of this tree form a fairly narrow, domed head. Most soils are suitable, although the ideal is a well drained but moisture-retentive loam. Other maples with attractive bark include the snake-bark species and varieties, such as *A. A. capillipes* and *pensylvanicum*.
　Atmospheric pollution – Autumn foliage.

Additional plants with ornamental bark that are featured elsewhere in this book

○ sun
CUPRESSUS glabra: 13.5-18 m (p. 156)
CRYPTOMERIA japonica 'Elegans': 6-7.5 m (p. 189)

○ [◑] sun (or partial shade)
PLATANUS×hispanica: 21-30 m (p. 92)
EUCALYPTUS gunnii: 15-21 m (p. 164)
QUERCUS ilex: 15-18 m (p. 87)

○ ◑ sun or partial shade
CARPINUS betulus: 15-21 m (p. 130)
BETULA pendula 'Youngii': 5.4-7.5 m (p. 95)
PARROTIA persica: 3- 5.4 m (p. 193)
DEUTZIA scabra e.g. 'Plena': 2.4-3 m (p. 96)

Twigs

SALIX daphnoides
[Violet Willow]

○ ◑
type of plant: HT
flowering season: e. spring
flower colour: silvery yellow
height: 6-9 m/20-30 ft
twigs purple with white bloom

The youngest shoots of this fast-growing tree are covered with a white bloom, but slightly more mature growths are a rich, dark, shiny purple and they contrast well with the pale catkins. With age, the violet willow's upright, broadly columnar head of branches spreads considerably. All moisture-retentive soils, including those that are damp or wet, suit this plant and it will thrive beside rivers and natural ponds.
　Clay – Damp and wet soils – Atmospheric pollution.

SALIX alba 'Chermesina' (syn. *S. a.* 'Britzensis')
[form of White Willow]

○ ◑
type of plant: HT
flowering season: l. spring
flower colour: greenish yellow
height: 3-4.5 m/10-15 ft
grown as a pollarded specimen, twigs orange-red

When pruned hard every or every other spring, this plant produces very brightly coloured young shoots on top of a limited amount of old wood. Unpruned specimens soon form large, upright, wind-resistant trees with slender leaves which look pale and rather grey from a distance. However, the new wood of these plants is much less strongly coloured than the shoots of specimens that have been pollarded. *S. a.* 'Chermesina' will grow particularly well in damp or wet soils.
　Clay – Damp and wet soils – Seaside – Atmospheric pollution – Grey, etc. leaves.

CORYLUS avellana 'Contorta' [Corkscrew Hazel]

○ ◖
type of plant: HSh
flowering season: l. winter
flower colour: yellow
height: 2.4-3 m/8-10 ft
twigs twisted

The extraordinary twigs of this slow-growing shrub are hung with slightly twisted catkins in the last weeks of winter. The leaves appear later, in spring, and they too are coiled and twisted; they turn yellow in autumn. Other plants with twisted branches and twigs include the not very widely available 'contorted willow' (*Salix matsudana* 'Tortuosa'), which grows slowly to about 12 m/40 ft. Soils of most types suit *C. a.* 'Contorta'. Its curly twigs form a rounded shape overall.

Clay – Containers – Autumn foliage – Winter-flowering plants.

CORNUS stolonifera 'Flaviramea' [form of Dogwood or Cornel]

○ ◖
type of plant: HSh
height: 1.8-2.4 m/6-8 ft
twigs greenish yellow

In large gardens this vigorous, suckering shrub is sometimes planted beside one or other of the red-barked dogwoods (such as the easily available form shown below). It must be cut back, almost to ground level, each spring if it is to produce large quantities of young, greenish-yellow shoots. Although other moisture-retentive soils are also suitable, this shrub grows best in damp and wet soils. In ideal conditions it may form thickets over 2.4 m/8 ft wide.

Clay – Damp and wet soils – Atmospheric pollution.

LEYCESTERIA formosa

○ ◖
type of plant: HSh
flowering season: summer
flower colour: white + claret
height: 1.8 m/6 ft
twigs green

The youngest of this plant's bamboo-like stems are the most vividly coloured, and removing older growths in spring encourages plenty of new shoots to grow. The claret-coloured bracts, which surround the flowers, persist while the dark, purple fruits ripen (birds normally find these fruits very attractive). *L. formosa* is easily grown in all reasonably well drained and fertile soils. In the colder parts of the United States, the stems will die back to the ground each winter, but the plant will make new growth from the base in spring.

Atmospheric pollution – Fruit.

CORNUS alba 'Sibirica' [form of Red-barked Dogwood]

○ ◖
type of plant: HSh
height: 1.5-2.4 m/5-8 ft
twigs red

Similar in many respects to *C. stolonifera* 'Flaviramea' (see above) and requiring the same growing conditions, *C. alba* 'Sibirica' has bright crimson-red stems. The foliage quite often becomes tinged with red and orange in autumn. As well as plain, green-leaved varieties, such as *C. a.* 'Sibirica' and the less familiar, scarlet-stemmed *C. a.* 'Westonbirt', there are a few variegated forms of *C. alba*. The commonest of these are *C. a.* 'Elegantissima' (see p. 72) and *C. a.* 'Spaethii' (with red stems and yellow-variegated foliage).

Clay – Damp and wet soils – Atmospheric pollution – Autumn foliage.

ARUNDINARIA nitida (syn. *Sinarundinaria nitida*)★ [species of Bamboo]

◖[○]
type of plant: HP (Ba)
height: 2.4-3 m/8-10 ft
E, canes purplish

A. nitida produces spreading clumps of dark, purplish canes. As they age, the canes arch outwards. In hot sun and in cold, windy sites this plant's masses of narrow leaves are apt to become scorched and desiccated. A moist or damp soil in a sheltered site will produce the best results. Other bamboos with attractively coloured canes include *Phyllostachys nigra* 'Boryana' (see p. 68), which has yellow stems marked with purple, and *Arundinaria murieliae* (see p. 183), the young canes of which are a very bright green.

Damp or wet soils – Green foliage.

Additional plants with ornamental twigs that are featured elsewhere in this book

○ sun
LARIX leptolepis: 24-30 m (p. 28)
PHYLLOSTACHYS nigra 'Boryana': 2.4-3.9 m (p. 68)
SPARTIUM junceum: 2.1-3 m (p. 56)
EUONYMUS alatus: 1.8-2.4 m (p. 190)
CYTISUS scoparius e.g. 'Andreanus': 1.8 m (p. 57)
CYTISUS scoparius e.g. 'Firefly': 1.5-2.1 m (p. 92)
CYTISUS × praecox: 1.2-1.8 m (p. 57)
CYTISUS scoparius e.g. 'Cornish Cream': 1.2-1.8 m (p. 86)
GENISTA hispanica: 60-90 cm (p. 99)
GENISTA lydia: 45-75 cm (p. 92)

○ [◖] sun (or partial shade)
EUCALYPTUS niphophila: 6-7.5 m (p. 209)
ARUNDINARIA japonica: 3-4.5 m (p. 182)

○ ◖ sun or partial shade
SALIX × chrysocoma★: 13.5-18 m (p. 72)
ARUNDINARIA murieliae: 1.8-3 m (p. 183)
KERRIA japonica 'Pleniflora': 1.8-3 m (p. 243)
CORNUS alba 'Elegantissima'★: 1.8-2.7 m (p. 72)
KERRIA japonica: 1.2-1.8 m (p. 96)
VACCINIUM corymbosum: 1.2-1.8 m (p. 193)
COTONEASTER horizontalis: 60 cm (p. 194)

◖ [○] partial shade (or sun)
KERRIA japonica 'Pleniflora': 1.8-3 m (p. 243)
KERRIA japonica: 1.2-1.8 m (p. 96)

Plants with flowers suitable for cutting (including flowers or seed-heads suitable for drying)

Sometimes it seems as if there are just two types of gardener: those that cannot bear to cut anything they have grown, and those that treat the whole of their gardens as picking beds. To the first type of gardener the following list will obviously be irrelevant, while the second type of gardener will think that it is ridiculously short and that its entries have been chosen on a decidedly unadventurous basis. However, for the majority of gardeners this list will provide a wide range of plants that are both attractive and long-lasting when cut.

Of course some flowers, notably chrysanthemums of various sorts, last particularly well in water, and they are popular material for cutting for this reason. Where the choice of varieties of long-lasting flowers is very wide, only those varieties that are most useful for cutting have been included. In some cases a flower may last well in water, but its bloom may be so large that it looks quite out of scale in anything but the biggest arrangements. The large-flowered hybrid gladioli, for example, might look splendid in the garden, but the general appearance and the size of the smaller-flowered hybrids, make them much more useful as cut flowers.

At the other end of the scale, some plants with flowers that might last well in water have been excluded from this list because their overall size is very small. With short stems there is little opportunity to achieve as many differences in height as one might wish for in arrangements. In addition, cutting the stem of a small plant several times, in order to get exactly the right line, can often lead to the stem becoming so short that it is useless. However, flowers from small plants are very effective in certain arrangements and, particularly where no similar, larger, varieties or species are available, small plants are included in this list.

Some gardeners are very wary of cutting shrubs and trees for flower arrangements. A few woody plants respond badly to being cut, and there are others that either grow so slowly or take so long to produce flowers in any quantity that they are impractical sources of cut flowers. Nevertheless, many shrubs and some trees provide beautiful material for indoor arrangements, in quite large quantities and with no detriment to the general health of the plants.

The majority of the trees and shrubs that appear in this list flower profusely or produce their blossom in dense clusters, so that it is only necessary to cut quite small pieces to obtain enough flowers for most arrangements. For descriptions of a wide range of shrubs and trees and their suitability for cutting, see Sybil Emberton's *Shrub Gardening for Flower Arrangement* (published by Faber and Faber).

Plants in this list that are suitable for drying are marked 'Dr'. Some so-called everlasting plants retain their shape and colour particularly well when dried. However, certain other plants produce seed-heads that do not bear a very close resemblance to the flowers which precede them.

Like everlasting flowers, seed-heads can be dried simply by hanging them upside-down in an airy place. Details of the preserving method for flowers which can be preserved only by drying agents such as silica gel and borax powder will be found in general books on flower arranging as well as publications dealing specifically with the subject of dried flowers.

In planning arrangements of dried flowers for the winter months, it is sometimes easy to forget that many seed-heads can be just as decorative in the garden as in the house. The varieties of *Erica cinerea* (bell heather), for instance, are really too small to be useful in many arrangements, but the russet-brown of their faded flowers is a considerable asset to any garden in late autumn and early winter. Similarly, the seed-heads of astilbes, which are often used in arrangements of dried material, can make interesting shapes oudoors and at a time when many other plants have died back to below ground level.

A considerable proportion of this list is made up of plants that either require or prefer a sunny site. As a general rule, sunshine encourages the production of flowers. Some plants, such as *Jasminum nudiflorum* (winter jasmine) and the forsythias, will grow healthily in both sun and shade, but they will not usually flower very freely in shady positions. In this particular list, plants of this sort are included in one or other of the 'sun' categories only, ○, ○ [◑] or ○ ◑. Plants that appear in the last two 'shade' categories, ◑ and ◑ ●, require at least some shade; they should not normally be planted in sunny positions.

For plants that do not provide good cut flowers, but which do have ornamental seed-heads or seed-pods, see the list entitled 'Plants with ornamental fruit'.

LATHYRUS odoratus e.g. 'Air Warden' sc NA [form of Sweet Pea]

○

type of plant: HACl
flowering season: summer to e. autumn
flower colour: orange-cerise
height: 1.8-3 m/6-10 ft

With their long, strong stems and large flowers, the varieties 'Air Warden' and 'Mrs R. Bolton' are good illustrations of why sweet peas are such popular cut flowers. The former variety is unusually well scented for a cerise coloured sweet pea; *L. o.* 'Mrs R. Bolton' (see right) is only slightly scented. For examples of particularly fragrant sweet peas which are also suitable for cutting, see p. 255. Some seedsmen offer a few, so-called 'picotee' sweet peas (such as *L. o.* 'Rosy Frills'). These plants have petals which are edged in a different colour from the main body *(contd)*

LATHYRUS odoratus e.g. 'Mrs R. Bolton' sc NA [form of Sweet Pea]

○

type of plant: HACl
flowering season: summer to e. autumn
flower colour: almond pink
height: 1.8-3 m/6-10 ft

See preceding plant.

(contd)
of the flower; they can look exceptionally pretty in certain kinds of arrangements. Sweet peas grown for cutting will produce the largest number of big blooms if they are given a really fertile, well prepared soil.

Climbers – Containers – Fragrant flowers (*L. o.* 'Air Warden' only).

CORTADERIA selloana (syn. *C. argentea*, *Gynerium argenteum*) [species of Pampas Grass]

○

type of plant: HP (Gr)
flowering season: autumn
flower colour: cream
height: 1.8-2.7 m/6-9 ft
E, mainly Dr

For large-scale dried flower arrangements there are few ingredients as impressive as the plumes of this pampas grass; they also look well in the garden. A smaller variety, *C. s.* 'Pumila', is about 1.5-1.8 m/5-6 ft high. All forms of *C. selloana* grow healthily in fertile soils that are either well drained or slightly damp – but not wet. They also require sheltered sites. In the United States, they are not hardy north of Washington DC.

Damp and wet soils.

LATHYRUS odoratus e.g. 'Galaxy Mixed'
[form of Sweet Pea]
○
type of plant: HACl
flowering season: summer to e. autumn
flower colour: mixed – salmon, cream, blue,
pink, scarlet, orange
height: 1.8-2.4 m/6-8 ft

Where plenty of cut flowers of various colours are
wanted, the vigorous and free-flowering Galaxy
strain of sweet peas is an excellent choice. Cutting
the blooms of this plant encourages it to produce
more of its large, long-stemmed flowers. A few
seedsmen's catalogues list separate colours of
Galaxy sweet peas. The mixtures include some
scented flowers. A rich, well drained soil is
essential for the best growth and the most
numerous blooms.
    Climbers – Containers.

ROSA (Hybrid Musk/Modern Shrub) e.g. 'Will
Scarlet'
[form of Rose]
○
type of plant: HSh
flowering season: summer to e. autumn
flower colour: scarlet
height: 1.5-1.8 m/5-6 ft

The bright flowers of this strong-growing and
bushy plant (which is variously classified as a
hybrid musk and a modern shrub rose) are lightly
scented. When fully open, they may be a vivid
pink rather than scarlet. The orange-red fruits
ripen late and are a decorative winter feature. *R.*
'Will Scarlet' is excellent for cutting. It needs only
light pruning.
    Fruit.

HELIANTHUS decapetalus 'Loddon Gold'
[form of Sunflower]
○
type of plant: HP
flowering season: midsummer to e. autumn
flower colour: yellow
height: 1.5 m/5 ft

The annual forms of sunflower, with their huge
blooms, are well known. This is one of the
perennial varieties and its deeply coloured, double
flowers are of a rather more manageable size –
about 8-10 cm/3-4 in across. They last well in
water. This plant needs a substantial, well drained
soil and plenty of sun for optimum growth, but
even quite shallow, chalky soils produce good
results. It must be staked.
    Chalk.

ROSA floribunda 'The Fairy' NA
○
type of plant: HSh
flowering season: nearly all summer
flower colour: light pink
height: 1.5 m/5 ft

An attractive, repeat-blooming rose with small,
double flowers. The shrub is less pest-prone than
hybrid teas and most floribundas and
architecturally it combines well in mixed borders
with a wide range of plants. No special care is
required.

DAHLIA (Semi-cactus) e.g. 'Hit Parade'
○
type of plant: HHTu
flowering season: l. summer to autumn
flower colour: scarlet
height: 1.35 m/4½ ft

This is one of many possible examples of so-called
'semi-cactus' border dahlias. The flowers of this
plant are about 15-20 cm/6-8 in in diameter. Most
dahlias are prolific providers of long-lasting cut
flowers. Despite their general name, border
dahlias are best grown in rows or in beds of their
own. In such circumstances, the necessary
enriching of the soil, staking, pinching out of
shoots, dead-heading, possible disbudding, and,
finally, lifting of the tubers for winter storage can
be carried out most conveniently. As well as being
rich, the soil for dahlias must be well drained, and
these plants need plenty of water both when
coming into flower and when flowering.

ROSA (Hybrid Tea) e.g. 'Pascali'
[form of Rose]
○
type of plant: HSh
flowering season: summer to mid-autumn
flower colour: white
height: 1.2-1.8 m/4-6 ft

In a dry season, the many lovely blooms produced
by this erect and vigorous rose will last well, both
in the garden and as cut flowers. In a wet summer,
however, they are likely to be damaged soon after
opening. Despite this drawback and the lack of
any pronounced scent, *R.* 'Pascali', remains a very
attractive rose. It needs the usual diet of a good,
fertile soil that is at least reasonably well drained.
    Atmospheric pollution.

ACHILLEA 'Gold Plate', (syn. *A. eupatorium* 'Gold Plate', *A. filipendulina* 'Gold Plate')★ **[form of Yarrow]**

○

type of plant: HP
flowering season: summer
flower colour: yellow
height: 1.2-1.5 m/4-5 ft
Dr

The flowers of this strong-stemmed plant are arranged in flat, 15 cm/6 in diameter heads which are outstandingly decorative and long-lasting. When dried, they keep almost all their deep yellow colour. *A.* 'Coronation Gold' (see p. 58) is a similar, but shorter plant with rather smaller flower heads. Both varieties need well drained soils.

Chalk – Hot, dry soils.

CHRYSANTHEMUM (Early-flowering: reflexed decorative) e.g. 'Tracy Waller' sc NA

○

type of plant: HHP
flowering season: e. autumn
flower colour: pink
height: 1.2-1.5 m/4-5 ft

The range of early-flowering chrysanthemums is large and constantly increasing. This particular variety is a popular, pink-flowered form which may easily be superseded in future years. For illustrations of a further nine early-flowering chrysanthemums, see later pages in the ○ (sun) section of this list. All these plants should be grown in a fertile, moisture-retentive soil. They need staking. Except in mild districts, they must be lifted in autumn and stored in a cold frame or greenhouse during the winter months.

DAHLIA (Decorative) e.g. 'Glory of Heemstede' sc NA

○

type of plant: HHTu
flowering season: l. summer to autumn
flower colour: lemon yellow
height: 1.2-1.35 m/4-4½ ft

The 'decorative' dahlias have what many people think of as the classic, dahlia flower shape. This particular variety is a well established favourite. Its blooms are normally about 10-15 cm/4-6 in in diameter; they have unusually neat, upturned petals. (For general remarks about dahlias and their cultivation, see *D.* 'Hit Parade' on the previous page.)

ASTER novae-angliae e.g. 'Harrington's Pink' [form of Michaelmas Daisy]

○

type of plant: HP
flowering season: e. autumn
flower colour: rose-pink
height: 1.2 m/4 ft

Some of the varieties of *A. novae-angliae* have flowers that remain unattractively half-open when cut but neither the form illustrated here nor *A. n.-a.* 'September Ruby' (see p. 46) have this fault. Both these Michaelmas daisies are easily grown plants, needing only sunshine, moisture-retentive soil and some staking to produce plenty of blooms suitable for cutting.

Clay – Damp and wet soils.

CHRYSANTHEMUM (Early-flowering: intermediate decorative) e.g. 'Evelyn Bush' sc NA

○

type of plant: HHP
flowering season: l. summer to e. autumn
flower colour: white
height: 1.2 m/4 ft

For general remarks about early-flowering chrysanthemums and their cultivation, see *C.* 'Tracy Waller', above. The blooms of the variety shown here are usually about 12 cm/5 in in diameter.

DAHLIA (Semi-cactus) e.g. 'Hamari Bride' sc NA

○

type of plant: HHTu
flowering season: l. summer to autumn
flower colour: white
height: 1.2 m/4 ft

D. 'Hamari Bride' has particularly long and slender, pure white petals which make the 15-20 cm/6-8 in wide flowers seem less solid and stiff than those of many other dahlias. General comments about dahlias appear under *D.* 'Hit Parade' on the previous page.

TITHONIA rotundifolia (syn. *T. speciosa*)
'Torch'
[form of Mexican Sunflower]

○

type of plant: HHA
flowering season: midsummer to mid-autumn
flower colour: orange-scarlet + yellow
height: 1.2 m/4 ft

This bright, free-flowering plant grows quickly and strongly in rich, well drained soils and sheltered sites. The flowers appear in succession and are very long-lasting in water. When being cut and arranged, however, they must be handled carefully, as the stems have a tendency to snap just below the flower heads.

DAHLIA (Decorative) e.g. 'Chinese Lantern'
sc NA

○

type of plant: HHTu
flowering season: l. summer to autumn
flower colour: orange-red
height: 1.05-1.2 m/3½-4 ft

Although the 10-15 cm/4-6 in wide blooms of this plant are quite small compared with those of the giant and large 'decorative' dahlias, their brilliant colouring makes them very striking both in the garden and in flower arrangements. (See *D*. 'Hit Parade', p. 213, for general comments about these plants.)

HELIOPSIS scabra e.g. 'Golden Plume'

○

type of plant: HP
flowering season: summer
flower colour: yellow
height: 1.05-1.2 m/3½-4 ft

The richly coloured flowers of this sturdy plant are hardly plume-like, but they are produced over a long period and they do last well in water. Most soils are suitable, and staking is not usually necessary.

KNIPHOFIA e.g. 'Royal Standard'
[form of Red Hot Poker]

○

type of plant: SlTP
flowering season: midsummer to e. autumn
flower colour: red + yellow
height: 1.05-1.2 m/3½-4 ft

Good drainage and warmth are important for this plant but, if it is to flower well, it must not be allowed to dry out completely. The great flower spikes, so warmly bicoloured, do not need staking, even in fairly windy seaside gardens. There are kniphofias in quieter colours and smaller sizes (see for instance, *K*. 'Maid of Orleans', p. 5), and these may suit some flower arrangers better.
    Chalk.

CHRYSANTHEMUM (Early-flowering: spray)
e.g. 'Golden Orfe' sc NA

○

type of plant: HHP
flowering season: l. summer to e. autumn
flower colour: yellow
height: 1.05 m/3½ ft

Spray chrysanthemums are rather easier to arrange with other flowers than the large and formal 'decoratives' illustrated earlier in this list. The blooms of *C*. 'Golden Orfe' are only 5-8 cm/2-3 in wide; there are usually at least four or five of them to each stem. (General comments under *C*. 'Tracy Waller', p. 214, apply in this case too.)

DAHLIA (Pompon) e.g. 'Bianco' sc NA

○

type of plant: HHTu
flowering season: l. summer to autumn
flower colour: white
height: 1.05 m/3½ ft

The five dahlias illustrated in this and the following four photographs all need the growing conditions and general care outlined under *D*. 'Hit Parade' (see p. 213). *D*. 'Twiggy' is a further, prettily coloured and small-flowered example of a popular, 'decorative' dahlia. *D*. 'David Howard' has even smaller blooms (about 8 cm/3 in in diameter), and they are an interesting, caramelized colour. The foliage of this plant is dark bronze-green. Rather different in flower shape are the pompon dahlias (*D. D*. 'Bianco' and 'Moor Place'). Both these plants have fairly small blooms. In comparison, the flowers of *D*. 'Apple Blossom' are large – about 15-20 cm/6-8 in wide (*contd*)

DAHLIA (Cactus) e.g. 'Apple Blossom' sc NA

○

type of plant: HHTu
flowering season: l. summer to autumn
flower colour: pink
height: 1.05 in/3½ ft

See preceding plant.

DAHLIA (Decorative) e.g. 'David Howard' sc NA

○

type of plant: HHTu
flowering season: l. summer to autumn
flower colour: burnt orange
height: 1.05 m/3½ ft

See *D*. 'Bianco', previous page.

DAHLIA (Pompon) e.g. 'Moor Place' sc NA

○

type of plant: HHTu
flowering season: l. summer to autumn
flower colour: purple
height: 1.05 m/3½ ft

See *D*. 'Bianco', previous page.

(*contd*)
(for further examples of cactus dahlias see pp. 220 and 228).
　Red, etc. leaves (*D*. 'David Howard' only).

DAHLIA (Decorative) e.g. 'Twiggy' sc NA

○

type of plant: HHTu
flowering season: l. summer to autumn
flower colour: rose-pink + yellow
height: 1.05 m/3½ ft

See *D*. 'Bianco', previous page.

CENTAUREA macrocephala

○

type of plant: HP
flowering season: summer
flower colour: yellow
height: 90-150 cm/3-5 ft
Dr

The long-lasting flowers of this sturdy plant are borne on strong stems; they are followed by knob-like seed-heads which are an additional source of attractive material for arrangements. *C. macrocephala* should be given a well drained and, preferably, alkaline soil.
　Chalk.

CHRYSANTHEMUM (Early-flowering: reflexed decorative) e.g. 'Early Red Cloak' sc NA

○

type of plant: HHP
flowering season: l. summer to e. autumn
flower colour: red
height: 90-150 cm/3-5 ft

The incurved petals of *C*. 'Primrose Evelyn Bush' (see following page) create a solid head of yellow some 10-12 cm/4-5 in across. However, many flower arrangers prefer the similarly sized, but more openly arranged flower heads of 'reflexed decorative' chrysanthemums such as 'Early Red Cloak' and 'Grace Riley' (illustrated here and on the following page respectively). There are a very large number of varieties of both types. They need the treatment outlined under *C*. 'Tracy Waller' (see p. 214).

CHRYSANTHEMUM (Early-flowering: reflexed decorative) e.g. 'Grace Riley' sc NA

○

type of plant: **HHP**
flowering season: **l. summer to e. autumn**
flower colour: **bronze**
height: **90-150 cm/3-5 ft**

See preceding plant.

CHRYSANTHEMUM (Early-flowering; incurved decorative) e.g. 'Primrose Evelyn Bush' sc NA

○

type of plant: **HHP**
flowering season: **e. autumn**
flower colour: **pale yellow**
height: **90-150 cm/3-5 ft**

See C. 'Early Red Cloak', previous page.

ASTER novi-belgii e.g. 'Fellowship' sc NA [form of Michaelmas Daisy]

○

type of plant: **HP**
flowering season: **autumn**
flower colour: **pink**
height: **90-120 cm/3-4 ft**

Varieties of *A. novi-belgii* are not exactly disease-free plants, but they are popular for their late flowers which last well in water. There are single, semi-double and double-flowered forms in a wide range of colours and heights. *A. n.-b.* 'Fellowship' has large, double blooms. It should be given a fertile, moisture-retentive soil.

Clay – Damp and wet soils.

DAHLIA (Collerette) e.g. 'Collerette Mixed'

○

type of plant: **HHTu**
flowering season: **l. summer to autumn**
flower colour: **mixed– yellow, red, pink, orange, cream**
height: **90-120 cm/3-4 ft**

The Collerette dahlias are most often available as a mixture, but separate varieties can be obtained from specialist growers. Although much less densely petalled than the 'decorative', 'cactus' and 'semi-cactus' dahlias illustrated earlier in this list, the flowers of the Collerettes are still rather formal. They should be cultivated in the same way as other border dahlias (see general comments under *D*. 'Hit Parade', p. 213).

DELPHINIUM (Belladonna Hybrid) e.g. 'Blue Bees'

○

type of plant: **HP**
flowering season: **summer**
flower colour: **light blue**
height: **90-120 cm/3-4 ft**
Dr

There are white-flowered and pink-flowered forms of Belladonna delphiniums as well as varieties, such as 'Blue Bees', with classic colouring. They are all elegant, branching perennials requiring only light support. When picked for arrangements, they must immediately be given a long soaking in deep water. Fertile, well prepared and properly drained soil is needed to grow good specimens of Belladonna hybrids. Unless dissuaded, slugs and snails devour the young shoots of these plants.

HELIANTHUS annuus e.g. 'Autumn Beauty' [form of Sunflower]

○

type of plant: **HA**
flowering season: **midsummer to e. autumn**
flower colour: **mixed – yellow, chestnut, maroon, brown, bicolours**
height: **90-120 cm/3-4 ft**

Most of the annual sunflowers have blooms far too big for anything other than making the neighbours gasp. However, the flowers of this particular variety are relatively small (about 15 cm/6 in wide) and they can be used in some large arrangements. A rich, constantly moist soil and a warm position produce really strong growth and plenty of flowers but, for most purposes, well drained soils of all types are suitable.

Chalk.

ROSA gallica 'Versicolor' (syn. *R. g.* 'Rosa Mundi')
[form of Rose]

○

type of plant: HSh
flowering season: e. summer
flower colour: crimson + white
height: 90-120 cm/3-4 ft

The bushiness and density of this bristly rose make it a good hedging plant, but its outstanding feature is the showy colouring of its flowers, which are very freely produced – if only for a fairly brief period. *R. g.* 'Versicolor' is an easily grown plant and most soils are suitable, but this rose should, ideally, be given a rich, medium loam.

Hedging.

DELPHINIUM (Belladonna Hybrid) e.g. 'Pink Sensation'

○

type of plant: HP
flowering season: summer
flower colour: pink
height: 90-105 cm/3-3½ ft
Dr

This is the only pink-flowered delphinium of the Belladonna type which is generally available. For an example of a form with blue flowers, see the previous page. Both these plants make pretty cut flowers but they need soaking in deep water immediately after they have been picked. They should be grown in deep, fertile, well drained soil. Slugs and snails can damage the young growths irreparably if they are not deterred.

ECHINACEA purpurea (syn. *Rudbeckia purpurea*)
[species of Purple Coneflower]

○

type of plant: HP
flowering season: l. summer to e. autumn
flower colour: purplish red
height: 90-105 cm/3-3½ ft

Like many daisy-flowered plants, *E. purpurea* lasts well when cut. Each of the 10 cm/4 in wide blooms has a prominent, orangey-brown centre and the petals are vividly coloured – too vividly, perhaps, for some flower arrangers, who may prefer the quieter tones of *E. p.* 'White Lustre'. Both the species and the variety need a rich, well drained soil.

IRIS (Bearded Hybrid) e.g. 'Jane Phillips'★ sc NA

○

type of plant: HP
flowering season: e. summer
flower colour: pale blue
height: 90-105 cm/3-3½ ft

Although bearded hybrid irises are tough plants, they produce the largest number of blooms for cutting if they are given a really sunny position and a well drained, limy soil; they should also be divided fairly frequently. *I.* 'Jane Phillips' is of a particularly lovely blue; its flowers have a soft, sweet scent. The variety 'Party Dress' (see right) has the frilled kind of fluffiness that looks attractive in some sorts of arrangements. Specialist nurseries offer dozens of varieties of bearded irises in a wide range of colours.

Chalk – Fragrant flowers (*I.* 'Jane Phillips' only).

IRIS (Bearded Hybrid) e.g. 'Party Dress' sc NA

○

type of plant: HP
flowering season: e. summer
flower colour: pink + tangerine
height: 90-105 cm/3-3½ ft

See preceding plant.

ACIDANTHERA bicolor murielae★

○

type of plant: HHC
flowering season: l. summer to e. autumn
flower colour: white + purple
height: 90 cm/3 ft

The lovely flowers of this plant last well in water, especially if they have been picked when still in bud. They have a very sweet fragrance. Only in the mildest districts of Britain can the corms be left in the ground during winter; in most areas it will be necessary to lift, dry and store them. Full sun, a sheltered site and well drained soil encourage this plant to be at least reasonably free-flowering. (*A. b. murielae* is occasionally listed as *Gladiolus murielae*.)

Fragrant flowers.

ALLIUM aflatunense

○

type of plant: HBb
flowering season: l. spring to e. summer
flower colour: lilac
height: 90 cm/3 ft
Dr

Whether dried or fresh, the great, globular blooms of *A. aflatunense* look striking on their long stems. Each starry flower is about 8 cm/3 in diameter. The strap-shaped leaves are much less remarkable than the flowers, and they soon die back. This is an easy plant to grow in any well drained soil.
   Chalk.

ALSTROEMERIA aurantiaca
[species of Peruvian Lily]

○

type of plant: SlTP
flowering season: summer to e. autumn
flower colour: orange
height: 90 cm/3 ft

This clearly coloured plant can be invasive once it has settled down in a rich, well drained soil. Despite this fault, it is quite popular, since its flowers last very well in water and they have strong, wiry stems. For details of the more softly coloured and less spreading Ligtu hybrid alstroemerias, see p. 223.

ANTIRRHINUM majus e.g. 'Madame Butterfly Mixed'
[form of Snapdragon]

○

type of plant: HHA
flowering season: summer to mid-autumn
flower colour: mixed– yellow, red, orange, white, pink
height: 90 cm/3 ft
Dr

Although antirrhinums have a decided preference for dry and stony soils, when grown for cutting they are best given richer, moister conditions. They are very popular plants, especially for summer bedding, but they are, unfortunately, prone to several diseases including rust. Some rust resistant varieties are available. They are usually less than 50 cm/20 in high (for an example, see p. 10). *A. m.* 'Madame Butterfly Mixed' is a tall variety with sturdy stems.

ASTER novi-belgii e.g. 'Marie Ballard'
[form of Michaelmas Daisy]

○

type of plant: HP
flowering season: autumn
flower colour: light blue
height: 90 cm/3 ft

Such is the range of *A. novi-belgii* varieties offered by specialist nurseries, that this particular plant is only one of many possible examples of blue-flowered forms. It is, however, a famous variety, and one that has fully double flowers, the appearance and lasting qualities of which often appeal to flower arrangers as well as gardeners. Any moisture-retentive soil is suitable, particularly if it is quite fertile.
   Clay – Damp and wet soils.

CHRYSANTHEMUM maximum e.g. 'Wirral Supreme'★
[form of Shasta Daisy]

○

type of plant: HP
flowering season: summer
flower colour: white+yellow
height: 90 cm/3 ft

Varieties of *C. maximum* are much more at home in mixed or herbaceous borders than the early-flowering forms illustrated elsewhere in this list, and yet they are just as suitable for cutting – and much less trouble to grow. *C. m.* 'Wirral Supreme' has double flowers; single and semi-double forms are available. *C. m.* 'Esther Read' (see p. 225) is a shorter growing, double-flowered cultivar. All these plants like fertile, preferably alkaline soils, and good drainage prolongs their lives.
   Chalk.

COSMOS (syn. *Cosmea*) bipinnatus e.g. 'Sensation Mixed'★

○

type of plant: HHA
flowering season: midsummer to e. autumn
flower colour: mixed – crimson, pink, white
height: 90 cm/3 ft

Although the sizzling flower colours and pretty foliage of this annual look well in the garden, it is as a cut flower that this plant is most popular. It thrives in light, rather dry soils. The blooms last longest in water if they are picked when only half-open. Some catalogues list separate colours of this strain of cosmea.
   Chalk – Hot, dry soils – Green foliage.

DAHLIA (Cactus) e.g. 'Doris Day' sc NA

○
type of plant: HHTu
flowering season: l. summer to autumn
flower colour: burgundy red
height: 90 cm/3 ft

This richly coloured dahlia, with its neat, 10 cm/4 in flowers, has long been a favourite. It is often very free-flowering. For brief comments on the growing of border dahlias, see *D.* 'Hit Parade', p. 213.

DELPHINIUM consolida e.g. 'Stock-flowered Mixed'
[form of Larkspur]

○
type of plant: HA
flowering season: summer
flower colour: mixed – blue, rose, lilac, scarlet, white, salmon
height: 90 cm/3 ft
Dr

The stock-flowered type of annual delphinium is very popular for cutting. It lasts well if given a long soak after it has been picked. It is, however, quite tall and the flower spikes are easily damaged if the plant is not staked with thick canes. Most soils are suitable, but if they are deep and well drained, flowering and general growth are particularly good.

GYPSOPHILA paniculata e.g. 'Bristol Fairy'
[form of Chalk Plant or Baby's Breath]

○
type of plant: HP
flowering season: all summer
flower colour: white
height: 90 cm/3 ft
Dr

The clouds of tiny flowers produced by this deep-rooted plant are the classic accompaniment of sweet peas. They are also attractive with many other flowers, and they may be dried too. The pink-flowered form, *G. p.* 'Rosy Veil' (see p. 14), is a considerably smaller plant and therefore less useful for cutting. *G. p.* 'Bristol Fairy' lives longest on light, limy soils.
    Chalk – Hot, dry soils.

PENNISETUM alopecuroides

○
type of plant: SlT/HHP (Gr)
flowering season: autumn
flower colour: dark purple
height: 90 cm/3 ft
Dr

P. alopecuroides is not a plant for a cold, wet garden, but in a sheltered position and well drained soil it forms a dense tuft of foliage and bears plenty of bristly flower heads, each one up to 15 cm/6 in long. These are an interesting addition to either fresh or dried flower arrangements.
    Ground-cover.

SCABIOSA atropurpurea e.g. 'Cockade Mixed'
[form of Sweet Scabious or Pincushion Flower]

○
type of plant: HA
flowering season: midsummer to e. autumn
flower colour: mixed – pink, red, lavender, blue, maroon, white
height: 90 cm/3 ft
Dr

Despite one of its common names, this hybrid form of *S. atropurpurea* is only very slightly scented. It is, however, an excellent cut flower which lasts very well in water. The seed-heads remain intact when dried and make nice, solid shapes for winter arrangements. *S. atropurpurea* grows especially successfully on chalky soil. Tall varieties, like 'Cockade Mixed', usually need light staking.
    Chalk.

CHRYSANTHEMUM (Early-flowering: spray)
e.g. 'Pennine Pink' sc NA

○
type of plant: HHP
flowering season; e. autumn
flower colour: pink
height: 75-105 cm/2½-3½ ft

More and more varieties of spray chrysanthemums are being produced, in a wide range of colours, to meet the demands of flower arrangers who find plants like *C.* 'Pennine Pink' much easier to use in mixed arrangements than the large, stiff blooms of some other types of early-flowering chrysanthemum. The cultivation of both sorts of plants is, however, similar (for brief details see *C.* 'Tracy Waller', p. 214).

GLADIOLUS (Butterfly Hybrid) e.g. 'Melodie'

○

type of plant: HHC
flowering season: summer
flower colour: pink + salmon-red
height: 75-105 cm/2½-3½ ft

The two plants illustrated in this and the following photograph have the closely packed, 5-10 cm/ 2-4 in florets characteristic of butterfly gladioli. Each flower spike is roughly 45 cm/18 in long. Many gladioli of this type have strong throat markings, like those of the variety 'Melodie'. On first opening, G. 'Page Polka' has quite a green tinge to its petals, but the flowers become yellower as they age. For an example of a butterfly gladiolus with lastingly green flowers, see p. 280. The corms of these plants need to be lifted for winter storage in all but the very mildest areas of Britain. If plenty of flowers suitable for cutting are wanted, then gladioli should be grown in well prepared (*contd*)

GLADIOLUS (Butterfly Hybrid) e.g. 'Page Polka'

○

type of plant: HHC
flowering season: summer
flower colour: pale yellow
height: 75-105 cm/2½-3½ ft

See preceding plant.

(*contd*)

and properly drained, fertile soil. It is often most satisfactory to plant them in rows by themselves. Treated in this way they need only light support.

ROSA (Hybrid Tea) e.g. 'Blue Moon'
[form of Rose]

○

type of plant: HSh
flowering season: summer to mid-autumn
flower colour: lilac
height: 75-105 cm/2½-3½ ft

Flower arrangers clamour for a blue rose and the breeders try to oblige, but 'Blue Moon' is not really blue. It is, however, an unusual colour and its large blooms are both freely produced and freshly fragrant. Despite its vigour, this rather erect rose has a tendency to succumb to rust. It needs the fertile, loamy soil required by most roses.
    Fragrant flowers.

AGAPANTHUS 'Headbourne Hybrids'★
[form of African Lily]

○

type of plant: SlTP
flowering season: summer to e. autumn
flower colour: light blue to violet blue
height: 75-90 cm/2½-3 ft
E, Dr

Straight, thick stems support the handsome flower heads – and subsequent seed-heads – of these virtually hardy plants. The name 'Headbourne Hybrids' refers to what is, in effect, a mixture and some differences in height and flower colour must be expected. A rich, well drained soil and a sheltered site are most suitable. These plants should be given plenty of water during their growing season.

AMARANTHUS caudatus
[Love-lies-Bleeding]

○

type of plant: HA
flowering season: midsummer to e. autumn
flower colour: crimson
height: 75-90 cm/2½-3 ft
Dr

Given a good, rich soil and some shelter, this plant grows strongly and becomes draped in 45 cm/18 in tassels which look plush enough to be decorating a velvet-covered sofa. Both the species and its green-flowered form (*A.c.* 'Viridis', see p. 280), are popular for cutting. They dry well too.

ASTER×frikartii★
[form of Michaelmas Daisy]

○

type of plant: HP
flowering season: l. summer to mid-autumn
flower colour: lavender blue
height: 75-90 cm/2½-3 ft

After all the bright glories of the popular *novi-belgii* asters, the sparse petals and gentle colouring of this healthy plant shine out in cool elegance. *A.×frikartii* has an exceptionally long flowering season, during which numerous long-lasting blooms can be picked. It deserves to be given the good drainage and fertile, moisture-retentive soil that it prefers, although it will grow in drier and poorer conditions.
    Chalk.

COREOPSIS grandiflora e.g. 'Mayfield Giant'
[form of Tick-seed]

○

type of plant: **HP**
flowering season: **summer**
flower colour: **golden yellow**
height: **75-90 cm/2½-3 ft**

This tough and unfussy plant will grow almost anywhere. Indeed a fertile soil is not an advantage, and most forms of *C. grandiflora* are short-lived perennials which produce the largest number of flowers over the longest period when they are given a rather light, poor soil. The bright, long-stemmed blooms last well in water.

    Chalk.

GAILLARDIA e.g. 'Wirral Flame' sc NA
[form of Blanket Flower]

○

type of plant: **HP**
flowering season: **summer to mid-autumn**
flower colour: **deep red + gold**
height: **75-90 cm/2½-3 ft**

When grown specifically for cutting, this plant must be staked. Really well drained soils are most suitable; in moist conditions general growth is poor, relatively few blooms appear and the whole plant needs replacing after a fairly short period.

    Chalk – Hot, dry soils.

HELICHRYSUM bracteatum e.g.
'Monstrosum Double Mixed'
[form of Straw Flower]

○

type of plant: **HHA**
flowering season: **midsummer to e. autumn**
flower colour: **mixed – pink, red, yellow, orange, white**
height: **75-90 cm/2½-3 ft**
mainly **Dr**

Even when fresh, the petal-like bracts of these flowers feel dry and, when dried, the brightness of their colours is such that they look fresh. They are easy to grow in all well drained soils. If they are to be used in dried arrangements, the flowers should be picked before their central, yellow discs are visible.

    Chalk.

LAVATERA trimestris e.g. 'Loveliness'
[form of Mallow]

○

type of plant: **HA**
flowering season: **midsummer to e. autumn**
flower colour: **rose-pink**
height: **75-90 cm/2½-3 ft**

Since it is so much bushier than most annuals of its size, *L. t.* 'Loveliness' usually needs no staking to protect its large flowers from being damaged before they are picked. The variety 'Tanagra' has even bigger blooms of a brighter pink, and there are also forms, such as *L. t.* 'Mont Blanc', with white flowers. They are all easily grown plants.

RUDBECKIA hirta e.g. 'Tetra Gloriosa'
[Gloriosa Daisy, form of Black-eyed Susan]

○

type of plant: **HHA/HB**
flowering season: **l. summer to mid-autumn**
flower colour: **mixed – shades of yellow, red-brown, bicolours**
height: **75-90 cm/2½-3 ft**

The flowers of this plant may be rather too large and glorious for some people's tastes – many of the blooms are 15 cm/6 in wide – but they last very well in water, they appear in large quantities and their stems are long and sturdy. There is a double, yellow form of this plant in which the shiny, central cones are partially hidden by the petals. *R. h.* 'Irish Eyes' is a clear yellow variety with prominent, green centres. All forms of *R. hirta* grow well in ordinary garden soil.

CHRYSANTHEMUM × spectabile e.g.
'Cecilia' sc NA

○

type of plant: **HA**
flowering season: **all summer**
flower colour: **white + yellow**
height: **75 cm/2½ ft**

The large and strikingly banded blooms of *C. × s.* 'Cecilia' are particularly good for cutting, since not only do they last well in water, but they also have long stems. The length of the stems does mean, however, that staking is essential. A light and fertile soil suits this plant best.

    Chalk.

CROCOSMIA masonorum (syn.
Tritonia masonorum)

○

type of plant: SlTC
flowering season: l. summer
flower colour: reddish orange
height: 75 cm/2½ ft
Dr

C. masonorum is now known to be an almost
completely hardy plant. Its intensely coloured
flowers last a long time in arrangements, and the
arching sprays of seed-heads can also look
attractive. Its broad, pleated leaves rise from
spreading roots. Heavy soils are not recommended
for this plant, but it does need plenty of moisture
in summer.
    Ground-cover.

ROSA (Floribunda) e.g. 'Allgold' sc NA
[form of Rose]

○

type of plant: HSh
flowering season: all summer
flower colour: yellow
height: 75 cm/2½ ft

Even though there are newer yellow roses, this
relatively old variety remains a firm favourite. It is
an exceptionally neat, vigorous and healthy plant
and, unusually for roses of this colour, its petals
are a strong, clear yellow until they drop. This
means that even fairly well expanded blooms are
suitable for cutting. The more fertile and loam-like
the soil, the better the growth of this and most
other floribunda – or cluster-flowered – roses.

STIPA pennata
[Feather Grass]

○

type of plant: HP (Gr)
flowering season: summer
flower colour: creamy buff
height: 75 cm/2½ ft
Dr

The long and distinctively slim plumes of this
plant dry well. They are produced most prolifically
in warm positions and on soils that drain freely.
    Hot, dry soils.

ALSTROEMERIA 'Ligtu Hybrids'★
[form of Peruvian Lily]

○

type of plant: SlTP
flowering season: summer to e. autumn
flower colour: mixed – pink, red, orange, yellow
height: 60-90 cm/2-3 ft

The beautifully veined blooms of these plants are
arranged in large heads and carried on tall stems.
They are long-lasting cut flowers. The plants begin
to die back towards the end of summer, so they are
not suitable for the edges of borders. In a fertile,
well drained soil and a sheltered site these plants
usually become established fairly quickly.

CHRYSANTHEMUM 'Korean Hybrids
Mixed'

○

type of plant: HP
flowering season: l. summer to autumn
flower colour: mixed – pink, red, yellow, bronze
height: 60-90 cm/2-3 ft

These perennial plants can easily be grown from
seed. They are normally regarded as hardy, but
gardeners in cold districts sometimes prefer to lift
them and to store them under cover during the
winter. They are very free-flowering plants which
are excellent for cutting and bushy enough to be
used in mixed borders. They need a well drained
soil that is fertile. Only the main colours of the
flowers are mentioned above; there are many
intermediate shades.

DIANTHUS (Border Carnation) e.g. 'Beauty of
Cambridge' sc NA

○

type of plant: HP
flowering season: summer
flower colour: yellow
height: 60-90 cm/2-3 ft
E

Border carnations are not, in fact, particularly
suitable for planting in most borders since, if they
are to produce a reasonable number of well shaped
blooms for cutting, they require firm – and usually
obtrusive – staking and a certain amount of
disbudding. They tend also to be rather short-
lived plants. However, they make lovely, lasting
cut flowers and many of the very numerous
varieties are beautifully scented (see, for example,
D. 'Salmon Clove', p. 258). All of them must be
given well drained, alkaline soil. (*contd*)

DIANTHUS (Border Carnation) e.g. 'Fiery Cross' sc NA

○
type of plant: HP
flowering season: summer
flower colour: scarlet
height: 60-90 cm/2-3 ft
E

See preceding plant.

(*contd*)
Yellow-flowered border carnations, such as *D.* 'Beauty of Cambridge', are virtually scentless. *D.* 'Harmony' (see right) is a popular, striped form, and the variety 'Fiery Cross' (illustrated above) is a particularly strong grower.
  Chalk – Grey, etc. leaves.

DIANTHUS (Border Carnation) e.g. 'Harmony' sc NA

○
type of plant: HP
flowering season: summer
flower colour: grey + cerise
height: 60-90 cm/2-3 ft
E

See *D.* 'Beauty of Cambridge', previous page.

EREMURUS bungei (syn. *E. stenophyllus bungei*) [species of Foxtail Lily]

○
type of plant: HP
flowering season: e. summer
flower colour: yellow
height: 60-90 cm/2-3 ft

Most of the foxtail lilies are very tall plants; *E. bungei* is a welcome exception, especially for gardeners with limited space. The leaves of the plant are usually dead by midsummer. Any soil approaching the ideal of a rich, sandy loam will give good results.
  Chalk.

GLADIOLUS (Primulinus Hybrid) e.g. 'Columbine' ★ sc NA

○
type of plant: HHC
flowering season: summer
flower colour: pink
height: 60-90 cm/2-3 ft

The primulinus hybrids are, perhaps, the prettiest of all the readily available gladioli for flower arranging. Their florets are less tightly packed than those of the butterfly and miniature hybrids and the flower spikes are only about 40 cm/15 in long. *G.* 'Columbine' and 'Rutherford' (for the latter plant see right) are just two examples from quite a wide range, which includes most colours except blue. For the cultivation of these plants, see *G.* 'Melodie', p. 221.

GLADIOLUS (Primulinus Hybrid) e.g. 'Rutherford' ★ sc NA

○
type of plant: HHC
flowering season: summer
flower colour: crimson
height: 60-90 cm/2-3 ft

See preceding plant.

MALOPE trifida 'Grandiflora'

○
type of plant: HA
flowering season: summer to e. autumn
flower colour: rose-purple
height: 60-90 cm/2-3 ft

Looking much more substantially bushy than many other annual plants, *M. t.* 'Grandiflora' is also very free-flowering and its 8 cm/3 in blooms will last at least a week in water. It is easy to grow in any sunny site. A light, rich soil produces the best specimens. This plant is often available as a mixture of pink, rose-purple and white-flowered forms.

ACHILLEA ptarmica 'The Pearl'
[form of Sneezewort]

○

type of plant: HP
flowering season: midsummer to e. autumn
flower colour: white
height: 60-75 cm/2-2½ ft

The bright, white bobbles of this plant appear in clusters at the top of stiff stems. They last very well when picked and placed in water. Good drainage ensures that plenty of flowers are produced.

Chalk – Hot, dry soils.

AVENA sterilis
[Animated Oats]

○

type of plant: HA/B (Gr)
flowering season: summer
flower colour: buff
height: 60-75 cm/2-2½ ft
Dr

When moved even slightly, the daintily spread spikelets of this grass jiggle. When still, they look light and graceful. They contrast well with the dense inflorescences of plants like the popular *Lagurus ovatus* or hare's tail grass (see p. 237). *A. sterilis* can be grown in almost any soil.

CENTAUREA cyanus e.g. 'Blue Diadem'
[form of Cornflower]

○

type of plant: HA
flowering season: summer to e. autumn
flower colour: blue
height: 60-75 cm/2-2½ ft

C. c. 'Blue Diadem' is a particularly large-flowered and deeply coloured variety of cornflower. It is an erect plant and it usually needs some support, as do other tall, double cornflowers. These plants are often available as mixtures which normally include pink, mauve, white and rose-coloured forms, as well as forms with blue flowers. They all like a light, rich and, preferably, alkaline soil.

Chalk.

CHRYSANTHEMUM maximum e.g. 'Esther Read'
[form of Shasta Daisy]

○

type of plant: HP
flowering season: summer
flower colour: white + yellow
height: 60-75 cm/2-2½ ft

This is a fully double form of Shasta daisy, a little shorter than some other varieties but just as good at remaining fresh and crisp-looking when cut. It grows best in well drained, alkaline soils of reasonable fertility.

Chalk.

KNIPHOFIA galpinii
[species of Red Hot Poker or Torch Lily]

○

type of plant: SITP
flowering season: l. summer to mid-autumn
flower colour: orange
height: 60-75 cm/2-2½ ft

Often overlooked in favour of some of the better-known hybrids with their denser flower heads, this plant is, nevertheless, quite readily available and, being so much shorter than most kniphofias, easier to fit into gardens of average size. Young plants, in particular, need winter protection, and well drained soil is essential. The cut flowers last well in water.

Chalk.

LIATRIS spicata
[species of Blazing Star or Gayfeather]

○

type of plant: HP
flowering season: l. summer to e. autumn
flower colour: pink-purple
height: 60-75 cm/2-2½ ft

Both the leaves and the flowers of this plant are arranged strikingly around the stalks or stems. The flowers are very long-lasting and good for cutting. *L. spicata* is a robust plant which will grow in well drained soil and in moist, boggy conditions.

Damp and wet soils.

PYRETHRUM roseum (syn. *Chrysanthemum coccineum*) **e.g. 'Brenda'**

○

type of plant: HP
flowering season: e. summer
flower colour: bright cerise
height: 60-75 cm/2-2½ ft

P. r. 'Brenda' and other related varieties of *P. roseum* thrive in light, fertile soils with good drainage. They are excellent for cutting, though, to keep their strong stems straight, these rather 'thin' plants need support. The forms illustrated here are single-flowered; some double-flowered cultivars are available, and both types of plant come in various shades of pink, red and white. *P. r.* 'E. M. Robinson' (see the following photograph) is an outstanding, vigorous variety which may easily exceed the height given here when well suited. The synonym given *(contd)*

PYRETHRUM roseum (syn. *Chrysanthemum coccineum*) **e.g. 'E. M. Robinson'★**

○

type of plant: HP
flowering season: e. summer
flower colour: pink
height: 60-75 cm/2-2½ ft

See preceding plant.

(contd)
here is the correct botanical name, and the name more commonly used in the United States.
Chalk.

SAPONARIA vaccaria (syn. *Vaccaria segetalis*) **e.g. 'Pink Beauty'**

○

type of plant: HA
flowering season: summer
flower colour: rose-pink
height: 60-75 cm/2-2½ ft

The sprays of freely produced flowers borne by this plant have a delicacy which makes them useful for putting with other, more solidly shaped blooms in arrangements. Most well drained soils are suitable.
Chalk.

TULIPA (Lily-flowered) e.g. 'White Triumphator'
[form of Tulip]

○

type of plant: HBb
flowering season: mid-spring
flower colour: white
height: 60-75 cm/2-2½ ft

This elegantly slim-flowered tulip has long stems which make it an attractive variety both for cutting and for spring bedding displays. The length of the stems does mean, however, that this is not a plant for an exposed and windy site but, given some shelter and a well drained soil, *T.* 'White Triumphator' will grow strongly and bloom freely.
Chalk – Hot, dry soils.

ZINNIA elegans e.g. 'Dahlia-flowered Mixed'

○

type of plant: HHA
flowering season: midsummer to e. autumn
flower colour: mixed – red, pink, orange, purple, white
height: 60-75 cm/2-2½ ft

Most zinnias have fairly thick stems, but in tall forms with large, fully-double flowers – and the blooms of this particular variety may be up to 12 cm/5 in across – the stems can easily break in strong winds. In a sheltered site, however, plenty of long-lasting 'dahlias' will appear and remain undamaged, especially if there are no periods of heavy rain during the flowering season. The best plants are grown in warm positions and rich soils.

ASTER amellus e.g. 'King George'
[form of Michaelmas Daisy]

○

type of plant: HP
flowering season: l. summer to e. autumn
flower colour: violet
height: 60 cm/2 ft

The *novi-belgii* types of aster are much more popular than the *amellus* varieties, but in catalogues with a large 'hardy perennials' section the latter plants will be offered too. They tend to live longer and be much less prone to disease than the *novi-belgii* forms. They also have rather larger and often somewhat simpler flowers. *A. a.* 'King George' is a notably free-flowering variety. Most soils are suitable, especially if they retain some moisture during summer and early autumn.

ASTER amellus e.g. 'Sonia'
[form of Michaelmas Daisy]

○

type of plant: HP
flowering season: l. summer to e. autumn
flower colour: pink
height: 60 cm/2 ft

See preceding plant.

CALLISTEPHUS chinensis e.g. 'Duchesse
Mixed'
[form of China Aster]

○

type of plant: HHA
flowering season: autumn
flower colour: mixed – white, yellow, mauve,
red, blue, pink
height: 60 cm/2 ft

Although the common name would suggest
otherwise, the blooms of this late-flowering plant
are much more like chrysanthemums than asters,
and this is true of a number of other varieties of
C. chinensis. This particular strain is fairly resistant
to wilt disease, which can be a serious problem
with China asters. The dense flowers last well in
water. Their stems need support in the garden. A
fertile loam with good drainage is ideal for this
plant.

CATANANCHE caerulea
[species of Cupid's Dart]

○

type of plant: HP
flowering season: summer
flower colour: blue
height: 60 cm/2 ft
Dr

This is not a long-lived plant, even when supplied
with the light, rather dry soil it prefers, but its
flowers are excellent for cutting and, later, for
using in so-called 'everlasting' arrangements. In
windy gardens, some staking may be necessary.
   Chalk.

CENTAUREA moschata
[Sweet Sultan]

○

type of plant: HA
flowering season: summer to e. autumn
flower colour: mixed – yellow, white, purple,
rose
height: 60 cm/2 ft

The musk-scented flowers of the sweet sultan
should be picked when only partially open. Their
long, stiff stems make them easy to use in
arrangements. The larger flowered *C. imperialis,*
or giant sweet sultan, is also available from
seedsmen. Both plants thrive in well drained,
alkaline soils.
   Chalk – Fragrant flowers.

CHRYSANTHEMUM (Early-flowering:
pompon) e.g. 'Cameo'

○

type of plant: HHP
flowering season: l. summer to e. autumn
flower colour: white
height: 60 cm/2 ft

For those who like neatly shaped flowers for
arranging, the pompon chrysanthemums provide
plenty of long-lasting material with relatively little
trouble. Only the growing tips need be pinched
out; no stopping and disbudding is necessary. In
most districts, however, the plants must be lifted
and stored under cover during the winter months.
Fertile soil and a steady supply of moisture give
good results. The variety illustrated here has
flowers approximately 4-5 cm/1½-2 in wide.

CHRYSANTHEMUM carinatum (syn.
C. tricolor) **e.g. 'Double Mixed'**

○

type of plant: HA
flowering season: all summer
flower colour: mixed – red, pink, yellow, white,
mauve
height: 60 cm/2 ft

In well drained, preferably alkaline soil and a
sunny position this plant will produce a mass of
flowers suitable for cutting, especially if the
earliest buds have been removed. Varieties like
C. c. 'Monarch Court Jesters' (see p. 9) have
flowers which are much more prominently marked
than the blooms of this mixture.
   Chalk.

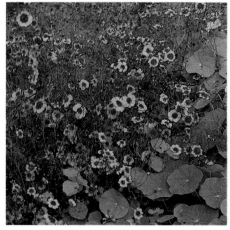

CLARKIA elegans e.g. 'Double Mixed'
○
type of plant: HA
flowering season: midsummer to e. autumn
flower colour: mixed – white, pink, scarlet,
  purple, orange
height: 60 cm/2 ft

As long as the soil is not heavy or badly drained, varieties of *C. elegans* will produce plenty of flowers. The blooms remain fresh for some considerable time in water. Individual stems should be cut soon after the lowest flower has opened. Early staking is essential.

COREOPSIS drummondii (syn. *Calliopsis*
drummondii)
[species of Tick-seed]
○
type of plant: HA
flowering season: summer to e. autumn
flower colour: yellow + crimson
height: 60 cm/2 ft

The various species and forms of *Coreopsis* grow well in the grimy air of cities and industrial areas. They also make good cut flowers, especially if picked in bud. *C. drummondii* needs staking, and it does best in a light soil and full sun. If dead-headed regularly, it will flower a second time in mid- or late autumn.
  Chalk.

DAHLIA (Cactus) e.g. 'Border Princess' sc NA
○
type of plant: HHTu
flowering season: l. summer to autumn
flower colour: salmon-orange
height: 60 cm/2 ft

The soft colouring of varieties like 'Border Princess' is a useful alternative to the fiery tones of many other dahlias. This particular form is unusually low-growing and it does not look out of place amongst other plants in a bed or border. It should be cultivated in the same way as *D.* 'Hit Parade' (see p. 213).

DELPHINIUM ajacis e.g. 'Giant
Hyacinth-flowered Mixed'
[form of Larkspur]
○
type of plant: HA
flowering season: summer
flower colour: mixed – blue, pink, white, violet
height: 60 cm/2 ft
Dr

Dwarf forms – approximately 45 cm/1½ in high – of this type of larkspur are available, but the taller varieties, such as the mixture illustrated here, are more useful for cutting. They all need a good, rich soil and protection from slugs and snails for the most satisfactory results. Tall varieties also need staking. All delphiniums need to be soaked in deep water, immediately after they have been picked, if they are to last well as cut flowers.

GLADIOLUS byzantinus
○
type of plant: HC
flowering season: e. summer
flower colour: magenta
height: 60 cm/2 ft

This daintily shaped, but strongly coloured species of gladiolus is hardier and much easier to grow than the commonly listed hybrids. In a light, fertile soil and full sun it will increase quite freely. Its long-lasting blooms and wiry stems make it a good cut flower.
  Chalk.

LIMONIUM latifolium (syn. *Statice latifolia*)
[species of Sea Lavender or Statice]
○
type of plant: HP
flowering season: midsummer to e. autumn
flower colour: lavender
height: 60 cm/2 ft
E/½E, Dr

All the popular sea lavenders have persistent parts to their flowers which look decorative when dried. This perennial species also has large, leathery leaves which are arranged in a ground-covering rosette. Any well drained soil will meet the needs of this plant.
  Ground-cover.

PAPAVER nudicaule e.g. 'Champagne Bubbles' ★
[form of Iceland Poppy]

○
type of plant: **HB**
flowering season: summer
flower colour: mixed– orange, yellow, red, white, bicolours
height: **60 cm/2 ft**
Dr

Beautiful though they are, the flowers of most poppies are not suitable for cutting. With some care, however, Iceland poppies can be made to last quite well in water. They should be picked in bud and the stem ends dipped in boiling water for about thirty seconds. A well drained soil suits these plants best, but they must not be allowed to dry out. The familiar, poppy seed-pods look attractive both when green and when dried.
  Chalk.

RUDBECKIA hirta e.g. 'Rustic Dwarfs'
[form of Black-eyed Susan]

○
type of plant: **HHA/HB**
flowering season: l. summer to mid-autumn
flower colour: mixed – shades of yellow, red-brown, bicolours
height: **60 cm/2 ft**

The large and strong-stemmed blooms of this late-flowering plant are of appropriately autumnal shades. They can last as long as a fortnight in water. Most garden soils are suitable and reasonable drainage is an advantage.

SALPIGLOSSIS sinuata e.g. 'Bolero'

○
type of plant: **HHA**
flowering season: midsummer to e. autumn
flower colour: mixed – yellow, red, pink, blue, orange, bicolours
height: **60 cm/2 ft**

Although picking and arranging the flowers of this plant can be a somewhat sticky business, the shapeliness and beautiful veining of the blooms make them most attractive for cutting. A rich, crumbly soil is needed, and *Salpiglossis* requires warmth and shelter too. Some staking is advisable.

TAGETES erecta e.g. 'Orange Jubilee'
[form of African Marigold]

○
type of plant: **HHA**
flowering season: midsummer to mid-autumn
flower colour: orange
height: **60 cm/2 ft**

The frilled globes of this plant are produced in large quantities and they are often at least 10 cm/4 in in diameter. African marigolds will tolerate poor, dry soils but, for the best results, a fairly fertile soil and a warm site are necessary. Some older varieties of *T. erecta* have unpleasantly scented leaves which make them unsuitable for picking. The flowers of all forms are, however, long-lasting.

TULIPA (Parrot) e.g. 'Fantasy'
[form of Tulip]

○
type of plant: **HBb**
flowering season: spring
flower colour: pink+green
height: **60 cm/2 ft**

The extravagantly fringed and feathered Parrot tulips are very popular with flower arrangers. In common with many other tulips of this type, the variety 'Fantasy' has large blooms; the green markings on the outer petals are also characteristic. Really good drainage is important, and the plants last longest if lifted each year and replanted in late autumn.
  Chalk – Hot, dry soils.

XERANTHEMUM annuum 'Mixed'
[form of Everlasting Flower or Immortelle]

○
type of plant: **HA**
flowering season: midsummer to mid-autumn
flower colour: mixed – white, red, pink, purple
height: **60 cm/2 ft**
mainly Dr

The flowers of this plant are quite small but they are very numerous. If they are cut just as they begin to open and then hung upside down in a dark and airy place, they provide pretty dried flowers for winter. A light, fertile soil is ideal, but this is not a difficult plant to grow in most soils.

GLADIOLUS (Miniature Hybrid) e.g. 'Pink Elf'

○

type of plant: HHC
flowering season: summer
flower colour: pink
height: 45-75 cm/1½-2½ ft

Miniature gladioli need to be grown in the same way as the larger flowered hybrids illustrated earlier in this list (for details, see p. 221). Each floret of the variety shown here is about 4-5 cm/1½-2 in wide. There are some green-flowered forms of miniature gladioli: an example, *G.* 'Greenbird', appears on p. 281.

**TRICHOLAENA rosea
[Ruby Grass]**

○

type of plant: HHA (Gr)
flowering season: summer
flower colour: reddish brown changing to
    purplish
height: 45-75 cm/1½-2½ ft
Dr

As grasses become more and more popular for cutting and drying, so it becomes easier to obtain individual species rather than 'choice' – but usually unspecified – mixtures. *T. rosea* is quite often listed as a separate item in seed catalogues. It will grow in most soils, but it prefers a light loam. It should be watered well in dry weather.

**AMARYLLIS belladonna★
[Belladonna Lily]**

○

type of plant: SlTBb
flowering season: l. summer to e. autumn
flower colour: pale pink
height: 45-60 cm/1½-2 ft

By the time the beautiful and sweetly scented flowers of this plant appear, the leaves have been and gone – having first emerged in winter. A really warm, sheltered position is needed both to ripen the bulbs and to protect the young foliage. Deep, fertile soil is also required, and it is important to water the plants freely in summer. The stems are stout and the flowers last well in water.

Fragrant flowers.

**ANAPHALIS yedoensis
[species of Pearly Everlasting]**

○

type of plant: HP
flowering season: l. summer to e. autumn
flower colour: white
height: 45-60 cm/1½-2 ft
Dr

This plant is less commonly grown than *A. triplinervis* (see p. 161), but its 'everlasting' flower heads are rather more conspicuous; it is also a taller and more erect plant. The best specimens of *A. yedoensis* are grown in well drained soils that remain moist during summer.

Chalk – Grey, etc. leaves.

**CALLISTEPHUS chinensis e.g. 'Bouquet
Powder-puffs Mixed'
[form of China Aster]**

○

type of plant: HHA
flowering season: midsummer to e. autumn
flower colour: mixed – pink, red, blue, purple,
    white
height: 45-60 cm/1½-2 ft

The Bouquet Powder-puffs strain of China asters is resistant to the wilt disease which so often attacks forms of *C. chinensis*. The centre of each large bloom is tightly packed with quilled petals, and the whole flower is less prone to damage from rain than the flowers of some other varieties of *Callistephus*. Well drained, fertile soil is needed and light staking should be provided. The photograph above shows a plant on which the flowers are just beginning to open fully.

CENTAUREA dealbata e.g. 'Steenbergii'

○

type of plant: HP
flowering season: summer
flower colour: deep rose
height: 45-60 cm/1½-2 ft

Particularly if its long-lasting flowers are wanted for cutting, it is safest to stake this plant. It is easily grown in any well drained soil, and it may become invasive in the dryish, alkaline conditions it prefers.

Chalk.

DIANTHUS barbatus e.g. 'Auricula-eyed'
[form of Sweet William]

○

type of plant: HB
flowering season: summer
flower colour: mixed – red, pink,
    white + contrasting zones
height: 45-60 cm/1½-2 ft

The conspicuous, white eyes of this plant are a
familiar sight in florists' shops, which indicates
how well the flowers last in water. There is a
clove-like scent to the blooms, but it is not very
pronounced. Shorter forms of sweet william, such
as *D. b.* 'Indian Carpet' (see p. 262), are available
and most seedsmens' catalogues list some separate
colours. All these plants should be given a well
drained, alkaline soil.

    Chalk – Fragrant flowers.

ERIGERON speciosus e.g. 'Darkest of All'
sc NA
[form of Fleabane]

○

type of plant: HP
flowering season: summer
flower colour: deep violet-blue
height: 45-60 cm/1½-2 ft

Both the varieties of fleabane shown here are very
free-flowering and easy to grow. A reasonably
steady supply of moisture ensures successful
results. The blooms remain fresh for a long time
once cut and placed in water.

ERIGERON speciosus e.g. 'Felicity' sc NA
[form of Fleabane]

○

type of plant: HP
flowering season: summer
flower colour: pink
height: 45-60 cm/1½-2 ft

See preceding plant.

IRIS (Dutch) e.g. 'Lemon Queen'

○

type of plant: SlTBb
flowering season: e. summer
flower colour: yellow
height: 45-60 cm/1½-2 ft

Among the somewhat similar English, Spanish
and Dutch irises, the last are the first to flower.
These plants prefer a light, fertile soil; in very cold
districts or rather heavy soil, the bulbs must be
lifted (in late summer), dried and then replanted in
early autumn. The flowers are slightly smaller than
those of the English irises; they last very well in
water. As well as the varieties illustrated here (see
the following page for *I.* 'Wedgwood') there are
forms with purple and with white or orange or
bronze flowers.

IRIS (English) e.g. 'Mixed Varieties'

○

type of plant: HBb
flowering season: midsummer
flower colour: blue, purple, pink, white
height: 45-60 cm/1½-2 ft

The so-called English, bulbous irises are hardier
and much more tolerant of heavy soils than the
Dutch irises, examples of which are also illustrated
here. Indeed, a moisture-retentive soil is essential
for good growth and English irises sometimes do
well in quite damp places. Their robust flowers are
excellent for cutting.

IRIS (Bearded Hybrid) e.g. 'Scintilla' sc NA

○

type of plant: HP
flowering season: l. spring
flower colour: ivory + beige
height: 45-60 cm/1½-2 ft

The ice cream and caramel sauce colours of this
plant look fresh and pretty in flower arrangements
and they stand out well in the garden too. A good,
light, alkaline soil is most suitable and, since this is
a tall intermediate iris, some shelter from strong
winds is necessary to prevent wind rock.

    Chalk.

IRIS (Dutch) e.g. 'Wedgwood'
○
type of plant: SlTBb
flowering season: e. summer
flower colour: light blue
height: 45-60 cm/1½-2 ft

See *I*. 'Lemon Queen', previous page.

NERINE bowdenii★
○
type of plant: SlTBb
flowering season: autumn
flower colour: pink
height: 45-60 cm/1½-2 ft

Distinctively curled and brightly coloured, the petals of this very nearly hardy plant stay fresh for a long time when the flowers have been picked and placed in water. The largest number of blooms appear when *N. bowdenii* is grown in sharply drained soil against a south-facing wall. The leaves die back, rather untidily, before the flowers open.

NIGELLA damascena e.g. 'Miss Jekyll'★
[form of Love-in-a-Mist]
○
type of plant: HA
flowering season: summer
flower colour: blue
height: 45-60 cm/1½-2 ft
Dr

After the beautiful, blue blooms have gone, this plant produces attractive seed-pods which are striped in red. The flowers, with their wispy, green appendages, are good for cutting, and the whole plant looks well in beds and borders because of its mass of very finely cut foliage. *N. d.* 'Miss Jekyll' has no special soil requirements.

Green foliage.

SCHIZOSTYLIS coccinea e.g. 'Mrs Hegarty'★
[Kaffir Lily]
○
type of plant: SlTP
flowering season: autumn
flower colour: pink
height: 45-60 cm/1½-2 ft

The Kaffir lilies, including this prettily coloured variety, are excellent, very long-lasting cut flowers. They like a moderately moist, fertile soil and a warm position. Under these conditions they usually increase quickly and need to be divided every few years.

Damp and wet soils.

AGROSTIS nebulosa
[Cloud Grass]
○
type of plant: HA (Gr)
flowering season: summer
flower colour: buff
height: 45 cm/1½ ft
Dr

A. nebulosa can be used, either fresh or dried, in much the same way as the annual and perennial gypsophilas are, to soften the outlines of more solidly shaped flowers. Most soils are suitable for growing this plant. It does well in rather sandy loams.

ALLIUM albopilosum (syn. *A. christophii*)
○
type of plant: HBb
flowering season: e. summer
flower colour: pale mauve
height: 45 cm/1½ ft
Dr

The globular blooms of this plant are often 25 cm/10 in in diameter. When fresh, each star-like flower shines. Even when dried, the whole round head keeps its shape well and some purplish colouring is retained in the stalks of the individual florets. This plant is easily grown in all fertile, well drained soils.

Chalk.

BRIZA maxima
[Pearl Grass]

○

type of plant: HA (Gr)
flowering season: l. spring to midsummer
flower colour: greenish
height: 45 cm/1½ ft
Dr

This plant is sometimes known as the large quaking grass, since its typically heart-shaped spikelets tremble whenever they are moved and they are about twice the size of the spikelets of *B. media* (see p. 236). Both plants will grow in any well drained soil; they thrive on chalk. They are easy to dry successfully.
    Chalk – Green flowers.

DIDISCUS caeruleus (syn. *Trachymene caerulea*)
[Blue Lace Flower]

○

type of plant: HHA
flowering season: midsummer to e. autumn
flower colour: lavender blue
height: 45 cm/1½ ft

A warm site and light soil are needed to grow this plant well outdoors. The flowers are good for cutting and they are carried on long, stiff stems but, since the overall habit of this plant is rather sparse, it often needs at least some support.

GYPSOPHILA elegans e.g. 'Covent Garden'

○

type of plant: HA
flowering season: l. spring to e. autumn
flower colour: white
height: 45 cm/1½ ft

There is a pink-flowered form of this plant (see p. 9) but the white varieties, such as the one illustrated here, are more popular. They are a common sight in florists' shops. Well drained, preferably alkaline soils are most suitable but, provided conditions are not wet, these are easily grown plants.
    Chalk – Hot, dry soils.

IXIA Hybrids
[forms of African Corn Lily]

○

type of plant: HHC
flowering season: e. summer
flower colour: white or yellow or red or blue or
    mixed
height: 45 cm/1½ ft

Warmth and sunshine are essential when growing these plants outdoors. Even in mild areas of Britain, a protective covering of leaves or sand is usually needed in winter, and the flowers must be in full sun to open properly. Only the yellow and white blooms are fragrant, but all the differently coloured flowers – with their thin and wiry stems – last very well in water.
    Chalk – Fragrant flowers.

LIMONIUM sinuatum (syn. *Statice sinuata*) **e.g.**
'Art Shades Mixed'
[form of Sea Lavender or Statice]

○

type of plant: HHA
flowering season: midsummer to e. autumn
flower colour: mixed – salmon, white, lavender,
    red, orange, pale pink, blue, yellow
height: 45 cm/1½ ft
Dr

Although the various forms of sea lavender are popular 'everlastings', some of the brighter colours of the fresh blooms fade a little when the flowers are dried. The variety *L. s.* 'Art Shades Mixed' contains an unusually high proportion of pale colours, while *L. s.* 'Market Growers' Blue' (see right) is an example of a more traditionally coloured form. The pink spikes of *L. suworowii* (see following page) are often over 30 cm/12 in long and, like the flower sprays of *L. sinuatum*, *(contd)*

LIMONIUM sinuatum (syn. *Statice sinuata*) **e.g.**
'Market Growers' Blue'
[form of Sea Lavender or Statice]

○

type of plant: HHA
flowering season: midsummer to e. autumn
flower colour: deep blue
height: 45 cm/1½ ft
Dr

See preceding plant.

(contd)
they are good for cutting and drying. Most well drained soils are suitable for these plants.

LIMONIUM suworowii (syn. *Statice suworowii*)
[species of Sea Lavender or Statice]

○

type of plant: HHA
flowering season: midsummer to e. autumn
flower colour: rose-pink
height: 45 cm/1½ ft
Dr

See *L. sinuatum* 'Art Shades Mixed', previous page.

SALVIA horminum e.g. 'Monarch Bouquet
Mixed'
[form of Clary]

○

type of plant: HA
flowering season: summer
flower colour: mixed – blue, pink, white
height: 45 cm/1½ ft
Dr

The flower colours given here for this mixture of *S. horminum* refer both to the tiny blooms and to the conspicuous, leaf-like bracts. The bracts retain their colour for several months when dried. Separate colours are available from most seedsmen. A light, rich soil is ideal for growing varieties of *S. horminum*.
    Chalk.

TAGETES erecta e.g. 'Gay Ladies'
[form of African Marigold]

○

type of plant: HHA
flowering season: midsummer to mid-autumn
flower colour: mixed – yellow, orange, gold
height: 45 cm/1½ ft

Like many of the modern African marigolds, this dwarf variety produces numerous large flowers on neat and uniform plants. It blooms a little earlier than other, similar forms. The flowers last well in water and, in contrast to some of the older varieties of *T. erecta*, the foliage does not smell offensive. Quite dry and poor conditions are suitable for this plant, but well drained, fertile soils produce better growth and larger blooms.

TULIPA (Rembrandt) e.g. 'May Blossom'
[form of Tulip]

○

type of plant: HBb
flowering season: l. spring
flower colour: cream + maroon
height: 45 cm/1½ ft

The unusual streaks of colour on the so-called Rembrandt tulips appeal to many flower arrangers, as do the elegant curves of lily-flowered varieties, such as *T.* 'Queen of Sheba', and the large, feathered blooms of Parrot tulips like *T.* 'Orange Favourite'. The flowers of this last plant are sweetly scented. All these tulips need really well drained soil and plenty of sun. They should be lifted in the summer and replanted towards the end of autumn if they are not to die out quickly.
    Chalk – Hot, dry soils – Fragrant flowers (*T.* 'Orange Favourite' only).

TULIPA (Parrot) e.g. 'Orange Favourite'
[form of Tulip]

○

type of plant: HBb
flowering season: spring
flower colour: orange-scarlet + green
height: 45 cm/1½ ft

See preceding plant.

TULIPA (Lily-flowered) e.g. 'Queen of Sheba'
[form of Tulip]

○

type of plant: HBb
flowering season: mid-spring
flower colour: orange-red + yellow
height: 45 cm/1½ ft

See *T.* 'May Blossom', second left.

CHEIRANTHUS cheiri e.g. 'Fire King' sc NA
[form of Wallflower]

○

type of plant: HB
flowering season: spring to e. summer
flower colour: orange-red
height: 40-45 cm/15–18 in
E

There are many varieties of *C. cheiri*; the commoner forms are available in shades of red, orange and yellow. *C. c.* 'Fire King' is of a particularly vivid colour. It has the characteristic warm fragrance of wallflowers, and it needs the usual well drained, alkaline soil to grow strongly. It makes an attractive cut flower.

Chalk – Hot, dry soils – Fragrant flowers.

GODETIA grandiflora e.g. 'Sybil Sherwood' ★
sc NA

○

type of plant: HA
flowering season: summer
flower colour: salmon pink
height: 40-45 cm/15-18 in

The beautifully and delicately coloured blooms of this bushy plant are usually produced in large numbers on any well drained and not too rich soil. Once the flowers have full expanded, they do not last very long, but this is a good plant for cutting since its numerous buds will open in water. Double and semi-double varieties, such as *G. g.* 'Azalea-flowered Mixed' (see p. 236), make even better cut flowers.

LAYIA elegans
[Tidy Tips]

○

type of plant: HA
flowering season: summer to e. autumn
flower colour: yellow + white
height: 40-45 cm/15-18 in

It is easy to overlook this plant in the pages and pages of more popular, but often more difficult annuals in seedsmen's catalogues. With minimum attention and in any reasonably well drained soil, *L. elegans* will bear plenty of very long-lasting flowers over its grey-green foliage. Each white-tipped 'daisy' is softly fragrant and quite large.

Grey, etc. leaves – Fragrant flowers.

CALLISTEPHUS chinensis e.g. 'Lilliput
Mixed'
[form of China Aster]

○

type of plant: HHA
flowering season: l. summer to e. autumn
flower colour: mixed – pink, red, mauve, white
height: 40 cm/15 in

Small though this variety of China aster is in comparison with, for instance, *C. c.* 'Duchesse Mixed' (see p. 227), it is still useful for cutting, since its flowers last well in water and they are not easily damaged by rain and wind. Fertile loams produce the best results, but the Lilliput strain of *Callistephus* usually blooms freely in well drained soils of most types.

CHRYSANTHEMUM (Early-flowering:
pompon) e.g. 'Denise' sc NA

○

type of plant: HHP
flowering season: l. summer to e. autumn
flower colour: yellow
height: 40 cm/15 in

The densely packed petals of pompon chrysanthemums remain fresh for a week or more in water. Varieties like 'Denise' and 'Fairie' (see here and right respectively) are also useful for growing amongst other plants, either in borders or in pots and tubs, since they are quite small overall and very floriferous. (See *C.* 'Tracy Waller', p. 214, for a brief outline of the cultivation of these plants.)

CHRYSANTHEMUM (Early-flowering:
pompon) e.g. 'Fairie' sc NA

○

type of plant: HHP
flowering season: l. summer to e. autumn
flower colour: pink
height: 40 cm/15 in

See preceding plant.

GODETIA grandiflora e.g. 'Azalea-flowered Mixed'

○

type of plant: HA
flowering season: summer
flower colour: mixed – pink, red, salmon, white
height: 40 cm/15 in

All the medium or tall varieties of *Godetia* make good cut flowers, but semi-double forms, such as the mixture shown here, last the longest in water. They are easy plants to grow, requiring only reasonably fertile soil. A very rich soil and wetness both produce unsatisfactory growth.

NARCISSUS (Poetaz) e.g. 'Geranium' [form of Daffodil]

○

type of plant: HBb
flowering season: mid-spring
flower colour: white + orange-red
height: 40 cm/15 in

This plant's clusters of broad-petalled flowers emit a fragrance which some people find rather too strong and sweet. However, even if it is not used for cutting, *N.* 'Geranium' makes an excellent garden plant, since it is vigorous and grows well in most soils.

Fragrant flowers.

ARCTOTIS × hybrida e.g. 'Large-flowered Hybrids' [form of African Daisy]

○

type of plant: HHA
flowering season: midsummer to e. autumn
flower colour: mixed – white, cream, yellow, orange, red
height: 30-45 cm/1-1½ ft

Full sun and really good drainage encourage these grey-leaved plants to flower freely for many weeks. Although the blooms are not particularly long-lasting in water, they have strong stems and they are usually available in large quantities. On overcast days and during the afternoon in summer, the flowers stay closed, but in autumn they remain open throughout the day.

Grey, etc. leaves.

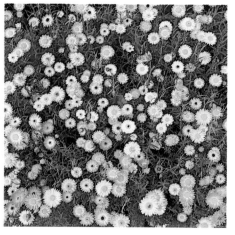

BRIZA media [Quaking Grass]

○

type of plant: HP (Gr)
flowering season: summer
flower colour: greenish
height: 30-45 cm/1-1½ ft
Dr

This sparsely leaved plant is quite common on the chalky grasslands of southern England. Its tiny, purple-tinged spikelets quiver at the slightest movement. They look pretty both in dried and in fresh arrangements. (See also *B. maxima*, p. 233.)

Chalk – Green flowers.

GOMPHRENA globosa 'Mixed' [form of Globe Amaranth]

○

type of plant: HHA
flowering season: midsummer to e. autumn
flower colour: mixed – purple, white, yellow, pink, orange
height: 30-45 cm/1-1½ ft
mainly Dr

Dwarf forms of globe amaranth (such as the purple-flowered *G. g.* 'Buddy') are often grown as pot plants and *Gomphrena* therefore appears in the greenhouse section of some seed catalogues. The flowers are long-lasting and carried on straight stems. They are easy to dry. Provided a warm site is available, most well drained soils will give good results.

HELIPTERUM roseum (syn. *Acroclinium roseum*) e.g. 'Large-flowered Mixed' [form of Everlasting Flower or Immortelle]

○

type of plant: H/HHA
flowering season: summer
flower colour: mixed – rose, pink, white
height: 30-45 cm/1-1½ ft
mainly Dr

Each long, thin stem of this plant carries a single flower which, if picked when only partly open, will dry well. Light soils – both fertile and poor – will produce plenty of flowers and fresh green leaves.

Chalk – Hot, dry soils.

LAGURUS ovatus★
[Hare's Tail Grass]

○

type of plant: HA (Gr)
flowering season: summer to e. autumn
flower colour: white
height: 30-45 cm/1-1½ ft
mainly Dr

Among the commonly available annual grasses, *L. ovatus* has distinctively dense and fluffy flower heads and these look just as decorative in the garden as in dried arrangements. The whole plant has an attractive, soft appearance since the leaves as well as the inflorescences are hairy. Most soils are suitable.

MUSCARI comosum 'Monstrosum' (syn. *M. c.* 'Plumosum')
[Feather Hyacinth, Tassel Hyacinth]

○

type of plant: HBb
flowering season: spring
flower colour: blue
height: 30-45 cm/1-1½ ft

Because the frizzy, tangled-headed flowers of this plant are sterile, they are very long-lasting. *M. c.* 'Monstrosum' is easy to grow in any well drained soil.
 Chalk.

PENNISETUM orientale

○

type of plant: HHA/SITP (Gr)
flowering season: midsummer to mid-autumn
flower colour: pinkish mauve or mauve-grey
height: 30-45 cm/1-1½ ft
Dr

Short-lived through this grass is in all but the warmest of areas, its attractive, hairy flower spikes and neatly radiating habit of growth make it well worth raising each year, if necessary. The flowers dry to a greyish, buff colour. A well drained soil increases the chances of this grass surviving a number of winters.

STOKESIA laevis (syn. *S. cyanea*)
[Stokes' Aster]

○

type of plant: HP
flowering season: midsummer to e. autumn
flower colour: blue or lilac
height: 30-45 cm/1-1½ ft
E/½E

Some gardeners would find this too pretty a plant outdoors to cut its flowers for use in the house. However, it blooms continously over many weeks and the 8 cm/3 in flowers stay fresh in water for a considerable time. It is easily grown in any well drained soil.

GAILLARDIA pulchella e.g. 'Lollipops'
[form of Blanket Flower]

○

type of plant: HHA
flowering season: midsummer to mid-autumn
flower colour: mixed – cream, yellow, crimson,
  bicolours
height: 30-40 cm/12-15 in

In a light, warm soil, this strain of blanket flower will produce many densely petalled, weather-resistant blooms which will last for about a week when cut and placed in water.
 Chalk – Hot, dry soils.

ZINNIA angustifolia (syn. *Z. haageana*, *Z. mexicana*) e.g. 'Persian Carpet'

○

type of plant: HHA
flowering season: summer
flower colour: mixed – yellow, orange, red,
  maroon, mahogany, bicolours
height: 30-40 cm/12-15 in

Although the popular forms of *Z. elegans* produce much bigger flowers than varieties of *Z. angustifolia*, they are not so free-flowering or so successful at withstanding damage from rain. In any case, some gardeners and flower arrangers will find the 2-5 cm/1-2 in blooms of cultivars like 'Persian Carpet' a positive attraction rather than a disadvantage. Ideally, these plants should be given a rich, well drained soil. They need plenty of water when they are growing fastest.

DIANTHUS × allwoodii e.g. 'Doris'★
[form of Pink]

○
type of plant: HP
flowering season: summer and e. autumn
flower colour: pink
height: 30 cm/1 ft
E

D. × a. 'Doris' is, perhaps, the most famous and certainly the most popular pink of its type. It is beautifully scented with shapely flowers on strong stems. It makes a good cut flower. Pinks of all sorts grow particularly well on chalky soils but, whether the conditions are alkaline or acid, good drainage and full sun are essential.

Chalk – Hot, dry soils – Grey, etc. leaves – Fragrant flowers.

HORDEUM jubatum
[Squirrel-tail Grass]

○
type of plant: HA (Gr)
flowering season: e. summer
flower colour: silvery grey changing to light brown
height: 30 cm/1 ft
Dr

The bristles which fan out elegantly from the inflorescences of this grass may be as much as 8 cm/3 in long. Most well drained soils are suitable, and *H. jubatum* will tolerate quite long periods of drought.

Hot, dry soils.

LYCHNIS viscaria (syn. *Viscaria vulgaris*)
'Splendens Plena'
[form of Catchfly]

○
type of plant: HP
flowering season: summer
flower colour: bright pink
height: 30 cm/1 ft

The sticky stems of this plant may not be pleasant to handle, but they are straight and strong and topped by vividly coloured, double flowers which last well when cut. *L. v.* 'Splendens Plena' will grow in any reasonably good garden soil.

RANUNCULUS asiaticus 'Mixed'

○
type of plant: HHTu
flowering season: l. spring to e. summer
flower colour: mixed – red, pink, orange, yellow, white
height: 30 cm/1 ft

The mixtures of *R. asiaticus* offered in most bulb catalogues produce variously coloured double or semi-double flowers which are excellent for cutting. In all but the very mildest areas, the tubers need lifting after the foliage dies; they should be replanted, in spring, in a warm site and rich, well drained soil.

TAGETES patula e.g. 'Naughty Marietta'
[form of French Marigold]

○
type of plant: HHA
flowering season: summer to mid-autumn
flower colour: golden yellow + maroon
height: 30 cm/1 ft

Most of the French marigolds are so low-growing that they are more useful for summer bedding than for cutting. However, a few varieties, including the form shown here, have relatively long stems. In general, these easily grown and bushy plants are very free-flowering and, if dead-headed regularly, they will bloom over many weeks. *T. p.* 'Naughty Marietta' has flowers which are unusually large for marigolds of this type; they are often well over 5 cm/2 in across.

NEMESIA strumosa e.g. 'Carnival Mixed'

○
type of plant: HHA
flowering season: summer
flower colour: mixed – bronze, red, pink, orange, yellow, white
height: 23-30 cm/9-12 in

The various forms of nemesia grow most successfully in light, rather acid soils that retain moisture throughout the summer. The bushiness and the bright and pretty colours of these annuals make them good bedding plants. In addition, their flowers last well in water. The Carnival strain produces exceptionally large blooms. For a further example of a variety of nemesia see the following page.

SPARAXIS tricolor 'Mixed'
[form of Harlequin Flower]

○

type of plant: HHBb
flowering season: l. spring to e. summer
flower colour: mixed– orange, yellow, red,
**   purple, white, with contrasting 'eyes'**
height: 23-30 cm/9-12 in

Unless they can be given a warm and sheltered site and a light, rich soil, these plants will not grow satisfactorily outdoors. Under the right conditions, however, they will provide long-lasting cut flowers in quite sizeable quantities – and for a considerable number of years, if the bulbs are lifted in late summer and replanted towards the end of autumn.

NEMESIA strumosa e.g. 'Blue Gem'

○

type of plant: HHA
flowering season: summer
flower colour: blue
height: 23 cm/9 in

See *N. s.* 'Carnival Mixed', previous page.

Additional plants with flowers suitable for cutting that are featured elsewhere in this book

○ sun

PRUNUS subhirtella 'Autumnalis': 6-7.5 m (p. 274)
ACACIA dealbata: 4.5-7.5 m (p. 253)
MAGNOLIA grandiflora 'Exmouth' ★: 4.5-7.5 m (p. 253)
ROSA (Climber) e.g. 'New Dawn': 4.5-6 m (p. 120)
ROSA (Rambler) e.g. 'Albertine': 4.5 m (p. 120)
HALESIA carolina: 3.6-5.4 m (p. 29)
COBAEA scandens: 3-6 m (p. 120)
LATHYRUS latifolius: 2.4-3 m (p. 121)
ROSA (Rambler) e.g. 'Albertine': 2.1 m (p. 120)
EREMURUS robustus: 2.1-3 m (p. 3)
LATHYRUS odoratus e.g. 'Leamington' ★: 1.8-3 m (p. 255)
LATHYRUS odoratus e.g. 'Noel Sutton': 1.8-3 m (p. 255)
LATHYRUS odoratus e.g. 'White Ensign': 1.8-3 m (p. 133)
LATHYRUS odoratus e.g. 'Winston Churchill': 1.8-3 m (p. 121)
ESCALLONIA e.g. 'Donard Radiance': 1.8-2.4 m (p. 125)
ESCALLONIA e.g. 'Apple Blossom': 1.8 m (p. 86)
ONOPORDUM acanthium: 1.5-1.8 m (p. 158)
ROSA (Rugosa Hybrid) e.g. 'Blanc Double de Coubert': 1.2-1.8 m (p. 129)
ROSA (Hybrid Tea) e.g. 'Peace' ★: 1.2-1.8 m (p. 92)
ROSA (Rugosa) e.g. 'Roseraie de l'Hay': 1.2-1.8 m (p. 256)
ROSA (Hybrid Tea) e.g. 'Wendy Cussons': 1.2-1.5 m (p. 256)
ROSA (Hybrid Tea) e.g. 'Prima Ballerina': 1.05-1.35 m (p. 256)
ASTER novae-angliae e.g. 'September Ruby': 1.05-1.2 m (p. 46)
CLEMATIS recta: 90-120 cm (p. 257)
ECHINOPS ritro ★: 90-120 cm (p. 4)
ERYNGIUM giganteum: 90-120 cm (p. 158)
EUPHORBIA wulfenii: 90-120 cm (p. 158)
HELICTOTRICHON sempervirens: 90-120 cm (p. 159)
IRIS (Bearded Hybrid) e.g. 'Dancer's Veil': 90-105 cm (p. 4)
IRIS (Bearded Hybrid) e.g. 'Frost and Flame': 90-105 cm (p. 4)
IRIS (Bearded Hybrid) e.g. 'Olympic Torch': 90-105 cm (p. 5)
KNIPHOFIA e.g. 'Maid of Orleans': 90-105 cm (p. 5)
HELENIUM autumnale e.g. 'Butterpat': 90 cm (p. 47)
HELENIUM autumnale e.g. 'Coppelia': 90 cm (p. 47)
HELENIUM autumnale e.g. 'Moerheim Beauty': 90 cm (p. 47)
PHYGELIUS capensis: 90 cm (p. 58)
STIPA calamagrostis: 90 cm (p. 58)
GLADIOLUS (Butterfly Hybrid) e.g. 'Green Woodpecker': 75-105 cm (p. 280)
ROSA (Floribunda) e.g. 'Elizabeth of Glamis' ★: 75-105 cm (p. 257)
ROSA (Hybrid Tea) e.g. 'Fragrant Cloud': 75-105 cm (p. 258)
ACHILLEA 'Coronation Gold': 75-90 cm (p. 58)
AMARANTHUS caudatus 'Viridis': 75-90 cm (p. 280)
COSMOS sulphureus e.g. 'Sunset': 75-90 cm (p. 58)
PHLOX maculata e.g. 'Alpha': 75-90 cm (p. 258)
ACHILLEA millefolium 'Cerise Queen': 75 cm (p. 6)
ANTHEMIS tinctoria e.g. 'Grallagh Gold': 75 cm (p. 6)
ANTHEMIS tinctoria e.g. 'Wargrave Variety': 75 cm (p. 6)
ERYNGIUM tripartitum: 75 cm (p. 58)
SCABIOSA caucasica e.g. 'Clive Greaves': 75 cm (p. 6)
DIANTHUS (Border Carnation) e.g. 'Salmon Clove': 60-90 cm (p. 258)
ASTER novi-belgii e.g. 'Carnival': 60-75 cm (p. 47)
CHRYSANTHEMUM rubellum e.g. 'Clara Curtis': 60-75 cm (p. 258)

TULIPA (Viridiflora) e.g. 'Greenland' ★: 60-75 cm (p. 281)
ACHILLEA 'Moonshine' ★: 60 cm (p. 159)
ERICA×darleyensis e.g. 'Arthur Johnson' ★: 60 cm (p. 100)
HELIANTHUS annuus e.g. 'Dwarf Sungold': 60 cm (p. 7)
INULA hookeri: 60 cm (p. 47)
LATHYRUS latifolius: 60 cm (p. 121)
MOLUCCELA laevis: 60 cm (p. 281)
TULIPA (Cottage) e.g. 'Dillenburg': 60 cm (p. 8)
ZINNIA elegans e.g. 'Envy': 60 cm (p. 281)
ERYNGIUM alpinum: 45-75 cm (p. 8)
GLADIOLUS (Miniature Hybrid) e.g. 'Greenbird': 45-75 cm (p. 281)
LYCHNIS coronaria: 45-75 cm (p. 159)
LYCHNIS coronaria 'Alba': 45-75 cm (p. 159)
CALLUNA vulgaris e.g. 'H. E. Beale': 45-60 cm (p. 100)
CENTAUREA dealbata e.g. 'John Coutts': 45-60 cm (p. 8)
COREOPSIS verticillata: 45-60 cm (p. 9)
NIGELLA damascena e.g. 'Persian Jewels': 45-60 cm (p. 181)
SCHIZOSTYLIS coccinea: 45-60 cm (p. 69)
SEDUM× 'Autumn Joy' ★: 45-60 cm (p. 9)
SEDUM maximum 'Atropurpureum': 45-60 cm (p. 170)
CALLUNA vulgaris e.g. 'Peter Sparkes': 45 cm (p. 30)
CHEIRANTHUS cheiri e.g. 'Blood Red': 45 cm (p. 9)
CHEIRANTHUS cheiri e.g. 'Cloth of Gold': 45 cm (p. 259)
CHRYSANTHEMUM carinatum e.g. 'Monarch Court Jesters': 45 cm (p. 9)
ERICA vagans e.g. 'Lyonesse': 45 cm (p. 30)
ERICA vagans e.g. 'Mrs D. F. Maxwell': 45 cm (p. 100)
GYPSOPHILA elegans e.g. 'Rosea': 45 cm (p. 9)
SALVIA horminum e.g. 'Blue Bouquet': 45 cm (p. 170)
SCABIOSA atropurpurea e.g. 'Dwarf Double Mixed': 45 cm (p. 10)
ANAPHALIS triplinervis ★: 30-45 cm (p. 161)
ASTER novi-belgii e.g. 'Audrey': 30-45 cm (p. 47)
HELIPTERUM manglesii: 30-45 cm (p. 60)
IRIS graminea: 30-45 cm (p. 260)
IRIS (Spanish) e.g. 'King of Blues' ★: 30-45 cm (p. 260)
LATHYRUS odoratus e.g. 'Bijou Mixed': 30-45 cm (p. 260)
NARCISSUS (Jonquil) e.g. 'Trevithian': 30-45 cm (p. 260)
ASTER novi-belgii e.g. 'Snowsprite': 30 cm (p. 70)
CENTAUREA cyanus e.g. 'Jubilee Gem': 30 cm (p. 11)
DIANTHUS×allwoodii e.g. 'Robin': 30 cm (p. 12)
DIANTHUS plumarius e.g. 'Mrs Sinkins': 30 cm (p. 261)
HELICHRYSUM bracteatum e.g. 'Hot Bikini': 30 cm (p. 12)
IRIS (Bearded Hybrid) e.g. 'Green Spot': 30 cm (p. 282)
IRIS unguicularis ★: 30 cm (p. 275)
LYCHNIS×haageana: 30 cm (p. 13)
RESEDA odorata e.g. 'Red Monarch': 30 cm (p. 261)
VERBENA×hybrida grandiflora e.g. 'Royal Bouquet': 30 cm (p. 261)
FREESIA 'Outdoor Hybrids Mixed': 25-40 cm (p. 261)
IRIS (Bearded Hybrid) e.g. 'Carilla': 25-40 cm (p. 13)
DIANTHUS chinensis e.g. 'Heddewigii Double Mixed': 23-30 cm (p. 14)
RESEDA odorata e.g. 'Machet': 23-30 cm (p. 262)
IBERIS umbellata e.g. 'Dwarf Fairy Mixed': 23 cm (p. 15)
ARMERIA maritima 'Vindictive': 15-23 cm (p. 102)

SYRINGA vulgaris e.g. 'Madame Lemoine'★
[form of Common Lilac]
○[◐]
type of plant: HSh
flowering season: l. spring
flower colour: white
height: 3-4.5 m/10-15 ft

Most lilacs with pure white flowers are popular for
cutting, but the variety 'Madame Lemoine' is a
favourite because of its particularly large and
dense panicles of attractively scented, double
blooms. It is a tough, rather broad, but upright
shrub which grows well in fertile soils; it thrives on
chalk. A sunny site should be chosen if plenty of
flowers are wanted. The double-flowered lilacs
make good tub plants when they are trained as
standards with clear stems.
    Chalk – Atmospheric pollution – Containers
(*grown as a standard, 1.8-2.4 m/6-8 ft*) – Fragrant
flowers.

ARTEMISIA lactiflora
[White Mugwort]
○[◐]
type of plant: HP
flowering season: l. summer to mid-autumn
flower colour: creamy white
height: 1.2-1.5 m/4-5 ft

This sturdy plant requires a rich, moist soil. Its
plumes of tiny flowers and its deeply indented
leaves are pleasantly scented. The former are
suitable for cutting when they are fully developed.
    Aromatic leaves – Fragrant flowers.

PHLOX paniculata 'Sir John Falstaff' NA
○[◐]
type of plant: HP
flowering season: summer to e. autumn
flower colour: salmon pink, with deeper eye
height: 1.2 m/4 ft

This is a long-blooming cultivar with unusually
large florets. If the terminal clusters of faded
flowers are removed, a second, lesser flowering
will take place in the leaf axils. Mildew can be
controlled with a systemic fungicide.

PHLOX carolina 'Miss Lingard' NA
○[◐]
type of plant: HP
flowering season: e. summer
flower colour: white
height: 1.05 m/3½ ft

This is an old cultivar with glossy, lance-shaped
leaves and trusses of clear white flowers which
come out several weeks before those of summer
phlox (*P. paniculata*). Moist but well drained soil
rich in organic matter gives the best results.

LYCHNIS chalcedonica
[Maltese Cross, Jerusalem Cross]
○[◐]
type of plant: HP
flowering season: summer
flower colour: scarlet
height: 90 cm/3 ft

As vividly coloured as most plants of its genus,
L. chalcedonica bears its fiery red flowers in
distinctively dense and flat heads which can
measure as much as 12 cm/5 in across. It grows
most strongly in slightly damp, fertile soils.

RUDBECKIA 'Goldquelle'
[form of Coneflower]
○ [◐]
type of plant: HP
flowering season: l. summer to mid-autumn
flower colour: chrome yellow
height: 75-90 cm/2½-3 ft

The single-flowered and the double-flowered forms of *Rudbeckia* are excellent for cutting. The double-flowered varieties, which include *R*. 'Goldquelle', tend to last longest in water. They should all be given a fairly moist and substantial soil for preference, but any fertile soil will do.
  Clay.

SOLIDAGO×hybrida e.g. 'Goldenmosa'
[form of Golden Rod]
○ [◐]
type of plant: HP
flowering season: l. summer to e. autumn
flower colour: golden yellow
height: 75-90 cm/2½-3 ft
Dr

The whole of this plant has a yellowish cast to it, since both the flowers and the flower stalks are yellow and the foliage is a light, warm green. Heavy, moisture-retentive soils are, perhaps, most suitable, but this is not a fussy plant. The pretty flower plumes can be air-dried as well as used fresh.
  Clay.

CAMPANULA persicifolia e.g. 'Telham Beauty'★
[form of Peach-leaved Bellflower]
○ [◐]
type of plant: HP
flowering season: summer
flower colour: blue
height: 60-90 cm/2-3 ft
E

Among all the lovely campanulas the peach-leaved varieties – including the exceptionally large-flowered form illustrated here – are outstanding. They are in bloom for many weeks (particularly if they are regularly dead-headed) and the flowers, on their thin, wiry stems, last well when cut. These plants should be given a fertile soil with good drainage.

LILIUMב×'Enchantment'
[form of Lily]
○ [◐]
type of plant: HBb
flowering season: e. summer
flower colour: orange-red
height: 60-90 cm/2-3 ft

L.×'Enchantment' is one of the easiest lilies to grow. It is so healthy and vigorous that, in most well drained and reasonably fertile soils, it will increase quite rapidly and produce a good supply of attractive cut flowers. It may also be used for naturalizing.

MORINA longifolia
○ [◐]
type of plant: SITP
flowering season: summer
flower colour: white changing to crimson
height: 60-90 cm/2-3 ft
mainly Dr

Some gardeners will find the long, fragrant, basal leaves of this plant more attractive than the smallish flowers, but when the latter have faded, the stems are set – at decreasing intervals – with clusters of soft green 'cups', which look interesting and decorative when dried. A deep, well drained soil and a sheltered site are advisable.
  Green foliage – Aromatic leaves.

CROCOSMIA×crocosmiiflora (syn. *Montbretia crocosmiiflora*) e.g. 'Jackanapes'★
[form of Common Montbretia]
○ [◐]
type of plant: SIT/HC
flowering season: l. summer to e. autumn
flower colour: orange-red + yellow
height: 60-75 cm/2-2½ ft
Dr

The colour combination in this plant's flowers may be a bit too eye-catching in certain situations, but more softly coloured varieties, such as *C.*×*c.* 'Citronella' (see p. 105), are also available. Whatever their colouring, however, these plants are first-rate as cut flowers and, in the warm and rather moist conditions which suit them best, their stiff leaves will be dense enough to give good ground-cover.
  Ground-cover.

CAMASSIA quamash (syn. *C. esculenta*)
[Common Quamash]
○ [◐]
type of plant: HBb
flowering season: summer
flower colour: blue or white
height: 45-75 cm/1½-2½ ft

A heavy, moisture-retentive soil is needed to
support this very large-bulbed plant. There is
some confusion in trade catalogues over the
naming of plants in the genus *Camassia* and, as a
further complication, *C. quamash* varies
considerably in the colour of flowers it produces.
However, plants offered under either of the
botanical names given above are good both for
cutting and for naturalizing. Unfortunately, they
normally die down and leave an awkward gap in
beds and borders at the end of the summer.
  Clay.

HEUCHERA sanguinea e.g. 'Red Spangles'
[form of Coral Bells]
○ [◐]
type of plant: HP
flowering season: l. spring to midsummer
flower colour: crimson
height: 45-60 cm/1½-2 ft
E, Dr

The various forms of *H. sanguinea* are useful as
well as pretty perennials. Provided they are
planted deeply in well drained soil and divided
every few years, their dark, evergreen leaves cover
the ground densely and they produce plenty of
attractive flowers. These last well when cut and
they are also suitable for drying. Most heucheras
have red or pink flowers, but white and green
varieties are available too.
  Ground-cover.

**MATTHIOLA incana (Ten Week) e.g. 'Column
Mixed'**
[form of Stock]
○ [◐]
type of plant: HHA
flowering season: summer
flower colour: mixed – pink, red, blue, white
height: 45-60 cm/1½-2 ft

All the readily available forms of Ten Week stocks
can be used for cutting, but the Column strain is
particularly suitable, since it produces single stems
– of a practical length – which are closely set with
flowers. *M. i.* 'Giant Perfection Mixed' (see below)
has a branching habit and very large blooms; it too
is a good cut flower. Both these plants are best
when grown in a rich, light soil. They have the
warm and full fragrance characteristic of
summer-flowering stocks.
  Fragrant flowers.

**MATTHIOLA incana (Ten Week) e.g. 'Giant
Perfection Mixed'**
[form of Stock]
○ [◐]
type of plant: HHA
flowering season: summer
flower colour: mixed – pink, red, mauve, white
height: 45-60 cm/1½-2 ft

See preceding plant.

**PHLOX drummondii e.g. 'Large-flowered
Mixed'**
○ [◐]
type of plant: HHA
flowering season: midsummer to e. autumn
**flower colour: mixed – violet, pink, red, white,
  lavender**
height: 30 cm/1 ft

As the flowers of this plant fade, they become
rather unpleasantly scented but, when fresh, they
are quite inoffensive. The mass of buds opens over
a fairly long period in water. A well drained, but
moisture-retentive and fertile soil is most suitable.

ANEMONE coronaria e.g. 'De Caen Mixed'
[form of Poppy Anemone]
○ [◐]
type of plant: SlTTu
flowering season: spring
**flower colour: mixed – red, pink, blue, mauve,
  white**
height: 15-30 cm/6-12 in

Tight bunches of these jewel-coloured flowers can
be seen in most florists' shops in winter and early
spring. The less prolific, double-flowered 'St
Brigid' strain (illustrated on the following page) is
not often grown for sale. Both varieties need a
warm site and a rich, light and well cultivated soil
to perform satisfactorily. They are not long-lived
plants.

ANEMONE coronaria e.g. 'St Brigid Mixed'
[form of Poppy Anemone]

○ [◑]
type of plant: SlTTu
flowering season: spring
flower colour: mixed – red, pink, blue, mauve, white
height: 15-30 cm/6-12 in

See preceding plant.

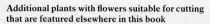

Additional plants with flowers suitable for cutting that are featured elsewhere in this book

○ [◑] sun (or partial shade)
SYRINGA×josiflexa 'Bellicent': 3.6-4.5 m (p. 21)
SYRINGA vulgaris e.g. 'Katherine Havemeyer': 3-4.5 m (p. 264)
SYRINGA vulgaris e.g. 'Primrose': 3-4.5 m (p. 22)
SYRINGA vulgaris e.g. 'Souvenir de Louis Spaeth': 3-4.5 m (p. 93)
PHILADELPHUS e.g. 'Virginal': 2.4-3 m (p. 93)
PHILADELPHUS coronarius: 1.8-3 m (p. 66)
SYRINGA microphylla 'Superba': 1.8-2.4 m (p. 264)
PHILADELPHUS e.g. 'Beauclerk'★: 1.5-2.1 m (p. 265)
ASPHODELINE lutea: 90 cm (p. 265)
IRIS sibirica e.g. 'Perry's Blue': 90 cm (p. 70)
IRIS sibirica e.g. 'White Swirl': 90 cm (p. 71)
ZANTEDESCHIA aethiopica 'Crowborough': 75-90 cm (p. 71)
RUDBECKIA fulgida e.g. 'Goldsturm': 75 cm (p. 49)
SOLIDAGO×hybrida e.g. 'Lemore': 75 cm (p. 49)
CAMASSIA cusickii: 60-90 cm (p. 49)
CROCOSMIA×crocosmiiflora e.g. 'Citronella': 60-75 cm (p. 105)
HEUCHERA sanguinea e.g. 'Scintillation': 60 cm (p. 105)
BUPHTHALMUM salicifolium: 45-60 cm (p. 49)
FILIPENDULA hexapetala 'Flore Pleno': 45-60 cm (p. 23)
MATTHIOLA incana (Ten Week) e.g. 'Beauty Mixed': 45 cm (p. 265)
MATTHIOLA incana (Brompton) e.g. 'Double Brompton Mixed': 40-45 cm (p. 265)
MATTHIOLA incana (East Lothian) e.g. 'East Lothian Mixed': 30-40 cm (p. 266)
SOLIDAGO×hybrida e.g. 'Golden Thumb': 30 cm (p. 49)
APONOGETON distachyus: 8-10 cm (p. 266)

HYDRANGEA paniculata 'Grandiflora'

○ ◑
type of plant: HSh
flowering season: l. summer to e. autumn
flower colour: white changing to pink
height: 1.8-3 m/6-10 ft
mainly Dr

With hard pruning each spring, and in a rich, loamy soil, the flower heads of this arching shrub can be over 30 cm/1 ft long. They maintain their shape well when dried and they can also be used in arrangements of fresh flowers.

KERRIA japonica 'Pleniflora' (syn. *K. j.* 'Flore Pleno')
[form of Jew's Mallow]

○ ◑
type of plant: HSh
flowering season: spring
flower colour: orange-yellow
height: 1.8-3 m/6-10 ft

In almost any soil and site, this erect and suckering shrub will produce plenty of long-lasting, double blooms on numerous, bright green stems. The flowers of the species – *K. japonica* (see p. 96) – are single and less suitable for cutting, but some gardeners prefer their simplicity to the conspicuous fluffiness of *K. j.* 'Pleniflora''s blossom.

Atmospheric pollution – Bark and *twigs*.

CHOISYA ternata★
[Mexican Orange Blossom]

○ ◑
type of plant: SlTSh
flowering season: mainly spring
flower colour: white
height: 1.8-2.4 m/6-8 ft
E

The sweetly fragrant flowers and the shiny, sharply aromatic leaves of this rounded shrub look well in arrangements. The foliage lasts an exceptionally long time when cut. In a really warm and sheltered site and on well drained soil, *C. ternata* will thrive in partial shade. In cold gardens, however, it must be given a sunny position.

Containers – Green foliage – Aromatic leaves – Fragrant flowers.

THALICTRUM dipterocarpum★
[species of Meadow Rue]

○ ◑
type of plant: HP
flowering season: summer
flower colour: rosy lilac
height: 1.2-1.8 m/4-6 ft

The flower heads of this graceful plant are held well clear of the lovely, ferny foliage and this means that they should be either sheltered from wind or given some support. They are good for cutting and are largest and most impressive in a moist but well drained soil that is also fertile.

Green foliage.

CHAENOMELES (syn. *Cydonia*)×superba e.g.
'Knap Hill Scarlet'
[form of Flowering Quince]

○ ◐

type of plant: HSh
flowering season: spring
flower colour: orange-scarlet
height: 1.2-1.5 m/4-5 ft

Although a sunny position will produce the
greatest number of flowers on this bushy plant, it
will bloom freely almost anywhere and in a wide
variety of soils (extreme alkalinity is, however,
best avoided). When grown against a wall, it will
exceed the maximum height given here and
flowering may begin in late winter. The blooms
should be cut when only partially open if they are
to be used in flower arrangements. The golden
yellow fruits are fragrant and edible.

Clay – Atmospheric pollution – Fruit.

ROSA (Floribunda) e.g. 'Iceberg' ★
[form of Rose]

○ ◐

type of plant: HSh
flowering season: summer to mid-autumn
flower colour: white
height: 1.2-1.5 m/4-5 ft

This famous rose is vigorous and free-flowering.
Its very slightly fragrant blooms are of an
unusually pure white. They are excellent for
cutting. In any reasonable soil this rose grows
strongly. Its upright shape makes it suitable for
hedging.

Atmospheric pollution – Hedging.

LILIUM×'Harlequin Hybrids'
[forms of Lily]

○ ◐

type of plant: HBb
flowering season: midsummer
flower colour: mixed – pink, lilac, rose, red,
purple, white, yellow
height: 1.2 m/4 ft

The strains of lilies shown in this and the following
photograph are particularly good as cut flowers.
They are also vigorous and less prone to virus
diseases than some other lilies. The Harlequin
hybrids have slightly wider flowers (about
10 cm/4 in across) than those produced by the
Citronella strain, but there are usually fewer of
them to each stem. These plants need excellent
drainage.

LILIUM×'Citronella Strain'
[form of Lily]

○ ◐

type of plant: HBb
flowering season: midsummer
flower colour: yellow+black
height: 90-120 cm/3-4 ft

See preceding plant.

LUPINUS Hybrid e.g. 'My Castle'
[form of Lupin or Lupine]

○ ◐

type of plant: HP
flowering season: l. spring to e. summer
flower colour: brick red
height: 90-105 cm/3-3½ ft

None of the large-flowered lupins are especially
long-lasting, either in the garden or when cut and
placed in water. However, they are popular plants
– with British gardeners in particular. Mixtures of
the Russell hybrids (see p. 35) are very readily
available, but flower arrangers may find varieties
in separate colours, such as the form illustrated
here, more useful. All lupins need a well drained
and an acid or neutral soil.

Acid soils.

LILIUM×'Mid-Century Hybrids'
[forms of Lily]

○ ◐

type of plant: HBb
flowering season: e. summer
flower colour: mixed– shades of yellow, orange,
red
height: 90 cm/3 ft

Most bulb catalogues will list both a mixture of
these hybrids and separate, named forms
(including *L.*×'Enchantment', see p. 241). These
plants are not difficult to grow, as long as they are
given good drainage. Their blooms last well when
cut.

PHLOX paniculata e.g. 'Prince of Orange'

○ ◑

type of plant: HP
flowering season: midsummer to e. autumn
flower colour: salmon-orange
height: 90 cm/3 ft

Magnificent through their trusses of flowers are, varieties of *P. paniculata* with red or orange blooms – like both the strong-growing forms shown here – have little or no scent. Some modern white-flowered cultivars, such as *P. p.* 'Mother of Pearl' (see p. 269) are, however, fragrant and there are a few, scented purple or mauve varieties. A moisture-retentive, fertile soil with reasonable drainage is most suitable for these plants. They all last quite well in water.

PHLOX paniculata e.g. 'Starfire'

○ ◑

type of plant: HP
flowering season: midsummer to e. autumn
flower colour: deep red
height: 90 cm/3 ft

See preceding plant.

AQUILEGIA e.g. 'McKana Hybrids' ★
[forms of Columbine]

○ ◑

type of plant: HP
flowering season: e. summer
flower colour: mixed – red, blue, white, cream, yellow, pink, mostly bicolours
height: 75-90 cm/2½-3 ft

The only drawback to these beautiful plants and other long-spurred columbines is that they are short-lived. However, they are easily grown in any moist, well drained soil; they thrive when provided with plenty of leaf-mould or peat. The long, wiry stems need no support and they help to make these plants excellent as cut flowers. The light green, fern-like foliage is also quite attractive.

PHLOX paniculata e.g. 'Hampton Court'

○ ◑

type of plant: HP
flowering season: midsummer to e. autumn
flower colour: rosy violet
height: 75-90 cm/2½-3 ft

A few of the varieties of *P. paniculata* have interesting foliage as well as decorative flowers. The leaves of *P. p.* 'Hampton Court', for example, are exceptionally dark and they set off the bluish flowers most satisfactorily. There are also forms with cream-variegated leaves, of which the best is the purple-flowered *P. p.* 'Harlequin'. The need for moisture in the soil is particularly important in the case of these cultivars, since relatively few leaves will be produced on dry soils. The flowers of *P. p.* 'Hampton Court' are suitable for cutting, but those of the variety 'Harlequin' are less attractive than the variegated foliage.

Green foliage.

PHYSOSTEGIA virginiana e.g. 'Summer Snow'
[form of Obedient Plant]

○ ◑

type of plant: HP
flowering season: midsummer to e. autumn
flower colour: white
height: 75-90 cm/2½-3 ft

The individual blooms of this plant can be pushed from side to side on their hinged stalks and they will stay in the position they have been moved to – hence the common name. They last well in water. Growth is best in soils that retain moisture during the summer months. For details of a smaller, pink-flowered form of *P. virginiana*, see p. 248.

PAEONIA lactiflora (syn. *P. albiflora*) e.g. 'Karl Rosenfeld'
[form of Peony/Paeony]

○ ◑

type of plant: HP
flowering season: e. summer
flower colour: wine red
height: 75 cm/2½ ft

All the sumptuous, double-flowered paeonies are popular for cutting. They are also splendid, long-lived garden plants with handsome foliage. In spring, the leaves of most varieties emerge from the earth a red-brown colour. *P. l.* 'Karl Rosenfeld' is one of the commoner, dark-flowered forms; specialist growers will list many more examples. A well dug, fertile soil is needed to produce good plants.

Green foliage.

TROLLIUS × cultorum e.g. 'Orange Princess'
[form of Globe Flower]

○ ◑

type of plant: HP
flowering season: l. spring to e. summer
flower colour: orange
height: 75 cm/2½ ft

Ideally, this plant should be grown in boggy
ground or near water, but it will do well in any
moisture-retentive soil. The lovely, fat flowers are
excellent for cutting, and the fingered leaves make
a good, ground-covering clump.
  Damp and wet soils – Ground-cover.

CAMPANULA glomerata 'Superba'
[form of Bellflower]

○ ◑

type of plant: HP
flowering season: summer
flower colour: violet blue
height: 60-90 cm/2-3 ft

The 'superb' feature of this plant is the strikingly
deep colour of its rounded flower heads. These last
well when cut and they are borne on good, straight
stems. *C. g.* 'Superba' will grow strongly – and
spread quite rapidly sometimes – in fertile, well
drained soils that retain moisture easily.

NICOTIANA alata (syn. *N. affinis*) e.g.
'Sensation Mixed'
[form of Tobacco Plant]

○ ◑

type of plant: HHA
flowering season: summer to e. autumn
flower colour: mixed – crimson, pink, purple,
  white, yellow
height: 60-75 cm/2-2½ ft

Many flower arrangers are particularly fond of
N. a. 'Lime Green' (see p. 282) but the mixture
shown here is also useful for cutting. Whether it is
grown in sun or light shade, its blooms remain
open throughout the day. Its sweet fragrance is,
however, most pronounced in the evening. It
should be given a warm position and a rich,
moisture-retentive soil with good drainage.
  Fragrant flowers.

PAEONIA officinalis e.g. 'Alba Plena'
[form of Peony/Paeony]

○ ◑

type of plant: HP
flowering season: l. spring to e. summer
flower colour: white
height: 60-75 cm/2-2½ ft

The cultivars of *P. officinalis* illustrated in this and
the following two photographs show the colour
range of these appealingly old-fashioned plants. Of
the three, *P. o.* 'Rubra Plena' is the most popular
variety. The brightness of the blooms of *P. o.*
'Rosea Plena' tends to fade with age; *P. o.* 'Alba
Plena's' flowers are often tinged with pink on first
opening. All these plants have attractive leaves
which remain fresh-looking long after the flowers
have past. Well cultivated, fertile soils give good
results. The 10-12 cm/4-5 in wide blooms are
excellent for cutting.
  Green foliage.

PAEONIA officinalis e.g. 'Rosea Plena'
[form of Peony/Paeony]

○ ◑

type of plant: HP
flowering season: l. spring to e. summer
flower colour: pink
height: 60-75 cm/2-2½ ft

See preceding plant.

PAEONIA officinalis e.g. 'Rubra Plena'
[form of Peony/Paeony]

○ ◑

type of plant: HP
flowering season: l. spring to e. summer
flower colour: deep crimson
height: 60-75 cm/2-2½ ft

See *P. o.* 'Alba Plena', second left.

AQUILEGIA 'Crimson Star'
[form of Columbine]

○ ◐

type of plant: HP
flowering season: l. spring to e. summer
flower colour: red + white
height: 60 cm/2 ft

Most of the long-spurred forms of columbine are available as mixtures, but a few separately coloured forms, like *A.* 'Crimson Star', are also listed. They are all short-lived, but easily grown plants for moisture-retentive soils with good drainage. They make most attractive cut flowers.

CALENDULA officinalis e.g. 'Geisha Girl'
[form of Pot Marigold]

○ ◐

type of plant: HA
flowering season: summer to e. autumn
flower colour: orange
height: 60 cm/2 ft

Pot marigolds are some of the easiest of all plants to grow. Even polluted air and poor soils do little to deter their performance. When grown for cutting, however, they should be given a reasonably fertile and well drained soil. The blooms of this particular variety have distinctively incurved petals; they last well in water, especially if they have been picked when only half open. Pot marigolds are also available as mixtures and in shades of yellow and cream.

CHELONE obliqua
[species of Turtle-head]

○ ◐

type of plant: HP
flowering season: l. summer to e. autumn
flower colour: rose-pink
height: 60 cm/2 ft

The rigid, upright stems of this plant usually need no staking. For the flowers to last well in water, almost all the large, dark green leaves should be removed. A light, rich loam suits this plant best.

PAEONIA mlokosewitschii★
[species of Peony/Paeony]

○ ◐

type of plant: HP
flowering season: mid-spring
flower colour: yellow
height: 60 cm/2 ft

Although this plant has a fairly short flowering season and the petals of its blooms drop quickly if it is in too warm a position (either indoors or outdoors), it has several features which make it desirable. Apart from its lovely, simple flowers, there are its handsome leaves – pinkish at first, then softly grey-green and, finally, orange and yellow in many autumns. In autumn too, there are eye-catching, red and blue seed-pods. This is a long-lived plant which should be provided with a deep, fertile and well dug soil from the start.

Grey, etc. leaves – Autumn foliage – Fruit.

RANUNCULUS acris 'Flore-Pleno'
[Yellow Bachelor's Buttons]

○ ◐

type of plant: HP
flowering season: l. spring to e. summer
flower colour: yellow
height: 60 cm/2 ft

The shiny little 'buttons' of this plant are densely petalled and long-lasting. Most soils are suitable, including those that are quite damp and heavy.

CALENDULA officinalis e.g. 'Art Shades'
[form of Pot Marigold]

○ ◐

type of plant: HA
flowering season: summer to e. autumn
flower colour: mixed – pale yellow, apricot, cream, orange
height: 45-60 cm/1½ ft

The unusually pale colours of this particular strain of pot marigold appeal to those flower arrangers who find the bright oranges and strong yellows of varieties like 'Radio' and 'Golden King' too strong. If cut when only partially open, these flowers last well in water. Pot marigolds are very easy to grow in any soil, though they do have a preference for good drainage.

CYNOGLOSSUM amabile
[species of Hound's Tongue]

○ ◑

type of plant: HB/A
flowering season: summer
flower colour: blue
height: 45-60 cm/1½-2 ft

When grown in the light and fertile soils that suit it best, this plant will often seed itself freely. If wanted for cutting, a fairly sunny position should be chosen, and any dead blooms should be removed quickly to ensure a long flowering season. The foliage of this plant is greyish green and it has a rough texture.

Grey, etc. leaves.

GEUM chiloense e.g. 'Lady Stratheden'
[form of Avens]

○ ◑

type of plant: HP
flowering season: summer to e. autumn
flower colour: yellow
height: 45-60 cm/1½-2 ft
E

In most sites, vigorous young plants of the two varieties of geum shown in this and the following photograph will produce enough foliage to support their long, branching flower stems. The bright blooms appear in large quantities and over a long period, provided that division of the plants is carried out every other year. A fertile, moisture-retentive soil gives the best results.

GEUM chiloense e.g. 'Mrs Bradshaw'
[form of Avens]

○ ◑

type of plant: HP
flowering season: summer to e. autumn
flower colour: scarlet
height: 45-60 cm/1½-2 ft
E

See preceding plant.

NICOTIANA × sanderae e.g. 'Crimson Bedder'
[form of Tobacco Plant]

○ ◑

type of plant: HHA
flowering season: summer to e. autumn
flower colour: red
height: 45-60 cm/1½-2 ft

Unlike *N. alata* (see p. 268) and most of its varieties, the flowers of this plant have practically no scent. They are, however, richly coloured, and they have the elegant, tubular shape characteristic of the blooms of tobacco plants. *N. × sanderae* and its varieties need warmth and a rich, moist soil to do well.

PHYSOSTEGIA virginiana e.g. 'Vivid'
[form of Obedient Plant]

○ ◑

type of plant: HP
flowering season: l. summer to mid-autumn
flower colour: deep pink
height: 45-60 cm/1½-2 ft

The flowers of this variety of obedient plant may be compliant (in so far as each little bloom will stay in whatever position it has been turned to) but the roots are occasionally less biddable. With a constant supply of moisture and a fertile soil, *P. v.* 'Vivid' can spread quite rapidly. These conditions will also ensure, however, that numerous flowers are produced for cutting.

NARCISSUS (Small-cupped) e.g. 'Barrett Browning'
[form of Daffodil]

○ ◑

type of plant: HBb
flowering season: mid-spring
flower colour: white + orange-red
height: 45 cm/1½ ft

All but the smallest daffodils make good cut flowers but, among all the varieties listed by specialist bulb growers, some have particularly attractive features for arrangements indoors. The small-cupped forms, for example (including the free-flowering 'Barrett Browning', illustrated here, and the richly coloured 'Chungking' – see the following page), have a neatness and delicacy which the large-cupped varieties often lack. However, the flower size and the vigour of cultivars like 'Carlton' and 'Sempre Avanti' (see next page) make them good dual-purpose *(contd)*

NARCISSUS (Large-cupped) e.g. 'Carlton'
[form of Daffodil]

○ ◑
type of plant: HBb
flowering season: e. spring
flower colour: yellow
height: 45 cm/1½ ft

See preceding plant.

(contd)
plants, since they are excellent for cutting and will
also naturalize well in grass. (The blooms of N.
'Sempre Avanti' are particularly long-lasting.)
Some gardeners may not consider white daffodils
and those with double flowers 'proper' daffodils at
all, but varieties like the magnificent 'Mount
Hood' (second right), the fluffy-flowered
'Cheerfulness' (right) and 'Mary Copeland' (the
following page) are popular with flower (contd)

NARCISSUS (Double) e.g. 'Cheerfulness'
[form of Daffodil]

○ ◑
type of plant: HBb
flowering season: l. spring
flower colour: white + cream
height: 45 cm/1½ ft

See N. 'Barrett Browning', previous page.

(contd)
arrangers. These varieties are also good garden
plants, and 'Cheerfulness' is sweetly scented.
When grown for cut flowers, daffodils need a well
dug, fertile soil and they should be lifted and
divided every few years. Applying a liquid
fertilizer to the leaves after flowering can be of
particular benefit in feeding these plants.
    Fragrant flowers (N. 'Cheerfulness' only).

NARCISSUS (Trumpet) e.g. 'Mount Hood'
[form of Daffodil]

○ ◑
type of plant: HBb
flowering season: mid-spring
flower colour: white
height: 45 cm/1½ ft

See N. 'Barrett Browning', previous page.

NARCISSUS (Large-cupped) e.g. 'Sempre
Avanti'
[form of Daffodil]

○ ◑
type of plant: HBb
flowering season: mid-spring
flower colour: cream + orange
height: 45 cm/1½ ft

See N. 'Barrett Browning', previous page.

DORONICUM e.g. 'Spring Beauty'
[form of Leopard's Bane]

○ ◑
type of plant: HP
flowering season: mid-spring to e. summer
flower colour: deep yellow
height: 40-45 cm/15-18 in

If D. 'Spring Beauty' is grown in a very sunny
position, its double flowers may fade to quite a pale
shade of yellow. However, the plant itself will
thrive in sunshine, provided that the soil is fairly
substantial and retains moisture easily. Both
single- and double-flowered varieties of leopard's
bane last well when cut. For an example of a
single-flowered variety, see p. 51.
    Clay.

NARCISSUS (Small-cupped) e.g. 'Chungking'
[form of Daffodil]

○ ◑
type of plant: HBb
flowering season: e. spring
flower colour: yellow + red
height: 40 cm/15 in

See N. 'Barrett Browning', previous page.

NARCISSUS (Double) e.g. 'Mary Copeland'
[form of Daffodil]

○ ◑

type of plant: **HBb**
flowering season: **mid-spring**
flower colour: **white + orange**
height: **40 cm/15 in**

See *N.* 'Barrett Browning', previous page.

NARCISSUS (Triandrus) e.g. 'Silver Chimes'★
[form of Daffodil]

○ ◑

type of plant: **HBb**
flowering season: **mid-spring**
flower colour: **cream + pale yellow**
height: **40 cm/15 in**

Each of this daffodil's strong stems usually carries at least four beautifully shaped blooms which are excellent for cutting and which emit a slight fragrance. General remarks about the cultivation of daffodils for cut flowers appear beneath *N.* 'Cheerfulness' (see previous page).

CALENDULA officinalis e.g. 'Fiesta Gitana'
[form of Pot Marigold]

○ ◑

type of plant: **HA**
flowering season: **summer to e. autumn**
flower colour: **mixed – creamy yellow, gold, orange**
height: **30 cm/1 ft**

This variety of calendula is exceptionally small, but its firm flower stalks are still long enough to make it useful for cutting. It is also popular for bedding displays where its low, spreading shape looks neat and tidy. All pot marigolds are very easy to grow. They will perform quite well in poor soils, but more fertile conditions result in a greater number of blooms.

Additional plants with flowers suitable for cutting that are featured elsewhere in this book

○ ◑ sun or partial shade

MAGNOLIA × soulangiana: 6-7.5 m (p. 33)
MAGNOLIA × soulangiana e.g. 'Alexandrina': 6-7.5 m (p. 95)
MAGNOLIA × soulangiana e.g. 'Lennei': 6-7.5 m (p. 95)
ROSA (Climber) e.g. 'Danse du Feu': 3.6 m (p. 123)
CAMELLIA reticulata e.g. 'Captain Rawes'★: 3-4.5 m (p. 34)
CORNUS mas: 3-4.5 m (p. 276)
GARRYA elliptica★: 2.4-4.5 m (p. 282)
HAMAMELIS mollis: 2.4-3.6 m (p. 276)
FORSYTHIA × intermedia 'Lynwood': 2.4-3 m (p. 24)
FORSYTHIA × intermedia 'Spectabilis': 2.4-3 m (p. 96)
FORSYTHIA suspensa: 2.4-3 m (p. 50)
JASMINUM nudiflorum: 2.4-3 m (p. 277)
VIBURNUM tinus: 1.8-3 m (p. 277)
RIBES sanguineum e.g. 'Pulborough Scarlet': 1.8-2.7 m (p. 80)
RIBES sanguineum e.g. 'King Edward VII': 1.5-2.1 m (p. 96)
CHAENOMELES speciosa e.g. 'Nivalis': 1.2-1.8 m (p. 96)
KERRIA japonica: 1.2-1.8 m (p. 96)
CHAENOMELES × superba e.g. 'Rowallane': 1.2-1.5 m (p. 130)
ASTILBE taquetii 'Superba': 1.2 m (p. 106)
ACANTHUS spinosus★: 90-120 cm (p. 184)
LUPINUS e.g. 'Russell Hybrids Mixed': 90-120 cm (p. 35)
LUPINUS Hybrid e.g. 'The Governor': 90-105 cm (p. 35)
PAEONIA lactiflora e.g. 'Festiva Maxima': 90 cm (p. 268)
PAEONIA lactiflora e.g. 'Sarah Bernhardt'★: 90 cm (p. 268)

THALICTRUM aquilegifolium: 90 cm (p. 166)
LYSIMACHIA clethroides: 75-90 cm (p. 51)
NICOTIANA alata: 75-90 cm (p. 268)
PAEONIA lactiflora 'White Wings': 75-90 cm (p. 193)
PHLOX paniculata e.g. 'Mother of Pearl': 75-90 cm (p. 269)
DORONICUM plantagineum e.g. 'Excelsum': 75 cm (p. 51)
TROLLIUS ledbouri 'Golden Queen': 75 cm (p. 74)
CHAENOMELES speciosa e.g. 'Simonii': 60-90 cm (p. 52)
DIGITALIS grandiflora: 60-90 cm (p. 52)
MONARDA didyma e.g. 'Cambridge Scarlet': 60-90 cm (p. 199)
MONARDA didyma e.g. 'Croftway Pink': 60-90 cm (p. 52)
NICOTIANA alata e.g. 'Lime Green'★: 60-75 cm (p. 275)
TROLLIUS europaeus 'Superbus'★: 60-75 cm (p. 75)
JASMINUM nudiflorum: 60 cm (p. 277)
LUPINUS Hybrid e.g. 'Dwarf Lulu': 60 cm (p. 35)
EUPHORBIA robbiae: 45-60 cm (p. 81)
LEUCOJUM aestivum 'Gravetye'★: 45-60 cm (p. 75)
RANUNCULUS aconitifolius 'Flore Pleno': 45-60 cm (p. 75)
ALCHEMILLA mollis★: 45 cm (p. 108)
EUPHORBIA polychroma: 45 cm (p. 108)
NARCISSUS (Poeticus) e.g. 'Old Pheasant Eye': 40 cm (p. 269)
NICOTIANA alata e.g. 'Dwarf White Bedder': 30-45 cm (p. 269)
NARCISSUS (Cyclamineus) e.g. 'February Gold'★: 30 cm (p. 277)
GALANTHUS elwesii: 15-25 cm (p. 277)
GALANTHUS nivalis: 10-20 cm (p. 278)
VIOLA odorata e.g. 'Princess of Wales': 15 cm (p. 270)

LILIUM 'Bellingham Hybrids'★
[forms of Lily]

◐ [○]
type of plant: HBb
flowering season: midsummer
flower colour: mixed – yellow, orange,
   red + brown
height: 1.5-2.1 m/5-7 ft

Given a lightly shaded position and a moist, leaf-mouldy soil the vigorous Bellingham hybrids are amongst the easiest of all lilies to grow well. Some named forms of these hybrids will be listed in the catalogues of specialist bulb nurseries. The very strong-growing variety 'Shuksan', which has pale orange, brown-spotted blooms, is particularly popular. All lilies of the Bellingham strain make very long-lasting cut flowers.
   Acid soils.

ASTRANTIA maxima (syn. *A. helleborifolia*)
[species of Masterwort]

◐ [○]
type of plant: HP
flowering season: summer
flower colour: pink
height: 60 cm/2 ft

Unless this plant is grown in a soil that is at least reasonably moisture-retentive, and this is particularly important if a sunny site is chosen, its lobed leaves will not form a really dense, ground-covering clump. Nor will its branching heads of long-lasting, 'collared' flowers be produced in large quantities. When growing well, however, this is a most attractive plant.
   Ground-cover.

DICENTRA spectabilis
[Bleeding Heart]

◐ [○]
type of plant: HP
flowering season: l. spring to e. summer
flower colour: pink + white
height: 45-75 cm/1½-2½ ft

The elegance and prettiness of this plant – with its arching stems and strings of heart-shaped buds – make it attractive both to gardeners and to flower arrangers. To complement its distinctive blooms, it has handsome, grey-green foliage which, unfortunately, dies down in midsummer. Ideally, *D. spectabilis* should be grown in deep, cool, well drained soil to which moisture-retaining substances, such as peat and leaf-mould, have been added if necessary.
   Grey, etc. leaves.

ANTHERICUM liliago
[St Bernard's Lily]

◐ [○]
type of plant: HP
flowering season: e. summer
flower colour: white
height: 45-60 cm/1½-2 ft

This plant's grassy leaves grow thickly enough to suppress most weeds, but it is for its slim spikes of cool white flowers, rather than its foliage, that *A. liliago* is usually grown. Most soils are suitable, as long as they do not dry out in warm weather.
   Ground-cover.

×HEUCHERELLA 'Bridget Bloom'★

◐ [○]
type of plant: HP
flowering season: l. spring to e. summer
flower colour: pink
height: 45 cm/1½ft
E

Although the attractive brown markings on the young leaves of this plant soon fade, the mature foliage makes good ground-cover throughout the year. The main flowering season is noted above but, quite often, more blooms appear as autumn approaches. ×*H.* 'Bridget Bloom' will flower freely in light soils. Its flower spikes are good for cutting.
   Ground-cover – Variegated leaves.

DIGITALIS purpurea e.g. **'Excelsior Strain'**
[form of Foxglove]

◐
type of plant: HB/P
flowering season: summer
flower colour: mixed – purple, pink, yellow,
   white, cream
height: 1.5 m/5 ft
Dr

This particular strain of foxglove is easier to deal with in flower arrangements than some other types, because the blooms surround the stems and do not hang from one side alone. *D. p.* 'Foxy' (see p. 54) is somewhat similar to the Excelsior foxgloves, but it is much smaller. All these plants grow well on clay, since they appreciate moisture, but the Excelsior hybrids will be perennials only if they have moisture *and* good drainage.
   Clay.

POLYGONATUM×**hybridum (syn.**
P. multiflorum)★
[Solomon's Seal, David's Harp]

◐ ●
type of plant: HP
flowering season: l. spring to e. summer
flower colour: white + green
height: 75-90 cm/2½-3 ft

Beautiful and accommodating, this plant will grow
anywhere there is sufficient shade. It will thrive
and increase slowly in cool, peaty soil, where its
arching stems will form quite dense thickets. The
largish leaves and the small, hanging flowers are
attractive individually and they make a most
graceful combination indoors and outdoors.

Chalk – Clay – Dry shade – Dense shade –
Ground-cover – Green foliage.

**Additional plants with flowers suitable for cutting
that are featured elsewhere in this book**

◐ [○] partial shade (or sun)
CAMELLIA japonica e.g. 'Adolphe Audusson'★:
    1.8-3.6 m (p. 36)
LILIUM speciosum rubrum: 1.5 m (p. 37)
HYDRANGEA macrophylla (Hortensia) e.g.
    'Altona': 1.2-1.8 m (p. 37)
HYDRANGEA macrophylla (Hortensia) e.g.
    'Générale Vicomtesse de Vibraye': 1.2-1.8 m
    (p. 98)
HYDRANGEA macrophylla (Hortensia) e.g.
    'Madame E. Moullière': 1.2-1.8 m (p. 137)
CAMPANULA latifolia e.g. 'Alba': 1.05-1.2 m
    (p. 26)
FILIPENDULA purpurea: 90-120 cm (p. 77)
MAHONIA aquifolium: 90-120 cm (p. 112)
SKIMMIA japonica 'Rubella': 60-90 cm (p. 39)
ASTILBE×arendsii e.g. 'Fanal': 60 cm (p. 184)
ASTILBE×arendsii e.g. 'Rheinland'★: 60 cm
    (p. 113)
ASTILBE×arendsii e.g. 'White Gloria': 60 cm
    (p. 78)
ASTRANTIA major: 60 cm (p. 283)
MERTENSIA virginica: 30-60 cm (p. 40)
PRIMULA vulgaris elatior e.g. 'Giant Bouquet':
    23-30 cm (p. 40)
PRIMULA vulgaris elatior e.g. 'Pacific Strain':
    23-30 cm (p. 40)
CONVALLARIA majalis: 15-23 cm (p. 272)

◐ partial shade
ENKIANTHUS campanulatus: 2.4-3.6 m (p. 194)
PIERIS formosa forrestii: 1.8-3 m (p. 42)
PIERIS 'Forest Flame': 1.8-2.4 m (p. 173)
PIERIS japonica 'Variegata': 1.8-2.4 m (p. 142)
CIMICIFUGA racemosa: 1.2-1.5 m (p. 185)
DIGITALIS purpurea e.g. 'Foxy': 75-90 cm (p. 54)
MILIUM effusum 'Aureum': 60-90 cm (p. 177)
ASPERULA orientalis: 23-30 cm (p. 273)

◐ ● partial or full shade
HELLEBORUS lividus corsicus: 60 cm (p. 283)
BRUNNERA macrophylla: 45 cm (p. 116)
HELLEBORUS niger★: 30-45 cm (p. 279)
EPIMEDIUM grandiflorum 'Rose Queen':
    20-30 cm (p. 117)
EPIMEDIUM×youngianum 'Niveum': 15-23 cm
    (p. 187)

Plants with fragrant flowers

The first reaction of many people, after looking briefly at an unfamiliar flower, is to smell it – and to express some disappointment if it has no scent. Among familiar flowers, those that are sweetly scented enjoy a special popularity. The names alone of well loved plants like lily of the valley, honeysuckle and lilac evoke memories of distinctive and delicious fragrances.

Although the following list includes plants that spring readily to mind when fragrant flowers are considered, there are others that, though attractively scented, are less easily remembered. Some of these plants that are overlooked have had so much attention paid to the form or colour of their flowers, that any fragrance which they might have tends to be disregarded. Very few descriptions of modern varieties of petunia refer to the scent emitted by most of the blue and purple flowered forms. In the same way, the sweet fragrance of the popular Gleam strain of nasturtiums is hardly ever mentioned.

Certainly, the attractive scent of some species is either absent or much less noticeable in many of their cultivated varieties. The most popular varieties of *Scabiosa atropurpurea* (sweet scabious or pincushion flower), for example, are so slightly scented that they have not been included in this list. However, the species itself, and some of its much less commonly offered varieties, such as 'King of the Blacks', have a marked fragrance.

Perhaps the absence of fragrance in many cultivated varieties of sweetly scented species accounts for the quite erroneous view that modern roses, and particularly hybrid teas and floribundas, have no scent. This list can only include a few examples of recently introduced roses which are fragrant, but the catalogue of a specialist rose nursery will provide many more names.

This list does not include some plants, such as the oval-leaved privet and its varieties, the scent of which most people find cloying and unpleasant. Plants with flowers which are generally regarded as only slightly scented have also been excluded. Many of the most popular flowering crabs, such as *Malus* 'Profusion', and the modern varieties of antirrhinum or snapdragon, for example, have fragrances which are only barely perceptible to most people.

The attractiveness of a flower's fragrance is, however, a highly personal matter. *Lilium auratum* (golden-rayed lily; gold-band lily in the United States) is included in this list, but it is one of a number of plants with a fragrance about which opinions are sharply divided: most people find this lily's penetrating scent very attractive, but there are others who find it offensive.

The strength, as well as the quality, of a fragrance can also be very differently perceived. Some people notice fragrances in plants that are usually considered odourless. However, there is the complicating factor that, in certain cases, very similar plants – some scented and others unscented – may be being confused.

If a species or genus and its varieties are grown mainly for the fragrance of their flowers, only the most strongly scented examples are included in this list. It can be distinctly disappointing to grow a variety of hyacinth or sweet pea, for example, and find that it is only slightly scented. Unfortunately, some of the most fragrant varieties of certain plants are not very readily available. For example, the single-flowered varieties of *Cheiranthus cheiri* (wallflower) are attractively scented, but the double forms, such as 'Harpur Crewe', are even more fragrant. While every sizeable seed catalogue has plenty of examples of single-flowered wallflowers, the choice of double-flowered wallflowers is much more limited. (The variety 'Harpur Crewe' is sterile and therefore has to be propagated from cuttings; it is available from certain nurseries dealing mainly in perennial plants.)

When choosing strongly scented flowers for cutting, it is worth bearing in mind that the scent of these plants will probably be intensified in a confined space. Certain popular, strongly scented flowers, such as the Old Pheasant Eye narcissus, make good cut flowers, but they smell so overpoweringly strong to a few people that their effect is nauseating, and particularly so indoors.

WISTERIA sinensis (syn. *W. chinensis*) 'Alba'★ [form of Chinese Wisteria]

○

type of plant: HCl
flowering season: l. spring to e. summer
flower colour: white
height: 18-30 m/60-100 ft

As dramatic in its flower form as *W. sinensis* itself (see p. 119), *W. s.* 'Alba' is even more strongly and sweetly scented. Like the species, it requires the same ample supply of moisture and shelter from late frosts. It should be pruned in summer and in winter to produce the best results.

Clay – Climbers – Containers (*grown as a standard, 90-150 cm/3-5 ft high*).

ACACIA dealbata (syn. *A. decurrens dealbata*) MC [Mimosa, Silver Wattle]

○

type of plant: HHSh
flowering season: e. spring
flower colour: yellow
height: 4.5-7.5 m/15-25 ft
*E

Where the necessary warmth and shelter can be provided, *A. dealbata* grows fairly quickly into a spreading shrub. In the warmest areas it becomes a tree. The sweet fragrance of the flowers in earliest spring is, perhaps, the main attraction of this plant, but the feathery, grey-green foliage is a source of additional, delicate beauty throughout the year.

Acid soils – Grey, etc. leaves – Cutting.

MAGNOLIA grandiflora 'Exmouth'★ sc NA MC

○

type of plant: SlTSh/T
flowering season: summer to e. autumn
flower colour: creamy white
height: 4.5-7.5 m/15-25 ft
E

The sumptuous, sculptural flowers of this magnolia may be as much as 20 cm/8 in wide. They are deliciously lemon-scented and are produced on even quite young plants. The leathery foliage is backed with a rust-coloured felt. In Britain, this plant is usually grown against a wall. Unlike many magnolias, it will tolerate some lime. Many cultivars have been named in California and the southern United States, and two of the most widely grown are 'St Mary' and 'Samuel Sommer'.

Acid soils – Atmospheric pollution – Green foliage – Cutting.

BUDDLEIA alternifolia
○
type of plant: HSh/T
flowering season: e. summer
flower colour: lilac
height: 3.6-5.4 m/12-18 ft

Even when this quick-growing shrub is not covered in strings of almond-scented flowers, its arching growth makes it interesting, particularly if it has been trained as a standard tree. This plant can, however, become ungainly and messy unless plenty of old wood is removed after flowering. It is less tolerant of shallow, chalky soils than the cultivars of the familiar *B. davidii* or butterfly bush.

AZARA microphylla MC
○
type of plant: SlTSh
flowering season: spring
flower colour: yellow
height: 3.6-4.5 m/12-15 ft
E

Except in the very warmest of British gardens, this gracefully branched shrub must be grown against a wall. In all cases, it needs a well drained soil. The flowers are small and not very conspicuously displayed amongst the fans of glossy leaves, but they have a strong, vanilla-like fragrance.
    Green foliage.

CYTISUS battandieri★
[species of Broom]
○
type of plant: SlTSh
flowering season: summer
flower colour: yellow
height: 3-4.5 m/10-15 ft

The freely produced blossom of this upright and quick-growing plant emits the sweet fragrance of ripe pineapples. The attractive leaves are large and silvery. Neither very acid nor very alkaline soils suit this shrub, but it grows well in dry and even poor soils. The protection of a wall is desirable in most districts and essential in colder areas.
    Hot, dry soils – Grey, etc. leaves.

BUDDLEIA globosa MC
[Orange Ball Tree]
○
type of plant: SlTSh
flowering season: l. spring to e. summer
flower colour: orange-yellow
height: 2.4-3.6 m/8-12 ft
½E

While some gardeners may find the vivid pompons of this erect shrub rather too reminiscent of a certain type of Christmas decoration, the sweet scent of the flowers is certainly an attraction. *B. globosa* may be grown in alkaline soils but very thin, dry soils should be avoided.

ROSA (Climber) e.g. 'Golden Showers'
[form of Rose]
○
type of plant: HCl
flowering season: summer to mid-autumn
flower colour: yellow
height: 2.4 m/8 ft

A susceptibility to black spot mars this otherwise excellent climbing rose. The flowers are large (often 10 cm/4 in wide) and fragrant, and they are produced continuously over a long period. *R.* 'Golden Showers' is particularly suitable for growing over pillars, pergolas and fences.
    Climbers.

VIBURNUM × burkwoodii
○
type of plant: HSh
flowering season: spring
flower colour: pink changing to white
height: 2.4 m/8 ft
E

Although this wide-spreading plant will grow well in a little shade, it is usually given a warm, sunny position to induce early flowering. Against a south-facing wall it may begin to flower in late winter and it will exceed the height given here. In more exposed positions it may be as little as 1.2 m/4 ft high. When its pink-budded flowers open they exude a fragrance as full and sweet as that of its parent *V. carlesii* (see p. 268). All moisture-retentive soils are suitable.
    Clay.

CARPENTARIA californica MC

○

type of plant: SlTSh
flowering season: summer
flower colour: white
height: 1.8-3 m/6-10 ft
E

This bushy plant is prone to some winter damage (mainly of a superficial nature) which leaves it looking rather unsightly, at least for a short period. In suitably sheltered sites – against south-facing walls, for instance – the beautiful, anemone-like flowers, with their sweet fragrance, usually compensate for any drabness during the colder months of the year.

LATHYRUS odoratus e.g. 'Leamington' ★
sc NA
[form of Sweet Pea]

○

type of plant: HACl
flowering season: summer to e. autumn
flower colour: lavender
height: 1.8-3 m/6-10 ft

The rich, yet fresh fragrance of sweet peas is many people's favourite flower scent. Like most blue or blue-tinged sweet peas, *L. o.* 'Leamington' and the variety 'Noel Sutton' (see right) are beautifully scented. Both of these tendrilled climbers have long flower stems, which make them particularly suitable for cutting but, if they are grown for that purpose, a well cultivated, fertile soil is especially important.
　　Climbers – Containers – Cutting.

LATHYRUS odoratus e.g. 'Noel Sutton' sc NA
[form of Sweet Pea]

○

type of plant: HACl
flowering season: summer to e. autumn
flower colour: blue
height: 1.8-3 m/6-10 ft

See preceding plant.

ROSA (Spinosissima Hybrid) e.g.
'Frühlingsgold' ★
[form of Scotch Rose or Burnet Rose]

○

type of plant: HSh
flowering season: l. spring to e. summer
flower colour: creamy yellow
height: 1.8-3 m/6-8 ft

During its rather short flowering season, *R.* 'Frühlingsgold' produces a mass of richly fragrant blooms on long and gracefully arching stems. This vigorous plant has a preference for light, well drained soils, and it can be grown successfully in shallow soils over chalk as long as the conditions are not actually hot and dry.
　　Chalk – Hedging.

ROSA (Modern Shrub) e.g. 'Fritz Nobis'
[form of Rose]

○

type of plant: HSh
flowering season: summer
flower colour: salmon pink
height: 1.8 m/6 ft

Each of this strong-growing rose's profusely borne and beautifully scrolled buds opens out into a shapely flower which emits the warm scent of cloves. The shrub itself is bushy and has arching branches. *R.* 'Fritz Nobis' produces hips, but these are small and not particularly colourful.

ROSA (Bourbon) e.g. 'Madame Pierre Oger' ★
[form of Rose]

○

type of plant: HSh
flowering season: summer to e. autumn
flower colour: pale pink changing to rich pink
height: 1.8 m/6 ft

The fragrant and voluptuously cup-shaped blooms of this rose deepen in colour when warmed by the sun. They are produced continuously over a long period. Unfortunately, this erect, rather open plant is susceptible to black spot.

ROSA (Hybrid Musk) e.g. 'Penelope'
[form of Rose]

○

type of plant: HSh
flowering season: summer to e. autumn
flower colour: creamy pink changing to cream
height: 1.8 m/6 ft

The sweet, musk-like scent of this rose can be perceived some considerable distance from the plant. Since *R.* 'Penelope' is rather more densely branched than many hybrid musk roses, it is especially suitable for hedging. The foliage is greyish. Pink hips – which are covered with a grey bloom – ripen in autumn.

Hedging – Fruit.

ROMNEYA coulteri MC
[species of Tree Poppy]

○

type of plant: SlTP/Sh
flowering season: midsummer to e. autumn
flower colour: white
height: 1.5-2.1 m/5-7 ft

Once established in a suitably sunny site and well drained but moisture-retentive soil, this suckering sub-shrub can become invasive. It is, therefore, best planted where at least some of its roots can be contained – at the base of a south-facing wall, for example. The spectacular flowers are up to 12 cm/5 in wide and they have a pronounced, sweet fragrance. The leaves are a bluish grey-green.

Ground-cover – Grey, etc. leaves.

PHILADELPHUS 'Silver Showers' NA

○

type of plant: HSh
flowering season: l. spring
flower colour: white
height: 1.5 m/5 ft

This is a dense grower with profuse single, large white flowers.

ROSA (Rugosa) e.g. 'Roseraie de l'Hay' ★
[form of Rose]

○

type of plant: HSh
flowering season: summer
flower colour: crimson-purple
height: 1.2-1.8 m/4-6 ft

The strongly clove-scented blooms of *R.* 'Roseraie de l'Hay' are produced continuously throughout the summer months. This plant is vigorous, dense and bushy; it needs little or no pruning. It may be used for informal hedging. Light soils suit it particularly well. No hips are produced but the leaves turn rich yellow in autumn.

Chalk – Seaside – Atmospheric pollution – Hedging – Autumn foliage – Cutting.

ROSA (Hybrid Tea) e.g. 'Wendy Cussons' ★
sc NA
[form of Rose]

○

type of plant: HSh
flowering season: summer to mid-autumn
flower colour: cerise-red
height: 1.2-1.5 m/4-5 ft

This vigorous, reliable rose produces its large and very fragrant flowers from unusually early in June until the first frosts.

Atmospheric pollution – Cutting.

ROSA (Hybrid Tea) e.g. 'Prima Ballerina' sc NA
[form of Rose]

○

type of plant: HSh
flowering season: summer to mid-autumn
flower colour: pink
height: 1.05-1.35 m/3½-4½ ft

R. 'Prima Ballerina' is one of the most strongly scented roses of its type. It forms an upright, rather slender plant which is vigorous and generally resistant to disease. Even in a poor summer, it flowers freely.

Atmospheric pollution – Cutting.

LILIUM candidum
[Madonna Lily]
○
type of plant: HBb
flowering season: summer
flower colour: white
height: 90-150 cm/3-5 ft

The clusters of very sweetly scented flowers borne by this lily are famous for their glistening beauty. Unfortunately, *L. candidum* is sometimes difficult to establish, and the fungal disease, botrytis, can affect it seriously. It has a preference for alkaline soils, and plenty of sunshine is essential. This does not mean, however, that it can be grown under hot, dry conditions.

LILIUM regale ★
[species of Lily]
○
type of plant: HBb
flowering season: midsummer
flower colour: white
height: 90-150 cm/3-5 ft

This is one of the easiest and one of the loveliest lilies, with its rich, pervasive fragrance and elegantly funnelled flowers. Given good drainage, it is tolerant of a wide range of soil types and, when growing well, it increases fairly quickly. It is sometimes attacked by botrytis disease.

CLEMATIS recta
○
type of plant: HP
flowering season: summer
flower colour: white
height: 90-120 cm/3-4 ft

Herbaceous clematis are rather less well known than the varieties and species with persistent, woody stems. This particular example of the herbaceous type bears its fragrant flowers – and, subsequently, its fluffy seed-heads – in generous quantities. It can be grown over small or medium-sized shrubs or it may be supported with twiggy pea-sticks. It prefers an alkaline soil. There are purple-leaved forms of this plant, and other herbaceous clematis sometimes offered include the blue, bell-flowered *C. integrifolia* 'Hendersonii'.
  Cutting.

GALTONIA candicans (syn. *Hyacinthus candicans*)
[species of Summer Hyacinth, Spire Lily or Cape Lily]
○
type of plant: HBb
flowering season: l. summer to e. autumn
flower colour: white
height: 90-120 cm/3-4 ft

This usefully late-flowering plant grows well in any reasonable soil – where it may seed itself freely. Its long, bare stems and large leaves are best concealed amongst other plants. Some people find that the sweet fragrance of the flowers is only just perceptible.

LAVANDULA spica (syn. *L. officinalis*)
[Old English Lavender]
○
type of plant: HSh
flowering season: summer to e. autumn
flower colour: grey-blue
height: 90 cm/3 ft
E

Some lavenders may have more colourful flowers than this grey-leaved species, but few of them are as well scented. At its best as a young plant, *L. spica* can be most easily kept neat and hummocky when it is grown in a light, preferably alkaline soil and full sun. It should be cut back hard in spring and trimmed after flowering.
  Chalk – Hot, dry soils – Hedging – Grey, etc. leaves – Aromatic leaves.

ROSA (Floribunda) e.g. 'Elizabeth of Glamis' ★
sc NA
[form of Rose]
○
type of plant: HSh
flowering season: summer to mid-autumn
flower colour: terracotta-salmon or orange-pink
height: 75-105 cm/2½-3½ ft

This popular rose has many good qualities: it makes a neat, upright plant; it grows strongly; it flowers well, even during a wet season; and, above all, perhaps, its beautifully shaped flowers emit an exceptionally attractive, soft, yet full fragrance. It does not, however, perform satisfactorily in cold and windy gardens.
  Cutting.

ROSA (Hybrid Tea) e.g. 'Fragrant Cloud' sc NA
[form of Rose]

○

type of plant: HSh
flowering season: summer to mid-autumn
flower colour: coral-red
height: 75-105 cm/2½-3½ ft

The exceptionally strong scent of this well branched and bushy rose is often at its most intense in the flowers produced during autumn. Black spot may sometimes affect what is otherwise a disease-free plant.

Cutting.

PHLOX maculata e.g. 'Alpha'

○

type of plant: HP
flowering season: l. summer to e. autumn
flower colour: pink
height: 75-90 cm/2½-3 ft

P. m. 'Alpha' is a sweetly scented and elegantly erect change from the more commonly seen *P. paniculata* varieties. Like all phloxes for the herbaceous border, however, this plant requires moisture-retentive soil and plenty of water in dry weather. It usually needs no staking.

Cutting.

DIANTHUS (Border Carnation) e.g. 'Salmon Clove'

○

type of plant: HP
flowering season: summer
flower colour: salmon pink
height: 60-90 cm/2-3 ft
E

The richly clove-scented flowers of this carnation appear in large quantities on young plants. In general, the orange and yellow-flowered varieties have little or no scent. Other, popular, fragrant plants of this type include 'Imperial Clove' (violet-carmine) and 'Robin Thain' (white, marked crimson). They all make long-lasting cut flowers. They should be given an alkaline soil which drains readily. The staking and disbudding which they require is most conveniently carried out if they are grown in beds of their own.

Chalk – Grey, etc. leaves – Cutting.

MIRABILIS jalapa
[Marvel of Peru]

○

type of plant: HHA
flowering season: midsummer to e. autumn
flower colour: mixed – yellow, red, white, pink
height: 60-90 cm/2-3 ft
flowers fragrant in late afternoon and at night only

In cool weather, the heavily scented flowers of this quick-growing plant may open earlier in the day than usual (generally, they open in late afternoon). A warm, sheltered site and rich soil are necessary. When growing well, *M. jalapa* makes a rounded, spreading mass of dark foliage and bright flowers.

CHRYSANTHEMUM rubellum e.g. 'Clara Curtis'

○

type of plant: HP
flowering season: l. summer to e. autumn
flower colour: clear pink
height: 60-75 cm/2-2½ ft

C. rubellum and its varieties provide cut flowers which are just as useful and long-lasting as those of the early-flowering, florists' chrysanthemums. Moreover, the bushy habit of plants like *C. r.* 'Clara Curtis' and their very free-flowering nature make them much better choices for mixed or herbaceous borders. Their blooms are softly fragrant.

Chalk – Cutting.

CRINUM × powellii MC

○

type of plant: SlTBb
flowering season: l. summer to e. autumn
flower colour: rose pink
height: 60 cm/2 ft
E

The base of a south-facing wall is the ideal site for this plant, but it should be borne in mind that plenty of water is needed during the growing season. The leaves are long and rather unsightly. However, the flowers are so beautifully shaped and sweetly fragrant that this shortcoming seems unimportant.

VERBENA rigida (syn. *V. venosa*)

○

type of plant: SITP
flowering season: midsummer to mid-autumn
flower colour: violet-purple
height: 45-60 cm/1½-2 ft

Because this plant has a very long flowering season, it is often used in bedding schemes, having been raised each year from seed. In mild areas, however, it is perennial and almost hardy. Its upright stems are covered in dense foliage and its blooms have a light, sweet scent. *V. rigida* should be grown in a well drained soil.

CHEIRANTHUS cheiri e.g. 'Cloth of Gold'
sc NA
[form of Wallflower]

○

type of plant: HB
flowering season: spring to e. summer
flower colour: yellow
height: 45 cm/1½ ft
E

Like all wallflowers, this large-flowered and richly fragrant variety prefers an alkaline soil. Further examples of varieties of *C. cheiri* are listed in the unillustrated section of this list. Additional colours include orange, purple and white.

Chalk – Hot, dry soils – Cutting.

HELIOTROPIUM peruvianum e.g. 'Royal Marine'★
[form of Heliotrope or Cherry Pie]

○

type of plant: HHA
flowering season: summer to e. autumn
flower colour: dark violet
height: 45 cm/1½ ft

As well as having the characteristic sweet, 'cherry pie' fragrance of the species, this variety of heliotrope produces foliage which is exceptionally dark and a decorative adjunct to the richly coloured flowers. The growing tips of young plants should be pinched out fairly frequently to encourage bushiness. Good specimens are produced in rich soils which are both well drained and moisture-retentive.

Green foliage.

MENTZELIA lindleyi (syn. *Bartonia aurea*)

○

type of plant: HA
flowering season: summer
flower colour: golden yellow
height: 45 cm/1½ ft

In sunny weather the flowers of this easily grown and bushy plant open fully and emit a soft, sweet scent. The long toothed leaves are an added – though minor – attraction.

TULIPA (Double Late) 'Eros'
[form of Tulip]

○

type of plant: HBb
flowering season: mid-spring
flower colour: pink
height: 45 cm/1½ ft

Few people associate large-flowered tulips with attractive scent, but this hybrid is only one of several, possible examples from the various classifactory divisions. Although *T.* 'Eros' has sturdy stems, its fragrant flowers are so large that some shelter is necessary to prevent decapitation. When sheltered, however, the flowers are unusually long-lasting. As with all tulips, a freely draining soil is an important requirement.

Chalk – Hot, dry soils.

CHEIRANTHUS × allionii (syn. *Erysimum asperum*) e.g. **'Golden Bedder'**
[Siberian Wallflower]

○

type of plant: HB
flowering season: spring to e. summer
flower colour: deep yellow
height: 40 cm/15 in
E

The spicily fragrant Siberian wallflower and its varieties form denser, rounder plants than the cultivars of *C. cheiri* (for an example of which, see above); they also flower a little later. Confusingly, perhaps, seedsmen list the Siberian wallflower under its botanical name and *C. cheiri* under 'wallflower'.

Chalk – Hot, dry soils.

TULIPA sylvestris
[species of Tulip]

○

type of plant: HBb
flowering season: mid-spring
flower colour: yellow
height: 40 cm/15 in

Establishing this graceful tulip can be difficult
sometimes but, once established, it flowers freely
and it may increase rapidly. It is suitable for
naturalizing in grass. In bud, the flowers are
pendant but, when fully open, they become
upright and emit a sweet scent.

    Chalk – Hot, dry soils.

IRIS graminea

○

type of plant: HP
flowering season: e. summer
flower colour: rosy purple + violet
height: 30-45 cm/1-1½ ft
flowers 23 cm/9 in high

The delicious scent of newly cooked plums
emanates from this plant's small flowers as they
bloom amongst the clump-forming foliage.
I. graminea is easy to grow in any reasonable soil
and, unlike the more commonly seen bearded
hybrid irises, it does not require frequent lifting
and dividing.

    Ground-cover – Cutting.

IRIS (Spanish) e.g. 'King of Blues'

○

type of plant: SlTBb
flowering season: e. summer
flower colour: deep blue
height: 30–45 cm/1–1½ ft

This outstanding hybrid is one of a number of
Spanish irises with attractive scent; in this case the
fragrance is reminiscent of violets. The popularity
of bulbous, hybrid irises – including Spanish irises
– as commercial cut flowers is a good indication of
their ability to last well in water. They thrive in full
sun and light soils.

    Chalk – Hot, dry soils – Cutting.

LATHYRUS odoratus e.g. 'Bijou Mixed'
[form of Sweet Pea]

○

type of plant: HA
flowering season: summer to e. autumn
flower colour: mixed – pink, salmon, red,
    mauve, blue, maroon, white
height: 30-45 cm/1-1½ ft
pastels fragrant

In recent years, sweet peas suitable for bedding,
rather than for exhibition or solely for cutting,
have become popular. The stems of this variety are
not as long as those of the Spencer cultivars, nor
are all the blooms as sweetly scented as those of the
old-fashioned Grandifloras, but they are suitable
for cutting and they do have some fragrance. *L. o.*
'Bijou Mixed' occasionally needs to be supported
with twiggy sticks, but this is often unnecessary.

    Cutting.

NARCISSUS (Jonquil) e.g. 'Trevithian'
[form of Daffodil]

○

type of plant: HBb
flowering season: e. spring
flower colour: yellow
height: 30-40 cm/12-15 in

The heavy scent of jonquilla narcissi, including *N.*
'Trevithian', seems overwhelmingly rich and
strong to some people. However, those who find it
attractive will be delighted to know that this
variety is vigorous and, as a cut flower, long-
lasting.

    Cutting.

TULIPA (Single Early) e.g. 'General de Wet'
(syn. *T.* 'de Wet')
[form of Tulip]

○

type of plant: HBb
flowering season: mid-spring
flower colour: orange + orange-scarlet
height: 30-40 cm/12-15 in

Tulips of this shape usually conjure up visions of
geometric bedding schemes in public places and
the fact that some of these plants are richly fragrant
is often overlooked. The flowers of this particular
variety are large and they have a sweet scent.
Really good drainage ensures that the bulbs of this
plant ripen well each summer, and this leads to
plenty of blooms in subsequent springs.

    Chalk – Hot, dry soils.

DIANTHUS plumarius e.g. 'Mrs Sinkins'
sc NA
[form of Pink]

○

type of plant: HP
flowering season: e. summer
flower colour: white
height: 30 cm/1 ft
E

This well loved plant has a full, strong fragrance. Its grey-green leaves are sufficiently dense to make it a good choice for edging, but there are other members of this genus that create better ground-cover. The variety 'White Ladies' is sometimes recommended as a stronger growing and less blowsy substitute for 'Mrs Sinkins'. It can be obtained from specialist nurseries.

Chalk – Hot, dry soils – Grey, etc. leaves – Cutting.

RESEDA odorata e.g. 'Red Monarch'
[form of Mignonette]

○

type of plant: HA
flowering season: summer to e. autumn
flower colour: red + yellowish green
height: 30 cm/1 ft

The flowers of most forms of mignonette may not be interestingly shaped or brightly coloured, but their sweet, penetrating fragrance certainly *is* remarkable. In general, the redder the flower spikes, the less powerful the scent: *R. o.* 'Red Monarch' is less fragrant than, for example, *R. o.* 'Machet' (see the following page) and *R. odorata* itself. An alkaline soil is most suitable for all these plants, but it must be rich and, if possible, well manured for the best results.

Cutting.

VERBENA × hybrida grandiflora e.g. 'Royal Bouquet'

○

type of plant: HHA
flowering season: summer to mid-autumn
flower colour: mixed – blue, white, red, purple, pink + white
height: 30 cm/1 ft
pastels most fragrant

'Royal Bouquet' is an example of one of the taller-growing and less spreading varieties of *V.* × *hybrida*. Its extra height means that it is suitable for cutting as well as for bedding displays. The flowers are produced over a long period; their scent is reminiscent of cloves. This plant will grow well in most soils, but it will not bloom freely in wet seasons.

Cutting.

FREESIA 'Outdoor Hybrids Mixed'

○

type of plant: HHC
flowering season: midsummer to e. autumn
flower colour: mixed – yellow, red, pink, orange, white
height: 25-40 cm/10-15 in

Success with these deliciously fragrant plants depends on a really warm, sheltered site, a light but rich soil and plenty of water during the flowering season. Prepared corms, such as 'Outdoor Hybrids Mixed', will flower outside in their first year. Then they must be lifted and dried or given greenhouse shelter during winter. Only in very mild districts can ordinary, unprepared corms be grown outdoors from year to year.

Cutting.

BRACHYCOME iberidifolia 'Mixed'
[form of Swan River Daisy]

○

type of plant: HHA
flowering season: summer
flower colour: mixed – blue, white, pink, purple
height: 23-30 cm/9-12 in

In sunny weather, these well branched plants, with their fine, deeply cut foliage, are covered in blooms; far fewer flowers are produced in wet weather. A light, rich loam suits these annuals best.

PETUNIA × hybrida e.g. 'Dwarf Resisto Blue'

○

type of plant: HHA
flowering season: summer to e. autumn
flower colour: blue
height: 23-30 cm/9-12 in
blue and purple petunias most fragrant, particularly in evening

The Resisto strain of petunias has been specially developed to withstand damage from wind and rain. Many blue and purple petunias, including this particular variety, emit a vanilla-like scent. They all need a fairly rich, moisture-retentive soil to grow well.

RESEDA odorata e.g. 'Machet'
[form of Mignonette]

○

type of plant: HA
flowering season: summer to e. autumn
flower colour: red+yellowish green
height: 23-30 cm/9-12 in

Compared with *R. o.* 'Red Monarch' (see the previous page), this variety of mignonette has even less interesting flowers, but its sweet scent – which is attractive to bees – is particularly strong. A rich, preferably alkaline soil is required for good growth. *R. o.* 'Machet' has dark green foliage which can look well beside more brightly coloured plants.
Cutting.

HYACINTHUS orientalis e.g. 'City of Haarlem'
[form of Hyacinth]

○

type of plant: HBb
flowering season: spring
flower colour: yellow
height: 23 cm/9 in

Although the catalogues of bulb specialists will list a considerable number of 'wonderfully fragrant' varieties of hyacinth, some are more strongly scented than others. *H. o.* 'City of Haarlem' and the two varieties illustrated right and below all have a pronounced, rich fragrance. The very large flower spikes of 'L'Innocence' need staking. 'Myosotis' is strong-growing and beautifully fragrant. 'City of Haarlem' blooms a little later than most hyacinths. They all require a well drained soil.

HYACINTHUS orientalis e.g. 'L'Innocence'
[form of Hyacinth]

○

type of plant: HBb
flowering season: spring
flower colour: white
height: 23 cm/9 in

See preceding plant.

HYACINTHUS orientalis e.g. 'Myosotis'★
[form of Hyacinth]

○

type of plant: HBb
flowering season: spring
flower colour: pale blue
height: 23 cm/9 in

See *H. o.* 'City of Haarlem', above.

DIANTHUS barbatus e.g. 'Indian Carpet'
[form of Sweet William]

○

type of plant: HB
flowering season: summer
flower colour: mixed – red, pink, white
height: 20-30 cm/8-12 in

Where the taller growing varieties of sweet william would look out of scale or where wind might damage them, *D. b.* 'Indian Carpet' and similarly compact forms are preferable. The clove-scented flowers of these plants last well in water, but the shortness of their stems makes them suitable for only very small arrangements. All varieties of sweet william appreciate well drained, alkaline soil.
Chalk.

MUSCARI armeniacum e.g. 'Heavenly Blue'
[form of Grape Hyacinth]

○

type of plant: HBb
flowering season: spring
flower colour: blue
height: 20-25 cm/8-10 in

This popular form of grape hyacinth is easy to grow. Indeed, it can increase so rapidly that it becomes a nuisance. Each little flower head gives out a sweet, soft scent. Unfortunately, as the flowers open, the leaves become straggly and rather unsightly.
Chalk.

HYACINTHUS orientalis albulus
[Roman Hyacinth]

○

type of plant: HBb
flowering season: spring
flower colour: white
height: 15 cm/6 in

Those gardeners who find the smell of the
large-flowered, hybrid hyacinths attractive, but
who object to the solidity and stiffness of the flower
spikes, may like the much more graceful and
equally fragrant Roman hyacinths. The form most
often available is white, but there are also pink-
and blue-flowered varieties. Most well drained
soils are suitable.

NYMPHAEA e.g. × 'Marliacea Albida' sc NA
[form of Water-lily]

○

type of plant: HPAq
flowering season: summer to e. autumn
flower colour: white
height: 10-15 cm/4-6 in

Although both the examples of fragrant
water-lilies shown in this and the following
photograph are hardy, the combination of bold
green foliage, shapely flowers and sweet scent
gives them an exotic, tropical air. *N.* × 'Marliacea
Albida' needs water about 25-60 cm/10-24 in deep
to grow well. It may produce large quantities of
leaves. In which case, frequent division will
restore the balance between foliage and flowers.
N. × 'Sunrise' (see right) flowers best in warmer
districts. It should be planted in water
25-45 cm/10-18 in deep.
　　Green foliage.

NYMPHAEA e.g. × 'Sunrise'
[form of Water-lily]

○

type of plant: HPAq
flowering season: summer to e. autumn
flower colour: yellow
height: 10-15 cm/4-6 in

See preceding plant.

**Additional plants with fragrant flowers that are
featured elsewhere in this book**

○ sun
TILIA platyphyllos: 24-36 m (p. 89)
WISTERIA sinensis: 18-30 m (p. 119)
TILIA × euchlora: 12-18 m (p. 90)
PAULOWNIA tomentosa: 9-12 m (p. 179)
ROBINIA pseudoacacia e.g. 'Bessoniana': 9-12 m
　(p. 90)
ROBINIA pseudoacacia e.g. 'Frisia': 7.5-10.5 m
　(p. 174)
MAGNOLIA denudata: 7.5-9 m (p. 28)
WISTERIA floribunda e.g. 'Macrobotrys': 6-9 m
　(p. 133)
ROSA (Rambler) e.g. 'Wedding Day': 6-7.5 m
　(p. 120)
ERIOBOTRYA japonica: 4.5-7.5 m (p. 180)
PITTOSPORUM tenuifolium: 4.5-7.5 m (p. 180)
PRUNUS (Japanese Cherry) 'Amanogawa':
　4.5-7.5 m (p. 2)
GENISTA aetnensis: 4.5-6 m (p. 56)
ROSA (Climber) e.g. 'New Dawn': 4.5-6 m (p. 120)
ROSA (Rambler) e.g. 'Albertine': 4.5 m (p. 120)
ROSA wichuraiana: 4.5 m (p. 101)
CORDYLINE australis: 3.6-9 m (p. 180)
CLERODENDRON trichotomum: 3-4.5 m
　(p. 202)
ERICA arborea: 2.4-3.6 m (p. 29)
MYRTUS communis: 2.4-3 m (p. 132)
BUDDLEIA davidii e.g. 'Black Knight': 2.1-3 m
　(p. 2)
BUDDLEIA davidii e.g. 'Royal Red': 2.1-3 m
　(p. 2)
CHIMONANTHUS praecox: 2.1-3 m (p. 274)
SPARTIUM junceum: 2.1-3 m (p. 56)
ROSA (Rambler) e.g. 'Albertine': 2.1 m (p. 120)
LATHYRUS odoratus e.g. 'Air Warden': 1.8-3 m
　(p. 212)
BUDDLEIA fallowiana 'Alba': 1.5-2.4 m (p. 157)
CEANOTHUS × 'Gloire de Versailles': 1.5-2.1 m
　(p. 91)
LUPINUS arboreus: 1.5-1.8 m (p. 86)

DAPHNE odora 'Aureomarginata' ★: 1.2-1.8 m
　(p. 146)
ROSA (Rugosa Hybrid) e.g. 'Blanc Double de
　Coubert': 1.2-1.8 m (p. 129)
ROSA (Spinosissima Hybrid) e.g. 'Stanwell
　Perpetual': 1.2-1.5 m (p. 3)
ROSA (Rugosa Hybrid) e.g. 'Schneezwerg': 1.2 m
　(p. 87)
YUCCA filamentosa: 90-180 cm (p. 57)
HEBE 'Midsummer Beauty': 90-150 cm (p. 87)
IRIS (Bearded Hybrid) e.g. 'Jane Phillips':
　90-105 cm (p. 218)
ACIDANTHERA bicolor murielae: 90 cm (p. 218)
ROSA (Hybrid Tea) e.g. 'Blue Moon': 75-105 cm
　(p. 221)
CENTAUREA moschata: 60 cm (p. 227)
IRIS pallida e.g. 'Argenteo-variegata': 60 cm
　(p. 147)
LAVANDULA spica 'Vera': 60 cm (p. 100)
AMARYLLIS belladonna: 45-60 cm (p. 230)
DIANTHUS barbatus e.g. 'Auricula-eyed':
　45-60 cm (p. 231)
LAVANDULA spica 'Munstead': 45-60 cm
　(p. 197)
CHEIRANTHUS cheiri e.g. 'Blood Red': 45 cm
　(p. 9)
ERICA × darleyensis 'Silver Beads': 45 cm (p. 275)
IXIA Hybrids: 45 cm (p. 233)
ROSA wichuraiana: 45 cm (p. 101)
TULIPA (Parrot) e.g. 'Orange Favourite': 45 cm
　(p. 234)
CHEIRANTHUS cheiri e.g. 'Fire King': 40-45 cm
　(p. 235)
LAYIA elegans: 40-45 cm (p. 235)
CHEIRANTHUS × allionii: 40 cm (p. 59)
NARCISSUS (Poetaz) e.g. 'Geranium': 40 cm
　(p. 236)
LAVANDULA spica 'Hidcote' ★: 30-60 cm
　(p. 126)

TROPAEOLUM majus 'Golden Gleam': 30-40 cm
　(p. 60)
CHEIRANTHUS cheiri e.g. 'Golden Bedder':
　30 cm (p. 11)
DIANTHUS × allwoodii e.g. 'Doris': 30 cm
　(p. 238)
IRIS unguicularis: 30 cm (p. 275)
ROSA (Miniature) e.g. 'Yellow Doll': 30 cm
　(p. 134)
CHEIRANTHUS cheiri e.g. 'Tom Thumb
　Mixed': 15-23 cm (p. 63)
LIMNANTHES douglasii: 15-23 cm (p. 140)
DIANTHUS gratianopolitanus ★: 15-20 cm (p. 16)
IRIS reticulata: 15 cm (p. 17)
VERBENA × hybrida e.g. 'Sparkle Mixed': 15 cm
　(p. 140)
ALYSSUM maritimum e.g. 'Little Dorrit':
　10-15 cm (p. 64)
ALYSSUM montanum: 10-15 cm (p. 140)
CROCUS imperati: 8-10 cm (p. 275)

JASMINUM officinale ★ MC
[Common White Jasmine]
○ [◐]
type of plant: HCl
flowering season: summer to e. autumn
flower colour: white
height: 9 m/30 ft
fragrance strongest in evening and at night

The strong, sweet fragrance of this vigorous
climber is one of the most popular of all scents.
Particularly large numbers of flowers are produced
when the plant is grown against a warm wall. In
mild districts, the common white jasmine may be
semi-evergreen. A larger flowered, pink-tinged
variety, *J. o.* 'Affine', and a form with yellow-
variegated leaves, *J. o.* 'Aureo-variegatum', are
sometimes offered by specialist nurseries. Any
well drained soil will suit these twining climbers.
 Atmospheric pollution – Climbers – Containers.

SYRINGA vulgaris e.g. 'Katherine Havemeyer'
[form of Common Lilac]
○ [◐]
type of plant: HSh
flowering season: l. spring
flower colour: purple-lavender changing to
  lilac-pink
height: 3-4.5 m/10-15 ft

For large quantities of headily fragrant blooms,
S. v. 'Katherine Havemeyer' should be grown in
full sun. Like most varieties of the common lilac, it
has a rather limited flowering season. All fertile
soils with good drainage will suit this broad,
openly branched shrub and it will flourish on
chalk.
 Chalk – Atmospheric pollution – Containers
(*grown as a standard, 1.8-2.4 m/6-8 ft*) – Cutting.

CORYLOPSIS sinensis NA
[Chinese Witch Hazel]
○ [◐]
type of plant: HSh
flowering season: e. spring
flower colour: light yellow
height: 3 m/10 ft

Refined, pale yellow floral bells appear on this
loose, open-growing shrub a week or two earlier
than forsythia. It is best grown at the edge of a
wood, in good deep loam with plenty of room for
expansion.

OSMANTHUS delavayi (syn.
Siphonosmanthus delavayi) ★
○ [◐]
type of plant: SlTSh
flowering season: mid-spring
flower colour: white
height: 1.8-2.4 m/6-8 ft
E

The small but abundant flowers of this
slow-growing shrub are of an especially elegant,
tubular shape; they are very sweetly scented.
Protection from cold winds is advisable and,
although this plant will do well in any reasonably
fertile soil, it tends to be short-lived on shallow,
chalky soils. The arching stems eventually form a
dense, wide-spreading mound, and several plants
can be used to create an informal hedge or screen.
 Atmospheric pollution – Hedging.

SYRINGA microphylla 'Superba'
[form of Lilac]
○ [◐]
type of plant: HSh
flowering season: l. spring to mid-autumn/l.
  spring, occasional repeats (NA)
flower colour: rose-pink
height: 1.8-2.4 m/6-8 ft

In small gardens, where the more common forms
of lilac might be too large and their flowering
season too short, this variety would be preferable.
S. m. 'Superba' tends to produce its fragrant
blossom in two main flushes – the first in late
spring and early summer, the second in late
summer and autumn. In the United States, the
shrub has an occasional repeat bloom in the
summer. A well drained, fertile soil and a sunny
site suit this spreading shrub best.
 Chalk – Atmospheric pollution – Hedging –
Cutting.

LONICERA fragrantissima
[species of Shrubby Honeysuckle]
○ [◐]
type of plant: HSh
flowering season: midwinter to mid-spring
flower colour: creamy white
height: 1.8-2.1 m/6-7 ft
½E

This densely twigged shrub may not look very
decorative for most of the year, but the penetrating
scent of its winter flowers make it well worth
planting in an out-of-the-way corner. Ideally, the
flowers should have some shelter to prevent them
being damaged by frost. Some gardeners prefer
the related and similar *L. × purpusii* (see p. 267) to
L. fragrantissima.
 Chalk – Winter-flowering plants.

CLETHRA alnifolia 'Paniculata'
[form of Sweet Pepper Bush]

○ [◐]
type of plant: HSh
flowering season: l. summer to e. autumn
flower colour: white
height: 1.8 m/6 ft
※

The arching stems of this bushy shrub are held erectly and they bear sweetly fragrant flower spikes at their tips. Moisture is essential for good growth and some shade should be provided if the soil is at all likely to dry out. The foliage of this plant sometimes turns an attractive, if unobtrusive yellow in autumn.

Acid soils – Damp and wet soils – Atmospheric pollution.

LILIUM auratum
[Golden-rayed Lily, Gold-band Lily (NA)]

○ [◐]
type of plant: HBb
flowering season: l. summer to e. autumn
flower colour: white + yellow + red
height: 1.5-2.1 m/5-7 ft
※

There may be as many as thirty 20-30 cm/8-12 in wide blooms on each of this lily's stems, and the size and profuseness of the flowers are matched by their sumptuously spicy scent. Unfortunately, *L. auratum* is short-lived and susceptible to virus diseases. Some bulb specialists may stock *L. a. platyphyllum* which is more vigorous than the species. Both plants need an acid soil that drains freely.

Acid soils.

PHILADELPHUS e.g. 'Beauclerk' ★
[form of Mock Orange]

○ [◐]
type of plant: HSh
flowering season: summer
flower colour: white
height: 1.5-2.1 m/5-7 ft

The mock oranges (which are often called syringas, although, confusingly, *Syringa* is the botanical name for lilacs) are easily grown plants with very fragrant flowers. The particular variety illustrated here makes an arching, spreading shrub. Amost any soil is suitable (good drainage is an advantage, but it is not essential). The flowers will last longest in water if the stems have had at least some of their leaves removed.

Chalk – Atmospheric pollution – Cutting.

ASPHODELINE lutea (syn. *Asphodelus luteus*)
[King's Spear]

○ [◐]
type of plant: HP
flowering season: summer
flower colour: yellow
height: 90 cm/3 ft

The erect flowers of this glaucous-leaved plant are sweetly scented. In autumn, they are replaced by spikes of round seeds which make attractive material for dried arrangements. *A. lutea* should be given a well drained soil and a site that is either sheltered or in full sun.

Grey, etc. leaves – Cutting.

MATTHIOLA incana (Ten Week) e.g. 'Beauty Mixed' sc NA
[form of Stock]

○ [◐]
type of plant: HHA
flowering season: summer
flower colour: mixed – yellow, red, pink, white, lavender
height: 45 cm/1½ ft

Both this form of stock and the form illustrated in the following photograph are upright, bushy plants with flowers which have a full, aromatic fragrance. Varieties of *M. incana* are at their best when grown in a warm place and in a rich, light, loamy soil. Seedlings with dark green leaves are normally discarded, since the single flowers which they produce look lanky and insignificant compared with the doubles.

Cutting.

MATTHIOLA incana (Brompton) e.g. 'Double Brompton Mixed' sc NA
[form of Stock]

○ [◐]
type of plant: HB
flowering season: spring
flower colour: mixed – red, pink, lavender, mauve, white
height: 40-45 cm/15-18 in

See preceding plant.

MATTHIOLA bicornis
[Night-scented Stock]

○[◐]

type of plant: HA
flowering season: summer
flower colour: lilac
height: 40 cm/15 in
fragrant in late evening and at night only

This untidy, small-flowered plant makes up for all its shortcomings in appearance by being powerfully and deliciously scented. The fragrance is emitted towards the end of the day and at night. Since the tiny flowers are not interesting enough for cutting, *M. bicornis* can be grown in drier and less rich soils than the large-flowered, hybrid stocks also illustrated here.

Chalk.

MATTHIOLA incana (East Lothian) e.g. 'East Lothian Mixed' sc NA
[form of Stock]

○[◐]

type of plant: HB
flowering season: midsummer to e. autumn
flower colour: mixed – red, pink, lavender, mauve, white
height: 30-40 cm/12-15 in

The East Lothian strains of *M. incana* produce their richly scented blooms as the flowers of other stocks start to fade. Like the 'Dwarf Double' Brompton types (see right), they form compact, well branched plants which are suitable for sites where wind would make staking of taller stocks essential. Both mixtures require the growing conditions described under *M. i.* 'Beauty Mixed' (see previous page).

Cutting (*M. i.* 'East Lothian Mixed' only).

MATTHIOLA incana (Ten Week) e.g. 'Dwarf Double Mixed' (syn. *M. i.* 'Park Mixed')
[form of Stock]

○[◐]

type of plant: HHA
flowering season: summer
flower colour: mixed – red, pink, lavender, white, yellow
height: 23-30 cm/9-12 in

See preceding plant.

APONOGETON distachyus sc NA
[Water Hawthorn]

○[◐]

type of plant: HPAq
flowering season: l. spring to mid-autumn
flower colour: white
height: 8-10 cm/3-4 in

As its common name suggests, *A. distachyus* produces flowers which have a hawthorn-like fragrance (fortunately, none of the fishier overtones of hawthorn are present). The roots of this plant should be placed in rich mud below a maximum of about 45 cm/18 in of still or very slow-moving water. Full sun encourages the strongest growth and ensures that plenty of flowers appear. (The faded flowers are completely green.)

Cutting.

CYCLAMEN cilicium

○[◐]

type of plant: SlTTu
flowering season: autumn
flower colour: pink
height: 8-10 cm/3-4 in

Although many of the familiar, large-flowered, florists' cyclamens have no scent, several of the hardier species, including *C. cilicium*, are fragrant. To grow well, this exceptionally pretty plant must have shelter from cold winds (amongst trees and large shrubs, for instance) and good drainage. Each of the delicately twisted petals has a red spot at its base. The leaves have silvery markings.

Variegated leaves.

Additional plants with fragrant flowers that are featured elsewhere in this book

○[◐] sun (or partial shade)
SYRINGA × josiflexa 'Bellicent': 3.6-4.5 m (p. 21)
SYRINGA vulgaris e.g. 'Madame Lemoine': 3-4.5 m (p. 240)
SYRINGA vulgaris e.g. 'Souvenir de Louis Spaeth': 3-4.5 m (p. 93)
ELAEAGNUS pungens 'Maculata': 2.4-3 m (p. 150)
PHILADELPHUS e.g. 'Virginal': 2.4-3 m (p. 93)
OSMANTHUS heterophyllus: 1.8-3 m (p. 126)
PHILADELPHUS coronarius: 1.8-3 m (p. 66)
ARTEMISIA lactiflora: 1.2-1.5 m (p. 240)
ULEX europaeus 'Plenus': 90-180 cm (p. 66)
SYRINGA velutina: 90-150 cm (p. 22)
PHILADELPHUS e.g. 'Manteau d'Hermine': 90-120 cm (p. 22)
MATTHIOLA incana (Ten Week) e.g. 'Column Mixed': 45-60 cm (p. 242)
MATTHIOLA incana (Ten Week) e.g. 'Giant Perfection Mixed': 45-60 cm (p. 242)
LYSICHITUM camtschatcense: 23-30 cm (p. 71)
MALCOMIA maritima 'Mixed': 15-23 cm (p. 143)

HOHERIA glabrata (syn. *Plagianthus lyallii*)
sc NA MC

○ ◑

type of plant: SlTSh
flowering season: summer
flower colour: white
height: 3-4.5 m/10-15 ft

A warm and sheltered position (preferably against a south- or west-facing wall) ensures that this erect shrub produces its glistening, fragrant flowers in profusion. The large, heart-shaped leaves, with their toothed edges, are quite attractive in themselves and they make a good background for the clusters of blossom.

Chalk.

ROSA (Bourbon) e.g. 'Zéphirine Drouhin'
sc NA
[form of Rose]

○ ◑

type of plant: HCl
flowering season: l. spring to e. autumn
flower colour: cerise-pink
height: 2.4-3.6 m/8-12 ft

The blooms of this thornless rose have a ripe, raspberry-like scent. They are often most abundant towards the end of the long flowering season. *R.* 'Zéphirine Drouhin' is, unfortunately, liable to attacks of mildew. These are generally less of a problem when the plant is treated as a free-standing shrub (which will grow about 1.8-2.4 m/6-8 ft high), than when it is trained against some sort of support.

Climbers.

CORYLOPSIS willmottiae

○ ◑

type of plant: HSh
flowering season: spring
flower colour: yellow
height: 2.4-3 m/8-10 ft

Since the cowslip-scented flowers of this open, twiggy shrub are produced very early in spring, they often need protection from frost and cold winds. A warm wall or light woodland are both suitable, sheltered sites. In good years, *C. willmottiae*'s dying foliage turns a mixture of warm colours in which yellow often predominates.

Acid soils – Autumn foliage.

×OSMAREA burkwoodii

○ ◑

type of plant: HSh
flowering season: spring
flower colour: white
height: 1.8-3 m/6-10 ft
E

Only if this neatly shaped shrub is used for hedging does it require any regular pruning. Otherwise, no special treatment and little attention are needed. The flowers of this plant are sweetly and strongly scented. They are conspicuously pale amongst the lustrous, dark green foliage.

Chalk – Atmospheric pollution – Hedging.

LONICERA×purpusii
[form of Shrubby Honeysuckle]

○ ◑

type of plant: HSh
flowering season: l. winter to e. spring
flower colour: cream
height: 1.5-2.4 m/5-8 ft

The intensely fragrant flowers of this shrubby honeysuckle are carried on more or less bare twigs. Overall, *L.×purpusii* makes a not very impressive, twiggy plant with rather ordinary foliage. The same is true of *L. fragrantissima* (see p. 264), which is one of the parents of *L.×purpusii*. *L.×purpusii* has the advantage of being a slightly more free-flowering plant. Both these shrubs grow best in fertile, well drained soils. In exposed positions, their flowers often become damaged by icy winds and frosts.

Chalk – Winter-flowering plants.

PAEONIA×lemoinei e.g. 'Souvenir de Maxime Cornu'
[form of Tree Peony/Paeony]

○ ◑

type of plant: HSh
flowering season: l. spring to e. summer
flower colour: bright golden yellow + pink
height: 1.5-1.8 m/5-6 ft

Few of the so-called tree paeonies are really easily grown, trouble-free plants, but this hybrid and other, related varieties – such as *P.×l.* 'Chromatella' – are less difficult than some. In general, tree paeonies require deep, fertile, well dug soil. A site that is sheltered from early morning sun in spring is ideal. The flowers of this particular variety are large and beautifully fragrant.

Green foliage.

CORYLOPSIS pauciflora

○ ◑

type of plant: HSh
flowering season: spring
flower colour: yellow
height: 1.2-1.8 m/4-6 ft

Like the larger *C. willmottiae* (see previous page), this shrub flowers early in the year, and protection from frost damage is, therefore, important. *C. pauciflora* consists of a spreading – though neat – mass of slender branches, along which the numerous blooms appear. These flowers have a sweet, nut-like scent. In autumn, the leaves often become brightly coloured in a mixture of yellow and orange.

Acid soils – Autumn foliage.

VIRBURNUM carlesii

○ ◑

type of plant: HSh
flowering season: spring
flower colour: white
height: 1.2-1.8 m/4-6 ft

V. carlesii is a slow-growing, rounded shrub with flowers that are richly clove-scented. As the foliage of this plant dies, it usually turns deep red and yellow. *V. c.* 'Aurora' is a slightly more vigorous variety of the species. It has pink flowers which open from red buds. Both the species and its variety need fertile, moisture-retentive soil.

Clay – Autumn foliage.

DEUTZIA × elegantissima

○ ◑

type of plant: HSh
flowering season: e. summer
flower colour: pale purplish pink
height: 1.2-1.5 m/4-5 ft

The most popular deutzias are cultivars of *D. scabra*. In comparison, the shrub shown here is much more graceful, with arching growths on rather upright branches. Its numerous flowers (which retain their colour longest in partial shade) are sweetly fragrant; the flowers of the commoner plants are unscented. *D.* × *elegantissima* is easily grown in any well drained soil.

Chalk – Atmospheric pollution.

PAEONIA lactiflora (**syn.** *P. albiflora*) **e.g.**
'Festiva Maxima'
[form of Peony/Paeony]

○ ◑

type of plant: HP
flowering season: e. summer
flower colour: white + crimson
height: 90 cm/3 ft
most white paeonies fragrant

After a slow start, the herbaceous paeonias make magnificent and very long-lived plants. They need to be grown in deep, rich soil and, apart from an annual mulching with compost or manure, they should be left undisturbed. Both the varieties illustrated here have fragrant flowers: 'Festiva Maxima' is delicately and freshly scented, while the fragrance of 'Sarah Bernhardt' (see right) is fuller and more pronounced. Both plants produce flowers which are excellent for cutting. The stems of 'Festiva Maxima' are stronger than (*contd*)

PAEONIA lactiflora (**syn.** *P. albiflora*) **e.g.**
'Sarah Bernhardt' ★
[form of Peony/Paeony]

○ ◑

type of plant: HP
flowering season: e. summer
flower colour: pale pink
height: 90 cm/3 ft

See preceding plant.

(*contd*)
those of many cultivars, but the large blooms and sweet scent of 'Sarah Bernhardt' make it a particularly popular choice for flower arrangements.

Green foliage – Cutting.

NICOTIANA alata (**syn.** *N. affinis*)
[species of Tobacco Plant]

○ ◑

type of plant: HHA
flowering season: summer to e. autumn
flower colour: white
height: 75-90 cm/2½-3 ft
unless grown in shade, flowers open and are
fragrant in evening only

Although there are varieties of this plant that are more interestingly coloured (such as *N. a.* 'Lime Green', p. 282) and forms that have flowers which stay open all day long (instead of opening just in the evening), few of them are quite as fragrant as the species itself. A well drained but moisture-retentive and fertile soil and a warm position produce the ideal conditions for this plant.

Cutting.

PHLOX paniculata e.g. 'Mother of Pearl'
○ ◑
type of plant: HP
flowering season: midsummer to e. autumn
flower colour: white flushed pink
height: 75-90 cm/2½-3 ft

Many modern varieties of *P. paniculata* are not
nearly so well scented as the original species.
However, this cultivar has a pronounced, sweet
fragrance which is most attractive – at least until
the flowers begin to fade. The healthiest plants
with the largest number of blooms are grown in
cool, moist, well drained soils. Some shade helps
to prevent undesirable drying out on light soils.
  Cutting.

DAPHNE × burkwoodii 'Somerset'
○ ◑
type of plant: HSh
flowering season: l. spring to e. summer
flower colour: pale pink
height: 60-90 cm/2-3 ft
½E

This unusually fast-growing daphne can make
quite dense, rounded mounds of foliage if it is
pinched back fairly regularly. The flowers have a
very sweet scent. They are most freely produced in
sunny sites, but in such positions it is particularly
important that the requirement for moisture, as
well as good drainage, is not overlooked.

HESPERIS matronalis 'Mixed'
[form of Sweet Rocket, Dame's Violet or
Damask Violet]
○ ◑
type of plant: HB/P
flowering season: l. spring to midsummer
flower colour: mixed – white, purple, lilac
height: 60-75 cm/2-2½ ft
fragrant in evening

Sweet rocket is one of those unspectacular 'cottage
garden' plants whose redeeming feature is their
fragrance. It is easily grown in a moist, preferably
alkaline soil. Although it is a perennial, it is usually
short-lived and best when treated as a biennial.

NARCISSUS (Poeticus) e.g. 'Old Pheasant Eye'
(syn. *N. poeticus recurvus*)
[form of Daffodil]
○ ◑
type of plant: HBb
flowering season: l. spring
flower colour: white + yellow + red
height: 40 cm/15 in

The very strong, sweet scent of this exceptionally
late-flowering daffodil makes some people feel ill,
but to others it is most attractive. *N.* 'Actaea', a
Poeticus daffodil of similar appearance and
fragrance, is sometimes considered a better garden
plant, since it is more vigorous and larger flowered
than the pheasant's eye narcissus.
  Cutting.

NICOTIANA alata (syn. *N. affinis*) e.g. 'Dwarf
White Bedder'
[form of Tobacco Plant]
○ ◑
type of plant: HHA
flowering season: summer to e. autumn
flower colour: white
height: 30-45 cm/1-1½ ft
particularly fragrant in evening

The flowers of most forms of tobacco plant remain
closed during the day (unless they are grown in a
shady site, when flowering may not be particularly
profuse). However, *N. a.* 'Dwarf White Bedder'
produces blooms which stay open and diffuse their
sweet scent night and day. A rich, moist soil and a
sheltered site suit this plant well.
  Cutting.

DAPHNE cneorum 'Eximia' ★
[form of Garland Flower]
○ ◑
type of plant: HSh
flowering season: l. spring to e. summer
flower colour: rich pink
height: 23-30 cm/9-12 in
E

This semi-prostrate variety of garland flower can
make a carpet of foliage up to 90 cm/3 ft wide, and
when it is covered with intensely fragrant flowers
the effect is quite remarkable. *D. c.* 'Eximia' grows
slowly. It is easiest to establish as a young plant in
well drained soil to which plenty of
humus-forming material, such as well rotted
compost or manure, has been added.
  Ground-cover – Containers.

Additional plants with fragrant flowers that are featured elsewhere in this book

○ ◑ sun or partial shade
CLEMATIS montana: 6-10.5 m (p. 122)
CLEMATIS montana rubens: 6-10.5 m (p. 122)
MAGNOLIA × soulangiana 'Lennei': 6-7.5 m (p. 95)
EUCRYPHIA × nymansensis 'Nymansay': 4.5-9 m (p. 33)
ROSA (Climber) e.g. 'Mme Alfred Carrière' ★: 4.5-6 m (p. 123)
BUXUS sempervirens: 3.6-4.5 m (p. 127)
PRUNUS lusitanica: 3-6 m (p. 127)
ELAEAGNUS × ebbingei: 3-4.5 m (p. 128)
HAMAMELIS mollis ★: 2.4-3.6 m (p. 276)
VIBURNUM × bodnantense 'Dawn': 2.4-3.6 m (p. 276)
BUXUS sempervirens e.g. 'Aureovariegata': 2.4-3 m (p. 152)
MAGNOLIA stellata: 2.4-3 m (p. 96)
CHOISYA ternata: 1.8-2.4 m (p. 243)
ROSA (Bourbon) e.g. 'Zéphirine Drouhin': 1.8-2.4 m (p. 267)
DAPHNE mezereum: 90-150 cm (p. 277)
OENOTHERA biennis: 75-90 cm (p. 67)
HEMEROCALLIS e.g. 'Marion Vaughn': 75 cm (p. 52)
NICOTIANA alata e.g. 'Lime Green': 60-75 cm (p. 282)
NICOTIANA alata e.g. 'Sensation Mixed': 60-75 cm (p. 246)
CLEMATIS montana: 60 cm (p. 122)
CLEMATIS montana rubens: 60 cm (p. 122)
NARCISSUS (Double) e.g. 'Cheerfulness': 45 cm (p. 249)
BUXUS sempervirens 'Suffruticosa': 30-60 cm (p. 128)
PRIMULA auricula e.g. 'Mixed Hybrids': 15-23 cm (p. 35)

VIOLA Hybrid 'Arkwright Ruby'
[form of Garden Pansy]

○ ◑
type of plant: HB/P
flowering season: l. spring to e. autumn
flower colour: crimson + black
height: 15-20 cm/6-8 in

There are very few large-flowered violas or pansies with any perceptible scent. This glowingly coloured variety is a welcome exception. Its sweet fragrance is, however, disappointing when compared with the scent of *V. odorata* and its forms (for an example of which, see the following illustration). As with most plants in this genus, dead-heading prolongs the flowering season considerably.

VIOLA odorata e.g. 'Princess of Wales'
[form of Sweet Violet]

○ ◑
type of plant: HP
flowering season: spring
flower colour: violet-blue
height: 15 cm/6 in
E

As well as being sweetly scented, *V. odorata* and some of its varieties – including the present example – make good ground-cover. They are especially suitable for covering rose-beds, since they flower before most roses do, but they are not so vigorous that they deprive the roses of moisture and nutrients. *V.* 'Princess of Wales' has long stems which make it a good cut flower.

Ground-cover – Paving – Cutting.

LONICERA × americana (syn. *L. grata*) ★
[form of Honeysuckle]

◑ [○]
type of plant: HCl
flowering season: summer
flower colour: creamy white + purple
height: 7.5-9 m/25-30 ft
½E/D

Once established, *L. × americana* blooms profusely and its fingery flowers emit a full, slightly spicy fragrance. The vigour of this plant's twining growth can be partially contained by pruning in early autumn or winter. All the honeysuckles illustrated here are best grown in moist, fertile soil and, if they are not lightly shaded, their roots, at least, should be out of direct sunlight. They may be used to cover north-facing walls.

Climbers.

LONICERA japonica halliana (syn. *L. halliana*)
[form of Honeysuckle]

◑ [○]
type of plant: HCl
flowering season: summer to mid-autumn
flower colour: cream changing to buff
height: 7.5-9 m/25-30 ft
E/½E, particularly fragrant in evening

This very vigorous plant, which can easily cover an unsightly shed or outhouse with its slender, twining stems, also makes good ground-cover. When pegged down, the long shoots root as they lengthen, building up into a 15-20 cm/6-8 in high carpet of greenery that will remain dense if clipped occasionally. Although the flowers are not very conspicuously borne, they are beautifully and freshly fragrant. For general comments on the cultivation of honeysuckles see the preceding plant.

Ground-cover – Climbers – Containers.

LONICERA periclymenum 'Belgica'
[Early Dutch Honeysuckle]

◑ [○]
type of plant: HCl
flowering season: l. spring to e. summer and often l. summer to e. autumn
flower colour: yellow + pink
height: 4.5-6 m/15-20 ft
particularly fragrant in evening

Between them, the early and the late Dutch honeysuckles flower over a considerable period. Both of these plants have long, twining growths, sweetly scented flowers and, in the cooler parts of the country, clusters of bright red berries. When used for ground-cover, they are about 15-20 cm/6-8 in high, although they can become bush-like and over 60 cm/2 ft high. For a brief outline of the cultivation of honeysuckles, see *L. × americana*, second left.

Ground-cover – Climbers – Fruit.

**LONICERA periclymenum 'Serotina'
[Late Dutch Honeysuckle]**

◑ [○]

type of plant: HCl
flowering season: midsummer to mid-autumn
flower colour: yellow + red
height: 4.5-6 m/15-20 ft
particularly fragrant in evening

See preceding plant.

MAHONIA japonica★

◑ [○]

type of plant: HSh
flowering season: l. autumn to e. spring
flower colour: yellow
height: 2.1-3 m/7-10 ft
E

The rich, lily of the valley fragrance of this shrub is only one of its many good features. It also has large, bold whorls of spiky foliage (which are borne on erect stems and which occasionally turn bright red before finally dying); its flowering season is unusual; and it is an extremely tough and hardy plant. Almost any soil is suitable, but moisture and some shade produce the best results.

Atmospheric pollution – Containers – Green foliage – Winter-flowering plants.

**RHODODENDRON (AZALEA) e.g.
'Narcissiflorum'**

◑ [○]

type of plant: HSh
flowering season: l. spring to e. summer
flower colour: yellow
height: 1.5-2.4 m/5-8 ft
*

The daffodil-like flowers of this azalea are quite small, but they usually appear in large numbers and they have a sweet, honey-like fragrance. Most of the Ghent hybrids – of which *R.* 'Narcissiflorum' is an example – form upright, twiggy bushes. They are very hardy plants which will thrive in open-textured, lime-free soils that remain cool and moist throughout the growing season. Many of them colour well in autumn.

Acid soils.

SKIMMIA japonica (syn. *S. oblata*)

◑ [○]

type of plant: HSh
flowering season: spring
flower colour: white
height: 90-150 cm/3-5 ft
E, male forms fragrant

When fertilized by a male plant, female forms of this dense, rounded shrub bear splendid, red berries which are exceptionally long-lasting. However, it is the male forms which produce the most attractive flowers. These are larger, more numerous and much more fragrant than the blooms of the female plants. (*S.j.* 'Fragrans' is a particularly well-scented, male variety.) The most suitable growing conditions for all these plants are moist, rather acid loams and partially shaded positions.

Atmospheric pollution – Ground-cover – Fruit – Cutting.

**LILIUM speciosum album
[form of Lily]**

◑ [○]

type of plant: HHBb
flowering season: l. summer to e. autumn
flower colour: white
height: 90-120 cm/3-4 ft
*

This half-hardy lily is often grown under glass but, in mild districts and with some natural shelter, its sweetly fragrant blooms can be borne quite profusely outdoors. Although it needs warmth, this plant should, ideally, have some shade as well, so that its roots remain moist and its flowers are not all produced at once and for a brief period of time only.

Acid soils.

**HOSTA plantaginea
[species of Plantain Lily]**

◑ [○]

type of plant: HP
flowering season: autumn
flower colour: white
height: 45-60 cm/1½-2 ft

In common with other hostas, this species has handsome foliage. Its ribbed leaves are of a beautifully fresh, yellowish green throughout the growing season. *H. plantaginea*'s special attraction, however, is the sweet smell of its flowers (for an indication of the shape of these flowers, see *H.* 'Thomas Hogg', p. 78). A warm, sheltered position ensures that the blooms are produced in reasonable quantities and that they are not damaged by frost. A moist soil is necessary for good, lush growth.

Damp and wet soils – Ground cover – Green foliage.

ENDYMION non-scriptus (syn.
Hyacinthus non-scriptus, Scilla nutans)
[Bluebell, Wild Hyacinth]

◐ [○]
type of plant: HBb
flowering season: l. spring
flower colour: violet-blue
height: 23-30 cm/9-12 in

Ideally, bluebells should be grown in moistish
ground, but their presence near large, mature trees
with extensive root systems shows their tolerance
of quite dry conditions. The soft, almost aromatic
scent of the flowers of these plants is strongest on
sunny days. Bluebell bulbs should be replanted as
soon as possible after being lifted from their
original site.
    Dry shade.

CONVALLARIA majalis
[Lily of the Valley]

◐ [○]
type of plant: HP
flowering season: l. spring
flower colour: white
height: 15-23 cm/6-9 in

When established, lily of the valley can become so
prolific that it is a nuisance, but this drawback is
usually overlooked because of the beautiful scent
of its flowers. The plants are best when grown in
cool shade and a moisture-retentive soil, but they
will tolerate a wide range of inhospitable
conditions. The red, poisonous berries are not
produced very often in Britain. *C. m.* 'Rosea' is a
pink-flowered and less vigorous form of lily of the
valley.
    Dry shade – Dense shade – Ground-cover –
Cutting.

**RHODODENDRON Hybrid e.g. 'Loderi King
George'★**

◐
type of plant: HSh
flowering season: l. spring
flower colour: pale pink changing to white
height: 4.5-6 m/15-20 ft
*E

The huge flowers of this magnificent
rhododendron are richly fragrant. They normally
appear in impressively large numbers, and some
blooms can be over 15 cm/6 in wide. The plant
itself is vigorous and forms a big, spreading shrub
which should be given a site – in light woodland,
for example – where it is sheltered from cold
winds.
    Acid soils.

RHODODENDRON Hybrid e.g. 'Albatross'
sc NA

◐
type of plant: HSh/T
flowering season: e. summer
flower colour: white
height: 3.6-4.5 m/12-15 ft
*E

Like the related plant in the previous illustration,
this hybrid makes a large, open shrub or,
occasionally, a small tree. It too has fragrant
flowers and these are often 12 cm/5 in wide. It
grows most satisfactorily in the south and west of
Britain, provided that it has a cool, moist, acid soil
and shelter from cold winds.
    Acid soils.

CARDIOCRINUM giganteum (syn. *Lilium*
giganteum)★
[species of Giant Lily]

◐
type of plant: HBb
flowering season: summer
flower colour: white
height: 1.8-3 m/6-10 ft

The superb, purple-throated flowers of this stately
plant have a full, sweet fragrance. They are
followed by smooth seed-pods that ripen from pale
green to yellow. A rich, well drained but
moisture-retentive soil and a sheltered position are
essential for the best results. A rather smaller
variety, *C. g. yunnanense*, is listed by some bulb
specialists. Its young foliage is bronze-green.
    Acid soils.

LILIUM henryi
[species of Lily]

◐
type of plant: HBb
flowering season: l. summer
flower colour: orange-yellow
height: 1.5-2.4 m/5-8 ft

This vigorous and hardy lily carries numerous,
sweetly scented flowers on each of its arching
stems (these stems nearly always need to be
staked). Where adequate moisture can be
provided, *L. henryi* grows well in limy soils. If it is
attacked by virus diseases, it is usually strong
enough to continue flowering quite adequately, for
a short time at least.

ASPERULA orientalis (syn. *A. azurea*,
A. azurea setosa)

◐

type of plant: HA
flowering season: summer
flower colour: lavender blue
height: 23-30 cm/9-12 in

The number of annual plants that can be grown in
shady sites is quite small, and exceptions like
A. orientalis can, therefore, be particularly useful.
The flowers of this plant are long-lasting and
sweetly scented. A moist soil produces good
growth.
　　Cutting.

CYCLAMEN europaeum

◐

type of plant: HTu
flowering season: midsummer to e. autumn
flower colour: deep pink
height: 8-10 cm/3-4 in

Among the cyclamen suitable for growing
outdoors, this species is both exceptionally hardy
and exceptionally fragrant. Each tuber produces a
mass of blooms which emits a strong, sweet scent.
The leaves remain green throughout the winter
months; they have delicate, silvery green
markings. Some shade and moisture are needed
for *C. europaeum* to grow strongly and to flower
prolifically.
　　Variegated leaves.

SARCOCOCCA humilis
[species of Christmas Box or Sweet Box]

◐ ●

type of plant: HSh
flowering season: l. winter
flower colour: inconspicuous, white
height: 30-60 cm/1-2 ft
E

The flowers of this dense, glossy-leaved plant are
very small and almost completely hidden amongst
the foliage, but their rich, vanilla fragrance is
strong and particularly welcome in winter. The
black fruits which follow are large for the size of
plant and a minor attraction where there is enough
light to make them shine. *S. humilis* spreads slowly
in all reasonably fertile soils, and it will grow quite
well in a variety of difficult circumstances.
　　Chalk – Dry shade – Dense shade –
Atmospheric pollution – Ground-cover – Fruit –
Winter-flowering plants.

**Additional plants with fragrant flowers that are
featured elsewhere in this book**

◐ [○] partial shade (or sun)
MAHONIA × 'Charity': 2.1-3 m (p. 278)
RHODODENDRON luteum: 1.8-3 m (p. 194)
PRIMULA florindae: 75-120 cm (p. 77)
SKIMMIA japonica 'Rubella': 60-90 cm (p. 39)
LONICERA japonica halliana: 15-20 cm (p. 270)
LONICERA periclymenum 'Belgica': 15-20 cm
　(p. 270)
LONICERA periclymenum 'Serotina': 15-20 cm
　(p. 271)

◐ partial shade
FOTHERGILLA monticola: 1.8-2.4 m (p. 194)
CIMICIFUGA racemosa: 1.2-1.5 m (p. 185)
FOTHERGILLA gardenii: 60-90 cm (p. 194)
SMILACINA racemosa: 60-90 cm (p. 186)
LEUCOJUM vernum ★: 15-20 cm (p. 55)
CYCLAMEN repandum: 10-15 cm (p. 155)

◐ ● partial or full shade
BUXUS sempervirens: 3.6-4.5 m (p. 127)
BUXUS sempervirens e.g. 'Aureovariegata':
　2.4-3 m (p. 152)
PHILADELPHUS coronarius 'Aureus': 1.5-2.1 m
　(p. 178)
BUXUS sempervirens 'Suffruticosa': 30-60 cm
　(p. 128)
PACHYSANDRA terminalis: 23-30 cm (p. 117)
PACHYSANDRA terminalis 'Variegata': 23 cm
　(p. 155)
CONVALLARIA majalis: 15-23 cm (p. 272)

Winter-flowering plants

If the thought of your garden in winter conjures up visions of slippery paths, depressingly large areas of lumpy, brown earth and the occasional snowdrop, then the following list should suggest some ways in which this bleak state of affairs could be altered. Gardeners who have some plants in flower at every season of the year are often regarded with awe by those whose gardens are filled with flowers for fewer months.

Yet, as this list shows, the range of winter-flowering plants is quite large: there are trees, shrubs, perennials, bulbs and tubers which flower in winter and these plants vary in height, flower colour and the amount of sun or shade they need. As a bonus many plants which flower in winter also look attractive either during some other season or throughout the year: for instance, the rich purple leaves of *Corylus maxima* 'Purpurea' are a striking feature in spring and summer, *Parrotia persica*'s leaves become brilliantly coloured in autumn, while the handsome, evergreen foliage of the camellias and mahonias in this list not only complements their flowers in winter but is decorative throughout the year.

Unfortunately, the average British winter hardly encourages the appreciation of flowers from close quarters outdoors. For this reason, the fact that many winter-flowering plants make attractive – though not necessarily longlasting – cut flowers is particularly welcome, and especially so since many are sweetly scented. Winter flowers also present the flower arranger with a good range of form and size, from the yellow spiders of *Hamamelis mollis* and long green catkins of *Garrya elliptica* to the expansive, summery look of *Iris unguicularis*' blue petals. As a final bonus point, almost every flower colour appears in this list of winter flowers.

If you are looking for foliage to put with your cut flowers in winter, it is worth remembering that, apart from the leaves of evergreen plants, there are a few plants which produce particularly attractive, marbled foliage in winter. (They do not, however, appear in this list since they are not winter-flowering.)

They include: *Arum italicum* 'Pictum' (see p. 154) and *Cyclamen neapolitanum* (see p. 81).

Of course, even if your garden contained every one of the plants mentioned in this list, winter would not necessarily be a time of prolific blossom in the garden and armfuls of flowers in the house. Plants which flower during winter often need the encouragement of a mild spell for many flower buds to open at any one time; winter jasmine (*Jasminum nudiflorum*) and autumn cherry (*Prunus subhirtella* 'Autumnalis') are two of many possible examples. For this reason many winter flowers are best picked (or, in the case of *Iris unguicularis*, pulled to prevent the base of the plant rotting) in bud and brought into the warmth of the house. Indeed, one spring-flowering shrub – *Skimmia japonica* 'Rubella' – has winter flower buds so striking that they are considered features in themselves. Picking winter flowers in bud also helps to fight the battle against frost which, in certain districts and some seasons, can be severe enough to reduce potential flowers to sad, brown lumps. In cold, exposed areas some winter-flowering plants may need the protection of a wall (preferably not east-facing) or an evergreen hedge to give many undamaged flowers. The following plants make suitably tough hedges for shelter against cold winds: *Ilex aquifolium*, *Rhododendron ponticum*, *Ulex europaeus* 'Plenus', *Taxus baccata* and *T. b.* 'Fastigiata'.

Although the definition of the term 'winter' must vary from year to year and district to district, it is used here to cover the months of December, January and February. In a late winter some autumn-flowering plants will still be blooming in December, while an early spring will produce flowers which are usually associated with March during February.

For additional winter interest, see also list of 'Plants with ornamental bark and twigs', list of 'Plants with ornamental fruit', and evergreens in lists of plants with coloured, variegated or decorative, green foliage.

PRUNUS subhirtella 'Autumnalis'
[Autumn Cherry]

○

type of plant: HT
flowering season: l. autumn to e. spring
flower colour: white
height: 6-7.5 m/20-25 ft

This plant eventually forms a sizeable tree with spreading branches. The flowers, which appear on the leafless twigs, are usually produced profusely; they are sometimes tinged pink, especially when first emerging from bud. The main flowering season is late autumn and early winter, but later mild spells will encourage further blossom.

  Atmospheric pollution – Cutting.

CHIMONANTHUS praecox (syn. *C. fragrans,* *Calycanthus praecox*)
[species of Winter Sweet]

○

type of plant: HSh
flowering season: winter
flower colour: yellow
height: 2.1-3 m/7-10 ft

C. praecox makes a bushy, twiggy shrub which is generally hardy. However, it flowers best and matures quickest when grown against a south- or west-facing wall, and this is an important consideration since only plants that are several years old produce their sweet-scented flowers in any quantity. The leaves are an unexceptional mid-green and willow-like; they appear after the flowering season is over.

  Chalk – Fragrant flowers.

FORSYTHIA ovata NA
[Early Forsythia]

○

type of plant: HSh
flowering season: l. winter to e. spring
flower colour: yellow
height: 1.2 m/4 ft

A rounded shrub with flowers a week or two before other forsythias, this species is important because of its hardiness. In the colder parts of the United States, where *Forsythia × intermedia* is not a dependable bloomer, *F. ovata* and its cultivars can be relied upon. The cultivars include 'Ottawa' and 'Tetragold', both with good flower colour.

ERICA × **darleyensis** (syn. *E. mediterranea hybrida*) e.g. 'Silver Beads' (syn. 'Silberschmelze') **MC**
[form of Heath or Heather]

○

type of plant: **HSh**
flowering season: l. autumn to l. spring
flower colour: white
height: 45 cm/1½ ft
E

Most varieties of *E.* × *darleyensis* make good ground-cover but the vigorous 'Silver Beads' is among the best. It will tolerate some lime, as long as the soil also contains plenty of leaf-mould or peat. The delicately honey-scented flowers are most numerous towards the end of this plant's flowering season.

Acid soils – Ground-cover – Containers – Fragrant flowers.

IRIS unguicularis (syn. *I. stylosa*) ★ **MC**
[Algerian Iris]

○

type of plant: **HP**
flowering season: winter to e. spring
flower colour: lavender blue
height: 30 cm/1 ft
E

Although the choice of winter-flowering plants is quite wide, few look as summery as this species of iris. The flowers, and their honeysuckle-like scent, are best appreciated indoors, where frost and winds cannot spoil them. The flower stems, which are overtopped by the rather untidy – but ground-covering – leaves, should be gently pulled rather than picked. Sharp drainage and plenty of sun are essential; a poor, rubbly soil gives good results.

Chalk – Hot, dry soils – Ground-cover – Cutting – Fragrant flowers.

ERICA carnea e.g. 'King George'
[form of Heath or Heather]

○

type of plant: **HSh**
flowering season: winter
flower colour: dark rose-pink
height: 15-23 cm/6-9 in
E

Of all the species of *Erica* this is perhaps the best in limy, though humus-rich soils. The variety 'King George' is particularly neat and early-flowering. Its tiny leaves create a dense, ground-covering carpet.

Acid soils – Ground-cover – Containers.

IRIS reticulata e.g. 'Harmony' ★

○

type of plant: **HBb**
flowering season: l. winter to e. spring
flower colour: sky blue
height: 15 cm/6 in

This is a more robust and brightly coloured version of *I. reticulata* itself (for an illustration of which, see p. 17). Given good drainage and full sun, it is as easy to grow, but the outstanding violet fragrance of the species is, sadly, only just perceptible in the variety.

Chalk.

IRIS histrioides 'Major'

○

type of plant: **HBb**
flowering season: winter
flower colour: deep blue
height: 10 cm/4 in

Some gardeners find that the shortness of the stems of this plant make it seem unattractively dumpy. However, the intensity of the flower colour, the ability of the petals to withstand severe weather unscathed and, of course, the earliness of the flowering season are all appealing features. The leaves lengthen up to 45 cm/18 in in spring. Sun and good drainage are needed, and an alkaline soil is preferable.

Chalk.

CROCUS imperati

○

type of plant: **HBb**
flowering season: winter
flower colour: buff + violet
height: 8-10 cm/3-4 in

In winter sunshine, the outer, buff-coloured petals of this crocus open up, to a width of 8-10 cm/3-4 in, revealing the rich violet of the inner petals. Some warmth also brings out this plant's sweet and delicate fragrance. A dry, sunny site is most suitable.

Chalk – Hot, dry soils – Fragrant flowers.

IRIS danfordiae

○

type of plant: HBb
flowering season: l. winter to e. spring
flower colour: yellow
height: 8-10 cm/3-4 in

Many of the more common, winter-flowering
irises with bulbous rootstocks have blue or purple
flowers, so *I. danfordiae* might be regarded as a
welcome exception. It is, however, rather more
difficult to grow than, for instance, *I. reticulata* and
its varieties (for an example of which, see previous
page). A really warm site and good drainage are
most likely to ensure success but, in any case, this
rather squat and only slightly scented iris is likely
to flower well the first year after planting and then
to break up into numerous, tiny bulblets, which
take some time to reach flowering size.

Chalk.

**CROCUS tomasinianus 'Whitewell Purple'
sc NA**

○ [◐]

type of plant: HBb
flowering season: midwinter to e. spring
flower colour: violet-purple
height: 8-10 cm/3-4 in

The outer, deeply coloured petals of this crocus
can be seen at the very beginning of the year; the
paler, inner petals are revealed a little later. Its
free-flowering nature, its hardiness and its
cheapness all make this plant understandably
popular. It grows well in grass. *C. tomasinianus*
itself is also widely available. It has pale lilac
flowers.

Chalk – Hot, dry soils.

CROCUS ancyrensis (syn. *C.* **'Golden Bunch')**

○ [◐]

type of plant: HBb
flowering season: l. winter to e. spring
flower colour: golden yellow
height: 5-8 cm/2-3 in

The warmly coloured flowers of *C. ancyrensis* are
produced prolifically at a chilly time of the year. It
is often recommended as a companion for
C. imperati (see previous page). However, this
combination works well only if both plants are
given a position in full sun, since the colourful
inner petals of *C. imperati* are not visible unless the
warmth of winter sun is present.

Chalk – Hot, dry soils.

**CORNUS mas
[Cornelian Cherry]**

○ ◐

type of plant: HSh
flowering season: l. winter to mid-spring
flower colour: yellow
height: 3-4.5 m/10-15 ft

This is one of a number of winter-flowering shrubs
that carry their flowers on bare twigs. The plant
itself is usually bushy and spreading but,
particularly in warmer areas, it may eventually
form a small tree. Some warmth is required too for
the red, cherry-like fruits to be produced, and they
are not a notable feature of this plant in Britain.
Occasionally, the leaves become tinged with
bronze in autumn if the preceding summer has
been good and if the plant has been grown in poor
soil.

Chalk – Cutting.

**HAMAMELIS mollis★
[Chinese Witch Hazel]**

○ ◐

type of plant: HSh/T
flowering season: midwinter to e. spring
flower colour: yellow
height: 2.4-3.6 m/8-12 ft

Robust and very sweetly scented flowers appear in
large numbers on the naked twigs and branches of
this outstanding winter-flowering plant. Although
the blooms last well in water, *H. mollis* should be
cut sparingly as it does not renew growth readily.
This spreading and often suckering shrub or small
tree grows best in neutral or acid soils that are well
drained. In autumn, its leaves turn yellow.

Acid soils – Autumn foliage – Cutting –
Fragrant flowers.

VIBURNUM×bodnantense 'Dawn'

○ ◐

type of plant: HSh
flowering season: l. autumn to e. spring
flower colour: pinkish white
height: 2.4-3.6 m/8-12 ft

The colour of this shrub's frost-resistant flowers is
perhaps too reminiscent of icy hands. Any
chilliness in colouring is, however, more than
made up for by the sweet warmth of the flowers'
fragrance. The plant has an upright, somewhat
gaunt habit of growth and coarse, dull green
foliage.

Clay – Fragrant flowers.

JASMINUM nudiflorum ★
[Winter Jasmine]

○ ◑

type of plant: HSh
flowering season: l. autumn to e. spring/l. winter
  to e. spring (NA)
flower colour: yellow
height: 2.4-3 m/8-10 ft

Winter jasmine is the most popular winter-flowering shrub. The yellow flowers look exceptionally cheerful against the slender, bright green branches. This is a scandent plant, rather than a true climber, and it requires support to grow upright. Walls of all aspects are suitable but, to prevent frost damage to the flowers, an east-facing wall is best avoided. *J. nudiflorum* may be allowed to sprawl along the ground, when it will form a spiky mass of rooting twigs about 60 cm/2 ft high.

Ground-cover – Climbers – Containers – Cutting.

VIBURNUM tinus MC
[Laurustinus]

○ ◑

type of plant: HSh/SlTSh (NA)
flowering season: l. autumn to e. spring
flower colour: white
height: 1.8-3 cm/6-10 ft
E

This is a tough and tolerant shrub whose dense, bushy form is a feature of many gardens. For the best results, *V. tinus* should be grown in moisture-retentive soil. Some gardeners consider this plant's foliage too 'dead' a green, but it makes a good background for the pink-budded flowers and for the flowers and leaves of other plants.

Clay – Seaside – Atmospheric pollution – Hedging – Containers – Cutting.

DAPHNE mezereum
[Mezereon]

○ ◑

type of plant: HSh
flowering season: l. winter to e. spring
flower colour: purple-red
height: 90-150 cm/3-5 ft

Any temptation to cut the stiff, upright branches of this plant when they are covered in sweetly fragrant flowers should be avoided, since *D. mezereum* resents any sort of pruning. It is, in addition, a slow-growing shrub. It does well in alkaline soils, but shallow soils over chalk are too hot and dry to produce good growth. The scarlet berries are poisonous.

Atmospheric pollution – Fruit – Fragrant flowers.

NARCISSUS (Cyclamineus) 'February Gold' ★
[form of Daffodil]

○ ◑

type of plant: HBb
flowering season: l. winter to e. spring
flower colour: yellow
height: 30 cm/1 ft

N. 'February Gold' is a miniature – but much prettier – version of the all-yellow trumpet daffodils so commonly planted in gardens. Despite its dainty appearance and exceptionally early flowering season, this is a robust plant which increases quite readily. It is suitable for naturalizing.

Cutting.

GALANTHUS elwesii
[species of Snowdrop]

○ ◑

type of plant: HBb
flowering season: winter
flower colour: white + green
height: 15-25 cm/6-10 in

This is one of a number of species of snowdrop which closely resemble the common type (for an illustration of which, see the following page). The main differences in this case are that the flowers are larger with darker green markings and the leaves are broader and longer.

Clay – Cutting.

VIOLA Hybrid 'Winter-flowering Mixed'
[form of Garden Pansy]

○ ◑

type of plant: HB/P
flowering season l. autumn to spring
flower colour: mixed – red, bronze, yellow,
  violet-blue
height: 15-23 cm/6-9 in
intermittently through winter if mild

Compared with some of the other hybrid pansies, the winter-flowering strains have fairly small flowers. Some gardeners will find this an advantage and, in any case, the flowering season will make these plants attractive to many people. (The flowers appear in appreciable quantities mainly in autumn and spring, unless a warm spell and a sheltered site combine to encourage a display in winter.) As usual, regular dead-heading ensures the production of plenty of blooms over a long period.

GALANTHUS nivalis
[Common Snowdrop]
○ ◑
type of plant: HBb
flowering season: winter
flower colour: white + green
height: 10-20 cm/4-8 in

Once established, the familiar and well loved
snowdrop can form large colonies. Since the leaves
are produced and receive light so early in the year,
it is suitable for planting beneath deciduous trees
and shrubs. The bulbs should be planted as soon as
possible after flowering. Bulb specialists'
catalogues usually list a number of varieties of the
common snowdrop, including the double-
flowered form 'Flore-pleno' and the vigorous and
sweetly-scented hybrid 'Sam Arnott'.
  Clay – Cutting.

ANEMONE blanda 'Atrocoerulea' (syn. *A. b.*
'Ingramii')
○ ◑
type of plant: HTu
flowering season: l. winter to mid-spring
flower colour: deep blue
height: 10-15 cm/4-6 in

The neat, daisy-like shape of this plant's flowers is
unexpected in winter, but the flower colour is,
perhaps, in its own intense and beautiful way,
more in keeping with chilly weather. Good
drainage, including that provided by competition
from the roots of other plants, is required to grow
this plant well.
  Chalk.

SCILLA tubergeniana
[species of Squill]
○ ◑
type of plant: HBb
flowering season: l. winter to e. spring
flower colour: pale blue
height: 10 cm/4 in

S. tubergeniana has flowers of a much more delicate
colour than most of the other squills. At close
quarters, a tiny stripe of deeper blue can be seen on
each petal. The flowers open almost as soon as the
stems emerge from the ground, but they are
eventually carried several inches high.

MAHONIA×'Charity' sc NA MC
◑ [○]
type of plant: HSh
flowering season: l. autumn to winter
flower colour: yellow
height: 2.1-3 m/7-10 ft
E

An eye-catching plant with dramatic spokes of
scratchy leaflets and great, thick wands of globular
blossom, *M.×*'Charity' is, sadly, much less
strongly scented than one of its parents –
M. japonica (see p. 271). Although it is tolerant of
quite a wide range of soils and sites, this stiff,
upright plant is best in some shade and a
moisture-retentive, leaf-mouldy soil. In some
years – and in some plants – the main flowering
season is nearly over by early winter.
  Atmospheric pollution – Containers – Green
foliage – Fragrant flowers.

RHODODENDRON×'Praecox'
◑ [○]
type of plant: HSh
flowering season: l. winter to e. spring
flower colour: rosy lilac
height: 1.2-1.5 m/4-5 ft
*E/½E

Those gardeners who flinch at the very thought of
a hybrid rhododendron should contemplate the
delicate little blossoms which are liberally
sprinkled over this bushy, small-leaved plant.
Unfortunately, the exceptionally early flowering
season does mean that these pretty flowers are
susceptible to frost damage. A site which is
sheltered – from cold winds, in particular – is,
therefore, advisable. The dark leaves of this plant
emit a refreshing fragrance when bruised.
  Acid soils – Hedging – Aromatic foliage.

ERANTHIS cilicica
◑ [○]
type of plant: HTu
flowering season: l. winter to e. spring
flower colour: yellow
height: 5-8 cm/2-3 in

E. cilicica is a somewhat sturdier relation of the
more familiar *E. hyemalis* (see p. 54). Like all
plants of this genus, however, it dies back and
disappears by early summer. Its tiny leaves are a
coppery green when young. Moisture, especially
during spring, seems to be essential for success
with this plant, and there is usually a better chance
of establishing it if the tubers are still growing
when they are transplanted.

RHODODENDRON lutescens

◑

type of plant: HSh
flowering season: l. winter to mid-spring
flower colour: yellow
height: 1.8-3 m/6-10 ft
°E

Like several early-flowering rhododendrons, this rather loose-limbed shrub is a hardy plant, but it needs the shelter of, for instance, light woodland to ensure that its freely produced flowers do not become damaged by frost. The shiny bronze of the new leaves is an extra decorative feature of this already attractive shrub.

Acid soils – Red, etc. leaves.

HEPATICA nobilis (syn. *H. triloba*, *Anemone hepatica*)

◑

type of plant: HP
flowering season: l. winter to mid-spring
flower colour: usually mauve-blue
height: 10 cm/4 in
½E

A year or two after being transplanted, this most attractive perennial settles down and begins to produce its variably coloured flowers. The catalogues of rock plant specialists will list double-flowered forms of *H. nobilis* as well as forms of particular colours – including white. Although this plant enjoys a limy soil, it must be remembered that it also requires some moisture to do well.

CYCLAMEN coum

◑

type of plant: HTu
flowering season: midwinter to e. spring
flower colour: pink or carmine or white
height: 8-10 cm/3-4 in

The colours of the flowers and the leaves of this plant vary a good deal. Shades of pink and carmine red are the most usual flower colours; the leaves are commonly dark green and glossy. The foliage is produced in late winter.

Green foliage.

HELLEBORUS orientalis Hybrids
[forms of Lenten Rose]

◑ ●

type of plant: HP
flowering season: l. winter to spring
flower colour: white or pink or purple or mixed
height: 45-60 cm/1½-2 ft
E/D

H. orientalis varies considerably in flower colour, mainly because it hybridizes easily with itself. (Nurseries specializing in perennial plants usually sell selected colour forms, as well as mixtures.) Once planted, *H. orientalis* and its hybrids should be left undisturbed, except for an occasional dressing of leaf-mould in late spring. They may, eventually, need division because of overcrowding.

Dense shade – Ground-cover.

HELLEBORUS niger
[Christmas Rose]

◑ ●

type of plant: HP
flowering season: winter to e. spring
flower colour: white
height: 30-45 cm/1-1½ ft
E

Although the flowers of this plant appear on numerous Christmas cards, *H. niger* is not often in bloom on 25 December (however, the much less commonly available *H. n.* 'Altifolius' usually is). To make the flowers last well in water, the stems should be dipped in boiling water, and incisions made from near the flower heads to the stem tips; stems and flowers should then be soaked in water for a few hours. *H. niger* appreciates a well drained but moist soil.

Dense shade – Cutting.

Additional winter-flowering plants that are featured elsewhere in this book

○ sun
POPULUS tremula: 9-15 m (p. 68)
CORYLUS maxima 'Purpurea': 3 m (p. 169)
DAPHNE odora 'Aureomarginata'★: 1.2-1.8 m (p. 146)
ERICA×darleyensis e.g. 'Arthur Johnson': 60 cm (p. 100)
ERICA carnea e.g. 'Springwood White'★: 23 cm (p. 102)
ERICA carnea e.g. 'Vivellii': 15-23 cm (p. 191)
IRIS reticulata: 15 cm (p. 17)
IRIS reticulata e.g. 'Cantab': 10-15 cm (p. 19)

○ [◑] sun (or partial shade)
LONICERA fragrantissima: 1.8-2.1 m (p. 264)
CROCUS chrysanthus e.g. 'Blue Pearl': 8-10 cm (p. 67)
CROCUS chrysanthus e.g. 'E. A. Bowles': 8-10 cm (p. 67)

○ ◑ sun or partial shade
PARROTIA persica: 3-5.4 m (p. 193)
CAMELLIA reticulata e.g. 'Captain Rawes': 3-4.5 m (p. 34)
GARRYA elliptica: 2.4-4.5 m (p. 282)
CORYLUS avellana e.g. 'Contorta': 2.4-3 m (p. 211)
CAMELLIA×williamsii e.g. 'Donation'★: 1.8-2.4 m (p. 34)
CAMELLIA×williamsii e.g. 'J. C. Williams': 1.8-2.4 m (p. 135)
LONICERA×purpusii: 1.5-2.4 m (p. 267)
JASMINUM nudiflorum★: 60 cm (p. 277)
NARCISSUS×'W. P. Milner': 15-25 cm (p. 53)
NARCISSUS cyclamineus: 10-20 cm (p. 36)
ANEMONE blanda 'Mixed': 10-15 cm (p. 26)

◑ [○] partial shade (or sun)
MAHONIA japonica★: 2.1-3 m (p. 271)
CAMELLIA japonica e.g. 'Adolphe Audusson': 1.8-3.6 m (p. 36)
CAMELLIA japonica e.g. 'Alba Simplex': 1.8-3 m (p. 137)
ERANTHIS hyemalis: 8-10 cm (p. 54)

◑ partial shade
LEUCOJUM vernum: 15-20 cm (p. 55)

◑ ● partial or full shade
JASMINUM nudiflorum★: 2.4-3 m (p. 277)
HELLEBORUS lividus corsicus: 60 cm (p. 283)
JASMINUM nudiflorum★: 60 cm (p. 277)
SARCOCOCCA humilis: 30-60 cm (p. 273)

Plants with green flowers

This is the only list in this book which is devoted to flowers of a single colour. Green flowers are treated separately for two reasons. First, these flowers enjoy a special popularity, mainly among flower arrangers, and second, they are sufficiently unusual to make searching for them under 'flower colour' in the larger lists tedious and time-consuming.

Giving useful and accurate descriptions of the colours of flowers is always a difficult task, and the problem is made worse when any particular colour is singled out for special attention. Although all the plants in the following list bear green flowers, there is quite a wide range of shades: *Zinnia elegans* 'Envy', for instance, is a fairly strong lime green, while *Fritillaria acmopetala*'s outer petals are a much paler, jade-like green. There are also several plants with yellowish green flowers, or flowers which are an almost equal mixture of yellow and green. How green some flowers look often depends upon the colour of surrounding materials. A yellow background will heighten the greenness of flowers which are on the borderline of yellow and green (for plants with yellow or yellow-green leaves see p. 174).

Although many plants in this list have subtly coloured flowers, it does not follow that most green flowers are dull. Neither *Garrya elliptica*'s catkins nor the drooping tassel-like flowers of *Amaranthus caudatus* 'Viridis' (a variety of love-lies-bleeding) are a particularly conspicuous colour, but in shape and length they are outstanding; the flowers of the Corsican hellebore, *Helleborus lividus corsicus*, are a pale apple-green, but they contrast most attractively with the foliage and are usually borne in large, prominent clusters.

Green flowers are, in a way, a compromise between flowers and foliage: flowers in form, foliage in colour. While this makes them unusual and interesting, it does mean that, if they are arranged with green foliage and flowers of stronger colours, there is a tendency for them to merge with the foliage. This problem can be overcome either by using flowers of subtle or pale colours – green and white arrangements are often particularly successful – or by using only green flowers and foliage. 'All-green' arrangements can be extremely elegant, and the very restricted range of colour concentrates the eye upon the differences in form, which are so easily overlooked in the more normal, multi-coloured arrangements.

If you are looking for extra material for these all-green arrangements remember that, before they ripen into more dramatic colours, most berries are green; many unripe seed-pods, such as those produced by the various poppies, are also suitable material. In addition, there are a number of white flowers which are marked with green. These markings are not conspicuous enough for the flowers to be described as green but their presence makes the flowers particularly compatible with green material. Plants with basically white flowers which are lightly marked with green include snowdrops, *Polygonatum* ×*hybridum* (Solomon's seal or David's harp) and the semi-evergreen azalea 'Palestrina'. Many white flowers are also greenish when still in bud, while hydrangeas grown in shade often take on green hues while fading, and these are yet further sources of material for green arrangements.

You may find references – usually in botanical, rather than horticultural, descriptions – to green flowers being borne by plants which appear elsewhere in this book. These plants have not been included here because their flowers are inconspicuous. A borderline case, which has been included, is *Gunnera manicata*. The flowers of this plant are olive green in the early stages of their development but, although they become at least partly obscured by the foliage, the dense, cone-shaped panicles of flowers are of such an impressively large size that the adjective 'inconspicuous' seems misleading.

As usual in these lists, the term 'flowers' covers flower-like parts of inflorescences as well as true flowers. Both Moluccella laevis *(bells of Ireland, shell-flower) and* Euphorbia wulfenii *(a species of spurge), for instance, have very small flowers but much larger and more conspicuous green calyces and bracts respectively.*

ALLIUM siculum

○

type of plant: HBb
flowering season: l. spring to e. summer
flower colour: green + pink
height: 90 cm/3 ft

Both the colouring of this plant and the arrangement of the flowers in loose – though sizeable – heads make this one of the subtlest and most attractive alliums. As a bonus, the flowers fade to interesting seed-heads, in which the individual bells no longer hang, but face upwards. *A. siculum* grows well and may increase quickly in well drained, fertile soils.
  Chalk.

GLADIOLUS (Butterfly Hybrid) e.g. 'Green Woodpecker' sc NA

○

type of plant: HHC
flowering season: summer
flower colour: yellowish green + red
height: 75-105 cm/2½-3½ ft

Gladioli are, of course, outstandingly popular cut flowers. The combination of lasting well in water and having green petals makes some of them, such as 'Green Woodpecker', particularly attractive to many flower arrangers. When grown for cutting or for exhibition, gladioli usually need considerable attention in the form of staking, fertilizing and thorough soil preparation.
  Cutting.

AMARANTHUS caudatus 'Viridis'
[form of Love-lies-Bleeding]

○

type of plant: HA
flowering season: midsummer to e. autumn
flower colour: pale green
height: 75-90 cm/2½-3 ft

The long, drooping tassels of love-lies-bleeding contrast well in form with most other flowers. This green-flowered variety is both interestingly shaped and subtly coloured. Much of the colour is retained when the flowers are dried for winter decoration. For the best results this plant should be grown in a rich soil and given a sheltered site.
  Cutting.

TULIPA (Viridiflora) e.g. 'Greenland' ★
[form of Tulip]

○
type of plant: HBb
flowering season: l. spring
flower colour: green + pink
height: 60-75 cm/2-2½ ft

Specialist bulb growers now offer quite a large number of tulips with green flowers or green markings on their petals; this variety is one of the most readily available. Its exceptionally pretty combination of colours makes it a popular choice for spring flower arrangements. Good drainage is important when growing this and other tulips.

    Chalk – Hot, dry soils – Cutting.

MOLUCCELLA laevis
[Bells of Ireland, Shell-flower]

○
type of plant: HHA
flowering season: l. summer
flower colour: green + white
height: 60 cm/2 ft

The tiny, white flowers of this annual are surrounded by large calyces which look well in fresh flower arrangements; they are also attractive when dried. The seed of this plant seems to require some light for successful germination. It should, therefore, either be given a very light covering of compost or left uncovered. Most soils are suitable.

    Cutting.

ZINNIA elegans 'Envy'

○
type of plant: HHA
flowering season: midsummer to e. autumn
flower colour: lime green
height: 60 cm/2 ft

Few green flowers are so sharply coloured as this variety of zinnia, and it can be used in arrangements and bedding schemes where a more delicate green would be lost. All zinnias benefit from being grown in rich soil. The taller varieties, including *Z. e.* 'Envy', also require some shelter from wind.

    Cutting.

GLADIOLUS (Miniature Hybrid) 'Greenbird'
○
type of plant: HHC
flowering season: summer
flower colour: sulphur green + red
height: 45-75 cm/1½-2½ ft

Like nearly all gladioli, this hybrid is long-lasting when cut. Its particular colour ensures its popularity with flower arrangers. For plenty of well formed flower spikes, the ground needs to be prepared carefully before planting and fertilizer should be applied after the young shoots have appeared.

    Cutting.

PHALARIS canariensis
[Canary Grass]

○
type of plant: HA(Gr)
flowering season: summer
flower colour: creamy green
height: 45-60 cm/1½-2 ft

The roots of this grass are rather weak – unlike those of the related and rampant gardener's garters or ribbon grass (*P. arundinacea* 'Picta'). The neat little flower heads contrast most attractively with the copious quantities of fresh green foliage.

EUCOMIS bicolor
[Pineapple Plant]

○
type of plant: HHBb
flowering season: l. summer
flower colour: green + purple
height: 45 cm/1½ ft

Although the broad, basal leaves of this plant can look rather untidy, they provide a strongly shaped background for the dense heads of starry, purple-edged flowers and the brown-spotted stems. The jaunty topknot of leaves on each flower spike gives the plant its common name and completes its eye-catching appearance. *E. bicolor* is suitable only for warm, sheltered sites.

HERMODACTYLUS tuberosus (syn.
Iris tuberosus)
[Snakeshead Iris, Widow Iris]
○
type of plant: HTu
flowering season: spring
flower colour: olive green + black
height: 30-40 cm/12-15 in

As one of the common names would suggest, the
flowers of this plant are somewhat gloomily
coloured. Nevertheless, the combination of one
subtle and one very dark colour is interesting and –
if the plant is given a sufficiently prominent
position – quite conspicuous. *H. tuberosus* thrives
in sharply drained soil.
Chalk – Hot, dry soils.

IRIS (Bearded Hybrid) 'Green Spot' sc NA
○
type of plant: HP
flowering season: l. spring
flower colour: white + green
height: 30 cm/1 ft

Despite an increase in the range of colours
available among the recently introduced, smaller
bearded hybrid irises, few varieties of any size have
the unusual colouring of *I.* 'Green Spot'. Like
most of those smaller irises, however, this is a good
garden plant which increases well when given
freely draining soil and an open, sunny position.
Chalk – Cutting.

GARRYA elliptica★ MC
○ ◑
type of plant: SlTSh
flowering season: midwinter to e. spring
flower colour: silvery green
height: 2.4-4.5 m/8-15 ft
E

The shape and colour of this shrub's flowers make
it popular with flower arrangers, but its unusual
flowering season, its tolerance of both dirty and
salt-laden air and its suitability for north walls
mean that it is generally well liked. The plant itself
is bushy and quick-growing. In exposed positions
in colder districts, its leathery foliage can become
unattractively 'burnt'. Female plants have shorter
flowers than male plants but, if fertilized, they
produce purplish fruits.
Seaside – Atmospheric pollution – Fruit –
Cutting – Winter-flowering plants.

NICOTIANA alata (syn. *N. affinis)* **e.g. 'Lime**
Green'★
[form of Tobacco Plant]
○ ◑
type of plant: HHA
flowering season: summer to e. autumn
flower colour: yellowish green
height: 60-75 cm/2-2½ft

This is one of the few readily available,
green-flowered plants that are attractively scented
(in this case, the fragrance emitted is a delicate and
sweet one). The site should be warm and the soil
rich and well drained to produce good specimens
of this annual.
Cutting – Fragrant flowers.

FRITILLARIA acmopetala★
[species of Fritillary]
○ ◑
type of plant: HBb
flowering season: mid-spring
flower colour: pale green + brown
height: 30-45 cm/1-1½ ft

Its rather sophisticated colouring and graceful
shape might suggest otherwise, but this is one of
the easiest fritillaries to grow, particularly in
Britain. A moisture-retentive but well drained soil
containing plenty of leaf-mould produces the best
results.

ORNITHOGALUM nutans
○ ◑
type of plant: HBb
flowering season: spring
flower colour: pale green + white
height: 30-40 cm/12-15 in

This unfussy and extremely pretty plant will
normally increase quickly. It is suitable for
naturalizing. The range of heights given here is an
average one, but *O. nutans* can be as small as
15 cm/6 in and as large as 45 cm/18 in high.

ASTRANTIA major
[species of Masterwort]

◑ [○]

type of plant: HP
flowering season: summer
flower colour: pale pinkish green
height: 60 cm/2 ft

The distinctive arrangement of tiny florets surrounded by papery ruffs is the main feature of this plant, but the tripartite leaves are also quite attractive and they make good ground-cover. The plant spreads, in an admirably restrained fashion, by means of underground runners.

Ground-cover – Cutting.

HELLEBORUS lividus corsicus (syn. *H. argutifolius*, *H. corsicus*)★
[Corsican Hellebore]

◑ ●

type of plant: HP
flowering season: l. winter to spring
flower colour: pale green
height: 60 cm/2 ft
E

Every part of this shrubby perennial is beautiful. That the Corsican hellebore should be at its best in the early months of the year is a bonus indeed. When cut, individual blossoms may be floated, stemless, in shallow containers of water, or whole clusters can be used if their stems are split along almost their entire length. Rather poor, even stony, soils seem to produce the longest-lived plants.

Dense shade – Green foliage – Cutting – Winter-flowering plants.

Additional plants with green flowers that are featured elsewhere in this book

○ sun
LIRIODENDRON tulipifera: 21-30 m (p. 179)
EUPHORBIA wulfenii: 90-120 cm (p. 158)
STIPA calamagrostis: 90 cm (p. 58)
GLYCERIA maxima 'Variegata': 60 cm (p. 147)
BRIZA maxima: 45 cm (p. 233)
BRIZA media: 30-45 cm (p. 236)

○ ◑ sun or partial shade
CARPINUS betulus: 15-21 m (p. 130)
GUNNERA manicata: 1.8-2.7 m (p. 183)
EUPHORBIA robbiae: 45-60 cm (p. 81)
ALCHEMILLA mollis: 45 cm (p. 108)

◑ [○] partial shade (or sun)
ANGELICA archangelica: 1.2-2.4 m (p. 199)
TELLIMA grandiflora: 45-60 cm (p. 113)

◑ ● partial or full shade
EUPHORBIA robbiae: 45-60 cm (p. 81)

Addresses of suppliers

Many of the more popular plants in these lists will be readily available from quite small nurseries and garden centres. However, if you cannot obtain a particular plant from such sources, one or other of the suppliers listed below will almost certainly stock it. Plants and seeds may be obtained by mail order from all these firms.

Although this is a small selection of suppliers, between them they sell an extremely wide range of plants, including many items that it was not possible to include in these lists. Apart from some quite rare plants, these suppliers will also sell many more varieties of certain plants than could be mentioned here.

Except in the rare cases of plants involving two or more synonyms, alternative botanical names have been repeated when several varieties of a species follow each other directly in the lists. This is to lessen the likelihood of synonyms being overlooked. It is most annoying to search for a plant through the different sections of a large catalogue, only to find, by chance, and some time later, that the plant does appear in the catalogue – under a synonym. In certain cases, it is important to note the common name too, since, in seedsmen's catalogues in particular, certain popular plants, including sweet peas, wallflowers and stocks, rarely appear under their botanical names.

Each of the suppliers mentioned below deals mainly in a few types of plants. These plant types are noted, in the abbreviated forms used throughout this book, beneath the supplier's name and address. If a supplier carries a reasonably wide range of some additional types of plant, these appear in italics, after the word 'also'. (Here, the abbreviation 'P' refers to perennial plants *apart from* aquatics, bamboos, grasses and herbs, which are noted separately, and the abbreviation 'Cl' denotes woody, perennial climbers.)

Nurseries
Walter Blom & Son Ltd, Leavesden, Watford, Herts WD2 7BH.
Bb, C, Tu, *also A, B, P*.

Bressingham Gardens, Diss, Norfolk IP22 2AB.
P (including bog plants), *also Ba, Co (mainly dwarf or slow-growing), F, Gr, Herb (decorative varieties), Sh (mainly small, including wide range of heaths and heathers)*.

de Jager, The Nurseries, Marden, Kent TN12 9BP.
Bb, C, Tu, *also P*.

Hillier Nurseries (Winchester) Ltd, Romsey Road, Winchester, Hants SO22 5DN.
Cl, Co, Sh, T (all exceptionally wide range), *also Ba, Bb, C, F, Gr, Herb (including decorative varieties), P (including bog plants), Tu*.

W. E. T. Ingwersen Ltd, Birch Farm Nursery, Gravetye, E. Grinstead, West Sussex RH19 41E.
Bb, C, P, Tu (all mainly rock garden or alpine), Co (dwarf or slow-growing), Sh (small).

Kelways Nurseries, Langport, Somerset TA10 9SL.
Bb, C, P (including wide range of paeonies and bearded hybrid irises), Tu, *also Gr*.

Perry's Hardy Plant Farm Ltd, Theobalds Park Road, Enfield, Middx EN2 9BG.
Aq, F, P (including bog plants).

Sunningdale Nurseries Ltd, London Road, Windlesham, Surrey GU20 6LN.
Cl, Sh (including wide range of rhododendrons, azaleas, roses), T, *also Co, F, Gr, P (including some bog plants)*.

Unusual Plants, White Barn House, Elmstead Market, Colchester, Essex CO7 7DB.
P (including bog plants), *also Gr, Herb (including decorative varieties), Sh (mainly small)*.

Seedsmen
Samuel Dobie & Son Ltd, Upper Dee Mills, Llangollen, Clwyd LL20 8SD.
A, B, P, *also Bb, C, Gr (annual only), Tu*.

Suttons Seeds Ltd, Hele Road, Torquay, Devon TQ2 7QS.
A, B, *also Bb, C, P, Tu*.

Thompson & Morgan (Ipswich) Ltd, London Road, Ipswich, Suffolk IP2 0BA.
A, B, Co, P, Sh, T, *also Bb, Gr*.

All the firms above sell seeds of herbs, but variegated or unusually coloured forms of these plants are not available from seedsmen.

For a comprehensive list of suppliers, see either *Shopping by Post for Gardeners* by Joy Montague (Exley Publications) or Veronica Crichton and Maud Crawford's *Green Pages: a guide to the nurseries and garden centres of the British Isles* (Granada Publishing) which includes a section devoted to plant sources.

Index of botanical names

Page numbers in *italics* denote synonyms.

Index of common names